NEOS

G U

D0836351

# GREEK ISLANDS
# ATHENS

MICHELIN
Travel Publications

## Note to readers

This guide covers the capital of Greece as well as the archipelagos of the Aegean: the Saronic Gulf Islands, the Sporades, the Cyclades, the North Aegean Islands, Crete, Rhodes and the Dodecanese. These areas are highlighted on the map on the inside front cover. The other Greek islands (Euboea, Thássos and the Ionian Islands) are covered in the guide to "Mainland Greece".

**Practical information** – The information given in the "Practical information" section applies to the country as a whole and is intended to help you prepare for your trip. Further practical information can be found at the end of each section in "Exploring Greece" (eg, "Making the most of Amorgós", page 224), such as how to get there, useful addresses, accommodation, eating out, things to do, shopping, etc. In order to help you choose hotels and restaurants, we have listed our recommended establishments by price categories (shown in euros). However, please remember that some of the addresses given may have changed since the date of publication, as may the opening times of certain sites or museums.

**Maps and plans** – For ease of reading, the sights indicated on the maps and plans are shown in English (when a translation exists), whereas landscape features (rivers, bays, mountains, etc.) are given in the local language.

The symbol ■ indicates possible overnight stops on the itineraries suggested in the text.

Every effort has been made to provide accurate information in this guide. However, discrepancies in the spellings of various place and proper names may occur, owing to the difficulties inherent in transcribing from the Greek to the Latin alphabet, and to the linguistic dichotomy that exists within the country itself.

Michelin Travel Publications
Published in 2001

# ◄NE⊙S►

N ew – In the NEOS guides emphasis is placed on the discovery and enjoyment of a new destination through meeting the people, tasting the food and absorbing the exotic atmosphere. In addition to recommendations on which sights to see, we give details on the most suitable places to stay and eat, on what to look out for in traditional markets and where to go in search of the hidden character of the region, its crafts and its dancing rhythms. For those keen to explore places on foot, we provide guidelines and useful addresses in order to help organise walks to suit all tastes.

E xpert – The NEOS guides are written by people who have travelled in the country and researched the sites before recommending them by the allocation of stars. Accommodation and restaurants are similarly recommended by a 🏠 on the grounds of quality and value for money. Cartographers have drawn easy-to-use maps with clearly marked itineraries, as well as detailed plans of towns, archaeological sites and large museums.

⊙ pen to all cultures, the NEOS guides provide an insight into the daily lives of the local people. In a world that is becoming ever more accessible, it is vital that religious practices, regional etiquette, traditional customs and languages be understood and respected by all travellers. Equipped with this knowledge, visitors can seek to share and enjoy with confidence the best of the local cuisine, musical harmonies and the skills involved in the production of arts and crafts.

S ensitive to the atmosphere and heritage of a foreign land, the NEOS guides encourage travellers to see, hear, smell and feel a country, through words and images. Take inspiration from the enthusiasm of our experienced travel writers and make this a journey full of discovery and enchantment.

## Practical information

B. Pérousse/MICHELIN

# GREECE

**Official name:** Hellenic Republic
**Area:** 131 944km$^2$
**Population:** 10.6 million
**Capital:** Athens (Athína)
**Currency:** euro (formerly drachma)

# Setting the scene

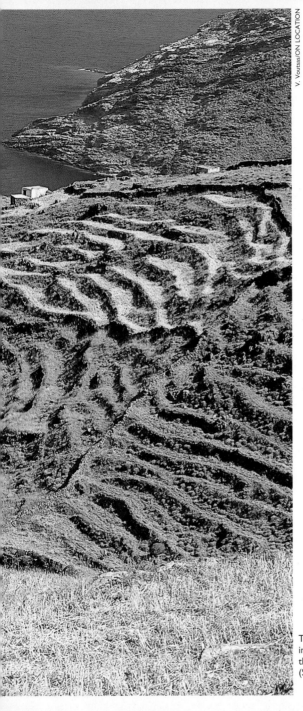

Terraces carved
into the hillsides:
the Greek islands
(Sérifos)

# BETWEEN MOUNTAIN AND SEA

With a surface area of nearly 132 000km², Greece is a small country, a little over half the size of the United Kingdom. However, its exceptional geographical location in the heart of the Mediterranean Sea, its hospitable climate and historical reputation make it one of the top destinations for holidaymakers, drawing archaeology enthusiasts and sun-seekers alike. The jagged contours of Greece form the southern extremity of the great Balkan Peninsula with a particularly fragmented relief. If you look at a map of Greece, you will immediately be struck by the fact that there are mountains everywhere, covering almost 80% of the country and even extending to the islands. The mountains are mostly part of the **Dinaric Alps**, a range which rises far to the north, then crosses Croatia, Bosnia and Herzegovina, Montenegro and Albania. However, although many of the summits in Greece exceed 2 000m, the legendary **Mt Olympus**, the highest of them all, peaks at only 2 917m. On the other hand, some massifs do stand out on account of abrupt changes of level and dramatically steep slopes. Consequently, very little room remains for the rare **plains** in Greece, which are to be found mainly in the north (Thessaly, Thrace and Macedonia). But although the mountains stand proudly for all to admire, it is the sea which seems to cast an irresistible spell upon visitors, who are drawn to it as if by the call of the Sirens. We are referring here, of course, to the **Aegean Sea**. For, despite the extensive western coastlines facing the Ionian Sea and the Sea of Crete in the middle of the Mediterranean, when the Greeks talk of the sea, they are almost invariably thinking of the Aegean and its countless islands. Even the country's loss of the territories in Asia Minor did little to undermine the feeling that the sea is Greek to the core, since all of the islands bordering the Turkish coast except for two were annexed by Greece over a century ago.

## A land in constant movement

The rather unusual landscape of Greece can be explained by two great tectonic phenomena. First of all, at the beginning of the Tertiary Period, a movement of the earth's crust gave birth to the **eastern Hellenidic ranges**. This structural mass of limestone with its regular folds forms the spine of Greece, with the peaks of the **Epirus**, **Pindus**, and **Peloponnese** ranges and the **mountain ridge of Crete** running from north to south. Erosion then set to work, carving out a karstic landscape sprinkled with caves, plateaux and inland basins, such as peaceful Arcadia in the heart of the Peloponnese. The history of eastern Greece and the Aegean Islands (except for Crete) is somewhat different: they are connected to an ancient primary substratum which fragmented, causing both **subsidence**, allowing the Aegean Sea to flood in, and **upthrusts**, of which the most striking remains are Mt Olympus in the north of Thessaly, **Pelion**, in the south-east of the same region, and above all the **Aegean Islands**.

As for the great arc of the Hellenic islands, its curvature can be attributed to the African plate moving under the European plate: the friction between these two titans is the cause of the **earthquakes** and **volcanic activity** which have been going on in the Aegean since time immemorial, in particular around the island of Santoríni, home of the legend of Atlantis (*see page 309*).

## The heart of Greece

Like a giant four-fingered hand, the **Peloponnese Peninsula** marks the southern tip of mainland Greece, a strange appendage linked to Attica by the Isthmus of Corinth and separated from the north by the narrow gulf of the same name. This peninsula became an island upon the construction of the **Corinth Canal** (1882-93), a two-millennia-old project which was finally completed at the end of the 19C. The Peloponnese, where some of the most famous ancient sites are to be found, is an extremely mountainous area with three peninsulas extending from its southern end.

Backed by farmland, most of its large towns stand near the coast on the plains of **Elis** to the west, **Achaia** and **Corinthía** to the north, **Messinía** and **Lakonía** to the south, and **Argolis** to the east. The only exception to this rule is the town of Trípoli, which is set in the heart of the pasturelands of **Arcadia**.

Further south, the rugged **Taíyetos** mountain range culminates in the **Máni** Peninsula, an arid landscape dotted with astonishing villages of tall square towers. The population in these villages is dwindling, and indeed some have been completely abandoned, because, despite the region's attractiveness to tourists, it provides a difficult living environment.

To the north of the Peloponnese lies **central Greece**, the heart of the country, which stretches down into the famous **Attica** Peninsula, forever dominated by the imposing city of Athens. Bounded by the peaks of **Mt Parnes**, **Mt Pentelikon** and **Mt Hymettus**, the vast urban centre of Athens, which has been the capital city since 1834, today boasts a population of over 3 million, almost one third of the country's total population.

Running parallel to the coastline of Attica and Boeotia is the island of **Euboea**, separated from the mainland by a narrow channel. This very mountainous island stretches out in a long ridge with sheer eastern slopes that offer no natural harbour on the Aegean. The island compensates for this handicap by turning more towards the mainland and making the most of its proximity to the capital.

The two vast and fertile plains of **Boeotia**, watered by the Kifisós and Asopós rivers, extend to the north of Attica. It was from their wealth that the ancient city of Thebes drew its strength to become the main city of the Boeotian League. Today, however, this old rival of Sparta and Athens is no more than a small commercial town of no great importance.

To the west, the mountains once again stake their claim, marking the boundary with **Phocis** and some of the most significant places in Greek mythology, including **Mt Parnassus** (2 457m), which was home to Apollo and his nine Muses. Its slopes are today the privileged domain of hikers and skiers, but also of the countless tourists who come to explore the illustrious oracular shrine at **Delphi**, dedicated to Apollo.

### The border country

The peaks of Phocis mark the beginning of the imposing **Pindus Chain** which, from north to south, isolates **Epirus** from the rest of the country. With rainfall levels much higher than the national average, the Pindus range, culminating in **Mt Smólikas** (2 637m), is cloaked in thick coniferous forests which make access to the hinterland difficult. These wooded mountains moreover served for a long time as a natural barrier against the advance of the Ottomans. They are now mainly inhabited by wolves, bears and a whole range of wildlife which, for a number of years now, has been able to flourish undisturbed in the two large **national parks** north of **Ioánnina**. To the west of this wall of rock, a few small plains with market gardens and orchards are scattered around the **Gulf of Árta** (to the south). Further northwards, a thin strip of coast heads up to the Albanian border, leading to the majestic site of **Párga**, with its coves, clear blue water and sandy beaches. Not far from here, on the once marshy **Acherón** estuary, is where the ancients situated the Gates of Hell, from where Charon ferried the souls of the deceased to the realm of Hades (*see page 48*).

### Fertile plains

East of the Pindus, **Thessaly** presents a different aspect of the country. This is Greece's main agricultural region, stretching out in an immense plain, surrounded on all sides by the highest mountains. To the south, Timfristós and Óthris, to the west the impenetrable Pindus chain, to the north, **Mt Olympus**, the country's highest peak and realm of the gods, without forgetting, to the east, Óssa and Pelion, which the Giants of mythology wanted to pile on top of each other to compete with their divine neighbours. Irrigated by the River **Piniós** and its numerous tributaries, the fertile lands of the Thessalian plain are ideal for cultivating cereals and raising cattle. In a curious contrast with the surrounding plain and Pindus massif, the **Metéora**, huge pillars of rock created by erosion, stand like sugar loaves set down there by some eccentric god. Perched on their summits are several Byzantine monasteries dating back to the 14C and 15C.

To the north of Thessaly, between Olympus and Óssa, the narrow Vale of Tempe leads up to **Macedonia**, birthplace of **Philip II** and of his son **Alexander the Great**. Here the mountains give way to alluvial valleys, all of them agricultural basins. Cotton fields extend over the plain, which is fed by the Axiós and Aliákmonas rivers and culminates in a marshy delta.

Further westwards, the foothills of **Mt Vérmio** are covered in vineyards and fruit trees, while to the east lies the great port of **Thessaloníki** (Salonika), the second largest city in Greece. Thessaloníki guards the entrance to **Chalcidice**, a broad three-pronged fork covered in forests, which juts out into the sea. Although the sandy beaches of Sithonía and Kassándra attract many a holidaymaker, the **Mt Athos** Peninsula is a land apart, timeless territory of the biggest monastic city in Europe, which is more than ten centuries old and off-limits to women.

Beyond Thessaloníki, eastern Macedonia's fields of **cotton** and especially tobacco, provide a foretaste of the landscapes of **Thrace**. Fragmented by the southern reaches of the **Rhodope Mountains**, which lie mainly in Bulgaria, the Thracian plains are also bathed in the reddish-brown colour of the **tobacco** leaves which are left to dry on long wooden pikes. Near the border with Turkey, which is separated from Thrace by the River **Évros**, the region takes on an oriental flavour: mosques, bazaars and women in headscarves are to be seen in the villages, and Turkish can already be heard in the streets.

## "Thálassa", or the Greek islands

No fewer than 437 islands, over 150 of which are inhabited, are scattered all around Greece, like pearls that have fallen from a broken necklace, with Crete being lost near the shores of the African continent. And this is without counting the islets, reefs, plain old rocks, or Scylla and Charybdis.

The most Greek sea of all, the **Aegean** boasts the greatest number of these islands, including the sun-drenched archipelago of the **Cyclades**, a favoured travellers' destination. It is a strange sight to see these almost bare and arid islands whose population increases tenfold in summer. Here you will be dazzled by the colours: the clear blue of the sea, the brilliant white of the houses and the ochre of the bare hills.

Just as mountainous, the "twelve islands" of the remote **Dodecanese** are barely any greener. Only **Kos** and prestigious **Rhodes** enjoy a more gentle climate, with sufficiently fertile land and enough rainfall to produce fruit and cereals.

The **north-eastern islands**, even closer to the Turkish coast, are blessed with a more lush vegetation. The island of **Sámos** even has expanses of dense pine forests and the flourishing Mediterranean scrubland known as garrigue.

Heading southwards, **Crete**, the last frontier before Egypt, is the largest and most populated of the Greek islands. Here, the land is fertile, producing an abundance of cereals, fruit, vegetables, vines and olives. But it is also just as mountainous as the rest of Greece, consisting of a long rocky ridge culminating in **Mt Ida** (2 456m), into which erosion has carved numerous basins, cirques and caves steeped in legend.

On the western side, the seven **Ionian Islands** hug the Greek coastline, facing Italy. Long occupied by the Venetians, they reflect a curious but attractive mixture of Hellenic and Latin influences. Although these islands have been hit by earthquakes many times throughout the centuries, they differ from the Aegean Islands in that they have a much higher population, more profuse vegetation and a greater capacity to accommodate tourists.

# A land of sunshine

For the most part, Greece has a **typically Mediterranean climate** with mild wet winters and hot dry summers. There are, however, considerable differences between the regions, mainly due to variations in altitude and latitude. In the north, in **Thrace** and especially in **Macedonia**, the temperatures are more bearable in summer, but the winters can sometimes be extremely harsh, with temperatures dropping to minus 20°C in eastern Macedonia. On the other hand, winter is practically non-existent in the south of the **Peloponnese**, and particularly in **Crete**, which even has some banana groves.

In autumn and winter, the **Ionian Islands** and **western coasts** suffer heavy rainfall which turns into snow on the higher ground, while the east of the country is protected by the mountain chain in the centre. Thus Corfu has an average annual rainfall three times greater than that of Athens.

Bougainvillaea,
flowers of the islands

H. Choimet/MICHELIN

But with the sunshine comes the drought. Raging through most of the country in summer, it often causes fires, fanned by the **meltem**, a hot dry wind which blows across the Aegean from May to September.

## Flora...

With over 6 000 plant varieties, Greece boasts a particularly rich and colourful flora. The mountainsides and the humid lands of Epirus are carpeted in **forests** of Aleppo pines, holm oaks, Greek firs, chestnut and beech trees. Below an altitude of 800m, the forests give way to a varied **maquis**, a scrubland vegetation of lentisk, carob, cistus, myrtle, heather, oleander and juniper, whose combined fragrances infuse the air with a balmy and delicious scent of sunshine.

The arid regions of the south and the Cyclades are mostly covered in a sort of low-lying garrigue called **phrygana**, which is just as fragrant. The omnipresent **olive trees** dominate the Greek countryside, painting the landscapes with their soft grey-green colour, so typical of the Mediterranean countries. In addition to **orange** and **lemon trees, vineyards** can still be found in many places, where grapes are culti-vated both for eating (notably producing the famous currants) and for **wine**.

## ... and fauna

Although perhaps not quite as abundant, the wildlife in Greece does spring a few surprises. A great variety of **birds** live, reproduce or make a stop on their long migra-tory journeys in the marshy deltas and other wetlands here: **geese, ducks** and **cormorants** cross paths with huge **white pelicans** and **Dalmatian pelicans**, and also with **white storks**, whose large nests can often be seen crowning church domes in Thessaly. **Birds of prey** reign over the higher reaches: various vultures and falcons, as well as the extremely rare **greater spotted eagle**, are to be seen gliding through the air before swooping down on their prey.

A few **brown bears**, lynx, wolves and wild cats inhabit the dense forests of Epirus, home of the Víkos-Aoós and Pindus nature reserves. Much greater numbers of **wild boar** roam the forests in search of berries, while various species of **lizard** live among the rocks. In Crete, the odd **chameleon** can be found hiding among the leaves.

**Flora and fauna**

# Five millennia of history

| Dates | Events | Places |
|---|---|---|
| 6000-3000 | Neolithic Period | *Sesklo, Dimini* |
| 3200-1900 | Cycladic civilisation | *Cyclades* |

**The Bronze Age in Crete** (3000-800 BC)

| Dates | Events | Places |
|---|---|---|
| 3000-2000 | Early Minoan. Early Bronze Age | |
| 2000-1570 | Middle Minoan. First palaces. | *Knossós* |
| | Linear A script | |
| 1570-1150 | Late Minoan. Disappearance of the Minoan civilisation on the mainland | |
| 2500-2000 | Early Helladic. Early Bronze Age | |
| 2000-1600 | Middle Helladic. Arrival of the Achaians | |
| 1600-1100 | Late Helladic. Mycenaean civilisation. | *Mycenae, Árgos* |
| | Linear B script | |
| Circa 1100 | Dorian invasions. | |
| | Colonisation of Asia Minor by the Ionian Greeks | |
| 1100-800 | The "Dark Age" | |

**Antiquity** (8C BC – 395 AD)

| Dates | Events | Places |
|---|---|---|
| 8C | Homer writes the *Iliad* and the *Odyssey*. | |
| | *Pólis* civilisation. Greek alphabet | |
| 776 | Creation of the Olympic Games | |
| 735-734 | Beginning of the colonisation of Italy and Sicily | *Náxos, Syracuse* |
| 734-680 | Lelantine War | |
| 680-660 | Colonisation of the Black Sea | *Byzantium* |
| 655-585 | Tyranny of Cypselus and Periander | *Corinth* |
| 595-586 | First Sacred War to gain control of Delphi | |
| 546-510 | Tyranny of Peisistratus and his sons | *Athens* |
| 546 | The Persians led by Cyrus impose their sovereignty upon the Ionian Greeks | |
| 499 | Beginning of the Persian Wars. | |
| | Revolt of the Ionian Greeks | *Sardis* |
| 490 | Battle of Marathon | |
| 480-479 | Battles of Thermopylae, Salamis and Plataea | |
| 449 | Peace of Callias | |
| 460-429 | The "Age of Pericles". | *Athens* |
| | Peloponnesian War. | |
| | Athens is conquered by Sparta | |
| 338 | Battle of Chaeronea. | |
| | Philip II of Macedon conquers Greece | |
| 334-323 | Alexander the Great builds his Empire | |
| 197 | Battle of Cynoscephalae. | |
| | Roman occupation of Greece | |
| 27 BC | Greece becomes the Roman province of Achaia | |
| 330 AD | Constantinople becomes capital of the Empire | |

**The Byzantine Period** (395-1453 AD)

| Dates | Events | Places |
|---|---|---|
| 395 | Beginning of the Byzantine Empire. | |
| | Invasion by Alaric and the Visigoths | |
| 467 | Invasion by Gaiseric and the Vandals | |
| 476 | End of the Roman Empire in the West | |
| 7C | Slav and Avar invasions | |
| 1054 | East-West Schism | |
| 1204 | Capture of Constantinople by the Crusaders. | |
| | Founding of the Latin Empire | |

| 1261 | Michael VIII Paleologus recaptures Constantinople | |
| 1402 | The Mongol Tamerlane defeats the Ottomans | *Ankara* |
| 1453 | Mehmet II and the Ottomans capture Constantinople | |

## The Ottoman Period (1453-1830 AD)

| 1521-66 | Reign of Süleyman the Magnificent | |
| 1522 | Rhodes captured by Süleyman | |
| 1571 | Conquest of Cyprus | |
| 1669 | The Venetians lose their last base in Crete | *Candia (Haniá)* |
| 1770 | Revolt in the Peloponnese. Turkish repression | |
| 1797 | Napoleon takes the Ionian Islands | |
| 1798 | Execution of Rígas Pheraíos | |
| 1821 | Beginning of the revolt in Greece | |
| 1825 | Intervention of the troops of the viceroy of Egypt, Mehmet Ali | |
| 1827 | Egyptian-Turkish fleet defeated by a combined Russian-British-French fleet | *Navarino* |
| 1829 | Signing of the Treaty of Adrianople | |

## Modern times

| 1830 | Treaty of London |
| 1831 | Kapodístrias assassinated |
| 1832-62 | Reign of Otto I of Bavaria |
| 1863-1913 | Reign of George I |
| 1878 | Congress of Berlin on the Balkans |
| 1897 | Defeat of Greek soldiers in Macedonia and Crete |
| 1912 | First Balkan War |
| 1913 | Second Balkan War |
| 1919-20 | Treaties of Neuilly and Sèvres, considerable territorial gains |
| 1922 | Mustafa Kemal's victory over the Greeks. Asia Minor and western Thrace become Turkish. Exodus of the population |
| 1924-35 | Unsuccessful attempt at a republic |
| 1936-41 | Dictatorship of General Metaxás |
| 1941-44 | German, Italian and Bulgarian occupation |
| 1946-49 | Civil War, victory of anti-Communist forces |
| 1947 | Restitution of the Dodecanese Islands |
| 1951 | Greece joins NATO |
| 1967-74 | Colonels' junta |
| 1974 | Turkish invasion of Cyprus |
| 1981 | Greece joins the EEC |
| 1992-94 | Crisis with the new Republic of Macedonia |
| 1995 | Kostis Stephanopoulos, ex-member of Karamanlís' party, elected President |
| 1997 | Election of the Socialist Kóstas Simítis, representative of the PASOK movement |
| February 2000 | Re-election of the Conservative Kostis Stephanopoulos by the Chamber of Deputies |
| April 2000 | Re-election of the Socialist Kóstas Simítis by popular vote |
| 1 January 2001 | Greece enters the European Monetary Union |

Five millennia of history

# THE CRADLE OF EUROPE

Like Egypt and a handful of other countries, Greece has the distinction of being profoundly marked by one period in its history. The exceptional appeal of Antiquity and the Hellenic civilisation should not, however, be allowed to outshine two millennia of history set in the heart of the Macedonian, Roman, Byzantine and Ottoman empires, which witnessed a succession of legendary characters such as Alexander the Great, Emperor Constantine, and Süleyman the Magnificent of Turkey.

The history of Greece is that of a country which, at the price of stubborn and often heroic resistance, managed to regain its freedom and independence and take a firm foothold in Europe and the modern age.

## The dawn of history
### (5000-1200 BC)

Traces of human life dating back to the Neolithic Period have been found at the sites of Sésklo and Dímini in Thessaly, and the remains of a very ancient settlement from the 5th millennium BC have also been found in the Cyclades. The discovery in Argolis (in the east of the Peloponnese) of 13 000-year-old tools made of obsidian from the island of Mílos, revealed that the islanders, as well as being experienced sailors, entertained relations with the mainland.

### The Cyclades, or a civilisation of idols

At the end of the 4th millennium BC, a veritable civilisation began to flourish in the Cyclades. Traces of its influence have been found as far afield as Portugal and the mouth of the Danube. Originally, the island settlements were built mainly along the coast, but the threat of piracy subsequently encouraged the islanders to take refuge in fortified villages in the higher reaches. Very little remains of these little cities, and it is the necropolises that have yielded the most information to archaeologists. Indeed, these generally mass graves contained a great many objects: crockery, jewellery, statuettes, but above all the famous marble "idols" *(see page 34)* with their very modern forms, which have become the symbol of this original civilisation. Soon, however, the rise of the Minoan civilisation in Crete swept the Cyclades up in its path, and another page of history was turned.

### From labyrinths to fortified cities

It was not until the Bronze Age that two great so-called palace civilisations began to develop. The earliest one, which was discovered in 1900 by **Sir Arthur Evans'** excavations on the site of Knossós, originated in Crete. It was named the **Minoan civilisation** after the legendary King of Crete, **Minos**, who is thought to have lived in the palace of Knossós. The Minoan civilisation really began to make its mark in 2200 BC, when the foundations of the first palaces were laid at Knossós, Phaistos and Mália. Veritable autonomous urban complexes, they contained shrines, shops, craftsmen's workshops and houses. These "palace-cities" contained a very hierarchical society, where the arts flourished and business prospered, with trade relations being established with the Cyclades, Syria, Egypt and the western coast of Asia Minor.

However, for some reason which is still a mystery – perhaps a volcanic eruption on Santoríni, an earthquake or invasions – this brilliant civilisation suddenly disappeared between 1450 and 1375 BC. It was superseded by another palace civilisation, this time developing on mainland Greece, the **Mycenaean civilisation**. Born from the mingling of the local populations with the **Achaians**, a seafaring people who had arrived from the north at the beginning of the 2nd millennium BC, it flourished towards 1600 BC around palatial centres such as Mycenae, Árgos and Tírintha in Argolis, and Pílos in Messinía. This warlike society, discovered by the German archaeologist **Heinrich Schliemann** between 1870 and 1890, constitutes the historical basis of all of the legends linked to the heroic age and the Homeric Trojan War. Upon contact with the Minoan civilisation, it gained **syllabic script** (known as Linear B), derived from Cretan script (Linear A), which the British architect **Michael Ventris** deciphered in 1952.

However, around 1200 BC, most of the palace-cities were destroyed, and the Mycenaean world in turn disappeared, for reasons which also remain unclear. Some speak of internal conflicts, caused purely by the bellicose nature of the Mycenaean people; others prefer the theory of an external cause, a new wave of invasions by an Indo-European people, the **Dorians**. Legend has it that they caused the Ionians of Attica and the island of Euboea to flee to the western coast of Asia Minor where they founded the **first Ionian cities**. Whatever the real reason, the fall of the Mycenaean civilisation marks a major turning point in the history of Greece. Not only were the main sites abandoned, but their script also disappeared, not to come to light again until three centuries later with the Phoenicians. However, after slowly maturing during this **Dark Age** (12C-9C BC), a new and totally transformed Greek society was to see the light of day in the 8C BC.

## Antiquity, or the Greece of legend
### (8C BC-4C AD)

### The golden age of the "pólis"

Gradually, a new social organisation emerged, the *pólis*, a **city state** consisting of an urban centre and the surrounding farmland. The *pólis* inhabitants formed a rigidly structured civic community harking back to distant ancestors, often mythical founders of the city. With the abandonment of the palaces, the real power subsequently passed to the aristocracy (*basileís*) in a large majority of cases, and the citizens regularly gathered together for ceremonies of their shared cults, in particular to worship the **god of the pólis**.

Bearing witness to its power, the *pólis* began to spread abroad: from the late 8C to the early 6C BC, Chalcis, Corinth, Megara, Miletus and many other cities set up **colonies** in Sicily (Syracuse, Catania), in southern Italy (Cumae, Tarentum) and in the south of

The frescoes of Firá (Santoríni), an exceptional portrait of life in the Cyclades around 1500 BC

Kraftt/J&V/HOA QUI

19

Gaul (Alalia in Corsica, Massalia / Marseille), up to the periphery of the Propontis (Byzantium) and the Black Sea, via the islands and promontories of Thrace and Macedonia.

## Organised warfare

Judging by the success of the great pan-Hellenic sanctuaries of Olympia, Delos and Delphi, one may be forgiven for thinking that perfect harmony reigned between the cities. But this was far from the truth; conflicts were rife. However, the face of war was changing: at the end of the 8C BC, the Lelantine War between Chalcis and Eretria was probably the last Homeric-type war, ie a ritualised combat where the use of arrows was not allowed and during which the champions fell one by one. In the 7C BC, a veritable military formation, the **hoplite phalanx**, appeared and continued to be used until the 2C BC. It consisted of several closed ranks of soldiers, the *hoplites*, advancing together, each equipped with greaves, breastplate and helmet made of bronze, a heavy shield of wood also set in bronze, a spear and short sword.

## From tyranny to democracy

**Sparta** was the hoplite city par excellence. With its power extending over the whole of the Peloponnese, its constitution spread far and wide, sweeping away in its path the **tyrants** who had been dominating the surrounding cities from the mid-7C BC. These despots (Cypselus in Corinth, **Peisistratus** and his sons in Athens, Orthagoras and Cleisthenes in Sicyon) took advantage of popular discontent to seize power unlawfully from the ruling aristocracy. Although they were often overthrown after one or two generations on account of their authoritarianism, the success of these tyrants highlighted the necessity for **democratic reform**. After the first measures taken by the legislator Solon early in the 6C BC, it was Cleisthenes, in 508 BC, and **Pericles**, around 450 BC, who eventually ensured the rule of democracy in Athens. This democracy was, however, very relative, concerning only 8% of the citizens.

## The Persian Wars

Since 546 BC, the Persians had been imposing their sovereignty over the Greek cities of Ionia in Asia Minor. In 499 BC, at the instigation of Aristagoras, the tyrant of Miletus, these cities revolted and burnt down Sardis, with the aid of Athens and Eretria. The revolt ended in 494 BC following a naval defeat and the sacking of Miletus. Three years later, the Persian **Darius** decided to take revenge, demanding earth and water from the Greeks as a symbol of submission. Of the big cities, only Athens and Sparta – which were allies for a time – refused to accept the Persian claims and, in 490 BC, Darius suffered a bitter defeat at the hands of the Athenians on the now famous Marathon plain.

In 480 BC, it was Sparta's turn to provide the heroes. This time it was **Xerxes**, the great new King of Persia, who was planning to subjugate the Greeks. With a con-

---

### Inter-city games

Created in 776 BC, the Olympic Games gave the city states the opportunity to measure each other's strength peacefully, through sports. In the stadium of Olympia, in the palestra or gymnasium, the winners of running races, pentathlons, wrestling sports and chariot races (quadriga) were awarded prizes and honours, their victories reflecting glory onto their "pólis". This highly political prestige, however, did not come without danger. On one notable occasion, the sons of Peisistratus, taking offence at the third quadriga victory of Cimon of Athens (528 BC), and in fear of losing their power, did not hesitate to have him assassinated.

---

### The battle of the champions

Around 546 BC a rather curious battle was fought between Sparta and Árgos, a combination of old-style – or Homeric – war and hoplite combat. In the long conflict between the two cities, 300 Spartans confronted 300 Argives. When the fighting was over, one single Spartan survivor found himself facing two Argives, who proclaimed victory and promptly fled... causing the Spartans to claim that victory was in fact theirs.

siderable army and a fleet of over 600 ships, he won a crushing victory over the Spartans at **Thermopylae**. But the heroism of **Leonidas** and his 300 men, who sacrificed their lives to slow the advance of the Persians, has gone down in history. Shortly afterwards, the great sea battle of **Salamis** dashed Xerxes' hopes completely. The Persian ships were overwhelmed by the Greek fleet under the command of the skilful Athenian strategist, **Themistocles**. This victory was confirmed on land the following year at the battle of **Plataea**.

## The Classical Period

It was only the alliance between Sparta and Athens which enabled Xerxes' army to be vanquished.

### The first Marathon

After landing at Eretria, the Persian army was preparing to go into battle on the Marathon plain. Warned by a trained runner, Pheidippides, who ran over 200km in 36hr (almost five times the distance of a modern marathon), the Spartans proffered the excuse of a religious festival for arriving when the battle was over. The 10 000 Athenians under the command of Miltiades therefore had to do without the Spartans, but with the help of 1 000 Plataeans, they managed to rout the enemy, forcing them to flee back to their ships. The Persians lost over 6 000 men, the Athenians only 192. This victory was the pride of Athens for generations to come, and, for a long time, there was considered to be no greater honour than to have been part of it.

However, this alliance was against nature. In 478 BC, Sparta had preferred to relinquish command of the fleet to the Athenians rather than share it. So in order to complete the liberation of the entire territory of Greece, Athens created the **Delian League**, which, in 466 BC, won the Battle of the Eurymedon before signing the **Peace of Callias** in 449 BC with Persia. Athenian hegemony was at its peak: at the head of an extremely powerful fleet, the city controlled the Aegean Sea and trade, and asserted its domination over the allied cities. After being sacked by the Persians in 480 BC, Athens had rebuilt its fortifications, which were linked to the port of Piraeus by two "Long Walls" of protection. Ambitious work was begun on the Acropolis, and with the enlightened cultural politics of **Pericles** (460-429 BC), Athens became the centre of Greece: this was the age of Sophocles, Euripides, the Sophists and **Socrates**.

This domination, however, riled and angered the other Greek cities which valued their freedom, particularly Athens' great rival, Sparta. Conflict was inevitable and came in 431 BC, when Sparta leapt to the defence of Corinth, which had taken a stand against Athens. Alliances were formed and soon the whole of Greece was in the grip of the Peloponnesian War. Athens managed to stand firm until the Peace of Nicias (421 BC), despite a terrible plague which killed almost one third of the city's population. Peace was, however, short-lived, and the failure of the expedition against Sicily (415-413 BC), undertaken on the advice of **Alcibiades**, marked a reversal of fortune from which Athens was never to recover. Despite a few resounding victories over the following years, the Athenian fleet suffered a disastrous defeat at the hands of the Spartan general, **Lysander**, in 405 BC. In 404 BC, Athens was forced to capitulate.

After a short period of calm, hostilities resumed and the next half-century witnessed successive attempts by Sparta, Athens and Thebes to gain hegemony over Greece. Signalling a serious decline in nationalism, these cities didn't hesitate to call on Persia to achieve their aims. The previously defeated Persia was quick to take advantage of the situation to seek revenge, imposing its authority when the peace treaties were signed.

### Sparta, the anti-Athens

A Dorian city, proud of its constitution which saved it from tyranny, Sparta was the archetypal hoplite State. The originality of the Spartan system lay in its dual monarchy: two kings from two families both claiming to be descendants of Heracles, with their power being supervised and counterbalanced by five ephors elected for one year. With its sights set mainly on war, the city also became a refuge for all the oligarchs of Greece.

## Alcibiades: portrait of an opportunist

Born into a great Athenian family, raised by Pericles, and a friend of Socrates, Alcibiades was handsome, rich, eloquent and intelligent. His flamboyance made him a magnet to women and men alike, he spent lavishly, and dazzled all and sundry with the success of his racing stables. A demagogue, he flattered the pride of the Athenians and secured the expedition against Sicily. However, his escapades also earned him many enemies. Accused of irreverence to the gods, he fled to Sparta where he did not hesitate to betray his birthplace by revealing Athens' weak points and sealing an alliance with Persia. However, kept at arm's length by the Spartans, Alcibiades betrayed them in turn, finally managing by way of intrigue, disavowals and clever speeches to return to Athens as a saviour. But not for long. He was stripped of all credit following the defeat of the Athenian fleet at the Battle of Notium (406 BC). He was removed from office, and his judicious advice to proceed with caution before the battle of 405 BC against Lysander was greeted with contempt. Following Athens' defeat, he took refuge in Phrygia, where the Spartans had him assassinated.

## Victorious – but Macedonian – Hellenism

Ironically, the new outburst of Hellenism in the face of Persian influence came from a region that the Greeks considered to be practically barbaric. But Macedonia had become united very early on, and had since then been unfailingly philhellenic. Under the command of **Philip II** (359-336 BC), it took the Macedonian army less than 20 years to conquer Greece, taking advantage of the division between the cities and the endless indecision of Athens. When resistance was finally organised, the allies were easily overcome by the Macedonian phalanxes equipped with sarissas (5 to 7m-long spears) at the Battle of Chaeronea in 338 BC. Victorious, Philip founded the **League of Corinth** in order to guarantee the freedom of the Greek cities and to fight Persia.

When Philip was assassinated in 336 BC, his son **Alexander III the Great** pursued his dream and managed to achieve the tremendous conquest of the Persian Empire (334-323 BC). However, on his death in 323 BC, the young Macedonian Empire was already breaking up and being divided between his generals – including the founder of the **Seleucid** dynasty – and Greece found itself placed under the protectorate of the kings of Macedonia. Its attempts to regain its freedom were unsuccessful in spite of the recurrent conflicts between Alexander's successors.

## A Roman province

After subjugating the Aetolians in 217 BC, Philip V sought to take control of the Adriatic and decided to support **Hannibal** in his campaign against Rome. Unfortunately, the Carthaginian was defeated, and the Romans waged two successive campaigns in Greece, culminating in their victory at **Cynoscephalae** in 197 BC. The following year, the consul, Flaminius, undertook to guarantee the freedom of the Greek cities. However, unsuccessful attacks led by the Seleucid King Antiochus III (192 BC), then the Macedonian King Perseus (168 BC), and in particular a rebellion by the Achaean League (headed by Corinth and severely quelled in 146 BC), tolled the knell of any hopes of independence.

Thereafter, the fate of Greece was inextricably linked to that of Rome. After claiming victory over Antony and Cleopatra at **Actium** (31 BC), Augustus annexed all of the Hellenic lands and turned Greece into the Roman **Province of Achaia** (27 BC). Greek civilisation nevertheless retained a great deal of prestige in the eyes of the Romans: the Romans demonstrated greater tolerance here in matters of both politics and religion than elsewhere in the Empire. Cities such as Ephesus, Alexandria and Athens were thus able to perpetuate the intellectual and cultural aura of Hellenism.

# Byzantine Greece (395-1453 AD)

From the 3C AD, the Roman Empire suffered successive waves of barbarian invasions, which were to destroy its unity. The Eastern Empire was under particular threat and required the almost permanent presence of the emperor at the frontier (the **limes**).

A first step towards division was taken in 325, when Constantine ordered a city to be founded on the walls of what had formerly been Byzantium. This city was named after him – **Constantinople** – and he proclaimed it the new capital of the Empire (330). The Empire was effectively divided in 395 upon the death of Theodosius I, who shared the territory between his two sons, Honorius and Arcadius. And so Arcadius inherited control of the Eastern Empire, which at that time included the Balkans, Asia Minor, Syria, Palestine, northern Mesopotamia and Egypt in addition to Greece.

## Alaric, or the Visigoth tornado
In an attempt to neutralise Alaric, Emperor Theodosius' successor, Arcadius, appointed him "master of the soldiers" in Illyricum and gave him Epirus. But this was all in vain: the Visigoth seized the opportunity to invade Italy and sow panic throughout the West (401-402). Driven back a first time by General Stilicho, he returned to Italy and sacked Rome in 410 but died before being able to invade Sicily.

## A land under constant threat
In Greece at this time, the traces of the sea expeditions of the Goths, Heruli and Scythians in the second half of the 3C had begun to fade away, and only the terrible **earthquake** of 21 July 365 disturbed a period of relative peace that was to last for over a century. Under the reign of Theodosius, **Christianity** became the State religion, pagan cults were banned and the Olympic Games abolished. Despite the preaching of St Paul, paganism remained very much alive in Greece. This resistance to State Christianity was perhaps not unrelated to the passivity of the imperial troops when Alaric's **Visigoths** invaded Macedonia, then Thessaly and Achaia in 395.

Thereafter followed an increasing number of invasions. Arriving from Africa, the **Vandals**, led by Gaiseric, pillaged Rome then ravaged Greece (467) but did not stay for long. Conversely, the successive and occasionally simultaneous invasions of the **Slavs and Avars**, beginning in the late 6C, brought about extensive and long-lasting demographic change. On the one hand, a considerable number of Greeks were forced to flee the Peloponnese, and on the other, a steadily increasing number of Slavs were settling all over Greece, to such an extent that Byzantium had to resort to force to impose its authority over the region (783 and 805).

A cause for even greater concern, while the **Muslims** occupied Crete in the 9C and 10C, mainland Greece was facing invasions by the **Bulgars** led by Simeon and Samuel (late 10C), as well as the threat of the **Normans** of Sicily (late 11C). In the face of these regular challenges to its existence, the Byzantine Empire buckled but did not break. At least not under the blows of a known enemy. In one of the paradoxes of history, it was to yield to the Christians who had come from the West to lend assistance against the Turks.

## The betrayal of the Crusaders
At the bidding of the French Pope, Urban II (1095), a tremendous spiritual impetus drove Western Christianity towards Jerusalem, which had been in Muslim hands since the 7C. The Byzantine emperors had indeed requested this intervention in the hopes of obtaining a reserve of men placed under their orders to help them reclaim

Byzantium, a Christian Empire (fresco from Mt Athos)

B. Kaufmann/MICHELIN

land which was historically theirs. However, unaware of these reasons, the European noblemen who had embarked on the Crusade kept all of the land taken from the Seljuq Turks for themselves, organising it according to the feudal system. **Latin States** began to flourish: the Kingdom of Jerusalem, the County of Edessa, the County of Tripoli and the Principality of Antioch, whose existence was to further poison relations between Byzantines and Westerners, already considerably damaged by the religious issues which had led to the Schism of 1054.

Moreover, in Constantinople the growing number of Latin merchants, Venetians in particular, was stirring up jealousy and rancour, eventually leading to a sinister pogrom in 1182. Although Greece was little affected by the first three Crusades, it was directly involved in the fourth (1202-04), a *Chronicle* of which was written shortly afterwards by the marshal of Champagne, **Geoffroi de Villehardouin**. This Crusade was, in fact, to cause the fall of the Byzantine Empire. The original aim of the Crusaders was to attack the Muslim Empire in Egypt. However, when the knights were unable to pay for the Venetian ships which were to ferry them across the Mediterranean, they paid off their debt by carrying out the wishes of the Doge of Venice. And so, ignoring the bans and excommunications of Pope Innocent III, the Crusaders headed for Constantinople on the pretext of restoring the overthrown emperor, Isaac Angelus, and his son, Alexius IV, to the throne. After a first intervention in the capital which went smoothly, a second one, caused by friction with the Byzantine aristocracy, ended in the mass pillaging of the city and the creation of the **Latin Empire** in 1204.

## The Franks in Greece

In truth, the Latin Empire of Constantinople pales in comparison with its predecessor. The unity which had been the strength of the Byzantine Empire was unable to withstand the diverging ambitions and infighting among the Crusaders. When the spoils were shared out, the Venetians took half of the capital, most of the Aegean Islands and a large number of strongholds in mainland Greece. Although **Baldwin of Flanders** could pride himself on being the first emperor of the Latin Empire, he had direct control only in the city of Constantinople and the surrounding regions, Thrace and Asia Minor. Elsewhere, he had to allow the main Crusade leaders to create their fiefs, following the purest feudal tradition. Boniface of Montferrat, who had led the Crusade, inherited the Kingdom of Thessaloníki. The Peloponnese, renamed **Principality of Morea** (or of Achaia), fell to Guillaume de Champlitte from Champagne. Through various vassals, the principality itself controlled a certain number of fiefs, including the powerful Duchy of Athens.

The Latin conquest of 1204 split the Byzantine Empire into four States: the Latin Empire of the East, the Byzantine Empires of Nicaea and Trebizond and, in Greece, the Byzantine Despotate of Epirus. The struggle between the Latins and the Byzantines thus commenced, barely delayed by a Bulgar invasion in Thrace. In 1224, the Byzantine Despotate of Epirus took possession of the Kingdom of Thessaloníki. At this time, the Franks were mainly concentrated in the Principality of Morea. Having fallen into the hands of the **Villehardouin** family, Morea gradually became suffused with French influence. In 1236, Geoffroi II Villehardouin saved the Latin emperor, Baldwin II, who was under siege in Constantinople, thereby asserting the strength of his principality. However, his successor, Guillaume de Villehardouin, bowed down before the *basileus* of Nicaea, the emperor **Michael VIII Paleologus**, thus sealing the fate of Constantinople (1261).

## Death of an empire

The fall of the capital and the restoration of the Byzantine Empire did not immediately rid Greece of the Latins. Guillaume de Villehardouin was set free shortly after the siege in exchange for four important fortresses in the Peloponnese, including the one at **Mistra**, which became the bridgehead of the Byzantine re-conquest in Morea. By accepting these conditions, however, Guillaume himself opened the floodgates to

## A chivalrous defeat

A rather curious family matter prefaced the fall of the Latin Empire. In 1259, the despot of Epirus, Michael Angelus Ducas and the basileus of Nicaea, Michael VIII Paleologus, both Byzantine, were fighting over Macedonia. After obtaining the aid of his son-in-law, Guillaume de Villehardouin, the despot of Epirus suddenly refused to do battle, leaving the Latins of Morea to fight alone for something that did not concern them. Although the Frankish knights knew that they were powerless against their much stronger adversary, they refused with dignity to abandon their foot soldiers. This was a chivalrous act, but with grave consequences: the absence of these men, defeated and taken captive, was decisive in the capture of Constantinople.

the evil that was to sweep through his fief. He tried to stem the tide by accepting the suzerainty of Charles I of Anjou, King of Sicily and brother of St Louis, but neither Anjou nor, subsequently, Navarre were able to prevent Byzantium from gradually subjugating the entire principality (1428).

Nevertheless, the restored Byzantine Empire was but a shadow of its former self. It was unable to put up any resistance to the invasion of Thessaly and Epirus by the **Serbian Empire** under Stefan IX Dusan (1331-55). Then, after defeating the Serbs at the Battle of Kosovo Polje in 1389, the **Osmanli Turks** proved even more dangerous. Arriving from Bithynia in Asia Minor, where they were rapidly shaking off Seljuq domination, they advanced into Europe, taking possession of Thessaly, pillaging Morea (1394) and steadily marching on towards Constantinople. Their surprise defeat at the hands of the Mongols under the command of **Tamerlane** in Ankara in 1402 was but a temporary setback. The Byzantine emperors made repeated appeals to the West, but to no avail. On 29 May 1453, Constantinople fell to the Ottomans under Sultan **Mehmet II** (1451-81). One by one, the last Latin and Byzantine strongholds crumbled. Only the Venetians put up any real resistance and delayed the advance of the Ottomans, but despite their efforts, Rhodes and the Dodecanese Islands were conquered in 1522, Chios in 1566 and Cyprus in 1571. Crete, the Venetians' last bastion in Greece, capitulated in turn in 1669.

## Ottoman Greece
### (1453-1830)

### Consensual occupation

Under Ottoman occupation, the Greek Christians, like all of the non-Muslim communities (*rayás*), were tolerated but considered inferior. They took particular exception not only to being more heavily taxed than the Muslims, but also to the fact that young Christians were being arbitrarily recruited to serve in the sultan's personal guard, the Janissaries.

21 December 1522:
Süleyman I at the walls of Rhodes
(16C manuscript, Bibliothèque
Nationale de Paris)

AKG Paris

However, although the intellectual elites had fled to Italy en masse upon the announcement of the fall of Constantinople, the weight of Ottoman rule on the Greek population should not be exaggerated. By comparison with the authoritarian and oppressive government of the Venetians in the Aegean Islands and in Crete, the Ottoman sultan showed great indulgence towards the non-Muslim population, leaving local administration up to the Greeks and demonstrating a broad

### The Janissaries, Christian soldiers

Originally made up of prisoners of war, this elite corps later gleaned its recruits from the Empire's Christian communities, converting children to Islam and training them in the arts of war. Although the method of recruitment was distressing, being chosen to become a future Janissary was often the only way for a large part of the Christian community to forge a career in the Ottoman administration. In the 17C, commissions in the Janissary corps (from the Turkish "yeni çeri", meaning "new troop") became hereditary, and corruption became rife as the soldiers began to act in their own interests. Extremely close to the seat of power, they eventually came to be a threat to the sultan, who ordered the corps to be totally disbanded in 1826 by having all of its members killed.

**religious tolerance**. Thus, far from banning the Orthodox clergy, the sultan confirmed the prerogatives of the Patriarch of Constantinople and even made him the representative of all the Christians in the Ottoman Empire and the guarantor of their loyalty (see also the chapter on "Religion", page 67). The attitude of the Church was certainly rather ambiguous: although it was thanks to the Church that Greek language and culture were able to survive, the patriarchs were constantly encouraging the faithful to consider the Ottomans as their protectors and condemning any movement of insubordination.

### The slow awakening of nationalism

Up until the 17C, the "Sublime Porte" (government of the Ottoman Empire) experienced a strong period of expansion, marked by the reign of **Süleyman the Magnificent** (1521-66). However, the subsequent decline of the Empire coincided with the emergence of a revival of Greek nationalism. Resistance to the Turkish occupation began with the growing success of the **klephts**, bands of robbers from the mountains who harassed the Ottomans. Indeed, the *armatoles*, Greek militiamen trained by the Turks to keep the klephts under control, often ended up joining forces with those whom they were supposed to be fighting!

However, there was to be no widespread national uprising in Greece until the 18C. On the contrary, taking advantage of the Muslims' reversal of fortune, some Greeks, mainly from the Phanar district in Constantinople (Istanbul), gradually infiltrated the wheels of the Empire, managing to obtain key positions in the sultan's entourage. These **Phanariotes** first of all helped themselves to the highest ecclesiastical magistratures and to an increasing part of the trade carried out by the Sublime Porte. Their extensive knowledge of European affairs soon led them to take charge of the diplomatic affairs of the Ottoman Empire and to secure certain offices, such as those of dragoman (official interpreter) of the Sublime Porte, dragoman of the fleet, or governor of the provinces of Moldavia and Walachia.

However, in spite of this infiltration of the Ottoman institutions, the idea of a revolution began to gain ground and came to fruition in 1770 when a revolt spread through the Peloponnese, emboldened by the promise of support from Catherine II of Russia. However, at the first sign of a setback, the small Russian fleet quickly turned tail, abandoning the Greeks to Turkish repression. But it did not stop there: the quest for freedom was encouraged by the rapid decline of the Ottoman Empire and also by the propagation of ideas from the French Revolution, and by the secession of the pasha of Epirus, Ali Pasha Tepelenë. In 1797, **Napoleon** took possession of the Ionian Islands. After falling into the hands of the Russians (1799-1800), then back to the French (1807-14) and lastly occupied by the British (1814-64), these islands embodied a refuge and hope for all of the Greek revolutionaries.

AKG Paris

The War of Independence: a philhellene camp
(painting by von Heideck, 1835, Karlsruhe)

In the early 19C, the elites who were fighting for the cause of independence tried to gain support in European circles. In Vienna, the poet **Rígas Pheraíos** thus founded a secret society (hetaireia) militating for an independent and multi-racial Greece. His activism, however, unsettled the Austrian authorities, who arrested him and handed him over to the Turks. His execution in 1798 turned him into a martyr and soon other secret societies were also springing up around Europe, in Paris, Athens and particularly in Odessa.

### The road to independence

Fomented with the support of Russia under **Alexander I**, on the initiative of his close Greek advisors, Alexander Ypsiliántis and Ioánnis Kapodístrias – also eminent members of the hetaireia of Odessa – the rebellion took shape in Moldavia and Walachia but rapidly failed (1821). But that was not the end of it: shock waves from the revolutionary movement spread throughout Greece. The Patriarch of Patras, **Germanós**, signalled the start of the revolt on 25 March 1821. Within a few months, klephts, armatoles and all the opponents of the occupation had driven the Turks out of the Peloponnese, central Greece and most of the Aegean Islands.

After this initial success, internal conflicts caused the revolution to grind to a halt, giving the sultan an opportunity to organise a counter-attack. Despite the intense feeling stirred up in intellectual circles in Europe, especially among the Romantics, the major powers did not intervene, in the name of the principle of the Holy Alliance, which gave priority to the maintenance of the status quo in Europe over becoming involved in national affairs. Only a few took a personal stand in favour of the Greek revolution, among them **Lord Byron**, who died at Missolonghi. In order to quell the rebellion once and for all, Sultan Mahmoud II called upon the viceroy of Egypt, **Mehmet Ali**, for assistance (1825). Led by the viceroy's son, **Ibrahim**, the Turko-Egyptian troops crushed the insurgents in Crete before reaching the mainland, where, after much bloodshed, they took the positions held by the Greeks.

The heroic defence put up by the insurgents, led by **Geórgios Karaïskákis** and **Theódoros Kolokotrónis**, and the massacre of tens of thousands of Christians, finally forced the European governments to react. Russia, Great Britain and France offered to mediate, exhorting the Sultan to grant the Greek territories an autonomous status under Ottoman sovereignty. Mahmoud II could not accept this, but his army was no longer in a position to resist, and the Turko-Egyptian fleet suffered a severe defeat at Navarino Bay (1827). While French troops were landing in the Peloponnese, the Russians were threatening Istanbul, forcing the Ottomans to sign the **Treaty of Adrianople** (1829) which established the autonomy of Greece. Elected president of the Republic in 1827, the authoritarian **Ioánnis Kapodístrias**, however, suffered from his reputation as a Russian agent and from an increasing difference of opinions with the leading citizens. His assassination in 1831 was the prelude to the application of the **Treaty of London**, which officially recognised the independence of Greece and established an absolute monarchy guaranteed by the contracting powers.

# The Greek State

## Greece under the Bavarian Otto I

Greece had gained its independence, but a great deal of frustration remained, so far removed did the new State turn out to be from the aspirations of the revolutionaries. Far from encompassing all the historic lands of Hellenism, the kingdom was limited to the Peloponnese, the south of central Greece and a certain number of islands close to the mainland: in all, barely 800 000 people gathered together in an impoverished, essentially agricultural and war-ravaged State. It is not difficult to understand, therefore, how the great Hellenistic project, the desire to bring all the lands that were historically or ethnically Greek together under one single nation, became the main axiom of Greek claims. The contracting powers had also chosen a Bavarian sovereign. Young **Otto**, who was still a minor when he came to the throne, caused further upset among his subjects by entrusting key positions in the government and army to his Bavarian compatriots. In 1843, a bloodless coup d'état compelled the monarch to promulgate a constitution adopted by the National Assembly. Bringing no major changes, this period of constitutional monarchy was marked in particular by great ministerial instability and the growing discontent of the population. Another coup d'état in October 1862 brought Otto's reign to an end, causing him to go into exile.

## The first successes of Greek irredentism

This time it was Great Britain whose influence was predominantly felt in the choice of the new dynasty of **George I**, youngest son of the King of Denmark, and also in allowing the return of the Ionian Islands. This time, the king no longer had absolute control, and the Government had to be supported by a **Parliament**, elected by universal suffrage. On a national level, the last quarter of the 19C, marked by the personality of the liberal prime minister Kharílaos Trikoúpis, coincided with a period of intense development: population growth, land reform (1871), the cutting of the Isthmus of Corinth by the construction of the **Corinth Canal** (1882-93).

After the **Congress of Berlin** (1878) on the Balkans question, the Ottomans were pressured by the major powers into giving up Thessaly and southern Epirus (1881). The Greeks' nationalist claims, however, remained largely unsatisfied and now had to withstand the territorial ambitions of the Bulgars and Serbs. So when **Crete** rebelled against the Turkish occupation (1897), the Greek authorities didn't hesitate to send in troops to support the rebels and even extended the conflict to Macedonia. But all in vain: in both cases, the Ottomans crushed their opponents, who were saved only by the mediation of Great Britain.

This defeat merely served to exacerbate Greek irredentism. When **Elefthérios Venizélos** of Crete proclaimed the island's unification with Greece (1908), the Government preferred to take no concrete action, despite popular pressure. But the following year, the **Goudi coup**, a rebellion staged by a group of radical officers, forced the King to call on Venizélos to form a government. The latter immediately made clear his determination to unite all Greek lands within one single nation and entered into an alliance with Serbia, Montenegro and Bulgaria to free the Balkans from Ottoman rule. Having emerged victorious from the **First Balkan War** (1912-13), the allied Christian countries argued over the partition of Macedonia at the London Conference. This caused Bulgaria to launch the **Second Balkan War** against Greece and Serbia, but, after suffering a rapid defeat, it was forced to sign the **Treaty of Bucharest** (August 1913). Greece gained a considerable amount of territory from both conflicts: Crete, southern Epirus, southern Macedonia and most of the islands in the Aegean Sea, except for the Dodecanese, which remained under Italian rule.

## A time of disillusionment

The outcome of the First World War allowed Greece to grow even more, satisfying practically all of the nationalists' hopes, despite the fact that Greece had only decided to side with the Allies late in the day. Succeeding his father George I, who had been assassinated in Thessaloníki in 1913, the new king, **Constantine I**, brother-in-law of the German Kaiser Wilhelm II, seemed to favour the Central European powers. Forced to resign by the King on account of his attempts to align with the Allies, the prime minister, Venizélos, formed a counter-government in September 1916 in Thessaloníki, which also served as a base for Allied operations from 1915 to 1918. Meanwhile, French naval fusiliers landed and overcame Constantine, who soon abdicated in favour of his second son Alexander I. Under the **Treaties of Neuilly** (1919) and **Sèvres** (1920), Greece gained western and eastern Thrace, the islands of Imbros and Ténedos, and a large part of the Aegean provinces of Asia Minor around Smyrna (Izmir) came under its administration.

However, Greek irredentism had now reached its limits. When the Turks under the leadership of **Mustafa Kemal** (Atatürk) refused to accept the Treaty of Sèvres, Venizélos decided to invade Anatolia. But the situation at home soon took a dramatic turn: the conflict cost the prime minister his office, and a plebiscite placed Constantine I back on the throne, left vacant following Alexander's sudden death. The Germanophiles' return to power immediately left the country without any support from abroad. Repeated military failures ensued. After two years of fighting, Mustafa Kemal managed to drive the Greeks out of Anatolia, and a second treaty (**Lausanne**, 1923) restored full Turkish sovereignty over all of Asia Minor, eastern Thrace, Smyrna, Trebizond, Erzurum and the Dardanelles. This heralded a mass **exchange of populations** between Turkey and Greece: 1.5 million Greeks from Asia Minor crossed paths with 500 000 Turks from Greece.

## From World War to civil war

The crushing military defeat, the exodus of the Greeks from Turkey and economic difficulties were to cause the successive abdications of Constantine I (October 1922), and of his son George II (December 1923). The **Republic** which was proclaimed in March 1924 was unable to stem the tide of discontent and become firmly established. Wracked by political and financial crises, it disappeared with the more or less tacit consent of the Republicans. And so, in March 1935, the monarchy was restored and George II reclaimed his throne. With his backing, General **Metaxás** set up a dictatorship along the lines of Italian fascism. However, despite the convergences with Mussolini's regime, the territorial ambitions of Il Duce caused Athens to side with the

### Decisive action

It was in Greece that the outcome of the Second World War began to take shape. By inflicting such a crushing and unexpected defeat on the Italian troops, the Greek army humiliated the Italian leader, Mussolini, who was forced to watch the Führer's soldiers come to the aid of his men. But more importantly, in order to come to the aid of the Italians, Hitler had to postpone his Russian campaign, Operation "Barbarossa", until June. This two-month delay may have prevented the Wehrmacht from reaching Moscow before the terrible winter of 1941-42, resulting in Hitler's first failure.

Allies. Although numbering twice as many, the Italian troops suffered a bitter defeat in 1940, forcing Hitler to send his army to their aid. In a blitzkrieg, the Wehrmacht swept through the Balkans and marched into Greece on 6 April 1941. Aided by a British force, the Greeks put up fierce resistance, which even impressed the German high command, but were unable to prevent the invasion or the partition of the country into three occupied zones: Italian, German and Bulgarian.

With the King and government in exile in Cairo, resistance against the occupier back home was organised around two large movements using guerrilla tactics. However, at the end of the war, the increasing friction between the monarchist EDES movement and the Communist EAM movement, which ceased to recognise the legality of the government in exile, turned into civil war (1946-49), the first embodiment of the **Cold War**. With the support of Yugoslavia and the USSR, the Communists, led by **General Márkos**, began to gain ground, but defeat became inevitable when the United States came to the aid of the lawful government and relations were broken off between Tito and Stalin.

### Democracy lost...
Under **Paul I** (1947-64), Greece, which had been given the Dodecanese Islands in 1947 and joined NATO in 1951, was in theory governed by moderate right-wing governments, but was in reality controlled by parallel extreme right-wing forces. When **Geórgios Papandréou**, who came to power in 1963 at the head of the Centre Union, proposed democratic reforms, he struck fear into these hidden forces and was rapidly asked to resign by the young King Constantine II (1965). This heralded a period of political crisis, resulting in the coup d'état of 21 April 1967 and the beginning of the **colonels' junta**. After a failed counter-coup attempt, Constantine II was forced to take exile in Rome. The military junta, led by Colonel **Papadópoulos**, set up an authoritarian and repressive government which alienated the people and attracted international disapproval, with the exception of the United States. In response to popular discontent and student demonstrations (1972-73), the regime applied martial law and created special courts.

### ...and found
Neither the proclamation of the Republic (July 1973) nor the replacement of Colonel Papadópoulos by General Ghizíkis could shake off this political deadlock. The Cyprus question was to serve as an epilogue to the colonels' junta. The junta's failed attempt to assassinate the President of Cyprus and the reaction of the Turks, who invaded 40% of the north of the island, led Ghizíkis to hand government over to the former right-wing prime minister, **Karamanlís** (July 1974). Shortly afterwards, a referendum confirmed the monarchy's replacement by the Republic, and a new constitution was promulgated in 1975. In 1981, the socialist party, **PASOK** (an evocative acronym meaning "cleaned up"), took over the reins of government under the leadership of **Andréas Papandréou**, marking the beginning of political alternation. In the same year, Greece joined the EEC. However, relations with neighbouring countries still remained turbulent; in the 1990s, not only did Greece have to contend with the recurrent conflict with Turkey, but it also came into conflict with **Albania** over control of northern Epirus and was faced with refusal by the Greeks to accept the name and flag of the new Republic of Macedonia.

# GREECE TODAY
## A YOUNG REPUBLIC

It is difficult to establish exactly when the Greek Republic came into being: it was proclaimed in 1973, but the colonels' junta did not come to an end until July 1974 and the new Constitution was only adopted in 1975. Despite its relative newness, the Republic with its tried and tested institutions now seems to have taken a firm foothold among the Greek population.

The **president of the Republic** is elected for five years by a two-thirds majority of Parliament. He is also head of the armed forces and appoints the prime minister, although this is purely a matter of form since the office automatically falls to the leader of the party with the majority of votes in Parliament. Moreover, he does not have actual executive power, which belongs to the **prime minister**. The latter heads a government which is collectively accountable to **Parliament**, an assembly composed of 300 members elected for four years and which holds full legislative power. Furthermore, the Constitution of 1975 guarantees freedom of religion, even though it paradoxically recognises the primacy of the Orthodox Christian religion.

At an administrative level, Greece is divided into **nine large regions**, which stems more from historical reality than from a desire to decentralise power. At the level below, **prefects** represent the government in each of the 52 districts or **nomí**. Lastly, both the municipalities with over 200 000 inhabitants *(demes)* and those with over 500 inhabitants *(municipes)* have a mayor and council, elected every four years by universal suffrage.

## A bipartite political context

Two large parties have monopolised the political scene from the beginning of the Republic. The left-wing Pan-Hellenic Socialist Movement, **PASOK**, which was founded in 1974 and has long been dominated by the personality of Andréas Papandréou, is well represented in rural areas and presents itself as a nationalist party, opposed to Social-Democratic and Communist policies. Its main aims concern the promotion of greater social justice and it stands against the influence of the major powers. The right of the political spectrum is dominated by Konstantinos Karamanlís' **New Democracy** party. Taking up where his National Radical Union left off before the junta, this party is pursuing the development of liberal policies in a European context. Other than these two influential parties, only the Communist party **(KKE)**, which is firmly rooted in working-class milieus, has enough support to be regularly represented in Parliament. Rather less successful, its "little brother", the **KKE Interior**, advocates reform and European integration.

For some years, a **left-wing ecological** coalition, Synaspismos, has managed to obtain a few seats. The same cannot be said of the **National Front**, however; the extreme right has never managed to become a serious contender in the political life of the nation.

## An economy on the move

Greece's membership of the **EEC** was decided in 1979 and became effective in 1981. Although previously not in favour of such a step, once PASOK came to power in 1981 under the leadership of Andréas Papandréou, it no longer questioned the participation of Greece in the construction of Europe. The Community's poorest country clearly had everything to gain by joining the European Union.

But despite progress made, the Greek economy is still trailing behind the European average. However, for some years now, the socialist government of **Kóstas Simítis** has been following a stringent budgetary and monetary policy and a privatisation programme, which have unquestionably caused the economy to move forward but have also produced an upsurge of discontent in the process. Thanks to this policy, the rate of inflation has fallen below 5%, the annual growth rate is bordering on 4%, and the country – originally refused entry into the economic and monetary union because of failure to satisfy the convergence criteria defined by the **Treaty of Maastricht** – has now gained entry into the euro zone. On the flipside of the coin, 10% of the population are unemployed, even though the Greeks' purchasing power has increased considerably and now stands at US$12 500 per capita per year.

## Agriculture and industry

Despite these encouraging results, much effort remains to be made in various economic areas. The **agricultural sector** still sustains almost 20% of the working population, with a production whose market value does not exceed 13% of the GDP. Although modern farming methods are gradually spreading, Greece still remains a country of smallholdings, with an average area of 4ha per inhabitant.

It is nevertheless to agriculture that **industry** owes a large part of its vitality, through the processing of agricultural products. **Construction** companies are the other major-league players in industry.

The country's **mining resources** are limited. **Lignite** extracted mainly in Ptolemaís fuels some thermal electric power plants, and there is an **oilfield** near the island of Thassos, but these are insufficient to meet the country's energy needs. Greece still has a little **nickel**, **zinc** and **magnesium**, but its greatest resource is **bauxite**, which is extracted from Mt Parnassus by the Pechiney group and used in the production of aluminium.

## Three essential blessings

The imbalance between the requirements of the population and the current economic performance of Greece lie at the root of a large deficit in its trade balance. The fact that the European Union absorbs almost half of the products exported by Greece and provides two-thirds of its imports bears witness to its successful integration into Europe. Fortunately, the trade deficit is partly offset by profits from the **merchant navy**, by income sent by Greeks who have emigrated abroad – 5.5 million strong, the **Greek diaspora** is indeed a significant factor (*see page 57*) – but above all, by revenue drawn from **tourism**. The combination of sun, sea, islands and the prestigious vestiges of Antiquity attracts almost 10 million tourists every year, which is as much as the country's entire population, and brings almost 4 billion dollars into the country.

An area in which Greece could probably make savings is in its rather onerous defence budget; with expenditure equal to 4.6% of its GDP in 1999, this is by far the highest rate of all the NATO countries.

Although Greek society is still archaic in many ways, progress has undeniably been made. The State notably plays quite a remarkable role in **education**, devoting a considerable amount of its budget to the development of public schools throughout the country and also to maintaining a high level of further education. A growing network of private schools is also flourishing alongside the public system.

### A nation of shipowners

In their day, the turbulent lives of the extremely rich shipowners Onássis and Níarchos, brothers-in-law and rivals, provided many a story for magazines the world over. Aristotle Onássis' love affairs with Maria Callas and Jackie Kennedy are legendary, and wild rumours still circulate about the suspicious circumstances of the deaths of his daughter, Christina, and the first wife of Stávros Níarchos. But alongside these great shipowners, who were also great patrons of the arts in the purest Greek tradition, is a myriad of other, more unassuming individuals, who hold a few shares in one or more ships and contribute, in their own way, towards endowing this little country with one of the world's most powerful merchant fleets. However, in recent years, this fleet has been sailing more often than not under flags of convenience.

# A small and unevenly spread population

With a little under 11 million inhabitants, Greece is small in comparison with other European countries. With a population density of around 80 inhabitants per square kilometre, ie three times less than in Germany or the United Kingdom, it even seems to be rather underpopulated. But it is difficult to make any real comparison, considering the country's extremely mountainous landscape.

The proportion of the population living in urban areas stands at almost 60%, which is a little lower than in the major developed countries; it is nevertheless quite considerable for a country with such a deep-rooted rural tradition. Over the last fifteen years, the mountains of the Peloponnese and the Pindus have witnessed a population exodus, as have many of the islands. But the gaps are being filled by immigrants from the Eastern European countries who have been flooding into Greece in successive waves since the fall of the Soviet empire.

With the main destination of the initial **rural exodus** being the capital city, **Greater Athens** is now home to over 3 million people, ie almost one third of the country's total population, although in 1821 the city was nothing more than a little town with 5 000 inhabitants.

## Uneven urbanisation

The influx of so many people within such a short period of time was bound to create problems. Some have been or are in the process of being solved, in particular the tricky question of supplying the capital with water, which has been solved by impounding the waters from Mt Parnassus. The saturation of Athens airport, which had been a problem for many years, has been eased by the recent inauguration of a new airport in Spáta, built with the aid of European subsidies. However, the air in Athens is still unbreathable on very hot days on account of the very high level of **air pollution**, in spite of the alternating traffic system set up by the municipal authorities.

Trailing far behind Athens, the Macedonian city of **Thessaloníki** has 700 000 inhabitants, while the country's third largest city, **Patras** (Peloponnese), has only 100 000. This uneven population distribution means that the centres of production are concentrated around Athens, and, more broadly speaking, along the Athens-Thessaloníki and Athens-Patras routes. Population figures are on the rise in these areas, but the growth rate remains relatively low, at +0.3%.

Platía Omónia, in the heart of modern Athens

B. Pérousse/MICHELIN

# ART AND ARCHITECTURE

Whether it be monuments with lofty columns still standing proudly on some rocky spur, or vestiges unearthed by archaeologists after centuries of oblivion, Greece yields a seemingly endless supply of relics from its illustrious artistic past, which are always a moving sight to behold. The art of Ancient Greece, above all, which already fascinated the Romans so long ago, obviously has its own special place. However, this chapter would be incomplete without a mention of the Byzantine, Latin and Ottoman civilisations which also left their imprint in Greece, allowing new artistic trends to flourish in a reflection of the strength of their culture.

*See also the lexicon and architectural plates at the end of this chapter.*

## The Bronze Age, or the art of the first palaces

As early as the Bronze Age, the city states of the two great Minoan and Mycenaean civilisations demonstrated an already highly-developed mastery of architecture and original artistic characteristics.

### The Cretan palaces

Veritable cities with a highly complex layout, the Cretan palaces of **Phaistos**, **Mália** and **Knossós** contained places of worship, shops, workshops for various different trades, and royal apartments. Set around a vast central courtyard – a prelude, perhaps, to the Greek agora – they spread over several levels (as many as five floors in Knossós), linked by countless passageways and staircases, which breathe life into the legend of the **labyrinth** *(see page 372)*.

Sweeping **frescoes** decorated the walls of the royal apartments, reception rooms and those devoted to worship in a powerful display of naturalism. They depicted dolphins, floral friezes, bouquets of reeds, and acrobats dancing on the backs of bulls, all enhanced by the most iridescent colours. In time, Minoan painting nevertheless began to focus increasingly on the representation of the human being, full-size figures or delicate faces, such as the charming *Parisienne* at the Herakleion Museum. This taste for realism paved the way for **relief painting**, murals with a low stucco relief which made the subjects even more life-like.

However, it was in the **minor arts** of **metalwork**, ceramics and marquetry that the Cretans excelled, as evidenced by the countless pieces of jewellery, figurines and everyday objects discovered in the royal necropolis of Mália. **Ceramic art** included magnificent jars and giant *pithoi* on which, after the dense geometric patterns, a whole world of sea creatures danced freely, with octopi, seaweed and fish undulating in red lines on the ochre of the terracotta.

### The Mycenaean cities: colossal undertakings

The Mycenaeans left little in the way of pictorial evidence, excelling more in the art of **fortification**, which undoubtedly betrays a more bellicose temperament. Unlike the Cretans, they built their cities on elevated sites protected by strong **Cyclopean**

### Cycladic art and idols

The brilliant civilisation which flourished at the end of the 3rd millennium BC in the Cyclades left behind a great deal of artistic evidence. This included painted and engraved ceramics, jewellery, elaborate weapons, but, above all, astonishing marble statuettes, the famous Cycladic idols, whose function still remains shrouded in mystery. They mainly represent women, their arms crossed over their naked bodies, with oval, flat and perfectly smooth heads and only a nose protruding. Some less common statuettes depict musicians, flautists or harpists sitting cross-legged. These truly remarkable and surprisingly modern works of art with their perfect proportions, bold curves and an acute sense of stylisation, influenced many 20C artists, starting with the Cubists.

**walls** composed of enormous perfectly-pointed blocks of stone, some weighing several tonnes. The best example of these colossal constructions – better still than Mycenae – is the city of **Tírintha** in Argolis.

However, their warlike character did not prevent the Mycenaeans from developing a highly refined **funerary art**, in particular in **metalwork**, as demonstrated by the fabulous treasure found in the nineteen royal tombs discovered in 1876 by the archaeologist Heinrich Schliemann (*see page 19*) at the site of **Mycenae**. It included gold masks, hundreds of filigreed gold plates, diadems, bracelets, rings, gold-plated silver sceptres with rock-crystal handles and damascened daggers.

An extraordinary wealth providing a stark contrast with the extreme material poverty that followed the disappearance of the Mycenaean civilisation.

## Ancient architecture

At the end of the Dark Age, the glorious Mycenaean civilisation fell into oblivion. Gradually a new society emerged in which each man belonged to a **city**. The importance of this civic community explains why Greek architecture lost interest in private houses and began to focus more on public buildings. However, at the height of the Archaic Period, the **agora** – public meeting place – was still nothing but a vast esplanade with no buildings; the first elements of civic architecture, **temples**, did not start to appear until the second half of the 8C BC. Indeed, until the 6C BC, the shrines devoted to the gods differed little in the way of architecture from residential buildings. A clay model of the Temple of Hera in Árgos (Peloponnese) shows the main characteristics: a large rectangular room **(megaron)** covered by a two-sided roof, with a small porch projecting at the front supported by two columns. Possibilities for innovation were still limited, however, by the materials used: clay, wood and stone blocks.

Cycladic purity: an idol from Páros (Musée du Louvre, Paris)

H. Lewandowski/RMN

### The birth of monumentality

A first step towards monumental architecture was taken at the Temple of Hera in Sámos at the turning point of the 8C and 7C BC, when the room devoted to the deity (the **cella**) was surrounded by a gallery supported by wooden columns **(peristyle)**. There was now a clear distinction between the houses of men and gods. But it was only when they began to use carved stone, particularly marble, that the Greeks were able to give free rein to their creative genius. Thus, in the 6C BC the first monumental structures appeared.

Two opposing styles immediately developed. In mainland Greece, the rather geometric **Doric style** obeyed rules of strictness and sobriety, with columns having plain capitals and no bases. In Asia Minor, the more decorative and lighter aspect of the **Ionic style** allowed architects greater freedom. Unlike the Doric order, the columns rested on moulded bases and the capitals boasted twin volutes.

The Temple of Artemis in **Corfu** was the earliest stone temple to be discovered and dates back to around 580 BC. Subsequent works were built on an ever-increasing scale. The Temple of Artemis in **Ephesus** - one of the Seven Wonders of the Ancient World – was 50m wide by 100m long, like Temple "G" at **Selinus**. The possibilities of these gargantuan undertakings were soon exhausted, and they also proved extremely costly. Such was the case of the gigantic **Temple of Olympian Zeus** in Athens (*see page 147*): begun by the Peisistratids and continued by their successors, it was not completed until six centuries later by the Roman emperor Hadrian.

## The Age of Pericles, or the golden age

The association of the sculptor **Phidias** and the architect **Ictinus** for the construction of the **Parthenon** in Athens (447-432 BC) marked the beginning of a new phase: the temple's originality lay not in its sheer size, but in the perfection of its proportions, the widening of the cella by the reduction of the lateral galleries, and in the refinement of the decoration. At the beginning of the 4C BC, in the **Temple of Athena Alea** in Tegea (south of Árgos, Peloponnese), the architect and sculptor, **Scopas**, accentuated this trend of embellishing the interior spaces by getting rid of the lateral columns and imposing the even more decorative **Corinthian order** with its curled acanthus leaves and volutes on the capital. But it is probably the very elaborate decoration of the **treasuries** which most clearly reveals the full extent of the Greeks' artistic talent. These little religious buildings dotted the Sacred Ways of the great pan-Hellenic sanctuaries – **Olympia**, **Delos** and, of course, **Delphi.** Built by a victorious city or a grateful family, they served simply as depositories for offerings. Enjoying greater freedom than they did with the temples, the artists decorated them with exquisite mouldings, paintings, carved friezes and caryatids, giving free rein to their imagination.

## Religion and prestige

The great wave of temple building that marked the 6C cannot be explained by technical progress alone or by a new religious fervour. At this time, the ruling tyrants had directed the spirit of competition ("agon") among the Greeks towards a sort of architectural rivalry. Indeed, the Greek cities were embellished under the tyrants' rule in an ostentatious display of their power and wealth, which also bestowed glory on the person commissioning the work. The aristocrats were quick to catch on and pursued this prestigious public patronage. When fire damaged the famous Temple of Apollo at Delphi, it was the Alcmaeonid family, in exile from Athens, who obtained the right to rebuild it. And, to make sure that they would not be forgotten, they added a pediment made from the finest Parian marble.

## The original theatre

Created for ceremonies of the cult of Dionysus, the Greek theatre ("théatron" is "a place of seeing") originally consisted of an area of beaten earth surrounded by wooden tiers. The chorus and dancers performed in the central area, where an altar to the god took pride of place. However, the theatre very soon stepped beyond these strictly religious bounds and also became a stage for the performance of tragedies. It became very popular in the 5C BC, but it was not until the following century that the first stone structures appeared, including the famous Epidaurus theatre, a perfect example of its kind. The tiers were now arranged in a semicircle ("cavea") backing onto a hillside, and, in the orchestra, the altar was moved so as not to stand in the way of the chorus. As drama evolved, the chorus began to interact with the actors. The "skene", a simple wooden structure (later made of stone) serving both as the wings and a backdrop, then acquired a "proskénion", a narrow platform projecting to the fore. It was subsequently replaced by a wider "skene", gradually gaining in depth to become the large stage of modern-day theatres.

## The spirit of Hellenism

Important changes took place in the 4C BC which were to leave an indelible mark on Greek architecture. Already in the 5C BC, **Hippodamus of Miletus** had begun to change the face of city planning in Greece by using a grid plan separating business and residential districts. Initially applied to Miletus (Asia Minor) and to Piraeus, the **Hippodamian plan** did not become widespread until much later on, when the conquests of Alexander the Great led to the building of many new cities. Among the great architectural innovations of the time was the increase in **ramparts** built around cities, **porticoes** (stoae) surrounding sanctuaries and agorae – pleasant shaded galleries with colonnades housing shops and offices – as well as the emergence and rapid success of the **theatre**.

The Hellenistic age was to witness a veritable revolution in ways of thinking. The centre of Hellenism shifted outside Greece and rivalries between the independent Greek kingdoms were expressed not only in the political arena but also in an **ostentatious architecture** made to serve royal ends. The greatest artists set to work for the rich sovereigns of Asia Minor, Syria and Egypt, where they developed a monumental art encompassing oriental techniques. Some of the most renowned Greek architects and sculptors were thus set to embellish **Halicarnassus** (Bodrum), the residence of the Persian satrap (governor) Mausolus; they built a monumental tomb for him there, the famous **Mausoleum**, which is also one of the Seven Wonders of the World.

But this great new development was not limited to sovereigns alone; it also reached into private homes, which had, up until that time, been deliberately austere. **Alcibiades** (*see sidebar page 22*) caused yet another great stir in the 5C BC by hiring Agatharcus to decorate his house. Indeed, the decline of civic sense in the 4C BC corresponded to a new desire of the wealthy to display their personal success. And where better to start than at home? Henceforth, luxuriously decorated, vast and beautiful houses were to be seen adorning the business districts and areas where the high-ranking officials lived in Alexandria, Pergamon and elsewhere.

## Ancient sculpture

The 7C BC marked the arrival of great Greek sculpture, inspired by Egyptian models, with one of the favourite themes of **Archaic statuary**, the kouros and the kore. They served a religious function and were placed in sanctuaries as an offering to the deity, and were also to be found adorning tombs to honour the memory of the deceased. As a result, they comply with strict conventions of representation. Carved from marble, limestone (*poros*) or bronze, the **kouros** represents a naked young man, standing with his left foot forward, his arms stretched down close to his sides, his fists clenched. In the second half of the 7C BC, the kouroi reached colossal proportions, before returning to a more human scale in the 6C BC. Their female counterpart, the **kore**, depicts a young girl, standing with her feet together, one arm stretched down by her side and the other crossed over her chest. Even more of a prisoner of the stone, the figure looks more like a pillar than a human body, the anatomy being suggested only by the movement of the drapery of the ceremonial robe.

Hygeia, Goddess of Health (National Archaeological Museum, Athens)

### The Classical Age, or the liberation of the body

After a so-called "Severe" transitional period, illustrated by the marvellous **Charioteer of Delphi**, the Classical Age gradually freed itself from the rigidity of the kouros model. In the 5C BC – the **High Classical Period** – Athens enjoyed absolute supremacy over the Greek world, attracting most of the great artists. Among them, the sculptor **Phidias**, whose figures displayed a flexibility, movement and majesty never seen before. Creator of the chryselephantine statue (made of ivory and gold) of the Olympian Zeus, which no longer exists but was, in its time, considered to be one of the Seven Wonders of the World, Phidias also decorated the Parthenon, creating in particular the wonderful **frieze of the Panathenaea**, which can now be seen in London and Paris.

T.A.P.

Another supremely talented sculptor, **Polyclitus**, emerged in Árgos. He created a canon of proportions according to which the total height of the body should be equal to seven times that of the head. Only Roman copies of his works survive, including the famous bronze **Doryphorus**, depicting a naked spear bearer.

In the **Late Classical Period** (4C BC), the Athenian **Praxiteles** departed from the hieratic style of the preceding period, injecting his works with a more natural and graceful quality: he was particularly adept at sculpting nude, sensual female bodies and carving his male subjects in languid poses.

The figures sculpted by **Scopas of Paros** were more expressive and tormented, triggering a movement towards realism which gathered great momentum in the Hellenistic Period. Subsequently, **Lysippus** of Sicyon produced many portraits of his protector, Alexander the Great, as well as bronze statues that had more slender forms than those of Polyclitus. Lysippus effectively created a new canon which held that the body equalled eight times the height of the head. His pupil, **Chares of Lindos**, adopted this model for his gigantic bronze statue of Helios (the Sun), the famous **Colossus of Rhodes**. This giant, over 30m high, another of the Seven Wonders of the World, sadly did not survive the earthquake of 227 BC intact.

## Greek vases, painting's living memory

Of the bright colours which once enhanced the architecture of the great monuments of Ancient Greece almost every trace has disappeared, worn away by time. Some beautifully decorated ceramics have however survived, to give us some idea of the evolution of painting as an autonomous art. Here again, the Dark Age swept away Mycenaean knowledge and, in the 9C BC, the decoration of vases was again reduced to simple bands of **geometric designs** around the body. Human and animal figures began to appear in the next century, although still in very schematic form: a circle was used to symbolise a man's head and a triangle his body. The main centre of geometrical ceramic production was in Attica, and particularly in **Athens**, with the most famous of them being the great funerary amphorae of the **Dipylon Master**.

### Black figures...

In the second half of the 8C BC, increasing contact with the Near East revolutionised this art. **Corinth** became a flourishing centre of production, inspired by **oriental models**. The geometrical motifs now gave way to palms, rosettes, lotus flowers, and lions, panthers and sphinxes. The black-figure technique moreover allowed the subjects to be depicted with much greater expression and realism: the figures were painted in black on the orange-red terracotta surface and the details were incised with a burin; white or red strokes were then added to emphasise the contours of the bodies. The famous **Chigi vase**, dating from around 650 BC, provides an unrivalled example of the possibilities afforded by this technique, with several friezes showing various scenes from ancient life and mythology, including a combat between hoplite soldiers accompanied by flute players, a lion hunt, a procession on horseback and the Judgement of Paris.

**"Opus tessellatum"**
Probably invented by the Sumerians, the earliest known mosaics, discovered in Mesopotamia, date back to the end of the 4th millennium BC. They consisted of small coloured cones of clay on a bitumen or cement base arranged in all sorts of patterns serving to decorate temple and palace façades. The art of mosaic was perfected in the Hellenistic Period, with the development of pavements made of pebbles and in particular of tesserae – small cubes of coloured stone, ceramic or glass paste – which were used to ornament temples and the homes of the wealthy. But it was the Romans who really turned it into a fine art, most notably in the Imperial Age when all buildings, public and private alike, were decorated with mosaics. This was when this art form reached its heights, with tiny tesserae as small as 4mm$^2$, yielding blends similar to painting. Byzantine artists also subsequently excelled in this art.

## ... and red figures

In the 6C BC, Attica in turn became the main production centre of black-figure pottery. Besides the inevitable scenes from mythology, the subjects mainly revolved around scenes from aristocratic life. Around 525 BC, the black-figure technique gradually gave way to the so-called red-figure technique: here, the outlines were painted in black, as was the background, but the figures were left in the red colour of the clay and the incision technique no longer used. The treatment of forms and faces in painting and sculpture developed along parallel paths: emotional expression intensified and bodies were revealed. **Polygnotus of Thasos** (5C BC) was a pioneer in this field and is also said to be the originator of the **notion of spatial depth** in painting, by placing his characters in settings composed of several planes.

As vase painting ran out of steam towards the end of the Classical Period, wall painting began to make an appearance. Like sculpture, it was to serve royal ends, and the painter **Apelles** made numerous portraits of Alexander the Great, depicting him as a conqueror and later as a god.

## Byzantine architecture, or the art of Christianity

Greece seemed to lose its artistic vitality when it fell under foreign domination. Henceforth, the only outlet for the talents of the Greeks lay in religious – Christian – architecture, where they were able to express original ideas in architectural design. But even then, a few centuries passed before they were really able to develop a style of their own, because initially (4C-6C AD) **basilica type** churches inspired by secular Roman architecture predominated.

In the 6C, the **dome**, already much appreciated in Rome, started to become the main element around which Byzantine churches were built. They became smaller in size, and gradually the **Greek-cross plan** took over: at the crossing of the transept, the dome rises from a drum adorned with windows, itself resting on four barrel vaults producing a cross with four arms of equal length. More often than not, this was contained within a square through the addition of lateral naves and apses; this type of plan is known as a **cross-in-square**.

Particularly well suited to this new architectural style, magnificent mosaic decorations depicted various scenes from the Gospels according to a well-defined liturgical arrangement: **Christ Pantocrator** in the dome, the **Virgin Theotókos** in the apse, scenes from the Life of Christ or the Virgin placed according to the feast days of the year in the nave or narthex. The **Dafní Monastery** (11C) in Attica thus contains a remarkable collection of mosaics enhanced with gold.

Byzantine masterpiece: the Dormition of the Virgin (Varlaam Monastery, Metéora)

B. Kaufmann/MICHELIN

Lastly, a rather curious but interesting combination of earlier architectural styles emerged in **Mistra**: a basilical plan at ground level, with a Greek-cross plan above (Aphendiko Church, at the Brontochion Monastery).

In the last great innovation of the Byzantine Period, the mosaics gradually gave way to frescoes, which, although they followed the exact same codes of representation as the mosaics, proved to be much less costly.

## Modern times

### Between Ottomans and Venetians

After the Turkish conquest, purely Greek art practically disappeared for four centuries. Mosques, Turkish baths, bazaars and caravanserais were soon to be seen dotting the Greek countryside. Great admirers of Byzantine churches, the Ottomans transformed the most beautiful of them into mosques. Besides adapting the Christian sanctuaries to the rites of Islam, the Turkish architects gave expression to their talent in a few grand creations, but most of the mosques in Greece were still relatively modest structures, consisting of a simple prayer room.

Under Ottoman domination, Christian art managed to persevere only on Mt Athos and in the Venetian enclaves of Crete and the Ionian Islands. Indeed the influence of Venice was very much in evidence here, particularly in **military architecture**; the Venetians built numerous fortified citadels in Corfu, Zacynthus and Cephalonia, and especially in **Crete**, which continued to hold out against Turkish assaults. The entrances to many of these strongholds are still guarded by **lions of St Mark**, the official symbol of Venice.

As for civil architecture, it inherited elegant **loggias**, such as the one in Herakleion which now houses the town hall, or the one in Réthimnon which has been turned into a library. And, of course, there are the **fountains** – symbol of the prosperity of those in power – whose refinement matches those of the Turks.

Venice also left its imprint on religious architecture, particularly in painting: the icons produced by some Greek artists, such as **Damaskinós**, reflect a skilful combination of Byzantine rigour and the sensual inspiration and more realistic forms of the Venetians. The most famous of these painters, Doménikos Theotokópoulos, is better known under the name of **El Greco** (1541-1614). After training in Crete, he moved to Spain where he gave expression to the full range of his talent alongside local and Italian masters. After Crete was captured by the Ottomans in 1669, many artists, such as **E Tzanès** (1610-90), settled in the Ionian Islands where they formed what is usually known as the **"Ionian School"**.

### Neo-Classicism, or the revival of Antiquity

The defeat of the Ottomans and the liberation of Greece in 1821 brought with them an overwhelming thirst for artistic renewal. Everywhere, the signs of Turkish domination were wiped out, submerged by a feverish desire to once again bring to the fore the monuments of Antiquity – proud symbols of the identity and prestige of Greece – and to re-endow the cities of the young nation with an authentic Greekness.

Already very fashionable in Western Europe, the neo-Classical style was therefore quickly adopted in Greece. Introduced by foreign artists, first of all Bavarian (following in the wake of King Otto), this trend, which was largely inspired by Antiquity, seemed to be the natural choice for the (re)construction of public buildings. **Athens** led this revival, with its University, National Library and Academy (*see page 149*).

## Modern painting and sculpture

Some painters, such as **Nikifóros Lytrás**, left to study in Munich, but all forms of artistic expression were still influenced by academism in the 19C. It was not until the turn of the century that the new artistic trends from Western Europe began to catch on in Greece, undoubtedly first introduced by the painter **Konstandínos Parthénis**, who was the first to take an interest in Impressionism and Fauvism.

**Konstandínos Dimitriádis** led the way in the field of sculpture, drawing inspiration from Rodin. Soon to follow suit were the expressionist painter **Giórgos Bouziánis**, the cubist **Níkos Ghíka** and the surrealist **Níkos Engonópoulos**. This modernist trend, however, did not win everybody over to its cause. A strong traditionalist movement, firmly rooted in the country's Hellenic, Byzantine and popular culture, persisted under the leadership of the painter **Spýros Vassilíou** and the architect **D Pikiónis**.

These traditionalist and modernist styles continued in the post-Second World War period; the painter **Yánnis Morális**, intent on rediscovering and respecting the roots of Greek culture, embodied the former, while some of his contemporaries sought to explore the new artistic trends of the Western world. Among them, the painters **Aléxandros Kontópoulos** and **Yánnis Spyrópoulos** became involved in abstract art. However, representational art soon made a graceful comeback under the aegis of the painter **Jánnis Ghaítis** and the sculptor **Giórgos Giorgiádis**. In a sign of the times, Greek artists were beginning to settle abroad and obtain international recognition. **Jánnis Kounéllis** rose to the fore in Italy in the Arte Povera movement, and Panayiotis Vassilakis, better known as **Tákis**, has worked in Paris for almost half a century. Specialising in technological art, his work explores the effects of magnetism, sounds and light, and the artist gained a certain reputation with his "electromagnetic sculptures", "light art" and "musical sculptures".

**Modern times**

# ARCHITECTURE OF ANTIQUITY

## THE TEMPLE

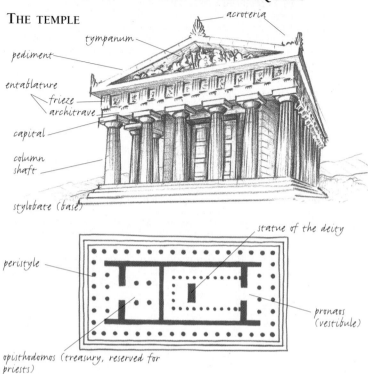

acroteria

tympanum

pediment

entablature

frieze

architrave

capital

column
shaft

stylobate (base)

statue of the deity

peristyle

pronaos
(vestibule)

opisthodomos (treasury, reserved for
priests)

## THREE CLASSICAL ORDERS

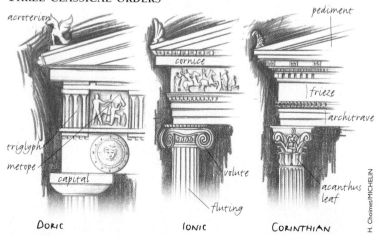

acroterion

pediment

cornice

frieze

architrave

triglyph

metope

capital

volute

fluting

acanthus
leaf

DORIC

IONIC

CORINTHIAN

H. Choimet/MICHELIN

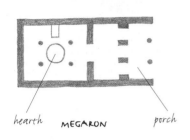

hearth    MEGARON    porch

THOLOS
(circular building)

## THE THEATRE

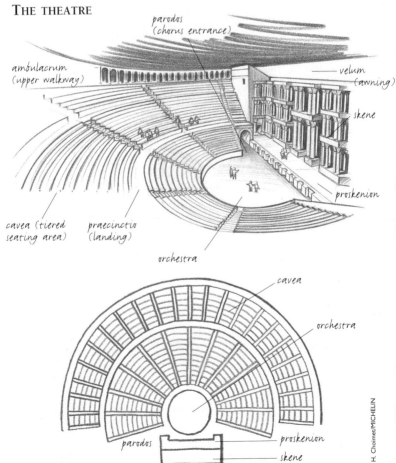

parodos
(chorus entrance)

ambulacrum
(upper walkway)

velum
(awning)

skene

proskenion

cavea (tiered
seating area)

praecinctio
(landing)

orchestra

cavea

orchestra

parodos

proskenion

skene

H. Choimet/MICHELIN

# BYZANTINE CHURCH

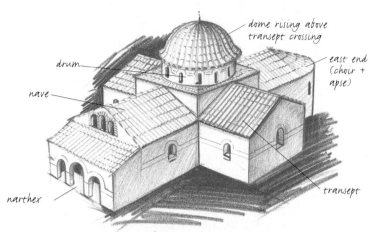

dome rising above transept crossing

east end (choir + apse)

drum

nave

narthex

transept

**GREEK-CROSS PLAN**

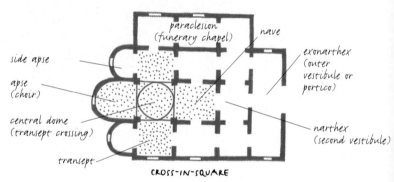

paraclesion (funerary chapel)

nave

side apse

exonarthex (outer vestibule or portico)

apse (choir)

central dome (transept crossing)

narthex (second vestibule)

transept

**CROSS-IN-SQUARE**

## DOMES

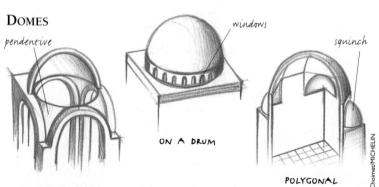

pendentive

windows

squinch

**ON PENDENTIVES**

**ON A DRUM**

**POLYGONAL ON SQUINCHES**

H. Choimer/MICHELIN

**Antiquity and general terms**

| | |
|---|---|
| Acanthus | Plant whose scalloped leaves served as a model for the decoration of the Corinthian capital. |
| Acropolis | The upper town of Greek cities, serving as a citadel and a place of worship. |
| Agora | An open space in Greek cities, used as a market place and political centre. |
| Altar | In a sanctuary, a small stone structure in the open usually in front of a temple, where offerings to the deity were placed. |
| Amphora | Two-handled vase used to store and transport oil and wine. |
| Anastylosis | Reconstruction of a ruined building using the fragments of the original. |
| Bond | Method of laying stones in a building (*opus* in Latin). |
| Bouleuterion | In Greece, the state council building (the council was known as the "boule"). It was a sort of small covered theatre, set in the agora and could also be used as an odeon. |
| Caryatid | A female statue used as a column. |
| Cella | The main body of a temple, usually housing the statue of the deity. |
| Dipteral | Term describing a monument with a double peristyle. |
| Exedra | Semicircular room containing a stone bench. Also more broadly denotes any apse or niche opening out into a larger space. |
| Gymnasium | Sports complex in Ancient Greece, comprising open-air grounds and various buildings: changing rooms, palaestrae, anointing rooms, etc. |
| Hexastyle | Describes a building with six frontal columns. |
| Hypostyle | A temple or palace with a roof supported by columns ("stylos" means "column" in Greek). |
| Lekythos | A small vase with a long, cylindrical body and a narrow neck, used for funerary offerings. |
| Megaron | From the Greek meaning "large room". An abode dating from the Neolithic Period and Bronze Age, with a porch and vestibule opening into a rectangular room with a central hearth. Greek temples were based on this plan. |
| Metope | A rectangular space, sometimes carved, between two triglyphs in a Doric frieze (*see this term*). |
| Mosaic | Assemblage of multicoloured tesserae, used to decorate the walls and pavements of buildings in Ancient Greece and subsequently in the Byzantine Period. |
| Nymphaeum | A small shrine dedicated to the Nymphs, built around a natural spring or fountain. |
| Octastyle | Describes a building with eight frontal columns. |
| Odeon | A small, usually covered theatre, used for concerts and lectures. |
| Oinochoe | A broad-bodied jug, with a vertical handle, used for pouring wine into goblets. |
| Opisthodomos | In a Greek temple, a room where offerings were laid out (treasury). |
| Order | Style of architecture defined by the decoration of the capital and entablature. |
| Palaestra | An exercise ground, set apart from or contained within a gymnasium, surrounded by a portico leading to changing rooms, washrooms, etc. |
| Peripteral | A term describing a monument surrounded by a single row of columns. |
| Peristyle | A gallery or colonnaded portico surrounding a temple or courtyard. |
| Pithos | Large jar, usually set in the ground, used for storing grain. |
| Portico | Covered gallery supported by a colonnade (*stoa* in Greek). |
| Proedria | In a theatre, a row of honour reserved for high-ranking citizens (the proedri). |
| Pronaos | Vestibule of a Greek temple, leading to the cella. |
| Propylaeum | Monumental entrance to an important public building, sanctuary, sacred precinct, generally in the form of a large porch. |

**Art and architecture**

| | |
|---|---|
| Prostyle | A term describing a temple which has freestanding frontal columns. |
| Prytaneion | Seat of the Prytaneis, Greek city officials who were in charge of convening the boule (see "bouleuterion"). |
| Stadium | Long open space mainly for running, but also used for wrestling, jumping and discus and javelin throwing. Approximately 180-190m long, the stadium was lined on three sides by earthen, wooden or stone terraces. The main remaining stadia are at Delphi and Olympia. A stadium was also a unit of length. |
| Stoa | See "portico". |
| Stucco | Plaster (gypsum) used in wall and ceiling decoration. |
| Temenos | A sacred enclosure around a sanctuary, where the faithful gathered. Sacred esplanade of an acropolis. |
| Tessera | Small cube of stone or glass used in the making of mosaics. |
| Tholos | Circular building with a conical roof or dome, for worship or funerary purposes. |
| Triglyph | Projecting rectangular part in a Doric frieze, with three carved vertical channels, between two metopes. |

## Byzantine Period

| | |
|---|---|
| Ambo | In Christian basilicas, a raised stone stand for the reading of the Gospels. |
| Aniconic | Without figurative images. |
| Apse | In a church, semicircular chapel at the end of the choir. |
| Archivolt | Continuous moulding ornamenting the extrados (outer face) of an arch. |
| Basilica | Civil building with three aisles used by the Romans as a court of justice or meeting place. Name given to the first Christian churches built according to this plan. |
| Bema | The raised part of an Eastern church, usually in front of the apse, containing the altar and the bishop's throne. |
| Chancel | Low balustrade in front of the choir in a church. |
| Diaconicon | The sacristy in Byzantine churches where the deacons kept their vessels and vestments. |
| Diptych | Two painted or carved panels hinged together. |
| Exonarthex | External vestibule preceding the narthex in some Byzantine churches. |
| Fresco | From the Italian "a fresco", painting on "fresh" plaster. The paintings in the first Byzantine churches were executed directly onto the stone, only partially covering the walls. The fresco technique, which provided a surface smoother than the wall and allowed a better reproduction of the colours, meant that artists could cover all of the church walls. |
| Iconostasis | A screen decorated with icons separating the nave from the choir in Eastern churches. |
| Narthex | Covered porch or vestibule in a church where penitents and catechumens assembled before they were baptised. |
| Pendentive | Triangular concave space between the four arches supporting a dome, enabling the transition from square to circular. |
| Post-Byzantine style | Synthesis between the traditional Byzantine iconography and the Italian manner which appeared in several Cretan monasteries during the 16C. |
| Prothesis | Sacristy located to the left of the apse, near the diaconicon, where bread and wine were prepared for consecration. |
| Synthronon | Tiered benches following the semicircular shape of the apse, reserved for the clergy in Byzantine churches. |
| Transept | Transversal separation of the nave and choir, forming the arms of the cross. Not all churches have a transept. |
| Triptych | A work comprising three painted or carved panels, whose outer sections can be folded over the central section. |

Art and architecture

# GREEK MYTHOLOGY

We are all familiar with Greek mythology, that vast compilation of narratives and legends about the gods and heroes of Antiquity which has become such a part of our shared culture. It has provided an endlessly fascinating source of inspiration for the greatest authors, from Homer to James Joyce, Euripides to Mary Shelley, Virgil to Cocteau. However, although many episodes of mythology remain etched in our memory, they often give the impression of being a rather disjointed and obscure collection, because either we have forgotten or were never aware of the "links" which would allow us to appreciate their unity and complexity. Because mythology has a meaning. A wealth of meanings, in fact. Hidden behind the countless characters and multitude of situations lies a whole world of symbols, an amazing reflection of historical events, philosophical thoughts and timeless proverbs.

Of this vast, variable and almost boundless "compilation", we shall simply try to lay out the principles and trace the outline, in the knowledge that the poets of ancient times produced a myriad variations – sometimes quite considerable – each having their own version of the love affairs or tribulations of a certain god or hero.

## The birth of gods and man

The origin of the universe, first of all, is a matter of myths per se: **theogonic** myths recount the origin of the gods, while **cosmogonic** myths deal with the creation of the world and mankind.

### The pre-Olympian deities

In the beginning there was **Chaos**, shortly followed by **Gaea** (the Earth) then **Eros** (Love). Alone, Gaea produced **Uranus** (Heaven), then the Mountains, the Nymphs and the barren Sea.

Uranus and his mother Gaea ruled the world together, and together gave birth to the second divine generation, the **Ouranides**. These included the **twelve Titans**, six boys and six girls, then the three **Cyclopes** and lastly the three **Hecatoncheires** (Hundred-Handed).

However, Uranus hated his offspring and imprisoned them in the depths of the Earth, in Tartarus. This eventually led to his downfall: Gaea could not bear such treatment being inflicted upon her children and started plotting with **Cronus**, the last-born of the Titans. With the aid of his brothers and sisters, who held down their father, the young Titan cut off his testicles. However, in the process, some of his seed spilt onto Gaea, who soon gave birth to the **Erinyes**, goddesses of vengeance, the **Giants** and the **Meliads** (Nymphs of the ash-trees). According to some authors, **Aphrodite**, the goddess of love, was also born as a result of this occurrence, after some sperm became mixed with foam from the Sea.

Cronus then began to rule in his father's place and married his sister Rhea with whom he planned to continue the family line. However, when a terrible prediction informed him that one day he would be dethroned by one of his children, he did not think twice about swallowing them as soon as they were born. Hestia, Demeter, Hera, Hades and Poseidon thus passed directly from their mother's belly into their father's. However, as in the previous generation, the danger was to come from the last-born of his children. **Zeus** managed to escape the sad fate of his brothers and sisters thanks to his mother, Rhea, who hid her newborn in a cave in Crete before tricking Cronus into swallowing a stone wrapped in swaddling clothes. When he reached adulthood, Zeus set his brothers and sisters free and, from the top of Mt Olympus, began to wage battle with them against Cronus and the Titans, who had taken refuge on Mt Óthris. This **Battle of the Titans** lasted for ten years until the Olympians finally claimed victory, aided by the Cyclopes and the Hecatoncheires, but resulted in no deaths, since it was fought between immortals.

But before finally becoming rulers of the world, the gods of Olympus still had to tackle the **Giants** (gigantomachia), whom they overcame thanks to the arrows of the mortal **Heracles**. Zeus then had to endure a long and merciless struggle with the terrifying monster, **Typhon**.

## The birth of man

According to **Hesiod**, the first humans – all male – were directly produced by Gaea. They had a happy and carefree existence alongside the gods, fearing not even death, which took them by surprise in their sleep. This perfect harmony was disturbed by **Prometheus**, a descendant of the Titan Iapetus: during a banquet, he was caught favouring men over the gods when sharing out the meat of an ox. Annoyed by such trickery, Zeus decided to deprive man of fire. But Prometheus once again dared to defy the omnipotent god by stealing fire and returning it to man. The wrath of Zeus knew no bounds: Prometheus was chained to the summit of Caucasus and his immortal liver endlessly devoured by an eagle.

And in order to punish mankind, Zeus created woman, "an evil to men, with a nature to do evil". Endowed with a different quality by each of the Olympian gods, **Pandora**, "the gift of all the gods", was thus offered to Epimetheus, Prometheus' brother. Once on Earth, Pandora discovered a strange jar and, unable to contain her curiosity, opened it, allowing all the evils of the world to escape and leaving hope alone inside. And so mankind was punished.

## The main gods of Olympus

High up in the mists of Olympus, the main deities convened in a "Council of the Gods", made up of twelve members. The actual members, however, vary according to the author and time of writing, with the only constant being that Zeus and his five brothers and sisters were definitely part of it.

Following their victory over the Titans, Cronus' three sons divided the world between them. **Zeus** took Heaven and quickly gained pre-eminence over his brothers. As master of the universe – although subject to Destiny – he was the protector of families and cities, and was devoted to ensuring the rule of justice and equity. Wisest of the wise, he is often depicted enthroned in limbo on Olympus, sporting a large beard, with a sceptre in one hand and a thunderbolt in the other. His notorious weakness, however, was his great appetite for women (and incidentally for men). Thus, in addition to his official wives, the goddesses Metis, Themis, Eurynome, Mnemosyne and **Hera**, he had many affairs with both goddesses and mortals, with whom he had a vast divine progeny.

Zeus' brother, **Poseidon**, ruled over the seas, although he was also able to make the Earth tremble. His palace was hidden in the ocean depths, which he occasionally left, riding on a sumptuous chariot, trident in hand and accompanied by a cortege of sea monsters (Tritons).

**Hades**, Zeus' second brother, inherited the underworld and the kingdom of the dead. Wearing a helmet that made him invisible, he kidnapped **Persephone**, the daughter of Zeus and Demeter, then married her.

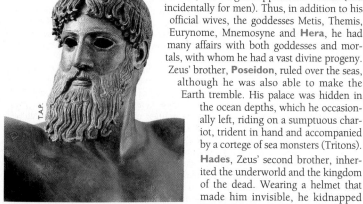

The powerful bronze Poseidon of Artemision (National Archaeological Museum, Athens)

**Hestia**, goddess of the domestic hearth and of the public hearth of the Prytaneis *(see page 46)*, was the eldest of Zeus' three sisters. Despite the advances made by Poseidon and Apollo, she remained a virgin and never left Olympus.

Zeus' sister **Demeter** had no such scruples and had an affair with him. Goddess of agriculture, and wheat in particular, she left the harvests to rot out of grief when Hades stole her daughter away. She eventually managed to arrange for Persephone to live with her for six months of the year, from the first growth of spring until sowing time in September.

Zeus' legitimate and permanent wife, **Hera**, vehemently detested all of her unfaithful husband's lovers and their offspring. So it is entirely natural that she should be the deity of marriage, protectress of conjugal fidelity and mothers. She was also goddess of vegetation.

Eight other gods and goddesses, all children of Zeus possessing outstanding powers and influence, can also lay claim to a place in the "Council of the Gods". The eternally young and handsome **Apollo** is a complex

Athena mourning
(Acropolis Museum, Athens)

deity, with many strings to his bow: god of poetry, music and song, he led the chorus of the Muses and played the **lyre**. Protector of fields and herds, he was blessed with healing powers but could also spread epidemics with his bow. But despite his great beauty, he had an unhappy love life.

**Hephaestus**, lame since the day Zeus threw him off the top of Olympus, was married to Aphrodite, who betrayed him with Ares. The crippled god took his revenge by laying a trap for the two lovers and exposing them to the view of all the gods. God of **smiths** and of metalwork, he created Pandora, the first woman, on the orders of Zeus.

The antithesis of **Ares** – the rough, brutal and cruel god of war who was intensely disliked by the Greeks – **Athena** was perceived as a warrior goddess full of good counsel. She was also the protectress of cities, women's work and peace, despite her appearance: iconography shows her emerging fully armed from Zeus' head, wearing a helmet, carrying a lance on one arm and her father's shield on the other. This shield (or her breastplate) bears the head of **Medusa** (one of the **Gorgons**) with its tresses of snakes. The head of this terrible creature, who turned to stone anyone who met her gaze, was given to Athena by Perseus.

Armed with a bow and arrow like her twin brother Apollo, **Artemis** had no qualms about killing anyone outright if they offended her. She spent the rest of her time hunting with her dogs. Although an eternal virgin, she personified fertility, a quality which she shared with the goddess of love and beauty, **Aphrodite**, who was said to have had countless lovers, including the handsome **Adonis**. In order to make sure that Paris would name her the most beautiful goddess rather than Hera or Athena, she immediately promised him the hand of the fair Helen, thus causing the Trojan War (*see below*). God of wine, ecstasy and fertility, **Dionysus** set out to conquer the East on a chariot drawn by panthers, with a kantharos full of wine in his hand and a cortege of daemons, including **Bacchants** and **Satyrs**. With his winged sandals, **Hermes** was the messenger of the gods, and carried the **caduceus** (herald's staff). Inventor of the lyre and panpipes (or syrinx, the shepherds' pipe), he was also portrayed as the god of travellers, trade, shepherds and sport, and his cunning spirit also made him the protector of thieves!

## The great legendary cycles

### A tireless labourer

Six of Heracles' Labours were performed in the north of the Peloponnese: the hero choked the reputedly invincible Nemean lion with his bare hands before using its skin as a coat. Then he used a sling to kill the man-eating birds of the Stymphalian lake. South of Árgos, he cut off the nine heads of the Hydra of Lerna. Next, he ran the ferocious wild boar of Mt Erymanthus to ground, after hunting it for months. It took him a year to capture the hind of Cerynea, which moved faster than air, but just one day to clean the stables of Augeas by diverting two nearby rivers. The other Labours consisted of capturing a mad bull in Crete, taming man-eating horses in Thrace, killing a three-bodied and three-headed king near the Strait of Gibraltar, capturing Cerberus, the hound that guarded the gates of Hell, and taking, in turn, the golden girdle of the Queen of the Amazons and the golden apples from the Hesperides' garden.

Alongside the myths lies a whole catalogue of cycles composed of countless stories portraying heroes, gods and incredible monsters, their unity being formed by one of the characters or their descendants. Here are some of the most well known:

### The adventures of Heracles

Son of Zeus and the mortal Alcmene, half god, half man, Heracles was endowed with extraordinary strength and performed a multitude of brilliant feats, conducting as many love affairs. Despised by Hera, Zeus' legitimate wife, he was provoked into killing his own children in a fit of madness sent by the goddess. To atone for these murders, he was ordered to carry out **Twelve Labours**, which he accomplished in the same number of years. Heracles performed several other feats before meeting his death after putting on a poisoned coat. However, the gods allowed him into Olympus, where he became immortal. And so justice was done.

### Jason and the Argonauts, or the quest for the Golden Fleece

Upon the death of his royal father, the young Jason's throne was usurped by his uncle Pelias. The latter agreed to return it to him on condition that his nephew bring him the Golden Fleece which was kept in Colchis on the Black Sea by King Aeetes. Pelias knew this was an impossible task, but Jason was not to be discouraged and set sail on board the **Argo**, a mighty ship built by Argos, a man with several pairs of eyes. Accompanied by his fifty **Argonauts** - including Heracles, the twins **Castor and Pollux**, and the musician **Orpheus** – he was to face many incredible ordeals throughout his voyage. He was aided not only by the precious powers of his companions, but also by the beautiful sorceress **Medea**, Aeetes' own daughter, whom he fell in love with and married. It was thanks to her powers that Jason was eventually able to secure the precious fleece.

### Theseus and the Minotaur

The great Athenian hero, Theseus, son of the King of Athens, **Aegeus**, accomplished feats similar to those of his contemporary Heracles. One of these, his fight with the **Minotaur**, is particularly famous. Son of Minos, King of Crete, this monster – half man, half bull – lived in his father's palace, a labyrinth designed by the brilliant architect **Daedalus**. Every nine years, Minos demanded that Athens, which he had just subjugated, send him seven young men and seven young women to be fed to the creature. Theseus volunteered to go and, when he arrived in Crete, managed to kill the beast. Thanks to the thread given to him by **Ariadne**, Minos' own daughter who had fallen in love with him, Theseus was able to find his way out of the labyrinth and return to Athens. But as he neared the shores of Attica where his father was watching for his return, he forgot to raise the white sails in a sign of victory. Believing his son to be dead, Aegeus threw himself from the top of the cliffs of the Acropolis.

A model labourer: Heracles
(5C BC, Musée du Louvre)

## The cycle of the Theban legends

This cycle traces the history of the origins of the city of **Thebes**, which was founded by King **Cadmus** on the spot where, as predicted by Apollo, a heifer collapsed from exhaustion. After a long reign, the elderly Cadmus passed his throne down to his descendants, **Laius** and his wife **Jocasta**. With them began one of the most famous and tragic episodes of the Theban legends, that of their son Œdipus. After being abandoned at birth, as a young man, he unwittingly fulfilled the terrible prediction of the **Delphic oracle** by killing his father and marrying his mother. It was during this episode that he rid the city of the **Sphinx**, a monster – half lion, half woman – which was devouring all the passers-by who were unable to solve the riddle it put to them.

**A riddle from the Ancient World**
Which creature walks on four feet in the morning, two at midday, and three in the evening, and, contrary to the laws of nature, is the weakest when it has the most legs? – "Man", replied Œdipus to the Sphinx. It was the right answer. Vexed, the monster threw itself to its death from the rock on which it had been perching.

The Theban cycle came to an end shortly thereafter with the quarrel between Œdipus' two sons, Eteocles and Polyneices, who killed each other, then with the tragic end of their sister, **Antigone**, who was immured alive for trying to give Polyneices a symbolic burial. The following generation was to witness the destruction of Thebes by the Argives.

## The Trojan War

Made famous by Homer, the story begins with Hera, Athena and Aphrodite assembling on Mt Ida in Crete where, under the auspices of the goddess of discord, a competition was to take place to choose the most beautiful goddess. The prize – a golden apple – was to be handed to the winner by the handsome **Paris**, the youngest son of **Priam**, the King of Troy. However, perfidious Aphrodite bribed the young man into choosing her by promising him the love of the most beautiful mortal, **Helen**, the wife of King **Menelaus**. Paris took her at her word and kidnapped the young woman, whom he brought back to Troy, thus causing war to break out.

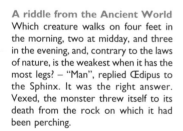

On one side, the Achaeans, led by **Agamemnon**, King of Mycenae and ally of Menelaus. On the other, the Trojans, aided by **Aeneas**, Aphrodite's son. The siege lasted nine years. Homer's account, the *Iliad*, actually recounts only one of the last episodes, that of the famous **Trojan horse**. Since the Trojans were holding out, Agamemnon decided to play a trick, offering Priam a magnificent wooden horse in which he was hiding with his best men, **Achilles**, **Odysseus** and **Ajax**. The horse entered the city, the enemy along with it, and Troy fell at last.

Homer also relates the quarrel that took place between Agamemnon and Achilles before the horse made its appearance, and the heroic deaths of the warriors Patroclus and Hector, then Achilles, who was wounded in the heel – his only vulnerable point – by a poisoned arrow.

## The return of Odysseus

Back from Troy, Odysseus set off for his kingdom, the Ionian island of Ithaca. During this ten-year voyage, which is related in the *Odyssey*, the hero encountered innumerable dangers: **Giants**, the sorceress **Circe**, the treacherously sweet song of the **Sirens**, as well as the monsters **Scylla** and **Charybdis**, not to mention the **cyclops Polyphemus**, son of Poseidon, whose murder brought the wrath of the god of the Sea down upon Odysseus and his companions. After finally returning to Ithaca twenty years after he left, the warrior was recognised by his wife, the faithful **Penelope**, because he was the only one able to string his bow and shoot a single arrow through twelve axes standing in a row.

These legendary cycles are as exciting as they are numerous. You are sure to come across many others on your travels, such as the tragic fate of the Atreids who haunt the ruins of Mycenae, and you will find them in the relevant sections of this guide.

## From Greek to Latin

| Greek name | Latin equivalent | | |
|---|---|---|---|
| Aphrodite | Venus | Hephaestus | Vulcan |
| Apollo or Phoibos | Apollo or Phoebus | Hera | Juno |
| Ares | Mars | Heracles | Hercules |
| Artemis | Diana | Hermes | Mercury |
| Asklepios | Aesculapius | Hestia | Vesta |
| Athena | Minerva | Erinyes | Furiae |
| Cronus | Saturn | Leto | Latona |
| Demeter | Ceres | Persephone | Proserpina |
| Dionysus | Bacchus | Poseidon | Neptune |
| Eros | Cupid | Rhea | Cybele |
| Hades | Pluto | Zeus | Jupiter |

Bellerophon and Pegasus; red-figure kantharos (National Archaeological Museum, Athens)

Greek mythology

# Meeting the people

The kafenío, or
the art of relaxation

# A HOMOGENEOUS NATION

"Where do you come from? Which village? Which family?" these questions are frequently asked when Greeks first meet. Solidarity and a willingness to help each other often best define relations between compatriots. This is because regionalism has always been synonymous with cultural and social identity since well before the notion of national identity began to develop under the yoke of Ottoman rule. Despite the country's small size, the regional disparities of modern Greece are quite considerable: Epirus has a distinct Balkan flavour, and a fisherman from Santoríni has very little in common with a wealthy shipowner from Athens living on European time. Nevertheless, the 10.7 million inhabitants of Greece have managed to form a homogeneous nation, built up over the centuries around the **language** and the **Orthodox Church**.

**National colours**
Although all Greeks acknowledge the same flag – five blue bands and four white, with the white cross of the Greek Orthodox Church in one corner – they don't all agree on the meaning of its colours. For most people, the blue represents the sky and the sea, and the white the struggle for independence. For others with more poetic leanings, the blue bands symbolise the sea and the white ones its foam. But the religious maintain that the blue is the colour of wisdom, the white representing the purity of the soul.

## The origins of the Greek world

To be Greek is to be the living memory of the country's wealth of history: the grandeur of Ancient Greece, the splendour of the Byzantine Period, the suffering of the Ottoman invasion and the pride of present-day Greece, which is busily trying to catch up with the rest of Europe while preserving and honouring a certain ideology of the past.

### The first Greeks: the Hellenes
The Hellenes, a group encompassing various Indo-European peoples considered to be the first Greeks, first appeared in the 2nd millennium BC. After 2000 BC, the early inhabitants of the Hellenic Peninsula, the **Pelasgi**, were forced to flee as the **Ionians** advanced. The latter were followed by the **Achaeans**, mariners from the north who mixed with the local populations and gave birth to the Mycenaean civilisation *(see page 18)*. This civilisation was to disappear, in turn, around 1200 BC in the face of the **Dorian** invasion. It was this last Indo-European wave which drove the Greeks towards the western shores of Asia Minor (Aeolis, Ionia, Doris), bringing them into contact with the eastern civilisations.

### Settlers from abroad
After 395 AD, the history of Greece merges with that of the Byzantine Empire, the heir to Rome and Hellenism. Further invasions beginning in the late 6C brought about considerable demographic change. While many Greeks were forced to flee the Peloponnese, **Slavs** began to settle throughout the territory. They were followed by the **Vlachs** (or **Aromani**), an Indo-European people who originated from a region corresponding to what is now Romania, and who still inhabit the mountains of Epirus, Thessaly and Macedonia.

Then came the **Arab** occupation of Crete in the 9C and 10C, the arrival of the **Gypsies** in the 9C, the **Bulgar** incursions (late 10C) in mainland Greece, and the attempted conquests of Sicily (late 11C) by the **Normans**. Very early in the 13C, the Greek islands fell into the hands of the **Venetians**, whose presence still persists in the small Catholic communities of the Cyclades. Lastly, the capture of Constantinople by the **Ottomans** in 1453 was to have an important impact on demographic makeup, particularly in the north.

It is also important to note the presence of a small **Jewish community**, consisting mainly of the descendants of Jews driven out of Spain and Portugal in the 15C, who were taken in by the Ottomans. Of the 80 000 Jews living in Greece in 1940 (50 000 of them in Thessaloníki), 62 500 were deported by the Nazis during the Second World War.

## The Greeks and the world

The Greeks have a very revealing expression which helps to better understand the link which binds them to their homeland, which they call the "centre of the world": when Greeks set out to travel abroad, they say "I'm going outside" (*"exoterikó"*), in other words, they are leaving their home to venture into the intrinsically hostile unknown; 400 years of Ottoman occupation have deeply marked the collective subconscious. Moreover, a feeling of latent insecurity – Greece still feels itself surrounded by enemies – continues to affect its relations with other countries.

### The Greek diaspora
Greece's historical importance and geographical location have encouraged its inhabitants to venture beyond their borders. Overpopulation and poverty in the early 20C generated a strong wave of emigration between 1906 and 1915, when over 250 000 Greeks (out of a total population of 3 million) took the road to exile. An estimated 5.5 million Greeks now live abroad in Egypt, Central Europe, around the Black Sea, in the Middle East – regions where Greek communities settled in very ancient times – and particularly in the **United States**, where there are currently thought to be over 3 million of them. **Michael Dukakis**, the Democratic candidate in the 1988 American presidential elections (running against George Bush), is a good example of the Greeks' successful integration on the other side of the Atlantic. In recent times, emigrants have headed for other industrialised countries such as Canada, Australia, South Africa and Germany.

### Status of minorities
A Greek citizen is an individual who practises the Orthodox religion (mention of religion has only just been removed from identity cards) and speaks Greek, which is the case of 97% of those living on Greek territory. However, within its present borders, which were stabilised after the Second World War, the country unites Greeks from all sorts of backgrounds, some of them from populations who have been moved at some point in their history.

The largest minorities include nationals from the border countries who are no longer in their own homeland for historical, economic or political reasons. Under the 1923 **Treaty of Lausanne** (*see page 30*), 500 000 Muslims left for Turkey and 1.5 million Greeks flooded in from Asia Minor where there had been a Greek presence for thousands of years. However, approximately 60 000 **Turks** managed to avoid this painful exchange of population and still live in Greece, while Istanbul has only a very small Greek community.

Greece also has some 120 000 **Pomaks**, Bulgarian-speaking Muslims who live mainly in western Thrace, **Macedonians** in northern Greek Macedonia, and **Albanians** from Epirus who remained in Greece when the borders were being mapped out, hence the presence of Orthodox Christians in Albania, which is at the root of the strained relations between the two countries.

From 1975, Greece became a country of immigration as thousands of Poles, Filipinos, Kurds, Romanians, Iraqis, Pakistanis, Ethiopians, Egyptians, people from the former Yugoslavia and particularly from the countries of the old **Soviet Union** began to flood into Greece looking for work. An estimated 7% of the Greek population are therefore immigrants, including a large proportion of "illegals". The State eyes these minorities with suspicion and officially recognises only one of them, the Muslims of Turkish origin, in accordance with the Treaty of Lausanne.

# DAILY LIFE

At the dawn of the third millennium, Greece is keen to renew its image and take its place in the modern world. The prospect of holding the Olympic Games of 2004 in particular has transformed the capital city into a huge building site, injecting life into many projects which had long remained on the backburner. Athens is getting a makeover: it is polishing up and restoring its ancient relics, extending its metro, renovating and developing its road network, working to reduce pollution and creating pedestrian zones. In short, it is making every effort to be worthy of its future guests, who will be coming from all over the world and from the Europe of tomorrow, to which it now also belongs.

This metamorphosis is, however, only visible in the cities. The mountains and islands of rural Greece are still largely unaffected by this technological revolution, and the rural exodus *(see page 33)* is only serving to widen the gap between town and country. While Internet cafés are mushrooming in cities all over the country, some mountain folk still communicate with their neighbours in the next village by using an elaborate whistling code. But mobile phones have made their appearance here too...

## Family portraits

### In Kifissiá, an upmarket district of Athens

Nícos Papadópoulos lives with his wife Hélena and their two children in an elegant neo-Classical house in Kifissiá, an upmarket district in the north of the capital. Nícos and Hélena met when they were very young. Their respective fathers had shared business and financial interests, and the marriage of their children served to strengthen their partnership. Since then, Nícos has taken over as manager of his father's company. Hélena, who has never worked, spends her spare time shopping and making every effort to be the "perfect woman", with frequent trips to the hairdresser and beautician. In the evening, the couple like to meet up with friends at a restaurant or in the chic *bouzoúkia (see sidebar page 77)* of the capital.

Their children, Geórgos and Anastasía, attend one of the best private schools in Athens, reserved for the children of the capital's "upper crust". They are taught in both Greek and English and are studying for an international baccalaureate which will allow them to go to university abroad. Lessons begin at 8am and the children are back home at around 3.30pm, where a copious lunch prepared by the maid awaits them. They spend the rest of the afternoon at the **frondistírio**, a private institute which fills the gaps of both public and private teaching.

### In Trípoli, a small town in the heart of the Peloponnese

Theódoros and Dímitra call each other *Papoú* and *Yayá*, like all of the grandfathers and grandmothers of Greece. They left their mountain village after their wedding to live in Trípoli, the nearest town. There, Theódoros found a job and a better environment in which to raise their two children in the way they wanted. Now a retired post office worker, he has a modest pension and devotes his spare time to the upkeep of the church in the village where he grew up, which gives him the opportunity to chat with lifelong friends. He also grows vines, which produce a pleasant rosé wine. Dímitra has never worked, but during the civil war she did much to help the locals and is still actively involved in the life of the community. She still finds time to take care of her kitchen garden, diligently watering it each morning before the council cuts off the public water supply, which it does every day until the evening.

### In Heliópolis, a working class district of Athens

Danáï, 20 years old, and Vassilis, 28, are engaged to be married. Vassilis has opened a computer shop with two of his school friends, tapping a rapidly expanding market. As for Danáï, she is busy with the wedding preparations under the watchful eye of her mother. The big day will, of course, begin with the church ceremony, and then it will be party time. But first of all, she must take care of the *"príka"*, the dowry: like all brides-to-be in Greece, Danáï must provide her husband with a furnished apartment where the couple will, at last, be able to live together. And since Danáï doesn't know how to cook, it is her mother, who lives on the floor below, who will take care of the cooking and the education of her future grandchildren. While waiting for their new life to begin, the two lovebirds often go out together in the evening. After an early-evening siesta, they will join their friends in a café or nightclub, unless the *paréa* (group of friends) prefers to go to a taverna, as is often the case at the weekend.

### In Shinoússa, an island lost in the middle of the Cyclades

In winter, Shinoússa has only 90 inhabitants, who all live in the village. In the low season, there are fewer connections by boat and the inhabitants have to rely on community spirit to cope with the isolation and hardship of winter. At the primary school, all of the children are taught together in one class by one single teacher. The oldest ones have to go and live with their cousins on the neighbouring island of Náxos in order to attend the secondary school. But with the holidays comes the time for family reunions: the children, along with all the other family members living far away, return to live on the island, and the population multiplies by ten. The first tourists herald the return of summer and, along with it, a radical change in atmosphere: the solidarity and conviviality of the islanders gives way to competition, a necessity of business. But this is just until the summer holidays come to an end, when the island becomes tranquil once again.

**What's in a name?**
During your travels, you may be surprised to find yourself constantly coming across the same first names – Níkos, Geórgos, Kóstas, etc. It is traditional in Greece for boys to be given the same name as their grandfather, which means that first names skip a generation but always reappear. The same goes for girls although, unlike for boys, some exceptions are tolerated on condition, however, that the name comes from the Orthodox calendar.

## Slices of life

### At the "laïkí", the market

The meeting place par excellence of all housewives, the *laïkí* is an open-air market, whose countless stalls, just like an oriental souk, take up the whole street. A constantly bustling bazaar with a friendly atmosphere, where grocers, market gardeners, fishmongers and ironmongers mingle in a medley of fragrances, colours and sounds. But remember, the *laïkí* is made up of two parts: on one side, fresh and dried fruit and vegetables, flowers and fish – sold directly by the fishermen – and on the other, an amazing variety of hardware stalls, often run by Póntii, Greek immigrants from Pontus Euxinus (the Black Sea), alternating with stalls selling lingerie and tourist souvenirs, not forgetting

G. de Benoist/MICHELIN

Donkey, goat, and Greek

Yássas (Cheers!)

the Africans with their alarm clocks, watches and radios. The *laïkí* are mainly frequented by Greek women, who love to meet up there and share their opinions on the latest fashions or the quality of the tomatoes, for which they never tire of bargaining.

## At the "kafenío": coffee and komboloï

Women at the *laïkí*, men at the *kafenío*. Impregnable bastion of the gentlemen – moustaches trimmed and caps firmly in place – every self-respecting kafenío must possess a television set, placed high on an oilcloth-covered shelf so that it can be seen by all. The Greeks go there at any time of day, for no particular reason, with the events of the day and the activity in the streets providing endless topics of conversation. Sitting in front of a Greek coffee or glass of ouzo (always served with a large glass of water), they discuss the TV news and football, criticise the latest law passed by Parliament, enthuse about the stock market, or chat, just as seriously, about donkeys and goats. Some play cards or **távli**, a very traditional board game (similar to backgammon) inherited from the Byzantines; others sit alone on the terrace watching the world go by, lacing their *komboloï* through their fingers. And so they pass the time peacefully until dinner time, when they all go home to enjoy the culinary delights prepared by their wives or mothers.

The picture would be incomplete without a mention of the **komboloï**, a curious "rosary" which all of these men, regardless of age and social background, hold in their hands and click through their fingers at their own pace. Some women have also taken to doing this – the actress Melína Mercoúri was one notable example – but in their case, it is considered to be more of a feminist statement. The first traces of this object date back to prehistory, to the famous caves of Altamira in Spain. They were originally made of animal knucklebones, the number and quality of which corresponded to its owner's rank within the tribe. A symbol of power among wise men, then gradually becoming considered as sacred through the centuries, they had various functions. In Greece, the *komboloï* have no religious significance, a rare thing in this country. Of plastic or precious materials and threaded, one by one, through the fingers all day long, the beads are of mainly sentimental value, tinged with a certain sensuality. But this does not prevent the inhabitants of some country areas from also attributing to the *komboloï* the power to ward off the "evil eye".

## A buzzing night-life

Like almost everywhere else around the Mediterranean, night-life in Greece is long and lively. It gets going around 11pm and carries on until dawn. Every night of the week, the night-clubs and *bouzoúkia (see page 76)* are full to bursting, the former attracting mainly young people, and the latter a greater mix of generations. People go to bouzoúkia to listen to their favourite singers, throw them flowers and get into the swing by dancing on the tables, if not joining them on stage! Then, of course, there are the restaurants, where *parées* (groups of friends) like to meet up, but not before 11pm.

At the most touristy sites and beaches in the high season (in Greece, summer begins at Easter and finishes in October), the nights come alive with the noise and lights of all these bustling places where the holidaymakers party together until the early hours of the morning. Which means that you'll find the biggest traffic

### An outdoor social life
The Greeks rarely entertain at home, preferring to meet up with their friends elsewhere. Although the "laïkí" is assiduously frequented by housewives, and the "kafenío" by married or retired men, the street remains the most popular meeting place: influenced by Western fashion, cafés and fast-food outlets are very popular with the younger generation, who meet up with their "parées" there.

jams – cars and backfiring two-wheelers – between 9pm and 4am. So if you're hoping to sleep peacefully, make sure you avoid rooms which give on to the street!

## At school
Whether public or private, all Greek schools are obliged by law to teach Orthodox theology, and at the beginning of every month, the parish priest comes to say a prayer to the schoolchildren.

School is compulsory between the ages of 6 and 15 and the school day has a minimum of five hours of lessons. However, insufficient funding means that many public establishments are unable to provide a fuller education and since there are not enough of them to educate all of the children, the State has imposed a system of half-day sharing of premises: the pupils go to school either in the morning or in the afternoon, so the establishment is fully occupied all day long. Likewise, schoolbooks are often terribly out of date, with some schools still using editions which are 30 years old. This explains why it is not uncommon to find words of warning in some history books advising children to "be wary of foreigners in general, and Turks in particular"!

The wealthiest families therefore often choose to send their children to private school, where they receive a fuller education, which includes learning several foreign languages and sports. But this remains a very expensive privilege, with some monthly instalments costing more than the equivalent of the Greek minimum wage.

## Religion, part of everyday life

As the State religion *(see the chapter on this subject page 67)*, Orthodox Christianity touches every aspect of Greek life and dictates a good many customs. At birth, for example, children are given a provisional name – *Baby* for boys, *Béba* for girls – until their baptism, when their godfathers give them their proper name, which, for the boys, is traditionally their grandfather's.

Every event, whether private or public, has to receive the **ayasmó**, the inevitable blessing of the Church. Depending on the occasion, it is the Orthodox priest or the archbishop who officiates (in return for payment, of course): the prelate to bless the election of a new president of the Republic or the forming of a new Parliament, the priest for the purchase of a house, a car or the opening of a shop.

As a mark of devotion to God, the **sign of the cross** - which contrary to the Catholic practice goes from right to left – is made on every occasion: children do it every morning at school before entering the classroom, and when passing a holy place it should be made three times.

Officially recognised by the State, **weddings at the Orthodox Church** suffice in themselves and couples are not required to go to the registry office as well. The number of registry office weddings, which are uncommon and unpopular, is estimated at less than 3%. Indeed, to many Greeks, a refusal to comply with religious traditions reminds them of Communism and civil war, the dark memory of which still lurks at the back of peoples' minds.

# Family ceremonies

The Greeks certainly know how to party, and weddings and baptisms bring family and friends together in the most festive atmosphere. If, during your travels, you come across such an occasion in a village, don't hesitate to join in: you will certainly be made to feel welcome, and these moments of joyful celebration are sure to leave you some wonderful memories.

### Baptism (váptisi)

The sacrament of baptism marks the entry of the faithful into the fold of the Church, and is the occasion on which the child is given its first name, chosen by its godfather (*O Nonós*) and godmother (*I Noná*). Holding the baby in their arms, they undress it and cover it all over with holy (olive) oil, before handing the child over to the priest, who then immerses it totally in water in a large tub three times in succession. The child is then dried and given **new clothes** which have never been worn before, so that it can enter life with "a new body, new spirit... and new clothes" – this special notion of "newness" is very important to Orthodox Christians. After this, the child is placed back in the arms of its godparents, who walk around the altar with it three times. Lastly, the priest cuts a **lock of hair** from the child, the first offering to God by the new member of the flock, in thanks for its consecration.

### Marriage (gámos)

The wedding ceremony is an even more colourful affair than a baptism. At the church, the congregation is free to move around during the liturgy, so family and friends greet one another, and introductions, hugs and congratulations abound as gleeful children run around in all directions. On this occasion, the congregation is exceptionally allowed to approach the altar on the other side of the iconostasis in order to follow the event more closely. Standing just behind the future husband and wife, the witnesses each hold a **crown of flowers** (*Stephánia*) above their heads, as a symbol of purity. Then all four of them walk around the altar three times under a shower of rice and flower petals as the cheers of the guests echo throughout the church. When they finally leave the church, the newlyweds and their respective families are congratulated by one and all with the words *"Na zíssete"* (long may you live), while the witnesses are wished *"Pánda áxios"* (be always worthy). Incidentally, divorce and remarriage are accepted by the Orthodox Church.

### Funerals (kidía)

The death of a loved one is obviously also an important time. In the villages, it is customary for the corpse of the deceased to be laid out at his or her home until the funeral so that everyone – family members and villagers – can go and pay their last respects. For the religious ceremony, the coffin is set down at the centre of the church surrounded by the deceased's family who, in some regions, still wear the black armbands of mourning. The Orthodox priest talks about the life of the deceased and of their being called to God while awaiting the resurrection of body and spirit. On leaving the church, the family hands out slices of cake which are supposed to ease the pain. The funeral cortege then forms to accompany the coffin to the cemetery. After the burial, the mourners gather around a copious meal served with wine, brandy and coffee. Finally, forty days later, one last mass is celebrated in memory of the deceased, the *Mnimósyno*.

## Family spirit... and women of today

Shaped by long centuries of Ottoman (Muslim) culture and a strict Orthodox tradition, the status of women in Greece still remains bound by many family customs and ancient social conventions.

But times are changing. In the villages, although the oldest grandmothers, bowed by hard work, still wear headscarves and dress in black from head to toe, their granddaughters are wearing makeup with tight T-shirts and trousers and hanging out at the cafés in town with their groups of friends. These two facets of Greek women symbolise the paradox of present-day society: a sincere attachment to tradition on the one hand, and a fierce desire to move into a new era, on the other.

Since 1952 when Greek women were finally given the right to vote (in Turkey it was in 1923), many laws have been introduced which have changed the status of women. Abortion has been legalised, divorce has rapidly become widespread and Greek women now have the right to keep their maiden name after marriage. On the other hand, although the **dowry** which the wife was supposed to give her husband has been officially abolished, the tradition has remained alive and it is still done for brides to provide their husbands with furnished accommodation as a wedding present.

In fact, most families continue to live together under the same roof, with parents and children dividing the storeys between them, and it is customary for parents to build or buy a house with as many apartments as they have daughters. This social convention has naturally caused a **very strong family bond** to develop, in which help from the parents plays a fundamental part. Furthermore, grandmothers still raise their grandchildren and are in charge of cooking for the entire household, with their daughters dropping in every day to pick up the dishes they prepare.

Far from disappearing, this family tradition is actually very well suited to the lives of women today. Women are now staking a claim to very different lives from those of their mothers and grandmothers, according more importance to building a career than a family. As a result, more and more women aim to have only one child or two at the very most, and head into the cities in search of greater social and personal fulfilment.

**Family spirit**

A short break at the kafenío between masses

V. Voutsas/ON LOCATION

# SOCIAL ETIQUETTE

Greece welcomes over 8 million visitors every year, a source of profit which certainly warrants special attention from the inhabitants. But beyond such business considerations, the Greeks have a real sense of hospitality, remaining true to the tradition which holds that a traveller should be welcomed like a guest. This idea is reflected in the double meaning of the word *xenos*, which means both "foreigner" and "guest". As soon as you arrive, you will appreciate the spontaneity with which the Greeks welcome you, eager to help make your stay easier in any way they can or to give you directions using whatever foreign words they know. In return, remember to thank them with a warm *"Evharistó poli"*, and you will see in their smiles the genuine pleasure they take in being able to give you a helping hand.

## A strong temperament

Like all true Mediterranean peoples, the Greeks have a **passionate** temperament and a fierce individuality, and are quickly carried away by their feelings. This character trait comes to the fore in all circumstances whenever personal or professional issues are at stake. They will fall into each other's arms and frantically embrace, just as they will argue and lecture each other at the slightest disagreement, gesticulating wildly. As you walk through a square, past a market stall or restaurant, you may even become unwittingly involved in such a spirited conversation yourself. Neighbours and passers-by will also join in to mediate or give their opinion before the altercation ends in front of a glass of ouzo to the accolades of a crowd satisfied with the show. You may be rather surprised by this excess of gestures and decibels, at times almost theatrical, but it is rarely of any great consequence.

The Greeks are **fervent patriots** and extremely proud of their roots, culture and land – hardly surprising for a people forced to endure four centuries of foreign domination. Thus they also care a great deal about what travellers think of their country.

## How to mix with the locals

### A wish for every occasion

Popular tradition holds that people should wish each other all sorts of good things not only when a major occasion arises, but also throughout the day, the seasons, and with the passing of time. For the Greeks, this is actually a way of keeping the "evil eye" at bay (*see page 74*). So there is a saying for every occasion, and you are sure to please if you can slip one in at the right time. Here are a few examples:
- *Na sas zíssi* on the birth of a child, which literally means "may he (or she) live long",
- an ill person should be wished a *Perastiká*, a good recovery,
- for expectant mothers, one hopes for a *Kalí eleftheria*, literally a "good freedom",
- on the patron saint's day, the whole family is wished *Hrónia pollá*, which means "many years", the equivalent of our "many happy returns".

Wishes are also exchanged at the beginning of every season, month and week:
- *Kaló himóna*: have a good winter,
- *Kaló kalokaíri*: have a good summer,
- *Kaló mína*: have a good month,
- *Kalí evdhomáda*: have a good week.

The best way to get fresh fish (Hydra harbour)

And of course every day starts with a lively *Hérete!*, lasting until the end of the afternoon when it gives way to the customary *Kalispéra* (have a good evening), then to the bedtime greeting *Kali nihta*.

Lastly, if you want to flatter a friend, congratulate a child or shower a newborn baby with praise, it is customary to finish with an emphatic *Ftoussou*, a magic formula which protects the loved one from the "evil eye".

## Sign language

- If, in answer to a question, your interlocutor throws their head back, raising their chin, it means no. However, if they incline their head slightly to the side, they are saying yes.
- You can clap your hands to attract a waiter's attention in a restaurant without being considered rude.
- Be warned: raising your hand with your five fingers spread (palm facing forward) is considered an insult.

## Do's and don'ts

As in all countries, it is good form to adapt your behaviour to suit the occasion. Being a religious people, the Greeks like visitors to respect their **holy places**: it is highly improper to enter while eating, and visitors must be suitably attired. Many monasteries and churches will allow women and girls to enter only if they are wearing below-the-knee skirts or dresses and their shoulders are covered. Likewise, men may be required to wear long trousers, heat wave or not!

**In the country**, or in regions where few tourists venture, the inhabitants may appear reserved or even distant. Each village effectively has its own customs and traditions, and the arrival of visitors in these peaceful and unchanging micro-societies can cause them to become particularly withdrawn. So if you want to **take photographs** of someone, be sure to ask their permission first with a smile.

If you are invited to a **family home**, you will soon discover that they don't stand on ceremony. In particular, at mealtimes, where the servings are often very copious, don't feel that you have to finish what is on your plate. These large servings are a counter-reaction to all the deprivation of the dark years and the lady of the house will not be offended, merely surprised by your "small appetite".

Lastly, when you meet people, remember to avoid certain **sensitive subjects** which are likely to put a dampener on the atmosphere. Be sure, in particular, to avoid any comparison with or even reference to **the Turks**. Resentment against Turkey, which is still being fuelled by the Cypriot question, remains very much in the hearts of the Greeks, despite the efforts of the Foreign Minister, Papandréou. A more conciliatory approach, however, appears to have emerged since the earthquake of summer 1999, which hit both countries in succession and resulted in spontaneous offers of mutual aid from Ankara and Athens.

It is also advisable to avoid raising any discussion about the events in **Kosovo**, since the Greeks, who are pro-Serb, very clearly opposed the attitude of the West, and the United States in particular.

In any event, although the Greeks love to discuss politics among themselves, they prefer to broach much lighter subjects with a *xenos* (foreigner) and laud the treasures of the "most beautiful country in the world".

# RELIGION

Orthodox Christianity is the official religion of Greece and unites 97% of the population. Since there has been no separation between Church and State, the president of the Republic is sworn in on the Bible, every public event unfailingly takes place in the presence of a representative of the Church, and the compulsory reference to religion on the national identity card – the only country in the whole of Europe to do this – has only recently been abolished. It is also important to remember that, in the early 19C, the clergy took an active part in the fight for independence which brought four centuries of Ottoman domination to an end. All in all, the Orthodox religion plays a major role in the national consciousness and is a fundamental part of Greek identity. If you're in any doubt, just attend one of the big religious festivals which dot the calendar and you will experience all the fervour of the Greek people at first hand *(see page 71)*.

## Orthodox Christianity, a State religion

### The Great East-West Schism

At first united by their genesis and doctrine, the paths of **Orthodox Christianity** and **Catholicism** began to diverge in the 5C, eventually resulting in the greatest schism in the history of Christianity. This rupture became official in July 1054 with the definitive separation of the Western Latin Church and the Eastern Church. Two worlds drew apart, and Byzantium, proclaiming itself the sole heir to Rome, became the new symbol of Hellenism. The main causes of the Great Schism – which are as numerous as they are complex – resulted, very basically, from two different readings of the Trinity or **"filioque"** (Latin, meaning "and from the son"): for the Catholics, the Holy Spirit came, in effect, from the Father and from the Son, while for Orthodox Christians, it came from the Father alone.

There is also the fundamental question of **language**: loyal to Rome, the Catholics held mass in Latin, while the Orthodox Christians, heirs to the Byzantine tradition, used ancient Greek with a vocabulary which yields a different interpretation of the Apostles' teachings.

Caught in a stranglehold between two Churches (although still mainly under Roman rule at the time), the Greek cities hesitated between East and West. Shaken by historical events, Greece wavered in its religious convictions for a long time, with the successive waves of invaders serving only to add to the confusion, first of all with the arrival of Arabic Islam in the 7C, then the intrusion of the Latins and Mongols in the 13C, followed by four centuries of Turkish Islam beginning in the 15C.

### A Christian enclave in a Muslim land

"Better the Ottoman turban than the Latin mitre" was the Patriarch of Constantinople's reaction when the Pope offered to send his soldiers to stave off Mehmet II's army, which was already standing at the gates of the city (1453). In one of the paradoxes of history, the Turks actually worked in favour of Orthodox Christianity gaining supremacy in Greece: under the aegis of the Patriarchate of Constantinople, they turned the conquered land into a **millet**, a community administered by the Orthodox Church, thus imposing Orthodox Christianity as the religion of Greece. The sultan's strategy was a clever one, allowing him to undermine the Pope's authority in the country while waiting for the last embers of Byzantium to die down in turn.

This privilege naturally meant that heavy tributes had to be paid to the Ottoman crown. What was initially considered to be a victory of Hellenic thinking over the Turkish occupant was gradually revealed as a compromise. And so, as the years of occupation turned into centuries, Orthodox Christians gradually turned their backs

## An ecumenical century?

It was not until the 20C that a dialogue was struck up again between the Catholic and Orthodox Churches. First in Jerusalem in 1964, then in 1967, when Pope Paul VI met the Patriarch of Constantinople, Athenagoras I. The first tangible signs of a reconciliation at last began to appear after centuries of cold opposition. The separation of Church and State is another recurring debate in Greece and a constant source of concern to the Orthodox Christians, since the Church has always played an important part in the country's affairs.

on the Patriarch of Constantinople, in favour of the parish priests, who were more in touch with the people and their expectations. The capture of Constantinople by the Turks served only to consummate the split. The millet system thus disappeared at the end of the 18C when the Greek bourgeoisie was casting off the political yoke of the Patriarchate, leaving it with nothing more than an ecumenical role. Today, only the Dodecanese and Crete – which joined Greece much later on – and Mt Athos still depend, at least in theory, on Constantinople.

## The heir to the Byzantine Church

It was the Church of **Byzantine rite** which gave itself the epithet of "Orthodox", ie "conform to doctrine". It represents the faith of the Fathers of the Church and considers itself to be the loyal heir to the writings of the Apostles. Although the Orthodox Church acknowledges the Pope, it does not consider him to be St Peter's successor, but merely a bishop.

The **Holy Synod** is the governing body of the Orthodox Church; the ecumenical patriarchate, the archdioceses and dioceses, and the parishes.

Despite being autonomous entities, the **patriarchates** all recognise the honorary primacy of the Patriarchate of **Constantinople**, the great historical patriarchates being those of Rome, Antioch (Antakya), Jerusalem, Aleppo and Alexandria.

The Greek Orthodox Church is independent. Since 1835 it has been an **autocephalous church**, governed by its own head bishops, having split away from the Patriarchate of Constantinople. Thus demonstrating a certain spiritual independence, it aims to be less of an institution and more the expression of a united and holy church, present even in the country's smallest villages and in touch with the people. This choice is reflected in various media initiatives, so it is not at all unusual to see the Patriarch of Athens on television commenting on current affairs in social-oriented statements.

In a remarkable departure from the Catholics, the Orthodox Church allows certain low-ranking secular priests to marry. **Orthodox priests** are therefore entirely at liberty to start a family and frequent the same places as any other citizen. So don't be surprised if you come across one of these honourable defenders of the Byzantine faith – long black *rasa* and grey beard under the inevitable *kalimavci* – wandering around a supermarket or sitting in a *kafenio,* talking away on his mobile phone!

## The icons, or images of the Kingdom of God

Another significant feature of Orthodox Christianity is the importance accorded to

### Mt Athos, sanctuary of the Byzantine faith

Spiritual and intellectual bastion of the purest Orthodox Christianity, the community of Mt Athos has, since the 10C, been the closed domain of hermits and monks living according to a tradition of strict discipline introduced by St Athanasius the Athonite. Although many pilgrims manage to gain entry to these monasteries, members of the fair sex are never to be seen there, since Athonite rules forbid any form of female presence – animal or human – on their territory. Since 1926, Mt Athos has had an autonomous administrative status, placed under both the canonic jurisdiction of the Patriarch of Constantinople and the political protectorate of the Greek government. In the 16C there were around 15 000 monks on Mt Athos but there are now only 1 500.

The iconostasis: splendour and mystery of the Byzantine church

**images** (icons) evoking the Kingdom of God, and the profound and mystical intensity of the liturgical vocabulary. In the churches, a high screen covered in icons – the **iconostasis** – separates the nave from the sanctuary, isolating the officiating Orthodox priest from the worshippers during consecration (the central doors are opened and closed according to the different stages of the ceremony), creating an atmosphere shrouded in mystery. The word

**A holy icon**
After the iconoclastic crisis which caused the loss of thousands of masterpieces from the world of art, it was the Empress Theodora who, on 11 March 843, reinstated the icons and their role in Byzantine churches. Since then, this date has been celebrated each year in all of the Orthodox parishes in Greece. The revered icon of the Virgin Mary on the island of Tínos attracts thousands of pilgrims, especially on the Day of the Assumption. According to tradition, this icon was the work of St Luke himself and is also said to possess miraculous powers, as evidenced by the countless crutches piled up in a corner of the church.

**mystery** is also used by Orthodox Christians to describe what other Churches call sacraments (baptism, marriage, etc). In the Orthodox religion, the images of the saints play a very special part. However, contrary to the thinking of the iconoclasts of the 7C-8C, these icons are not in themselves objects of worship linked to idolatrous practices, but symbolic images devoid of any realism, which comply with strict conventions established right from the outset. Each character can thus be recognised by its attributes, the colour of the clothes and so forth, thereby creating a visual language that allows everyone, literate or not, to identify the saint to whom they are praying.

## Religious minorities

In Greece, the religious minorities are gathered together under the high patronage of the Orthodox Church. In practice, this means that for the renovation or construction of a church, mosque or synagogue, for example, they have to obtain permission from the relevant Orthodox bishop.

## Catholics

The Greek Catholic community numbers approximately 45 000, but despite this relatively low figure, it has encountered strong resistance from the Orthodox Church. Although the archbishoprics of Corfu, Thessaloníki and Tínos have been officially recognised by the Greek State, this is still not the case of the archbishopric of Athens, founded in 1880, ie almost 60 years after the War of Independence.

The same distance exists in civic affairs: marriages between Catholics are recognised by the Greek State, but matters are complicated when the husband and wife do not share the same faith. In the event of a "mixed" marriage, Catholics recognise and tolerate the Orthodox party and accept the union without any particular requirements. But there is no reciprocity, and the Orthodox Church only acknowledges the marriage if it is celebrated within its fold. The future husband and wife are, however, free to hold a Catholic wedding beforehand.

Furthermore, in order to avoid conflicts between the followers of different faiths during Lent or feast periods, Greek Catholics have agreed to celebrate Easter according to the Julian calendar, like the Orthodox Christians.

## Muslims

The Muslims of Greece are still living with the memory of the dramatic and difficult **exodus** which followed the end of the First World War. Once independence was proclaimed, the Greeks immediately set about eradicating every trace of Ottoman domination from their territory. The last bastion of Islam in the country, **Thrace** (north-east Greece) is today home to 120 000 Muslims, and the region's cities are still dotted with minarets.

This minority has acquired a special position and status within the Greek State and is even represented in Parliament by two elected authorities, guaranteeing the Muslims a certain number of rights and provisions. This presence at government level enables, among other things, the national recognition of Koranic schools (medrese), the official teaching of Turkish, and the integration of Muslim students into Greek universities. Thrace is divided into three prefectures and governed by a **mufti**, an elected administrator in charge of religious affairs and the administration of the Islamic clergy of the region.

## Jews

Greece has experienced several waves of Jewish immigration, the first one as long ago as very early Antiquity when merchants left Israel c 2300 BC to set up trading posts around the peninsula. Since they spoke Greek, they had no difficulty in mixing with the local populations, who subsequently began to call them **Romaniotes**, ie Jews of Greco-Roman origin.

In the 15C, a large **Sephardic** community found refuge in Greece after being driven out of Spain by the Inquisition in 1492. They were followed five years later by Jews from Portugal, then from Central Europe and southern Italy. The community thus increased extensively, bringing a know-how and culture that the Ottoman occupiers were quick to put to use, seeing it as a providential instrument to reduce Christian opposition. And so the Turks granted the Sephardic Jews a number of privileges (the Romaniote Jews were considered to be less "educated", more boorish), and for several centuries helped this community to settle in Greece. The Second World War, however, decimated this community in the most tragic fashion. Originally numbering 77 000 individuals, the Jewish community, which is mainly based in Macedonia, has been reduced to a mere 5 000.

# TRADITIONAL FESTIVALS

Since religion is firmly imprinted in daily life, dictating many cultural and social customs, most of the major festivals in Greece correspond to the liturgical calendar. However, while certain celebrations are steeped in a pious atmosphere of purely Orthodox contemplation, particularly in the islands and villages, other occasions combine the holy and the profane – hovering somewhere between a mass and a village fête – in a mixture of deep piety and pagan rituals, the undying legacy of ancient times. This provides the Greeks with a multitude of opportunities to celebrate life and the seasons with their all-consuming and ever-colourful fervour.

## Let the festivities begin...

The most ecumenical festival of all is, of course, **New Year's Day**, but this does not stop people from going to church on this day too. In the evening of 31 December, the whole household gathers together around the traditional *Vassilópita* **(St Basil's Cake)**, which contains a gold medal or coin. As the twelve strokes of midnight ring out, the head of the family cuts the cake with great solemnity, following a very specific ritual: after cutting it into four – in the sign of the cross – he then cuts it into as many pieces as there are guests, not forgetting to leave a piece for God and for absent friends and to set aside other pieces to ensure the protection of the home, for good luck or to make a wish come true. Once the cake has been handed out, the person who finds the hidden coin or medal will have good luck and happiness in the coming year.

### The major dates in the liturgical calendar

All Greeks, be they devoutly religious or sceptic, celebrate the main religious occasions. This is because, beyond their liturgical bases, these festivals also have a national dimension which unites the whole population, Orthodox Christianity being part of the cement which bound the Greek nation together after it was freed from the yoke of Islam under the Ottomans.

In 1923, the church officially adopted the **Gregorian calendar**, with the exception of Easter, which is still celebrated according to the **Julian calendar**.

• **Epiphany**, 6 January, commemorates the baptism of Jesus in the River Jordan, with a blessing of the waters. After the church service, the Orthodox priest traditionally throws a cross into the sea, which the local boys race in to retrieve.

• The three weeks before the beginning of Lent (the period of fasting leading up to Easter) is a very festive time, when adults and children alike parade around the streets in **carnival** (or **Lent Announcement**) costumes. This respite in the heart of winter gives each town an opportunity to organise its own festivities, and Patras, for example, is renowned for its superb parades of decorated floats.

• Forty days before Easter, **Clean Monday** (Katharí deftéra) marks the beginning of Lent, a period of partial fasting during which several types of food are forbidden (mainly meat and milk, but also some fatty foods), and the skies are filled with fluttering kites.

• During **Holy Week**, various events herald the Resurrection, the most important one being Good Friday, with the procession of **epitáphios,** large liturgical cloths representing the shroud of Jesus on which he is depicted surrounded by weeping angels. They are covered in flowers, marking the arrival of spring, and in some villages, photographs of those who passed away during the previous year are also attached to them. Every church has its *epitáphion,* which is carried on high through the streets of the town, followed by a crowd of worshippers holding lighted candles in their hands. The most spectacular epitáphios are in Athens and in the churches of Kifissiá, Corfu and the island of Mýkonos.

• Much more so than Christmas, **Easter** is the main festival of the year, and is a time of great celebration throughout Greece. As well as being a religious festival, it is also an exaltation of spring. The celebrations begin on the morning of Easter Saturday and reach their high

**One single flame for one single god**
Each year at Easter, the same small flame passes throughout almost the entire country. It is flown over from Jerusalem, landing in Greece on Easter Saturday, ready to light all the candles in the country.

point at midnight when, after a long mass, the Orthodox priest emerges from the church holding a lighted candle to announce the resurrection of Christ: "*Christós Anésti!*". The crowd awaits him on the square, each person holding an unlit candle. The priest then lights one of the candles with his flame and, within minutes, the square is alight with a myriad of small flickering flames, while the bells ring out long and loud. Back home again, the head of the family draws the sign of the cross with the smoke from his candle on the embrasure of the front door (this is also customary when blessing a new house). Everybody can then sit down for **Easter dinner**, with, on the menu, soup made with the intestines of milk-fed lambs, and roast meat and potatoes, all much appreciated by the guests after the long period of Lent. At the end of the meal, eggs painted red (symbolising the blood of Christ) are handed around and broken with one's neighbour. At dawn the next day, the master of the house lights the fire under the Easter lamb and *kokorétsi*, brochettes of tripe. Throughout the day and well into the following night, relatives and friends come to eat and drink to the resurrection of Christ. A communal meal is usually also organised in the village square to give everybody the chance to celebrate Easter properly, regardless of social standing.

• 15 August is the feast of the **Assumption**, commemorating the ascent of the Virgin Mary (*Panagía*, the "All-Holy") into heaven after she fell asleep for the last time (Dormition). Celebrations are held by all the churches and many pilgrimages take place in the towns and villages, in particular on the island of Tínos.

• The last major festival of the year is **Christmas**, celebrating the birth of Christ. In Greece, it is not celebrated to the same extent as in the rest of Europe since the Orthodox faith attaches much greater importance to the symbol of the resurrection. Children traditionally go carol-singing from house to house.

## National festivals...

In addition to the religious festivals, the Greeks celebrate two historic dates, which are of the utmost importance for this nation of patriots: **25 March**, commemorating the beginning of the Greek War of Independence, and **28 October** or "No! day" ("*Óchi* day"), in remembrance of the rejection of the Italian ultimatum in 1940 (*see page 30*).

**"Panigíri", or festivals every day**
In Greece, saints' days are celebrated with even greater enthusiasm than birthdays. These are the panigíri, and the most important are celebrated in style, such as that of the patron saint of Greece, St George (Ágios Geórgios), whose name is one of the most common in the country (along with Ioánnis, Constantínos and Eléni – or John, Constantine and Helen). On this occasion, travelling salesmen – often gypsies – and tradesmen set up shop at the numerous fairs which are held throughout the country. The villagers flock there to rummage through the displays and make their purchases in preparation for winter, buying hardware, tools, animals, hi-fis, records, clothes, household linen, toys, trinkets, and much else besides. Musicians from the surrounding areas come to play and encourage the locals to dance a few steps.

These two commemorative festivals are celebrated in a similar way. Every town or village organises its **parréllassi** (parade) of all the important local figures. Soldiers, representatives of the Church in ceremonial dress, local dignitaries, the best students and sports club members march by to the sound of the brass band. In a moderately nationalistic speech, the mayor usually recalls the heroism of the Greeks, who emerged victorious from these episodes of history, and the national flag can once again be seen flying in every public place.

In Greece, where the month of May can always be counted on to keep its promises of sunshine, **Labour Day** is also the **Flower Festival**. On 1 May, city-dwellers go out to picnic in the countryside, and in the villages, garlands of flowers adorn the front doors.

## ... and regional festivals

In summer (July and August) numerous **wine festivals** are scattered throughout the mainland and in the islands, but the dates and venues can vary from year to year. In a lively atmosphere, revellers can sample as much of the year's wine as they like and dance until dawn. The most popular festivals are at **Loubarda** in Agía Marína (near Cape Soúnion), **Dafní** (near Athens), Piraeus and all over **Crete**.

Another more unusual celebration, the **Anastenariá** (from the word *"anastenázo"*, meaning "to groan"), takes place on 21 May in **Macedonia** and **Thrace** in commemoration of a particular event – the rescue of icons from a burning church in the 13C – which has been stigmatised by the Church. Certain villagers (men or women) bearing icons, dance barefoot on burning coals groaning loudly to evoke the panic caused by the incident.

Still in northern Greece, some villages have taken the original step of instituting the equivalent of a **"Women's Day"** on 8 January. To celebrate this **gynaecocracy** (gynaikokratía), men and women swap roles for a day, giving the ladies free rein to spend the day on the café terraces while their dearly beloved stay home to do the housework.

Village festivities: a traditional wedding in Arkasa, Kárpathos

E. Slatter/HEMISPHERES

# HUMOUR AND SUPERSTITION

The Greeks love to have fun, all the more so since the country's recent history did not really encourage this trend. So they are often to be found gathering together in *parées* (small groups of friends) around a drink or meal, telling the latest jokes or spreading, for better or for worse, the latest gossip. Although the Greeks willingly laugh at the expense of their peers, they are not overly fond of being the butt of other people's jokes themselves. So beware of teasing them about certain subjects – humour is not always compatible with national pride and self-esteem!

## Karaghiózis, the Greek puppet show

Like the Indonesians and the Turks, the Greeks have their own **shadow theatre**. Using silhouettes cut out of painted leather and mounted on sticks, the stories are enacted before a lighted canvas. The comparison is not purely by chance, since the Javanese *Wayang kulit*, which was imported into Egypt by the Arabs, probably inspired the Turkish Karagöz from the 16C, then the Greek Karaghiózis. Others, however, maintain that Karagöz is of purely Turkish origin and dates back to the 14C. The two main heroes, Karagöz and Hacivat, were hired as workmen on the building site of a mosque in Bursa. However, the two cronies worked only half-heartedly, preferring to spend their time entertaining their fellow workers. To punish and make an example of them, Sultan Orhan had them hanged, but the townspeople missed them so much that a certain Seyh Küsteri came up with the idea of making puppets in their effigy, using them to perpetuate their stories. This, so it is said, is how the Turkish shadow theatre, and subsequently its Greek counterpart, were born. The Karaghiózis puppet is a **caricature of the Greek man in the street**. With his big "black eyes" – literal translation of the Turkish word *Karagöz* – his hunched back and his inordinately long arm, the hero of Greek shadow theatre is hideously ugly. The incarnation of the Evil One, a truly artful character, he is quick in repartee, with a ready wit and a consummate knack for storytelling and trickery in which he sometimes gets almost inextricably caught up himself. He is facetious, irreverent, sometimes generous, sometimes dishonest, but always patriotic and, above all, constantly famished. He has turned his hand at every trade, taken all sides, and meddled in every love affair and political or financial intrigue. His adventures are a joyful combination of history – especially Ottoman domination – everyday life and Greek mythology, with never a care for anachronism. The other protagonists represent various figures from late 19C Greece. The vain and garrulous Athenian is represented by **Morphonios** ("the Educated" in a pejorative sense), whose enormous head symbolises the intellectual. **Hadziavatis**, the Turk, is the double of Karaghiózis, his accomplice, often his victim, and always the butt of his jokes. Although the Karaghiózis shadow theatre seems to be dying out, the spirit of his character lives on a little in every Greek man who loves his country but detests the State, who respects knowledge but lampoons scholars and who can, on every occasion, make a mockery of the things he reveres the most.

## Popular superstitions

### The evil eye

The legacy of centuries of Ottoman invasion, the **mati** (literally the "eye") borders on the obsessive among the Greeks, who live in constant fear of becoming *mati-assmeni* (being hit by the evil eye). People suffering from flu, nausea or colds, in particular, often say that they are *matiassmeni*. And so, to ward off any malediction, everyone carries a small glass eye set in turquoise blue. They can be seen pinned onto clothes and babies' cradles, hanging around the necks of children and adults, inside houses, cars, shops and any other inhabited place. The "guardian angel" eye is said to provide protection against the treacherous and jealous spirits which lie dormant in all people.

Compliments should never be made to a child or newborn baby unless immediately followed by a **ftoussou**: this movement of the lips, which is actually rather like spitting, in-

**Lacheío! Lacheío!**
The Greeks like to gamble and are great believers in their good fortune. This spirit of speculation has resulted in a great proliferation of games involving chance and luck. In particular, "propó" and "loto" – ordinary or sports – "xistó" (scratch card), "lacheío" (numbered tickets), along with a multitude of variations. Every district in every town has a shop exclusively devoted to selling these lucky tickets and officially recording bets and lottery cards. They can also be bought from street vendors who walk around the streets shouting: "Lacheío! lacheío!".

dicates that the praise is sincere and devoid of any feeling of hidden jealousy. In maternity wards, there are countless signs saying that it is forbidden to "ftoussou" on the infants, for reasons of hygiene!

If, in spite of these precautions, a person does fall under a spell, certain people "in the know" – often the grandparents – claim that they hold a miraculous formula which, with the aid of a glass of water and a drop of olive oil, will deliver the afflicted from the evil eye in an act of "purification" which can even be carried out by telephone.

## A mixed blessing
In the country, the building of a house, factory or any other place for living or working, sometimes begins with a ceremony during which a cockerel's throat is cut. Under the watchful eye of the family, friends or workers, the Orthodox priest sacrifices the creature before giving it to the poor. In the towns, instead of this ritual, it is still customary to seal a gold or silver cross in the building's foundations.

## Proskinitario, chapels of remembrance
On your travels, you are bound to notice the tiny chapels which stand at the side of roads, motorways or country lanes, often not far from a bend in the road. These remarkable little constructions are to give thanks to the Lord for an accident in which no-one was killed or, on the contrary, to honour the memory of the deceased. Enthroned inside is an icon of the patron saint, illuminated by a small oil lamp – often just a glass filled with olive oil – along with a few offerings and a bouquet of faded flowers cloaked in dust.

P. Texier/HOA QUI

**Popular superstitions**

75

# MUSIC AND DANCE

A few friends, a glass of ouzo and high spirits are the basic ingredients of any impromptu party. The Greeks rarely pass up an opportunity to listen to music and dance a few steps of the *syrtáki*, *bálo* (in the islands) or *zeïbékiko*, which are popular with men and women of every generation.

## From classical music to music of the classes

Very little is known about the music of Ancient Greece, other than that a prestigious operatic art existed in the 5C BC, mainly in the cities of Delphi, Sparta and Athens. Music subsequently seems to have rapidly fallen by the wayside, leaving the more potent force of poetry to take centre stage.

The revival of Greek music did not take place until the mid-19C, when two very different trends emerged; on the one hand, classical music mainly influenced by Italian works, and, on the other, popular **(laïkí musikí)** and folk **(dimotikí musikí)** music, which were closer to the lives and preoccupations of the people.

### Classical music

The composer of the national anthem, **Nikólaos Mantzaros** (1795-1872), was the pioneer of the classical music movement which continued in the following generation under the leadership of Manólis Kalomíris – composer of the first Greek opera, *The Masterbuilder*, in 1915 – and Níkos Skalkottás.

**Iánnis Xenákis** (1922-2001) was undoubtedly the most innovative Greek musician of the 20C. Noted and recognised by his peers well beyond the borders of Greece, this trained mathematician and architect became an eminent composer of contemporary stochastic music, which applies probability theory and random variables to music. Mention should also be made of **Géorges Apérghis** (b 1945), who helped to introduce the "musical theatre" genre.

### Rembétika: popular songs and music

In the late 19C, in the slums of Smyrna (now Izmir), Istanbul, Athens and Piraeus, a new form of music, *rembétika*, was beginning to emerge, and a whole social and political movement along with it. Often compared with blues music, *rembétika* flourished in the 1920s among the Greeks from Asia Minor and the country folk who had come to look for work in the cities. In this milieu of misfits, the musicians organised secret gatherings (*stéki*) to dance, play the music "of the poor townspeople" (*ipokosmos*), smoke hookahs and throw plates. The *rembétis* (*rembétiko* singers) lived on the fringe of society, taking a certain pride in their non-conformism. But they were poets nonetheless, and their texts, which were often written in slang and railed against injustice, abuse and inequality, also recount stories involving drugs and women of loose morals. Although its roots were in Asia Minor, a truly Greek style of music began to emerge thanks to the work of musicians such as **Vassílis Tsitsánis** (1915-84). The movement spread very rapidly, despite – or perhaps because of – the contempt of the bourgeoisie, who preferred more Western styles of music. With the revival of nationalism in the post-war period, record companies took the opportunity to bring *rembétika* out of the shadows, turning it into a huge success.

But what would the lyrics of *rembétika* be without the **bouzoúki**? Originally known to the bourgeoisie as the "devil's instrument", the story goes that this mandolin was subsequently upstaged by the *baglamás*, a smaller version which could be hidden inside a coat!

**The Greek music revival** – Two renowned contemporary artists, **Míkis Theodorákis** (b 1925) and **Mános Hadzidákis** (1925-94), were intent on preserving and exploiting the musical legacy of Greece. The former, in addition to his commitment to politics which has made him a real living legend in his country, also composed scores for films such as *Z* and *Zorba the Greek*, which achieved great success abroad. Hadjidakis also worked in films and notably composed songs for Nana Mouskouri. Other talented contemporary singers include Yórgos Daláras, Háris Alexíou and Eleftheria Arvanitáki.

## Folk music (dimotiki musiki)

Every town and village has its own brass band, which the Greeks rather ambitiously call "philharmonic orchestras". These formations are composed of musicians of all ages, who are mostly self-taught and perform at every festival.

**Say it with flowers**
The "bouzoúki" also gave its name to a type of night-club where, every evening, the popular musicians of the moment come to perform in front of an audience of people from every generation and social class. Although the musical background of these singers has little in common with the rembétika of the 1920s, the enthusiasm of the crowd is just as fervent. And the plates which the public used to throw as a sign of their appreciation have now been replaced by flowers.

The music and the instruments on which it is played vary from region to region, and even from one town to the next, but a certain unity can be found in the essence of the pieces. The *cantáta* (cantatas) of the Ionian Islands, for example, are love stories and local tales set to violin and guitar music, which resemble melodies from southern Italy, whereas the *miroloï* and *pípiza* variations in Epirus are more doleful, recalling the suffering of a people in exile.

## Folk dancing

Every *rembétiko* or *dimotiki musiki* orchestration is accompanied by figures that are not governed by any choreographic rules as such, but rather by a tradition of harmony between the body, the mind and facial expression. This explains the regional variations which you may see in dances that are performed throughout the land. Among the most common is the **hassápiko** ("butchers' dance"), which dates back to the Byzantine era when it was performed by the butchers of Constantinople for their guild festival. A simplified and slower version of this dance, the **syrtaki**, was made famous the world over by the film *Zorba the Greek*, released in the 1960s. The **zeïbékiko** – a dance associated with *rembétika* – originated in Asia Minor. It was originally performed by a single dancer surrounded by an audience which would crouch and clap along in a very specific rhythm.

Others which are also worthy of mention are the **mandíli kalamatianó** ("handkerchief dance"), the wedding dance par excellence, and the **tsiftetéli**, named after the two-stringed violin which used to provide the accompaniment in times gone by. This belly-dance performed by women stems from ancient fertility rituals from Asia Minor.

### Traditional instruments

| | |
|---|---|
| Baglamás | small bouzoúki (also found in Latin America) |
| Bouzoúki | long-necked mandolin with three or four pairs of strings |
| Daoúli | wooden cylinder with a taut skin membrane at each end |
| Défi | tambourine |
| Floyéra | a shepherd's flute made of reeds or wood |
| Gáida | bagpipes (mainland Greece) |
| Láouto (lagouto) | lute with four pairs of strings |
| Lýra | a three-stringed viol played with a bow |
| Miroloï | long rough-sounding flute |
| Oúti | short-necked lute |
| Pípiza | high-pitched oboe |
| Sandoúri | zither played by striking the strings |
| Toumbeléki | tambourine |
| Tsaboúna | bagpipes (Greek islands) |
| Zournás | oboe (often accompanied by the daoúli) |

Folk dancing

# LITERATURE AND CINEMA

The legacy of Greek literature has shone out like a beacon since ancient times, providing a model for the Western world. Plato's philosophy, Sophocles' plays and Homer's epic poems have been passed down through the ages and civilisations. Their legendary heroes have not aged a bit and continue to haunt the modern world which they helped to shape: the Ulysses of James Joyce's novel walks the streets of Dublin in 1904, while the Ulysses brought to celluloid life by the Coen brothers, directors of the film *O Brother, Where Art Thou?*, lives in the United States of the late 20C. And these are just two examples of the countless adaptations of Homer's *Odyssey*. Three thousand years of literature have passed since this epic was written, and modern literature – free of the vast legacy of Ancient Greece, but enriched by it – is very much alive in Greece, as evidenced by the Nobel prizes awarded to two Greek poets Giórgos Seféris and Odysséus Elýtis.

## Birth of a pleiad of styles

Ancient Greek literature covers a very long period, stretching from the *Iliad* and the *Odyssey* (9C-8C BC) to the fall of the Byzantine Empire (1453). The most beautiful pages in its history were written during the Age of Pericles (5C BC), after which it fell into gradual decline under Roman domination. With the arrival of Christianity, Byzantium closed the academies, marking its end. A certain neo-Classicism did continue to exist as Byzantine literature developed, but as soon as the Gospels were written in Greek, a new Gnostic form of Greek "literature" began to emerge. Until the 3C, the Christian doctrine was conveyed in this language, before Latin began to prevail as the language for religious works and the teaching of the Christian faith throughout the Mediterranean basin.

### The Iliad and the Odyssey: the origin of Greek literature

The earliest known expression of Greek literature dates back to the 9C or 8C BC, when **Homer** wrote his two **epic poems**, the *Iliad*, which relates the last episodes of the Trojan War (Ilion), and the *Odyssey*, which narrates Odysseus' (Ulysses') long journey back to Ithaca. These major works, which in all likelihood were based on a longstanding oral tradition, tackle the founding myths, depicting the origins and fate of the Greek people under the supervision of the gods *(see page 51)*.

At around the same time, a farmer by the name of **Hesiod** penned a prose work, the *Works and Days*, in which he promoted his vision of how life in the countryside should be lived. He is also credited with writing the *Theogony*, a document of great importance since it was the first to address the issue of the origins of the world and the genealogy of the gods. Of the numerous authors who followed in the footsteps of these pioneers, many were to fall into oblivion, but others, such as **Sappho**, the famous poetess of Lesbos *(see page 452)*, carved their names in stone.

### Aesop's fables

The very existence of Aesop (6C BC) is still shrouded in mystery. According to some, he was a Greek slave from Thrace, whose spirit and perspicacity earned him his freedom. Subsequently gaining popularity at the court of King Croesus, this supremely gifted fabulist went on to achieve great literary success. However, one day he accused the priests of the oracle of Delphi of plundering the worshippers' offerings. Not one of his better ideas, this denunciation was to cost him his life and he was condemned to death in 564 BC. The 350 fables which are attributed to him today, provided a great source of inspiration for the 17C French author, Jean de la Fontaine.

### The success of the theatre

In the 5C BC, the theatre really began to come into its own and amphitheatres were filling with a growing number of spectators *(see*

An undying art: a performance at the Odeon of Herodes Atticus, Athens

*page 36)*. Of religious origin, this literary genre is associated with the cult of Dionysus. Indeed, theatres were generally to be found near the temple devoted to the god, where certain rites were carried out during performances. To compose their masterly tragedies, **Aeschylus**, **Sophocles** and **Euripides** delved into mythology, depicting human nature in all of its excesses, with incest, parricide or madness taking pride of place in their plays. **Aristophanes**, for his part, became a master in the art of **comedy**, never hesitating to combine clever puns or vulgar farces with philosophical thought.

## Making History

Thanks to the great traveller **Herodotus** of Halicarnassus, nicknamed the "Father of History", the 5C witnessed the birth of a new literary genre concerned with recording factual events and sticking as closely as possible to the truth. History, with a capital H, was born. **Thucydides** was one of the greatest of these ancient historians and is particularly renowned for his political analysis of the Peloponnesian War, which was supported by various eyewitness accounts.

## The invention of philosophy

In the cities, as the art of oratory began to generate cohesion at meetings, the role of the word took on increasing importance. The collective nature of decisions – specific to cities – effectively led to a certain "publicity" of knowledge which could no longer be confined to discussion between those in the know, but must, on the contrary, be disclosed and explained. Although philosophy is a tradition in Greece, it was not until the 4C BC that it really began to make its mark.

Through dialogue, **Socrates** (470-399 BC) endeavoured to lay bare the falsehoods distorting public opinion, refute politicians' claims and reveal their ignorance. This midwife's son, an expert in the art of maieutics (eliciting new ideas from people who had not been aware of them), left no written documents, but his teachings were passed down through the generations thanks to his disciple, **Plato** (428-347 BC). Plato devoted part of his work to the memory of his master, using the same analysis to denounce the violence, immorality, injustice and disorder which were gradually

## The father of geographers

It was in Nyssa (Turkey) that the Greek geographer Strabo (58 BC-circa 22 AD) studied history and geography. With his diploma in his toga pocket, he set to work on two voluminous essays, "Historical Sketches" and "Geography" (only the latter is still extant). Little known during his lifetime, his work was rediscovered during the Renaissance and was of great interest to Leonardo da Vinci. Although two thousand years old, Strabo's "Geography" with its reflections on the origins of peoples, the history of empires and, above all, man's relationship with his natural environment, is still a remarkably relevant work which merits greater attention.

taking hold of the cities. Plato subsequently became the master of the philosopher and scholar **Aristotle** (384-322 BC), whose philosophical and scientific thinking were to greatly influence the Western world, particularly in the field of logic. Other philosophers, representing various schools of thought (Stoicism and Epicureanism, to name but a few), succeeded them, but very few of their writings have survived the passage of time.

## The quest for Greek identity

Modern Greece steadfastly celebrates its mythology and classical literature with numerous summer festivals held in ancient theatres. But the country is not content to rest on its laurels. Influenced by literary trends similar to those which have spread through Europe since the 15C, Greece has also managed to cultivate its own individuality, producing a generation of modern, internationally renowned writers.

### Greek literature during the Ottoman Empire

In the 10C, the characters of a modern Greek literature began to emerge with the great cycle of epic-style folk ballads celebrating the exploits of **Digenis Akritas Basileios**, the legendary hero of the Byzantine Empire's struggle against the Arabs on the Euphrates frontier. This new form of literature really began to flourish with the fall of the Byzantine Empire in 1453, when several styles emerged, varying from one region to the other in the wake of the Ottomans' advance.

Some islands which were spared the Turkish invasion for longer than the mainland (until 1669 in Crete, for example), were effectively able to demonstrate a certain originality in their literary creations. The Dodecanese, Chios, Cyprus, Crete and the Ionian Islands became important centres of island literature, greatly influenced by Western occupiers, such as the Venetians or the Genoese. **Vitzéntzos Kornáros** of Crete is thus remembered as the author of the epic poem *Erotókritos*, the last large-scale work before the Ottoman invasion.

On the mainland, however, the arrival of the Turks put a considerable damper on literary creation, causing many scholars to emigrate to the West from the 15C onwards. The scholars from **Phanar** (a quarter of Constantinople) in the late 17C, were thus to be the last representatives of Hellenism on Turkish soil.

It was not until the 19C that a veritable revival of Greek literature was brought about by the Greek Enlightenment movement, whose most famous representative was **Koraïs** who studied and lived in France, and the Ionian school, influenced by Italy.

### The emancipation of Greek literature

After the Greek War of Independence, the Turks withdrew from the peninsula, leaving behind a traumatised people in search of a national identity. This mass disorientation did not spare the novelists either who, badly in need of inspiration, turned either towards the West with its Enlightenment and modernity, or to the Christian East, land of the Byzantine tradition.

During the dispute over language (*see page 83*) which was stirring up Greek society at the time, divisions in society were reflected in the balancing act between classicism and progressivism. Falling between the popular and the scholarly language, *katharévoussa* was chosen as a compromise between the classical form and modern usage advocated by **Adamántios Koraïs** (1748-1833). The defence of the common vernacular was taken by poets such as **Dhionísios Solomós** (1798-1857), who is considered to be the first poet of modern Greece. The leader of the **Ionian School** (or Heptanesian School), he stood in opposition to the **Athenian School**, which favoured extreme romanticism, before turning to symbolism. In the late 19C, the intellectuals decided to use Demotic in their works, one of the most staunch "demoticists" being **Yánnis Psicháris** (1854-1929), whose narrative *My Journey* was partly a manifesto against a language that was too scholarly and elitist.

## Pastures new
After the "Great Catastrophe" of 1922 *(see page 30)*, which sketched out the geographical outline of modern Greece, writers were plunged into an era of total defeatism. Greek literature was pulled out of this painful and pessimistic period by the **1930s generation**, which decided to drop the linguistic controversy and focus on the substance, propelling Greece into the world of modern literature. This new wave brought with it such prestigious authors as the 1963 Nobel prize-winner, **Giórgos Seféris** (1900-71), who opened the way to surrealism, and the 1979 Nobel prize-winner, **Odysséus Elýtis** (1911-96), one of the leading poets of this new narrative technique, which gathered a good many writers in its train. Mention should also be made of the poet **Constantine Caváfy** (1863-1933), a Greek from Alexandria who represents the Hellenism of the famous Greek centres of the late 19C. Greek literature was subsequently taken far beyond the country's borders by **Vassílis Vassilikós** (b 1934), author of *Z*, and **Níkos Kazantzákis** (1883-1957) who penned *Zorba the Greek* and *The Last Temptation of Christ*, works which, oddly enough, gained a better reception abroad than in Greece.

# Cinema

Heavily influenced by popular Italian comedies and burlesque theatre, Greek cinema really began to come into its own in 1949 at the end of the civil war.
The 1950s, marked by Italian neo-Realism, were dominated by two great directors: **Michális Cacoyánnis**, who made the comedy *Windfall in Athens*, then *Stella* – his biggest film, starring Melína Mercoúri – and **Níkos Koúndouros** with *Magic City* and *The Ogre of Athens*. But it was not until the following decade that one could really start talking about a "golden age" of the cinema: encouraged by relative political stability, the studios were able to boost production. This was the era of the light comedies starring Alíki Vouyoukláli, Lámbros Konstandáras and Georgía Vassiliádou, which are still today the very epitome of insouciance.

## The emergence of "auteur" films
With the arrival of television in people's homes and the creation of the first national Greek television channel (ERT), the public began to turn their backs on the cinema in favour of the small screen. In the 1970s, with the dictatorship in full swing, the commercial cinema was plunged into its first big crisis. The new directors were indulging a more introspective, rather obscure, genre, while most cinemagoers were looking for escapism. This yawning gap between the cinema and its public eventually led to the studios' collapse.
The fall of the colonels' junta in 1974 coincided with the beginning of the **new Greek cinema**, headed by **Theódoros (Theo) Angelópoulos**. This director's long film career was studded with international awards, including the Golden Lion at the Venice Film Festival for *Alexander the Great* (1980), the award for the best screenplay in Cannes for *Voyage to Cythera* (1984), the Silver Lion at the Venice Film Festival for *Landscape in the Mist* (1988), the Grand Jury Prize at the Cannes Film Festival for *Ulysses' Gaze* (1995) and lastly the *Palme d'Or* at Cannes for *Eternity and a Day* (1998).

## Return to a wider public

With the spectacular development of video clubs in the 1980s, the **Greek Film Centre**, which was the only investor at that time, became caught in the stranglehold of its increased politicisation, and dragged the auteur movement down with it in its fall. In 1989, the private television channels (Antenna and Mega) burst onto the scene, tolling the knell of Greek cinema. In the face of European and Hollywood productions, the few Greek films which were still being screened fell by the wayside. It was not until the middle of the 1990s that the Greek Film Centre changed its position, agreeing to give financial backing to commercial films with more Western-style screenplays, more in tune with cinemagoers' expectations. For its part, Parliament passed a law subjecting television channels to a fee to subsidise film production. The new generation of producers is now striving to give a fresh lease of life to Greek cinema by making films with greater public appeal, as you will see if you take a trip to the **Thessaloníki Film Festival** in October, where the year's films are presented.

### Open-air cinemas

A summer tradition and THE place to go to start your evening out, open-air cinemas show the previous winter's hits in a friendly atmosphere. The screen looms above an area filled with tables and chairs, where spectators can have a drink while watching the film, which always has an interval.

"Never on Sunday"

CAT'S Collection

MELINA MERCOURI
Grand Prix d'interprétation au Festival de Cannes
JULES DASSIN dans **Jamais le Dimanche**
Scénario et mise en scène de JULES DASSIN
avec GEORGES FOUNDAS · TITOS VANDIS
Musique de MANOS HADJIDAKIS
Directeur de la Photographie JACQUES NATTEAU
Une Production MELINAFILM Distribués par LES ARTISTES ASSOCIÉS

# LANGUAGE

Despite the long centuries of Turkish occupation, the Greeks managed to preserve their language, the symbol of national identity. Around 97% of the country's inhabitants speak Greek, while the minorities still use their mother tongue, which means that Turkish, Albanian, Bulgarian, Romany, etc, are also spoken in certain areas (see page 57). So, Modern Greek is spoken throughout the land by over 10 million people, and in Cyprus by 500 000. Not forgetting the vast Greek diaspora, 5.5 million people living in countless communities spread all over the world. Moreover, the Greeks pride themselves on being able to travel without having to learn another language, since they are always sure to meet one of their compatriots wherever they go. *Also see the glossary page 115.*

## The road to Modern Greek

A vector of Greek philosophical and scientific thought, language of the Gospels and the Church, and also the official language of the Byzantine Empire, Ancient Greek testifies to the exceptional influence of one of the greatest civilisations of the planet. Suffice it to say that its modernisation was no mean feat...

### The birth of Greek
After having gradually imposed their Indo-European language in Greece during the latter half of the 2nd millennium BC, the Hellenes, who came from the North, soon borrowed the script of the **Phoenicians**, who had also settled in the Mediterranean area. In all likelihood, the adaptation of the Phoenician alphabet for use by the Greeks around the 8C BC resulted in the Greek alphabet such as we know it. This borrowing was coupled with a revolutionary innovation, **vowels**, which the Greeks substituted for certain Phoenician consonants for which they had no equivalent sounds in their language.

### A bitter linguistic controversy
The gap gradually began to widen between **classical Greek** and the **common vernacular**, *koiné*, which was mostly based on the dialect of Attica and incorporated words of foreign – mainly Turkish – origin. When the sensitive issue of the future national language arose in the late 18C, right in the middle of the turmoil caused by the independence movement, this marked the beginning of a long dispute which was to rage between classicists and modernists over the next two centuries, and which has still not been resolved.

In fact, this linguistic controversy was merely one facet of a much wider debate concerning the position and prestige of the nation: the decision to continue or to break away from classical Greece.

For the *Phanariótes*, the administrative nobility of the 18C (originally established in the Greek quarter of Phanar, in Constantinople), maintaining classical Greek guaranteed them control of the cultural and political life of the country, in particular over the bourgeoisie and the working classes. It wasn't until the early 19C that the intellectuals took up the issue, launching a pitched battle between the partisans of a pure language and those of a "vulgar" language.

Following the War of Independence, the solution advocated by **Adamántios Koraïs** (1743-1833), leader of the Greek Enlightenment, won out and a clever compromise between the classical form and modern usage, **Katharevusa** (*katharos* meaning pure) was born. Although it was adopted as the official language of the country, it remained alien to the people, who continued to use **Demotic** (demotikí) (*démos* meaning people), the popular language of oral tradition. Demotic was supported by authors such as **Dhionísios Solomós** (1798-1857), who is regarded as the first great poet of modern Greece and who, incidentally, wrote the national anthem.

In the late 19C, rebelling against this scholarly and elitist language, some intellectuals again decided to use *demotiki* rather than *katharévoussa* in their works of literature. At the heart of an increasingly political conflict, the supporters of Demotic fiercely opposed the conservatism of the *katharévoussa* partisans. Notable examples of subsequent champions of popular culture include poets such as **Giórgos Seféris** (1900-71) and **Odysséus Elýtis** (1911-96), both winners of the Nobel Prize for literature.

## Modern Greek: a simplified language

In the end, it was the colonels' junta which took *katharévoussa* down with it when it fell in 1974. In order to emphasise the break with the previous regime, Karamanlís' government decreed Demotic to be the official language. However, its linguistic simplifications are still the subject of many a debate: from one ministry to the next, between the Ministry of Education and the highways department (in charge of road signs), for example, discussion still continues on whether to use the *y* or the *i*, and whether or not to keep the *h*, and so on.

Be that as it may, while Ancient Greek had five genders, Modern Greek has only three: masculine, feminine and neuter. Demotic has also passed through various stages of development, the most remarkable undoubtedly being the "ee-ification", consisting of replacing the pronunciation of numerous vowels or diphthongs from Ancient Greek by an "ee" sound.

# Give-and-take

With its considerable linguistic heritage, Greek vocabulary reveals a highly complex system of declensions and syntax as well as myriad possibilities for creating neologisms. Over the centuries it has also been further enriched by numerous foreign influences.

## Contributions from abroad...

Although Greek vocabulary forms the basis of the theological, philosophical, scientific and technical terminology of the West, it itself contains a certain number of words borrowed from various invaders – the most obvious being words of Turkish origin – and from foreign languages, especially French, the language of a society which enjoyed great prestige in the late 19C and early 20C. Influences from nearby Italy and the English-speaking world can also be detected.

## ...and vice versa

In addition to Latin (which gave us *vice versa*), Greek constitutes one of the main bases of many languages, including English, to which it has given innumerable prefixes. Here are just a few of the most common: *micro* (small) has given us the microscope, microwave and micrometry, *megalo* (big) megalopolis, megalomania, megahertz, and *kiclos* (round) has mutated into cycle, cyclic, cyclone, etc.

Likewise, Greek has provided us with a whole catalogue of suffixes, including *logia* and *logos* (theory, speech), which are used to designate all of our sciences (geology,

### Foreign flavours

Many English and French words which have passed into the Greek language belong to specific areas. Greek football terminology, for example, has borrowed several words from English, such as "máts" (match), "fáoul" (foul), "off-sáit" (offside), "kórner" (corner), "jkól" (goal). And many a French word has, unsurprisingly, slipped into the field of gastronomy, for example, millefeuilles, gratins, "volovène" (vol au vent), "quislorène" (quiche lorraine) and "bessamél" (bechamel).

biology, etc), *graphein* (to write) giving us the telegraph, *philos* (friend) anglophile, and its opposite, *phobia* (fear) xenophobia, claustrophobia, etc.

Countless English words thus stem from Ancient Greek in an endless combination of prefixes and suffixes. Other words derive from a whole word, including all medical terms: paediatrician (*pediatros*) comes from the word *pediá* (children), gynaecologist (*gynekológos*) from *gynéka* (woman), and podiatrist (*podólogos*) from *pódia* (feet), to name but a few.

# THE GREEKS AT HOME

From the islands to the mainland, Greece contains a great variety of housing ranging from drystone dwellings to big bourgeois homes with neo-Classical façades, and small fishermen's cottages tucked away at the foot of rugged hillsides. This diversity can be explained by the country's contrasting geography, which embraces all kinds of different environments: mountains, sea and agricultural plains, with varying amounts of rainfall and sunshine. Although the archetype of the Cyclades – those charming white houses with blue shutters which make such beautiful postcards – is so emblematic of Greece, the architecture on the mainland is undoubtedly a better reflection of the country's cultural legacy, with its combination of Byzantine and Ottoman traditions. But the differences have been levelled out in recent times, with breeze-blocks and concrete becoming sadly ever more commonplace throughout the country, like everywhere else in the Mediterranean.

## In the cities

Shortly after stepping off the plane at Athens airport and hopping into a bus for the city, visitors are plunged into the capital's notorious traffic jams. The kilometres of teeming avenues are lined with unattractive six- or seven-storey apartment buildings all sporting concrete balconies covered in flowers which hide the flaking paint. Below, the ground-floor "arcades" house shops, offices, banks and cafés. This rather grim architecture has sadly shaped the face of present-day Athens.

### Reinforced concrete...

Until the early 1950s, detached houses still largely dominated the urban landscape of the Greek metropolis, except for the centre. However, the following decade witnessed the propagation of reinforced concrete, and a uniform type of structure built in a slap-dash manner began to spread chaotically throughout the country like a plague.

In addition to constant **demographic pressure**, it was the pressing necessity of establishing an urban infrastructure which led to this unbridled transformation of Athens.

After the war, a law was passed under which anyone who owned a house or piece of land could hand it over to an entrepreneur for the construction of an apartment building, gaining some of the apartments in exchange. This led to many of the historic quarters being destroyed by a combination of anarchic initiatives and public decisions, in a total lack of concern for preserving the national heritage. Over the last twenty years, however, new regulations have been introduced to protect and restore the surviving old traditional or neo-Classical houses.

But concrete has also started creeping into some of the villages and, in recent years, an increasing number of arson attacks in the countryside, ridding the land of its vegetation, have left the way open to property developers.

### Unfinished business

In Greece, building is a must. Although less prevalent than before, the tradition which holds that parents should build a house for their daughters as a dowry still stands. Consequently, wherever you go, you are sure to come across houses or buildings cast in concrete, terraces one atop the other with their iron skeletons poking out. Not one village in Greece has been spared these unfinished constructions, which are constantly awaiting the unlikely addition of an extra storey. This phenomenon has been encouraged by two laws. The first one stipulates that an illegal construction can be torn down only if the offender is caught in the act. However, given that controls are carried out only during the day, many sections of wall are raised during the night and are still wet at dawn. The second law states that as long as a construction has not been roofed and the iron rods are still exposed, the owner cannot be taxed. Between aesthetics and taxes, most Greeks make the same choice.

### ...and bourgeois houses of yesteryear

But rest assured, the 19C charm of the towns and villages has not totally disappeared. A few shining examples of the urban architecture from the age of King Otto still remain in Athens and in the **hóra** (capitals) of the islands. Torchbearer of the Hellenic revival and reclaimed independence, European neo-Classicism rapidly found a home in Greece. Embodying the new trend of optimism after four centuries of Ottoman occupation, so-called **neo-Hellenic architecture** aimed to resuscitate the golden age of Ancient Greece *(see page 126)*. This trend was reflected in a mushrooming of opulent villas, imposing one- or two-storey houses with façades which followed the broad outlines of Ancient architecture but were also influenced by the Italian Renaissance and, in particular, 17C French classicism: on the ground floor, Doric columns and pilasters stand against walls or jut out to frame the **porch**, and the first floor is decorated with Ionic columns between the bays containing **high windows**. A small **balcony** enhances the central bay window beneath a broad tiled roof set off by acroteria and antefixae. During the golden years of the merchant navy, the wealthiest shipowners of the islands even went so far as to erect small pediments decorated with bas-reliefs or statues of chimeras.*

Behind these elegant façades, prosperous members of the middle class live Western-style in vast, high-ceilinged and well-lit rooms decorated with wainscoting, paintings and period furniture. The kitchen is on the ground floor and several small outbuildings stand nearby.

The same style of construction can also be found in the towns, where various **apartment buildings** boast equally elaborate façades.

However, this neo-Classical architecture was used mainly for the great public monuments and the private residences of the wealthy. Alongside these bourgeois homes, families forced into exile from Asia Minor in 1922 and country folk coming to the towns to look for work hurriedly built much more modest houses, urban versions of their country homes with whitewashed walls of stone blocks or rendering. They usually consisted of one single room on the ground floor serving as a kitchen, dining room and living room, with, depending on the family's means, two bedrooms on the first floor.

## Rural homes

With their ochre roughcast or whitewashed walls, and terrace or Roman-tiled timbered roofs, rural homes of the past were mainly built according to principles of functionality, depending on the climate and activity. Although modern conveniences – electricity, telephones and running water – are now widespread, those age-old houses that have managed to survive earthquakes and have not been abandoned for more modern constructions, are still extremely rustic. Here you will find the traditional **living room**, with perhaps another storey, covered by a **roof adapted to the climate**: a flat terrace roof in the sun-drenched islands, a four-sided roof in the regions with higher rainfall or snow, as in the north of the country.

### The "archontiká" or house of prosperity

Reflecting commercial prosperity and a mixture of influences, the "archontiká" are the residences of the local dignitaries. Typical examples of these opulent one- or two-storey mansions are to be found on the island of Hydra with its great families of shipowners *(see sidebar page 176)*. Under a roof of tiles or flat stone slabs, the stone or roughcast walls are studded with narrow windows fitted with leaded glass panes which filter the light even more. Above the stone-built ground floor, the upper floor made of wood and daub juts out in an overhang to form a sort of loggia (*hagiátsi* or *xostego*), thus creating a more spacious interior, the **sarái** or reception room. A bench resembling a Turkish sofa skirts the room and the walls and floor are swathed in warm fabrics and carpets. Decorated with carved and painted motifs whose refinement reflects the wealth of the household, the ceiling (*tavani*) is the main ornament

F. Guiziou/HEMISPHERES

Ottoman houses in Réthimnon

of the room. Many of these beautiful buildings influenced by Ottoman architecture are still to be found in the towns and villages of **Macedonia**, Thessaly and **Epirus** (Ioánnina, Métsovo), some of them complete with garden.

## A Greek's house is his castle

In regions which were often subject to attack by pirates or other foreign invasions, **pirgóspito** (from *pirgos*, meaning "tower") began to appear. These large austere dry-stone buildings in the shape of round or square towers with narrow loophole-type windows, rise several storeys high like watchtowers, heirs to the Hellenistic towers. The **Máni** Peninsula, in particular, in the south of the Peloponnese, abounds with these tower houses, most of them built in the 15C, which make the villages look like medieval citadels. The towers were built by local noblemen and provided a place of refuge for the villagers in times of conflict – which was frequent – with their neighbours. The living quarters proper occupied the first floor, while the ground floor was used as a stable and barn. Various outhouses were attached to the main building, the whole ensemble of buildings being protected by a surrounding wall.

# Island life

## In the Aegean Sea

The small whitewashed cube-shaped houses which are so typical of the Greek islands look as if they have been painted with sunshine. They generally spread out over two or three split levels, following as closely as possibly the lie of the land, which is often uneven. The overall impression is one of a picturesque chaos of cell-like structures lining a maze of narrow streets. In the Cyclades, this seeming disorder does, however, comply with a well-defined **defence plan**, whereby houses are set as close as possible to each other in order to form a sort of rampart. For the same reason, doors and windows mainly open towards the interior of the village and are small in size, thus allowing the houses to remain cool inside. The villages are usually laid out around one single narrow street paved with cobbles or large paving stones, which winds its way to the main square.

On account of the climate and lack of wood in these arid islands, flat roofs are more common than pitched ones, but the indoor ceilings are vaulted, since this makes them more resistant to earth tremors. The islands have one particularly distinctive feature: the furniture is built into the structure of the houses. A **stone bench** skirts the walls, and the seats, beds and couches, which are all whitewashed, are likewise an extension of the walls or floor. This traditional heritage which makes the islands so charming, is fortunately very well adapted to the new anti-seismic standards and to the ever-increasing demands of the hotel trade, thereby ensuring its preservation.

## Italian influences

Influenced by nearby Italy, the **Ionian Islands** boast luxurious mansions with impressively elaborate façades, the **palazzi**, directly inspired by Venetian palaces. These elegant homes respect a very precise architectural symmetry, both as regards the façade, in iridescent pastel shades of yellow, orange or ochre, and the internal layout. Many ordinary houses also look more Italian than Greek.

Other islands steeped in an Italian atmosphere include **Rhodes**, which reflects a happy combination of Venetian and Ottoman influences, and **Crete**, most notably in Haniá, where houses with overhanging upper storeys alternate with the flat façades of the Venetian palazzi subtly enhanced by Ancient Greek and Renaissance motifs.

### Krokalia

In the islands – the Cyclades in particular but also the Dodecanese (Rhodes) – many houses still have beautiful "krokalia" paving, arrangements of black and white pebbles used to decorate both the outdoor courtyards and the floors of the rooms inside. They come in a variety of geometrical, aquatic or animal designs, not forgetting the "méandros", a sort of decorative frieze passed down from Antiquity which symbolises the continuity of life.

# GREEK CUISINE

It will come as no surprise that, in such an old melting pot as Greece (see page 56), the cuisine has been flavoured by the many peoples who formed or passed through the country. But it remains, above all, a **cuisine of the sun**, full of the flavour of olives, resin and honey.

## "Horiátiki", or the national salad

The proper name for what is commonly known as a "Greek salad" is **horiátiki** (or choriatiki) meaning "the rustic". This national dish, full of authentic flavours, contains all the basic ingredients from a Greek village: delicious sun-ripened tomatoes mixed with slices of firm cucumber and red onion, all covered by a slice of feta and seasoned with oregano, a few olives and a dash of olive oil from Kalamáta. A very simple but inimitable combination.

## Meze galore

Mezé are served at the *mezedopolio* and *ouzeri* (ouzo bar). This Turkish word designates an infinite variety of hot or cold side-dishes made with meat, fish, cheese or vegetables. They range from the very simple – a few olives with a slice of feta – to the more complicated, such as stuffed mushrooms in wine

### Ancient Greek gourmets

The notion of gastronomy, of course, dates back to Ancient Greece. The Athenian philosophers, great thinkers that they were, were also experienced gourmets who were already glorifying "pleasant living". In the 5C BC, cooking competitions were even organised with large prizes – often pecuniary – being handed out to the winners. The Athenian cook, Archestratus, caused a stir with his delicious oven-baked fish wrapped in a fig leaf. This exquisitely simple recipe served merely to confirm the ancient proverb that the mark of a good cook ("archimágeiras") lies in the way he cooks fish.

sauce, and are served with white wine, beer, ouzo or rakí. Although some ouzo bars offer only around twenty kinds of meze and could almost be mistaken for kafenía, others have around one hundred on the menu. There are far too many to mention, there being probably as many *mezé* as there are cicadas, but here are a few to whet your appetite: **saganáki**, fried or flambéd cheese, courgette and aubergine fritters (*melidzánes*), which can be seasoned with **skordaliá**, a garlic and potato purée, and **dolmádes** and **dolmadhákia**, dainty pâtés of meat and rice wrapped in vine or cabbage leaves, which can be eaten hot or cold.

If you're more than a little peckish, you may prefer a few of the more filling **keftédes**, fried meat or vegetable balls. The island of Santoríni has developed its own version of this recipe, **tomatokeftédes**, tomato and melted cheese balls.

The Greeks are also great fans of **pulse** salads: haricot beans (*fassólia*) or lentils (*fakés*), mixed with slices of onion, parsley and a hint of olive oil.

## Grilled meats...

For a quick snack, there is nothing better than a little **gíros**, Greek counterpart of the Turkish *döner kebap*, lamb roasted on a vertical spit from which thin slices are cut as it cooks. You may, nevertheless, prefer the **souvlákia**, small brochettes of pork or chicken which line the refrigerated displays of all the tavernas. Gíros and souvlákia are served in a *pita* filled with tomatoes, onion and *tzatzíki*, covered by a generous sprinkling of paprika. Or you could allow yourself to be tempted by a traditional **tirópita** or **spanakópita**, tasty pasties, one stuffed with cheese, the other with spinach.

The tavernas have all sorts of grilled or roast meats on the menu – lamb, pork, beef, poultry and even goat – which are generally served with potatoes, the most common vegetable in Greek cuisine. And if you are partial to a lamb chop, you are sure to appreciate the **païdhákïa**, which are served by the kilo!

Greek cuisine

**The gíros, or the oriental-style roast**
Turkish folklore has it that in the late 19C a man named Iskender (Alexander) had the novel idea of placing lamb's meat vertically on a spit to roast it. And so the famous "döner", or "gíros" in Greek, was born (literally meaning "which constantly revolves").

A few **traditional family dishes** have now become regular restaurant fare, such as the world-famous **moussaká**, a gratin of aubergines and minced meat in tomato sauce covered with bechamel. But you may not be as familiar with **kokinistó kréas**, a highly flavoured stew (the islands of Sífnos and Tínos in the Cyclades are renowned for their meat specialities, among others), or **pastíchio**, a gratin of macaroni in tomato sauce with a generous covering of bechamel. These dishes can all be found on the menus of certain tavernas, but they may well disappoint gourmets in the more touristy areas, since they are frequently swimming in oil and have been reheated once too often...

## ...and fish
Surrounded by 15 000km of coastline, Greece has access to a wide variety of fish and seafood. The fishermen, who mainly come from the islands, sell their catch directly to the restaurateurs, so the products are very fresh. If you are a connoisseur, you can ask to choose your fish straight from the refrigerators in the kitchen; otherwise, ask the chef what he recommends. A few delicious suggestions to try: fried or grilled **barboúni** (red mullet), and the exquisite **grouper** (*sforos*), which is fished not far from the shore. You could also try the **sole** (*glóssa*), which, although it generally comes from fish farms, is a true delight, or common bream (*fagrí*) and bream (*sférida*). And there is always the **octopus** (*octapódi*) and squid, which you will see everywhere hanging from hooks in the tavernas. Fished from the coastal reefs, they are served grilled, perhaps with a dash of olive oil, or marinated in white wine.

Waiting for the octopi to dry

G. de Benoist/MICHELIN

### Oriental sweetmeats
Greek meals do not include dessert. But, if you have a bit of a sweet tooth, don't worry: cakes and other delicacies are served at all hours of the day, and can be enjoyed with a glass of cool lemonade. However, you won't find any purely Greek specialities: Greek pastries are the most obvious example of the famous culinary "borrowings", and although the recipes have been somewhat modified, their origins are betrayed by their names, which are often oriental: *baklavá*, *kataífi* and *loukoumádes* from Asia Minor, are just as full of honey, almonds and pistachios as the original versions. But you may be surprised to find the *millefeuilles* and *profiteroles* which are so dear to France, or *tiramisu* and *panaccotas* from Italy!

## Pines and wines

In Plato's famous *Symposium*, Socrates talks of the importance of the pleasure of the palate, devoting a large place to wine. Indeed, the sunshine and the shade of the pine trees are encapsulated in the aroma of **retsína**, which is made with pine resin. However, it can be an acquired taste and you may prefer the wines with more classical flavours. Greece and its islands produce a wide variety of pleasant red and white wines, some of which deserve a mention. Among the whites, **mandinia** from Arcadia and **roditis** from the island of Límnos are two very flavourful wines. The wines of **Santoríni** are also renowned for their special aroma, which is said to come from the island's volcanic soil.

## The art of ouzo

A national emblem of Greece, the ouzerí is a veritable institution with its own set of rules, without which the ritual would lose its essence. First of all, there are no individual place settings on the tables and ouzo drinkers usually require at least two or three chairs to make themselves really comfortable – one to sit on, an elbow resting on the back of a second and a leg on the bars of a third. This all underscores a certain detachment with respect to the food, and facilitates cursory and nonchalant gestures. The varied meze must be served in small portions and chosen in order to maintain a balance between the taste of the ouzo and a blend of garlic, salt, vinegar and spice flavours. Lastly, this is no place for serious conversation or sharp comments; quips and anecdotes are much better suited to the ouzo atmosphere. Once comfortably ensconced, it is easy to while away the hours.

As for red wines, there are some very respectable **Cabernet Sauvignons**, both in the north of Greece and in the Peloponnese. More typically local wines, **agiorítiko** from Neméa and **xinómavro**, are also quite full-bodied.

And, of course, no trip to Greece could ever be complete without a small glass of **ouzo**, an aniseed-flavoured drink which originated from French pastis. Friends gather together to savour its delights at **ouzerí** (ouzo bars) – where else? – and pick at a delicious assortment of meze.

## The taverna, or a taste of sunshine

A restaurant of the people... and of travellers, the *tavérna* is the ideal place to sample the local cuisine. Here you will find simple traditional dishes, and the service is usually fast. Each taverna, nevertheless, has its own specialities, depending on the chef's home region and savoir-faire. Consequently, some of them offer mainly fish and seafood (*psarotavérna*) while others specialise in grilled meats (*psistariá*). You will, however, find certain dishes wherever you go, even beyond the borders of Greece: what better to have with your aperitif than a spot of **taramosaláta**, a purée of fish eggs finely mixed with breadcrumbs, olive oil, lemon, garlic or onion, or **tzatzíki**, a creamy sauce made with yoghurt, garlic and cucumber. Not forgetting **melizanosaláta** (or "aubergine caviar") made with tender grilled and seasoned aubergine flesh.

The waiter will bring you the menu (*catálogos*), but it is often a good idea to ask him what is readily available. This way, he will be able to recommend the freshly made dishes of the day, avoiding products that require defrosting. And don't be shy to go into the kitchen to make your choice directly from the pans or traditional refrigerated displays where all the goods are laid out. Allowing yourself to be guided by the various aromas is by far the best way of discovering specialities whose names you don't know.

**Greek cuisine**

# HANDICRAFTS

Although the Greeks have no great crafts tradition, some tradesmen have managed to adapt certain typically regional creations to foreign tastes. Most of the items marked as "traditional", and intended exclusively for tourists, do not necessarily come from local craftsmen. But you may well be able to unearth some "authentic" objects in the villages off the beaten track.

## Woodwork

Some islands, the **Northern Sporades** in particular, are renowned for their traditional furniture, which includes beds, sideboards, trunks (*kasséla*), benches (*nissiótikos kanapés*), dressers (*piatothíki*), tables and chairs, painstakingly fashioned out of chestnut, fruit trees, oak or mahogany.

The Peloponnesian town of **Vitina** is known for its objects in walnut, cherry-wood or pine, ranging from hair slides to salad bowls, bread boards, cutlery and the ever-popular water pitchers.

## Jewellery

In the 1950s, **Ilias Lalaounis** started a trend in jewellery-making by copying precious objects from Ancient Greece. A school and workshops were founded under his patronage to train craftsmen in the techniques of working with **gold**. These workshops still produce wonderful pieces inspired by the Minoan, Macedonian, classical Greek and Byzantine civilisations, and such pieces are now also produced by other jewellers. Although it is not always easy to differentiate between individually made and industrial productions, the difference in price is often a good indicator.

In tourist areas, shops offer a large selection of metalwork, jewellery and charms, often beautiful copies of ancient or modern pieces. Even if they were not made by a craftsman, the – often original – pieces of gold jewellery are good value for money, although still rather expensive. People on smaller budgets will have to settle for **silver** jewellery, which is a speciality of the town of Ioánnina.

## Leather and fur

Leather products are produced mainly in northern Greece. A wide range of handbags, rucksacks and travel bags, sandals, leather flip-flops and belts are sold at reasonable prices in all tourist spots.

During your travels, you may be surprised by the rather impressive number of fur shops. The skin trade, which is encouraged by tourism, is particularly traditional in **Kastoriá**, Epirus.

## Carpets and fabrics

Most carpets, which are in the Ottoman tradition, are woven mechanically in the numerous factories of the Thessaloníki region. But some fabrics from Crete, Delphi and Epirus merit special attention on account of their weave and designs – often with stripes or checks – which have remained unchanged for several generations.

In times gone by, young girls prepared their trousseau by embroidering **kendímata**, fabrics with colourful designs representing flowers, animals, seascapes or landscapes as well as scenes inspired by mythology. It is still possible to unearth some true masterpieces in a few rare villages off the usual tourist trail, for example in northern Greece or Kárpathos, one of the Dodecanese Islands.

## Souvenir shops

As well as all the usual objects, you may want to bring back a **távli** (a board game of Ottoman origin), **flitzanáki** (small white porcelain coffee cups), **keramiká** (pot, pitcher or any other ceramic object from Sífnos, Rhodes and the neighbouring islands), **bouzoúki** (*see page 76*) or one of the famous **komboloï** (*see page 60*).

P. Frilet/HOA QUI

Traditional trades: a bootmaker in Kárpathos

# Practical information

B. Pérousse/MICHELIN

Following in the
wake of Odysseus
(arriving at
Santoríni)

# Before going

• **Time difference**

Greece is 2 hours ahead of Greenwich Mean Time (GMT) and 7 hours ahead of Eastern Standard Time (EST). The time is the same throughout the country, from the islands to the mainland.

• **International dialling**

Dial international + 30 + the number you wish to call without the first 0 of the area code.

For regional area codes, see page 104.

**International information:** if you are searching for a phone number in Greece, dial 32 12 for information (applicable throughout the country).

• **When to go**

Unless you are hoping to find a crowd, it is obviously preferable to avoid the summer months, particularly from mid-July to the end of August. The first 20 days of August are the busiest, as the Greeks, who for the most part spend their summer holidays in their own country, add to the already considerable number of foreign visitors. Accommodation is full and restaurants are overcrowded. As a result prices increase and the service given to guests a few weeks earlier becomes slack due to high demand. Everything from lodging to restaurants to rentals is therefore more difficult and more expensive. Also keep in mind that in August the wind (the *meltém*) sometimes blows violently across the Aegean Sea. While it may seem a refreshing change from the scorching heat, at the same time it makes the beaches much less enjoyable. If you plan to visit archaeological sites you will also want to avoid the high tourist season, if possible, when the museums and sites are jam-packed.

The month of June (as well as the end of May and the beginning of July) is THE ideal season to visit. You'll benefit from summer weather without the high temperatures or the violent winds and some of the spring colours can still be found. Accommodation is half price and it is not necessary to make reservations. Hoteliers are attentive and in a good mood at the beginning of the season.

**September** is also an auspicious month to visit. The first week of the month is still considered summer, even if the Greeks say *"Kaló himóna"* ("have a good winter"). September is a perfect time for anyone who likes warm water as the sea reaches its maximum temperature at this time. This mild autumn weather lasts until mid-November although many of the hotels and restaurants close at the end of October. Afterwards, the days become noticeably shorter and the rain from the storms revives the colour of the vegetation.

Although brief and intense, **spring** is a splendid season throughout Greece where all the colours are at their peak. The mountains, as well as the islands, are covered with gorgeous blossoms, however the sea is still a bit cool.

In **winter** the country has two contrasting faces. In the north and at high altitudes, thick snow blankets the countryside, while in the south and on the islands the sea tempers the winter weather. The average temperature is 11°C (52°F) in Athens and 12°C (54°F) in Herakleion in January. It is possible to ski on slopes two hours away by car from Athens and dine on the capital's outdoor terraces (warmly dressed, of course) on bright days.

• **Packing list**

*Clothing*

In the summer, plan to bring light clothing (cotton rather than synthetic) and don't forget a hat and **sunglasses**, essential everywhere in the country. If you are travelling in the spring, bring one or two light jumpers, as evenings can still be a bit cool depending on the region, and a raincoat for the north of Greece. In winter, be sure to bring your coat – a heavy one for the north and a lighter one for the south.

In summer, bring a light **windcheater** that you can roll up and stick in your bag. This is ideal for high altitude cold, especially if you plan to travel by bicycle or motorcycle (if you return after the sun sets, it can be quite chilly). It will also be useful when you're on a boat or when the meltem occurs. Don't forget that nights by the sea are quite cold, even in the middle of summer. If you plan to rough it, a sleeping bag or warm clothes are a must. Finally, if you visit **monasteries** and other sacred sites, women should plan to wear something to cover their legs. A skirt that is easy to put over shorts will do the trick.

## • A trip for everyone

### Travelling with children

You will have no trouble finding lodging if you are travelling as a family. Tourist rentals include many studios or furnished apartments equipped with small kitchens. They're often even more economical than two double rooms.

### Travelling alone

A woman travelling on her own should fear nothing more than the legendary Greek *kamáki* (literally the "harpoon"). In other words, the Greeks may try to seduce you but they're not aggressive.

### Disabled travellers

Unfortunately there is still little in the way of facilities catering for disabled persons outside Athens. You'll be able to count more on the kindness of the locals than on appropriate facilities.

## • Address book

### Tourist information

**United Kingdom –** 4 Conduit Street, London W1R ODJ, ☎ (020) 7734 5997, Fax (020) 7287 1369.

**USA –** Olympic Tower, 645 Fifth Avenue, New York, NY 10022, ☎ (212) 421 5777, Fax (212) 826 6940.

**Canada –** 1300 Bay Street, Toronto, Ontario, M5R 3K8, ☎ (416) 968 22 20, Fax (416) 968 65 33.

1233 rue de la Montagne, Suite 101, Montreal, Quebec, H3G 1Z2, ☎ (514) 871 15 35, Fax (514) 871 14 98.

**Australia –** 51-57 Pitt Street, Sydney, NSW 2000; PO Box R203 Royal Exchange NSW 2000 ☎ (2) 9241 1663 / 4 / 5 or 9252 1441, Fax (2) 9235 2174.

### Cultural centres

**The Hellenic Centre –** 16-18 Paddington Street, Marylebone, London W1U 5AS, ☎ (020) 7487 5060, Fax (020) 7486 4254, www.helleniccentre.com

**Hellenic American Union –** Massalías 22, 10680 Athens 368-0000, www.hau.gr

### Web sites

Surfers may find the following websites useful:

**Greek Tourism Organisation**: www.gnto.gr
**Maritime schedules**: www.gtpnet.com
**Greek Cultural Heritage**: www.culture.gr
**Travel information**: www.travelocity.com
**Hellenic Resources Network**: www.hri.org
**Hellas**: www.greece.org provides useful information about Greece and discusses Greek issues.

### Embassies

**United Kingdom – IA Holland Park, London W11 3TP,** ☎ (020) 7229 3850, Fax (020) 7229 7221.

**USA –** 2221 Massachusetts Avenue NW, Washington, DC 20008, ☎ (202) 667 3169, 939 5800, Fax (202) 939 5824.

**Canada –** 76-80 MacLaren Street, Ottawa, Ontario, K2P 0K6, ☎ (613) 288 62 71, Fax (613) 238 56 76.

**Australia** – 9 Turrana Street, Yarralumla, Canberra 26000, ☏ (62) 733 158 / 733 011, Fax (62) 732 620.

### • Modern Greek courses

**Hellenic College of London** – 67 Pont Street, London SW1X 0BD, UK, ☏ (020) 7581 5044, Fax (020) 7589 9055, www.ukstudies.gr
**International Center for Language Studies, Inc (ICLS)** – 727 15th Street NW, Suite 400, Washington, DC 20005-2168, USA, ☏ (202) 639 8800, english@icls.com

### • Specialised bookshops

**The Hellenic Bookservice** – 91, Fortess Road, London NW5 1AG, UK, ☏ (020) 7267 9499, Fax (020) 7267 9498, hellenicbooks@btinternet.com, www.hellenicbookservice.com

### • Formalities

*ID, visas*

For nationals of states belonging to the European Union, a passport (even one that has expired less than 5 years ago) or valid identity card is sufficient. Americans and Canadians must show a valid passport. For all other nationals, check the Greek consulate in your country for entry requirements.

*Customs*

Regulations with regards to imports (alcohol, cigarettes, etc.) are the same throughout the European Union. Cars are exempt from customs duties for up to 6 months. After that time, you must either take your vehicle out of the country or request temporary registration.

*Health regulations*

There are no particular health regulations governing entrance to Greece.

*Vaccinations*

No vaccinations are required.

*Driving licence*

If you plan to drive in Greece (either cars or motorcycles), UK citizens must have their national driving licence and proof of insurance. For US, Canadian and Australian nationals, an international driving licence is obligatory. *(See the section above on ID).*

### • Local currency

*Cash*

The euro became the official currency of Greece in 2001. However, the Greek **drachma (Dr)** will remain in circulation during the changeover period until 2002. At the time of writing, €1 is worth approximately US$0.9 and Dr340.

*Currency exchange*

It's better to change your money once you arrive as commissions are lower. In the cities, there are many exchange offices. You can change money at the airport or post office, as well as in banks and hotels. Keep in mind that hotels will offer worse exchange rates.

*Travellers' cheques*

Use of travellers' cheques is still limited to the tourist areas and large cities. You can, however, change them easily in all the banks.

*Bank cards*

Cash dispensers (ATMs) for international bank cards are available in all cities, on most islands and at the main tourist sites. In some cases, banks will provide cash upon presentation of a bank card with an approximate 3% commission added on. Most large hotels accept payment by bank cards and an increasing number of establishments are starting to do so. On the other hand, this is not very common in small hotels or guesthouses.

## • Spending money

Be it accommodation, food or shopping, life in Greece is not as cheap as it used to be. While the quality of **accommodation** has increased, so have the prices. Of course, rooms in local homes (with shared bathroom facilities) remain reasonably priced, but owners prefer to improve the level of comfort so they can raise their rates, and competition for reasonably priced lodging is very tough. Moreover, prices vary considerably depending on the period you visit; they practically double between low and high season depending on the place. In high season, a double room with private bath can rarely be negotiated for less than €23.

It's a different story with family-operated local **restaurants**. You can easily find little *tavérnas* that offer delicious meals at a modest price. *Souvláki* (around €1) is one nutritious solution and is well worth trying. If you travel during the warm season, you may also want to consider having a picnic; tomatoes, fruit from the markets, local cheese and freshly baked bread are good choices. This is still the cheapest way to eat and there are plenty of lovely places to enjoy these feasts.

Entrance to **archaeological sites** and small **museums** is usually around €1.50 or €7.50 for the most expensive. As far as **public transport** is concerned, buses are more reasonable than trains, which also serve fewer destinations, and ferries are a better deal than hydrofoils, which are double the price.

Hotels in **Athens** are slightly more expensive. You should plan to spend around €45 for a good quality room (although there are some decent ones for €30-38) and €7.50-15 is necessary for a good meal. You should therefore plan to spend around €68-75 per day including your transport costs and the obligatory bottle of water or soda to counter the scorching heat.

In short, with a daily budget of €60 per person (based on two people travelling together), you will have a very enjoyable holiday equipped with an economy rental car, without depriving yourself. For those on a tighter budget, €23-30 (based on double occupancy) will suffice if you travel by bus, dine on "souvláki" and "tirópita" (around €7.50 for both meals) and stay in small, modest hotels.

## • Booking in advance

Advanced booking is necessary if you travel to tourist areas in high season on an average budget. Decent accommodation at standard rates is subject to tough competition. As soon as you arrive in Athens, reserve your next stop, and, if possible, ask the staff at your hotel to negotiate the deal in Greek. Before 15 July and after the end of August, there are fewer problems and you can arrive without advance notice.

## • Travel / health insurance

Consider taking out repatriation insurance before leaving home if travelling independently. Many tour operators already include repatriation insurance in the price of your trip (be warned, this can be very expensive). Contact your local insurance company for information on obtaining this.

# GETTING THERE

## • By air

In the summer, be sure to book your flight at least 2 months in advance. The weight and the number of authorised bags vary according to the airline company and the class you select. As a general rule you can check in up to 20kg of luggage on regularly scheduled flights and 15kg on charter flights.

*Scheduled flights*

**From the UK**

**British Airways** – Waterside, PO Box 365, Harmondsworth UB7 OGB, ☎ (08457) 733377. Daily flights from various cities in the UK to Athens via London.

**Cronus Airlines –** Reservations, ☎ (020) 7580 3500, info@cronus.gr
**Olympic Airways –** 11 Conduit St, London W1R OLP, ☎ (0870) 6060460, Fax (020) 7629 9891, email@olympicairways.co.uk or at Heathrow Airport, Terminal 2, ☎ (020) 8745 7339 / 8759 5884, Fax (020) 8897 0279.

**From the USA**
**Delta Air Lines –** Hartsfield Atlanta International Airport, Atlanta, GA 30320, ☎ (1 800) 241 4141 or (404) 715 2600. Daily departures from New York's JFK to Athens.
**Olympic Airways –** Olympic Towers, 645 Fifth Ave, New York, NY 10022, ☎ (212) 735 0200, Fax (212) 735 0212.

*Charter flights*
Other companies have weekly charter flights from major cities. Obtain information from travel agencies or the Internet, and don't forget that some large companies provide charter rates on their regularly scheduled flights.
**Lambda World –** 350 Fifth Avenue, Suite 3304, New York, NY 10118, USA, ☎ (212) 439 5268, info@lambdaworld.com, has flights from NYC to Athens and Thessaloníki.
**Avro –** Wren Court, 17 London Road, Bromley, Kent BR1 1DE, UK, ☎ (020) 8695 4440, Fax (020) 8695 4004, reservations@avro.co.uk Flights from numerous cities in the UK to Athens, Corfu, and Herakleion.

*Confirmation*
To be on the safe side, confirm your return flight at least 48hr before departure.

*Airport taxes*
Airport departure tax in Greece has gone up to about €20. However, this is generally included in the price of your plane ticket.

● **By train**

Only those who really love to travel by train will want to choose this form of transport (travel time from London to Brindisi, Italy, takes more than 25hr). From there you still have to cross by ferry to Patras before climbing aboard a Greek train to your selected city. There are daily departures from London to Paris aboard the Eurostar (to the Gare du Nord). You must then change stations (Gare de Lyon) and take a night train to Milan or Turin. From there, you will connect to Brindisi. A combined ferry / train ticket is not available and you will need to reserve the crossing from Brindisi to Patras through a maritime company (see the section "By boat").

● **By bus**

Needless to say, this is also a very time-consuming way to travel (at least 55hr from London to Athens) but what an experience for those who have the time! The price war among airline companies, however, gives little reason to use this type of transport. Check that the connection (which operates only during the summer) is working.

● **By car**

A driving licence is sufficient for European Union nationals. You must, of course, provide documentation for your vehicle and be sure to verify that your insurance contract covers any damage incurred in Greece.
It's possible to travel to Greece by car passing through Eastern Europe (plan at least 5 days if travelling from London). However, the political instability in the Balkans may make crossing through certain states difficult if not impossible. A (long) detour via Hungary, Romania and Bulgaria is highly recommended. Contact the embassies of these countries for information on entry conditions. For a shorter trip, go via Italy instead and take the ferry *(see below)*.

● **By boat**

Book at least 2 months in advance during the summer, especially if you plan to bring your car.

G. de Benoist/MICHELIN

*Via Italy*

Leave from an Italian port (Venice, Ancona, Bari, Brindisi or Trieste). To reserve a passage (for you and / or your vehicle), contact:

**Paleologos SA** – Odós 25 Avgoústou 5, 71202 Herakleion, Crete, ☎ (081) 346185 / 330598, Fax (081) 346208, www.greekislands.gr, info@greekislands.gr Provides reservations for all the main ferry lines connecting Italy to Greece

**ANEK Lines** – www.anek.gr, booking@anek.gr

**Minoan Lines** – www.minoan.gr, info@minoan.gr

Information on most of the ferry companies operating in Greece can be found at www.ferries.gr

*Length of crossing*

Travel time from Venice to Patras is approximately 36hr, 20hr between Ancona and Patras, and around 10hr for a connection from Brindisi or Bari to Patras.

• **Package deals**

*Generalists*

**Anemone House** – 109 Myddleton Road, London N22 8NE, UK, ☎ (020) 8889 9207, Fax (020) 8889 1127, holidays@anemone.co.uk

**Odysseys Unlimited** – 85 Main Street, Suite 101, Watertown, MA 02472, USA, ☎ (888) 370 6765 or (781) 370 3600, Fax (781) 370 3699, corp@odysseys-unlimited. com Small group travel for 12-24 passengers.

**Tourlite International** – 120 Sylvan Ave, Englewood Cliffs, NJ 07632, USA, ☎ (800) 272 7600 or (201) 228 5280, Fax (201)228 5281, tourlite@tourlite.com

*Greece specialists*

**Avenir Travel & Adventures** – 2029 Sidewinder Drive, PO Box 2730, Park City, UT 84060, USA, ☎ (1 800) 367 3230 or (435) 649 2495, Fax (435) 649 1192, info@AvenirTravel.com

**Destination Greece** – 195 West Como Avenue, Columbus, OH 43202, USA, ☎ and Fax (614) 261 8444, Operations@DestinationGreece.com

**Intersky Holidays** – 407 Green Lanes, London N4 1EY, UK, ☎ (020) 8341 9999, Fax (020) 8341 1153, Info@InterSkyHolidays.co.uk

**Sunvil Holidays** – Sunvil House, Upper Square, Old Isleworth, Middlesex TW7 7BJ, UK, ☎ (020) 8568 4499 / 8232 9797, Fax (020) 8568 8330, greece@sunvil.co.uk

**Tourcom** – 53 Condict St, Jersey City, NJ 07306, USA, ☎ (888) 868 7266 or (201) 395 9401, Fax (201) 395 9403, tour@tourcom.com

**Ya'll Tours USA, Inc** – 4711 SW Huber Street, Portland, OR 97219, USA, ☎ (1 800) 644 1595 or (503) 977 3758, Fax (503) 977 3765, inquire@greecetraveltours.com

*Cultural trips*

**Educational Tours & Cruises** – 94 Prescott St, Medford, MA 02155-3750, USA, ☎ (800) 275 4109, Fax (718) 396 3096, edtours@aol.com

**OPA Tours Greece** – 137 Genoa Street, Suite B, Arcadia, CA 91006, USA, ☎ and Fax (800) 672 7155, opatours@aol.com

**Westminster Classic Tours, Ltd** – Suite 120, 266 Banbury Road, Summertown, Oxford OX2 7DL, UK, ☎ (01865) 728565, Fax (01865) 728575, info@wct99.com

*Adventure trips*

**Country Walkers** – PO Box 180, Waterbury, VT 05676, USA, ☎ and Fax (802) 244 5661, ☎ (888) 886 4075, info@countrywalkers.com Walking tours of Crete and the Peloponnese.

**ExperienceGreece** – 4595 Westmore, Montreal, QC H4B 2A1, Canada, ☎ (888) 317 8622 or (514) 489 2722, Fax (450) 451 3358, contactus@experiencegreece.com Provides walking tours in Greece.

**ExperiencePlus! Specialty Tours, Inc** – 415 Mason Ct #1, Fort Collins, CO 80524, USA, ☎ (800) 685 4565, Fax (970) 484 8489, tours@ExperiencePlus.com Bicycle and walking tours.

# THE BASICS

## • Address book

*Tourist information*

All of the tourist centres, regardless of their size, have their own tourist information office. These usually provide good documentation and have competent staff to help you. Don't hesitate to visit them. If there is no tourist information office available, local travel agencies often provide the same services (accommodation, transportation, etc). **Greek National Tourism Organisation (EOT)**, open 9am-7pm, Saturday 10am-3pm; closed Sunday. Odós Amerikís 4 (near Sýndagma), ☎ (01) 331 05 61 / 2 / 5. Lots of information is available here, not only on Athens but also on all types of transport in Greece (including schedules and rates) to the islands, Attica, the Peloponnese or the north of the country. The staff are often overworked but very friendly.

*Embassies and consulates*

**United Kingdom** – Odós Ploutárchou 1, 106 75 Athens, ☎ (01) 727 2600, Fax (01) 727 2720, info@athens.mail.fco.gov.uk

**United States** – Leofóros Vassilíssis Sofías 91, 101 60 Athens, ☎ (01) 721 2951

**Canada** – Odós Ioánnou Gennadíou 4, 115 21 Athens, ☎ (01) 727 3400, Fax (01) 727 3480

**Australia** – Odós Dimitríou Soútsou 37, Ambelókipi 11521, Athens ☎ (01) 645 0404, Fax (01) 646 6595, ausembgr@hol.gr

## • Opening and closing times

Government offices, public offices (post office and telephone) and banks are closed in the afternoon.

*Banks*

Banks are open Monday to Friday 8am-1.30 or 2pm. They are closed Saturdays and on public holidays. Staff will serve customers who have arrived before the doors close, so if you are in a queue, be patient. Be sure to take a ticket to await your turn.

*Post offices*

Post offices are generally open Monday to Friday from 7.30am-2pm. In main post offices you will also need to take a number before you queue up.

The basics

### OTE (telephone) offices

OTE offices are open from 8am-2pm, with the exception of some of the Athens offices: Odós Stadíou 15, which is open daily around the clock and Odós Athinás 50, open 24hr a day during the week and from 7am-10pm on Saturday and Sunday.

### Shops

In the cities, shops are open Monday, Wednesday and Saturday from 8 or 9am-3pm (on Saturday, supermarkets stay open until around 6pm), and Tuesday, Thursday and Friday from 8am-8pm. Some shops (particularly grocery stores) close for one to two hours in the afternoon. On Sundays, bakeries and stores selling wines, spirits, soda, ice cream, etc, are open, some of them until about 8pm.

### Kiosks

A mainstay in Greek daily life, kiosks, or **períptero**, never really close; or rather, there is always at least one open in every neighbourhood. In addition to buying their main product, tobacco (in Greece, smokers never lack anything), you can buy newspapers, cold drinks, and snacks. Most kiosks also sell emergency items, such as aspirin, stamps and envelopes, film, condoms, shampoo and thousands of other useful little things.

### Restaurants

Opening hours vary depending on the restaurant, but they generally stay open and serve meals (whatever is left, of course) until late. Except in small, isolated hamlets with fewer than twenty houses, it's quite common to find a **psistariá** open nearby where you can sample souvláki, chips, a salad and a beer or a glass of *retsina*.

### • Museums, monuments and archaeological sites

#### Opening times

Notable efforts have been made to standardise opening hours. Despite this, variations still remain, some of them logical (sites undergoing excavation must close earlier), others less so. As a general rule, in the summer, archaeological sites and museums open at approximately 8am and close at either 3pm or 7pm (earlier in winter). Monasteries and small art and folklore museums keep variable hours; however, even if the opening times are indicated, they are not always respected.

#### Churches

Diocesan churches (where Orthodox priests celebrate the liturgy daily) are open in the morning and sometimes at the end of the afternoon. The more important ones stay open all day. On the other hand, private churches (the countless chapels scattered across the countryside and Greek towns) are closed more often. This is unfortunately also the case with historic churches and monasteries. The *panigíri* (religious or village festivals) often provide the chance to explore these buildings. You will, however, find small chapels open to passers-by (especially on the islands).

#### Entrance fees

Ticket prices range from €1.50-3 as a general rule. The large museums in Athens and the Acropolis are more expensive (€6). Student discounts are given at the larger sites and museums upon presentation of an international student identification card.

### • Post offices

You'll easily recognise Greek post offices by their yellow sign with the word **ELTA** and a profile of the god Hermes. In addition to the standard-priced stamp, the Greek postal service offers an "express" rate, which is cheap and quick (a letter sent from the Sýndagma post office in Athens will arrive in London in 2 days for approximately €1.50). You can also buy stamps (*gramatóssima*) at the períptero (kiosk) for postcards. Money can be exchanged at the post office, however there are no public phones.

Finally, you can receive all types of mail through poste restante upon proof of identification.

## ● Telephone (OTE)

Telephone booths are everywhere and you can get phone cards (*kárta tilephónou*) in any períptero. International phone calls from Greece can be quite costly. If you're planning to call overseas, make sure you have several phone cards or go to an OTE office to make the call. You can also make calls from the períptero.

*International calls*

To make an international call, dial **00 + country code + number** (without the first 0 of the area code). To call the UK, dial 00 44; for the US and Canada, 00 + 1; for Australia 00 + 61.

*Local calls*

Each district (be it a village, an island or a district) has its own area code (between parentheses) composed of 1 to 3 numbers preceded by a 0. For example, Athens (01), Thessaloníki (031), Réthimnon (0831), etc. The phone numbers themselves consist of between 5 and 7 digits according to the place. For a local call within the same region, you only need to dial the main number. If calling another region, first dial 0, followed by the code for that region (3 digits everywhere except Athens) and the number you want to call.

Mobile phone numbers are longer and their area code varies according to the operator, but all begin with 09. If you call these numbers from abroad, dial the international dialling code from your country + 30 for Greece + the number you are trying to call without the 0.

*Useful numbers*

**For all OTE services**, ☏ 134.
**Telephone directory services**, ☏ 131 (in Attica), ☏ 132 (in the rest of Greece)
**International telegrams**, ☏ 165.
**International phone calls**, ☏ 161.
**To obtain international codes** (in English), ☏ 169.

## ● Public holidays

| | |
|---|---|
| **1 January** | New Year's Day. |
| **6 January** | **Epiphany**. Blessing of the sea. In every port, regardless of its size, young people dive into the water to recover the cross that is ceremoniously thrown in by the Orthodox priest. |
| **Clean Monday** | *Katharí deftéra*: 41 days before Orthodox Easter (dates vary), the first Monday of Lent. The *koulouma* is celebrated in the countryside, weather permitting, and the menu consists of fish and seafood. |
| **25 March** | **Greek Independence Day and Annunciation**. A military parade in Athens and Thessaloníki and school parades all over Greece. |
| **Easter** | On Good Friday, all the churches prepare an *epitáphion* decorated with flowers, the symbol of Christ's shroud that the faithful follow in a procession. Celebrations for the Resurrection start Saturday at midnight with fireworks. On Sunday, traditional lamb from the spit is eaten. |
| **1 May** | **Labour Day.** |
| **28 October** | *Óchi* Day when Greeks said "No" and rejected the Italian ultimatum in 1940. Military parade. |
| **25-26 December** | Christmas. |

The basics

# GETTING AROUND

## • By car

### Car rentals

There are many car rental agencies, both local and international, in Athens and all over Greece. Some hotels and travel agencies also provide this service. Rates vary according to the place, season, number of days, and the type of vehicle. For example, a lower-range car rented in Athens at a major rental company costs around €55. The same car will cost €68 in Mýkonos in August.

### Road network

The quality of the roads is not bad but some of the **main roads** are not wide enough to handle the heavy traffic. On the hilly islands the main roads are often narrow and sinuous. You will often find yourself stuck behind a large truck with no chance of overtaking for miles. In this case, it's common for the emergency breakdown lane (when there is one) to become an extra lane for slower vehicles, while the regular lane is used for overtaking. As the railway network is not well developed, almost all travel is done by road. Motorways are multiplying on the mainland and very soon you should be able to travel from Patras to Thessaloníki via Athens exclusively by toll motorway.

Additionally, the country preserves countless **trails**, which are sometimes impassable without a four-wheel-drive vehicle.

Off the beaten path, road signs are often rudimentary and are only in Greek. You may therefore want to familiarise yourself with the Greek alphabet as soon as possible. Finally, on country roads and in villages, be careful of the sheep and goats, either in flocks or alone, which can hold up traffic.

### Driving

While driving rules may be similar to those in other European countries, police patrols tend to be more infrequent.

### Fuel

Fuel stations are scattered throughout the country, although these are a bit harder to find in the mountains and remote areas. Fuel tends to be a bit less expensive than in most European countries. Be aware that very few stations accept credit cards. There is no self-service in Greece and an attendant will pump the fuel for you.

### Parking in town

There is no metered parking in the centre of Athens, and spaces are difficult to find during the day. If you park illegally, an officer will confiscate one of the licence plates to ensure that the offender comes to the police station to pay the fine.

### Accidents

A report must be written up by a police officer in due form and you will need to obtain a copy. After this you will be able to repair your vehicle at a garage.

## • By taxi

Taxis are yellow in Athens and grey or burgundy in the rest of the country.

## • By train (OSE)

The railway network is not well developed but it is inexpensive. Trains run frequently and you can get to the main Greek cities easily from Athens. Some examples of rates and travel time (for **intercity trains**) are: Athens-Patras, 3hr30min, around €9; Athens-Náfplio, 3hr, around €6; Athens-Thessaloníki, 5hr30min (by express train), approximately €24. Be sure to make advance reservations if you want a seat on the train between Athens and Thessaloníki. Note that the two railway stations in Athens are now connected by the metro.

Two routes that are particularly picturesque: the line from Kalávrita (in the Peloponnese) by rack railway and the "aerial" route from Livadiá to Lamía which passes by impressive viaducts.

## • By bus

Bus services are well developed in Greece and are reliable (with numerous departures), inexpensive compared to trains, and generally faster as well. They more than make up for the lack of a comprehensive railway network. Bus lines connect Athens with the Ionian Islands (via boat) and this is the best means of exploring northern Greece. It is however inconvenient that the long-distance bus terminals in Athens (that go further than Attica) are more difficult to get to than the railway stations.

## • By boat

All inhabited islands in Greece have a **ferry** service, however the frequency of crossings varies enormously. There are several departures daily for Páros and Santoríni but only one ferry a week for Koufoníssi. Overall, the Cyclades have a better service than the islands of the Dodecanese or the Sporades.

Keep in mind that the unexpected can always happen when travelling by sea. If there is a storm warning only the large ferries will operate. The most modern ones are equipped with stabilisers, however if you are prone to seasickness, you should plan to stay below deck. Although the Mediterranean is a landlocked sea, it nonetheless tosses boats around in a very unpleasant manner.

**Hydrofoils** are highly susceptible to wind and if you choose this form of transport, you may want to confirm that it will operate the evening before or the morning of your departure. Boats that are equally as fast but larger and more reliable during bad weather are now available: the **Highspeed** and **Seajet** (sometimes called **catamarans** because of their shape). These heavy boats with their enclosed and air-conditioned binnacles are more comparable to trains (or planes) than boats. Their main advantage is their speed which is practically double that of a classic ferry – but they are also double the price.

*The large ports*

The port at **Piraeus** (*see details in the "Making the most of Piraeus" section, page 163*) operates services to the islands of the Saronic Gulf, the Cyclades, the Dodecanese, Lesbos and Crete. The port at **Rafina** provides a service to the Cyclades and Euboea (Káristos and Marmári). The port at **Lávrio** serves the island of Kéa (Tziá). The port at **Patras** serves the Ionian Islands and Italy. The port at **Igoumenítsa** serves the islands of Corfu and Paxós as well as Italy. And the port at **Kilíni** serves the islands of Zacynthus (Zákinthos) and Cephalonia.

*Rates*

Tickets can be purchased at shipping agencies at the port or on-board ship. A ticket check is carried out systematically once the ship is at sea. There are several classes available on board; first class or sleeper berths are only worthwhile for trips of 10hr or more. Some sample rates (in economy class) are: Piraeus-Herakleion, around €21.50; Piraeus-Mýkonos, around €15; and Rafína-Ándros, approximately €7.50.

*Information*

The EOT office in Athens provides thorough information on these three means of transport (routeing, frequency of departures, hours) and even rates for the bus and train.

## • Renting two-wheel vehicles

You can rent a two-wheel vehicle (up to a capacity of 125cc) upon presentation of your driving licence. The rental agencies rarely supply **helmets**, often considered superfluous in Greece, particularly in the summer. For your own safety, ask for one (even if you only get a relic from the 1970s) especially if you plan to travel on winding roads. The daily rate for a 50cc vehicle is approximately €11-15.

Be sure to specify if the length of rental time is for the day (from morning to evening) or for 24hr as rental agencies are sometimes evasive about this matter. Also quickly verify the **state of your vehicle** (tyres, lights and the amount of fuel in the tank, as the gauges are often unreliable).

Getting around

If there are two of you riding on the same vehicle, you may want to consider the traditional **papáki** (literally "little duck"). These are three-speed mopeds without a clutch and are thus named due to the noise they make when they slow down. While they are less glamorous than motor scooters, these rustic machines, often used in the Middle East and in Asia, are nonetheless solid, relatively powerful and manage the road

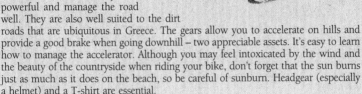

G. de Benoist/MICHELIN

well. They are also well suited to the dirt roads that are ubiquitous in Greece. The gears allow you to accelerate on hills and provide a good brake when going downhill – two appreciable assets. It's easy to learn how to manage the accelerator. Although you may feel intoxicated by the wind and the beauty of the countryside when riding your bike, don't forget that the sun burns just as much as it does on the beach, so be careful of sunburn. Headgear (especially a helmet) and a T-shirt are essential.

• **Domestic flights**

**Olympic Airways** no longer has a monopoly on internal flights even if it remains the primary Greek company going to certain islands, such as Mýkonos, Santoríni, Páros, etc. Some small private companies also operate internal services, and the proliferation of flights to Crete and Thessaloníki has lowered fares. Addresses in Athens:

**Cronus Airlines**, Odós Óthonos 10, ☎ (01) 33 15 502-4.
**Aegean Airlines**, Leofóros Vouliagménis 572, ☎ (01) 99 88 350.
**Olympic Airways**, Odós Filelínon 15, ☎ (01) 92 67 444.

• **Organised tours and excursions**

Greece has been a popular tourist destination for a long time now. You'll be able to find whatever you're looking for, from cruises to archaeological tours, resort holidays to all sorts of hikes and treks and any possible combination of these different components.

# BED AND BOARD

Hotel provision in Greece is very well developed with lots of variety, ranging from deluxe hotels to small hotels to rooms to let. The quality of accommodation has also improved considerably and you will find it to be clean and comfortable no matter what category. On the other hand, it's not always that easy to track down hotels of charm; the 1960s and 70s produced a large number of concrete boxes. The current tendency, however, is to return to a more traditional architecture. This can either be authentic, when restoration or new construction is carried out with care using the old materials, or pseudo, particularly prevalent in the Cyclades, where walls are merely painted white and shutters blue and a few concrete arches are provided. This is nonetheless more pleasant than a standard rectangular block.

In short, good clean accommodation with that little extra touch is mostly to be found in the middle category. If you want to combine charm and comfort with reasonable rates, you should plan to come in the low season, in June or September, when these establishments offer reduced rates.

If you're travelling with family or friends, an interesting option is to rent a studio with a kitchenette. This type of lodging is widespread in Greece and can be a good alternative not only for its high quality (in comparison to rooms) but also for the price. Breakfast costs at least €4.50 daily and fewer meals in restaurants will more than compensate for the additional cost of this type of accommodation.

### Rates

The rates mentioned in this guidebook are calculated on the basis of double occupancy in high season or the price of a studio apartment for two people. Be sure to barter in low season or in less touristy areas, especially if you plan to stay for several days, as there is often a sliding scale.

## • Various categories

### Hotels

The Greek National Tourism Organisation **(EOT)** classifies hotels, studios and rooms into six categories: Deluxe, A, B, C, D, and E. These categories are determined by a set of criteria: the service provided, the facilities, the size of the rooms, their decor, available staff, etc. You will have to be the judge of the charm, the view, the quality of the furniture and additional services. For your information, we have listed below some daily rates based on double occupancy in high season, from the cheapest to the most expensive.

- E: €13-33
- D: €18-35
- C: €36-100
- B: €75-122
- A: €82-152
- Deluxe: €90 and up

These rates are not enforced. They vary from one establishment to another, according to the season and how touristy the site is. With this in mind, a new C category hotel can be more expensive that an old hotel that has a B ranking. D and E category hotels don't systematically include private bathrooms or breakfast. EOT classified lodgings have a small blue and yellow plaque and post their rates. They are itemised at local tourist information offices and travel agencies.

### Rooms to let

The hotel categories don't apply to rooms to let, which are undeclared. On certain islands, the owners come to welcome the visitors at the port when the boats arrive. If this isn't the case, you can either telephone when you arrive (the reply will be in Greek or very rudimentary English) or just show up at the house which is the best means to judge the quality of the lodgings. Signs marked *Rooms* or *Domátia* will indicate where to go. You can also shop around; in Greek villages, a good number of the houses are almost always empty. To find this out, go to the *kafenío* (café) or the village bar and ask *"Psáhno dhomátio sto horió"* ("I'm looking for a room in the village"), after giving the respectful greeting *("Yá sas")*. Keep in mind however that you will not always find philanthropists. Make sure you have a budget and know that it's always easier to negotiate a lower rate for five nights than for two.

### Camping

In principle, camping in the wild is forbidden but every island and tourist area has at least one campsite. All have relatively good facilities (mini-markets, bathrooms, etc.) and are often pleasantly shaded. A site for two people with shower costs about €12 per day.

### Youth hostels

Youth hostels have never been particularly widespread in Greece, given the low rates charged by small hotels and for rooms to let.

**Youth Hostel Association of Greece**, Odós Dragatsaníou 4, Athens, ☎ (01) 32 34 107.

G. de Benoist/MICHELIN

## • Eating out

There is no shortage of places to eat out and you can find something for every taste and budget. We can distinguish five broad categories of restaurants. For both standard cuisine or fish and seafood, **tavérnas** are popular restaurants that serve simple traditional Greek dishes that are inexpensive for the most part. **Ouzeris** (ouzo bars) and *mezedopolio* differ from tavernas by their menus, which offer meze (*see page 89*) rather than cooked or meat dishes. The term **psistariá** (literally "steakhouse") stands for small, inexpensive restaurants (with or without tables) where you can buy *souvlákia* (brochettes) and other grilled meats (chicken, lamb, etc), served with chips and sometimes a tomato salad. **Kafenía** are Greek cafés par excellence and also serve some meze to nibble on. You'll also find cafeterias which serve as cafes and provide breakfasts and some dishes. Naturally there are lots of multi-service establishments. As for **restaurants** (*estiatório* in Greek), you can find both Greek and international cuisine, and even elaborately prepared gourmet dishes. The decor and service are generally meticulous and prices are higher than elsewhere. Hotel restaurants – even well-established ones – are generally expensive and disappointing, particularly in Athens, with the exception of some famous gourmet restaurants.

*Prices*

Obviously prices vary according to the place and the menu. Keep in mind however that you will need to spend €7.50-11 per person for a decent meal in an ordinary taverna. Fish, on the other hand, is very expensive. Although Greece is surrounded by water, its resources of seafood are unfortunately diminishing rapidly and prices reflect this (around €30 per kilo for a top-category fish).

# SPORTS AND PASTIMES

## • Sports activities

*Hiking*

If you are a rambler, you will be in heaven. Greece is covered with paths, trails, unusual sites and nature parks (especially in the north of the country) which make for wonderful walking. Whether you're an avid hiker or simply enjoy a peaceful walk, there is something for everyone, particularly those who like to combine nature, history and finding out about the local way of life.

In some areas or islands, the local tourist information office distributes more or less reliable maps of paths and trails. You'll find all the necessary information at tourist information centres in Athens or abroad for skiing, golf, horse riding (still undeveloped for tourism), hiking in the mountains, and caving (Greece has a large number of sites that already have their followers).

## • The sea

### Sailing

Boating indisputably offers one of the most pleasant ways of exploring the Greek coast and its numerous islands. This type of tourism is booming but today is encountering difficulties due to the insufficient mooring space in the ports and marinas. It is common to have long queues alongside the quay in the middle of August. Once again, it's better to travel in the spring, in June or September.

### Addresses

**Anemos Tours –** 12-10 Astoria Park South, Long Island City, NY 11102-3704, USA, ☎ (718) 777 5050, Fax (718) 721 8043 or (520) 569 1479, info@anemos.net
**Hellenic Professional Yacht Owners Association**, Zéa Marina (Piraeus), Greece, ☎ (01) 45 26 335, 42 80 465, Fax (01) 45 26 335.
**Minotaur Charters –** 204 Altham Grove, Harlow, Essex CM20 2PW, ☎ (01279) 830478 (in the UK) or (0645) 92027 (in Greece), Fax (01279) 830478 (in the UK) or (0645) 92845 (in Greece), infor@minotaurcharters.com
**Sailing Paradise –** 59 Bark Ave, Central Islip, NY 11722, USA, ☎ (888) 864 SAIL(7245) or (631)342 0219, sparcom@sailingparadise.com

### Scuba diving

Take advantage of your stay in Greece to learn how to scuba dive or to perfect your style. The depths of the Aegean or Mediterranean may not be as attractive as some of the warmer seas but it is always pleasant to come across sea turtles, dolphins and large groupers, or even the remains of an ancient wreck (which must absolutely be left alone). Local agencies have appropriate equipment and certified instructors available.
**Eurodivers Club –** Paríkia (Punda), Páros Island, ☎ and Fax (0284) 92071, mobile (093) 233 6464, info@eurodivers.gr, www.eurodivers.gr
**Vikings Yacht Cruises –** 4321 Lakemoor Dr, Wilmington, NC 29405, USA, ☎ (800) 341 3030 or (910) 350 0100, Fax (910) 791 9400, cocco44a@prodigy.net or greek@gicc.net (in the USA) or ☎ (01) 8980 729 / 8949 279, Fax (01) 8940 952, vikings@vikings.gr (in Greece), www.vikings.gr

### Surfing, windsurfing and water-skiing

On the islands and at beach resorts, those who thrive on big thrills will revel in the choices between windsurfing, water-skiing or even jet-skiing. The best surfing areas can be found on Páros (in the Cyclades). Avoid weighing yourself down with your own equipment. Local clubs rent it out, particularly on Páros, Mýkonos and Santoríni.

## • Night-life

### Summer cinemas

Enjoy the pleasure of an open-air cinema. Devout film lovers will, however, be somewhat discouraged – the sound is not very good quality, your neighbour may be nibbling loudly on a snack and there will be a 15min break in the middle of the film. Nonetheless it's an original way to see repeats of American and European blockbusters from the past year. (*See also page 82.*)

### Bars and discos

Night-owls will find plenty of things to occupy the warm summer nights. Greeks certainly don't drink iced coffee until 10pm and go home to bed afterwards. In tourist areas, you will find all kinds of music. Keep in mind though that a club that plays techno can just as easily switch to Greek music at 4 or 5 in the morning if there is a local crowd. This is the opportunity to discover the *tsiftetéli*, melodies and a sort of oriental dance to contemporary music.

- **Cultural activities**

In addition to the large cultural summer festivals, particularly dance and theatre (in Athens, Epidaurus, Náfplio and Réthimnon), and big religious festivals like 15 August, each village celebrates its saints during the merry *panigíri*. You can get information on site but don't forget that the meal and the evening activities always take place the day before the actual holiday. During this time there is a commemorative mass. For more details, see the practical information in each section.

# SHOPPING

- **What's on offer**

*Culinary specialities*

Epicureans will find all sorts of products to bring home so they can prolong their holiday with the tastes and aromas of the country. There is a wide choice ranging from honey from Kalamáta or Attica (thyme honey), fig or cherry jam, *amigdalotá* (a type of macaroon), *kourabiédes* (almond pastries), pistachios (a speciality of Égina), *halvá* (a type of sesame paste, sometimes stuffed with pistachios), *pastéli* (a honey and sesame macaroon), retsína from Attica, red wines from the Peloponnese or Thessaly, white wines from Santoríni, Léros, the Peloponnese and Thessaly, liqueur wines (muscatel from Sámos and Mavrodaphni), spirits (*Plomári* ouzo from Mitilíni, Lesbos, or rakí and tsípouro from Thessaloníki), not to mention olive oil from Crete.

*Handicrafts*

You'll find examples of some of the best and the worst items in the souvenir shops, from antique reproductions to T-shirts. At the same time, some handicrafts of good quality (sometimes rather expensive) are sold in all the big tourist centres today. These range from pottery and ceramics to carpets and hand-woven fabrics, knitted goods, embroidered clothing, **lace**, **embroidery**, bedspreads, wool carpets (originally from Aráhova or Thessaly), furs from Kastoriá, sponges from Kálimnos, and gold **jewellery**, both contemporary pieces and styles reproduced from Antiquity. Some jewellers, such as Lalaounis or Zolotas, are internationally renowned. You'll also find traditional silver jewellery from Ioánnina and Macedonia, carved wooden objects, **marble** and **onyx** sculptures, and reproductions of **icons** (especially in the monasteries).
Kritsá and Haniá are known for their Cretan **leather** boots, and the island of Skíros for its painted furniture. In Athens and on all the islands you'll find a large selection of leather sandals and handbags, popular in the 1970s, which are cheap but poor quality. Lastly, don't bypass the famous **komboló**ï, the beads that Greeks are constantly threading through their fingers and which can be found in all the shops.

- **Bartering**

Bartering is no longer commonly practised in Greece and you'll risk causing offence if you try it. Negotiating room rates, however, can lead to a pleasant discussion. You can also negotiate the price of your purchases in tourist shops, jewellery stores and silver and goldsmiths. Your margin of negotiation will be the equivalent of the item's VAT. On the other hand, in grocery stores and tavernas, this is completely inappropriate.

- **Tax and payment**

The ΦΠΑ (FPA), the Greek VAT, is always included in all marked prices. In Greece, payment by bank card is not always welcome, except in tourist areas, because this is proof of income that can be easily checked by the State and subject to tax. Shopkeepers prefer cash and they will be more likely to negotiate prices if you pay by this method. Bear in mind that shopkeepers must always give you a receipt whenever you make a purchase.

# HEALTH AND SAFETY

## • Precautions

There are no diseases in particular which you need to worry about in Greece, but beware of sunstroke. In the summer, especially on the islands, the sun is scorching and if you stay in it for too long, you'll risk getting burned, nausea, or a headache. If you plan to travel by bicycle or motorcycle, be sure to protect your shoulders, likewise if you're driving a convertible or walking, and remember to wear a hat. Also make sure you drink plenty of water.

*Medical kit*

You'll find everything you need in Greece, however you may want to bring a small medical first aid kit with you. Some essential items include aspirin, sunscreen (crucial in the summer), plasters, cotton balls, and antiseptic lotion for small cuts. Also remember to bring some mosquito repellent.

## • Health

*First aid*

The small Greek hospitals are reliable but they are only equipped to handle minor illnesses. In the event of a serious problem, make sure you're transferred to Athens or repatriated (*see the section on "Travel / health insurance", page 99*).

*Pharmacies*

As Greeks are large consumers of medicine, you will find many pharmacies in Greece that sell all sorts of brand name pharmaceutical products. As in other countries, you will need a prescription for antibiotics.

*Doctors*

Most doctors (and pharmacists) speak a foreign language: English, French or Italian (many study in Italy). And there is almost always a doctor nearby.

*Reimbursement*

If you have health insurance at home, be sure to bring your insurance papers with you. Contact your local insurance company before leaving home for information on reimbursement procedures for medical or hospital services and medication in Greece.

## • Emergencies

Dial 166 anywhere in Greece.

# FROM A TO Z

## • Antiques

Exporting antiques is strictly forbidden. No object over 100 years old may be taken out of Greece and you risk a heavy fine if you attempt it. Don't ever pick anything up from an archaeological site or when diving, be it a fragment of stone or pottery, even if it appears to be insignificant. The laws are very severe for this type of theft.

## • Cigarettes

Smoking in public places or on public transport is prohibited. The Greeks respect the no-smoking laws concerning public transport, but elsewhere you will have to contend with smokers, who make up the majority of the Greek population.

## • Drinking water

Water is fit to drink throughout the country. When it comes from natural springs (in the Peloponnese, northern Greece and on some islands), it is even delicious. On the other hand, arid islands like Santoríni import water in tanks in the summer. Although it is fit for consumption, it doesn't taste very good.

## • Electricity
Electricity is 220 volts in Greece.

## • Laundry
You will find dry cleaners in the cities but very few self-service launderettes. Tourism has however caused some to open in tourist areas. Many hotels have their own laundry service and small hotels often provide a washing machine for their guests' use.

## • Newspapers
Most of the main foreign newspapers are available the day after publication. If you don't want to miss any local or international current events while you're travelling, read the *Athens News,* printed in English and available in Athens and tourist areas.

## • Photography
Unless you are partial to a special brand, you can buy film without any problem in Greece. You will, however, find print film more easily than slide film. Prices are also often cheaper than in many other countries. Make sure you check the expiry date and avoid purchasing film that has been displayed in the windows and exposed to the sun.

## • Radio and television
Since the State's monopoly on television disappeared, numerous private channels have emerged. Most of them focus on political debates and society, game shows, variety shows, or Mexican and American series. In short, the usual programmes found on regular channels. **ERT** (one of the three public channels) is unanimously considered to be the best. In some hotels that provide satellite TV, you will be able to pick up the BBC and CNN.

## • Safety
Athens and most of Greece are relatively peaceful. There are almost always lots of people out at night and this is your best guarantee for safety. Moreover, the State and shopkeepers are careful to preserve the tourist reputation in Greece. As a result, a lot of crime has been stamped out. Sometimes, however, the hordes of summer visitors still encourage a certain amount of moneygrubbing, but this is exceptional (and another good reason to avoid coming during the high season).

## • Tipping / gratuities
No one will ever ask for a tip but this is no reason not to give one. As in other parts of Europe, it's common practice to leave something (usually about 10% of the bill) in cafés or restaurants. As far as taxi drivers are concerned, as a rule you should round up the balance to their advantage.

## • Units of measurement
Greece follows the metric system.

Distances in this guide are given in kilometres. As a rule of thumb, one kilometre is five-eighths of a mile: 5 miles is therefore about 8 kilometres, 10 miles is about 16 kilometres and 20 miles is about 32 kilometres.

Consult the table below for other useful metric equivalents:

| Degrees Celsius | 35° | 30° | 25° | 20° | 15° | 10° | 5° | 0° | -5° | -10° |
|---|---|---|---|---|---|---|---|---|---|---|
| Degrees Fahrenheit | 95° | 86° | 77° | 68° | 59° | 50° | 41° | 32° | 23° | 15° |

1 centimetre (cm) = 0.4 inch
1 metre (m) = 3.3 feet
1 metre (m) = 1.09 yards
1 litre = 1.06 quart
1 litre = 0.22 gallon
1 kilogram (kg) = 2.2 pounds

## • Weather

Weather reports are broadcast daily on television and in the newspapers. You won't need to understand Greek; you only need to look at the small suns illustrated on the map of the country! In the summer, climatic uncertainty focuses only on the possibility and the intensity of scorching heat and on the strength of the wind (important if you plan to take a boat out).

# LOOK AND LEARN

## • History and archaeology

BULFINCH Thomas, *Myths of Greece and Rome*, Viking Press, 1981.

DREWS Robert, *The Coming of the Greeks*, Princeton University Press, 1994. Through history, archaeology and linguistics, this scholar delves into the origin of the Greeks.

FINLEY Moses I, *The Ancient Greeks*, Viking Press, 1992.

HAMILTON Edith, *The Echo of Greece*, 1964 and *The Greek Way*, (reprint 1993), WW Norton & Company. The pre-eminent scholar of the classical world explores the Greek world and culture.

KITTO Humphrey Davy Findley, *The Greeks*, Penguin USA, 1991.

PEDLEY John Griffiths, *Greek Art and Archaeology*, Harry N Ambrams, 1997.

SEKUNDRA Nicholas, *The Spartans*, Osprey Publishing Co, 1999. Provides background on Greek warfare.

STEPHANIDES Menelaos, *The Gods of Olympus*, Sigma, 1999. A world renowned study of Greek mythology.

WOODHOUSE CM, *Modern Greece: A Short History*, Faber & Faber, 2000.

## • People and culture

BLUNDELL Sue, *Women in Ancient Greece*, Harvard University Press, 1995.

KREMEZI Aglaia, *The Foods of Greece*, Stewart Tabori & Chang, 1999. This internationally renowned food expert shares 135 regional dishes from her homeland.

## • Literature

BERNIERES Louis de, *Captain Corelli's Mandolin*, Vintage Books, 1995. This bestselling novel that sheds light on the history of Cephalonia has been made into a film (starring Nicholas Cage).

FOWLES John, *The Magus*, Modern Library, 1998. Originally published in 1965, this spellbinding novel forays into the adventures of a young Englishman caught in a game of psychological intrigue on a Greek island.

PAPANDREOU Nicholas C, *A Crowded Heart*, Picador USA, 1998. An autobiographical novel that blends politics, Greek culture and American influences.

PRESSFIELD Steven, *Gates of Fire*, Bantam Books, 1998. A suspenseful historical novel about the Spartan War and *Tides of War: A Novel of Alcibiades and the Peloponnesian War*, Doubleday Books, 2000.

RENAULT Mary, *The Mask of Apollo*, Vintage Books, 1988. Set in the 4C BC, this novel is a must for anyone interested in the history of theatre.

STORACE Patricia, *Dinner with Persephone*, Vintage Books, 1997. A penetrating exploration of the complexities of contemporary Greek life, history and identity.

VALTINOS Thanassis, *Data from the Decade of the Sixties: A Novel*. Northwestern University Press, 2000. A chronicle on the transformation of Greece in the 1960s.

## • Travelogues

DURRELL Lawrence, *Prospero's Cell*, Marlowe & Co, 1996 (reprint). A memoir about Durrell's time spent on the island of Corfu.

FERMOR Patrick Leigh, **Mani**, Penguin, 1984.

KIZILOS Katherine, **The Olive Grove: Travels in Greece**, Lonely Planet, 1997.

MILLER Henry, **Colussus of Maroussi**, WW Norton & Company, 1988. An account of his travels in the 1930s and 40s, Miller depicts ancient and modern Greece in his flowing poetic style.

● **Films and documentaries**

DASSIN Jules, **Never on Sunday**, 1959. In Piraeus in the 1950s, a prostitute with a big heart meets an American who is trying to understand Greek society. Dassin directed Melína Mercoúri, his future wife, for the first time in this film.

CACOYÁNNIS Michális, **Stella**, 1955. The film that brought Melína Mercoúri to stardom. A tender and tragic evocation of the poor neighbourhoods in post-war Greece. **Electra**, 1962, and the famous **Zorba the Greek**, 1964, starring Anthony Quinn and adapted from the novel by Kazantzákis, give two spectacular portraits of the Greek soul.

COSTA-GAVRAS, **Z**, 1969. The film on the rise to power of the colonels' junta. A political thriller inspired by the Lambrákis affair, a leftist member of parliament is assassinated at the beginning of the junta (Z is the first letter of the verb "zóo" which means "to live").

ANGELÓPOULOS Theo, **The Suspended Step of the Stork**, 1991, **Eternity and a Day**, 1998. The recurrent themes of identity, boundaries and memory pervade the films of Angelopoulos, the only world-famous Greek filmmaker.

GILBERT Lewis, **Shirley Valentine**, 1989. A British housewife embarks on a spontaneous holiday to the Greek islands that will change her life.

● **Music**

THEODORÁKIS Míkis, **His best popular songs, The very best of Theodorakis**. Discover the mythical figure of Greek music.

Three aspects of Greek song:

ALEXÍOU Háris, Ψίθυροι ("Murmurs"), ARVANITÁKI Eleftería (Polygram) and DALÁRAS Geórgos, **Kalós tous** (Minos).

TITSÁNIS Vassílis, **Homage to Tsitsánis**. One of the great figures of rembétika.

REMBÉTIKA, Rembetica: Historic Urban Folk Songs from Greece (Rounder Records). **The Soul of Greece: 101 Strings** (Madacy Records).

**Folk music of Greece** (Topic World records). Traditional music from the four corners of the Greek world.

● **Maps**

MICHELIN, **Greece** (Map 980), 1/700 000.

# GLOSSARY

● **Pronunciation**

Here's a glance at the Greek alphabet and its pronunciation.

| | |
|---|---|
| A α | a |
| B β | v (van) |
| Γ γ | g (gate) before a consonant and the vowels a, o, and ou; y (yoghurt) when placed before the i sound (η, ι, υ, ε ε ι). The same rule follows for Georgos ("Yorgos"), because of the e. |
| Δ δ | th (the); transcribed by d. |
| E ε | e |
| Z ζ | z |
| H η | i |
| Θ θ | th (think) |

| | | |
|---|---|---|
| | i | k |
| | l | |
| | m | |
| | n | |
| | x (taxi) | |
| O o | o | |
| Π π | p | |
| P ρ | r | |
| Σ ς | s | |
| T τ | t | |
| Y υ | i | |
| Φ φ | f | |
| X χ | kh (as in "loch") | |
| Ψ ψ | the sound *ps* | |
| Ω ω | o | |

## Common expressions

| | |
|---|---|
| Good morning | Kaliméra |
| Good evening | Kalispéra |
| Greeting (at any time of the day) | Hérete |
| Hi (good day, goodbye, see you later) | Yássou (informal term) or Yássas (formal or polite form) |
| Please | Sas parakaló |
| Thank you | Evharistó |
| Yes | Nai |
| No | Óhi |
| Excuse me | Signómi (pardon), Me sinhoríte (formal or polite form) |
| OK, all right | Endáxi |
| I don't understand | Den katalavéno |
| I don't speak Greek | Den miláo helliniká |
| Do you speak English? | Miláte angliká? |
| I would like | Tha íthella |
| There is | Ipárhi |
| There isn't | Den Ipárhi |
| Me / you (informal) / he / she / us / you (formal) / them | egó / essí / aftós / aftí / emís / essís / aftí |

## Basic conversation

| | |
|---|---|
| How are you? | Ti kánete? |
| Where are you from? | Apo pou íssaste? |
| I am British / American | Íme ánglos / amerikános |

## Time

| | | | |
|---|---|---|---|
| What time is it? | Ti óra íne? | hour | óra |
| it is 7 o'clock | Íne eftá | day | méra |
| yesterday | kthés | week | evdomáda |
| today | símera | Monday | deftéra |
| tomorrow | ávrio | Tuesday | tríti |
| morning | proí | Wednesday | tetárti |
| evening | vrádi | Thursday | pémti |
| early | norís | Friday | paraskeví |
| late | argá | Saturday | sávato |
| night | níhta | Sunday | kiriakí |

## Common adjectives

| | | | |
|---|---|---|---|
| handsome / beautiful | oréo, ómorfo (person) | open | anigtó |
| expensive | akrivó | hot | zestó |
| inexpensive, cheap | ftinó | cold | krío |
| new | kainoúrio | good | oréo, kaló |
| old | pallió | bad | kakó |
| big | megálo | fast | grígoro |
| small | mikró | slow | argó |
| closed | klistó | | |

## Colours

| | | | |
|---|---|---|---|
| white | áspro, lefkó | black | mávro |
| blue | ble, galázios | red | kókino |
| yellow | kítrino | green | prássino |

## Finding your way

| | | | |
|---|---|---|---|
| here | edó | road | drómos |
| there | ekí péra, ekí | tourist information | touristikó grafío, |
| north | vória (B) | office | grafío tou EOT |
| south | nótia (N) | | (eótt) |
| east | anatoliká (A) | museum | moussío |
| west | ditiká (Δ) | church | eklissía |
| to the right | dexiá | hotel | xenodohío |
| to the left | aristerá | rooms | domátia |
| straight ahead | efthía | taverna | tavérna |
| where is? | Pou ínai? | restaurant | estiatório |
| village | horió | post office | tahidromío |
| What's the name | Pos to léne | entrance | íssodos |
| of this village? | aftó to horió? | exit | éxodos |
| square | platía | sea | thálassa |
| town centre | kéndro | lake | límni |
| street | odós | beach | paralía |
| avenue, boulevard | leofóros | | |

## Transport

| | | | |
|---|---|---|---|
| bus | leoforío (bus), | ticket | issitírio |
| | auto-car (luxury coach) | return ticket | issitírio mè epistrofí |
| car-ferry | karávi, plío, | car | aftokínito |
| | vapóri, féri | motorcycle | mihanáki |
| aeroplane | aeropláno | fuel station | venzinádiko |
| train | tréno | garage | synergío |
| bus station, stop | stássi | please fill | yémissé to |
| port | limáni | the tank up | |
| airport | aerodrómio | | |
| railway station | stathmós | | |
| | trénon | | |

## At the hotel

| | | | |
|---|---|---|---|
| passport | diavatírio | toilet paper | hartí iyías |
| luggage | valítses | ladies | yinekón |
| room | domátio | gentlemen | andrón |
| single bed | monóklino | sheets | sendónia |
| double bed | díklino | towel | petséta |

| | | | |
|---|---|---|---|
| room | domátio mé bánio | blanket | kouvérta |
| with private bath | | key | klidí |
| shower | dous | breakfast | proïnó |
| toilet, WC | toilétes | laundry | stegnokatharistírio |

## At the restaurant

| | | | |
|---|---|---|---|
| table | trapézi | eat | tróo |
| menu | catálogo | drink | píno |
| salad | saláta | knife | mahéri |
| grilled | psitó | fork | piroúni |
| meat | kréas | salt | aláti |
| chicken | kotópoulo | pepper | pipéri |
| fish | psári | rice | rízi |
| dessert | gliká | sugar | záhari |
| a drink | potó | rice | rízi |
| mineral water | fissikó metalikó neró | sugar | záhari |
| | | yoghurt | yaoúrti |
| fruit juice | himó | milk | gála |
| wine | krassí | egg | avgó |
| tea | tsái | olive | eliés |
| coffee | kafé | soup | soúpa |
| bread | psomí | the bill, please | to logariasmó sas parakaló |

## At the post office

| | |
|---|---|
| stamp | gramatóssima |
| Do you have stamps? | Éhete gramatóssima? |
| envelope | fákelo |
| letter | gráma |
| package | déma |
| send | stéllno |
| telegram | tilegráfima |
| telephone card | kárta tilephónou |

## Shopping

| | |
|---|---|
| How much is this? | Pósso káni? Pósso éhei? |
| It's too expensive | Ínai polí akrivó |
| It's very beautiful | Ínai polí oréo |
| money (change) | leftá |
| cigarettes | tsigára |
| credit card | pistotikí kárta |
| travellers' cheques | traveler's cheques |

## Emergencies

| | |
|---|---|
| It doesn't work | den litouryí |
| Call the police | Páre tin astinomía |
| There was an accident | Sinévike éna atíhima |
| doctor | yiatró |
| hospital | nossokomío |

## Numbers

| | | | |
|---|---|---|---|
| 0 | midén | 30 | triánda |
| 1 | éna | 40 | saránda |
| 2 | dío | 50 | penínda |
| 3 | tría | 60 | exínda |
| 4 | téssera | 70 | evdomínda |
| 5 | pénde | 80 | ogdónda |
| 6 | éxi | 90 | enenínda |
| 7 | eftá | 100 | ekató |
| 8 | októ | 200 | diakóssia |
| 9 | eniá | 1000 | híllia |
| 10 | déka | 1 million | ekatomírio |
| 20 | íkossi | | |

## • Non-verbal language or gestures

Whether or not you find it easy to speak Greek, communicating in gestures is always very useful. In a country where excess is the norm, gestures instantly translate the thoughts of the person you are speaking with as well as many nuances. It's therefore worthwhile to understand their meaning, especially when they are foreign to us. For example, to say "no", Greeks simply raise their head, or sometimes only their eyes, and lightly click their tongue. To say "yes" they lower their head and their eyes, sometimes recoiling slightly. These signs, which are barely perceptible to those who aren't used to them, are useful for repelling an aggressive salesperson or a taxi in search of passengers.

A light rotation of the hand translates into a gesture the onomatopoeia "po po po" which is the equivalent of "oh dear" or "goodness me" and signifies surprise. If the movement increases with the hand open, it becomes a matter of admiration. Greeks will be more than willing to give you information and if they can't help you out, they will hail a passer-by who will bend over backwards to help you.

**Glossary**

# Exploring Greece

J. Sierpinski/DIAF

Over the rooftops:
the Wine-dark Sea
(Póros)

# ATHENS ★★
## (ATHÍNA)
Capital of the country and of the district of Attica
Michelin map 980 fold 30 – Plans on following pages
Pop 3 million – Very hot climate in summer, temperate in winter

**Not to be missed**
The Acropolis and Greek Agora.
Strolling through the streets of Pláka and Monastiráki.
The National Archaeological Museum, the Benáki Museum and the Museum of
Cycladic Art.

**And remember...**
Adapt your activities to the climate: visit outdoor sites in the morning;
have lunch around 2pm, then choose between a nap or an air-conditioned museum;
go for a stroll in the evening and have a late dinner.

Athens stretches across a wide basin dotted with steeply sloping hills along the shores of the Saronic Gulf. From the majestic promontory of the Acropolis, the modern city spreads for miles in every direction and now numbers over 3 million inhabitants – a third of the country's population! Moreover, the millions of visitors who come every year to admire its monuments may have somewhat conflicting feelings about it. Indeed, one never gets tired of contemplating the Acropolis, of strolling through the colourful Pláka district, or of exploring the origins of Western civilisation in an elegant marble statue. Likewise, what could be more delightful than enjoying the cool evening air on a taverna terrace or sipping a glass of ouzo in the sun? But one might also be tempted to flee this hectic modern metropolis with its noise and pollution.

So, when in Athens, do as the Athenians do. For those who are observant of the little things in everyday life, the city has a lot more to offer than a mere voyage back in time, no matter how fabulous it may be. It is a real odyssey taking you deep into the history of the Mediterranean and of the Balkans on the border between Europe and the Orient.

## The city of Athena

The **Ionians** came from the North at the beginning of the 2nd millennium BC to settle in Attica, where their influence spread throughout the region. They founded the bustling city of Athens which gradually dominated the little principalities in the area during the Mycenaean Period (1600-1100 BC). Its solidly fortified acropolis was built in terraces and possessed a palace, placing it among the top three Mycenaean cities next to Tírintha and Mycenae itself.

Then history gets blurred with legend: the struggle between Poseidon and Athena for guardianship of the city ended in favour of the goddess. At the same time, Theseus went to the palace of Minos in Crete and slew the Minotaur (see page 372). Both myths symbolise the victory of Attica (Athena's territory) over the Minoan world (of the sea). As for Theseus, he was personified by **Cecrops,** the first king of Athens, who established the Greeks' sovereignty and independence on the mainland.

In the 11C BC, however, the monarchy was undermined by the collapse of the Mycenaean world, giving way to an aristocratic government composed of the chiefs of the region's four biggest tribes. The new Attica born from this alliance was unified by the 6C BC. It was a feudal territory, but the archon **Solon,** followed by the tyrant **Peisistratus** and his sons, were to tone down its land-based, seigniorial character in favour of the new business elite. Athens began to really blossom, focusing its commercial and political ambitions on the entire Aegean area. This was the start of a brilliant artistic flowering marked by the geometric style in ceramics, as well as by the birth of monumental architecture, skilful urban planning (water supply, sewers, road maintenance), and dazzling religious activity (Panathenaic and Dionysiac Festivals). Through this wealth of innovations, Athens rose to the stature of a 'capital'.

**The Golden Age** – Athens reached its high point in the 5C BC with a host of political, artistic and intellectual achievements which established it as the centre of Western civilisation. After a popular revolt in 508 BC, **Cleisthenes** created a democratic system for the city, whose institutions were established by his successor, **Pericles**. Re-elected every year for thirty years (460-430 BC), Pericles surrounded himself with the greatest artists and scholars of his day. Their works reflect one of the most brilliant phases in Hellenic civilisation, an era known as the Age of Pericles, which they passed on to posterity.

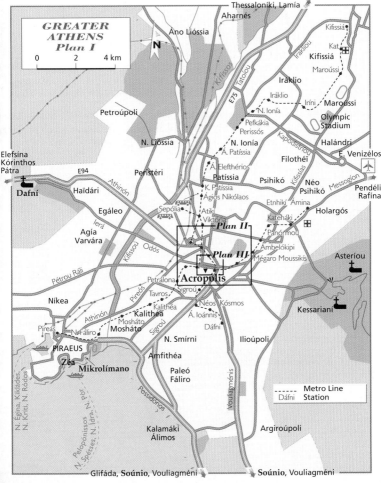

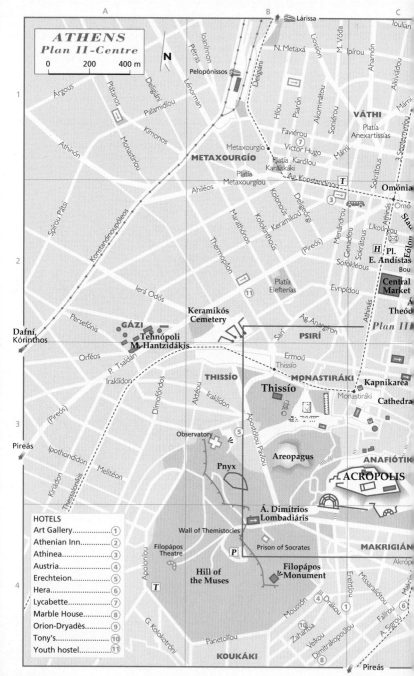

# ATHENS
## Plan II–Centre

0    200    400 m

**N**

### HOTELS

| | |
|---|---|
| Art Gallery | ① |
| Athenian Inn | ② |
| Athinea | ③ |
| Austria | ④ |
| Erechteion | ⑤ |
| Hera | ⑥ |
| Lycabette | ⑦ |
| Marble House | ⑧ |
| Orion-Dryadès | ⑨ |
| Tony's | ⑩ |
| Youth hostel | ⑪ |

Lárissa
Ioulian
N. Metaxá
Liossíon
M. Vóda
Ipírou
Acharnón
Alkiviádou
Márni

**VÁTHI**

Ioannínou
Petrás
Delianí
Lénorman
Peloponníssos
Ágrous
Plátanos
Palamidíou
Delianí
Deliamídíou
Kímonos
Monastiríou
Athinón

Hlíou
Psarón
Akominátou
Soniérou
Platía
Anexartissías

Faviérou
Victor Hugo
Márni
⑦

Metaxourgío
Platía Karólou
Karaïskáki

**METAXOURGÍO**

Ag. Konstandínou
**T**

Platía
Metaxourgíou
Ahiléos

Kolonoú
Deligeórgi
Menándrou
Genadíou
Sokrátous
**Omónia**
Omó

Marathónos
Kolokinthoús
Keramikoú
(Pireós)
Sofokléous
**H**
**Pl.**
**E. Andístas**

Spírou Pátsi
Konstandínoupóleos

Ieráa Odós
Thermopílon
⑪
Platía
Eleftherías
Evripídou
Bou

**Central
Market**
Á.
Theód

Persefónis
**GÁZI**
**Tehnópoli
M. Hantzidákis**

Keramikós
Cemetery

Sarí
**PSIRÍ**
Ag. Anargíron

*Plan III*

Dafní,
Kórinthos

Orféos
P. Tsaldári
Iraklídon

Dimofóndos
Aktéou
Iraklídon

**THISSÍO**

Ermoú
Thissío

**MONASTIRÁKI**
**Kapnikaréa**

Pireás

Ipothondídon
Melitéon

(Pireós)

**Thissío**

Monastiráki
**Cathedra**

Kríadon
Thessaloníkis

Apostólou Pávlou

Observatory
⑤

**Areopagus**

**ANAFIÓTIK**

**ACROPOLIS**

**Pnyx**

Apolloníou

Filopápos
Theatre
**T**

Wall of Themistocles
**P**

Á. Dimítrios
Lombadiáris

Prison of Socrates

**MAKRIGIÁN**

Akróp

**Hill of
the Muses**

G. Kolokotróni

**Filopápos
Monument**

Moussón
Drákou
Zahartsá
Panetolíou
Velkou
Dimitrakopoúlou
④ ①
⑩
⑧

Erehtíou
Missaralótou
Fálirou
A. Sigroú
⑥

**KOUKÁKI**
Pireás

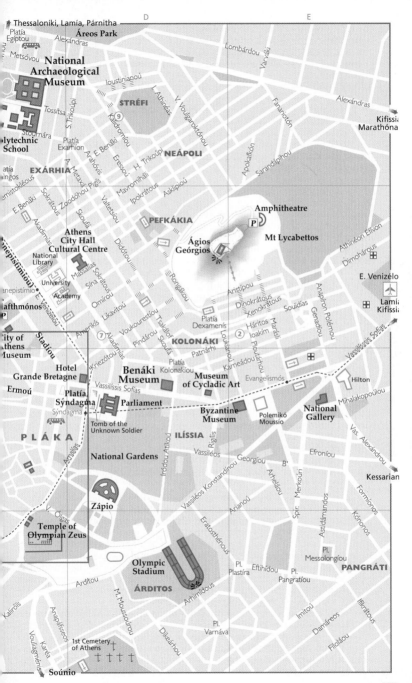

The Athenians' victory over **the Persians** (490-479 BC) put them at the head of the **Delian League**, an alliance which included all the cities from the Aegean Islands as well as from the coast of Asia Minor. Under Pericles, Athens subjugated its allies for its own profit within an economic and political framework that was more imperial than federal.

But this desire for hegemony over the Greek world was not to everyone's liking, and Athens soon earned the hostility of Sparta, Corinth and Euboea, leading to the Peloponnesian War (431-404 BC). **Sparta** won the war, triggering the political decline of Athens.

Yet despite this gradual decline, Athens remained the undisputed metropolis of Hellenic civilisation, whose new leaders, **Philip II of Macedon** and above all **Alexander the Great**, extended it all the way to the borders of Asia. Under **Lycurgus** – and thanks to the kings' favour towards the Hellenistic Orient – this civilisation experienced a great renewal between 350 BC and the late 2C BC marked by the construction of many monuments.

Athens regained its independence during a second golden age consolidated by the Roman victory over Macedonia (168 BC).

But this last gasp of prosperity was suddenly interrupted when the city was captured and sacked by **Sulla** (68 BC). Nevertheless, this *pax romana* enabled Greek culture to be disseminated on an unprecedented scale throughout the Mediterranean world, making Athens a kind of university city where part of the political, intellectual and artistic elite of the Roman Empire went to be educated.

**An outlying town** – Yet its decline was inevitable. After destruction in the barbarian invasions (the **Heruli** in 267 AD, the **Goths** in 396), the closing of the philosophy schools in the 5C AD and the transformation of pagan buildings into Christian basilicas put an end to over ten centuries of influence. Athens and Rome took a back seat to Constantinople as the Christian Hellenistic world moved back towards Eastern Europe, Asia Minor and the Middle East. Though still relatively densely populated, the Greek city was reduced to a small provincial town on the fringes of the Empire. The Byzantine churches and monasteries built after the expedition of Emperor Basil II to the Balkans (11C-12C) were the city's last sparkle before its long sleep, dramatically triggered by the **Saracen raid** in the late 12C.

From the 13C, Athens was passed from the Crusaders (1204-1311) to the Catalans (1311-87), then from the Florentines to the **Venetians** (1387-1456), before being handed over to the **Turks**, who settled on the Acropolis and its environs for four centuries (1456-1833). Just below the fortified town was a settlement of about 10 000 people, mostly Greeks and Albanians. When the ancient buildings weren't fortified or transformed for civil purposes, they were used as stone quarries for houses or as raw material for limekilns! In short, the city which European travellers passed through in the 18C was an unrecognisable place on its last legs.

**The reign of Otto, or the awakening of modern Athens** – The choice of Athens as the capital of the young Hellenic kingdom (*see page 28*) at the height of European neo-Classicism in 1834 signalled its revival. The challenge was a stimulus to the imaginations of the Greek and Bavarian architects charged with drawing up plans for the future new town. But not one of the numerous projects proposed was undertaken, and the city grew haphazardly. The urban fabric sprawled in an anarchic fashion, even gobbling up the archaeological area around the Acropolis. The government undertook some large-scale works, however, and even went so far as to periodically force people to leave their homes in order to inaugurate new streets, including wide avenues such as Alexándras and Sigroú (in the 1880s).

For want of any urban planning, a handful of architects – Kléanthis, Schaubert, the two **Hansen brothers**, **Ziller**, Boulanger, Kálkos and Kaftanzóglou – designed a number of neo-Classical structures, lining the straight avenues of the capital with imposing buildings with marble façades. Houses in a composite style blending elements of neo-Renaissance and Baroque were built for the upper classes in the area around Platía Sýndagma.

**Sprawling growth** – At the turn of the 19C and 20C, the population of Athens grew sharply – 453 000 inhabitants in 1928 compared to 110 000 in 1889. This phenomenon was due in particular to the massive arrival of **Greeks from Asia Minor** following the Treaty of Lausanne (1923), and prolonged after the Second World War by the huge **rural exodus**. Once distinctly separated from the capital by the countryside, the village of Maroússi to the north-west and Piraeus to the south-east were now connected by a continuous network of housing. In its colossal expansion, the urban area absorbed the two local rivers, the **Ílissos** and the **Kifisós**, which disappeared beneath boulevards.

Until the 1950s, however, space-consuming individual houses were still the dominant feature in the urban landscape of the Greek metropolis outside the city centre. But the following decade saw the spread of concrete constructions that were all identical with their superimposed apartments, graceless balconies and ground-floor galleries occupied by shops and cafés. This particularly dreary architecture has nevertheless shaped the face of the whole of present-day Áthens.

In recent years, however, preparations for the 2004 Olympic Games have in turn disrupted the capital. In addition to large-scale work on the metro and the road network, the city centre has acquired new pedestrian areas such as the large, paved Odós Ermoú. And, in a historical twist, the famous archaeological area that Kléanthis and Schaubert wanted in 1833 is finally on the verge of being created...

## Athens and its neighbourhoods

Upon arriving in Athens you will probably go through **Platía Sýndagma** (Plan II, D3), the city's nerve centre where banks, hotels and airline companies are lined up across from the Parliament. **Odós Ermoú** (Plan III, D2) cuts through the heart of the city, prolonging the square's central axis all the way to Piraeus. This great commercial thoroughfare is dotted with animated little squares and innumerable clothing shops. To the south-west, leading to the slopes of the Acropolis, is **Pláka**, the tourist area with a host of tavernas and souvenir shops in its old houses and winding alleyways. To the west near the **Greek Agora** lies **Monastiráki**, the old Turkish quarter that has preserved its atmosphere of a Balkan bazaar with its flea market. North of Sýndagma, the straight streets of **Kolonáki** hem in the wooded slopes of **Mount Lycabettos (Lykavitós)**. With its chic, trendy boutiques, this residential neighbourhood is an area frequented by the established local bourgeoisie and the intelligentsia. From Sýndagma, **Leofóros Stadíou** and **Leofóros Panepistimíou** feed into the north-west side of noisy **Platía Omónia** (Plan II, C2). Nearby stands the **National Archaeological Museum** in a part of Athens that has a neo-Classical feeling to it.

---

**If you have only one day to spend in Athens:**

The Acropolis and surrounding area. A walk through Pláka. The National Archaeological Museum. Have dinner in Exárhia or in Pláka.

**If you have a minimum of four days in Athens:**

| | |
|---|---|
| 1st day | **The Acropolis and surrounding area**. A walk on Filopápos Hill, the Pnyx. Dinner in Pláka. |
| 2nd day | **Pláka**. The Byzantine churches, the City of Athens Centre for Popular Arts and Traditions, Anafiótika, the Kanelópoulos Museum, the Tower of the Winds, the Roman Forum, Monastiráki. Dinner in Psirí or Gázi. |
| 3rd day | **In the heart of Athens**. The Greek Agora, Keramikós Cemetery, Psirí, Kendrikí Agorá (Central Market), the National Archaeological Museum. Dinner in Exárhia. |
| 4th day | **Around Sýndagma**. Hadrian's Arch, the Temple of Olympian Zeus, the Stadium, the National Garden, Odós Ermoú, the Benáki Museum and the Museum of Cycladic Art. Cocktails on Mt Lycabettos, and dinner there or in Kolonáki or Dexaméni. |

**Athens**

# The Acropolis*** (Acrópoli)

*Count on 2hr for your visit, more if you're feeling contemplative. Plan page 131.*

*There are two ways to go: from Pláka via the Perípatos, a long paved path that climbs up the north face of the Acropolis; the other access, via the rock's southern side, leaves from Odós Dionissíou Areopagítou where it intersects with Odós Apostólou. 8am-6.30pm. Entrance fee. The ticket includes the site and museum.*

Even if you are just passing through Athens, do not miss the Acropolis. The site and the collection of monuments and treasures exhibited in the museum are indeed among the most prestigious bequeathed to us by Antiquity. Visit it preferably early in the morning before the sun and marble become scorching. And if the crowds are already there, remember that in olden times the celebrations honouring Athena drew just as many people.

Due to construction work that has closed off traffic on large sections of Odós Dionissíou Areopagítou, you must make a detour on Odós Kalispéri if you are coming from Sýndagma or Pláka. A huge project is underway to turn the Acropolis and its surroundings into an **archaeological park**, a pedestrian space incorporating the Stadium (to the east) and including the collections from the Acropolis Museum, which is currently closed. The area will be served by the future Makrigiáni metro station, which is also under construction. Large signs placed at each end of Odós Dionissíou Areopagítou give an idea of the project, which is scheduled to be finished for the Olympic Games.

As you walk towards the Acropolis, take a short detour first up to the **Areopagos** (Ários Págos) (Plan III, A3), a wide rocky promontory overlooking the Agora *(shortly before the entrance to the Acropolis, on the right alongside the Perípatos)*. A bronze plaque at the foot of the boulder shows the way up via steps carved out of the rock *(be careful as the steps are rather steep and slippery)* and recalls that St Paul passed this way. It affords a splendid **view** of the site and the huge grey expanse of the city fading into the distant haze. The debris scattered on the ground spoils the ambience

The Athens Acropolis, the dawn of Western civilisation

a bit, but the lofty silhouette of the Acropolis makes you quickly forget the turpitude of modern life. Dedicated to Ares (the god of war), this hill (*págos*) gave its name to the oldest Council of Athens, the Areopagos, which was both a judicial tribunal and a political council at first and was later reduced to preserving customs and laws. It is said that the principle of a person's right to defence first arose within this assembly, and also that **St Paul** preached about the 'unknown god' here, converting one of its members, Dionysius, the future **St Dionysius the Areopagite** who was to become the first bishop of Athens.

## A site to match the mightiest city in Greece

The Athens Acropolis, whose name means 'the city summit' (Lycabettos is higher, but it was outside the city limits at the time) is a huge stone vessel that seems to float above the plain, occupying an exceptional site. Its flat summit is nearly 300m long by 156m at its widest, forming a vast 3ha esplanade that overlooks the lower city from a height of 115m. It was an ideal site for the Acropolis of the most powerful city in Ancient Greece.

Before viewing the monuments, take time to contemplate the fabulous **panorama\*\***. To the south-west (*with your back to the Parthenon*) it goes all the way to the **Saronic Gulf** (when the sky is clear enough), while to the south-east, to the north-east and to the north you can see, successively, **Mounts Hymettus (Imittós)**, **Pentelikon (Pentéli)** and **Parnes (Párnitha)**; not to mention **Filopápos Hill** (Plan II, B4) quite nearby (to the south-west), crowned with the monument of the same name.

Inside the ramparts (which date mainly from the 5C BC), a few vestiges go back to the Mycenaean Period (1400-1125 BC) but most of the visible monuments are from the great **Age of Pericles** (5C BC) of which they are a brilliant illustration. Admittedly, the air pollution, the earthquake in 1981 and clumsy measures taken in the past have altered their beauty and made it necessary to protect the stone and replace the remaining sculptures (*exhibited in the Acropolis Museum*) with copies. But the site has preserved all of its majesty, and indeed the inside of the Parthenon has been restored with Pentelic marble identical to the original.

**The Acropolis**

B. Kaufmann/MICHELIN

## In the footsteps of the Panathenaea

Now you can follow the path taken by the **Panathenaea** processions during which people went to the Acropolis to offer Athena the *péplos*, a tunic woven by young Athenian women. The ceremony, which took place every four years, heralded the end of a lavish festival of musical, athletic and equestrian contests dedicated to the city's tutelary goddess.

After a climb in the shade of the olive and pine trees, the procession reached the Propylaea via a series of ramps. The current path takes the little **Roman way** on the side overlooking on the left the pedestal of the **Agrippa Monument***, an edifice that supported the statue of the Emperor Augustus' son-in-law, raised up on a bronze chariot (178 BC). At its base, a projecting platform affords a fine **view*** of the surrounding area.

At the foot of the ramparts is an imposing wall topped by the slender columns of the Temple of Athena Nike. Opposite you are the steps of the Propylaea, while behind you lie the remains of the **Beulé Gate*** (from the name of its discoverer, archaeologist **Ernest Beulé**), unearthed in 1852-53 under the Turkish bastion. Dating from the early 3C AD, this edifice with its two adjoining towers was probably built to reinforce the Acropolis' defences.

### The Propylaea**

Now walk up the marble steps of the Propylaea, protected by wooden planks. This monumental entrance was equal to the grandeur of Pericles' sumptuous acropolis. After the Parthenon had been completed (a wide opening was needed to let the slabs of marble through as it was being built), the architect **Mnesikles** got to work on the Propylaea in 437 BC. He was intent on finding a harmonious solution to the problems posed by differences in level while still facilitating the passage of the Panathenaea. Devoid of any sculpted decoration, the complex includes a central body flanked by two asymmetrical wings, wide pavilions which the bishops and dukes of Athens made into their residence from the 12C to the 15C.

The **central part**, a huge rectangle built in the form of a staircase, was preceded by a **portico** of which six Doric columns remain. Beyond that lay the **vestibule**, framed by two lateral naves separated by six Ionic columns. The left wing, or **Pinakotheke**, the largest, was first a banquet hall, then a painting gallery (thus its name). The much smaller **right wing** seems to have been built above all to re-establish a sense of symmetry, yet without detracting from the Temple of Athena Nike close by. At the end of the vestibule were **five doors**, the wider middle one being used by the Panathenaea procession. These doors led to a last portico analogous to the one at the (partly preserved) entrance, giving onto the Acropolis area.

Once past the Propylaea, you emerge onto the vast plateau of the **temenos**, and are immediately drawn towards the lofty silhouette of the Parthenon standing imposingly on the right. But in the days of Pericles, your gaze would have landed first of all on the colossal **statue of Athena Promachos**, an impressive 9m-high bronze female warrior standing in its centre. Created by Phidias, it commemorated the Athenian victories over the Persians.

### The Parthenon***

*The inside and immediate surroundings of the temple are not accessible.* Nowadays visitors turn first of all to the Parthenon. And the majesty of this vision is no accident. Raised slightly and at an angle to the axis of the Propylaea, the temple offers you its best profile. But imagine this imposing façade with red, yellow and blue stripes! Indeed, buildings and statues were entirely painted; and the immaculate white marble to which the Renaissance and its taste for the ancient world accustomed us is only due to the wear and tear of time. Commissioned by Pericles, this temple to the glory of the goddess and her city was designed by the architect **Iktinos** under the direction of **Phidias**, who also supervised the making of the sculpted decorations. This jewel of Doric architecture – its yardstick, one could say – was apparently considered a masterpiece as soon as it was completed.

While the marble on the roof fell in the fire of 267, the monument preserved its columns, walls, roof and most of its internal spaces... until the Acropolis was bombarded by the Venetians in September 1687. Thus, the building was nearly intact when it was turned into a Byzantine church (the first one in the 6C). Afterwards, it became a cathedral under Frankish rule, then a mosque with a minaret adjoining the temple's south-west corner (some remains are still visible). At that time a large part of its sculpted decoration remained, until **Lord Elgin**, the British ambassador to Constantinople, removed the friezes between 1801 and 1803. The long job of restoration began as early as 1834, marked in particular by the difficult process of raising the columns, known as 'anastylosis', carried out by Greek archaeologists.

Built in Pentelic marble, the Parthenon stands on a thick **stylobate** (upper layer of the base), which itself lies on a limestone foundation. Almost none of the **sculptures**, **bas-reliefs** and **statues** that decorated the temple are visible on the site. You must go to the British Museum (whom Greece has been asking to return the friezes for years), to the Louvre and, closer by, to the Acropolis Interpretation Centre (*temporarily closed*), which has casts of nearly all of the building's statues. Use your imagination to reconstruct the Parthenon with the colours, bas-reliefs and gold that made it so beautiful.

Polychrome sculptures stood out against a blue background on the **pediments**. Phidias' genius consisted in using this highly constraining triangular space to his

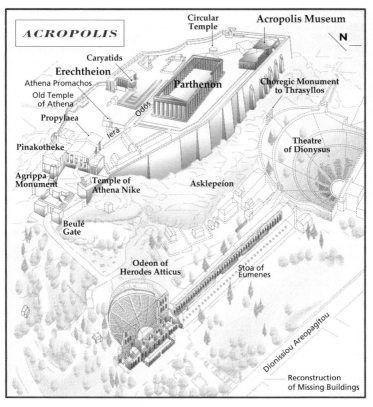

ACROPOLIS

Circular Temple
Acropolis Museum
N
Caryatids
Erechtheion
Athena Promachos
Old Temple of Athena
Propylaea
Pinakotheke
Agrippa Monument
Temple of Athena Nike
Beulé Gate
Parthenon
Choregic Monument to Thrasyllos
Theatre of Dionysus
Asklepeíon
Odeon of Herodes Atticus
Stoa of Eumenes
Iera Odós
Dionissíou Areopagítou

------ Reconstruction of Missing Buildings

## Phidias' secrets

Trying to attain visual perfection in the temple, Phidias strove to correct the optical illusions through a subtle use of lines. In choosing a peristyle with forty-six 10.43m-high columns (8 per façade, 17 for each side) he ensured the sanctuary a perfect balance between width and length. The shafts tapering upwards (1.90m in diameter at the base and 1.45m at the capitals) and their slightly inward curve, as well as the slight reinforcement of the corner columns and the imperceptible convexity of the horizontal elements, also contribute to the building's great harmony. Without these precautions the columns would indeed seem wider at the top than at the bottom, the corner columns would look less robust and the entablature would appear to be curved slightly inwards.

advantage: the figures are lying down, sitting, leaning or standing upright according to need. Besides the rare vestiges that remain, we know these works from the 200 drawings which the **Marquis de Nointel** had done in 1674.

In far better condition, the frieze★★★ was composed of 92 metopes (slabs sculpted in relief) between each triglyph on a red background featuring mythological scenes. Lastly, the architrave supported golden shields offered by Alexander the Great.

One went inside (*access is forbidden, but it is visible through the colonnade*) through a 10m-high door cut out of the **eastern portico**. This gave onto the pronaos, a vestibule preceding the holy of holies (*naos*) containing the **chryselephantine statue of Athena**, a huge 12m-high sculpture in gold and ivory (over a wood and marble frame) rising all the way up to the ceiling. A two-storey colonnade on each side marked the limits of the central space, complemented by an ambulatory. Behind this, the Parthenon itself housed the **treasury** of the Delian League led by Athens; behind the building you can still see the four Ionic columns that supported the ceiling. The famous **frieze of the Panathenaea** (preserved in part in Paris and in London) depicting the sacred procession ran along the outside wall of the *naos*, under the peristyle, forming a superb band of sculpture nearly 160m long.

As you cross the esplanade towards the Erechtheion, take a look (*on the right*) at the foundations of two temples dedicated to Athena built in the 6C and 5C BC. The first is known as the **Hecatonpedon** ('the Temple of 100 Feet') and the second as the **Old Parthenon**.

## The Erechtheion★★★

Walking along the northern façade of the Parthenon, the procession then reached the Erechtheion, another jewel of the Acropolis. Finished in 406 BC, this masterpiece of Ionic art successively housed a church, a palace, a harem and a powder magazine! Its restoration was begun in the 19C and completed in 1987.

Walk around the temple on the right in order to understand the way it was laid out and made more complex by the presence of several shrines inside, the largest of them dedicated respectively to **Athena**, to **Poseidon** and to **Erechtheos** and **Cecrops**, the two legendary kings of Athens.

In answer to the martial colonnade of the Parthenon, the famous porch of the korai or **Porch of the Caryatids★★★** responds with the grace and lightness of its six 2m-high statues of young women (*the originals are preserved in the Acropolis Museum*). The sensual bend in their knees and their nonchalant elegance are underscored by the parallel folds of their tunics evoking the fluting on the columns they replace. On the right, the six Ionic columns of the **eastern portico★** open onto the sanctuary containing the site's oldest **statue of Athena**, made of olive wood. The **western façade** was modified during the Roman era. An **olive tree** in the adjacent courtyard recalls the place where people came to worship the sacred tree of Athena (which explains why there is no roof).

This side of the Acropolis is where the Mycenaean settlement lay (1400-1125 BC), its rare vestiges of stone blocks scattered here and there around the Erechtheion. Continuing towards the eastern tip of the hill at its highest point, one discovers the remains of a **sanctuary dedicated to Zeus Polieus**. The Romans later built a **circular temple** next to it dedicated to Rome and Augustus, which can be picked out by its few standing columns and accompanying cypress trees.

The tip forms a slight promontory from which there is a **view★★** over the roofs of Pláka. By turning around you can see the back of the Parthenon (*watch out for the wind, which is sometimes very strong here*). It is particularly impressive when Athens is glowing in the sunset.

### The Acropolis Museum★★★

Cleverly hidden in a hollow, this richly endowed museum contains mainly sculptures and objects from the monuments and excavations on the site, in particular from its early buildings. On display in **Rooms 1 and 2** are **Archaic works★★** from the 7C and 6C BC, including fragments of **pediments★** in tufa which still show blue and red traces of their original colours. The Labours of Heracles, including his struggle with the Triton, are the subject of several sculptures. Of particular interest is the famous **Moscophoros★★★** or Calf Carrier (*Room 2*), unquestionably one of the most graceful statues from the Archaic Period.

**Room 3** boasts a stunning sculpture of a **bull★** being attacked by two lions, while **Room 4** has a prestigious **collection of korai★★**, as well as the **Rampin Horseman★**, another Archaic statue with a legendary smile.

**Room 5** contains a **group of sculptures★** from the old Temple of Athena featuring a remarkable gigantomachia (the Battle between the Olympian Gods and the Giants). Not to be missed in **Room 6**: the fine votive relief of **Athena mourning★★** (or 'pensive'), as well as the **Fair Head★★** of a young man, the **Kritios Boy** and the beautiful **Euthydikos kore★★**.

**Rooms 7 and 8** contain casts of **sculptures★★** from the Parthenon and the Temple of Athena Nike, as well as the **Caryatids★★★** from the Erechtheion – the real ones! – protected in glass cases. In the last room there is a **bust of Alexander the Great★**, a **statue of Procne★** by a student of Phidias, and a wonderful **head of a philosopher★**.

On leaving the museum walk along the southern edge of the hill for a **view★** over the Theatre of Dionysus and, further to the left, of the Temple of Zeus and the Stadium. The striking feature at the south-west tip of the temenos is the elegant **Temple of Athena Nike★** ('Victorious'). The building and surrounding area are closed for restoration, so you will have to contemplate its lovely Ionic façade completed in 410 BC from afar. It juts out like a watchtower in front of the Propylaea. From this rocky outcrop, from which you can see the coast, old **Aegeus** is said to have thrown himself into the sea that now bears his name. Indeed, he thought his son **Theseus** was dead when he saw a black sail – instead of a white one – hoisted on the mast of the ship bringing him home from Crete after having defeated the Minotaur. Since the temple is out of bounds, enjoy the **view★★** overlooking the amphitheatre of the **Odeon of Herodes Atticus★★** (Plan III, B4) (*only open during musical performances*).

## Around the Acropolis★★ (Plan III, C4)

### The Theatre of Dionysus★ (Dioníssou Théatrou)

*Access (hidden behind a fence): from Odós Dionissiou Areopagitou, 10m after the Makrigiáni bus stop at the top of the steps. 8am-6.30pm. Entrance fee.* To conclude (or precede) your exploration of the Acropolis, you may want to see the oldest theatre from Antiquity. It was also the most prestigious, because this is where the masterpieces from the classical repertory – by **Aeschylus**, **Sophocles**, **Euripides** and **Aristophanes** – were all staged in the 5C BC.

Born in the Athens Agora, **tragedy** was originally staged in simple wooden theatres before being moved in the 6C BC to this well-chosen site. Indeed, it already possessed a sanctuary dedicated to **Dionysus Eleutherios**, tutelary god of the dramatic arts, as the Dionysiac festivals included choruses, mime and dance. This basic set-up, probably a simple earthen embankment, was replaced by a real theatre with wooden tiers in the following century. While retaining the same structure and dimensions, the stone theatre dates from the time of **Lycurgus** (4C BC) and owes its current form to the Romans.

Only a few vestiges remain – from the wall and colonnades – of the vast **portico** that stood in front of the entrance to the theatre. Through their proportions, the **tiers★** create a feeling of both space and intimacy. Moreover the perfect shape of the cavea, built against the rock face of the Acropolis, ensured ideal **acoustics**. It could accommodate nearly 17 000 spectators (compared to 12 000 in Epidaurus in the Peloponnese), each of whom brought his own cushion.

Built under the reign of Nero (1C), the sculptures on the **frieze★** decorating the proskenion evoke the myth of Dionysus. Note the bearded Silenus, crouching in the position of Atlas, the only character whose head is intact. Grouped around the altar dedicated to Dionysus, the chorus stood in the middle of a **lozenge** formed by the marble paving. In the first row, slightly above the seats reserved for dignitaries, is the **seat** of the high priest of Dionysus. High on top of the tiers, two Corinthian columns mark the site of the **choregic monument to Thrasyllos** along with other honorific structures.

There is a splendid **view★** from on top of the tiers over the columns of the Temple of Olympian Zeus and the Stadium, below to the left. Closer by to the left of the amphitheatre lie the ruins of the **Odeon of Pericles**, mainly used for rehearsals and music competitions.

### The sanctuary of Asklepios (Asklepeíon)

Adjacent to the theatre, the rather disorderly ruins of this sanctuary dedicated to **Asklepios** (the god of medicine) are not exactly inspiring; but the walk through the cypress trees has a certain charm to it. From the upper part of the theatre, follow the path along the huge wall of the **portico of Eumenes**. Built in the mid-2C by Eumenes II, King of Pergamon, this monumental stoa was 163m long on one floor. You then reach (on your right) the terrace with the ruins of the **Asklepeíon**, which included two sanctuaries from different eras. At the foot of the rock face stand the remains of the first **portico**, a 50m-long Doric gallery (4C BC) where patients slept as they waited to have a dream in which the god would reveal what form of therapy they should follow. Adjoining the gallery, a **tholos** (circular temple) housed the sacred spring where patients came to purify themselves. Excavations have also unearthed fragments of a **basilica** devoted to Saints Cosmas and Damian, two Christian doctors of Arab origin – a sign that, while replacing the old gods, the new religion preserved the sanctuary's medical vocation. Further on are the ruins of an **Ionic portico** (circa 420 BC).

*Have a rest in the shady woods surrounding Filopápos Hill, or enjoy a gastronomic meal at the famed Dionysus restaurant at the foot of the hill – a real institution where you can taste the most refined dishes in Greek cuisine.*

### On the hill of the Muses★ (Mousseíon or Lófos Filopápou) (Plan II, B4)

A wide paved path leads through the trees to the foot of the Mousseíon, the hill dedicated to the muses. This piece of nature in the heart of Athens is among the most pleasant sites in the city. After the pretty **Ágios Dimítrios Loumbardiáris** Chapel, a path (on your right) follows along the line of the **wall of Themistocles** (built around Athens in 460-457 BC) and winds through the pine trees to the summit past a series of former **troglodyte cave-dwellings**, one of which was held to be **Socrates' prison** according to a fanciful tradition. Crowned by the **Filopápos monument★★**

(114-116 AD), from which the hill derives its name, the summit affords a magnificent **view**\*\* of the Acropolis, particularly at sunset. The monument, a giant stele, contained the remains of a prince of Syrian origin who became a Roman consul, as well as a citizen and benefactor of Athens. Its striking 10m-high **concave façade**\* preceded a funerary chamber containing the sarcophagus. The deceased is shown standing in a quadriga on the bas-relief.

Walking back down, take the last path on the left. It leads to the **Pnyx** (Pníka) (Plan II, B3), literally 'the place where people are squashed together', a natural amphitheatre where the **Assembly of the People** was held from the 6C to the 4C BC. During these democratic meetings, citizens discussed laws being proposed, and each man had the right to speak once. Attendance was so low by the 4C that the constabulary had to force people to go in order to reach the quorum of 5 000! On summer evenings the Acropolis **son et lumière** show is held here (*see page 162*).

## Pláka\*\* (Plan III)
*Allow a whole day*

You will love Pláka from your first step inside this maze of colourful, sometimes quiet and sometimes hectic streets dotted with churches, busy squares and autumnal-coloured houses. This neighbourhood with a provincial feel blends many eras, from Antiquity to the Ottomans. Its many vestiges bring alive the story of Greece, transporting you to a village in the Cyclades or to Arcadia. In short, this is the best place in the city to go for a stroll.

To begin your explorations, start with the **Church of Sotíra Lykodímou**\* (E3) (*on the corner of Odós Filelínon and Odós Souri*), the largest medieval building in Athens (11C). Partly damaged during the War of Independence, this former abbey-church was acquired by Czar Nicholas I who offered to have it restored for the Russian community in Athens. It is decorated with **frescoes** by the German painter Thiersch. From Odós Filelínon head into the heart of Pláka on Kidathinéon, a pedestrian street. Tall cypress trees herald the **Church of Sotíra tou Kotáki** (D3) (*on your right*), also known as **Agía Sofía**. Built in the 11C-12C, it has lost its beautiful brick face, which is covered over with an awful roughcast added when it was restored in 1908. But the admirable dome has remained intact.

Just opposite it is the **Museum of Greek Folk Art**\*\* (D3) (*10am-2pm; closed on Monday; entrance fee*) which contains a magnificent collection ranging from the mid-17C to the present. It features all of the country's traditions, including Balkan, Mediterranean and Oriental influences. The ground floor has a collection of **embroidery**\* often of Byzantine inspiration from the Dodecanese, Epirus, Thrace, Crete and Skíros. The mezzanine is devoted among other things to works in wood, metal and ceramics, as well as to the famous shadow theatre, **Karaghiózis** (*see page 74*). In addition to a room devoted to temporary exhibitions, the 1st floor contains paintings by the naive painter **Theóphilos Hatzimichaíl** (1868-1934). In his works, this representative of popular culture brings together figures such as Alexander the Great and Kolokotrónis, a hero from the War of Independence. The 2nd floor has a display of **silver and gold objects**, and the upper floor features textiles (costumes, weaving) and stone sculptures.

**Filomoússou Eterías**\* (D3), a pleasantly shady square, is a Mecca for gastronomic tourists with its countless restaurants in neo-Classical buildings. At rush hour (ie 1pm and 8pm) a tout holding menus in several languages is sent out by each establishment in the hope of enticing passers-by to stop off at its several-metre-long territory; then it is the turn of his colleague from the neighbouring taverna...

Follow Odós Farmáki (*on the left*) to the apse of **Agía Ekateríni**\* (D3) (11C-12C), one of Athens' most beautiful Byzantine churches, whose interior has just been renovated. Its square, shaded by tall palm trees, is distinctly lower than the rest of the district; at its far end are some Roman remains sunk almost 2m below the present-day street level – proof of the dynamism of urban development in this part of the city.

Only a few metres away stands the **Lysicrates monument**\* (D3) (erected in 334 BC), the sole survivor among the choregic monuments that dotted the route connecting the Theatre of Dionysus and the Agora. Standing at the end of Odós Tripódon – a name evoking the bronze tripods offered to winners of the Dionysiac contests, which they then displayed all along the way – this structure was restored by the French School of Archaeology in Athens in 1845 and used to be known as the **Lantern of Demosthenes**. Above its Corinthian columns is a frieze in which Dionysus can be seen transforming pirates into dolphins, presumed to be the subject of the drama contest won by Lysicrates.

Enjoy lunch or a short break here and cool off in the delicious shade of its large tree.

## Upper Pláka: Anafiótika\*\* (Plan III, C3)

Lined with pretty ochre-coloured houses, the little street of **Odós Epimenídi**\* (D4) takes you into a part of Pláka far from the madding crowd that has remained intact and quiet *(when you reach Thrassílou, the continuation of Strátonos, turn right towards Anafiótika)*. On your left, olive trees stretch out to the foot of the Acropolis cliffs crowned with its powerful fortifications, while far off to the right is the silhouette of Mt Lycabettos. In 1834, a law forbade all construction around the Acropolis. Despite this, the inhabitants of the island of **Anáfi** (east of Santoríni), who had taken refuge in Athens at the beginning of the War of Independence, settled on the side of the sacred hill, giving Athens a genuine village with low-lying houses. Later growth in Pláka spread to this world apart without penetrating inside it.

Stroll through this maze of narrow alleys fragrant with the sweet scent of ripe figs. Turn left, then left again after a set of stairs, to climb up to the highest houses in the 'village', where there is a beautiful **view**\* of Athens, particularly at sundown.

Disappearing into its maze of lanes, where the only creatures you will run into are napping cats (or lost visitors!), you will eventually find your way back to Odós Pritaníou by the Church of **Ági Anárgiri Kolokinthí**\* (C3) (17C) perched just above the Psaras restaurant.

## The Aérides Quarter\* (Plan III)

If you liked the Anafiótika quarter, then you ought to also enjoy Odós **Thólou**\* (C3) and Odós **Aretoússas**\* (C3) *(turn left onto Pritaníou)*. They delimit one of the most beautiful parts of Pláka, full of houses from the late 19C. However, they were badly damaged by the earthquake of 15 September 1999, and most of them are awaiting restoration.

At the beginning of Odós Thólou, first you will pass on your left the **Old University**\* (1833) or **Kléanthis House** (C3), recognisable by its rust-coloured rendering. Designed by the architect of the same name, it housed the first university of the young Greek government from 1837 to 1842.

The **Kanelópoulos Museum**\*\* *(8.30am-3pm; closed on Monday; entrance fee)*, created to preserve the treasures bequeathed to the State in 1976 by collectors Pavlos and Alexandra Kanelópoulos, stands at the corner of Odós Aretoússa and Odós Panós in a superb neo-Classical house built in 1884. It contains all kinds of works of art and archaeology – Cycladic, Minoan and Mycenaean clay figurines, Coptic textiles, Byzantine and post-Byzantine icons and funerary masks from Faiyum, bronzes and jewellery – from the Hellenic peninsula and archipelago, Asia Minor and the Middle East. The choice of objects was intended by the collectors to show the continuity and evolution in Greek art in time and space.

Have a break at the **Neféli café** *(at the end of Odós Aretoússa)* or at one of the tables at the **Diskoúron café**, tucked away at the end of little Odós Mitróou. These establishments on the edge of the Agora afford a beautiful **view**\*\* of Athens.

A few metres away *(via Odós Andokídou)* stands the **Tower of the Winds**\*\* (C2), a strange octagonal building each side of which features an *aéride*, or winged figure, representing one of the eight winds that blow in Athens. Boreas, the cold north wind, is shown in the form of a bearded man *(facing Odós Eólou)*, while flowers are blown from the cloak of gentle Zephyr on the western face. These **Aérides** gave their name to the district around the Roman Forum between Pláka and Monastiráki. Built to the east of the Roman Forum under the reign of Julius Caesar (1C BC), the tower served a double purpose: first it sported a weathervane indicating the direction of the wind, then it had a hydraulic clock hidden inside that was driven by the **Klepsidra spring** on the north slope of the Acropolis hill. Since then, the name clepsydra has designated this type of water clock device.

Music-lovers may want to pay a brief visit to the nearby little **Museum of Music**★ (C2) *(10am-2pm, Wednesday: 12pm-6pm; closed on Monday; free admission)*. Housed in a building dating from 1842, it has close to 1 200 folk music instruments from the 18C to the present, collected by musicologist Fívos Anoyanákis. Headphones *(commentary in Greek and in English)* placed in front of each case explain the various types of Greek instruments, from the bouzoúki to the sandoúri, as well as the cymbals and spoons. The museum also has a bookshop and a pretty garden (where concerts are held).

The **Plátanos taverna**, one of the most pleasant in Pláka with its shady terrace, awaits you only a few steps away on Odós Diogénous.

The flattened dome and columned porch behind the Tower of the Winds is the **Fetiye Djami Mosque**★★ (C2) (15C), or Victory Mosque (referring to Mehmet the Conqueror's taking of Constantinople), more prosaically nicknamed Djami tou Staropazarou, the 'wheat market mosque', by locals.

It adjoins the **Roman Forum**★ (B2) *(8.30am-3pm; closed on Monday; entrance fee)*, a wide quadrilateral where the city's commercial activity was concentrated, and which the Turks turned into a cereal market. It stretched all the way to the colossal **Gate of Athena Archegetis**★★ *(at the other end of the site, facing Odós Pikilis)*, and was framed by a **portico** dating from the 1C BC, the remains of which are still visible. Odós Dexípou provides a fine view over **Hadrian's Library** *(not open to the public)*, a vast complex built in 131-32 AD. A part of the wall is still standing *(on the right, in Odós Eólou)*, which formed the actual library wing and reading rooms. To the left, at the other end of the site, the west wall has preserved a fine group of columns. Have a look at the **frescoes**★ across the street in the **Taxiárhes Church**★ (B2) ('of the Archangels'), a building from the 11C-12C that was completely rebuilt in 1852. Nearby are the **wicker merchants** whose cluttered stalls overflow with treasures: how about a pair of bulrush slippers or a sumptuous flowerpot-holder made in China?

## Monastiráki★, the old Turkish bazaar (Plan III)
Walk down Odós Áeros, a traditional hangout for the last surviving hippies and others who feel nostalgic for those days. The whole range of seventies fashions – genuine hippie jewellery, embroidered purple tunics, military surplus accessories – stretches all the way to Platía Monastiráki a bit further up.

**Dzistaráki Mosque**★ (B2) (1759) contains a rich **ceramics collection**★ *(9am-2.30pm; closed on Tuesday; entrance fee except on Sunday)* from the Museum of Greek Folk Art. In addition to some beautiful decorative works by well-known ceramicists, a variety of early 20C pieces from Greek and Cypriot workshops are cleverly displayed so as to highlight the building's architecture, which is worth a visit in itself. Right next to it is Platía Monastiráki, the heart of the former Turkish quarter, which has unfortunately been encumbered with barriers while work is being done on the metro. On the right however you can see the fine **tower**★ of the **Church of Panagía Pandánassa**★ (C1). Nicknamed *Monastiráki*, the 'little monastery', it gave its name to the local bazaar which stretched all the way to the Roman Forum in Ottoman times. The **flea market**★★ (B1), a dense maze of alleyways, takes up all the space between Odós Adrianoú and Odós Ermoú. Formerly the domain of metalworkers,

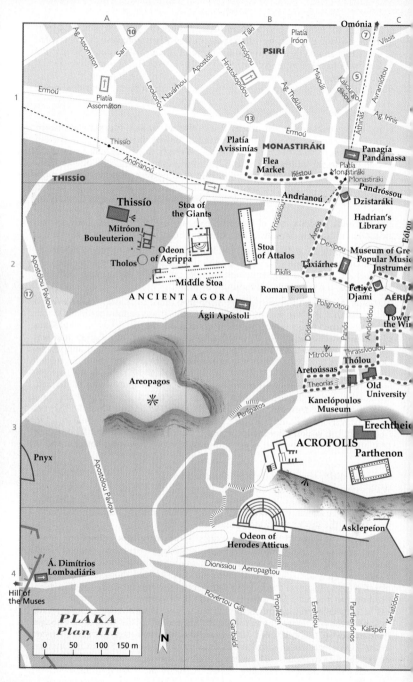

PLÁKA
Plan III
0    50    100   150 m

N

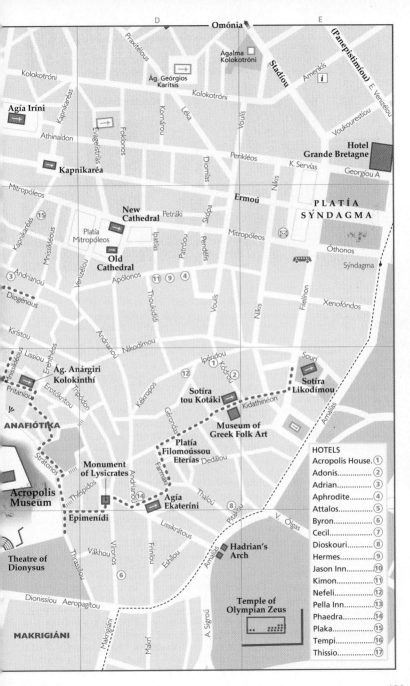

**Omónia**

Praxitélous

Kolokotróni

Ágalma Kolokotróni

**Stadíou**

 Amerikís

E. Venizélou

(Panepistimíou)

Ág. Geórgios Karitsis

Kolokotróni

Kapnikaréas

**Agía Iríni**

Athinaídon

Evangelistrías

Foklonos

Kornárou

Léka

Voulís

Voukourestíou

Peuklióou

**Hotel Grande Bretagne**

**Kapnikaréa**

K. Servías

Georgíou A

Mitropóleos

Diomías

Nikis

Kapnikaréas

Mnissikléous

15

**New Cathedral**

Petráki

Platía Mitropóleos

Venizélou

Ipatás

**Old Cathedral**

Pendélis

Voulís

Adrianóu

3

Diogénous

Apólonos

Thoukidídi

Nikis

Fileliínon

**Ermoú**

**PLATÍA SÝNDAGMA**

Mitropóleos

Óthonos

Xenofóndos

Síndagma

Kinístou

Andrianóu

Nikodímou

Mnissikléous

Lissíou

Erechthéos

**Ág. Anárgiri Kolokinthí**

Tripodon

Erotókritou

Pritaníou

Kékropos

Géronda

Ipéridou

Kódrou

1

2

Souri

Amalías

12

**Sotíra tou Kotáki**

**Sotíra Likodímou**

Kidathinéon

**ANAFIÓTIKA**

Strátonos

**Museum of Greek Folk Art**

**Monument of Lysicrates**

Thespídos

Andrianóu

Farnáki

**Platía Filomoússou Eterías**

Dedálou

**Acropolis Museum**

Epimenídi

14

**Agía Ekateríni**

Thaloú

Lissikrátous

8

Pikrodou

V. Ólgas

Amalías

**Theatre of Dionysus**

Thrassílou

Vákhou

Víronos

Friníou

Eshílou

6

**Hadrian's Arch**

Dionissíou Aeropagítou

Makrigiáni

Maví

A. Sígou

**Temple of Olympian Zeus**

**MAKRIGIÁNI**

| HOTELS | |
|---|---|
| Acropolis House. | ① |
| Adonis | ② |
| Adrian | ③ |
| Aphrodite | ④ |
| Attalos | ⑤ |
| Byron | ⑥ |
| Cecil | ⑦ |
| Dioskouri | ⑧ |
| Hermes | ⑨ |
| Jason Inn | ⑩ |
| Kimon | ⑪ |
| Nefeli | ⑫ |
| Pella Inn | ⑬ |
| Phaedra | ⑭ |
| Plaka | ⑮ |
| Tempi | ⑯ |
| Thissio | ⑰ |

P. Frilet/HEMISPHERES

Monastiráki, the flea market district

Odós Iféstou has been converted into more tourist-oriented trade: shoe and clothing shops of all kinds now compete with antique dealers and souvenir shops for space. The real second-hand goods dealers are to be found on **Platía Avissinías\*** (B1), which is particularly animated on Sunday mornings. The surrounding streets all the way to **Thissío** station echo with the sounds of languages from all over Central and Eastern Europe. This is where to find that pair of binoculars from the Red Army (complete with star, hammer and sickle) that you have always dreamed of. Then you can enjoy a break at one of the terrace cafés on Odós Adrianoú set up at the edge of the railway tracks.

If you still haven't found 'the' gift you were looking for after taking this route, there is one radical solution left: go back to Platía Monastiráki and plunge into narrow **Odós Pandróssou\*** (C2). This market, so touristy that it is amusing, features shops with jewellery, clothing, ceramics, leather and the most kitschy souvenirs packed one next to the other. And if that isn't enough, walk around Hadrian's Library and take **Odós Adrianoú\*** (B2) which crosses the entire Pláka from Platía Monastiráki to Agía Ekateríni Church. This beautiful paved street is also lined with a host of tourist shops selling natural sponges, leather goods (although the classic sandals from the 1970s are increasingly giving way to big sports name brands), and piles of hideous T-shirts, not to mention reproductions of various objects and masterpieces from Antiquity.

## In the heart of Athens\*\*
### Allow a whole day

Use the cool of the morning to explore the two other principal sites of ancient Athens: the Agora and Keramikós Cemetery, both as charming as they are rich in history. Continue your voyage back in time at the **Central Market** and the old shopping district around Odós Athínas and Odós Eólou between the central market and **Platía Omónia** (Plan II, C2), which was the heart of the capital in the 1930s. Don't miss the nearby National Archaeological Museum, a must for any visitor to Greece.

For lunch or a refreshing break, head for the **attractive Thissío quarter** (Plan II, B3) (in particular the pedestrian street, Iraklídon), while in the evening the lively streets of **Psirí** (Plan II, B2) offer the perfect setting for a delicious dinner.

**The Agora**★★ (Plan III, A2-B2)

*There are three ways to reach the Agora: at the end of Odós Polignótou (at the far end of the Roman Forum), at the bottom of Odós Adrianoú (in Monastiráki) and via Odós Apostólou Pávlou. 8am-3pm; closed on Monday. Entrance fee (the ticket is also valid for the museum). Allow 2hr.*

Take time to walk around in this city centre garden of stone, the heart of ancient Athens. It has been excavated since the 1930s by the **American School of Archaeology**, which is also responsible for replanting the area in order to beautify it and to evoke the ancient city's vegetation. At first glance, however, the place looks more like a chaotic maze of ruins; but the two **plans** – one at the Odós Adrianoú entrance and the other on the terrace in front of the façade of the Hephaisteion – give a good overall idea of the layout *(brochures are available at the ticket office)*.

The Agora was the focal point of life in the city, and the citizens of Athens spent a great deal of time here. Markets were held here, as well as certain religious festivals with their processions and theatrical or athletic contests. It was here, too, that citizens came to discuss public affairs and to listen to orators in the shade of the *stoas*, the long porticoes sheltering shops and administrative offices.

While the Agora was first laid out in the 6C BC, it did not take on its final form until the 2C BC. Bounded by various administrative buildings, temples and porticoes, it spread out over 2.5ha and was crossed diagonally by the **Panathenaic Way**. An open space was preserved in the centre, where, starting with Augustus, the Romans built temples to the glory of Rome as well as a monumental odeon.

Overlooking the ruins, the lofty façade of the **Theseion**★★★ (Thissío or Hephaisteion) *(100m from the entrance on Odós Apostólou Pávlou)* immediately catches your attention. Perched on a 65m-high mound, it is the best starting point for exploring the site and affords a striking **view**★ of the Acropolis. Dedicated to the worship of Athena and her brother **Hephaestus**, the god of smiths and metalworkers – of which there were many in the neighbouring area at the time *(now clustered around Odós Ermoú)* – this majestic Doric temple (449-444 BC) is one of the best preserved in the Greek world. While the **sculptures** on its two pediments have completely disappeared (there are a few fragments in the museum), it has kept the highly eroded **decorative motifs**★ from its metopes and outer frieze in Parian marble, evoking the adventures of Heracles and Theseus. Hence the old nickname Thissío (or Theseíon) given to the building and the nearby district. One rare feature was the **garden** that embellished the area around the sanctuary, scented with potted pomegranates, myrtle trees and vines. Another was the east portico, or pronaos, which has preserved its **coffered marble ceiling**★.

At the foot of the mound *(on the right)* stood the **tholos**, a circular building that housed the **Council of the Prytaneis**, a kind of executive branch of Athenian democracy, as well as the standard weights and measures. The **Council of Five Hundred**, the Assembly of Athens, was held in the nearby **bouleuterion**, while the **Metróon**, a temple to the Mother of the gods, was where state archives were kept. The statues in the centre of the esplanade indicate the site of the **Stoa of the Giants** that preceded the **Odeon of Agrippa**, a 1 000-seat performance hall. The rows of columns behind it give an idea of the size of the **Middle Stoa**. Don't miss the **frescoes**★ (the ones in the dome are from the 18C) in the **Church of Ágii Apóstoli**★ (the Holy Apostles) built in the late 10C and now fortunately rid of its 19C modifications.

Now imagine that you are a citizen of ancient Athens and stroll through the huge **Stoa of Attalos**★ (125-122 BC), a superb two-storey gallery that is 116m long by 20m wide. Offered to the city by Attalos III, King of Pergamon, it was reconstructed in 1956 by the American School of Archaeology to house the findings from its excavations, its archives and the researchers' workshops. The 'public antiquities' in the **museum**★ are open to the public. They include voting tokens, tools designed for picking court juries, weights and measures, etc, a striking testimony to the political, judicial and commercial life of the young Athenian democracy. In addition to these objects, there are all the artefacts discovered in the tombs and dwellings – a wide variety of **ceramics** – as well as sculptures that decorated the Agora. On the 1st floor there is an interesting **model★** of the Agora and the Acropolis.

Close by the Agora lies the old **Gázi district** (Plan II, A2), where the first stages of industrialisation in the capital took place between the late 19C and the early 20C. The area owes its name to the public gaslights installed there in 1877. It is now the site of the **Technópolis M Hantzidákis**, a cultural park where concerts and exhibitions are held. Artists' workshops, and a few trendy restaurants and bars show that this is one of the city's up-and-coming areas.

### Keramikós Cemetery★ (Plan II, B2)

*Odós Ermoú 148. Thissío metro station. 8am-3pm, 8.30am on Sundays and holidays; closed on Monday. Entrance fee (same ticket for the museum).* Less frequented than the Acropolis and the area around it, the site of the largest and oldest necropolis in Attica invites you to take a voyage in the shade of its olive and cypress trees beyond the Styx, the river of Hades; it features a whole range of Greek funerary art waiting to be explored.

Located outside the ancient city, the **necropolis** takes its name from the clay (*kéramos*) used in making the funerary vases and objects that were placed near the deceased. Beginning in the 6C, and depending on the fortune – and vanity – of the deceased, tombs were adorned with steles, stone vases, statues and even small chapels, structures that reached the height of luxury during the Age of Pericles.

To the left of the entrance is a **museum** containing some of the objects discovered on the site, while the path in front of you leads to the **Street of the Tombs★** (*on the left*), lined with plots belonging to rich Athenian families. On the right, a path leads to the **Sacred Gate** (5C BC), built as an extension of the Sacred Way connecting Eleusis and Athens.

Parallel to the Sacred Way, the **Academy Road** led to the **Dipylon★**, the main gate to Athens. This 'double gate' which had two towers – one facing the city and the other facing out – was part of the fortified wall around the city.

A stone's throw from Keramikós, you can plunge into the narrow streets of the **Psirí district★** (Plan III, B1) a colourful, charming and unpretentious area where old – often dilapidated – houses and soulless recent buildings rub shoulders. There are lots of little cafés tucked away, but the area is at its best in the evening, when you can stroll around before ending up on the terrace of a *mezedopolío* for a tasty dinner (on Platía Iróon, Odós Táki). In short, this is the ideal place to come after a day of sightseeing. Psirí has become quite a trendy place in recent years. It has a wealth of cafés, bars and restaurants, and not a week goes by without a new establishment opening its doors here. On Sundays, the exotic scent of the Far East permeates the atmosphere with the **Spice Market**, where the capital's Asian communities (Indians and Filipinos, among others) come to do their shopping.

### The Central Market District★ (Plan II)

Take **Odós Eólou★** (C1-2-3), a long, narrow pedestrian street lined with textile and inexpensive clothing shops that leads to the old Athens market. In the past, when the city was still of a reasonable size, this maze of winding streets was where its commercial heart beat most strongly. While it may not be as prosperous as in former times, the activity here is still frenetic.

In passing, have a look at the **Aiolou** café (a very good one) across from the white church of **Agía Iríni**; it has preserved its metal-framed **awnings** typical of the neighbourhood. In the same style of architecture – though on a much larger scale – the **central market★** (Kendrikí Agorá) (C2) *(closed on Sunday)* is lively, noisy and colourful, as well as being a place of strong smells (not recommended immediately after breakfast). In the wee hours of the morning, night owls gather in the little restaurants in the area to have some *patsá*, or tripe soup, the supreme remedy for stomachs that have been ill-treated by strong drink.

At night the area is also a hangout for homeless people of all kinds. It's a place of contrasts; by day, poverty gives way to speculators – large and small – on Odós Sofokléous where the **Stock Exchange** (krimatistírio) stands with its pompous Doric colonnade.

Further on, the large **Platía Ethnikís Andístassis** (National Resistance Square) (C2) contains the **Athens City Hall** (on the left) and the fine neo-Classical buildings of the National Bank of Greece (on the right). A number of examples of architecture from the beginning of the century are hidden among the modern buildings in the centre of Athens. Of particular note are the 1920 **frescoes★** on the building on the corner of Athinás and Likoúrgou.

**Platía Omónia** (C2) ('Concord' Square), a hectic, deafening place that is almost always congested – and devoid of all charm – is only a stone's throw away. It is hard to believe that during the Belle Époque, with its palm trees, groves, luxury hotels (now dilapidated) and chic cafés, it was as elegant as Platía Sýndagma. The intense traffic, the deterioration of neighbouring areas and a whole series of building works have reduced it to a mere place of passage where people take the metro. It also has an unsavoury night-time reputation.

But this is the way to the National Archaeological Museum (it is only 600m from Platía Omónia via Leofóros 28 Oktomvríou). On your way, have a look at the **façade★** of the **Polytechnic School** (C1) (1862-76, enlarged in the 1920s and 1950s) the work of the talented and prolific Kaftantzóglou.

### National Archaeological Museum★★★ (Plan II, C1)

*Open daily 8am-7pm, including Sundays and holidays, Mondays: 12.30pm-7pm. Entrance fee.* This is a must! Devoted to ancient art, from the Neolithic to the Roman Period, the Athens museum is one of the richest in the world, boasting innumerable masterpieces from the major Greek archaeological sites, with the exception of Delphi, Olympia, Crete and some Macedonian sites. Constructed between 1866 and 1889, the neo-Classical building was gradually enlarged according to need. Theoretically,

The central market in the heart of the modern Agora

R. Manin/HOA QUI

works are presented **in chronological order** and based on the materials used and private collections, but on top of the restoration and modernisation work on certain rooms, the earthquake in September 1999 completely disrupted this well-ordered plan. Thus, the 1st floor (ceramics, frescoes and ceramics from Santoríni) has been closed to visitors for an indeterminate period, and a significant part of the museum has been subjected to temporary arrangements which the official **catalogue** is hard put to keep up with. Apart from the recently remodelled rooms, the central part of the building has no air conditioning. With the heat and crowds in summer, be prepared for high temperatures; and given the large number of pieces displayed in each room, all it takes is two or three groups on a guided tour to spoil your pleasure. So don't hesitate to upset the chronology and look at objects randomly; or go when there are the fewest people – at opening and closing times. Finally, signs (not always very legible) and descriptive panels are in Greek and English.

■ Begin your trip through the past in **Room 5**, devoted to the **Neolithic Period**, containing **terracotta figurines** (nos 5894 and 5937) from Sesklo (Thessaly): a male idol with disproportionate genitals suggesting that it is a fertility god, and a female idol holding a child in her arms. Note the fine **vase** (no 5922) from Dimini (Thessaly), which already shows highly developed decoration.

■ **Room 6** has **Cycladic antiquities**★★ (3000-2000 BC), vases and marvellous **marble idols**. There are four exceptional pieces: the **goddess** of Amorgós (no 3978), the **Amorgós head** (no 3909) and the two **statuettes of musicians** (nos 3910 and 3908) with their harmonious lines.

■ **Room 4** contains the fabulous treasures from the **Mycenaean Period**★★★ (1600-1100 BC) that have made the museum's reputation. Most of the pieces on display come from Mycenae, excavated from 1876 onwards by Schliemann and his successors. It also has some precious objects unearthed at other Mycenaean sites such as Tírintha, Árgos and Pílos. The central cases contain some magnificent **gold funerary objects**, including the famous **mask of Agamemnon**★★★ (no 624) which Schliemann wrongly attributed to the 'king of kings', and which, perhaps due to its expressive power, is far superior to the others. Diadems, inlaid daggers, and engraved rings complete this incredible array, along with embossed metal goblets, a splendid **rhyton**★ (drinking vessel) in the shape of a bull's head, a duck-shaped vessel made of rock crystal, and small ivory objects attesting to the link between the Mycenaean world and the Orient. Don't miss the **warrior vase** (no 1426), the delicate **woman's head** in limestone (no 4575) and the frescoes, including the **Mycenaean woman**★ (no 11670), exhibiting a striking suggestion of perspective.

■ Return to the entrance hall to reach the rooms devoted to **Geometric and Archaic Art**★★ (10C-6C BC). The major piece in **Room 7** (next to the cloakroom) is the monumental **geometric amphora**★★ (no 804) from the mid-8C from a tomb in Keramikós Cemetery with a geometric pattern framing a funeral procession.

**Room 8** features a **Dipylon Head**★ (no 3372), found near the gate of the same name; it belonged to the oldest known kouros, which was standing on the tomb. The huge **votive kouros** (no 2720) stood in front of the temple to Poseidon at Cape Soúnion.

Gold funerary mask, or mask of Agamemnon (Mycenae)

T.A.P.

Room 9 contains the charming and graceful **kouros** and **kore** from the Cyclades and Attica. Of particular note is the **Phrasikleia kore** (*no 4889*) with its crown and dress decorated with flowers, as well as the **Winged Victory** (Nike) once placed as an acroterion on top of a temple (*no 21*).

In the centre of **Room 10** stands the very noble **Volomandra kouros★★** (*no 1906*), whose extremely fine face contrasts with the relatively rustic rendering of the body.

Go back to Room 8 to reach **Room 11**, where you must stop to look at the **funerary stele of Aristion★** (*no 29*), or 'the warrior of Marathon'. This sculpture of a warrior is by Aristokles, whose name can be seen on the base.

**Room 12** contains the strange **funerary stele of a running hoplite** (*no 1959*), so-called because it represents a hoplite (soldier) who is running; then again, it could be a dancer...

In **Room 13** is a superb **funerary kouros★** (*no 3851*) from Attica (530 BC). An inscription at the bottom says that the statue adorned the tomb of Kroisos. The **statue of Aristodikos** (*no 3938*), one of the last kouroi from the Archaic Period, shows the transition into classical art in which the body was freed from the stone. Two **bases of statues** (*nos 3476 and 3477*) discovered in Themistocles's wall are decorated with bas-reliefs showing youths doing athletic exercises, and an amusing fight between a dog and a cat. Among the votive and **funerary steles** in **Room 14**, don't miss the votive **relief** (*no 739*) in honour of a girl named Amphotto holding an apple, and the **Attic relief** (*no 3344*) of an Ephebe putting on a crown, illustrating the beginning of classical art.

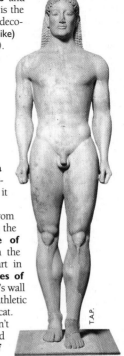

Kouros: an early depiction of the body

■ **Classical Art★★** (5C-3C BC):

**Room 15** contains two of the museum's masterpieces: the extraordinary **Artemision Poseidon★★** (*no 15161*) (c 460-450), a bronze statue salvaged in 1928 off the coast of Cape Artemision (at the northern end of Euboea). Standing in a superb pose, the god of the Sea wears a stern face above a powerful body, his right hand clasping what was once a trident. Another masterpiece is the wonderfully expressive **Eleusinian relief★★** (*no 126*) (c 440-430) with its solemn figures. Demeter (*on the left*), the goddess of fertility and patron of agriculture, is shown with her daughter Persephone giving an ear of corn to Triptolemos, son of the King of Eleusis, charged with teaching agriculture to mankind.

Outstanding among the many steles cluttering **Room 16** is the **great funerary lekythos** (*no 4485*), a narrow vase found in Platía Sýndagma. Hermes, in the centre, is taking a young woman to the Acherón, the river leading to the kingdom of the dead, while her family bids her farewell.

Of particular note in **Room 17**, devoted to **classical sculptures** and **votive reliefs**, is a **relief of Hermes★** (*no 1738*) with both sides sculpted, as well as one dedicated to **Dionysus** (*no 1500*).

In **Room 18**, **Hegeso's tombstone★★** (*no 3624*) shows a seated young girl studying a piece of jewellery taken from a case handed to her by her servant. This work of exceptionally elegant design, tinged with sorrow, is attributed to Kallimachos (c 410), one of Phidias' main students.

The following rooms have **classical sculptures**: statues from the 5C and 4C BC that are classical copies of the originals, including the famous (lost) chryselephantine **Athena** by Phidias that stood in the Parthenon.

**Room 21** contains the remarkable **Jockey of Artemision★** (no 15177), a Hellenistic bronze from the 2C BC, which was salvaged from the waves – like the statue of Poseidon – off Cape Artemision. The artist has captured the galloping horse and spirited young rider with great realism.

Go past Rooms 34 and 35, which have various sculptures and votive reliefs, to **Room 36** featuring the **Karapánou collection★** which includes figurines and small **bronze** objects from the 8C to the 3C BC. The most remarkable pieces are from the sanctuary of Zeus at Dodona (Epirus), in particular the delicate little bronze of **Zeus** (no 16546), a horse (no 16547), and a **statuette of a 'colonel'** (no 16727).

**Room 37** contains **objects** (8C-4C BC) from the islands, Thessaly and north-west Greece, Olympia, Crete and the Peloponnese; note the **Athena Promachos** from the Acropolis (no 6447).

*Go back to Room 21.*

Rooms 22 to 24, devoted to art from the 4C BC, have a series of **sculptures** from the tholos at the Temple of Asklepios in Epidaurus (*Room 22*), as well as **funerary monuments** (*Room 26*) and **votive reliefs** (*Rooms 25 and 27*).

There are three pieces of note in **Room 28**: a **high-relief★** (no 4464) of a spirited horse held by a black slave, which came from a funerary monument dating from the 2C BC that was found in Athens. The very lively and lifelike piece is a wonderful example of the transition between classical and Hellenistic art. The **Ephebe of Antikythera** (no 13396) is a bronze statue found in the sea off the island of Antikythera representing Paris giving the famous apple to Aphrodite. The **Head of Hygeia** (no 3602), the daughter of Asklepios, attributed to Scopas, is striking for its introspective expression and gentle contours.

■ **Hellenistic Art★★** (3C-2C BC):
The sculptures in **Room 29** include a fine **statue of a Gaul★** (no 247). **Room 30** features a colossal **statue of Poseidon★★** (2C BC) which dominates the entire space. Don't miss the two bronze heads, which are highly individualised and expressive portraits: a **head of a philosopher** (no 13400) (3C BC) and a **man's head** (no 14612) (c 100 BC), as well as the **group with Aphrodite**, Eros and Pan (no 3355, created c 100 BC).

■ Save up some energy for **Roman Art★**, illustrated by reliefs and statues produced in various Greek workshops in the 1C BC. In the centre of **Room 31** is the haughty **equestrian statue of Augustus** (fragment). The piece next to it is a group of funerary **portraits** from steles (2C-3C AD) discovered near the Tower of the Winds.

**Rooms 32 and 33** contain Greek pieces from the Roman Period (2C-3C AD), including a lovely **sleeping maenad★** (no 261) and numerous busts: the **philosopher Metrodorus** (no 368), a **head** (no 3085) from a funerary monument, another **head of a woman** (no 3087), and one of a **young man** (no 420). Note the museum director's thoughtful touch in putting side by side **Antinoüs** (no 417) and the **Emperor Hadrian** (no 249, see also no 3729), a reminder of the insatiable passion which the former inspired in the latter.

End your visit of the Roman section with the great **sarcophagus** (no 1497) from Attica and a **relief** representing a family portrait (no 3239).

■ If your legs are still willing, finish your tour with an African escapade in the **Egyptian antiquities collection★**. With its 7 000 pieces (only some of which are on display), the **Dimitriou collection★★** in **Rooms 40-41** covers the entire history of Ancient Egypt, from the pre-dynastic period to the Ptolemaic Era (5000-1C BC). Statues in wood, granite, clay, alabaster and bronze, as well as jars, vases, amphorae, knife fragments, votive reliefs, tablets covered in hieroglyphics, jewellery, masks and funerary statuettes illustrate the amazing consistency of Egyptian art throughout the centuries.

■ In the shadowy light of **Room 42** lies the sparkling **antique and Byzantine gold jewellery**★★ from the **Helene Stathátou collection**, from Macedonia and especially from Thessaly *(be careful not to brush against the cases, as the alarms go off at the slightest touch)*.

For a welcome break in a cool (but not air conditioned) place, you have a choice between the museum café (Museum Garden) located at the entrance to **Aréos Park**★ (Plan II, D1) – one of Athens' biggest green spaces – and Green Park. Or you might feel like a complete change of scene altogether, and go to Platía Exarhíon or Odós Kalidromíou. At the foot of **Stréfi Hill**, west of Lycabettos, **Exárhia** (Plan II, C1) is a lively and colourful area where students, fringe groups and dissidents of all kinds hang out. The area has many tavernas featuring simple, tasty and inexpensive food, making it a good place for an evening meal.

# Neo-Classical Athens★

## Around Platía Sýndagma (Plan II, D3)

What could they do to rebuild Pericles' prestigious city? The people who shaped modern Athens for a whole century (1830-1930) were obsessed by this dream. No building was to be without its marble colonnade! And what better choice as an introduction and model for this new city than the two ancient monuments to **Hadrian**, the philhellenic Roman Emperor?

A great admirer of Athens and of Greek culture, Hadrian stayed in the capital on several occasions and embellished it with numerous buildings. The Athenians honoured their powerful benefactor by erecting a sort of arch of triumph to him in the Roman style in 131 AD, at the point where Athens and the Roman quarter met. Inscriptions engraved on the frieze of **Hadrian's Arch**★ (Plan III, D4) proclaim, on the Pláka side: 'This is the town of Athens, the ancient city of Theseus', while the opposite side says: 'This is the city of Hadrian, not of Theseus'. By putting the mythological hero and the Roman Emperor on the same level, the Athenians acknowledged their noble visitor... and played up to his vanity.

## Temple of Olympian Zeus★★ (Plan III, E4)

*Go around Hadrian's Arch to the left to reach the entrance to the site (on your right at the beginning of Leofóros Vasillíssis Ólgas). 8.30am-3pm; closed on Monday; entrance fee.*

Paintings, drawings and stories all attest to the fact that no traveller ever passed through Athens without being moved by the fallen majesty of these powerful columns standing in the middle of a bare esplanade. More than the monuments on the Acropolis, which were remodelled by its various occupants and hardly recognisable, the Temple of Olympian Zeus was the ultimate ruin possessing the melancholy air so dear to European romantics. They were also moved by its colossal dimensions recalling an era of giants: with its **triple colonnade** of 104 Corinthian columns (in all), the building formed a 107.75m by 41.1m rectangle, making it one of the largest temples in the Greek world.

Pausanias thought that **Deucalion**, the mythical ancestor of the Greeks, was the originator of the sanctuary. On a more prosaic level, archaeologists estimate the oldest foundations to be from the era of the **Peisistratid tyranny** (546-510 BC). Abandoned with the rise of democracy, work was resumed in 174 BC thanks to the Seleucid King Antiochus IV and completed by Emperor Hadrian in 132 AD. The building's fate is uncertain, but there is no doubt that its huge quantities of marble were sent to the limekilns. When Cyriacus of Ancona visited Athens in 1436, there were only 21 columns left.

Near the entrance to the site, on the right, are the foundations of the **Baths of Hadrian**, whose actual baths have preserved their marble **mosaics**.

For a taste of the neo-Classical, go down Leofóros Vasillíssis Ólgas towards the **Olympic Stadium\*\*** (Plan II, D4), built for the first **Modern Olympic Games** in April 1896. Abandoning the original wooden stadium (330 BC), General Herodes Atticus gave the city (in 144 AD) a building in Pentelic marble more in keeping with the prestige of the Panathenaic athletic contests. The present stadium is a faithful replica of that building. It can accommodate 70 000 spectators, who come to admire the athletes or to enjoy the beautiful **view\*** of the National Garden and the Acropolis.

Leave the traffic on Leofóros Vassiléos Konstandínou for the quiet park opposite. At the end of a lovely tree-lined path stands the neo-Classical façade of the **Zappeion (Zápio)** (Plan II, D3) (1874-88), a huge **exhibition hall** designed by talented architects T Hanser and F Boulanger. It was above all the dream of one man, K Zappas, a rich Greek from Alexandria. He put his entire – substantial – fortune into trying to rebuild Athens through what had been its greatest glory: architecture, art and athletics.

Walk around the building on the left, then enter the cool shade of the **National Garden\*** (Plan II, D3), an oasis in the heart of the city that is open from dawn to dusk.

### Platía Sýndagma\* (Plan II, D3)

Leaving the garden via Leofóros Amalías, return to Platía Sýndagma, 'Constitution Square'. Swamped by the intense traffic that reigns all around it – most of Athens' buses and trolleybuses stop here – not to mention the countless bitterly fought-over taxis, it has lost its former charm from the days when it was lined with terrace cafés. However, the new green spaces and the fountain gushing forth in the centre by the brand new metro stop are very welcome additions. But with its banks and two huge fast-food restaurants, Sýndagma has turned into a mere place of passage, of feverish activity, which fills up and empties according to the rhythm of office hours.

At the foot of the old royal palace (1836-42), which became the **Parliament** (Voulí) in 1935, the *evzónes* wearing *foustanèlles* (pleated kilts that are the traditional Albanian costume which came into fashion with Otto) and *tsaroúchia* (pom-pom shoes) stand guard in front of the **Tomb of the Unknown Soldier**. The changing of the guard (*every hour*) is the occasion for a little **ceremony** – a kind of military dance – that has always been very popular with tourists.

The **Hotel Grande-Bretagne** (1843) on the right, undoubtedly the most prestigious in the city, probably has no memory of having housed the **French School of Archaeology** (now in Kolonáki) between 1856 and 1873.

### A stroll down Odós Ermoú

Take Odós Voulís to **Odós Ermoú**, a long pedestrian shopping street that forms a breach through the city from the colonnade of the Voulí all the way to Keramikós Cemetery.

When you reach Evangelistrías, a street running off at right angles, have a look (*on the left*) at the two cathedrals. The work of architects and a monarch, the **New Cathedral (Mitrópolis)** (Plan III, D2) built in 1842-62, flattens Platía Mitropóleos with its graceless mass. More interesting is its tiny neighbour, the **Old Cathedral\*\***, a lovely Byzantine chapel from the 12C dedicated to Panagía Gorgoepíkoos, the 'Virgin who answers (prayers) quickly'. Many elements dating from ancient and medieval times used in its construction can be seen in the outer walls.

Another treasure of Byzantine art, the **Church of Kapnikaréa\*\*** (Plan III, C1) (11C-13C) stands in the middle of Odós Ermoú, a few metres away. Its fine brick façade is set off by friezes and two elegant little marble columns.

A maze of narrow streets lined with shops of all kinds takes you to **Platía Klafthmónos** (Plan II, C2) and its verdant esplanade. In the shade cast by the trees, the **Church of Ágii Theódori\*** seems to have been placed here by some spell. Rebuilt in the 11C on the foundations of a 9C sanctuary, it has some striking patterns of Arab origin on its outer walls.

The little Byzantine Church of Kapnikaréa squeezed between modern buildings

Between 1836 and 1842, the Greek sovereigns resided at **Vouros Palace** (1834) on Odós Paparigopoúlou, the present location of the Museum of the City of Athens★ (Plan II, C2) (*9am-1.30pm; closed Tuesday and Thursday; entrance fee*), also called the Vouros-Eutaxia Museum. Paintings, drawings and engravings from the 17C-20C (*on the ground floor and 2nd floor*), as well as a large **model of Athens★** from 1842, recall the capital's urban history. On the 1st floor are Otto's and Amalia's furnished **salons**, which are livened up by a few historical pieces such as a copy of the **Treaty of London** in French signed by Talleyrand. The atmosphere is evocative of the bourgeois household of a small monarchy with fewer than one million subjects...

Head for **Panepistimíou★** (Plan II, C2) (officially called Eleftériou Venizélou, but no one uses that name). The University avenue has some of the finest of Greek neo-Classical buildings: from left to right, the **National Library** (1887-1902), the **University** (1839-64) and the **Academy** (1859-87). With its fine Ionic colonnade flanked by two high columns supporting statues of Athena and Apollo, the latter is perhaps the greatest of the three. These 'temples of culture' form a harmonious whole that is imposing without being too monumental. Financed by Greeks from the diaspora – the only ones capable of raising the kind of money needed for such projects – they were entrusted to two Danish architects living in Greece: the **Hansen brothers**, who left their mark on what is known as the neo-Hellenic style.

Relax in the cool shade (rather rare in this part of Athens) of the terrace café hidden in a corner of the **Athens City Hall Cultural Centre** (Plan II, D2) (*take the pedestrian street, Odós Massalías*), whose ground floor houses the **Theatre Museum** (*Monday-Friday, 9am-2.30pm; free admission*) devoted to modern Greek theatre. If you are getting hungry, try some meze at Athinaïkon or Andréas' on Odós Themistokléous.

# Kolonáki★ and the Museum District

*Leofóros Vassilíssis Sofías and its museums*
*are close to Platía Filikís Eterías (Kolonakíou).*

The preserve of intellectuals, politicians (the Prime Minister lives on Odós Anagnostópoulou), professional people, well-heeled foreigners, chic shops and cafés where people go to see and be seen, Kolonáki stretches out at the foot of Lycabettos, forming a regular grid of shady (and often congested) streets of which **Skoufá** and **Patriárhi Ioakím** are the backbone. It is also a district with a multitude of museums to be explored during the hottest time of day before going for a drink on top of the mountain.

## Benáki Museum★★★ (Plan II, D3)

*Access via Odós Neofýtou Doúka or via Leofóros Vassilíssis Sofías. 9am-5pm, Thursday 9am-midnight, Sunday 9am-3pm; closed Monday. Entrance fee).* Like the Kanelópoulos, this museum is first and foremost the work of one man, **Adonis Benáki** (1873-1954), who had a passion for all forms of expression of Hellenism throughout the ages. Born into a wealthy family from the Greek diaspora in Alexandria, Egypt, Benáki created the museum in 1930 as a showcase for his collections. Enriched with numerous later donations, they occupy the family home, a magnificent neo-Classical residence from the early 20C. Long closed to the public, the museum has been completely remodelled and is now open again. Everything has been very thoughtfully laid out, from the presentation to the reception, the shop, the rooftop terrace café and documentation *(bring a sweater, however, as the air conditioning is a bit on the chilly side).*

Presented in chronological order from prehistoric times to contemporary Greece, the many forms of expression of Greek identity gathered here – whether artistic or linked to everyday life – will take you on a fascinating voyage through the country's history. **Rooms 1 to 8** *(from prehistoric times to the 6C AD)* contain in particular an exceptional collection of **gold objects★** (3200-2800 BC) and **Hellenistic jewellery**, as well as a fine amphora in the geometric style and two portraits from Faiyum. **Rooms 9-12** *(Byzantine and post-Byzantine eras)* feature some delicate **rock-crystal pendants, illuminated manuscripts of the Gospels**, some very beautiful **icons★★**, in particular two early works by El Greco, and some sculpted wooden **iconostases**. On the 1st floor, **Rooms 13-24** *(the period of Ottoman and Venetian rule)* are the realm of precious fabrics, brocades and silks from Venice, a superb collection of **costumes★★** and jewellery from the 18C and 19C. They also contain **interior decorations★★** from various regions of Greece with wood panelling and furniture. Finally, the last two floors recall the War of Independence and some aspects of modern Greek history through paintings, weapons and various documents.

## Museum of Cycladic Art★★ (Goulandrís Foundation) (Plan II, D3)

*10am-4pm, Saturday 10am-3pm; closed Tuesday and Sunday. Entrance fee.* Created in 1986, this remarkable museum is devoted to Aegean civilisation, in particular the prehistoric Cyclades. The objects on display – over a thousand – cover a period ranging from 3000 BC to the 4C AD. Excellent explanatory texts with maps and sketches provide a better understanding of the collections and of Cycladic culture, its art and funerary customs.

Since 1991, the museum has been enlarged to include the **Stathátos Palace** *(the new wing is connected via a glass passageway)*, the elegant adjoining neo-Classical home which is now used for long-term exhibitions. For the time being, there is a fascinating exhibition entitled **'The city beneath the city'**, featuring 500 of the innumerable discoveries made while the metro was being built. A bronze head, marble sculptures, ceramics with black designs, and numerous lekythoi (narrow vases) with white bases are the finest pieces.

Back in the **main building**, white marble stairs – evoking the Aegean world – lead to the 1st floor and the famous **Cycladic idols\*\*\***. Whether large or small (from less than 10cm to 1.4m for the tallest), their simple forms and strikingly modern pure lines make these white marble figurines among the most precious in prehistoric art. While they have preserved some of their mystery, they are thought to have been connected to funerary worship (thus the folded arms) and lain down horizontally (perhaps near the deceased), which would explain their pointed feet.

The 2nd floor contains works of art and various utilitarian pieces dating from 2000 BC to the 4C AD. The most important pieces are the **bronzes**, red-figure **ceramics\*\*\*** and **large amphorae\*\*\***. Note the touching little **doll** with movable joints *(no 197)* taken from a child's tomb. The 4th floor (the 3rd floor houses temporary exhibitions) has the highly varied, excellent **Charles and Rita Polítis collection\*\*** (ceramics, Byzantine lamps, statuettes, helmets, swords, etc). Of particular note are the elegant **statuettes of women\*** *(no 73-76)*.

## Byzantine Museum\*\* (Plan II, E3)

*8.30am-3pm; closed on Monday. Entrance fee.* The museum is in a handsome neo-Renaissance house built in 1848 for the **Duchess of Piacenza**, an important figure in the philhellenic movement and in Athens society during the reign of Otto. While it is a very well-endowed collection, the presentation is unfortunately not of the same standard (it could use more space and better explanations). However, this may be remedied by the renovations currently being carried out.

Don't miss the two **reconstructions of churches\***: one of a **Christian basilica** from the 5C-7C *(Room 2)*, with a **sculpture of the good shepherd\*** *(on the right)*, and another of the **dome\*** of a Greek-cross church *(Room 4)*. Take time to admire the **icons\*\*** in Room 7, some of which are exceptional. In particular the **Archangel Michael\*\*\*** (14C), and the **Panagía Glikó Filoússa\*** (literally 'the Virgin who kisses sweetly'), not to mention the **mosaic of the Visitation** (14C) *(on the right at the end of the room)*. The next room has some pretty **frescoes** and small objects (jewellery, crosses, ceramics, rock-crystal glasses, metal utensils) from the early Byzantine era. The visit ends with various **silver and gold** objects and **clerical garments**.

## If you have any time left...

Art lovers may want to visit the **National Gallery\*** (Alexander Soútsos Museum) (Plan II, E3) *(across from the Hilton Hotel, Monday and Wednesday 9am-3pm and 6pm-9pm, Thursday, Friday, Saturday 9am-3pm, Sunday 10am-2pm; closed on Tuesday; entrance fee)* which has three paintings by **El Greco\*\***, including the famous *Concert of the Angels*, as well as Cretan and post-Byzantine icons. It also contains the most representative trends in **neo-Hellenic painting**, in particular 18C works from the Ionian Islands and those by the main masters of the Munich school (**Gýsis**, **Lytrás**, **Iacovídes**, **Volanákis**, etc). A room *(on the 1st floor)* is devoted to the painter **K Parthénis** (1878-1967), who had a decisive influence on 20C Greek art. There are also ten frescoes by the naïve painter **Theóphilos** and works by the sculptor **I Halepás** occupying two rooms and the garden.

## On Mt Lycabettos\*\* (Plan II, D2)

*By the road or the funicular (at the corner of Odós Aristípou and Odós Ploutárchou); leaves every 10 min, every day from 8.45am-0.15am, Thursday 10.30am-0.15am.* Why not end your exploration of Athens with the spectacular **panorama\*\*** over the capital and its environs from the top of Mt Lycabettos? Legend has it that Athena was carrying this huge 278m-high boulder to the Acropolis in order to lift up her temple and bring it closer to the heavens. But two black birds appeared in the sky, predicting bad news for her. Full of anger, the goddess dropped her boulder... and left it there. Ever since, the 'Hill of the Wolves' has stood right in the centre of the Athens basin which is bounded by far-off Pentelikon, Parnes and Hymettus. Completely

B. Pérousse/MICHELIN

Mt Lycabettos: a rock rising out of concrete

deforested during the Ottoman era, Lycabettos got back its fragrant pine and cypress trees at the end of the 19C. Standing like a lighthouse above the **open-air amphitheatre** is the little **Church of Ágios Geórgos**, which provides shade for the restaurant terrace. This is the ideal place to come at the end of the day to watch the city lit up by the rays of the setting sun, then sparkling with a thousand electric stars.

## Short excursions from Athens

If you have time before your boat leaves for the islands, or if you just want a bit of peace and quiet far from the hectic capital, try getting away for a couple of hours and exploring the surrounding area – either to Cape Soúnion *(allow 4-5hr)* or closer by to the Byzantine Monastery of Dafní *(allow 2hr30min)*, two of Attica's major sites.

### Dafní Monastery★★
*10km west of Athens on the road to Corinth. Take the A 16 bus from Platía Elefterías (Plan II, B2). Get off at the 'Psychiatricó' stop (the monastery is opposite a psychiatric hospital) and cross the road. 8am-3pm; closed on Monday. Entrance fee.*

This remarkable 11C Byzantine monastery close to the teeming city is hidden away in a delightfully quiet wooded area. Constructed in several stages in the Middle Ages, it has preserved its beautiful **Cistercian cloister★**, built during the Frankish occupation by disciples of St Bernard who lived here from 1211 to 1458. The wide dome of the **katholikón★★**, a masterpiece of Byzantine architecture, looms over the Greek-cross plan characteristic of mainland Greece. Its admirable **façades★★** are a fine combination of brick and stone. But plan on spending most of your time on the inside, which contains some superb **mosaics on a gold background★★★**, probably by the most famous artists in Constantinople. Characteristic of religious art in the late 11C, they frame the austere figure of **Christ Pantocrator★★** on the dome, forming a whole that is extraordinary for its fine design and harmonious colours.

## Cape Soúnion** (Akrotírio Soúnio)

*70km away, at the southern end of the peninsula. Take either a tour bus (through a travel agent), or the bus that leaves from Mavromatéon, in Aréos Park (Plan II, D1) (last departure at 6pm). By car, leave Athens via Leofóros Sigroú (Plan II, C4). Then, in Fáliro, take the expressway on the left that goes by the airport and follows the west coast, known as the Apollo Coast.*

To round off the day, there's nothing like a drive out to Cape Soúnion, a rocky promontory dominated by the superb **Temple of Poseidon**** *(10am-sundown; entrance fee)*. Built by order of Pericles, 16 of its 24 original columns are still standing, perched at the tip of the cape 60m above the sea. This gem of Doric architecture is at its most beautiful at sunset. The pretty little **beach** below, where there's a taverna, is a good place to relax in the shade of what Homer called the 'sacred sentinel'.

---

## Making the most of Athens

### COMING AND GOING

See also (page 163), 'Making the most of Piraeus'.

**By air** – The new **Elefthérios Venizélos** Airport was opened in April 2001 in Spáta (27km south-east of the city centre). The Greek capital's other two airports have been permanently closed and all air traffic is now concentrated at Venizélos, including international, domestic and charter flights. This huge airport hopes to become one of the most modern new hubs in Europe. Its first task will be accommodating the millions of visitors arriving for the first Olympic Games of the 3rd millennium. Services available – all brand new – include car rentals, travel agencies, shops, left-luggage lockers, hotels, restaurants, banks, money changers, etc.

**For information**, call: ☎ (01) 36 98 300 / 35 31 000. You might also want to have a look at the airport's very clear Web site: www.athensairport-2001.gr It features timetables for all flights and contact information for all domestic and international airline companies that have flights to Athens.

**Access**: Shuttle bus service 24 hours a day to the centre of Athens and Piraeus. The Athens shuttle leaves from Platía Sýndagma ('Airport-Spáta' bus).

To get to the airport by car: from Sýndagma, take Leofóros Vassilísis Sofías (alongside the Parliament) (see page 125 Plan II, D3-E3). This feeds into the new 6-lane expressway built for the airport.

Travel times vary according to traffic of course, so allow extra time (45min).

If you take a taxi, make sure the meter is working properly (rate 1 during the day, rate 2 after midnight, on Sundays and holidays).

**By train** – Athens has 2 railway stations, used by Hellenic Railways (OSE), right next to each other: the first, **Peloponnese Station** (Plan II, B1), Leofóros Theódorou Deligiáni (get off at Deligiáni station, line 2) is for trains going to southern Greece; the second, **Lárissa Station** (Plan II, B1), Platía Laríssis (get off at Lárissa station, line 2), is for northern Greece.

**By bus / metro** – Piraeus-centre is served by blue and yellow **bus 040**; departs from Platía Sýndagma (Plan III, E2), at the beginning of Odós Filelínon. To get to the main harbour of Piraeus, take metro line 1.

The KTEL company's orange buses serve Attica, in particular the ports of Rafína and Lávrio and the Soúnion site. The terminal is located on Platía Egíptou, Odós Mavromáteon, in front of Áreos Park (Plan II, C1) (5min from Victoria station on line 1).

**For the north and south**, go to bus terminal A, 'KTEL Kifissoú', 100 Odós Kifissoú (Plan II, C2). It is served by bus 051; the stop is on the corner of Odós Zínonos and Odós Menándrou, near Omónia. Buses go to the Peloponnese, the Ionian Islands, and Thessaloníki.

**For central Greece:** terminal B, 'KTEL Liossíon', Odós Liossíon 260, served by bus 024, the stop for which is on Leofóros Amalías (Plan II, D3). Buses go to Delphi, Galaxídi, Tríkala (Metéora), Vólos (Pelion), etc.

## FINDING YOUR WAY

An accurate and practical plan of the city is given away free at the information office, 4 Odós Amerikís. Other city plans, which vary in quality, are for sale at stands and in bookshops. The historical map of Athens published by the Ministry of Culture (€3) is by far the best, but its one-square-metre size makes it a bit unwieldy. It is available, along with others, at **Elefteroudákis** (Leofóros Panepistimíou 15), **Road Edition** (Odós Ipokrátous 39) and at the **National Archaeological Museum**. Don't be shy about asking your way (most people understand some English), as local people will be delighted to give you directions.

## GETTING AROUND

**By bus – Blue buses** (centre and outskirts), **mini-buses** (centre) and **trolleybuses** (centre) run from 5am to 0.30am. Tickets ('isitíria') are valid for buses and trolleybuses (but only for one trip; around 35 cents) and are sold at stands near stops, at Sýndagma (there is a ticket machine by the 040 bus stop) and at Omónia. Make sure you cancel your ticket when you get on the bus. Buses are crowded at rush hour (between 3pm and 5pm) and move slowly through the centre due to traffic jams. The map of Athens offered by the information office indicates the routes taken by the trolleybuses and 4 mini-bus lines.

**By metro –** Athens has 3 metro lines, open from 5am to 0.15am. The oldest line ('ilektrikó') runs between Piraeus and Kifissiá, via Thissío (Keramikós and the Agora), Monastiráki and Omónia (The National Museum is halfway between Omónia and Victoria, the next station). A ticket costs around 60 cents, or 75 cents if you plan to continue your trip on the other 2 brand new metro lines.

The 2 new lines, which cost around 75 cents, are linked by 3 connecting stations: **Omónia** connects lines 1 and 2; **Atikí** and **Sýndagma** connect lines 2 and 3. Opened in December 1999, this new network is not in full service yet, and some stations are still under construction. Some connections indicated on maps are not accessible yet, in particular Monastiráki station, which is only accessible via line 1 for the time being.

**By taxi –** Taxis are relatively inexpensive and numerous. Don't be surprised if your taxi lets on other customers during rush hour; this is an accepted custom. The driver must then deduct the cost of each passenger's trip (make sure he does it). Besides the 60 cent pick-up charge (or more if you reserve a car by telephone, and a small extra charge for baggage), there are 2 rates: **rate** (during the day) and **rate 2** (at night, midnight-5am, on Sundays and holidays, or outside the city limits, double rate 1). Finding a taxi on Platía Sýndagma, where the traffic is deafening, is a demanding sport that has at least two rules: go out to meet them, while avoiding the buses and trolleybuses, and clearly articulate your destination. If the taxi already has passengers, it will flash its headlights and slow down rather than coming to a complete stop. That's when you must state your destination out loud. A broad 'A' followed by your mouth closing around the sound $\Delta\rho$ ('drr') will signify 'aerodrómio', or airport, without fail.

**Car rentals –** Nearly all the companies, large and small, have offices on **Leofóros Sigroú** (at the beginning) (Plan II, C4). The lowest rates for renting a car run from €45 to €55 per day during peak season. Sliding rates are available depending on the length of rental. Small companies offer lower rates, but make sure you get the equivalent in terms of coverage for accidents and breakdowns.

**Hertz**, Leofóros Sigroú 12, ☎ (01) 922 01 02-04.
**Budget**, Leofóros Sigroú 8, ☎ (01) 921 47 71-73.
**Athens Car**, Odós Filelínon 10, ☎ (01) 323 37 83.

**Autorent**, Leofóros Sigroú 94 and Odós Vizándiou 11 (right angles to Sigroú), ☎ (01) 923 25 14 / 923 84 38.

**Roadside Assistance** – Contact **ELPA**, the Greek Automobile Touring Club, for any technical problems, ☎ 104.

ADDRESS BOOK

**Tourist information – EOT, the Information Bureau of the Greek National Tourism Organisation**, Odós Amerikís 4 (near Sýndagma) (Plan II, D2), ☎ (01) 331 05 61 / 2 / 5. 9am-7pm, Saturday 10am-3pm; closed on Sunday. They can provide a great deal of information not only about Athens, but also regarding all means of transport in Greece (schedules and rates): to the islands, Attica, the Peloponnese and northern Greece. The hostesses are very friendly even though they are often over-burdened with work. Free brochures and three magazines in English containing a wealth of information on cultural life in the city during the summer (performances, concerts, films, etc) are also available.

**Embassies / consulates –**
**United Kingdom**, Odós Ploutárchou 1, 106 75 Athens, ☎ (01) 727 2600, Fax (01) 727 2720, info@athens.mail.fco.gov.uk
**United States**, Leofóros Vassilíssis Sofías 91, 101 60 Athens, ☎ (01) 721 2951.
**Canada**, Odós Ioánnou Gennadíou 4, 115 21 Athens, ☎ (01) 727 3400, Fax (01) 727 3480.
**Australia**, Odós Dimitríou Soútsou 37, ☎ (01) 645 0404, Fax (01) 646 6595, ausembgr@hol.gr

**Cultural centres –**
**British Council**, Platía Kolonáki 17.
**The Hellenic American Union**, Massalías 22.
**The French Institute**, Sína 29 / Massalías 1.

**Travel agencies –** There are many travel agencies in the area between Sýndagma, Filelínon and Pláka. Tickets and schedules for ferryboats to the islands are available, and you can book rooms there.

**Airline companies – Olympic Airways**, Odós Filelínon 15 (Plan III, E2), ☎ (01) 92 67 444 / 92 67 555 / 92 67 663. Arrivals-Departures, ☎ (01) 93 63 363. International flights, ☎ (01) 96 94 111.
**British Airways**, Leofóros Vouliagménis 130, ☎ (01) 89 06 666 / 96 01 444.
**Air France**, Leofóros Vouliagménis 18 (Plan II, C4), ☎ (01) 96 01 100 / 96 01 444, Airport, ☎ (01) 35 30 110.
**Canadian Airlines**, Leofóros Sigroú 7 (Plan II, C4), ☎ (01) 92 12 470.
**Delta**, Odós Óthonos 4 (Plan III, E2), ☎ (01) 33 11 660.
**Swissair**, Odós Óthonos 4 (Plan III, E2), ☎ (01) 33 70 520, Airport, ☎ (01) 35 30 152.
**Sabena**, same telephone number as Swissair.

**Banks / Currency exchange –** There are cash dispensers all over Athens. All the major banks have branches at Sýndagma. Currency exchange bureaux are preferable to banks (closing time: 2pm), which take a higher commission and you might have to wait in line (especially at the National Bank). They are located in areas with many tourists such as Omónia, Monastiráki, Pláka, Sýndagma and the major avenues. **Eurocambio** (on the corner of Akadimías and Sína) offers the best rates with no commission.

**Post offices –** The **Sýndagma branch** (on the corner of Odós Mitropóleos) (Plan III, E2) is open 7am-8pm daily, Saturday 7.30am-2pm, Sunday 9am-1pm. The **Omónia branch** (100 Odós Aiolou) has the same hours.

**Internet –** Athens is full of Internet cafés.
**Gr Net**, on the corner of 28 Oktomvríou and Irakliou, near the National Museum.
**Sky Net Centers**, Odós Apóllonos 10, in Pláka.
**Bytes & Bites**, Odós Akadimías 78 (on the corner of Odós E Benáki).

**Media –** Newspapers and magazines can be purchased at news-stands on Platía Sýndagma and Platía Kolonáki. *Athens News*, the English daily, is available free at the information office.

**Emergencies** – In the event of a problem (health concerns, theft, mugging, accidents, etc) call the **tourist police**, ☎ 171 or **police emergency service**, ☎ 100.
**Emergency medical assistance**, ☎ 166.

**Bookshops** – **Compendium**, Níkis 28. **Elefteroudákis**, Leofóros Panepistimíou 15. The 1st floor has a large section with maps and tourist books (in Greek and English).
**Road Edition**, Odós Ipokrátous 39. This company, which publishes maps – the best – and guidebooks, has a small shop that is well-stocked with tourist literature.

**Laundry** – Launderettes are few and far between in Athens. Try a dry cleaner's ('stegnokatharístria'); some hotels provide this service.

#### WHERE TO STAY

Prices shown are for a double room at peak season including breakfast except where indicated to the contrary. Hotels will lower their rates for stays longer than 2 days. For those on a tight budget, the youth hostel is about the only place in Athens where you can stay for under €23; but it is usually taken by storm, and finding a bed there is a rare occurrence indeed. The best areas to stay in – combining a lively atmosphere, good facilities, and a practical location for getting to the major sites – are Pláka, Monastiráki and Eólou (very central and full of shops), Thissío and Exárhia (very lively in the evening, although a bit out of the way). Kolonáki is the most chic area.

• **Pláka** (Plan III)

*Between €25 and €30*
**Phaedra**, Odós Herefóndos 16, on the corner of Odós Lissicrátous, ☎ (01) 32 27 795 / 32 38 461 – 21rm. 🖋 ⚓ Shared showers, supplement for breakfast. Across from beautiful Agía Ekateríni Church. What this little hotel lacks in comfort is made up for by its location in the heart of Pláka.
**Dioskouri**, Odós Pitakoú 6, ☎ (01) 32 48 165 – 20rm. 🖋 ⚓ An old building with a worn-out façade, run

by an English-speaking couple. Youth hostel atmosphere, with a pretty inner courtyard full of flowers.

*Between €30 and €45*
**Kimon**, Odós Apóllonos 17, ☎ (01) 33 14 658 – 13rm. 🖋 🖋 ⚓ ⚓ The entrance isn't much to look at, but the rooms are decent and it has a pretty terrace with a view of the Acropolis.

*Between €60 and €75*
☺ **Adonis**, Odós Kódrou 3, ☎ (01) 32 49 737 / 32 49 741, Fax (01) 32 31 602 – 27rm. 🖋 ⚓ 📧 TV CC Extremely well-situated in the heart of Pláka, this handsome, comfortable hotel has all the amenities and very reasonable prices. Superb view of the Acropolis from its terrace, which has a little bar for a drink in the evening. Excellent value for money, and if you do without air conditioning they knock off €9.

☺ **Acropolis House**, Odós Kódrou 6-8, ☎ (01) 32 22 344 / 32 26 241, Fax (01) 32 44 143 – 19rm. 🖋 ⚓ 📧 TV CC This charming hotel (with antique furniture and murals) has all the modern comforts in a pretty, neo-Classical house. The proprietors are very welcoming. You can save €15 by doing without air conditioning.

**Aphrodite**, Odós Apóllonos 21, ☎ (01) 32 34 357-9, Fax (01) 32 25 244 – 84rm. 🖋 ⚓ 📧 CC The decor in this modern hotel is a bit dreary (the terrace could really do with some sprucing up), but the rooms are better than the 1970s-style marble lobby. Still, this establishment in the Pláka is good value for money.

**Ómiros**, Odós Apóllonos 15, ☎ (01) 32 35 486-7, Fax (01) 32 28 059 – 37rm. 🖋 ⚓ 📧 TV ⚓ CC This modern hotel is not particularly attractive, but it is comfortable. The terrace is a pleasant place to have breakfast.
**Nefeli**, Odós Iperídou 16, ☎ (01) 322 80 44-5, Fax (01) 322 58 00 – 18rm. 🖋 ⚓ 📧 CC Very well-situated on a quiet street in Pláka across from a beautiful (and, unfortunately, highly damaged) neo-Classical home. This pleasant little hotel has recently installed air conditioning and has consequently raised its prices a bit too much.

Athens

**Adrian**, Odós Adrianoú 74, ☎ (01) 32 21 553 / 32 50 454, Fax (01) 32 50 461 – 22rm. ♪ ⁿ⌂ 📧 TV 🍴 CC
In the heart of Pláka a few metres from the Tower of the Winds, this is another small hotel with impeccable comforts and a really beautiful shady terrace from which you can see the Erechtheion. The interior decoration is quite elegant. Ask for a room on the other side of the building.

*Between €75 and €90*

**Austria**, Odós Moussón 7 (Plan II), at the foot of Filopápos Hill, ☎ (01) 92 35 151-3, Fax (01) 92 47 350, austria@hol.gr – 37rm. ♪ ⁿ⌂ 📧 TV 🍴 CC A fine hotel located in one of the quietest areas in the city. Terrace and balconies with views of the Acropolis.

**Lycabette**, Odós Valaorítou 6 (Plan II), ☎ (01) 36 33 514-7, Fax (01) 36 33 518 – 39rm. ♪ ⁿ⌂ 📧 TV ✕ 🍴 CC In a quiet pedestrian street nestled between Stadíou and Panepistimíou. This clean and comfortable establishment above the elegant Florian café has rooms with balconies. Good value for money.

**Pláka**, Odós Kapnikaréas 7, ☎ (01) 32 22 096-8, Fax (01) 32 22 412, rofos@ath.forthnet.gr – 67rm. ♪ ⁿ⌂ 📧 TV ✕ 🍴 CC Comfortable and attractively decorated rooms. The ones facing the Acropolis are naturally more in demand. If they are already taken, try to get the price lowered a bit. There is always the terrace for the view.

**Byron**, Odós Víronos 19, ☎ (01) 32 30 327 / 32 53 554, Fax (01) 32 20 276 – 22rm. ♪ ⁿ⌂ 📧 🍴 CC This is one of the oldest buildings on the street, which says a lot. Fortunately, this hotel has recently been modernised so you will find all the comforts here, as well as a friendly welcome. From the terrace there is a view of the southern slope of the Acropolis and the roofs of Pláka.

**Hermes**, Odós Apóllonos 19, ☎ (01) 32 35 514, Fax (01) 32 32 073 – 45rm. ♪ ⁿ⌂ 📧 TV ✕ CC It's a pity this modern hotel doesn't have a terrace. But its rooms are large and all have balconies, some the size of verandas. This comfortable hotel – with all the amenities and well-kept communal areas – also doubles as a travel agency.

• **Athinás, Eólou, Monastiráki** (Plan III)

*Around €33*

**Témpi**, Odós Eólou 29, ☎ (01) 32 13 175 / 32 42 940, Fax (01) 32 54 179, tempihotel@travelling.gr – 24rm. ♪ ⁿ⌂ ✈ Very well-situated on Eólou, a traffic-free street at the entrance to Pláka, near Agía Iríni Church, an area that is quiet in the evening and lively during the day. Modest, but with a warm welcome; and there's a laundry in the hotel. Breakfast not served.

**Pella Inn**, Odós Ermoú 104, ☎ (01) 32 50 598 / 32 12 229 – 21rm. ♪ ⁿ⌂ ✈ 🍴 Hidden behind the construction work on the metro, this is a small, backpacker-style hotel with an outdated and gaudy decor. Modest comforts and reasonably clean. Ask for a room on Odós Karaïskáki, as Ermoú is noisy in the evening. They also offer services such as money deposits and a travel agency.

*Around €53*

**Attalós**, Odós Athinás 29, ☎ (01) 32 12 801-3, Fax (01) 32 43 124, atthot@hol.gr – 80rm. ♪ ⁿ⌂ 📧 TV CC Lovely rooftop terrace. At the beginning of Athinás just next to Monastiráki (a noisy, but very lively, area). Clean and comfortable. View of the Acropolis from the balconies.

⊛ **Cecil**, Odós Athinás 39, ☎ and Fax (01) 32 17 079 / 32 18 005 / 32 19 606 – 40rm. ♪ ⁿ⌂ 📧 🍴 CC This hotel in a beautiful neo-Classical building was recently renovated. The rooms, which have wooden floors, are charming, some noisier than others (ask for one on the little corner street). Warm welcome.

• **Thissío** (Plan III)

*Around €38*

**Erechtheion**, Odós Flamarion 8 on the corner of Odós Agías Marínas (Plan II), ☎ (01) 34 59 606 / 34 59 626, Fax (01) 34 62 756 – 22rm. ♪ ⁿ⌂ 📧 TV 🍴 A stone's throw from Agía Marína Church and the Observatory, on a very quiet street. Run by two very friendly ladies, this hotel has preserved its 1960s decor; but the rooms are clean and comfortable, and very quiet. It's a pity the terrace isn't really useable.

**Thissío**, Odós Apostólou Pávlou 25 on the corner of Odós Agías Marínas, ☎ (01) 34 67 634 / 34 67 655, Fax (01) 34 62 756 – 18rm. ✐ ⁿ⌐ ▤ ✈ ✗ ⇧ CC This building, a bit more modern than the previous one, is from the 1970s. The rooms are clean and comfortable, but the air conditioning is old and sometimes just as noisy as Odós Apostólou Pávlou. Pretty terrace. Good value for money.

*Around €55*

**Jason Inn**, Odós Assomáton 12, ☎ (01) 32 51 106, Fax (01) 32 43 132 – 57rm. ✐ ⁿ⌐ ▤ TV ✗ CC Right near the Agora and across from Keramikós, this modern hotel has every possible comfort at affordable prices. While standard, the decor is not lacking in taste. Every room has its own balcony.

• **Omónia, Exárhia** (Plan II)

Omónia and the area around the two railway stations is the cheapest part of Athens, but it is noisy. The lively nightlife in Exárhia is a particular attraction.

*Around €18*

**Youth Hostel Victor Hugo**, Odós Victoros Hugo 16, ☎ (01) 52 34 170, Fax (01) 52 34 015 – 138rm (2-4 people). A fairly recent (1994) and well-kept youth hostel. Rooms are light and soundproofed, with or without bathroom. Safes and lock-up cupboards, left-luggage lockers, communal kitchen. Breakfast is not served, but the hostel is expanding to include more services. A very good place, but it is often full.

*Around €27*

**Orion**, Odós Dryádon 4 (the first steep little street on the left after the intersection of Odós Benáki and Odós Kalidromíou), 25min from Pláka, ☎ (01) 38 27 362 / 38 20 191 / 38 27 116, Fax (01) 380 51 93 – 20rm. ✐ ✈ ⇧ While a bit out of the way, this establishment and the neighbouring Dryádes (see below) are worth mentioning. Built on a slope on the edge of little Strefi Park, they overlook the pleasant Exárhia district (cafés, bars and tavernas). Friendly welcome and 'glamorous' atmosphere (models of both sexes like to stay in both hotels). In both cases, avoid the rooms overlooking the neighbouring

basketball court, which gets noisy in the evening. The Orion has one shower for 2 rooms. They are clean and quiet, and some have lovely views.

*Between €45 and €55*

**Dryádes**, next to the previous hotel – 15rm. ✐ ⁿ⌐ ✈ ⇧ The same address and management as the Orion, but more comfortable. Try to get one of the 3 rooms on the top floor, which have magnificent views.

**Athinéa**, Odós Vilará 9, 5min from Platía Omónia and 15min from Pláka, ☎ (01) 52 43 884-5 / 52 45 737 – 42rm. ✐ ⁿ⌐ ▤ TV ✗ ⇧ CC This modern hotel is clean and comfortable, and is located on a quiet pedestrian street lined with cafés near the large Church of Ágios Konstandínos. Excellent value for money.

• **Kolonáki** (Plan II)

*Around €68*

⌂ **Athenian Inn**, Háritos 22, 10min from Pláka, ☎ (01) 72 38 097 / 72 39 552 / 72 18 756, Fax (01) 72 42 268 – 28rm. ✐ ⁿ⌐ ▤ CC In the heart of the chic Kolonáki district in a quiet street lined with shops, near the museums. The end of Odós Háritos is pedestrian (bars and an open-air cinema). This is a very comfortable little family hotel with well-designed decor (works by Greek painters) and a high standard of service. Laurence Durrell, the English writer who was a great connoisseur of Greece, is said to have stayed in this hotel whenever he was in Athens.

• **Koukáki** (Plan II)

*Around €43*

**Tony's**, Zaharísta 26, ☎ (01) 92 36 370 / 92 30 561 / 92 35 761 – 13rm. ✐ ⁿ⌐ ⇧ Breakfast not served. The rooms are clean and relatively comfortable, some with balconies.

⌂ **Marble House**, a cul-de-sac off Odós Zini, between Odós Dimitrakopoúlou and Odós Androútsou, ☎ (01) 92 34 058 / 92 26 461 – 8rm: ✐ ⁿ⌐ ▤ ⇧ CC 6rm: ✐ ⁿ⌐ ✈ ⇧ CC 6rm: ✐ ✈ ⇧ CC Depending on the category: €45, €40 and €33. A recent building at the end of a quiet alley. A large bougainvillaea brightens up the marble façade, and the decor inside is simple but elegant. Pretty terrace. Extra charge for breakfast.

**Athens**

*Around €53*

☕ **Art Gallery**, Odós Erehthíou 5, ☎ (01) 92 38 376 / 92 31 933, Fax (01) 92 33 025 – 21rm. ♫ ⁿ⁄ 🌂 Very near Pláka, but in an area that has its own charm thanks to the cafés and restaurants on Platía Gargarettas. In a fine house from the late 19C that belongs to an artist whose paintings adorn the walls. Remodelled by architects, the hotel has a simple but elegant decor with wooden floors. Warm welcome, pretty terrace for breakfast or for a drink in the evening. Dry cleaning service.

*Around €88*

**Hera**, Odós Fálirou 9, ☎ (01) 92 36 682 / 92 35 618, Fax (01) 92 47 334, hhera@hol.gr – 49rm. ♫ ⁿ⁄ 📋 TV ✕ 🌂 CC In the Makrigiáni district near the Acropolis and Pláka, this modern hotel has a terrace with a view of the Acropolis, lounges, and a pleasant bar and patio, in addition to the usual comforts for this category. The reception is quite friendly for an establishment of this standing.

**EATING OUT**

Depending on your appetite, you can pick a restaurant ('estiatório') or taverna, which serve traditional Greek dishes, or an ouzo bar (or 'mezedopolío') if you feel like snacking on meze. To help you make your culinary choices, see the chapter on Greek cuisine, page 89. Tavernas not catering to tourists are usually closed for lunch.

● **Kolonáki area** (Plan II)

*Under €12*

**Rozia**, Odós Aristípou 44 (E2). Closed on Sunday. This taverna serves simple, delicious food in a cool garden at the foot of Lycabettos.

**Rozalia**, Odós Valtetsíou 58 (E2). Open for lunch. This taverna frequented by regulars serves simple and very inexpensive dishes in a little courtyard beneath a leafy arbour. Choose your food inside and try the house rosé which is quite decent.

☕ **Athinaïkón**, Odós Themistokléous 2 (C2). Mezedopolío. Open for lunch. A pleasant air-conditioned room with traditional white marble tables. This is an ideal place to spend the hot early hours of the afternoon in a typically Athenian atmosphere.

**Andréas kai Yiós**, Odós Themistokléous 18 (C2) (in a cul-de-sac on the right). Mezedopolío. Open for lunch, closed on Sunday. It doesn't look like much, but they have delicious fish meze with ouzo or white wine to accompany them.

☕ **Dexaméni**, Platía Dexaméni (D2). Ouzo bar. Open for lunch. People come here at all hours to have a chat while snacking on a salad and some meze, or to quench their thirst with a cool beer under the shade of the trees lining the street; the atmosphere feels a bit like being out in the country.

*Around €23*

☕ **47 Maritsa's**, Odós Voukourestíou 47 (D2). Mezedopolío. Air-conditioned room and outdoor tables (very pleasant in the evening). Don't let the rather starchy look of the place put you off. The meze have an incomparable flavour. A simple plate of steamed courgettes with a dash of olive oil and a few drops of lemon juice can make a great dish, especially when it is accompanied by bits of grilled octopus.

● **Gázi** (Plan II)

*Between €12 and €15*

**Mamacas**, Odós Persefónis 41 (A2). Open for lunch. Venture into the Gázi district lined with old houses and enjoy some 'traditional nouvelle cuisine' there. In other words, Greek flavours with a touch of the exotic. This restaurant is located in a charming all-white little house with tables in the shade in front. Try the meatballs in cumin and tomato sauce.

**Kallixorou**, Odós Persefónis 31 (A2). This restaurant in a pretty pink-coloured house – with a decor that is both modern and rustic – offers a wide range of appetisers to get you started and some tasty dishes to complete your meal. Have dinner on the terrace in the evening.

● **Pláka** (Plan III)

*Under €11*

**Plátanos**, Odós Diogénous 4 (C2). Closed on Sunday, open for lunch. In the shade of a eucalyptus tree, a vine arbour and a plane tree, and a stone's throw from the Tower of the Winds. Platanos taverna is an old Pláka classic. Try the tasty moussaká with a salad and a refreshing beer in this delightful setting.

**Tripódon**, Odós Tripódon 14 (D3). Ouzo bar. Open for lunch. The two ladies of the house serve a wide assortment of meze on large platters – from which you choose the dishes you want – under a delightful pergola shaded by vines.

**Tó Kafenío**, Odós Epiharmou (D3), just beyond the previous establishment. Closed for lunch. The tables are set out on both sides of a pretty little street in Pláka with a charming neighbourhood atmosphere. Some good, simple dishes including fried aubergines ('melidzánes'), tzatzíki, 'saganáki' (cooked slice of cheese), 'keftedákia' (meatballs), and salad.

**Xinou**, Odós Angélou Gérondas 4 (D3). Taverna. Another Pláka 'classic', because of its garden and its moussaká, its spaghetti and meatballs lightly flavoured with cinnamon and its nostalgic music (in the evening).

**Glikis**, Odós Angélou Gérondas 2 (D3). Ouzo bar. Open for lunch. Choose between the 'pikilía' (assortment) for one, two or three people, or twenty or so meze. Covered in vines, the pergola is probably one of the most attractive in Pláka.

*Between €12 and €15*

🐌 **Tou Psará**, Odós Erehthéos 16 and Odós Erotókritou 12 (C3). Open for lunch. Located on a little square where several streets cross, the oldest taverna in Pláka has a charming setting and delicious food (don't miss the meat with sauce). Take time to mull over the abundant menu. One of the best places in Pláka.

**Kafé Avissinia**, Platía Avissinías. Mezedopolío (B1). For lunch. The inside is a bit like an old Parisian bistro. The owner brings out his tables as the antique dealers put away their wares. Excellent meze, and the rice pilaf with mussels won't disappoint you.

*Under €20*

**Dionysos**, Odós Rovértou Gáli 43 (B4). Restaurant. Terrace or air-conditioned room. Alongside its international menu (hence the tour buses parked all around), this restaurant has a solid reputation for Greek gastronomy. This is the place to taste some real 'dolmádes', light 'pítes' (flaky-pastry pies) and a deliciously oriental baklava.

● **Exárhia** (Plan II, D1)

*Under €11*

**Lefká**, Odós Mavromiháli 121. Closed on Sunday. A courtyard and a few huge wine casks make up the decor in this unpretentious taverna where the food is simple (salads, a few starters and grilled meats) and inexpensive.

**Ama Lahi**, Odós Kalidromíou 71 or Odós Methónis 66. Taverna. A neo-Classical house with a large, shady courtyard giving onto two streets. Try the 'moshári stamnáto', a tasty beef stew. This pleasantly cool place makes you want to linger, especially since the neighbouring bars are so inviting.

🐌 **Bárba Iánnis**, Odós E Benáki 94. Open for lunch. A taverna with tables set out on a pedestrian street in the heart of the Exárhia district. Try one of the cuts of meat with sauce and a good salad washed down with some retsína (on sale downstairs).

*Between €12 and €15*

**Stréfis to Stéki tis Xánthis**, Odós Irínis Athinéas 5, on the corner of Odós Poulherías. Closed on Sunday. A magnificent flower-decked terrace crowns this pretty neo-Classical house located at the foot of Stréfi Hill. An ideal place for a tête-à-tête, where taverna fare with a slightly more sophisticated touch is served.

● **Psirí**

*Under €12*

🐌 **Platía Iróon**, Platía Iróon 1 (Plan III, B1). Mezedopolío. In the heart of this old Athens neighbourhood where the evenings are lively. Tables on the square. For anyone who wants to learn about meze, the menu theoretically has 250 varieties! The service can be a bit slow, but it's worth it.

🐌 **Náxos**, Odós Christokopídou, next to the church (Plan III, B1). Mezedopolío. Open for lunch. Delicious grilled, fried or marinated fish meze. Psirí atmosphere, although a bit out of the way.

**Telys**, Odós Evripídou 86 (Plan II, B2). Closed on Sunday, open for lunch. Specialises in charcoal-grilled meats. Aside from a few salads and fries, the only fare is chops, rib steak, mutton, beef or pork fillet. A very inexpensive taverna.

• **Pagrati** (Plan II, D4)

*Around €9*

**Karavitis**, on the corner of Odós Arktinou and Odós Pafsanía, 5min from the stadium. This taverna – an institution – has 2 addresses: a winter one, and a summer one in a courtyard with a vine arbour, a very pleasant place to have something from the grill.

### HAVING A DRINK

July and August are not the best months for exploring Athens' night-life, because the numerous cabarets, theatres, cinemas, and many bars are closed. Apart from air-conditioned places, which aren't very pleasant in the evening, the only establishments that remain open are those with an outside area.

**Cafés, bars** – There is a semblance of activity around the large and small terrace cafés on Odós Tsakálof and Platía Filikís Etairías in Kolonáki, but the neighbourhood is quite deserted between 1 and 20 August. The most lively spots are the big cafés on Odós Iraklídon (pedestrian) and Odós Nileos in Psirí and Thissío:

**Clepsídra**, a small, intimate terrace on the corner of Odós Thrassívoulou and Odós Clepsídras (Plan III, C3), offers a welcome halt after exploring the Aérides quarter.

**Níkis**, Odós Níkis (Plan III, E2), a small street perpendicular to long Odós Ermoú. A little café for regulars with a few tables on the pavement, very near the many shops on Ermoú, but still quiet. Ideal for a coffee break. It has good music (jazz, Cuban, etc), a wood decor, and is unpretentious and very pleasant.

**Stavlos**, Odós Iraklídon 10, Thissío (Plan II, B3), a bar-restaurant with an exhibition area in a very beautiful old home.

**Tango**, Odós Anargíron 21-23, in Psirí (Plan II, B2). Pleasant bar that is also a restaurant.

**Dío epí Tría** ('2x3'), Odós N Apostóli, in Pláka (Plan III, B1), at the beginning of Odós Adrianoú. This place by the railway tracks is very pleasant in the evening.

In Exárhia (Plan II, C1-D1), there is a pleasant atmosphere in the cafés on Platía Exarhíon and in the bars on Odós Kalidromíou, in particular at **Mílos** and across the street at **55**, as well as at **Kalidromíou** (on the corner of the street of the same name and Odós Zossimadon).

**Open-air cinemas** – Open-air cinemas are naturally made for watching films, but a sandwich and a beer or a soft drink are all part of the experience, as is the break in the middle of the film (your chance to get another beer, soft drink...). And it's also an opportunity to see an old classic or a film from last year. In Greece, films are sub-titled in Greek, but never dubbed. The sound is usually not as loud for the second showing, for the neighbours' sake; so don't sit too far from the speakers. The programme for the cinemas is listed in Athens News (in English).

⚐ **Dexaméni**, Platía Dexaméni, Kolonáki (Plan II, A4). With its 2 bars, this is undoubtedly one of the nicest places in Athens. The sound is quite loud, except when the security team of the Prime Minister, who lives next door, makes it known that he would like to get some rest.

**Thissíon**, Odós Apostólou Pávlou 7 (Plan III, A3). Chairs with cushions, a view of the Acropolis and many cafés nearby where you can discuss the films afterwards.

**Ciné Paris**, Platía Filomoússou Etairías. On a terrace in the heart of Pláka. Photos from old films on sale at the entrance.

⚐ **Cine Psirí**, Odós Sarí 40-44, Psirí (Plan II, B2). The best screening conditions in one of the oldest areas of Athens.

### OTHER THINGS TO DO

**Athens Festival Office**, Odós Stadíou 4 (near Sýndagma) (Plan II, C2), in the Spyromilíou gallery, ☎ (01) 32 21 459. For information about performances at the Odeon of Herodes Atticus and Lycabettos, and about the Pnyx son et lumière show. Monday-Friday 9am-3pm, Saturday 9am-2pm.

**Son et lumière** – At the Pnyx site, every evening at 9pm. For information, contact the above-mentioned festival office. Shows in all languages.

**Traditional dancing** – *Dóra Strátou Theatre*, information available at: Odós Scholíou 8, in Pláka. Traditional Greek dance performances are held every night except Monday at 10.15pm on Filopápos Hill (main entrance on Platía Apoloníou in Koukáki). Additional performances at 8.15pm on Wednesday and Sunday.

### SHOPPING GUIDE

**Miscellaneous** – For classic souvenirs, go to Pláka where they have copies of everything ever produced by Greek civilisation from the Age of Pericles to modern times – from plaster statuettes of Athena to kombolóï (worry beads), not to mention natural sponges and the inescapable T-shirts. In the same vein, but much more chic, are the *reproductions of antiquities* from the capital's major museums. For the best deals, buy them straight from the workshop that supplies the museums... and sells them at better prices: *Arionas*, Odós G Drossini 19, Ilioúpoli, a 20min drive from the centre of Athens.

**Second-hand / flea market** – In the area around Odós Ermoú there are timeless shops where the standard items on sale, which haven't changed since 1880, now amount to second-hand goods. Hunt around at the flea market too, or in the shops in *Monastiráki*, where you might find a 'bríki', a little pot for making Greek coffee, a storm lantern, or a fine brass church censer.

**Culinary specialities** – In desperation you can also fall back on ouzo (the best brands are, among others, Barbayiánni, Plomario, Mini and Babatzim) and pistachios from Égina.

Athens

Polluted and overheated Piraeus (*Pireás*) (Plan I) is not exactly a resort destination. So you will most likely only go there if your boat to the islands casts off early in the morning, or if you get back to town late at night and don't want to go back to Athens before your flight takes off. Piraeus has three harbours: the **main harbour**, right by the metro station, where ferries leave for the islands; **Zéa Marina** reserved for hydrofoils, and **Mikrolímano**, a small sailing harbour that is very lively in the evenings.

### COMING AND GOING

**By bus – Coming from Athens**: from Sýndagma, take green bus no 40, which leaves every 15min, from 5am to midnight. Get off at Platía Grivas before the last stop (count on a 30min trip, more at rush hour). From Omónia: take bus no 49, get off at Platía Themostokléous in Piraeus, on the left as you come out of the metro station.

**Coming from the airport:** an express shuttle bus runs 24 hours a day. Get off at the 'Harbour' stop (approx 1hr).

**To go to the airport**: take the same bus from Platía Karaïskáki a few hundred metres on the left as you come out of the metro station. From the Piraeus metro station to Zéa Marina, take bus no 905 or trolleybus no 20.

**By metro –** Piraeus is the southern terminus for the Kifissiá-Piraeus line. Trains leave every 10min from 5am to midnight. (Count on a 20min trip from Monastiráki, 25min from Omónia.)

**By train –** Piraeus has 2 stations: **Peloponnese Station**, just to the right as you come out of the metro station, ☎ (01) 41 78 335, only serving cities on the peninsula, and the **station for northern Greece (Lárissa)**, across from the metro on the other side of the basin (go around the latter on the right), ☎ (01) 46 12 734.

**By taxi –** Ask the price of a trip before getting into a taxi (€15 on average to go to the centre of Athens). **To reserve by telephone**, ☎ (01) 41 35 888 / 49 33 811 / 41 15 200.

### GOING TO THE ISLANDS

Information about boat schedules is available at the **Piraeus main harbour police**, ☎ (01) 42 26 000, and for hydrofoils at **Zéa Marina**, ☎ (01) 45 25 315. Also on the Internet at www.gtpnet.com Tickets can be bought at the same price in any agency in the harbour, where they will tell you the name of the boat and the quay.

**Ferries –** When taking a taxi to the main harbour in Piraeus (where the ferries leave from), tell the driver which island you are going to so that he can drop you off at the appropriate quay. When arriving by metro, the quays (or 'Gates') on your right are, successively, B, A, then H; on the left is quay G, just next to the metro, then quays D and E.

These are the main destinations and names of the corresponding quays: A and B for islands in the North Aegean (Chios, Lesbos, Ikaría, Sámos); E for the Dodecanese Islands; G and E for the Saronic Gulf; A for Crete; B for the Cyclades (Kíthnos, Sérifos, Sífnos, Kímolos, Mílos, Astipálea, Folégandros); G and D for Síros, Mýkonos, Íos, Tínos, Santoríni, Irárklia, Schinoússa, Koufoníssi, Amorgós, Donoússa; G for Páros and Náxos.

**Hydrofoils –** They leave from Zéa Marina, except for the ones to Égina, which cast off from the main harbour of Piraeus.

### ADDRESS BOOK

**Banks / Currency exchange –** There are several banks (with cash dispensers) along the harbour: **National Bank** and **Eurobank** on the right as you come out of the metro, **Western Union** on the left.

**Post office –** ☎ (01) 41 71 584.

**Police –** Main harbour branch, ☎ (01) 42 26 000.

**Medical service – Hospital**, ☎ (01) 49 15 061.

### WHERE TO STAY

All the hotels in Piraeus are expensive, so those on a tight budget will have to stay in the capital. Choose your hotel based on its proximity to your embarkation quay, or because they agree to drive you to your boat, an invaluable service when you are loaded down with luggage. Do not blindly follow one of the young people waving brochures who advertise hotels at the metro exit. First ask them to show you on a map exactly how close the hotel is to your embarkation quay, and where the nearest bus stop is.

### • Piraeus Harbour

*€45*

**Eva**, Odós Notará 2, ☎ (01) 41 70 110, Fax (01) 41 70 350 – 🖉 📶 🗏 TV This hotel, which opened in the spring of 1999, is one of the most pleasant in Piraeus. The rooms are small, but comfortable and attractively decorated. The quietest ones are on the 6th floor. The only drawback is that breakfast is not served, and the closest café is three streets away.

**Zacharatos**, on the corner of Odós Notará and Odós Evangelístrias, ☎ (01) 41 78 830 – 59rm. 🖉 📶 🗏 ✕ TV Just across from the Hotel Eva, this older establishment is still clean and comfortable. There is always a fan to take over when the air conditioning gives out.

*Around €60*

**Anita-Argo**, Odós Notará 23-25, ☎ (01) 41 21 795, Fax (01) 41 22 420 – 57rm. 📶 🗏 TV This hotel behind the metro station in a dark but quiet little street is neither particularly cheery nor too well swept. They take you by minibus to the harbour, and even to the airport.

**Poseidónio**, Odós Chariláou Trikoúpi 3, ☎ (01) 42 86 651, Fax (01) 42 99 220 – 54rm. 🖉 📶 🗏 TV CC Although a bit far from the harbour, this clean and recently renovated 10-storey building has comfortable rooms with good facilities (hair dryer, mini-bar, etc). While it doesn't have a restaurant, guests can have cooked meals delivered.

**Noufara**, Odós Iróon Polytehníou 45, ☎ (01) 41 15 541, Fax (01) 41 34 292 – 84rm. 🖉 📶 🗏 TV CC As comfortable as the Poseidónio (which belongs to the same owner), this modern hotel has the advantage of being closer to the harbour, and thus easier for those planning to take a boat.

*Between €60 and €98*

**The Park**, Odós Kolokotróni 103, ☎ (01) 45 24 611, Fax (01) 45 24 615 – 80rm. 🖉 📶 🗏 TV ✕ 🍴 CC This hotel, usually frequented by businessmen and less than a 10min walk from the harbour, is a comfortable place to stay in the midst of the furnace of Piraeus. The flower-decked terrace crowning the building is quite delightful for breakfast too (continental or buffet). Nearly all of the rooms have a balcony, and 24 of them also have saunas.

### • Zéa Marina (Passalimáni)

*Between €57 and €60*

**Lilia**, Odós Zéas 131, ☎ (01) 41 79 108, Fax (01) 41 14 311 – 20rm. 🖉 📶 🗏 TV CC This small and quiet hotel in a pretty little street overlooks Zéa Marina, which is more elegant and lively in the evening than Piraeus harbour. Ask for a room overlooking the street (the others give onto a wall). Upon request, a free shuttle service will take you from the hotel to the harbour (in the morning) and from the harbour to the hotel (in the afternoon) if your schedule coincides.

### EATING OUT

It isn't easy to find a good restaurant in Piraeus when you're only passing through for one evening. The best establishments are only known to locals and are too far to reach on foot from the seafront. What is left along the harbour are fast-food joints and the usual greasy spoons with their paper tablecloths. However, there are a few pleasant surprises in the adjoining streets, mostly in the area around the municipal theatre. To get there from the main harbour, turn left when facing the seafront and follow Aktí Posidónios. Go past Holy Trinity Cathedral and continue down Leofóros Vas Giórgou for 100m until you reach the theatre, which stands on top of a flight of steps. Just behind it is a charming square full of cafés and tavernas where you can rest in a (nearly) cool place. Stay away from the tourist restaurants along Mikrolímano harbour, which are expensive and often dreadful.

## • Around Zéa Marina (Passalimáni)

*Between €7.50 and €9*

**To palió tis katsikis**, Odós Ipsilándou. This old taverna, which has been remodelled, is directly opposite the Olympiakos shop (a good spot for football souvenir-hunters). It's the kind of place where you go into the kitchen to choose your dinner and then enjoy it while watching the news on TV.

**Tá ennéa Adélphia** ('the 9 brothers'), Odós Sotíros. From Zéa Marina, go up Odós Lambrákis as far as the first street on the right. The taverna is hidden behind the trees on a little square. This institution, a local favourite, has a wide variety of well-cooked traditional Greek dishes to choose from. Its specialities include a perfectly tender veal with onions and delicious stuffed aubergines.

*Around €23*

**Pétrino**, on the corner of Odós Merahias and Odós Ipsilándou, ☎ (01) 89 45 861. Local people are very fond of this restaurant. Its fanciful decor (stone walls covered with photographs of famous people, an overdone ceiling, artificial flowers, etc) is matched by its interesting menu featuring a variety of Greek dishes, abundant meze and delicious desserts (on the house). As for the service, it is fast and friendly.

### HAVING A DRINK

If you are spending an evening in Piraeus, stay away from the harbour which is frankly rather grim at night. Head for the centre of town around the municipal theatre, or Zéa Marina (near the metro, bus no 905 or yellow trolleybus no 20). You could also take a taxi to delightful little **Mikrolímano harbour** where most of the town's trendy bars are located. Techno atmosphere guaranteed.

All aboard for the islands (Piraeus)

B. Pérousse/MICHELIN

The Saronic Gulf Islands on Athens' doorstep (Póros)

# THE SARONIC
# GULF ISLANDS

Just a few miles from the furnace of Athens a small chain of islands – also known as the **Argo-Saronics** on account of the proximity of the Argolid Peninsula – is generally thought of as a floating paradise. Whether rocky or covered in forest, the islands provide enough beaches, night-life and romantically charming ruins to entertain and inspire visitors. Hardly surprising then that Greeks from the capital rush there every weekend, or that when summer arrives, holidaymakers disembark in droves to spend an hour, a day, or more as the feeling takes them. Each island has its own history and personality. Nothing remains of the ancient past of Salamína, opposite Piraeus, as time and dismal housing estates have wiped out all trace. So there's no point looking for any vestiges of the naval battle that took place between the Greek and Persian fleets in 480 BC. On the other hand, the larger and greener island of **Égina** has managed to make something out of its historic heritage. This includes the neo-Classical houses around the harbour – reminders of the time when the island was the first capital of newly-free Greece in 1828 – and above all the Temple of Aphaia, one of the country's finest, rising impressively among the pines. **Póros**, with its Temple of Poseidon, lies only a short distance from the mainland. It is a more easily accessible island but is less well known. Only its little harbour, which could almost come from the Cyclades, fleetingly attracts passing tourists. Lastly, **Hydra** and **Spétses** are fashionable resorts popular with the international jet set. Tourism came late to these islands. For centuries they were inhabited by goats and pirates, and only began to develop in the 18C when their shipowners, who had become rich through shipbuilding and trade, engaged their merchant fleet in activities against the occupying Turks. While the shipping merchants' deeds are still celebrated as high points in Greek history, their lovely mansions or *archontiká* are today let out to well-to-do holidaymakers.

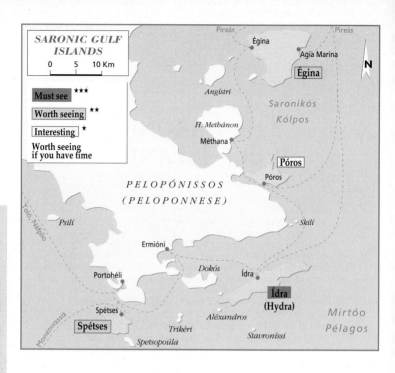

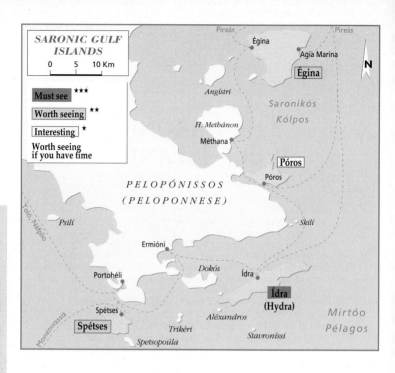

Map: SARONIC GULF ISLANDS — with legend:
Must see ***
Worth seeing **
Interesting *
Worth seeing if you have time

0    5    10 Km

Labels on map: Pireás, Égina, Agía Marína, Égina, Angístri, Saronikós Kólpos, H. Methánon, Méthana, Póros, Póros, PELOPÓNISSOS (PELOPONNESE), Psilí, Toló, Náfplio, Ermióni, Skilí, Dokós, Portohéli, Ídra, Ídra (Hydra), Spétses, Aléxandros, Mirtóo Pélagos, Spétses, Trikéri, Stavroníssi, Spetsopoúla, Monemvassía

## The Saronic Gulf

---

## Making the most of the Saronic Gulf

### COMING AND GOING

The Saronic Gulf Islands are very well served by a fleet of boats that link them to Athens at all times. Day cruises are also organised by all the travel agents in Athens.

**By ferry** – Starting at 7am, ferries leave on the hour from Piraeus harbour (Piraeus metro station). The crossing takes 90min for Égina, 2hr30min for Póros, 3hr for Hydra, and 5hr for Spétses.

**By hydrofoil** – Hydrofoils are more expensive than ferries, but faster. The crossing takes only 35min for Égina, 1hr for Póros, 90min for Hydra and 2hr30min for Spétses. Bear in mind that not all hydrofoils leave from the same

harbour. Those serving Égina collect passengers from **Piraeus**, near the dock for ferries to the islands. For Póros, Hydra and Spétses, hydrofoils leave from **Zéa Marina**, 3km west of Piraeus. To get there, take either a taxi, or bus no 904 or 905, on the left as you come out of Piraeus metro station. Before leaving, or on reaching your destination, it is best to check the return times for Athens to avoid disappointment.

**By caique** – Regular services provide links between the mainland and three of the islands. There are caiques between Póros and Galatás (very close, every 10min), Hydra and Portohéli, and Spétses and Kósta.

# ÉGINA ★★

Saronic Gulf – District of Attica – Michelin map 980 fold 30
83km² – Pop 11 639 – Allow 2 days

**Not to be missed**
The Temple of Aphaia.
Égina Town harbour and the Temple of Apollo.

**And remember...**
If you only have a few hours, take a bus or taxi straight to the Temple of Aphaia,
then return to Égina harbour for a meal.

Famous since Antiquity for its Temple of Aphaia, one of the finest in the Hellenic world – and one of the best preserved – Égina is a must for archaeology lovers. A mere 35min from Piraeus, it is also one of the green suburbs of the capital, where houses belonging to Athenians have sprung up like mushrooms in the shade of pines and pistachio trees. As a result of the exodus from the city, the hydrofoils look like suburban trains packed with commuting business people, and Égina Town, which was the first capital of free Greece in 1828, is stormed every weekend by Athenians seeking cooler temperatures.

## Pistachio paradise
Égina enjoys a dry and particularly mild climate, even in winter. Its fertile plains surrounded by pine-clad hills have been planted with **pistachio trees**. The first specimens were imported as ornamental trees from Iran and Egypt by British travellers in the early 20C. As the trees acclimatised, they soon produced plump, soft fruit, now thought to be the best in Greece.

## Europe's first coins
During the fourth millennium BC the first settlers came to Kolóna and Agía Marína, attracted by the island's location. In the third millennium they built up strong trade relations with the islands in the Aegean and with Crete. Égina prospered, and reached its height between the late 7C and the middle of the 5C BC. The island, which was rich and had a prestigious **school of sculpture**, prided itself on being the first place in Europe to mint its own coins. Silver coins bearing a tortoise were circulated in all the markets from Gibraltar to Egypt. But such power irritated Athens, which soon imposed a nine-month siege on the island, seized its fleet, forced the inhabitants to demolish the city walls and then expelled them. Before the 5C was out, what Pericles called "the spot that blinded Piraeus" had definitively ceased to overshadow its proud neighbour.

### The first Greek capital
After the War of Independence, Égina became the temporary seat of the first government of free Greece on 12 January 1828. Kapodístrias, the governor, was sworn in there and – with history repeating itself – had the new money for the young State minted there. The town then filled with opulent buildings and opened schools and printing works, which produced the first publications of modern Greece. On 3 October the capital was transferred to Náfplio, before being moved to Athens several years later.

## Égina Town ★★
*2hr are enough to take in the atmosphere of the town, visit the site of Kolóna and sunbathe on the beach below (water quality not all it should be).*

The white **Chapel of Ágios Nikólaos** stands at the entrance to Égina harbour. All along the lively seafront are fine **neo-Classical houses★** which recall the former power of the first capital of Greece. Their red-tiled roofs, ochre-coloured walls set off by painted shutters and their wrought-iron balconies lend the ensemble an undeniable note of nobility. The town itself, busy with shops and traffic, is less attractive.

Nonetheless, it is worth taking the time to see some of the monuments dating from the time of the first republic. Among them is the pink **Marcellus Tower**, probably a restored medieval fort, which for several months served as the headquarters of the new government.

### Kolóna and the Temple of Apollo★

*8.30am-2.45pm; closed Monday. Fee (including museum). Allow 45min.* Return to the harbour and follow the waterfront to the right. The town beach occupies the site of the ancient naval base, where parts of **submerged piers** may still be seen. The base was linked directly to a city sufficiently powerful to have been compared to Troy; its remains stand on a nearby hill covered in pines. Founded in 3000 BC, the city reached its height in the Classical Period, and was only abandoned in the 9C when its inhabitants moved to Paleohóra, which was less exposed to pirate raids. In the Middle Ages the Venetians named it Kolóna, after the one remaining upright column that had belonged to its main temple.

**Tour of the site** – The current excavations on the site add to the general chaos of the ruins. This means that you do not necessarily discover in chronological order the remains of **eleven successive cities**, jumbled together or built one of top of the other. To the right of the first flight of steps, you can make out behind the foundations of the houses, the enormous **protective wall**★ that was built in the 3C BC and stretched down to the harbour.

The **Temple of Apollo** dominating the site once had 30 Doric columns. The sole survivor seems to have been sharpened to a pencil point by erosion. The temple is a contemporary of the Temple of Aphaia (6C BC), and was built by the same craftsmen. To the west, in the direction of the sea, lie the levelled walls of two small **temples dedicated to Artemis and Dionysus**, as well as those of a **tholos**. Lastly, nothing remains of the main **theatre**, which the historian Pausanias compared to the one at Epidaurus (the museum now stands on its site).

**Archaeological Museum**★ – The museum is laid out like an ancient villa with an atrium flanked by a portico off which lead the rooms. It contains objects found on the island. A **scale model** in the hall shows one of the houses built at Kolóna in 3000 BC, whose two storeys testify to a high level of technology. There are rows of Hellenistic **funerary steles** on the patio, while the first room on the right contains **sculptures**★★ from one of the pediments of the Temple of Aphaia, depicting a battle of Amazons. A display case at the back on the left contains several pieces of **pottery** with black figures on a red background (10C-8C BC). The rest of the museum exhibits objects dating from the Neolithic to the Roman Period, including Archaic statues, a marble **sphinx**★ (5C BC), funerary bas-reliefs, as well as a fine collection of **geometric style pottery**★★.

## A drive to the north-east★

*Every 30min buses from Égina Town harbour leave for Agía Marína, via Ágios Nektários and the Temple of Aphaia. If you have a car, make the most of it to visit the north-east of the island (allow 2 to 3hr, including a swim).*

**Barbarossa and his works**

Only a few centuries of Paleohóra's history were lived in peace. In 1537 the terrible Turk known as Barbarossa took the town by force, cutting the men's throats and selling off the 6 000 women and children in slave markets in the Orient. In spite of the ordeals that continued to oppress Paleohóra, particularly under the Venetians, the town remained inhabited until 1800 when its citizens moved to the west coast, settling at the foot of ancient Kolóna.

■ On leaving Égina Town the road passes through a succession of villages lost among **pistachio orchards**. Six kilometres out of town it passes the monumental **Church of Ágios Nektários**, which was modelled on Ayasofya in Constantinople. More renowned for its size than its beauty, the church is dedicated to a local saint who died in 1920. His remains are kept nearby in the monastery of the same name.

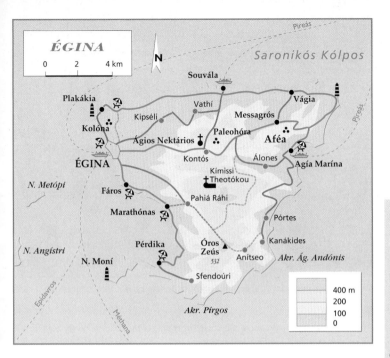

**ÉGINA**

0    2    4 km

N

*Saronikós Kólpos*

Pireás

Souvála

Plakákia

Vathí

Vágia

Kipséli

Messagrós

Kolóna

Paleohóra

Áfea

Ágios Nektários

ÉGINA

Kontós

Álones

Agía Marína

*N. Metópi*

Kímissi Theotókou

Fáros

Pahiá Ráhi

Marathónas

Pórtes

*N. Angístri*

Kanákides

Pérdika

Óros Zeús
532

Anítseo

*Akr. Ág. Andónis*

N. Moní

Sfendoúri

400 m
200
100
0

*Akr. Pírgos*

*Epídavros*

*Méthana*

■ 1.5km further along, on the left, are the scattered remains of the Byzantine city of **Paleohóra★**. This was built in 896 by the inhabitants of Kolóna who wanted to escape from attacks by Saracens, and was the main town on Égina until the early 19C. Its square medieval houses and 365 churches linked by a maze of alleyways once covered the slopes of a steep hill. Called with some exaggeration the "second Mistra", the ruined town's main interest lies in the melancholy beauty of its site and the restored churches decorated with frescoes, notably the **Cathedral★** whose iconostasis features a lovely icon of the Virgin (16C or 17C).

## ■ The Temple of Aphaia★★★ (Aféa)

*North-east of Égina Town. A cafeteria at the foot of the temple has a telephone booth from where you can call for a taxi for the return journey. 8.15am-7pm; closed Monday. Fee (ticket also includes the museum). Arrive preferably in the early morning to avoid the heat and the hordes of tourists. Arrange your tour (allow 1hr) around the inconvenient museum times (11am-11.15am / 12noon-12.15pm / 1pm-1.15pm).*

Beyond the market town of **Messagrós**, which specialises in traditional pottery-making, you can see the ochre outline of the Temple of Aphaia, standing watch at the top of a hill covered in pines. The road stops at its feet. The temple, which was built to form a "sacred triangle" with the Temple of Poseidon at Soúnion and the Parthenon, enjoys a dominating position with an **exceptional view★★** of the island and the Saronic Gulf. It was built in the early 5C BC, and was probably abandoned only a few decades later when the citizens of Égina were driven from the island by the Athenians.

**171**

The beginnings of the Doric style: the Temple of Aphaia, Égina

## Tour of the site

*A notice board at the entrance to the site in the middle of the pines shows the temple as it was in 490 BC.* Take the lane that climbs to the temple. Beyond five small steps and an earth platform, a flight of steps marks the beginning of the **Sacred Way** that led to the altar. It passed through the **propylaeum**, the monumental entrance gate carved out of the retaining wall that demarcated the sacred enclosure. Outside this area, on the right, there were once several **houses**, reserved for priests, built up against the wall.

The pale limestone columns of the exceptionally well-preserved **temple\*\*\*** were once covered in roughcast imitating white marble. The temple, measuring 32m by 16.50m, had six columns along the façade at ground level and twelve on each of the longer sides, while above, more modest colonnades provided support for the roof. Head towards the entrance. Slightly to the right lie the remains of a rectangular **altar** flanked by two **offerings rooms** (now in ruins). From there, people would enter the temple along a **ramp**. Even viewed from the outside (*you may not enter the temple*) the layout of the inside of the building is easy to understand. At the top of the ramp, two Doric columns marked the entrance to the vestibule, a long room lined on its main sides by five columns. It was here, in the **naos**, that the statue of the goddess once stood. Continue round the temple, towards the back, and you will see to the right of the altar, beyond one of the offerings rooms, a **cistern** and, just beside it, a truncated column that bore a monumental statue of a sphinx.

### To the glory of the "Invisible"

A local version of Athena the goddess of wisdom, the nymph Aphaia (the Invisible) was venerated on Égina. She was pursued for her beauty by Minos, King of Crete, but managed to escape from him by leaping into the sea. On being rescued by a fisherman from Égina, who in turn succumbed to her charm, she fled once again and disappeared into a forest. The temple dedicated to her was founded in the 7C BC on the site of a former place of worship dedicated to a prehistoric goddess. Two religious buildings, of which little remains (the second was destroyed by fire) preceded the present temple, built between the late 6C and early 5C BC.

## Museum★

*West of the temple. 15min.* The small Aphaia museum only consists of three rooms, which one visits without wasting any time, given the opening hours (*see above*). Go quickly through the first room, which is dedicated to the history of the excavations, so that you can spend more time in the others. They display reconstructions of the second temple of Aphaia – destroyed by fire in 510 BC – using some of the original pieces, in particular a **polychrome façade★**. However, most of the sculptures were sold in auction to Ludwig I of Bavaria and are now in the Glyptothek in Munich.

## Return along the north coast

A path (*marked with arrows, to the right as you leave the temple*) leads to **Agía Marína**, a 30min walk through the pines. The only attraction of the resort, which has been taken over by hotels, shops and tavernas, is its long **sandy beach**, although this is packed in summer. The coast to the south barely offers more of interest, so you would do better to return to Égina Town via the north coast, passing through **Vágia** with its beach and **Souvála**, the former harbour for Paleohóra. Beyond these villages the road runs alongside a jagged coastline punctuated by creeks and shipyards. It also goes through **Plakákia**, where the writer **Níkos Kazantzákis** (1883-1957) wrote his most famous novel, *Zorba the Greek.*

## The west coast and the centre

*The road south from Égina Town runs parallel to the shore for about ten kilometres. As the terrain is flat until 2km before Pérdika, this part of the trip can be done by bicycle.*

The southern suburbs of Égina Town cover a swampy area with reeds and eucalyptus, beyond which lie the resorts of **Fáros** and **Marathónas** (fine sandy beaches). Several hills covered in pines announce the approach to the fishing harbour of **Pérdika★**, one of the most charming on Égina, with its sailing ships and yachts in the harbour, and fish tavernas on the waterfront. Caiques from here take 10min to cross to the lovely beaches on **Moní islet** just opposite.

On returning to Marathónas, the more energetic visitor may like to climb **Mt Zeus** (Óros Zeús), the highest point on Égina (532m). After a 2hr climb (*quite steep*), you reach some ancient steps and scattered ruins – the remains of a 5C BC **temple dedicated to Zeus**. The steps lead on to a stony plateau with a **Byzantine church** and a beautiful panoramic **view★**.

## Making the most of Égina

### COMING AND GOING

**By boat – Sea Falcon** hydrofoils from Piraeus (not Zéa) provide links with Égina Town (30min), Souvála in the north (25min), and Agía Marína in the east (30min).

### GETTING AROUND

**By bus –** The **terminal** is near Égina Town harbour, ☎ (0297) 22 787 / 22 412. Regular services run between Égina-Marathónas-Pérdika, Égina-Ágios Nektários-Messagrós-Aphaia-Agía Marína (every 30min), and Égina-Kipséli-Vathí-Souvála.

**By taxi –** In **Égina Town** the taxi rank is on the left side of the harbour when facing the town, ☎ (0297) 22 635. In **Agía Marína**, ☎ 0944 950815.

**By car –** There are several rental agencies by the harbour at Égina Town. Avoid the Sklavenas agency, on the left when facing the town (poorly maintained vehicles).

**By boat –** Several daily shuttles between Égina Town-Souvála and Agía Marína, ☎ (0297) 22 328 / 25 734.

**By bicycle –** Bicycle rental by the harbour.

**Tourist information –** No official tourist office, but there are several private agencies in Égina Town, such as **Pipinis Travel**, Odós Kanari 2, opposite Flying Dolphins, ☎ (0297) 28 780 / 25 664, Fax (0297) 28 779, pipinis@hellasnet.gr Accommodation and car rental, boat bookings, currency exchange, cash dispenser.

**Bank / Currency exchange –** Most of the banks are at the harbour. Plenty of cash dispensers.

**Post office –** Platía Ethnegarsías, on the left side of the harbour when facing the town, ☎ (0297) 22 398.

**Telephone – OTE**, in Odós Aekon, which leads off from the harbour to the left of the Harbour Police, ☎ (0297) 22 599. In **Agía Marína**, in Odós Aphaia, ☎ (0297) 32 399.

**Internet –** In **Agía Marína** at **The Bell Inn** café, ☎ (0297) 32 049.

**Tourist police –** In Odós Leonárdos Ladá, which leads off to the right of Platía Ethnegarsías (on the left side of the harbour when facing the town), in a courtyard.

**Police –** Same address as the tourist police, ☎ (0297) 22 100.

**Medical service – Égina Hospital**, ☎ (0297) 22 209 / 22 251. **Agía Marína Medical Centre**, ☎ (0297) 32 175.

**WHERE TO STAY**

Apart from Agía Marína where there is a vast amount of modern accommodation, and some of the villages along the west coast, the island does not have much in the way of decent hotels. In Égina Town you will often find only noisy, antiquated rooms. At all costs, avoid the mediocre Miranda hotel where the cleanliness is doubtful, and the Egenitiko Archondiko, a fine old mansion where, alas, the rooms (and the clients) are neglected. The best places in Égina Town are grouped together beyond Kolóna. As good accommodation is rare, it is essential to book.

• **Égina Town**

*Around €45*

🏨 **Nafsika Hotel Bungalows**, Odós Kazantzáki 55, 500m north of the harbour, ☎ (0297) 22 333, Fax (0297)

22 477 – 34rm. 🍴 🅿 🖼 ☂ The bungalows with terraces, hidden among the bougainvillaea in the garden, are almost invisible from the road and have a faithful clientele of nature lovers and people seeking peace and quiet. The welcoming owners add to the charm of the place. Open from mid-April to mid-October. Book ahead.

*Between €60 and €68*

**Klonos**, 800m north of the harbour, ☎ (0297) 22 640 / 22 597, mobile 097 395947 – 20rm including 6 suites. 🍴 🅿 🖼 📺 ✕ ☂ ☂ ✗ 🆑 A little outside the town. A large new building and annexe with spacious, comfortable rooms. The garden contains a swimming pool for children adjoining one for adults.

• **Vágia**

*Between €45 and €55*

**Vagia**, ☎ (0297) 71 179 – 21rm. 🍴 ☂ 3km from the Temple of Aphaia and 200m from the beach. Two buildings in the old style with ochre-coloured walls and flower-filled pergolas have charming, clean rooms. The Égina-Aphaia bus stops nearby. Ideal for those seeking respite from the bustle of Agía Marína.

• **Agía Marína**

*Around €60*

**Apollo**, at the entrance to Agía Marína if you are coming from the Temple of Aphaia. At the end of a little road in the middle of trees, on the left. ☎ (0297) 32 271 to 4 / 32 281, Fax (0297) 32 688 – 107rm. 🍴 🅿 🖼 📺 ✕ ☂ ☂ ♨ ✗ 🆑 In spite of its massive appearance typical of 1970s architecture, the hotel is Agía Marína's pleasantest. The bright, cheerful rooms and the wide passageways were renovated in 1997. Pontoons have been laid out below the hotel so people can swim in the sea.

• **Moondy Bay**

*Between €60 and €75*

🏨 **Moondy Bay**, 2km north of Pérdika, on the west coast, ☎ (0297) 61 215 / 61 146 / 61 622, Fax (0297) 61 147. In Athens: (01) 38 03 745-6, Fax (01) 38 21 780 – 90rm and 2 suites. 🍴 🅿 🖼 ✕ ☂ ☂ ♨ ✗ 🆑 An attractive hotel complex consisting of chalets spread out over a pine-covered hill stretching down to the sea. Each well-designed studio has its own terrace with a view. Among the facilities are table tennis, crazy golf, bicycles and water sports, as well as an adventure playground for children. The bus for Égina and Pérdika stops in front of the hotel.

### • Pérdika
*Between €30 and €55*
**Antzi studios**, at the entrance to Pérdika harbour, on the right, ☎ (0297) 61 445 / 61 767 / 61 233, Fax (0297) 61 446 – 20 studios. ◦˥ 🖉 ☰ TV ⟍ CC A modern hotel without any special charm, but the rooms have kitchenettes and balconies. Pleasant swimming pool in the garden. If the receptionist is out, enquire at the Nondas taverna in the harbour.

### EATING OUT
The restaurants in Égina Town and Pérdika are renowned for their fish.

### • Égina Town
Near the covered market you can take pot luck and try grilled octopus in the small eating-houses frequented by stall-holders.
*Under €6*
**Dodoni**, by the harbour, just opposite the moorings for sailing boats. A self-service restaurant with decent *souvlákia* and mixed salads. Good choice of ice cream.
**Tropics**, in the harbour. Well-known for its inexpensive pita bread and other sandwiches.
*Around €7.50*
**To Spiti Tou Psara** ("House of the Fisherman"), to the right of the landing-stage. An ideal taverna for fried fish, fish fillets and steaks served with *skordaliá*, mashed potato with garlic. Avoid the taramosaláta, which comes out of a tin.
**Maridakis**, just beside the place above. This typically Greek establishment is packed every evening. Hence the somewhat hectic service.

### • Messagrós
*Between €9 and €12*
**Argyris**, on the main road out of the village, take the first road left just beyond the school, then the first on the right, ☎ (0297) 71 303. This taverna hidden among the greenery is mainly popular with local people, and serves very fresh grilled fish washed down with delicious local retsína. Try the spinach pie.

### • Álones
*Around €9*
South of Agía Marína, take the Álones road left. Two tavernas, **Takis** and

**Kostas**, serve authentic Greek fare beneath shady pergolas in a village atmosphere. Good meze and fish specialities.

### HAVING A DRINK

### • Égina Town
**Kavourina**, north of the harbour, beyond the bus station. A friendly ouzo bar with good meze (fried cheese, prawns, squid, etc).

🍴**Eakio**, in the middle of the harbour, sells the island's best cakes and ice creams.

### • Agía Marína
**Léo Club**, a disco lost among the pines near the Apollo Hotel.

### OTHER THINGS TO DO

**Outdoor pursuits** – In Égina Town and on the west coast. Scuba diving with the **Aegina Dive Center**, ☎ 0944 641571 / 0944 544 3675. For divers of all abilities. In Agía Marína various water sports are organised by the **Argo Hotel**, ☎ (0297) 32 266.

**Excursions** – There are numerous tours to Athens, the Argolid Peninsula and the neighbouring islands. You could also spend a day on **Angístri Island**. Smaller and quieter than Égina, the islet with many pines (but not many beaches) is accessible by boat from Égina Town harbour (20min crossing).

**Amusement park** – Fáros has a small **Water Park** with a swimming pool, giant slides, etc. Free entry for children up to 10 years old.

**Local festivals** – Around 9 November there is an important votive festival at Ágios Nektários Church.

### SHOPPING GUIDE

**Market** – Pleasant covered market in the town surrounded by modest bars and tavernas. In the harbour a small fruit and vegetable market is held in the caiques.

**Arts and crafts** – **Messagrós** has traditional pottery.

**Local delicacies** – Try the Égina **pistachio nuts** plain, crystallised or mixed with honey. Prices decrease the further you go from the landing-stage.

# HYDRA★★★
## (ÍDRA)

Saronic Gulf – District of Attica – Michelin map 980 fold 30
Regional map page 168 – 56km² – Pop 2 800

**Not to be missed**
A walk in Hydra Town.

**And remember...**
A day's excursion will give you a good idea of the harbour and its lively activities.
For a longer stay, book your accommodation in advance,
as Hydra is hugely popular in summer.

After a peaceful crossing through the blue waters of the Saronic Gulf, the boat enters the superb **Bay of Hydra★★**. Like a giant theatre, the compact harbour crowded with yachts and ferries forms the stage, while the tiers of houses rising up the surrounding hills make up the auditorium. Each fisherman's cottage, painted white or pastel, and each mansion with its austere grey façade, forms part and parcel of the set. Even the donkeys and mules, which replace motor vehicles that are banned on the island, form part of the cast.

In this opulent stage set it is a question of seeing and being seen. Yachts have replaced the former merchant fleet and the rich shipowners who first put Hydra on the map have given way to members of the international jet set.

### From trade to war

When the War of Independence broke out against the Turks in 1821, the Hydriot shipowners, still referred to as "captains", converted 130 of their merchant ships into warships, thus supplying Greece with two-thirds of its fleet! All the shipowners became involved, Tombázis, Tsamados, Koundouriótis – who was thought to be the richest man in Europe – and Andréas Miaoúlis, who destroyed enemy boats by launching "fire ships" towards them, old vessels packed with explosives. Victory was won at the price of much sacrifice, and also grief, as it cost Hydra its entire fortune. When steam replaced sails, the shipowners, now ruined, did not receive from Athens the help they were expecting to renew their fleet. Today, the island owes its newly found prosperity to tourism.

### A dry island

As you walk along the bare shores of the narrow island (4 to 5km wide) it is difficult to believe that there were once enough springs for it to be called Hydreia, meaning "rich in water". Never cultivated, and subjected to fires that destroyed most of its forests, Hydra is just a long strip of barren, mountainous land with rock outcrops everywhere. The large cisterns dug by the Hydriot shipowners to catch rainwater can no longer supply enough for the needs of the island, and so every day Hydra has to import around 4 000 tonnes of water by tanker from the Peloponnese coast.

### Renowned shipowners

For a long time Hydra was just a stopover for pirates and a grazing ground for goats. However, in the 15C the arrival of Albanian refugees fleeing the Peloponnese and Ottoman persecution changed its destiny. As the land had nothing to offer, these skilled sailors turned to the sea for most of their resources. Past masters in the art, they began to build ships on a large scale, and after obtaining from the occupying Turks the freedom to sail on all seas, they amassed colossal fortunes through international maritime trade that took them as far as America. Making the most of the situation, they slipped through the English blockade to supply France for considerable sums during the Napoleonic Wars, turning to piracy and contraband. In the 19C, the power of these matchless shipowners was such that Hydra, which was home to **Europe's first merchant navy training school**, was named "Little England".

# Hydra Town***
*Begin your walk with a tour of the harbour from east to west.*

To take in the whole town nestling in the curve of its bay, go to the end of the ferry quay where the **statue of Miaoúlis** stands on the esplanade. Note the tall mansions or **archontiká** dotted among the houses on the hillside stretching down to the harbour. There are also several windmills (currently being restored) on the heights, and, in the middle of the waterfront, the Clock Tower of the Monastery of the Assumption.

As you walk along the waterfront, take a look at the **Historical Archives Museum**★ *(9am-4.30pm except Monday; fee)*, which retraces the island's seafaring past. A room on the ground floor presents a **history of lighthouses** from the mid-19C to the present day. The more interesting first floor is entirely dedicated to Hydra and the memory of its sea captains. In the middle of a collection of portraits, sea charts, navigational instruments and figureheads is a funerary urn containing the heart of Miaoúlis. On leaving the museum, you pass alongside an imposing **archontiká** nearby that once belonged to the shipowner Tsamados. It is home to a section of the Greek Merchant Navy Captains' School.

## Powerful archontiká

The shipowners' mansions or "archontiká", built mainly in the late 18C, bear witness to the power of their owners. Their tall grey stone walls up to 1.30m thick, pierced with narrow windows covered in wire mesh, lend them a fortress-like air, commanding respect. Within the walls however, everything once exuded opulence. There were gardens planted with rare flowers imported from Europe, loggias inspired by Genoese architecture, and vast rooms with marble flooring and painted ceilings decorated with the Western furniture and paintings that the shipowners brought back on each of their voyages.

After passing jewellers' shops and café terraces you reach, in the middle of the waterfront, the **Monastery of the Assumption** whose large **Clock Tower** marks the entrance. It was built in 1643 and restored in the second half of the 18C after an earthquake. Its two courtyards bathed in the white glow of marble form a delicious

Hydra harbour retains memories of its former prosperity

Hydra

haven of peace. They contain busts of captains and a war memorial. In the basilica with three naves topped by a dome you can see an impressive marble **iconostasis★** and a **gilt icon★** of the martyr Constantine the Hydriot. Note also the **chandeliers**, decorated with ex-votos featuring ships.

On leaving the church take the steps up to a loggia that leads to a small **Byzantine Museum** (10am-5pm; closed Monday; fee) containing a collection of liturgical items, chalices, crucifixes, icons and embroidered vestments.

On either side of the monastery three large pedestrian streets lead off into the town. Full of shops at first, they then gradually become quieter the further you go from the harbour. They lead to the **Kiafa district★★★** above the hospital where Hydra's earliest houses are grouped together. An ideal spot for taking photos, this is the most appealing part of the town with its confusing tangle of alleyways and **covered passageways** where the inhabitants used to take refuge during pirate raids. In this silent world, the neo-Classical façades of the large **private houses★** restored in the 19C after an earthquake create a shimmering play of colour, with their white or pastel walls set off by the celadon green, light grey or blue of their doors and windows.

## Short tour of the island

*For short trips (less than 2hr) you can walk along the coast either side of the town. To explore the centre of the island, hire a donkey or leave on foot early in the morning with water and other supplies.*

### The north-east
*Go round the statue of Miaoúlis that closes off the harbour to the east, and follow the coast road, along which stand smart villas.*

■ After 20min on foot from the town centre you come to **Mandráki**, the only place where you will find a **sandy beach** worthy of the name. It belongs to the Miramare Hotel (but is open to the public).

■ If you enjoy harsh, barren landscapes, take a path to the right that leads up to the **Monastery of Agía Matronís** (45min walk), lost in the mountains. It is a fine example of local monastic architecture.

■ Well beyond the monastery, you reach the lonely **Zourvás Convent★** (16C), the easternmost one on the island (on foot, allow 3hr from Mandráki; by boat, ask to be dropped ashore at the foot of the Zourvás hill and allow for a 15min walk). The convent affords a superb **view★** of the island. The nuns who live here sell **needlework**: curtains, place mats, table cloths and carpets.

### The south-west
*From Hydra Town, go beyond the lighthouse west of the harbour and take the coast path. This trip to Mólos takes 90min on foot, and can also be done by caique.*

■ At **Spilias**, several minutes from the town centre, concrete pontoons protected by old cannon enable you to dive into the deep water. However, to find a beach (shingle), you must go through the hamlet of **Kamíni**, a small, easy-going fishing harbour (20min walk).

■ A little further on you come to **Vlichós**, another solitary little harbour whose red pebble beach contrasts with the whiteness of the houses.

■ Beyond, the broad **Bay of Mólos** opens up, with several yachts at anchor. From here you can climb through a wide wooded valley of pines to the hamlet of **Episkopí** where the remains of a **Mycenaean dwelling** have been discovered. You may prefer to go swimming in the clear water around **Cape Bísti**, in which case you would do better to take a caique.

## The centre of the island

By taking Odós A Miaoúli (*to the left of the Monastery of the Assumption*) you come to the top of the hill dominating the town, where the **view★** of the harbour is particularly beautiful at sunset.

■ By continuing on foot or by donkey, you reach (*in 1hr*) the **Monastery of Profítis Ilías**, hidden in a pinewood at an altitude of 500m. You will be able to see the cell in which Kolokotrónis, a hero of the War of Independence, was imprisoned for several months in 1825.

■ From there, you may either go on to the white **Convent of Agía Efpraxía**, where the nuns make silk fabrics by hand, or climb to the top of **Mt Éros** to enjoy the **panorama★★**. This takes in the Saronic Gulf on one side, the Mirtóo Sea on the other, and at your feet the rocky terrain of Hydra dotted with abandoned hamlets.

---

## Making the most of Hydra

### COMING AND GOING

See "Making the most of the Saronic Gulf", page 168.

### GETTING AROUND

**By donkey** – Mule-drivers around the harbour transport luggage to hotels and take people up into the mountains. Fix the price beforehand.

**By boat** – Caiques and water-taxis (more expensive) serve the beaches and take people on tours around the island.

### ADDRESS BOOK

**Tourist information** – *Saitis Tours* to the right of the landing-stage in the harbour ☎ (0298) 52 184 / 54 151, Fax (0298) 53 469, lets rooms, villas and yachts, organises excursions on Hydra and to neighbouring islands, and changes travellers' cheques. It has a detailed map of the island.

**Bank / Currency exchange** – Several banks to the right of the harbour landing-stage.

**Post office** – In Odós Ikonómou, at right angles to the harbour, near the market.

**Telephone** – **OTE**, behind the Monastery of the Assumption. Plenty of booths taking phone-cards.

**Police** – Just opposite the OTE.

**Medical service** – The hospital is in the first street to the right of the monastery, ☎ (0298) 53 150. There is a **pharmacy** in the same street, ☎ (0298) 52 059.

**Laundry** – In the town centre, in the vicinity of the fruit market. 9am-1pm / 5pm-9pm.

### WHERE TO STAY

Hydra has every category of hotel, from the average to the most sophisticated. You will have no difficulty finding standard accommodation with rooms at around €30-38, all much of a muchness. The addresses given below are at the upper end of the scale, combining comfort and refinement. Avoid the centre if you want peace and quiet. You will also find some charming places, elegant mansions that have been converted.

• **Hydra Town**

*Between €55 and €60*

🏨 **Miranda**, in the middle of Odós A Miaoúli, ☎ (0298) 52 230, Fax (0298) 53 510 – 15rm. ⌐⌐ ℰ 🍽 ✕ This superb old house converted into a hotel has kept its shady courtyard garden and its interior decoration typical of Hydriot architecture (coffered ceilings, neo-Classical furniture), which makes it look like a museum. The rooms, however, have varying standards of decoration. Some have fridges and televisions.

*Between €49 and €95*

**Miramare**, on the beach at Mandráki, ☎ (0298) 52 300, Fax (0298) 52 300, miramare@compulink.gr – 28rm. ⌐⌐ ℰ 🍽 ✕ 📺 ✕ 🌂 🜔 🆑 Cool bungalows with terraces and fridges look out onto the sand beach at Mandráki, 7min from the town centre by boat (shuttle service until 3am). Numerous water sports and a pool for children. Organised tours round the island in the hotel boat.

*Between €60 and €75*

**Mistral**, at the end of Odós Tombázis, on the left side of the harbour, ☎ (0298) 52 509, Fax (0298) 53 412 – 19rm including 1 studio for 4 people. ⌐| 🖉 ▤ 📺 🆑 A house built of traditional grey stone in a quiet street. The bright, clean rooms open onto a flower-filled patio where breakfast is served (included).

*Between €75 and €120*

**Bratsera**, in a quiet part of Odós Tombázis, not far from the centre, ☎ (0298) 53971, Fax (0298) 53 626 – 23rm. ⌐| 🖉 ▤ 📺 ✕ ⌐ 🆑 The hotel, converted from a former sponge factory whose stone walls, timbered ceilings and flagstone floors have been preserved, is certainly the finest on Hydra, if not on many other Greek islands. The tastefully decorated rooms are absolutely charming, from the smallest, perched atop a staircase, to the most spacious and refined (Virani suite). Meals are served on the patio beside the swimming pool. Open from Easter (Greek Orthodox calendar) to the end of October.

**Orloff**, take Odós Votsi to the right of the Monastery of the Assumption. Continue to the pharmacy beyond the public gardens and the hotel is just on the right. ☎ (0298) 52 564 and, in Athens, (01) 52 26 152, Fax (0298) 53 532 – 9rm for 2 to 4 people. ⌐| 🖉 ▤ 📺 🆑 This 18C mansion with its unobtrusive exterior will delight lovers of traditional architecture. In addition to the plainly decorated though comfortable rooms (mini-bars, hair dryers), are beautiful communal areas and a peaceful garden where breakfast is served (extra). Gracious reception.

EATING OUT

On Hydra you eat well, but meals are quite expensive.

• **Hydra Town**

*Between €7.50 and €12*

**To Steki**, a taverna a little way up the hill, offering full menus including ouzo and dessert at reasonable prices (wine is extra). Packed in the evening.

**Gitonikon**, in a quiet little street, at the back and to the right of the Xeri Elia taverna. The restaurant on two floors (with a terrace) is run by Christina and Manolis. Very fresh ingredients (fish, raw vegetables, grilled meats) and carefully prepared dishes. One of the best places in Hydra in terms of value for money.

*Between €11 and €14*

**Barba Dímas**, a traditional taverna in the heart of town (tables on the pavement) whose excellent cooking (grilled fish, fried prawns and *fáva*) is hugely popular with the Greeks. If you order in advance, you can try snails (*saligária*), a Hydriot speciality.

**Xerí Eliá (Douskos)**, in the town centre, giving onto a pretty square bordered by white houses. A decent establishment with tables set out beneath two hundred-year-old trees. Try the stuffed squid and wine from the barrel. Greek music.

*Around €15*

**Strophylia**, at the beginning of Odós A Miaoúli, on the left. A very fashionable ouzo bar whose old-style decor (sideboard, globe lamps, marble tables) explains the rather high prices.

*Between €23 and €38*

**Bratsera**, in the hotel of the same name. The smartest restaurant in Hydra, with magnificent decor. The menu offers traditional Greek fare as well as international dishes (tabbouleh, Caesar salad) and a wide variety of pasta. Pity about the limited choice of dessert.

• **Mandráki**

*Between €7.50 and €9*

**Mertazani zoi**, between the harbour and Mandráki. A small, unpretentious ouzo bar whose tomatoes come fresh from the vegetable garden and the fish from the sea below. A good place to stop, just above a small pebble beach.

• **Kamíni**

*Around €15*

**Kodylenia's**, a taverna at the entrance to Kamíni harbour. The terrace has a superb view of the sea, as you savour wonderfully fresh fish (grilled swordfish, crayfish).

## HAVING A DRINK

Most of the bars are grouped together around the harbour, THE place to go. Unfortunately, prices are exorbitant.

**Heaven**, on the west side of the harbour, above the Sunset. Perched high up, the night-club has an unrestricted view of the sea and the Peloponnese coast. For fans of rock and contemporary music.

**Amalour**, at the beginning of Odós Tombázis, opposite the landing-stage. Bar with jazz and Spanish music.

**Pirates**, on the other side of the harbour, for rock enthusiasts.

## OTHER THINGS TO DO

**Beaches** – Swimmers who would rather not walk as far as the beaches can use the concrete pontoons 10min from the town centre, towards the west. Otherwise, the nearest beaches are at Mandráki and Kamíni. Caiques go to the tree-lined Bísti and Limiónissa beaches on the south coast.

**Excursions** – 6hr excursions are organised around the island. Boats depart at 11am (except when there is a high wind). Bring your own picnic. There are also excursions from the harbour to Portohéli, Kósta and the theatre at Epidaurus.

**Open-air cinema** – In the harbour, in the first street to the right of the Emborikí Bank, tucked away among the tavernas. In summer, shows begin at 8.30pm and at 10.30pm.

**Local festivals** – A **carnaval** is held on the last Sunday before Lent. Good Friday: a ceremony at Kamíni in memory of those who died at sea. Late June: Navy Week or **Miaoulia** with boat races, demonstrations by the national fleet, dances and fireworks. 15 August: folk dancing. National holiday on 28 October: regattas between Athens and Hydra.

## SHOPPING GUIDE

**Market** – A permanent fruit and vegetable market is open daily in the town centre.

**Arts and crafts** – Linen items embroidered by the nuns at **Zourvás Convent**. Other traditional items are on sale at **Pan Asproúlis** in the town.

**Other** – Numerous **art galleries** around the harbour exhibit paintings and sculptures by artists from all over the world. The very best can be found next to the very worst.

# PÓROS★

Saronic Gulf – District of Attica – Michelin map 980 fold 30
Regional map page 168 – 33km² – Pop 3 600

**Not to be missed**
A walk through the old town of Póros.
Zoodóhou Pigí Monastery.
The Temple of Poseidon lost among the pines.

**And remember...**
Half a day is enough to explore Póros;
the best thing is to hire a car on your arrival in the morning.

While Póros is not the most spectacular of the Saronic Gulf Islands, its location – an hour from Athens by hydrofoil – means that it acts as a kind of bridge between the mainland and the islands, offering an introduction to the world of the Cyclades. You feel this as you disembark right in the heart of Póros Town. Its quay stretches out at the foot of two charming little hills covered in neo-Classical houses that form an elegant cascade of red roofs – a reminder of Attica – and the white façades which are one of the characteristics of the Cyclades. Beyond the town and its crowds of tourists is a magnificent pine forest that covers the rest of the island. This almost untouched area serves as the setting for the romantic remains of the Temple of Poseidon.

Póros, Zoodóhou Pigí Monastery

## Two islands in one, plus part of the mainland

A giant could step across the channel that separates Póros from the Attica coast without getting his feet wet. The island is so close that its modern suburb of **Galatás** has developed on the mainland shore for want of space, thus preserving the old island city from sprawls of unattractive housing. The island itself is divided by an isthmus into two parts, with the smaller, **Sfería**, being given over entirely to Póros Town. The much larger **Kalavría** makes up the garden of Póros, with a succession of pine-clad hills and lemon and olive groves bordered by pretty beaches.

The island's finest hour was in the 7C BC, when an important temple was founded and devoted to Poseidon. Along with six other towns in Attica, Boeotia and the Peloponnese, Póros formed part of an Amphictyony, a religious alliance, and participated in major sacrificial ceremonies in honour of the sea god up until the 3C BC.

## Póros Town★

Escape from the hordes of tourists around the harbour and climb the hill on which rises the tall blue **bell-tower** of the church, dominating the area like a lighthouse. In less than a quarter of an hour you will find yourself in a labyrinth of steps and alleyways lined with houses where every window seems to be observing your ascent. At the top there is a fine **view★** and you can watch in peace the endless coming and going of caiques between Póros and Galatás.

On returning to the harbour, turn left and walk round to the small **Archaeological Museum** in Platía Alexis Korizis (*8.30am-3pm, 9.30am-2.30pm weekends; closed Monday; free*), which contains some fine **architectural remains** unearthed on Póros

and in the ancient city of Troizen on the Argolid mainland. Enthusiasts will be charmed by the **tanagras** or terracotta statuettes (3C and 4C BC) and the collection of **pottery**.

*To leave Sfería, walk along the waterfront with the sea on your left and cross the isthmus that connects the town to Kalavría.* Note on the left, the **Naval School**, which occupies the buildings of an old Russian naval base built in 1806.

## Kalavría
*By car, allow a good hour without counting a stop at the beach.*

After the hectic pace of the town, it is good to breathe in the gentle atmosphere of the bucolic countryside, bathed in the scent of the pine, olive and lemon trees.

The first road left beyond the isthmus leads to excellent **sandy beaches at Mikro**\* and **Megálo Neório**\*, in a lovely verdant setting. Less than 5km further on, the road comes to a dead end in a little bay with calm water where sailing boats are moored *(pebble beach)*.

*Retrace your steps and continue straight ahead towards the east.*

Beyond **Askéli beach**, which is usually packed, take the time to visit **Zoodóhou Pigí Monastery**\*, lost in the pines *(4km; open until 4pm in winter, 9pm in summer; free; if you are unsuitably dressed, you will be lent appropriate clothing)*. The 18C monastery buildings enclose a courtyard in which several heroes from the War of Independence lie buried. Two immense cypress trees stand in front of the church, a domed basilica that contains an impressive **iconostasis**\* carved in gilt wood, together with several 18C icons. Below the monastery is a little **sandy beach** beside a taverna.

Beyond Zoodóhou Pigí the road disappears into the heart of the island, through 6km of lonely forest. If you are interested in archaeology, seek out the **Temple of Poseidon** *(8am-2.30pm; closed Monday; free)*. It is worth visiting not so much for the remains of the temple and the other ruins as for the beautiful **view**\* of the Peloponnese and, in fine weather, of Attica and Salamína.

## Making the most of Póros

COMING AND GOING
See page 168.

GETTING AROUND

**By bus** – All parts of Póros are served by bus. Station in the harbour, to the right as you disembark.

**By taxi** – Taxi rank on the hydrofoil wharf, ☎ (0298) 23 003.

**Car, bicycle and motorcycle rental** – Several firms in Galatás, on the mainland. In Póros Town harbour there are plenty of bicycle and motorcycle hire firms, but only one car hire firm (check the brakes): **Spheros**, to the right of the Flying Dolphins agent. Fuel station in the town.

**By boat** – **Caiques** leave the harbour every hour for the beaches at Neório, to the west, and Askéli and Zoodóhou Pigí Monastery, to the east. **Water-taxis** wait near the landing-stage.

ADDRESS BOOK

**Tourist information** – Several travel agents serve as tourist offices. In the harbour, on the left as you disembark, **Hellenic Sun Travel** lets rooms, hires out bicycles and motorcycles and sells tickets for boat trips and excursions. ☎ (0298) 25 901 to 903, mobile 0977 900471, Fax (0298) 22 697.

**Bank / Currency exchange** – On the right as you disembark, the **Emboriki Bank** has a cash dispenser.

**Post office / Telephone** – Beyond the Emboriki Bank, in a square. **OTE**, to the left of the landing-stage, a 5min walk.

**Tourist police** – To the left as you disembark, just beyond Kostas Bikes, by a flight of steps, ☎ (0298) 22 256.

**Medical service** – **Pharmacy** in the harbour, to the left of the landing-stage. **Emergencies**, ☎ (0298) 22 596 / 23 333.

## WHERE TO STAY

While the hotels in the town centre are convenient because they're near the harbour, they are also noisy. You will find pleasanter places to stay on the seafront (book in summer, as they are hugely popular with tour groups). The hotels in Galatás are less attractive and therefore cheaper.

### • Póros Town

*Between €45 and €55*

**Manissi**, in the harbour, almost directly opposite the ferry dock, ☎ (0298) 22 273, Fax (0298) 24 345 – 15rm. ⚏ ℱ 🍴 TV An elegant neo-Classical building with a yellow façade and a rather old-fashioned interior. Each room has a fridge and a balcony.

### • Neório Bay

*Between €49 and €60*

**Póros Hotel**, ☎ (0298) 22 216 or, in Athens (01) 94 00 580, Fax (01) 94 30 161 – 100rm. ⚏ ℱ ✕ 🛁 🕴 ⚱ CC A large hotel complex dating from the 1970s, without much charm, but very well located between the pinewoods and the beach (private), where boats may be hired. The rooms overlooking the sea have an unrestricted view of the harbour. Continental breakfast included. Open from mid-April to the end of October.

### • Monastiri Bay

*Between €73 and €111*

**Sirene**, on the road between Askéli beach and Zoodóhou Pigí Monastery, ☎ (0298) 22 741 to 743, Fax (0298) 22 744. ⚏ ℱ 🍴 TV ✕ 🛁 🕴 CC This recently renovated six-storey luxury hotel, the finest on Póros, stands on a cliff between the road and the beach. The rooms are prettily decorated and have balconies (the pleasantest overlook the sea). Beneath them are a restaurant, snack bar, dance hall, and, above the private beach, two swimming pools – one for adults and the other for children. Open from mid-April to the end of October.

## EATING OUT

The food in Póros is not the island's strong point. Only the **Seven Brothers** in the harbour stands out a little from the rest of the eating places. Briskly run by the tireless brothers, the restaurant serves good local cuisine accompanied in high season by performances of Greek singing and dancing.

## HAVING A DRINK

Apart from the address given above, there is the **Poseidon Music Club** between Póros and the Temple of Poseidon. The bar has a swimming pool and a magnificent view of the harbour and Galatás. Every evening in summer there are concerts of Greek and international music. Free bus from 9pm.

## OTHER THINGS TO DO

**Outdoor pursuits – Passage**, ☎ (0298) 23 927, mobile 0944 387759, Fax (0298) 24 433, passage@passage.gr, www.passage.gr, in peaceful Neório Bay is a centre for water-skiing and other water sports for adults and children (4 years and over). Friendly welcome. English spoken. Open all year round.

**Beaches** – The quietest are at **Neório**, in the west, and the most popular at **Askéli**. Several kilometres west of the Temple of Poseidon a dirt track leads to the lonely beach at **Vayonia**.

**Excursions** – There are organised tours to the ancient site of **Troizen**, which has the remains of a stadium and a temple dedicated to Hippolytus, as well as to the main archaeological sites in the Peloponnese.

From Galatás you can go to **Lemonodássos**, a huge lemon grove, which until about ten years ago was the largest in Greece.

**Cinema** – The **Cinema Café** on the west side of the harbour shows films every evening in summer.

**Local festivals** – In summer there is a water sports week, with various events including regattas and exhibitions.

# SPÉTSES★★

Saronic Gulf – District of Attica – Michelin map 980 fold 30
Regional map page 168 – 244km$^2$ – Pop 3 500

**Not to be missed**
A walk through the town, from Dápia to the old harbour.
A swim at Ágioi Anárgiri, Zogeriá or Paraskeví.
**And remember...**
You only need a few hours to visit the town and the old harbour,
but allow an extra day to tour the island.
Cars are banned on the island, but you can get around on foot
or hire a bicycle or motorcycle.

**The Saronic Gulf**

### The victory of the Spetsiot shipowners

Over the centuries, thanks to the impetus given by the Greek-Albanians who settled on the island in the 15C, Spétses acquired great expertise in shipbuilding and navigation. When the War of Independence broke out, the local shipowners were rich enough to convert about fifty merchant vessels into warships that could stand up to the Ottoman fleet. On 8 September 1822, they managed to destroy the enemy flagship which was passing through Spétses' waters to take supplies to Náfplio. The boat caught fire and sank off the island, marking a major victory for the Greek side. Since then the event has been celebrated on Spétses, on the nearest Saturday to 8 September, by setting alight a small boat symbolising a Turkish vessel.

A privileged holiday spot for rich Athenian and British summer visitors, the most southerly of the Saronic Gulf Islands has developed over the years into a well-to-do seaside resort. The shipowners' houses in the only settlement on the island have been converted into charming flower-bedecked residences, and the old shipyards, which brought fame to Spétses during the War of Independence, have made way for an international yacht harbour. The downside of all this is that the island has become very expensive and has also lost something of its traditional character. Nonetheless, it is still a very pleasant place to stop during a cruise around the gulf. With little motor traffic, the pace of life is ideal for relaxing, for simply taking it easy in the shade of the pine trees.

### Pine-tree island

There is only one settlement on the island, Spétses Town, which stretches along the coast facing the Argolid Peninsula. The rest of the island is practically uninhabited and is given over to a vast, deliciously fragrant forest of **Aleppo pines**, hence its ancient name of *Pityoussa*, "planted with pines".

## Spétses Town★★

*If you can only spare a morning, allow time to visit the museum, which closes in the afternoon. Allow a total of 2hr for a tour.*

### Dápia wharf

You will have barely disembarked before plunging into the colourful bustle of Dápia (or "fortified town" in Turkish), the waterfront crowded with shops, cafés and banks. In the 19C this was where the military leaders met, as is borne out by the **cannon** pointing seawards and a statue in honour of **Bouboulína**, Spétses' fighting heroine.

From Dápia, venture into the alleyways in the town centre. After a few hundred metres you will suddenly find yourself alone, or almost, in a peaceful area. This is where the **Mexis Museum★★** is located, in a splendid 18C mansion (*from Dápia,* head towards the centre and then turn left. *8.30am-2.45pm; closed Monday; fee).* The house once belonged to Hadziyannis Mexis, one of the Spetsiot leaders of the War of Independence and first governor of the island. The façade, flanked by two austere wings, has an elegant **arcaded loggia★** with two flights of stairs. You can go quickly through the ground floor where **antique remains** discovered in the waters of the gulf are displayed, to the first floor, which has kept its late-18C **interior decoration★**, a harmonious mixture of local, Ottoman and neo-Classical styles. A series of rooms shows in turn objects dating from prehistoric times (pottery), 18C utensils and furniture, as well as souvenirs from the War of Independence. One of the rooms contains the bones of **Bouboulína**.

*Return to the centre of Dápia.*

The only other shipowner's mansion open to the public is **Bouboulína's House★**, converted into a private museum by her descendants. The house stands in a charming square shaded by pines set slightly back from Dápia *(13 guided tours a day, in English and in Greek. Times shown at the entrance; fee).* The building is approached through a large courtyard paved with **Botsaloto cobblestones★** (also known as krokalia). In a rather formal atmosphere the first floor displays a collection of furniture, paintings and personal items that belonged to the heroine of the War of Independence.

A street to the left of Bouboulína's House climbs to the upper town *(15min)* to the top of **Kastéli Hill** which was once protected by fortifications that have now disappeared completely. If you cannot visit the three churches *(often closed)*, including the island's former **Cathedral**, you will at least enjoy a fine **view★** of the nearby Peloponnese coast.

## Bouboulína, a fighter for Independence

One of the great female figures in Greek history, Laskarína Boúboulis was born in 1771 in a prison in Constantinople where her mother had come to visit her husband who had been locked up for involvement in a plot. Married successively to two Spetsiot sea captains who lost their lives in naval combat, Bouboulína found herself alone with seven children. But she was sufficiently patriotic to use the considerable fortune she had inherited to further the cause of the revolution. She had several ships built, including the Agamemnon, the foremost Greek warship, and at the beginning of the War of Independence trained a corps of fighters to man her vessels. She had a strong personality, and took part in battles against the Turks, haranguing her men and, it is said, willingly taking them as lovers. Her end was less glorious. She died at the age of 54 a ruined woman, murdered by the family of a young woman whom one of her sons had abducted.

Bouboulína, a national heroine

E. Slatter/HEMISPHERES

## Botsaloto, the Spetsiot paving stone

The Botsaloto (or Krokalia) Spetsiot tradition, consisting of pretty mosaics of small black and white pebbles illustrating motifs often inspired by the sea or the island's military history, is a few centuries old. Originating in the 8C, the pebble pattern first served as paving for private houses and courtyards before spreading to streets and public places, and now covers nearly the whole of Dápia. The same decorative technique can be seen in Líndos, on the island of Rhodes.

## Along the waterfront

*Make your way down to the harbour, turn left and follow the waterfront heading north-east.* Topped by a dome, the majestic façade of the **Posidonion Hotel** faces the sea, flanked by two corner towers. The immensely wealthy Spetsiot Sotírios Anárgyros had the place built in 1914, thereby making Spétses a fashionable destination for the rich and famous. There followed the building of the coast road and the advent of **horse-drawn carriages** – one of the island's curiosities – not forgetting *(further north)* the opening of the **Anárgyros-Orgialénios College** for boys from the Greek aristocracy *(today a conference centre)*. The British novelist John Fowles, whose book *The Magus* was inspired by Spétses, taught at the college in 1951 and 1952. To reach it, take the corniche road along the coast, always busy with bicycles and horse-drawn carriages. This makes for a pleasant outing through one of Spétses' most exclusive residential areas,

Spétses, the magnificent mansion of the Anárgyros family

where fine mansions and their lovely gardens are hidden behind high walls – protection against Turks, pirates and erosion from the sea.

*Return to the waterfront, heading south-east (allow 1hr on foot, there and back, or take a carriage). If you have the time on the way back, it is just as pleasant to go through the alleyways in the town.*

## The old harbour★★ (Paleó Limáni)

Below the corniche road is an inviting little **pebble beach**, the nearest to the town centre, while to the right stands the bell-tower of the **Church of Ágios Nikólaos★**, now Spetses Cathedral. The war memorial with two cannons bears the motto of the Revolution, "Freedom or Death", and marks the place where the first flag of independent Greece was flown in 1821. The dimly-lit church interior creates a haven of peace and contains a fine **iconostasis** made of carved and gilded wood.

The church marks the entrance to the old harbour, where you will see a mixture of traditional fishermen's houses, tourist hotels and the modest remains of the 18C and 19C shipyards. On the way to **Agía Marína**, near the lighthouse, is the **Chapel of Panagía Armáta★**, recognisable by its white and yellow façade. It was built to commemorate the victory of 8 September 1822, and contains a large late-19C **painting** of the battle.

*Go into the town and, once past the houses, continue into the pines.*

At the end of the road *(15min on foot)* the **Agíon Pánton Convent** (8am-11.30am, 5pm-8pm) appears, nestling in the greenery on the heights. It was built by the widow of a Spetsiot sea captain who became Mother Superior after having taken part in the War of Independence. You may enter provided that you are decently dressed, and visit the church with its bell-tower and the convent buildings, all bathed in a serene atmosphere. However, the place is especially worthwhile for the **view★★** of Hydra and the Argolid coast.

# On the beach

Spétses has several fine (often pebble) beaches to choose from for swimming. You get to them by boat or on foot if you are a keen walker. However, it is worth noting that nearly all the island's beaches – among the best in the Saronic Gulf – are well provided with facilities (sun-beds, water-sports equipment, etc) and can get very crowded, not least when the tavernas start livening up in the evenings. Despite this, the little bays beyond **Agía Marína**, south of the old harbour, and the sandy beach at **Kaiki\*** *(1.5km north of the town)* are very attractive. But it is on the west of the island where you will find the best beaches, fringed by pines and scrubland. They include **Ágioi Anárgiri\*\*** (unfortunately very popular), **Agía Paraskeví\*\***, which is accessible by boat, or **Zogeriá\*\***, on the northern tip of the island *(2km from Agía Paraskeví)*.

## Making the most of Spétses

### COMING AND GOING

**By boat** – See also "Making the most of the Saronic Gulf", page 168. Spétses is 70min from Athens by hydrofoil. Ferries also cross to Kósta on the Argolid coast (15min crossing).
**Harbour Police**, in the second square left of the landing-stage, beside the Bouboulína ouzo bar, ☎ (0298) 72 245. Timetables for boats to Piraeus.
If you have a boat, there are moorings for yachts and sailing boats in the old harbour – where you can fill up with water and fuel – or on the mainland, in the bays of Portohéli and Toló.

### GETTING AROUND

**By bus** – Standing with your back to the sea, the terminal is on the left side of Dápia. 2 buses do the return trip to the beach at Ágioi Anárgiri, as well as to Kastéli.

**By bicycle and motorcycle** – This is the ideal way to tour the island. Plenty of bicycle, motorcycle and moped *rental agents* offer their services for the day or half day (it takes 2-3hr to do the 28km round the island). To hire a mountain bicycle, call the **Halcyon Bar**, ☎ (0298) 73 774.

**By horse-drawn carriage** – 35 carriages wait to the left of the landing-stage. If you are not put off by the price, take a ride at sunset; it is very pleasant trotting along the corniche road between Dápia and the old harbour.

**By taxi** – There's a taxi rank near the carriages. Convenient if you have á lot of luggage or if your hotel is far from the centre.

**By boat** – In Dápia harbour there are water-taxis and (less expensive) caiques that go round the island dropping people off at beaches.

### ADDRESS BOOK

**Tourist information** – There is no municipal office, but several private agencies to the left of the landing-stage rent out rooms, sell boat tickets and organise excursions. One such is **Melédon** and **Mimoza**, ☎ and Fax (0298) 73 427, and in Athens: ☎ (01) 68 22 026 / 68 48 590.

**Bank / Currency exchange** – In Dápia you will find plenty of banks that change money and have cash dispensers. The nearest to the harbour are **Ionian Bank** (Visa and Mastercard) and **Alpha Bank** (Visa, American Express).

**Post office** – In the street parallel to the waterfront, between the landing-stage and the museum.

**Telephone** – **OTE**, behind the Posidonion Hotel, ☎ (0298) 72 199.

**Internet** – **Delfinia Net-café**, just beyond the Roussos restaurant, on the road to the old harbour. An Internet café open all year round.

**Police** – 150m below the Mexis Museum, ☎ (0298) 73 100. The building also houses the Tourist Police ☎ (0298) 73 744.

**Medical service** – The Tourist Police provide telephone numbers for doctors on duty and emergency services. A first-aid post is open in the morning from Monday to Friday. ☎ (0298) 72 472.

**Pharmacy**, behind the harbour police, in the street running parallel to the sea. Open daily in the morning.

**Other – Laundry**, in a street parallel to the harbour, behind the Pisteos Bank. Washing, dry-cleaning and ironing.

### Where to stay

The Spétses hotels are in different areas depending on their category. The smarter ones are near the Posidonion, north-west of Dápia, while the guesthouses and cheaper places are in the old harbour. Luxury hotel complexes with swimming pools tend to be on the hillside, 10-15min on foot from Dápia.

#### • Dápia

The very lively Dápia area in the town centre is noisy. Here, however, are two quiet places:

*Between €30 and €55*

👒 **Villa Christina**, a hundred metres from Dápia in a quiet street (signposted), ☎ (0298) 72 218 – 14rm of which 2 are studios. An authentic Spetsiot house with pleasant rooms giving onto a garden with lemon trees and bougainvillaea where breakfast is served. Good value for money, and charming too.

**Villa Mimoza** behind Bouboulína's House, 200m from the harbour, ☎ (0298) 73 426, Fax (0298) 73 427 – 12rm. The rooms with fridges and balconies are tiny. But you can enjoy the large garden where barbecues are organised twice a week.

#### • South-east of Dápia

*Between €24 and €37*

**Villa Marina**, on the way to the old harbour, in a street heading off to the right of a kiosk, ☎ (0298) 72 646 / 660 – 16rm. While the house lacks charm, it is in a good position between the two harbours. Some of the rooms give onto the sea. Each has a fridge. You may make breakfast in the shared kitchen and enjoy it in the pleasant flower-filled courtyard.

#### • North-west of Dápia

*Between €55 and €66*

👒 **Posidonion**, on the waterfront, on the right side of Dápia, ☎ (0298) 72 308 / 72 006 – 43rm and 3 suites. Even if the place could do with a lick of paint, it is the ideal venue for savouring the luxury hotel atmosphere of the roaring twenties. There are marble staircases, rooms with high ceilings, and, on the waterfront, a spacious and inviting terrace shaded by parasols and palm trees where you can sip a drink. All that's missing are the boaters and crinolines. Delightful.

*Between €100 and €290*

**Nisia**, 500m from Dápia, beyond the Posidonion, on the waterfront, ☎ (0298) 75 000, Fax (0298) 75 012. Reservation in Athens (31 houses and studios): ☎ (01) 346 28 79, Fax (01) 346 53 13. If you want to be really extravagant! A very refined deluxe complex built in the local style. Each private house, superbly equipped and tastefully furnished, has a fireplace for winter and a private garden. Each studio has a terrace. The restaurant serves very good international fare and is one of the town's top places to eat.

### Eating out

Spetsiot restaurants favour quality. Try the local speciality, cod with tomatoes and garlic cooked in white wine.

#### • Dápia

**Politis**, not far from the Posidonion Hotel. A café that serves full breakfasts and is good value for money. It is also one of the best cake shops on the island (delicious almond cakes).

*Between €9 and €12*

**To Spezotiko**, decent cooking, less expensive than the neighbouring Roussos. Try the grilled octopus and the garlic-flavoured cream chicken with mushrooms, not bad at all.

**Roussos**, on the left side of Dápia, towards the old harbour. A good place, in spite of touting by the waiters. Homemade taramosaláta, flavourful Spetsiot fish and crisp chips done to perfection. Avoid the rather acidic carafe wine.

- **Old harbour**

*Between €13 and €15*

**Byzantino**, halfway between Dápia and the old harbour. A trendy place with an unrestricted view of the bay. Excellent assortment of meze washed down with a good white wine. Fish dishes are more expensive.

**Mourayo**, at the far end of the old harbour. This quiet, friendly restaurant with a terrace overlooking the sea offers cuisine of a high standard including fish cooked à la Spétses and French dishes. For night owls: Greek music and a piano bar from 2am.

- **Kastéli**

*Around €9*

**Lazaros**, in an old Spetsiot mansion at the top of the street leading from Bouboulína's House. This taverna is known for its speciality, goat in lemon sauce, which is served with the house retsína. Only open in the evening. Come early for a table.

- **Agía Marína**

*Around €11*

**Paradise**, on the beach of the same name. An excellent place with a view of the sea, where you can have freshly grilled fish between swims or before a night out in Dápia.

- **Ágioi Anárgiri beach**

*Around €14*

**Tassos Taverna**, one of the best places on Spétses for cooked dishes. Try the moussaká served in fondue dishes and the lamb with peppers.

**Bars / Night-clubs – Figaro**, ☎ (0298) 73 220. A pleasant disco in the old harbour.

**Papagayo**, also in the old harbour, ☎ (0298) 73 742. You can have dinner or just a drink while listening to music. Bands on Friday, Saturday and Sunday.

**Local delicacies –** A must: the little almond cakes sold in all the cake shops in town, particularly at **Politis** (see the "Eating out" section above), one of the best on Spétses.

OTHER THINGS TO DO

**Open-air cinema – Titania**, in the street that climbs from Bouboulína's House up towards Kastéli. 2 shows, at 8.30pm and 10.30pm every evening in summer.

**Outdoor pursuits –** All the beaches except the one in the old harbour have facilities for all kinds of water-based activities, including pedalos, water-skiing and parasailing. Horse riding, ☎ (0298) 72 533, mobile 0977 213690.

**Excursions –** There are boat tours of the island from Dápia harbour as well as day trips to the resort at Portohéli on the Peloponnese coast.

**Local festivals –** 26 July: traditional festival at the Church of Agía Paraskeví, on the beach of the same name. On the nearest Saturday to 8 September, the **victory of Spetsiot shipowners** over the Turks is commemorated with fireworks and dancing throughout the town.

**Making the most of Spétses**

Sime/DIAF

Alónissos: Vótsi Bay

# THE SPORADES

Beaches lapped by turquoise water, villages with white houses and shaded alleyways, Byzantine monasteries crammed with icons, small fishing harbours bursting with life... little wonder that the Sporades are particularly favoured by Greeks and tourists alike.

The islands have something for everyone, sun lovers, night-owls, boating enthusiasts, scuba divers and hikers.

Spreading out into the heart of the Aegean off the Pelion Peninsula and the island of Euboea, the islands live up to their name, meaning "scattered". The northern Sporades, Skiáthos, Skópelos and Alónissos, and their dependent islets lie close together, while Skíros occupies an isolated position to the south-east. Along with fishing and sheep rearing, the pine forests, olive groves, orchards and vineyards long provided the island inhabitants with all they needed for a prosperous life. But now the magnificent landscapes are focusing the interest more on tourism.

**Skiáthos**, a short distance off the Pelion Peninsula, has an impressive number of tavernas, bars, hotels and souvenir shops. What it has gained in liveliness it has lost in authenticity, but its fine sandy beaches are among the most beautiful in the country. However, if you want a taste of ageless Greece, you would do better to opt for **Skópelos**, the most fertile of the Sporades. It boasts a delightful harbour, a host of chapels and monasteries dotted about the verdant countryside, and myriad beaches and creeks. **Alónissos**, long sheltered from tourism, now sees a growing number of visitors who enjoy the friendly welcome and lovely beaches. A visit to the Marine Park may also provide the opportunity of seeing the last of the monk seals. Lastly, **Skíros**, wilder and more mountainous, has a character all of its own with its distinctive culture and village architecture: you are already in the Cyclades.

# ALÓNISSOS★

Sporades – Province of Thessaly – District of Magnissía
115km from Vólos – Michelin map 980 fold 18-19
65km² – Pop 3 000 – Allow 2 days

### Not to be missed
The old village of Alónissos and the beaches on the east coast.

Long neglected by tour operators, Alónissos now attracts an increasing number of visitors, who come not only for the beaches and the caique trips to creeks and underwater caves, but also for the island hospitality and the possibility of escaping from mass tourism. The island lies on the far eastern side of the Sporades, its long, tortured form stretching in a ridge from north to south, set off by a chain of pine-covered hills. Alónissos is also known for its Marine Park with crystal-clear water, home to a small community of monk seals, some of the rarest mammals in the Mediterranean.

## Tour of the island

### Patitíri, the Alónissos harbour
Patitíri and its harbour, the main town on Alónissos, has the usual range of hotels, restaurants and travel agents but not the hectic pace you find elsewhere in the Sporades. Indeed, the traditional siesta has not entirely given in to the needs of tourism. The modern town does not have much character but lies in a delightful setting in the curve of a bay dominated by a promontory covered in pines... and hotels. As for the vines that gave Patitíri its name ("wine press"), they have long since disappeared, wiped out by an epidemic of phylloxera.

*Two roads from the harbour go up into the village: Pélagon, on the left, leads to the old village of Alónissos, and Ikion Dolopon, on the right, leads to Vótsi and the east coast. Energetic visitors can go from Patitíri to Alónissos on foot (4km; 1hr walk), along a pretty path marked "Ecological Cultural Hiking Trail" (which begins near Galini guesthouse).*

### The old village of Alónissos★★★
Like a condensed version of ageless Greece, Alónissos displays its traditional white or blue houses with tile or slate roofs, its terraces shaded by plane trees and churches bathed in light. Fortunately, motorised vehicles have been banned, so you explore the winding alleyways on foot. Like a citadel perched on the heights, the village affords a splendid **view★★★** of the sea.

### Disruption through the ages
Alónissos has been developing apace over the last few decades. After the terrible earthquake in 1965, the government decided to move the capital close to the sea from its age-old location on the heights. Unwilling to abandon their village for uncomfortable military accommodation, the inhabitants long resisted the idea. But during the decade that followed, schools and administrative offices moved, thus causing an exodus of the population. Then, in the 1990s, rich foreigners set their hearts on the village and bought up and renovated the houses. Alónissos has regained all its character, but people there speak just as much English, German and French as they do Greek.

Several **beaches** are accessible from the village by car or on foot, including **Megálo Mourtiá**, **Mikro Mourtiá** *(45min walk)*, **Marpoúnda** and **Vrysítsa** *(35min walk)*.
To stay on the island you can also opt for one of the twin villages of **Rousoúm★** and **Vótsi★** *(15 and 30min on foot from Patitíri)*, both nestling in little bays with very small pebble **beaches**.

### A tour of the beaches
*Tracks of varying degrees of practicability head off to the beaches from the road that leads to the northern tip of the island. You can also get to the beaches by caique.*

The east coast has a series of pebble beaches, such as **Miliá Ialos**★, surrounded by wooded hills, and **Trotzi Yalo**★ and **Lefto Yalo**★★, fringed with olive groves. If you prefer sand, head for **Hrysi Miliá**★★ (*5km from Miliá Ialos*) or the less pretty **Kokkinokástro** (bar), opposite Vrachos islet.

**Stení Vála** fishing harbour (*11km*) is a pleasant place for a holiday, even though its beach is rather ordinary. The same goes for **Kalamákia** (*12.5km*), a little further along. It is protected by **Peristéra island**, with the water between them forming a kind of inland sea.

The long pebble beach at **Ágios Dimítrios**★ (*16km*) attracts few people. Just behind it is a small winter lake that serves as a nesting ground for migratory birds.

### North coast
The northern half of Alónissos has fewer woods and is less attractive, but if you are looking for solitude you are sure to find it at the pebble beach at **Gérakas**★ ("Sunrise") (*19km*), where the road ends (*bring your own provisions*).

As for the west coast, it is not accessible by road or by boat apart from the beaches at **Megáli Ámos** and **Tourkonéri**. It does, however, lend itself to beautiful **walks**★.

### The National Marine Park★★
In addition to the island of Alónissos, four main islets, **Pelagós**, **Gioúra**, **Psathoúra** and **Pipéri** make up the Marine Park that is home to a small community of **monk seals**. There are only about a hundred of these creatures still living in the Mediterranean. Among the other wildlife on these deserted islets are the wild goat, **Eleanora's falcon**, Audouin's gull and the shag. You need special permission to set foot in the park, but you can go on a boat excursion (*see "Making the most of Alónissos"*) and perhaps see some **dolphins**.

## Making the most of Alónissos

**COMING AND GOING**

**By ferry –** Patitíri is the only ferry dock on the island. In summer, ferries leave for Skópelos about three times a day (crossing time: 30min), for Skiáthos two to four times a day (2hr30min), usually stopping at Glóssa and Skópelos, and for Vólos every day except Wednesday (5hr30min). Ferries also serve the Pelion Peninsula, Chalcidice and Euboea.

**By hydrofoil –** Hydrofoils, numerous in summer, nearly all stop at Skópelos and Skiáthos. There are frequent connections with Skiáthos (crossing time: 70min), Skópelos (20min) and Vólos (about 2hr30min). For Skíros, there's a daily connection except on Wednesday and Saturday (85min). For Thessaloníki, one or two connections a day (4hr40min). There are also hydrofoils to the Pelion Peninsula, Chalcidice and Euboea.

GETTING AROUND

**By bus –** In summer, a bus runs every hour between Patitíri (opposite the dock) and Alónissos, from 9am to midnight, except between 3.25pm and 7pm. Tickets are valid for the whole day. Another bus goes twice a day to Stení Vála.

**By taxi –** The taxi rank is near the landing-stage. Rates are shown on a board.

**By bicycle –** Several hire firms in Patitíri, notably in Odós Ikion Dolopon.

**Motorcycle rental – I'M**, ☎ (0424) 65 010. 150m from the harbour, on the right in the street that leads to Alónissos. See also the travel agents given below.

**Car rental –** See the travel agents below. Negotiate rates in the low season.

**By water-taxi –** Caiques are a good means of getting to the beaches on the east coast. They leave from Patitíri harbour in the morning.

ADDRESS BOOK

**Harbourmaster's office –** Odós Ikion Dolopon, Patitíri, ☎ (0424) 65 595.

**Bank / Currency exchange – National Bank**, at the bottom of Odós Ikion Dolopon, Patitíri. Monday-Thursday 8am-2pm and Friday 8am-1.30pm. Cash dispenser.

**Post office / Telephone –** On the right hand side of Odós Ikion Dolopon, Patitíri. Monday-Friday 7am-2pm.

**Travel agents – Albedo**, Patitíri, to the right of the landing-stage, ☎ (0424) 65 804, Fax (0424) 65 806. Car rental, room reservations, ferry and plane tickets, currency exchange. Three other agents offer the same services: **Alónissos Travel**, ☎ (0424) 65 188, Fax (0424) 65 511. **Drossakis Travel**, take Odós Pélagon from the harbour, ☎ (0424) 65 225, Fax (0424) 65 719. **Ikos Travel**, Patitíri, in the harbour, ☎ (0424) 65 320, Fax (0424) 65 321. Organised walks and a cruise in the Marine Park.

**Police –** Near the National Bank, ☎ (0424) 65 205.

WHERE TO STAY

Alónissos has plenty of accommodation and is a little less expensive than Skópelos or Skiáthos. At the height of summer, guesthouses often require you to stay at least 2 or 3 days.

**Rooms to Let**, Patitíri, near the landing-stage, ☎ and Fax (0424) 65 577. This municipal service helps you find accommodation. Daily 10am-2.30pm / 6pm-10pm, from May to September.

• **Patitíri and environs**
As the hotels in the harbour are noisy, try those on Kavos hill, to the right of the creek.

*Under €30*
**Domátia Nikos Alexiou**, Patitíri, Odós Pélagon, ☎ (0424) 65 239 – 3rm. This little guesthouse has simple, unembellished rooms. Bathrooms upstairs.
**Domátia Georgios N Kalogiannis**, Vótsi, ☎ (0424) 65 273, Fax (0424) 65 822 – 34rm or studios. ⁌ ✕ A simple, friendly guesthouse set back from the harbour. Flowery decor.

*Between €30 and €45*
**Domátia Dimitris**, Vótsi, ☎ (0424) 65 035 – 8rm. ⁌ ⤱ ℘ A guesthouse perched above the harbour among trees. Studios and small but pleasant rooms with balconies overlooking the bay.
**Agalloy Konstandínos**, Rousoúm, ☎ (0424) 65 360, Fax (0424) 65 640 – 16rm. ⁌ Quite small though comfortable rooms with terraces. No view.
**Aristotelis**, Rousoúm Ialós, ☎ (0424) 65 380 – 10rm. ⁌ ℘ Set in a small white building on the promontory to the right of the harbour. An inexpensive guesthouse with a lovely view of the bay. Clean, comfortable rooms.
**Domátia Avra Dimitris & Maria**, Patitíri, in the harbour, ☎ (0424) 65 047 – 8rm. ⁌ Studios set above a cafeteria, and therefore a little noisy. The manager is planning to install kitchenettes and air conditioning.
**Pension Ninna**, Patitíri, ☎ (0424) 65 242 – 17rm. ⁌ This welcoming, well-run hotel overlooking the harbour provides comfortable accommodation in rooms or studios (kitchenette), with terraces. Breakfast extra.
**Kavos**, Patitíri, ☎ (0424) 65 216, Fax (0424) 65 083 – 22rm. ⁌ ℘ A welcoming hotel.

The Sporades

@ **Liadromia Hotel**, Patitíri, ☎ (0424) 65 521, Fax (0424) 65 096 – 20rm. ⌐| ℰ cc The hotel, located on Kavos promontory and run by a friendly manager full of information about the island, has real character. The rooms with balconies giving onto the harbour are very comfortable.

*Between €45 and €60*
**Alkyon Hotel**, in the harbour, ☎ (0424) 65 602, Fax (0424) 65 195 – 36rm. ⌐| ℰ ✗ Comfortable rooms with a view of the harbour (quite noisy). Rather cool reception.

**Hotel Gorgona**, Rousoúm, on the seafront, ☎ (0424) 65 317, Fax (0424) 65 629 – 26rm. ⌐| ⌣ ℰ April to October. Comfortable rooms, some of which look onto the bay. Relatively expensive studios with kitchenettes, but the price is negotiable.

*Over €60*
@ **Paradise**, Patitíri, on Kavos spur, ☎ (0424) 65 213, Fax (0424) 65 161 – 31rm. ⌐| ℰ ⌣ cc A luxury hotel open from May to October (booking is essential in summer). Very comfortable rooms. Breakfast is served on a terrace. Swimming pool with a view of the sea.

• **Alónissos**
*Between €30 and €45*
**Domátia Hiliadromia**, in the first square in the village, ☎ and Fax (0424) 65 814 – 12rm. ⌐| A charming guesthouse. Rooms and studios with a view.

• **East coast**
*Over €75*
@ **Milia Bay**, ☎ (0424) 66 032, Fax (0424) 66 037 – 12rm. ⌐| ⌣ ℰ TV ⌣ This new hotel perched on a hill among the pines has an unrestricted view of the bay. Luxury studios equipped with kitchens and verandas. Garden swimming pool with a pleasant bar.

**EATING OUT**
Alónissos has a wide choice of eating places, in Patitíri (avoid the restaurants in the harbour, which are expensive and not very welcoming), in the old village and on most of the beaches.

• **Patitíri and environs**
*Under €12*
**Garden Restaurant**, on the tip of the rocky Kavos headland. ⌂ A very

pleasant garden terrace facing the sea, serving Greek dishes and seafood. Fairly varied wine list. Closed at midday.

**Argo Restaurant**, on the tip of the rocky Kavos headland. ⌂ Not far from the Garden Restaurant, and similar in style.

**Babis**, on the road to Alónissos, just beyond the fuel station. A good restaurant with a lovely terrace overlooking the village. Rather dreary dining room.

• **Alónissos**
The restaurants are closed during the day, except in July and August.

*Under €12*
@ **Nikos Taverna**, at the entrance to the village, on the right. ⌂ A delightful terrace with trellised vines and a view of the sea. The restaurant is renowned for its grilled dishes and seafood.

@ **Paraport Taverna**, at the end of the village. ⌂ This has the finest view in the village. Good choice of Greek dishes.

**Kástro**, one of the two restaurants in the main street. ⌂ Unremarkable fare but pleasant setting.

**I Kyrá Nina**, opposite the Kástro. ⌂ Greek dishes and seafood.

**HAVING A DRINK**

**Cafés, bars – Aerídes**, Alónissos, in the first square in the village. ⌂ A very pleasant little bar, with a good choice of Western music. Cake specialities.

**Ostrio Café**, Rousoúm. A delightful café giving onto the beach.

**OTHER THINGS TO DO**

**Excursions –** Alónissos is a paradise for walkers. You can either go through a travel agent or buy a copy of the very useful "Alónissos on Foot".

**Ikos Travel**, see "Travel agents" above.
**Kassándra**, ☎ (0932) 524 180. This yacht does excursions into the Marine Park (departure at 11am, return at 5.30pm).

**SHOPPING GUIDE**

**Antiques, arts and crafts –**
**Gorgóna**, Alónissos, ☎ (0424) 65 104. A good shop selling antiques and ancient textiles.

**Ergastírio**, Alónissos, ☎ (0945) 31 27 96. Traditional jewellery and local arts and crafts.

# SKIÁTHOS

Sporades – Province of Thessaly – District of Magnissía
76km from Vólos – Michelin map 980 fold 18 – Regional map page 195
50km² – Pop 5 000

**Not to be missed**
A tour of Skiáthos Town and Kástro.
The beaches. A boat trip.

**And remember...**
Avoid Skiáthos in July and August, and book your accommodation beforehand.

Small fishing harbours, bays with turquoise water, seafood restaurants, burning sandy beaches, Skiáthos has many attractions, which people have known about for a long time. Hence the island's rating as one of the top tourist destinations in the country. Naturally, the development has not come about without its downside, and you will search in vain for signs of the traditional, gentle way of life, or a deserted beach. Skiáthos especially appeals to those who enjoy swimming, boat trips and night-life, and are not put off by crowds of holidaymakers.

## From the Chalcidians to Barbarossa

The first inhabitants of the island, long ago, were the Kares, who were succeeded by the **Chalcidians**, in the 8C BC. But it was in 478 BC that Skiáthos came into the picture historically speaking by joining the Athenian League. After the Peloponnesian War, it came under the yoke of Sparta, and then reverted to Athens before being conquered by the Macedonians. During the Middle Ages, under constant threat of attack by Barbarossa's pirates, the inhabitants of the island took refuge in Kástro, in the north. Then in 1204, the island was attached to the Duchy of Náxos. In 1538, the Turks took control and remained on the island until 1823. Several years later the inhabitants abandoned Kástro and gave their first capital a new name, Skiáthos.

## Tour of the island
*Allow 2 days on the island*

### Skiáthos Town*

*From the landing-stage, the main street Odós Papadiamántis (closed to traffic at 8pm), heads inland and cuts across Odós Evangelístrias at the post office.* Skiáthos is a picturesque town built on the slopes of two hills, with white houses with red roofs. It has kept much of its charm, and is further enhanced by the small, pine-clad **Boúrdzi peninsula** that separates the old harbour from the new.

Relatively peaceful in winter, Skiáthos becomes a completely different place in summer when the charter flights of tourists arrive. The countless souvenir shops, money changers, restaurants and hotels that have invaded the waterfront bear witness to the ever-growing industry. Every evening, the town comes joyfully to life until late, as the bay lights up with the incandescent reflections of the peninsula, and the water laps gently against the fishing boats.

For a more authentic atmosphere, leave the main thoroughfares and lose yourself in the maze of alleyways that burst here and there into colourful cascades of bougainvillaea. The tiny **Aléxandros Papadiamántis Museum** *(9am-1pm / 5pm-8pm, in the main street)*, set in the home of the poet and novelist, is of little interest, unless you want to fill a rainy afternoon.

### A short cultural tour...

Head north. A road near the airport leads to the **Evangelístria Monastery** *(allow 1hr on foot)*, which crowns the highest point on the island (438m) in a delightful setting of cypresses and pines. The church contains a beautiful wooden **iconostasis**.

The Sporades

Further north, near the coast, is the **Ágios Harálambos Monastery**, perched above a narrow strip of pebble beach called **Lalária** (*accessible by caique*), famous for its **pierced rock**.

Further west, you come to **Kástro***, the former capital (1540-1829). Perched on a dramatic rocky promontory overlooking the sea (*90min by caique, 4hr on foot, outward journey*), it occupies an impregnable site, which in the past sheltered it from pirates. A drawbridge across a precipice once closed off the entrance. Take the time to stroll through the ruined village and look at the two churches. One contains a lovely 17C wooden **iconostasis**.

## ...and lazing on the beach

The island has more than sixty beaches; most alas, are overcrowded. If you are looking for a little peace and quiet, head for the ones on the north coast, or those that are only accessible by boat. Whatever the case, however, don't count on finding anything deserted. We recommend the following:

From Skiáthos Town heading southwards, leave Megáli Ámos, Vassiliás and Ahladiá beaches and continue to the small one at **Nóstos** (*7km*) (taverna, water-sports club) or, 1km further on, that of **Kanapísta**, which is also family-friendly and offers the same activities.

Beyond this are the beaches on the headland, particularly **Vromólimnos** (tavernas), bordered by pine trees.

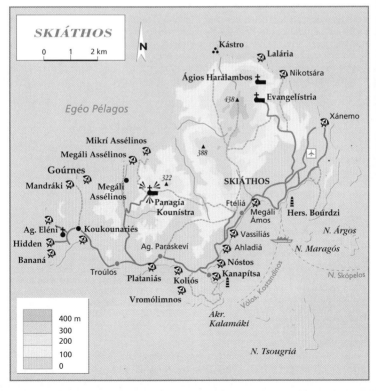

Not far from **Koliós** beach is the one at **Plataniás** (tavernas, water sports), which is longer, but just as crowded.

For a prettier setting, head for **Koukounariés**\* *(showers)*, considered to be one of Greece's most beautiful. Having been spared any concrete, apart from a marina and kiosks selling drinks, fried fish and English newspapers, the beach forms a little lagoon surrounded by pines, home to a protected ecosystem. However, Koukounariés pays for its success by attracting a large crowd.

Less packed because it is more difficult to reach, the attractive **Bananá**\* (Krassás) beach (taverna, water-sports clubs) on the south-west tip of the island is just as good an option. To reach it, go to the end of the lake, turn right along a track that goes through a pine forest, then head downhill through olive and fig trees. The **Small Bananá Beach** nearby is favoured by nudists.

Further north *(return to the main road and take the road near the Golden Beach Hotel)* you will find another pleasant beach, **Agía Eléni**\*, which is backed by pine trees and has a taverna. Off the coast, you can see the prow of a shipwreck emerging from the waves. A better option still is the tiny **Hidden Beach**\*\* (taverna) 1km away down a poor track, squashed-in at the foot of a hill covered in heather.

A winding track from the lake leads across a wild moor carpeted with heather to the west coast, and serves the less crowded northern beaches. You have a choice between **Mandráki**\* (Limáni Xérxi) (tavernas) with its beautiful fine sand and **Goúrnes**, a little further on.

A road from Troúlos leads directly to the west coast, to **Megáli Assélinos** *(after 2km, turn left at the fork)*, a large beach with a campsite and a taverna.

Keep the best part for the end of your trip: return to the fork and take the road left that winds up the hill to **Panagía Kounístra Monastery**, in the middle of sweet-smelling pines. The superb **panoramic view**\*\* stretches to the sea. The road then becomes a track and leads down towards the coast, running above it as far as **Mikrí Assélinos**\*\* (taverna), a delightful beach nestling in the heart of some of the island's most beautiful scenery.

## Making the most of Skiáthos

## GETTING AROUND

**By bus** – The **terminal** is at the end of the new harbour. Every 30min from 7.30am to 10.30pm a bus serves the beaches up to Koukounariés (travelling time: 30min). The bus is packed on the return journey towards the end of the day. There are fewer connections with Megáli Assélinos.

**By taxi** – Taxi rank to the right of the landing-stage, ☎ (0427) 21 460. Negotiate the fare beforehand.

**Motorcycle / car rental** – Negotiate a small reduction if you are hiring for several days. No matter what time you rent, you will pay for the whole day, up to 8pm.
**Autorent**, ☎ (0427) 21 797. **Avis**, ☎ (0427) 214 58, Fax (0427) 232 89. **Europcar**, ☎ (0427) 21 124. **Hertz**, main street, ☎ (0427) 23 706. **Mamaras**, at the end of Odós Papadiamántis, on the left, ☎ and Fax (0427) 21 777; cars and motorcycles. **Thanos**, main street, near the International Bank, ☎ (0427) 22 810; motorcycles. **Rent a Car, A & E Aivalioti**, to the right of the landing-stage, ☎ (0427) 21 246; cars and motorcycles.

**By boat** – Most of the beaches on the south coast can be reached by caique. The boats leave from the old harbour from 10am onwards and return from 4pm onwards.

### ADDRESS BOOK
There is no tourist office. Enquire at travel agents or at the harbourmaster's office.

**Tourist police** – At the top of the main street, on the right, ☎ (0427) 23 172. Daily, 8am-8pm.

**Harbourmaster's office** – Provides information on ferries and hydrofoils, ☎ (0427) 22 017.

**Bank / Currency exchange** – There are plenty of money changers, banks and cash dispensers.
**National Bank**, main street. Monday-Thursday, 8am-2pm, Friday, 8am-1.30pm.

**Post office** – Odós Papadiamántis, on the right. Monday-Friday, 7.30am-2pm. Poste restante.

**Telephone** – Local code: 0427. **OTE**, main street, 7.30am-2.30pm; closed Sunday.

**Internet** – **Skiáthos Internet Center**, coming from the main street, turn right at the post office into Odós Evangelístrias, then left into Odós Miaúli (11am-1am).

**Airline companies** – **Olympic Airways**, Odós Papadiamántis, ☎ (0427) 22 200.

**Travel agents** – **Alkyon Travel**, at the end of Odós Papadiamántis, ☎ (0427) 22 029.

**Heliotropo**, on the right when coming from the landing-stage, ☎ (0427) 22 430 / 21 538.

**Mare Nostrum Holidays**, Odós Papadiamántis 21, ☎ (0427) 21 463. The agent represents American Express and changes travellers' cheques without commission.

### WHERE TO STAY
In July and August, prices increase by 50 to 200% and hotels are often full.

#### • Skiáthos
*Under €45*
**Hotel Morfo**, coming from the main street, turn right at the National Bank, ☎ (0427) 21 737 – 16rm. ⌖ ℰ 🆑 Small, comfortable rooms decorated with wood trim, with a view either of the street or a garden. Friendly reception.
**Karafelas**, at the end of Odós Papadiamántis, on the left, ☎ (0427) 21 235 – 16rm. ⌖ ✕ Clean, simple, panelled rooms at a reasonable price. Some of the best value for money on Skiáthos.
**Meltémi Hotel**, new harbour, near the landing-stage, ☎ (0427) 22 493 – 18rm. ⌖ ✕ ℰ A comfortable, beautifully kept hotel with charming rooms giving onto the harbour.
**Hotel Pothos**, go up Odós Papadiamántis and turn left into Odós Evangelístrias, ☎ (0427) 22 694, Fax (0427) 23 242 – 22rm. ⌖ ▤ ℰ A good hotel with panelling in the lounge. The rooms are comfortable, but lack charm. Breakfast included.
**Christina**, new harbour, ☎ (0427) 22 747, Fax (0427) 21 466 – 26rm. ⌖ ℰ Comfortable though characterless rooms equipped with kitchenettes, with a view of the harbour. Prices rocket in summer.
**Hotel Mato**, in an alleyway above the old harbour, near the church, ☎ (0427) 22 186, Fax (0427) 23 105 – 9rm. ⌖ ▤ ℰ 📺 🆑 A charming

little hotel set among palm trees and bougainvillaea. The rooms have every modern comfort and breakfast (included) is served in a delightful room with a fireplace.

### • Ahladiá

*Under €45*

**Alexander & Pavlina Karvounis**, no 10 bus stop, ☎ (0427) 22 486 – 10rm. ⁜ 🏊 A pleasant, simple guesthouse with a garden and a view of the sea. Rooms and apartments are let for a minimum of 3 to 5 days. The beach is just below the rocks.

*Between €45 and €60*

**Vontzos**, no 10 bus stop, ☎ (0427) 22 875, Fax (0427) 21 285 – 23rm. ⁜ ✗ A modest, reasonable hotel rather lacking in character. Good value for money but unfriendly reception.

### • Kanapítsa

*Between €90 and €105*

🏠 **Cape Kanapítsa**, beyond the beach, no 12 bus stop, ☎ (0427) 21 752, Fax (0427) 22 170 – 34rm. ⁜ 🍽 🖉 📺 🏊 🏊 cc An elegant hotel set among the pines. Very pleasant rooms with flagstone flooring and balconies overlooking the sea. Apartments are also available. Closed from October to February.

**Plaza Hotel**, ☎ (0427) 21 971, Fax (0427) 22 109 – 80rm. ⁜ 🍽 / ✗ 🖉 ✗ 🏊 🏊 ⚓ cc A chic though characterless hotel in a quiet, pleasant setting 100m from the beach. The rooms are clean and comfortable (some have television). Ask for one with a balcony overlooking the sea. Open from May to October. Facilities include table tennis, adventure playground, billiards, waterskiing and windsurfing.

### • Agía Paraskeví, Koliós

*Between €45 and €60*

**Stefano's House**, no 14 bus stop, ☎ (0427) 49 322, Fax (0427) 49 493 – 9rm. ⁜ In a quiet setting near an olive grove and a private beach. The guesthouse lets studios and apartments equipped with kitchens, with a view of the sea. The rooms are rather hot.

*Between €75 and €90*

**Arco**, no 14 or 15 bus stop, ☎ (0427) 49 387, Fax (0427) 49 377 – 53rm. ⁜ 🖉 📺 ✗ 🏊 🏊 cc A hotel with a white marble hall and a garden planted with trees. Comfortable, impeccably-kept

rooms. Unfortunately you get a rather cold welcome and the prices are very high in summer.

**Magic Hotel**, ☎ and Fax (0427) 49 453 – 26rm. ⁜ 🍽 🖉 ✗ cc On a hillside, with comfortable rooms with balconies overlooking the sea (100m away, on the other side of the road). Warm welcome. Breakfast included.

*Over €150*

**Skiáthos Princess**, no 15 bus stop, ☎ (0427) 49 226, Fax (0427) 49 666 – 131rm. ⁜ 🖉 ✗ 🏊 🏊 cc A long white three-storey building with a garden facing the sea. The rooms with balconies are not particularly tasteful, though very comfortable. The hotel is ideal for families, offering stays with half-board. There is a gym, a jacuzzi and an adventure playground for children.

### • Plataniás

*Under €90*

🏠 **Atrium**, ☎ (0427) 49 345, Fax (0427) 49 444 – 78rm. ⁜ 🖉 ✗ 🏊 🏊 cc A luxury hotel clinging to the hillside at the end of a creek. It is a rather tough climb back from the beach, but the setting gives the place a superb view of the sea. The entrance, made of marble and stone, is attractively furnished and very elegant. Lovely rooms with balconies.

### • Troúlos

*Under €75*

**Troúlos Bay Hotel**, ☎ (0427) 49 390, Fax (0427) 49 218 – 43rm. ⁜ 🖉 ✗ 🏊 cc The irreproachably comfortable rooms (ask for one with a balcony overlooking the beach) are unfortunately rather small. Breakfast included.

### • Koukounariés

*Campsite (around €15)*

**Assélinos**, Megáli Assélinos, ☎ (0427) 49 250 – 1 000 pitches. ✗ 300m from the beach, in a quiet setting planted with trees. The only official campsite on the island. There is a mini-market. Open from May to October.

*Under €60*

**Villa Nikos**, ☎ (0427) 49 291 – 8rm. ⁜ Modest, basic rooms in a small hotel set back from the beach. The place is considered to be the oldest hotel in Koukounariés (1965). Apartments are also available. Open from July to September.

**Lake Hotel**, opposite the lake, ☎ (0427) 49 362 – 16rm. ⁕ Small, clean comfortable rooms. Avoid the rather dark ones on the ground floor. Breakfast included.

*Over €150*

**Skiáthos Palace**, 12km from Skiáthos, ☎ (0427) 49 700, Fax (0427) 49 666 – 254rm. ⁕ ℰ TV ✕ ☍ ☌ ☓ CC A renowned, undeniably comfortable establishment dating from the 1970s, with exorbitant prices. The hotel is 200m from the beach and has a superb swimming pool on the roof, with a view. Numerous services (shops, car rental, travel agents).

EATING OUT

• **Skiáthos**

You are spoilt for choice for places to eat in the town and along the waterfront, but quality and service are disappointing, and prices are high. Most of the island's beaches have at least one taverna.

*Under €15*

**Nikos**, main street, on the right, before the National Bank. A good place for breakfast, where you are given a friendly welcome and copious servings.

**George Taverna**, main street, opposite the Nikos. To be avoided, however, unless you have no choice. Unlike the Nikos, the service is not friendly and the portions are tiny.

**Taverna Ouzerí**, left of the landing-stage, opposite the peninsula. ☍ An enormous terrace, where salads, souvláki, fish, seafood and ice cream are served.

**Dionnissos**, main street. Turn right at the National Bank. ☍ Greek and Italian specialities served on an enormous, attractive terrace. Set menus at reasonable rates.

*Over €15*

**Mistral**, turn left off Odós Papadiamántis on the corner with the National Bank, and then left again at the end of the alleyway. ☍ A charming little restaurant (only open in the evening), where you are served Greek dishes in the shade of olive trees.

**Taverna Polikrates**, at the top of Odós Papadiamántis. ☍ One of the town's smartest establishments, where it is best to book. A pleasant terrace in spite of the throng, where you can try aubergine croquettes with cheese or veal in a cheese and basil sauce, among other delights.

**Psaradika**, on the waterfront, at the far end of the old harbour. ☍ A taverna slightly off the beaten track. Excellent grilled fish.

**Taverna Asprolithos**, at the top of Odós Papadiamántis turn right behind the school, then into the first street on the right, ☎ (0427) 21 016. ☍ Customers dress up to come to this smart, expensive restaurant. Good quality fare. Only open in the evening. Booking recommended.

**The Windmill**, in the upper town. This has become an institution in Skiáthos. Set at the foot of a windmill with an exceptional view. Original decor and refined cooking (European), but with prices to match.

HAVING A DRINK

**Cafés, bars** – Difficult to recommend a place as there are so many. **Kentavros Bar**, near the Papadiamántis Museum. This small bar has been an island institution "since 1978", featuring funk, acid jazz and blues.

**Bourzi**, on the peninsula. A romantic bar, where you can sip a drink on the terrace as you look out over the sea. Soft Greek music.

**Oasis**, at the end of the old harbour, on the right. Wickerwork armchairs and backgammon.

OTHER THINGS TO DO

**Excursions** – A boat in the old harbour does a **tour of the island** (departure 10am, return 5pm), with all sorts of stops. Another goes round the north coast (departure 10am, return 3pm).

**Outdoor pursuits** – Nearly all the beaches have their own water-sports club with windsurfing, water-skiing, etc.

SHOPPING GUIDE

**Antiques** – **Markos Botsaris**, near the Papadiamántis Museum, ☎ (0427) 22 163. A museum-like establishment in a kind of doll's house.

**Newspapers** – **Licos Line**, on the waterfront, to the right of the main street. English-language newspapers.

**Making the most of Skiáthos**

# SKÍROS ★★

Sporades – Province of Thessaly – District of Magnissía
46km from Kími (Euboea) – Michelin map 980 fold 19 – Regional map page 195
223km² – Pop 2 900

**Not to be missed**
The village of Skíros (Hóra) and its traditional houses.
The beaches on the northern peninsula and the desolate landscapes in the south.

**And remember...**
The most convenient way to tour the island is by motorcycle or car.

Even though Skíros, the largest of the Sporades Islands (223km²), offers the same deserted bays and turquoise waters as the others, it has a very different character, being both harsher and wilder. More than anything, it has managed to preserve its identity, which is apparent in its arts and crafts (carved and painted furniture, embroidery, carpets, basketwork and ceramics), and its strong traditions. The **carnival**, notably, is one of the local highlights. In the villages, you can still come across venerable old men dressed in the baggy blue trousers of yesteryear, thick gaiters and the *trohádia* sandals inherited from Antiquity.

### The carnival trio

The Skíros carnival is held in February to announce the beginning of Lent. It is a strange mixture of pagan rites connected with the cult of Dionysus, the memory of Achilles... and goats. Groups of three men sing, dance and recite poetry through the alleys of Hóra, making a great deal of noise. The main character in the unusual trio is the "Géros", played by an old man wearing the traditional clothes of a shepherd: a mask and a goatskin armed with heavy bells that clank and ring. He is accompanied by the "Kopéla", a young man dressed as a woman, in memory of an event in the life of Achilles, as well as the "Frángos", a comic character dressed in rags, representing... a foreigner!

### Two islands in one

Like a large butterfly, Skíros unfolds its wings on either side of an isthmus barely 2km wide. The two regions thus formed couldn't be more different. The northern one, known as **Méri**, is home to most of the island's population and cultivated land, while the more mountainous **Vounó**, in the south, is home to half-wild sheep and goats, and especially to a breed of small **native horses** whose origins are lost in the mists of time.

Successively colonised by the Carians, the Cretans and the Dolopians, Skíros is mentioned several times by Homer. Its name is connected through legend with the demigod **Achilles**, and with **Theseus**, the son of Aegeus, King of Athens. In the 5C, the island came under Athenian domination and remained so until the arrival of the Romans. A long period of instability began with the advent of the Middle Ages, marked by rivalry between Byzantines, Venetians and Ottomans. But Skíros was integrated into the young Greek State on its independence in 1821. For several decades, tourism has been developing harmoniously under the aegis of a local cooperative. The island has managed to avoid an exodus of its population, and its villages have not been sold to rich foreigners... much to the delight of visitors. The tradition of hospitality, or *philoxénia*, has remained intact.

## Tour of the island
*Allow 3 days*

### Skíros Town★★★ (Hóra)

The main settlement on the island is a superb sight, with its white houses cascading like little cubes down the steep slopes of a rocky outcrop crowned by a citadel. Through the inextricable maze of alleyways runs **Agorá**, a narrow pedestrian street lined with shops, bars and tavernas.

If by chance it is open, do not miss the **Traditional House** at no 992 *(from Halrondopanaya Church, climb up towards the Kástro to a little square with a large tree)*. With its finely carved wood furniture, and its copper and earthenware articles hanging on the walls, the house gives a good idea of a Skyrian interior.

Not far from here is the **Fortress of Lycomedes** (Kástro) *(March-August, 7am-10pm; September-February, 7.30am-6pm)*, an ancient Byzantine fortress, which later became Venetian, and was once one of the most powerful bastions in the Aegean Sea. Its bright walls stand on the site of a temple, where according to legend the young Achilles grew up dressed as a girl, among the daughters of King Lycomedes. He was thus attired so as to escape from death at Troy as announced by the oracle. The outcome proved otherwise.

Today the ruined Kástro is mainly visited for the **view\*\*\*** it affords of the village, the surrounding countryside and the sea.

As you leave, take a look at the **Monastery of St George** (Moní Ágios Geórgios) standing guard at the entrance. Its 10C church contains a fine **iconostasis**, **frescoes** and four columns that come from a temple to Dionysus *(bare legs and shoulders are not allowed)*.

Continue to the northern end of the town, to the **Faltaïts Museum of Folk Arts\*\*** *(summer, 10am-1pm / 6pm-9pm; winter, 10am-1pm / 5.30pm-8pm; fee)* laid out in a vast mansion belonging to the Faltaïts, a rich Skyrian family. Successfully recreating an 1830s interior, the museum displays furniture, kitchen utensils, ceramics, rich fabrics and costumes, as well as an outstanding collection of **old books**, letters and **official documents**. There is a wide choice of ceramics in the shop.

Complete your exploration of old Skíros with a visit to the **Archaeological Museum\***, just next door *(8.30am-3pm; closed Monday; fee)*. There are items from the Helladic and Roman Periods, particularly **pottery** from Palamári, an ancient site on Cape Kastráki, as well as **marble statues** from different periods. The section on Skyrian dwellings includes some magnificent **embroideries\*\***.

Skíros, the old town: a chequerboard of terraces

G. Guérard/MICHELIN

**Skíros**

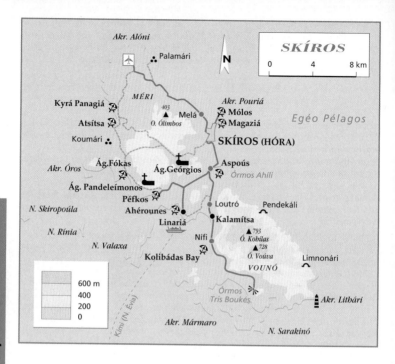

The **statue of Rupert Brooke** (1887-1915) standing on a nearby terrace is a memorial to the English poet who died of septicaemia off Skíros on his way to the Dardanelles. His **grave** is in the southern part of the island.

## The northern peninsula
*From Skíros, head north towards the airport.*

■ A long sweep of sand at the foot of Hóra stretches northwards as far as the eye can see, taking in the beaches at **Magaziá**★ and **Mólos**★ (1km). While these beaches suffer a little from their proximity to the town, you can nonetheless easily enjoy a swim in the sea, or a meal of grilled sea bream on a taverna terrace.

■ Continue now along the road, beyond Bina beach to **Cape Pouriá**. Strange **troglodyte chapels,** some half buried, appear here and there, dotted about a desolate landscape facing a small **windmill** that has lost its sails.

*Beyond Melá the road forks. Bear left, ignoring the road to the airport.*

■ The road avoids the north of the island and very soon reaches the west coast, beginning with the sand and pebble beach at **Kyrá Panagiá** (15km from Hóra, taverna). While the place has less charm than Magaziá or Mólos, it offers the advantage of having few visitors.

■ 2km further south you come to **Atsítsa**, a delightful fishing harbour guarded by a stone tower with its base in the water. There's a **pebble beach** beside the village (beware of sea urchins). However, it is better to swim at the beach 300m from the harbour, or at the little isolated one 2km to the south.

■ From the beach, a track *(practicable)* disappears for 5km into a superb **pine forest**★, bathed in the fragrance of resin, and comes out at a fine pebble beach, **Ágios Fókas**★ *(taverna)*.

■ The road then climbs a hill to the **Chapel of Ágios Pandeleímonos** (4km), a small building without any special charm, but which affords an exceptional **panoramic view**\*\* of the coast and surrounding mountains. Before heading down towards Péfkos, the road runs alongside an old **marble quarry** that was exploited during the Roman era.

■ **Péfkos**\*\* harbour (*3km, or 12km from Skíros*) lies at the foot of wooded hills in the curve of a little bay with a **beach** of fine sand. This haven of peace, barely troubled by the lapping of the waves or the cry of the gulls, is where you will find everything you need for a deliciously lazy time: beach, tavernas and *domátia*.

■ The atmosphere changes at **Linariá** harbour (6km, or 12km from Skíros). With its bars, restaurants and souvenir shops, it is a pleasant place to wander around while waiting for a ferry. However, if you have the time, go instead to **Ahérounes** (2km north), a resort tucked away in a creek with a sand and shingle **beach** (*tavernas, hotel*).

■ Lastly, heading back towards Skíros, you can enjoy **Aspoús beach** (taverna) on the east coast, although it is very exposed to the wind.

## A short trip south (Vounó)

The southern part of the island contrasts completely with the northern. The higher, more tormented relief forms a wild, bare area where you will see sienna-coloured goats melting into the rocky scrub.

■ From Skíros, the road that crosses the isthmus leads to **Kalamítsa** (11km), a small resort with several hotels, lying in the curve of a wide bay that opens out at the foot of some high hills. At the southern end of the bay there is a sand and pebble **beach**, where you will find tavernas and domátia. But if you are looking for solitude, head on, down to the beach at **Kolibádas Bay**\* (*5km*).

■ If you have a vehicle, it is worth heading further south. The landscape becomes breathtakingly barren. At the end of the road, at sunset, the view of the **cliffs**\*\*\* plunging into the sea takes you back to the dawn of time.

### COMING AND GOING

**By air** – The *airport* is on the northern tip of the island, ☎ (0222) 916 25. In summer, Olympic Airways has a return flight to Athens on Wednesday and Sunday (40min).

**By ferry** – The port is at Linariá, on the west coast. Buy your tickets on the spot or at Skíros. Two ferries a day for Kími (Euboea), travelling time: 2hr.
*Lykomidis Ticket Office*, Skíros, near Skíros Travel, ☎ (0222) 917 89, Fax (0222) 917 91.

**By hydrofoil** – Hydrofoils only serve Skíros from June to September. There is one connection a day except on Wednesday and Saturday with Alónissos (75min), Skópelos (1hr40min) and Skiáthos (2hr20min). For Vólos, departure on Tuesday (3hr50min); for Thessaloníki, departures on Monday, Thursday, Friday and Sunday (6hr).

### GETTING AROUND

**By bus** – The terminal is at the bottom of Odós Agorá. A bus goes to Linariá five times a day (travelling time: 20min) to meet the ferries and hydrofoils. There are plenty of buses for Magaziá and Mólos in summer.

**By taxi** – Taxi rank beside the main square, ☎ (0222) 916 66.

**Motorcycle rental** – *Moto Rent*, ☎ (0222) 912 23. *Moto Bagios*, take the alleyway opposite the town hall, ☎ (0222) 929 57.

**Car rental** – *Skíros Travel & Tourism* (see below).
*Pegasus Rent a Car*, Odós Agorá, near the Skíros agency, ☎ (0222) 911 23, Fax (0222) 921 23.

### ADDRESS BOOK

**Harbourmaster's office** – ☎ (0222) 914 75.

**Bank / Currency exchange** – Plenty of money changers in the main street. **National Bank**, Odós Agorá, near the terminal. Monday-Thursday, 7.30am-2pm, Friday, 8am-1.30pm. Cash dispenser.

**Post office** – In the first street on the right as you come up Odós Agorá from the bus terminal. Monday-Friday, 7.30am-2pm.

**Telephone** – Local code: 0222. **OTE**, turn right beyond the main square. Monday-Friday, 7am-2.40pm.

**Travel agents** – **Skíros Travel & Tourism**, ☎ (0222) 916 00, Fax (0222) 921 23. Plane and hydrofoil tickets, car rental. The agency organises boat trips to the south of the island, with visits to Geránia and Pendekáli caves, and a stop at Sarakinó (departure at 11am from Linariá, return 6pm).

## WHERE TO STAY

### • Skíros

Skíros has plenty of *domátia*. You will be approached with offers as soon as you arrive in Linariá. The prices indicated below – for a double room in summer – decrease by about half the rest of the year.

*Under €30*

**Pension Elena**, near the post office, ☎ (0222) 917 38 – 11rm. Modest rooms, some with private bathrooms, some with terraces. Reasonably comfortable and clean, but no more than that.

**Domátia Kaliope**, Skíros, near the Kástro, ☎ (0222) 922 93 – 2rm. ⌁ A little love nest with a terrace and an exceptional view of the sea, run by the delightful owner.

**Domátia Ienakaki**, Skíros. At the bottom of Odós Agorá, on the left, ☎ (0222) 914 59 – 6rm. Clean comfortable rooms with two or four beds, some with balconies giving onto an orchard.

*Between €30 and €45*

**Domátia Soula Panarjodou**, Skíros. Cross the main square and turn right, ☎ (0222) 928 27 – 3rm. ⌁ Small comfortable rooms with bathrooms and kitchenettes, run by the charming owner.

**Domátia Anna Kiriazi**, Skíros. At the top of Odós Agorá turn left at the fork and then climb up towards the

museums on the right, ☎ (0222) 915 74 – 1rm. A charming traditional house, with a mezzanine bedroom, fireplace, ceramics, and a terrace.

*Over €45*

**Nefeli**, at the entrance to the town, ☎ (0222) 919 64, Fax (0222) 920 61 – 23rm. ⌁ ▤ / ⤬ ♒ ⓉⓋ ✖ ⛱ ⒸⒸ One of the best places to stay on the island. Apartments or double rooms in an attractive white building with old-style fireplaces and wooden furniture. The bar near the swimming pool is particularly pleasant.

### • Magaziá and Mólos

*Under €30*

**Domátia Popi Fragoli**, Mólos, just before the fishing harbour, ☎ (0222) 910 93 – 5rm. ⌁ ♨ A small house with an annexe in a pleasant setting overlooking the beach with spacious, comfortable rooms.

**Pension Galini**, Mólos, 100m before the harbour, along the road set back from the beach, ☎ (0222) 913 79, Fax (0222) 929 70 – 10rm. ♨ A white building with small but cool rooms. Most have a terrace and a private bathroom. Go for the one on its own under the roof. Breakfast included.

**Domátia Georgia Tsakami**, Magaziá, ☎ (0222) 913 57 – 10rm. ⌁ ♨ Open from May to September. A family guesthouse with a little garden. Cool comfortable rooms with fridges. Free access to the kitchen.

*Between €30 and €60*

**Domátia Kabadzina Papastathis**, Magaziá, ☎ (0222) 913 22 – 10rm. ♨ This comfortable guesthouse is open all year and has a lovely view of the citadel. Most of the rooms have private bathrooms.

**Motel Hara**, Mólos, ☎ (0222) 917 63, Fax (0222) 921 24 – 22rm. ⌁ ♒ 100m from the beach. Accommodation in rooms or studios, with mezzanine layout. The large studios have televisions, kitchenettes and air conditioning.

**Pension Angela**, Mólos, ☎ (0222) 917 64, Fax (0222) 920 30 – 14rm. ⌁ ♒ 200m from the beach, with a lawn.

Spacious comfortable rooms with balconies. Some have fans and fridges (air conditioning is planned).

*Over €60*
**Skíros Palace Hotel**, Girísmata, north of Mólos, ☎ (0222) 919 94, Fax (0222) 920 70 – 18rm. ⚐ 🖉 ✕ ⚒ ♨ ⚔ [CC] A luxury complex in an isolated spot at the end of the road. Comfortable rooms with balconies, and a swimming pool surrounded by lawns. The rooms on the first floor have air conditioning. Open from May to September.
**Hotel Hydroussa**, Magaziá, ☎ (0222) 920 63, Fax (0222) 920 62 – 22rm. ⚐ ✕ ♨ The main hotel on the beach (former Xenia Hotel) is set in a very pleasant spot. All the rooms have balconies overlooking the sea.

● **Ágios Fókas**

*Under €45*
**Kalimanolis**, Ágios Fókas, ☎ (0222) 66 44 05 – 9rm. ✕ ♨ A small guesthouse in a charming location run by a very welcoming manager. Half board, with seafood, home-made cheese and local vegetables served beneath a climbing vine.

● **Atsítsa**

*Under €45*
**Adonis Kalimeris**, ☎ (0222) 929 90 – 20rm. ⚐ ✕ ♨ Open from May to September. The hotel with its small clean rooms with kitchenettes looks over the creek and has a taverna on the beach.

### EATING OUT

● **Skíros Town**

*Under €9*
**Chez Anemos**, Odós Agorá, not far from Skíros Travel. ☕ An ideal place for breakfast (yoghurts, croissants), a pizza or an ice cream.
🍴 **Taverna Sisyfos**, main street, on the left, 100m beyond the terminal. ☕ Varied, tasty dishes (lasagne, fresh vegetables, lentil soup), quick service and a very pleasant terrace in the shade, all at a modest price.
**Marietis**, main street, on the left beyond the main square. ☕ A wide choice of seafood, salads and grilled dishes that attract a local clientele.

**Papous**, at the top of Odós Agorá, on the right. ☕ A fashionable place renowned for its chicken and lamb dishes served in a sauce. Greek music.

● **Mólos**

*Between €9 and €15*
**Taverna Sargos**, ☕ A pleasant terrace on the beach. Fish and salads.
Mólos has other tavernas including **Thomas**, **Asteria**, and **Mylos**, which is set in an old windmill.

### HAVING A DRINK

**Bars, night-clubs – Café Iron**, Skíros, opposite the main square. Local clientele and Western music until late. Very pleasant rooftop terrace with a bar.
**Neoptolemos**, Skíros, Odós Agorá. A lively bar that stays open late, where you can listen to music.
**O Kavos**, Linariá. A very lively bar at the end of a creek overlooking the sea. Open until late. International pop music and a wide choice of cocktails and pastries.

### OTHER THINGS TO DO

**Excursions** – See **Skíros Travel & Tourism**.

**Outdoor pursuits** – **Skíros Institute**, contact in England: ☎ (020) 7267 4424 / 7284 3065, Fax (020) 7284 3063, connect@skyros.com, www.skyros.com This well-known centre organises alternative holidays with accommodation in traditional houses in Skíros Town and in Atsítsa, with courses including dance, yoga, climbing, drama, creative writing, and relaxation.

**Feasts and festivals** – If you come in February, don't miss the famous **Skíros carnival** (see sidebar).

### SHOPPING GUIDE

**Special purchases** – Odós Agorá contains a host of shops.
**Amerissa Ftoulis**, Skíros, at the top of Odós Agorá, just beyond the fork. Wide choice of embroidered goods.
**Stamatis Ftoulis**, Skíros, opposite Skíros Travel, ☎ (0222) 915 59. Ceramics from Magaziá.
**Stamatis Fergadis**, Skíros, Odós Agorá. Specialises in honey, sweets, etc.

# SKÓPELOS★★

Sporades – Province of Thessaly – District of Magnissía
107km from Vólos – Michelin map 980 fold 18 – Regional map page 195
97km² – Pop 5 000

### Not to be missed
Strolling through Skópelos Town and Glóssa.
Visiting the monasteries on Mt Paloúki.

### And remember...
Bring modest clothing to wear when visiting the monasteries.

The boat arriving from Skiáthos follows the Skópelos coast for some time, bringing into view a succession of beaches and bays dominated by wooded hills. Here and there, the dazzling white walls of a church or monastery suddenly loom up out of the dark green undulating countryside. A lot less tourist-orientated than its neighbour, the island has recently begun developing fast, but has still been able to keep its character. It is not unusual to come across women still wearing traditional dress – pleated silk skirts with flowery embroidery, velvet bodices and silk headscarves.

## The orchard of the Sporades
Little is known about ancient Skópelos, apart from the fact that a Cretan colony was founded there by Staphylos in the 6C BC. However, at some point, the citadel at **Peparithos** (the early name for Skópelos) was destroyed. Philip II of Macedon undertook its restoration in the 4C BC, as did the Venetians much later (1204). The island came under Ottoman control in 1532 and remained so until the independence of Greece in the early 19C, its powerful fleet (the seventh largest in Greece) having participated actively in the struggle against the occupying forces. Blessed with fertile soil, Skópelos was long considered the main island in the Sporades, its hills covered in olive and almond trees, vines – renowned since Antiquity – and above all **plums**, which are still prized throughout the country.

## Tour of the island
*Allow 2 days. There are two towns on the island: Skópelos, the main one*
*(in the south-east), and Glóssa (in the north), in the wildest part.*

### Skópelos Town★★
Built on a hillside, the superb town of Skopelos enjoys a peaceful existence sheltered by its sea wall, in the curve of a wide bay. Barely will you have left the ferry when you will be enchanted by the friendly atmosphere and the liveliness all along the waterfront (*no traffic allowed after 8pm*), among the cafés and souvenir shops. Choose an alleyway at random and go up into the inextricable maze of white houses, interrupted here and there by a church. In the upper part of the town, you should see the 9C **Chapel of St Athanasius★** with its beautiful polychrome **iconostasis★**. Higher still, from the **Venetian Kástro**, there is an unrestricted **panoramic view★** of the bay.

### The convents and monastery on Mt Paloúki★
*On foot (a long walk) or by car. From the landing-stage, take the road that skirts the shore to the other side of the bay, before climbing the hill. Turn left at the fork.*

■ A nun of indeterminate age, all in black, will open the doors of the **Evangelístria Convent** (*5km from Skópelos Town, 8am-1pm / 5pm-8pm; donation*). She will take you round, giving brief explanations in basic English. In addition to a superb **iconostasis★** in gilded wood hidden in one of the two chapels, the visit is thoroughly worthwhile just for the **view★★** of Skópelos Town, which stretches out in the distance below.

■ Go back down to the fork and turn left for **Metamórfossi Monastery**∗ (*8am-1.30pm / 5pm-8.30pm; donation*), whose immaculately whitewashed walls stand out among the cypress and olive trees. The monastery was built in the 16C and contains a chapel that stands in a flower-filled **courtyard**∗ set off by a wooden gallery.

■ **Pródromos Convent** (*10km from Skópelos Town, 8am-1pm / 5pm-8pm; donation*) seems less cut off from the world in spite of its position at the end of the road. Here also, a fine **chapel** stands in the middle of a courtyard, but it has suffered a little from restoration. The place is mainly worthwhile for the staggering **view**∗∗∗ of the wild, jagged coast.

■ For another lovely view, continue along the track (*which becomes increasingly rough and rocky*) to the top of **Mt Paloúki**, a 566m-high promontory that affords a magnificent **panorama**∗∗ of the mountains tumbling down to the sea.

## Shingle and sand
The island has some very beautiful beaches. However, for peace and quiet, you often have to opt for pebbles rather than sand.

■ The very popular **Stáfylos beach**∗ (*4km south of Skópelos Town*) has both, and occupies a delightful spot in the curve of a little bay backed by pines (taverna). Very close by, a discovery was made of the tomb of **King Staphylos** (meaning grape in Greek), who gave the island its early glory in the Minoan era. Items from the tomb, including gold weapons and offerings, can be seen in the Vólos Museum on the mainland.

A white castle on the mountain: Metamórfossi Monastery (Skópelos)

J. Gabanou/DIAF

■ Just as charming, **Velanió beach**\*, round the rocky headland (*to the east*), is popular with nude bathers.

■ Further west (*3km from Stáfylos*) is **Agnóndas beach**, a tiny pebble cove in a very steep-sided bay with yachts and fishing boats (taverna).

■ From here, a dead-end road leads to the sand beach at **Limnonári**\*, bordered by scrub (tavernas, hotel). Meanwhile, the main road affords superb **panoramic views**\* of the coast, then runs past a **Genoese tower** before disappearing into woods.

■ Nestling in a deep bay, the little resort of **Pánormos** (guesthouses, money changers, travel agents, tavernas) stretches out along a grey pebble **beach** bordered by pines. A small harbour on the left shelters yachts at anchor.

■ Lastly, further north, **Miliá pebble beach**\*\* (*3km*) is considered to be the island's finest. Lined with tavernas, guesthouses and a water-sports club it faces a rocky islet that sits imposingly in the middle of the bay.
If you prefer wilder surroundings, go to the next beach along, **Kastaria**\* (sand and pebbles), which has no tourist amenities.

■ The road continues to **Élios** (New Klíma), a resort with little in the way of interest (rather dull beach), where you can, however, stop for lunch.

## Glóssa and the north*

The bus stops in front of the main square, which, as might be expected, is flanked by a **church** and a taverna with a terrace. Quieter and more authentic than Skópelos Town, the island's main northern settlement has the same enchanting, brilliantly white houses and a maze of shaded alleys, deserted during siesta time. At a bend in a street you suddenly see a streak of blue sea, adding a touch of colour to the

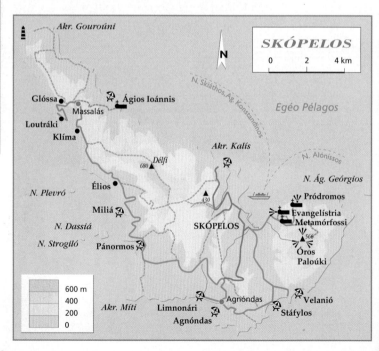

sparkling townscape. Here, life seems to follow the same undisturbed course as it has for centuries. But make no mistake: over the last few years, Northern Europeans have been moving in, buying and restoring houses.

A road leads down from Glóssa to **Loutráki**, Glóssa's **harbour**. Along the waterfront are several seafood restaurants, pleasant places to pass the time in.

Several kilometres south of Glóssa, you reach the village of **Klíma**, which was damaged by an earthquake in 1965. It has since been resurrected thanks to foreigners who fell in love with the island and restored the houses.

However, the loveliest excursion in the surrounding area is to the **Ágios Ioánnis Monastery**\* *(5km)* on the east coast. Perched on a narrow rocky promontory close to the shore, the little **chapel** at the top of a steep flight of steps continues to inspire countless post cards. For a last swim, you can try the neighbouring sandy **beach**\*, which stretches out below the cliffs plunging into the sea.

---

## Making the most of Skópelos

### COMING AND GOING

**By ferry** – The island's main port is Skópelos Town, although in summer, ferries also call at Loutráki, Glóssa's harbour on the west coast. The travelling times given below are from Skópelos Town.

**Nomicos Line** and **Lemonis Travel**, in the harbour, to the left of the landing-stage, ☎ and Fax (0424) 22 363. For Alónissos, around three connections a day (travelling time: 30min); for Skiáthos, three to six (90min); for Vólos, two to three (5hr, or 3hr40min without any stops); for Ágios Konstandínos, one or two (4hr30min).

**By hydrofoil** – **Madro Travel**, to the left of the landing-stage, ☎ (0424) 22 145, Fax (0424) 22 941. An agent for Minoan Flying Dolphins. Hydrofoils operate from May to October. Frequent connections with Alónissos (20min) and Skiáthos (1hr). For Vólos, five connections (2hr15min); for Ágios Konstandínos, three (2hr15min); for Skíros, one connection a day except on Wednesday and Saturday (1hr45min); for Thessaloníki, one or two connections (4hr15min).

### GETTING AROUND

**By bus** – The bus **terminal** is on the waterfront, 400m from the landing-stage. In summer, there are buses for Glóssa every 90min from 7.30am to 10pm (travelling time: 1hr). For Pánormos and Miliá, there are departures every hour from 7am to 10.30pm (travelling time: 30min); for Stáfylos and Agnóndas, frequent buses between 7am and 11pm (15min).

**By taxi** – The taxi rank is opposite the bus terminal. ☎ (0424) 22 566.

**Car, bicycle and motorcycle rental** – You are spoilt for choice in Skópelos. **Avis**, on the waterfront, ☎ (0424) 23 170, Fax (0424) 23 488. Motorcycle rental: **Madro Travel**, facing the landing-stage, ☎ (0424) 22 145, Fax (0424) 22 941. **Motor Tour**, ☎ (0424) 22 986, in the harbour. **Pánormos Travel Agency**, ☎ (0424) 23 380, Fax (0424) 23 748.

### ADDRESS BOOK

There is no tourist office but the travel agents provide all the necessary information. A small **municipal agency** in the harbour will help you find accommodation in private houses, ☎ and Fax (0424) 24 567.

**Travel agents** – **Madro Travel** and **Pánormos Travel**, see above under "Car, bicycle and motorcycle rental".

**Harbourmaster's office** – ☎ (0424) 22 180. Information on ferry timetables.

**Bank / Currency exchange –
National Bank**, on the waterfront.
Monday-Thursday, 8am-2pm, Friday,
8am-1pm. Cash dispenser and auto-
matic exchange machine.

**Post office –** To get to the post office,
take the street facing the bus terminal,
then the first left, the first right, the first
left and left again! Monday-Friday,
7.30am-2pm.

**Telephone –** Local code: 0424. **OTE**,
from the waterfront, go up the street to
the Armoloï shop and turn left beyond
the kiosk. Monday-Friday, 7.30am-3pm.

**Internet – Avia Electronics**, to the
right as you leave the OTE. From 10pm
to midnight only.

#### WHERE TO STAY

The summer rates given here are 50 to
100% higher than those in mid-season.

**• Skópelos Town**

*Under €45*

**Domátia Angela**, 50m from the OTE,
☎ (0424) 23 558 – 8rm. A pleasant,
modest, reasonably comfortable little
guesthouse. Warm family welcome. The
owner plans to equip the rooms with
private bathrooms.

🖈 **Kir Sotos**, in the harbour, on the
corner of the alley that leads up to the
OTE, ☎ (0424) 22 549, Fax (0424)
23 668 – 12rm. 🖈 ⊼ A charming,
comfortable, country-style hotel although the rooms are rather dark. Avoid
the ones giving onto the harbour on
account of the noise. You can have
breakfast on the terrace in the courtyard
(making it yourself in the kitchen).

**Hotel Élli**, Ring Road, at the top of Platanos village. From Skópelos Town, go
up the alleyway to the mini-market,
☎ (0424) 22 943, Fax (0424) 23 284 –
24rm. 🖈 𝒫 ⊥ CC An attractive hotel
with a garden and green flagstone flooring. The stylish, comfortable rooms have
balconies. Breakfast is included, making
the place good value for money.

*Between €45 and €60*

**Hotel Aegean**, at the far end of the bay,
on the road that leads up to the monasteries, ☎ (0424) 22 619, Fax
(0424) 22 194 – 15rm. 🖈 𝒫 TV A modest but comfortable hotel built on several

levels, with panelling and marble flooring. It is relatively isolated and enjoys a
superb view of the bay. Some rooms are
air-conditioned. Breakfast included.

**Hotel Agnanti**, at the far end of the bay,
☎ and Fax (0424) 227 22 – 12rm. 🖈
⊼ 𝒫 An attractive white building surrounded by plane trees. Decent rooms
and sea view.

**Hotel Regina**, behind the Hotel Adonis, ☎ (0424) 22 138 – 16rm. 🖈 ⊼ TV
A modest but friendly hotel with perfectly kept rooms (with fridges). Some
have a view of the sea. Good value for
money.

*Between €60 and €75*

**Hotel Adonis**, in the harbour, near the
terminal, ☎ (0424) 22 231, Fax
(0424) 23 239 – 8rm. 🖈 ▤ ✕ An
enormous building with balconies, facing the sea. Pleasant, well-kept rooms.

**Aperitton**, in the upper part of the
town, ☎ (0424) 22 256, Fax
(0424) 22 976 – 31rm. 🖈 ▤ 𝒫 TV ⊥
CC A clean, comfortable hotel, but
without any particular character. Immaculate white rooms with balconies.
Bar. Breakfast included.

*Over €75*

**Prince Stafilos**, at the far end of the bay,
☎ (0424) 22 775, Fax (0424) 22 885 –
64rm. 🖈 𝒫 ✕ ⊥ CC An elegant building with a slate roof set back from the
road, behind flower-beds. Charming
rustic hall with a craft shop. Pleasant
rooms. Breakfast included.

**• Pánormos**

*Between €60 and €75*

**Hotel Pánormos**, ☎ (0424) 22 711,
Fax (0424) 33 005 – 34rm. 🖈 ▤ ✕ Set
a little distance inland. Attractive hall
decorated with craft items. Small though
comfortable rooms. Ask for the ones
with balconies overlooking the garden.
Family atmosphere and warm welcome.

*Over €105*

🖈 **Hotel Adrina**, Adrina beach, 500m
beyond Pánormos, ☎ (0424) 23 373,
Fax (0424) 23 372 – 54rm. 🖈 ⊼ ✕ ⊥
⊶ CC An impeccable hotel with attractive furnishing in the hall and rooms giving onto the sea. The bungalows are
more expensive. The hotel has its own
small pebble beach, with a taverna.

**The Sporades**

- **Glóssa**

*Under €30*

**Domátia Nina**, take the alleyway that runs beside the church, ☎ (0424) 33 686 – 4rm. ⚲ A large family home with a garden and terrace and an exceptional view of the sea. The rooms are clean and are reasonably comfortable (double beds and kitchen area).

## EATING OUT

- **Skópelos Town**

*Under €12*

**Chez Greka**, from the landing-stage, take the alleyway near the Kir Sotos hotel and turn left towards the OTE. ☕ The only pancake restaurant on the island. Run by Greka, who may come and have a chat with you at your table.

**O Platanos**, near the post office. ☕ Open for lunch and dinner. A small restaurant serving standard food (kebabs, souvláki) on a terrace in the shade of a plane tree.

**Klimataria**, near the landing-stage. ☕ A terrace giving onto the harbour, ideal for a salad or seafood.

*Over €12*

**Taverna Finikas**, signposted from the OTE. ☕ A very pleasant place with a terrace overhanging the street. Apart from traditional fare, there are also several unusual dishes such as the delicious chicken with four different cheeses (copious!).

- **Glóssa, Loutráki**

*Over €12*

**Vrachos Taverna**, in Loutráki harbour, beyond the church. ☕ A place on the waterfront serving seafood and grilled specialities. There's another similar establishment just beside it.

## HAVING A DRINK

**Cafés, bars – Café International**, in the harbour. ☕ Specialises in Skópelos pastries (ice cream, walnut cakes). Ideal for breakfast or tea.

**Kafe Ermion**, from the OTE, follow the signs to Fimkas. ☕ A characterful place with a small, peaceful, shady courtyard. Perfect for a drink or breakfast (opens at 10am).

**Vraxos**, go up the steps near the National Bank. ☕ The terrace has the finest view of Skópelos Town. Huge choice of cocktails, and reggae music for the local youths.

**Platanos Jazz Club**, opposite the landing-stage. ☕ A terrace with bistro-style tables spread out in the shade of a plane tree. Copious yoghurts for breakfast. In the evening, the place becomes a lively bar with jazz in the background.

**Dimotiko Cafénio**, in the harbour. ☕ The town café, where local men come to discuss the day's events.

**Blue Bar**, from the waterfront, go up the street beyond the kiosk and turn right opposite the church. ☕ One of the town's trendy bars, small but lively.

**Ouzerí Anatoli**, in the Kástro. ☕ A superb view of the town. Concerts of Greek music in the evening at 11.30pm.

## OTHER THINGS TO DO

A boat goes to Glistéri beach, north of the town. Departures from 10am to 3pm, with trips back until 6pm (travelling time: 20min).

**Boat trip** – Vassilis Kouroutos offers a fascinating trip lasting one or two days around the Marine Park islands aboard his superb boat, the **Oceanis**. Enquire in the harbour at Madro Travel or on the boat itself. Expensive but unforgettable.

**Festivals** – The feast day of the patron saint of the island, **Ágios Riginos**, is on 25 February, and that of the Transfiguration of the Saviour is on 6 August.

## SHOPPING GUIDE

**Antiques – Ploumisti Shop**, from the harbour, take the street just beyond the kiosk and turn into the first on the right. An attractive shop selling fabrics, wooden window frames and jewellery.

H. Le Gac/MICHELIN

Hóra and the windmills of Mýkonos: the essence of the Cyclades

# THE CYCLADES

According to the legend, it was Poseidon who, with a blow of his trident, made the Cyclades rise up from the depths of the Aegean in the form of a rough circle (*kýklos* in Greek – hence the name of the archipelago) around the sacred island of Delos. And there is an almost divine quality about this group of islands despite the barren, rocky landscape and scrubland, buffeted remorselessly by Aeolus, the god of the winds who has been given the local name of *meltém*. The *meltém* sometimes blows so hard that no boat will venture out to sea, except possibly one belonging to an Odysseus or a Jason. Of the 39 islands of the archipelago, only 24 are inhabited – on the others, what water there is would barely quench the thirst of a few goats.

So what Siren song is it that compels travellers to visit these islands? There is nothing very remarkable about them, except the extraordinary light and a sea of infinite shades of blue: sometimes turquoise, sometimes almost green, or maybe midnight blue, or crystal clear. This great expanse of blue merges with the blue of the sky, forming a backdrop to the mountainous landscape. It contrasts vividly with the yellow ochre of the rocks, and even more starkly with the villages of white houses, a myriad small white boxes gleaming from one hill to another. In the harbour, the fishing boats paint the waves red, yellow and green. The heights above are studded with lonely little chapels, the occasional old monastery, and with ancient windmills, their sails long gone. They watch over the beaches of shingle or golden sand, and over the olive trees with their silvery green foliage on the hillsides and terraces. The aromas of olive, fig, lemon and almond trees perfume the air. A cat sleeps in the sun on a warm slab of marble, and the shrilling of the cicadas is heard everywhere.

# AMORGÓS★★

Aegean Sea – District of the Cyclades – Michelin map 980 fold 45
Regional map on the inside back cover – 121km² – Pop 1 632

**Not to be missed**
The Hozoviótissa Monastery.
The archaeological site at Minoa. Hóra and the village of Langáda.

**And remember...**
When purchasing your ticket for the boat, state at which harbour you wish to
disembark: Katápola in the south, or Egiáli in the north. This is particularly important
if you arrive at night (there is no bus service linking the two towns at night).

Having been long neglected by mass tourism due to its remoteness – it is about a
12hr boat ride from Piraeus – Amorgós has now emerged from obscurity. Without
any doubt, the fact that Luc Besson filmed key scenes of *The Big Blue* here has played
a role in its new-found fame. But you don't need to see the film to be seduced by the
charms of the most easterly of the Cyclades, a narrow strip of land 35km long and at
most barely 6km wide: in the mountains, the footpaths lined by drystone walls are
perfect for walking and, in the back streets of the dazzling white little villages, the
local songs, handed down from generation to generation, resound in the evening air.

## The island of idols
Between 3000 and 2000 BC, Amorgós was one of the most flourishing islands, with
about a dozen acropolises and a prolific artistic heritage which is perhaps best known
for its extraordinary white marble figurines, which this island, along with a few of

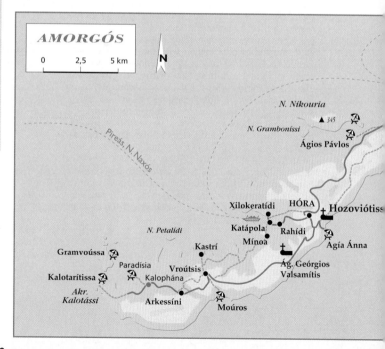

its neighbours, produced in abundance. The early examples of these statues being very abstract in form, the shape was more reminiscent of a violin than a woman. As the centuries passed, they acquired more figurative detail, and were sometimes enhanced with polychrome motifs. The head appeared first; then the arms, folded across the stomach; and finally the eyes and the breasts. The contours of the legs, the feet and the pubis were depicted with simple lines engraved using a sharp piece of obsidian. The exact purpose of these idols, the height of which varies from a few centimetres to 1.5m, has yet to be explained. Are they nymphs or dancers? Were they intended to replace human sacrifices or were these stone concubines slipped into tombs to sweeten the journey of the dead to the other world? To this day, the idols still guard their secret.

## Around Katápola

*About 20km. Allow a whole day at a relaxed pace.*

### Katápola★
Straddling the length of a deep bay, the port of Katápola today is really a conglomeration of three villages: **Katápola** itself, where the ferries and hydrofoils dock and where most of the tourist facilities are located, **Rahídi**, in the centre, which is still rather rural and poor, and **Xilokeratídi**, to the north, the fishermen's district, which is dotted with tavernas. This is where most of the island's visitors disembark, on their way to its pride and joy, the Hozoviótissa Monastery. But the town itself also has a certain charm, with its little white streets and its old churches dating from the time of early Christianity, for example **Panagía Katapolianí**, in the centre of Katápola, and **Taxiárhis**, on the road to Hóra.

But if it is swimming you are interested in, it is best to head out of the town. You can walk to the **beaches of Ágios Panteleímonas**, **Maltési** or **Plakès** (*reserved for nudists*), or hire a vehicle to get to the beaches in the south of the island (*not all of the beaches are served by buses*).

### Ancient Minoa★
*2.5km from Katápola. On foot: from the harbour, take the road that heads up the hill overlooking the bay (45min walk). By car: follow signs for Hóra for about 200m, then take the first right-hand fork along a road that soon turns into a stony lane. The site is closed because excavations are still in progress but it can be observed from the perimeter. Allow 30min.* Obviously, it is somewhat frustrating not being able to walk among the ruins, and it is difficult to imagine the size of this prosperous city, which was continuously inhabited from the 10C to the 4C BC. But it is worth climbing to the top of the hill of Moundoulia, for the **view★** of the Bay of Katápola, especially at sunset (*follow the path that runs along the edge of the site to the left*).

The excavations, which are still in progress, have not yet uncovered all the buildings on the south-eastern and southern slopes of the hill. In the lower part of the site, however, you can see the remains of successive **defensive walls** as well as the remains of a **gymnasium** dating from the 4C BC, which was altered during the Hellenistic Period. Through the fence, on the left, you can also see the ruins of a **Hellenistic temple**: the torso of a statue stands in the centre, surrounded by small devotional buildings. At the top of the hill are the foundations of a **sanctuary** from the Geometric Period, dedicated to Dionysus.

## Hóra★★

*By bus: depending on the season, between 10 and 16 a day from Katápola, and between 3 and 5 a day from Egiáli.* A **Venetian citadel** perched on the top of a sugar-loaf mountain, watching over the white houses huddled at the foot of the rock, a few **windmills without sails scattered on the ridge of a hill: Hóra** is a typical example of a Cycladic village. There is no better way to explore it than getting lost in its narrow streets, emerging from the shade of a vine or a vaulted passageway into the dazzling light of a little square bathed in sunshine...

The **Archaeological Museum** is housed in a fine example of a 16C nobleman's residence *(from the square where the bus stops, take the first alley on the right; 10am-2pm / 6pm-8pm in summer; no entrance fee).*

It contains various objects from the island, dating from prehistoric times to the Roman Period: there are a few statues and capitals in the patio, the remains of some ancient steles, and a small collection of pottery is displayed in a **large room with a wooden ceiling**.

On the other side of the street, a narrow lane climbs up to the **Loza** (from the Italian "loggia"), the elegant central square dominated by the **cathedral** (17C) *(on the right)* and the **town hall** *(on the left)*, the noble façade of which is adorned with plaques bearing the decrees of the old towns on the island. At the far end of the square, on the left, a passage leads to the **citadel** (kástro) which has fine **views★★**. Finally, in the northern part of the town, you can cool off in the shade of **three churches**. Built side by side in an identical style, they have vaulted roofs in the shape of an upturned ship's keel, a typical feature of local architecture.

## Hozoviótissa Monastery★★★

*3 buses per day from Hóra. By car, follow directions for Agía Ánna beach. Car park below the monastery which is reached by a fairly steep staircase (about a 10min climb). 8am-1pm / 5pm-7pm in summer, 8am-4.30pm from November to April. Try to visit the monastery in the early morning when the light is good but the heat is still bearable. At the entrance, there are garments available to cover up bare legs. Allow 30min.*

"A cupboard adhering to the bottom of an awful rock", was how the French writer Piton de Tournefort, described it during his visit to Greece in the early 18C... Another way of describing it would be to liken it to a book, pure white in colour, flattened by the wind against the ochre-coloured rock. A book scarcely 5m thick, hanging 300m above the waves, ready to detach itself from the rock and plunge into the void, the "place of the devil" as the faithful of the area used to call it. To compensate for its lack of depth, the building is eight storeys high, partly dug into the cliff, and partly overhanging the abyss. "Shining like the eye of a dragon", the monastery has hung here, suspended between the sky and the sea, for a thousand years...

**A monastery 1 000 years old** – According to local tradition, the first monastery (consisting of a few cells dug into cracks in the rock) was built in the 9C to house an icon of the Virgin Mary seized from the iconoclasts by a woman from Palestine. In 1088, Emperor Alexius Comnenus decided to expand the monastery, which

A white cupboard pinned to the rock: the Hozoviótissa Monastery, Amorgós

subsequently underwent numerous alterations and extensions right up to the 20C. And it was the building of this monastery that gave rise to the population of the island, with the arrival of craftsmen, builders and farmers employed on the land owned by the monks. As the 17C icon known as the "Prayer of Gennádios" testifies, for several centuries, the monastery was twinned with the monastery on Pátmos. A rare exception in the area, it never ceased to be inhabited, even during the periods of Venetian and Turkish occupation.

**Tour** – A staircase cut into the rock has replaced the old wooden ladder which used to provide access until the beginning of the 20C. Once through the **Venetian arch** of the entrance gate (15C), a staircase leads up through a tunnel in the mountain to the reception hall. Inside the **church** (katholikón) there are several splendid **icons\***. Do not miss the *Panagía Kozoviótissa* or "founder" (on the iconostasis), covered with engraved silver, or the *"Prayer of Gennádios"* depicting the miraculous salvation of the monks who were caught in a memorable storm between Pátmos and Amorgós.

On the ground floor is a **library**, containing **precious manuscripts\*** from the 10C to the 18C, a collection of embroidered clerical robes, and various liturgical objects. The library opens onto a small **terrace** with a vertical drop down to the sea, the only outside space in the monastery. At the end of the tour, the monks offer visitors the opportunity to taste Turkish delight, lemon liqueur or tea.

On leaving the monastery you could head for the **beach of Agía Ánna\*\***, in a delightful little rocky bay a few hundred metres below, with beautifully clear water. Perfect for relaxing after all that effort.

## The south

*About 30km round trip. By bus: there are two return services a day. By car: allow a whole day, including a stop for swimming.*

■ From Hóra, head south by the only road leading to the **kato méria** or "villages of the south". 4.5km from the Hozoviótissa Monastery, don't miss the road on the right leading to the **Ágios Geórgios Valsamítis Monastery\*** *(not signposted; allow 30min)*. Less impressive than its famous neighbour (to which it is linked), the building and its setting – a small white dot in the middle of a quiet valley, carpeted with cultivation terraces – are nevertheless worth a detour. Recently restored, the building (16C) has some 17C **frescoes** and a **miraculous spring** which, it is said, once cured some lepers who had disembarked from a pirate ship. Its name comes from a local species of mint called *valsam*, which once covered the valley where the people who had been cured discovered an icon of St George.

*Return to the main road and cross the only agricultural plain on the island.*

■ Just before **Vroútsis**, a road on the left leads to **Moúros**, a broad bay dotted with inlets with shingle beaches *(and a taverna)*, which are all very popular.

■ If you are a keen walker *(allow 40min to get there, on a downhill path)*, park the car at the church in Vroútsis and go and have a look at the old **Arkessíni\*** (or Kastri) *(allow a good 2 hours to walk there and back; NB: the village of Arkessini is the only one on the island to boast a hotel with a restaurant; simple rooms)*. The cobbled road soon gives way to a path leading down to the sea through a dry, rather desolate landscape. It emerges on a bare rocky promontory jutting out above the waves. Here lie the remains of a city founded in the 4C BC. Inhabited until the period of Venetian domination, it was destroyed by a pirate raid. You can still see the well-preserved **walls** of the acropolis, and the ruins of a defence tower, as well as some **ancient tombs**.

*If you have to retrieve your car, head back up the same path. Otherwise, walk back by the coastal path, which is longer, but very pleasant.*

■ The far south of the island also has several **beaches** which get fairly busy in summer (*to reach them, take the first road on the left coming out of Kalophána*). As you head towards the sandy beach of **Kalotarítissa**, look out (*on the right*) for the **wreck** made famous by the film *The Big Blue*, washed up on the shore. From the bay, a caique plies to and from the island of **Gramvoússa★**, known for its beach which is cleaner and even more beautiful than the nearby Paradísia beach.

## The north★

*About a 10km drive. Allow a whole day, including time for a swim. By bus: there are several daily services between Katápola and Egiáli (24km to the north) along a recently tarmacked road. On foot: from the Hozoviótissa Monastery, you can reach the village of Potamós by the road following the ridge (a 4hr walk), provided you leave early and ensure that it is not windy; the meltem can blow very hard higher up. Don't forget to wear good walking shoes and a hat, and take water as well as a map of Yorgos Kapsalis, vital if you are to avoid getting lost. Otherwise, follow the lines of telegraph poles. Find out bus times if you have to return to Katápola in the evening.*

Isolated from the rest of the island for many years, the community of Egiáli is now the second most important tourist centre of Amorgós after Katápola. For some years now, increasing numbers of tourists have been coming here, attracted by its beaches of white sand, but also by the Cycladic villages nearby, perched high above the harbour. The **Kríkelos** massif also attracts keen walkers.

From Katápola to Egiáli, the coast **road★** crosses a hilly, arid landscape, where herds of goats graze. About 2km from Egiáli, shortly after a ruined **Hellenistic tower**, a road leads down to the **Ágios Pávlos beach** (*dirty*), where a caique provides a service to the more pleasant beach on the nearby island of **Nikoúria** (*from the harbour of Egiáli, a caique leaves at 11.30am for Nikouria, but no return trip is guaranteed; you can either return on foot or catch the Katápola-Egiáli bus*).

■ **Egiáli** – It is hard to believe that fifteen years ago there was no harbour here given the tourist facilities that the seaside resort of Amorgós now offers. Fortunately, this rapid development has not blighted its pleasant atmosphere, so welcome after the hustle and bustle of Katápola, nor spoilt its sandy beaches, which can still be reached by caique (*expensive*).

Amorgós, pretty as a picture

B. Chabrol/MICHELIN

More specifically, staying in Egiáli is an opportunity to explore the three villages nestling among the mountains, three white dots in a rocky landscape: first, **Potamós\***, the most secluded of the three, a veritable balcony overlooking the Aegean; then to the west, **Tholária\***, known for its savoir-vivre, and particularly its cuisine. And lastly, the finest of them all: **Langáda\*\***, in the middle, and without a doubt the most typically Cycladic, especially during its religious festivals, when the streets are covered with chalk drawings.

Langáda is also the starting-point for wonderful walks in the mountains: especially towards Tholária, via the pretty hamlet of **Stroúmbos\*** *(1hr walk, if possible at sunset)*, hidden in the bottom of a green valley, or in search of the last windmills adorning the tops of the hills to the east *(1hr)*.

You can also visit the splendid **Church of Panagía Epanohorianí\*** *(20min)*, to the north, surrounded by fields (superb **view\*\***), or the **Ágios Ioánnis Theológos Monastery\*\*** *(fork right along a marked path; 90min)*, containing some remarkable **Byzantine frescoes\*** which have recently been restored. And if you are a keen walker *(and the wind isn't too strong)*, continue as far as **Stavrós\*** *(2hr30min)*, where the charming church is the focus of a village pilgrimage in September.

## Making the most of Amorgós

### COMING AND GOING

**By boat** – Amorgós is about 12hr by ferry from Athens. In summer, there are usually daily services to Piraeus, and less frequent services (2 or 3 days a week) to Rafína, via Náxos, Mýkonos, Síros and Tínos. Depending on the year, certain ferries continue their journey to Astipálea, Santoríni, Kálimnos and Rhodes. From Katápola, the little ferry called the "Skopelitis" provides services to Náxos, Mýkonos and the Lesser Cyclades (Irárklia, Schinoússa, Koufoníssi and Donoússa). Tickets can be purchased from the agencies at the harbours of Katápola and Egiáli.

**By hydrofoil** – Depending on the season (and the wind), there are several weekly connections between Katápola and Rafína, or Piraeus. (4hr30min journey).

### GETTING AROUND

**By boat** – You can go from Katápola to Egiáli on the ferries which stop at both harbours.

**By bus** – There are 8 services daily between Katápola and Egiáli; 16 between Katápola and Hóra (some buses go on to Hozoviótissa Monastery and the villages in the south). In the north, there are fewer than a dozen services between Egiáli, Tholária and Langáda.

**By rental car** – There are several car-hire firms in Katápola. Take extra care when hiring a moped or motorcycle and make sure it is in good condition (often they are not). In Egiáli, there is only one car-hire agency: **Aigialis Tours**, up the stairs on the left of the To Limáni bar. There are two fuel stations: one between Katápola and Hóra, the other in Egiáli, on the road to Tholária, behind the campsite.

### ADDRESS BOOK

**Tourist information** – There are some private tourist offices in Katápola, and there is one in Egiáli: **Aigialis Tours** (see below for address).

**Banks / Currency exchange** – In Katápola: the **Agrotikí** bank, opposite the quay, changes traveller's cheques and has a cash dispenser.

In Hóra, the post office changes notes and postal orders. In Egiáli, where there is no cash dispenser, you can still change money at the post office (in the street leading from the quay) and at the souvenir shop located between the bridge and the supermarket. If you are changing money, avoid Aigialis Tours, where commission is very high.

**Post office** – In Hóra: in the little square below the museum.

There are two post offices in Egiáli: in the little street leading off from the quay, and under the porticoes opposite the To Stéki restaurant, to the left of the supermarket. They change money (cash and travellers' cheques).

**Telephones – OTE** (telephones): the only agency on the island is located right at the top of Hóra. But all villages have public card-operated phone booths.

**Internet –** In Egiáli: **@morgos net café**, to the left of the To Limáni restaurant, up the stairs, ☎ (0285) 73 394.

**Medical service –** In Katápola: dispensary at the beginning of the road to Hóra; pharmacy at the harbour.
In Hóra: a surgery has opened 100m before the bus stop (road on the left); pharmacy near the bus stop.
In Egiáli, there is a dispensary on the road from Potamós, but no pharmacy.

**Laundry –** In Katápola, there is a launderette in a street off the main square.

## WHERE TO STAY
In August, booking is essential, since the accommodation capacity of Amorgós is insufficient to cope with the demand. Prices are rising rapidly...

### • Katápola
*Campsite (around €12)*
**Katápola municipal campsite**, ☎ (0285) 71 257, at Rahídi. Limited in terms of pitches and washing facilities.

*Between €30 and €45*
**Titika Rooms**, In the Xilokeratídi district, ☎ (0285) 71 660, mobile 0932 725076 – 10rm. ☏ Simple, clean rooms around a garden planted with flowers. The charming hostess provides a warm welcome.

**Minoa Hotel**, on the main square of Katápola, ☎ (0285) 71 480, Fax (0285) 71 003. ☏✕ Spacious, pleasant rooms. Those overlooking the garden are quieter.

**Castelopetra**, slightly further away from the harbour, on the road from Hóra, ☎ (0285) 71 269 / 71 042, Fax (0285) 71 360. ✐ ☏ TV A new hotel. Rooms have a kitchenette and a balcony overlooking the bay. On request, the owner will find you a boat.

### • Hóra
There are some rooms to let in the town. Ask at the **Giulia café**, in the square where the bus stops.
*Between €23 and €38*
**Pension La Hóra**, on the outskirts of Hóra (road to the left), on a rather windswept hillside, ☎ and Fax (0285) 71 882 – 10rm. ☏ A large, modern house with clean, spacious rooms with kitchenette and, in some cases, a balcony overlooking Hóra. A good place for people looking for peace and quiet.

### • Arkessíni
*Between €23 and €30*
**Marousso K Koveou Rooms**, below the road, on the right coming from Hóra ☎ (0285) 72 253 – 10rm. ☏✕ A small, unpretentious hotel. Four of the rooms have a kitchenette. Rather expensive (the price does not include breakfast).

### • Egiáli
Most of the new hotels are to be found on the hill leading up towards Potamós. Their owners come down to meet the boats.

*Campsites*
**Askas d'Aigiali**, ☎ (0285) 73 333, on the road to Tholária. It occupies a couple of acres of ground planted with trees. Some pitches have pergolas. Satisfactory washing facilities.

*Between €30 and €45*
**Pension Askas**, ☎ and Fax (0285) 73 333 – 18rm. ✐ ☏ ✕ On the road to Tholária, a hotel built in the traditional local style, with pleasant rooms looking onto the garden. The restaurant next to the campsite hosts various festivities with traditional singing and dancing every Saturday evening.

**Pension Lakki**, halfway along the beach, ☎ (0285) 73 505 / 6, Fax (0285) 73 244. ✐ ☏✕ ☒ CC Recently renovated, this group of bungalows is arranged in a large garden, separated from the beach by a few ancient tamarisk trees. Some contain flats for 4 to 6 people. The only disappointment is the catering facilities (self-service), which are a bit grubby.

*Between €53 and €75*
**Hotel Aigialis**, ☎ (0285) 73 393, Fax (0285) 73 395 – 30rm. ✐ ☏ ▤ ✕ ⬛ ▦ CC 2km from the harbour but on a bus route, this is the most com-

fortable hotel in Egiáli. The rooms are simple, but all of them overlook the Bay of Egiáli (unrestricted view). Meals are served on the panoramic terraces above the swimming pool (open to the public). Spacious communal areas with billiards, satellite TV, and the "Corte" night-club for people who like loud music.

● **Tholária**

*Between €30 and €45*
**Hotel Vigla**, ☎ (0285) 73 288 / 73 004 / 5, Fax (0285) 73332 – 25rm. *♪* ⌂ TV
✗ On the outskirts of the village, a new hotel built in the typical Cycladic style. Pleasant rooms with fridge and private balcony overlooking the Bay of Egiáli.

● **Langáda**

*Between €45 and €75*
*⊜* **Pagali**, below the main road, next to Níkos' taverna, ☎ (0285) 73 310 / 73 600, Fax (0285) 73 368 – 18rm. *♪* ♪ ✗ ⌂ The old hotel of the village, above the bar (6 noisy rooms), has added another 12 quieter well-designed rooms with a private or communal fridge, a balcony or terrace, and, in some cases, a kitchenette. Small garden with play area for children, and bus stop nearby. Níkos, the owner, will come to meet you off the boat (although he sometimes forgets!). He also lets out houses in the village and organises trips around the island in four-wheel-drive vehicles. His taverna, which extends over several small terraces, has a very cosmopolitan atmosphere in summer.

EATING OUT

● **Katápola**

*Under €7.50*
**Bitzéntzos**, on the outskirts of Xilokeratídi. A taverna in a charming position, right on the water's edge, with real home cooking.

*Between €11 and €23*
*⊜* **Mouráyo**, halfway along the seafront. Superb fish and seafood taverna. Since this is the best place to eat in town, the tables go fast!

● **Hóra**

*Between €11 and €15*
*⊜* **Liotriví**, in a narrow street to the right of the bus station. The best restaurant in town, serving delicious tradi-

tional (moussaká) or more original (casseroled rabbit) fare. Get there early.

● **Egiáli**

*Between €7.50 and €11*
**To Limáni**, on the main thoroughfare, run by the friendly Katína. Tables are set out on the street under the laurel trees or on the terrace on the 2nd floor. Sadly, the quality of the cuisine takes a dive in summer. But it is the best place to enjoy an ouzo and a game of "távli".

● **Langáda**

*Around €7.50*
**O Loudaros**, halfway down the main street. This taverna, with its terrace overlooking the street, is run by a charming couple who serve traditional Amorgós cooking.

● **Ágios Pávlos**

*Between €11 and €19*
The only taverna in town is a bit gloomy but serves exceptionally fresh seafood. To make the most of it, wait until the fishing boats have come in, after 10pm.

● **Tholária**

*Around €7.50*
*⊜* **Kalí Kardiá**, to the left of the church. A traditional taverna with tables arranged on the steps leading up to the village. Excellent cuisine and a particularly jolly Greek atmosphere.

*Between €7.50 and €15*
*⊜* **Panorama**, in the centre of the village. Although it doesn't live up to its name now that two houses obscure the view, this is one of the most popular places in Amorgós. Tasty "kokorétsi" (brochettes of tripe) and as tender a goat stew as you could wish. In summer, the local musicians come and play and the owner tells jokes (in Greek!). To be sure of finding a table, get there before 9pm.

HAVING A DRINK

● **Katápola**

Most of the cafés are clustered around the central square of Katápola. As a result, the prices are higher here. **Kafenío**, on the jetty (no name; look for the "Interamerican" sign). A real old-fashioned kafenío that has remained unchanged for decades. Service is rather nonchalant, but the "ouzo-kombolói" atmosphere is guaranteed.

**Bar du Grand Bleu**, at Xilokeratídi. Every evening the film of the same name is shown here, in English with Greek subtitles. Aimed at those with nostalgic tendencies, cinema fans and those who have not yet seen the film.

- **Egiáli**

**Frou-Frou**, in the little street leading to the harbour. A wonderful cake shop with a sea view. Serves breakfasts, cakes, crêpes and ice cream round the clock. It has a shop on the beach at Levrosos, near the Hotel Aigialis.

**Que**, discotheque halfway along the main beach. During the day, swimmers come here to eat under the trees. In the evening, Dimitris organises beach parties. But the disco atmosphere doesn't get off the ground until about 4am.

**Corte**, the discotheque at the Hotel Aigialis (see above).

- **Langáda**

**Loza**, the restaurant in the main square is not what you might call gastronomic but is a good place to go to enjoy this delightful little village square. The owner and her son are very hospitable.

The **Aigialis Tours agency**, in Egiáli (see above), organises all kinds of excursions (on donkeys) or boat trips around the island in caiques.

**Feasts & Festivals – Church of Panagía**, 1 500m north of Langáda: on 14 and 15 August, the church services are followed by a meal served in the square: a vegetarian meal in the evening of the 14th and a dinner of goat's meat at midnight on the 15th. There is no charge, but it is customary to leave a donation in the collection box inside the church. On these two evenings, there is traditional dancing in all the tavernas in Langáda.

**Festival of the Presentation of the Virgin**, on 21 November, at Hozoviótissa Monastery: this is your only chance to eat with the locals, in the refectory of the monastery.

**Local delicacies – Fáva** – dried pulses which are cooked in water and served as a warm purée, with a drizzle of olive oil. Why not try some?

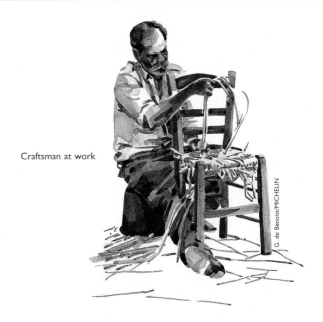

Craftsman at work

G. de Benoist/MICHELIN

Making the most of Amorgós

227

# ÁNDROS★★

Western Aegean – District of the Cyclades – Michelin map 980 fold 32
Regional map on the inside back cover – 374km² – Pop 8 781

**Not to be missed**
Hóra and the area around Steniés.
The Moussiónas region.

**And remember...**
For walks, bring sturdy footwear, a picnic, water and swimwear!
If you're travelling by motorcycle in the hills, it can get very cold
from the late afternoon onwards.

The third-largest island of the Cyclades and rather different in character, Ándros has a high mountain chain running the length of the island from north to south, culminating in Mt Profítis Ilías (997m). Rivers, streams and springs abound, resulting in forest cover that is unique in the archipelago. Oaks, plane trees, cypresses, pines, olive, almond and citrus trees ensure that Ándros is a green island in both summer and winter, especially in the south, where there are countless springs.

But the mountain also separates the island into two parts, preventing the rain from watering the north, where the more arid landscape consists of Cycladic garrigue with rocks in a hundred shades of ochre and brown. The undergrowth shelters a plethora of insects, reptiles, small mammals and birds including partridges and raptors such as falcons and the rare **Bonelli's eagle** which inhabits the hills.

Alongside these majestic wild spaces, the hills are sculpted with terraces, their drystone walls stretching out across the slopes. And there is any number of beauty spots for visitors with a taste for adventure and hill walking. The landscape is also wonderfully serene. For those who prefer less energetic pleasures, the island also has some fine beaches: the west coast, sheltered from the wind, is dotted with unspoilt ribbons of white sand, and the east coast boasts several rocky bays.

## An island apart

Ándros is also distinctive on account of its **architecture**. Naturally it has the same modern complexes typical of the Cyclades – with its standardised layout of white cube-shaped houses – the same old neo-Classical residences and Hellenistic towers. But it also has some unusual fortified houses, farmhouses embellished with strong walls and dovecotes, stone bridges and watermills. History has also left a legacy of fine monuments: there are still a few proud watchtowers dating from Ancient times, when the capital was **Paleópoli** (meaning "Old City"). There are buildings dating from the 11C and the Byzantine Period: numerous churches (the Taxiárhis at Ipsiloú, Melída and Messariá) and some interesting monasteries. The 20C bestowed formidable maritime prosperity on the island when **Dimitris Moraítis** opened up the route from America. The shipowners of Ándros were some of the most powerful in the country, and luxurious patrician residences were built on the island. In 1939, the merchant fleet of Ándros was the second-largest after that of Piraeus.

## On the west coast★
*Excursions starting from Gávrio*

Nestling at the heart of a little bay, the attractive harbour of **Gávrio** has everything you could possibly want in the way of tavernas, cafés, hotels and rooms to let to make it a comfortable place to stay. The **little streets** behind the seafront are especially charming and merit a stroll before dinner. Gávrio is also a good starting-point from which to explore the coast.

## Heading north

■ North of Gávrio, take advantage of **Felós beach**\*, near a small seaside resort, or the beach at **Limanáki**\*, at the end of a long track: solitary bathing is almost guaranteed here, with magnificent landscape all around.

■ Then head for the hills. A driveable track *(surfaced further on)* goes all the way to the magnificent mountain village of **Amólohos**\*\* *(6km from Gávrio)*, set deep in an arid landscape dotted with drystone walls. A pretty **fountain** welcomes you at the entrance to the village, while, lower down in the valley, are three **watermills** driven by the water from rivers flowing down from the hillside. On the outskirts of Gávrio, the **Ágios Kiprianós beach** is a delightful place for a swim and lunch *(taverna)*.

## Heading south\*

*From Gávrio, take the 1st road on the left after the fuel station (3km from the mountain road)*. The very winding coast road *(take care on the bends!)* climbs up through the majestic, rocky landscape between the mountain and the cliffs.

■ Three kilometres further on, a tall round tower appears on the right, together with a little white chapel that gave it its name, **Ágios Pétros**\*\* *(from the outskirts of the village walk down towards the tower following a path which is not always easy to make out)*. This is the finest example of a **Hellenistic tower** on the island, and is thought to have been used for three different purposes: as a forge, a watchtower and for sending smoke-signals. Nine metres in diameter, its five floors, which are almost intact, rise to a height of 20m.

■ The road then continues to **Kalokeriní** *(5km)*, the town before the **beaches of Vitáli**\* and **Gídes**\* *(at the end of a 4km driveable dirt track)*, which are very pleasant particularly if the wind isn't blowing *(taverna at Vitáli)*.

■ *From here, you can head back via the village of Yidès.* Beyond it are the large beaches of **Ágios Pétros**\*, **Psilí Ámos** and **Kipri**\*. As they are easy to reach and well sheltered from the wind, they tend to attract quite a few people.
From the third beach, a track leads up to the **Zoodóhou Pigís Monastery**\*, built in the 12C-14C *(open until 12am)*, where there are some **icons** and traces of ancient frescoes.

■ The main holiday resort on the island, **Batsí** has a lovely sandy beach which is very busy in the high season. The predominantly British holidaymakers stay in the modern hotels which are springing up everywhere around this old **fishing harbour.** But the place still has a certain charm: take a stroll through the **little village streets**\*, above the jetty on the edge of the bay, and absorb the typically Cycladic atmosphere.

■ **Paleópoli**\* (the "Old City"), the capital of the island in Antiquity, is now no more than a village perched on the side of the mountain. Inhabited since the early first millennium BC, the town was partly destroyed by an earthquake in the 4C BC. A section of concrete road and 1 039 steps lead down to the bottom of the **archaeological site**\*, where sections of the jetty and the ramparts can be seen just above the water. It is a delightful walk through the olive groves along a path that ends by a lovely **beach**\*.

■ A detour by way of another beach, **Halkolimióna**\*, is a possible way to end this tour.

## The north-east coast\*

*After 22km on the winding coast road from Batsí, there is a crossroads.*
*To the left, the road descends towards Hóra passing through the Messariá valley.*

Less enclosed by gently curving hills, the soft rural landscape of the **Messariá valley**\* is dotted with villages, isolated farms, olive groves, chapels and dovecotes. A few kilometres after the crossroads, on the left *(sign)* stands the magnificent white **Church of the Taxiárhis of Melída**\*\*. This fine building, which stands next to a cemetery, and dates from the 11C, houses some 12C **frescoes**\*.

**Ándros**

# ÁNDROS

0    3    6 km

N

Akr. Kambanós

Akr. Fása

Kalivári

Makrotándalo

Amólohos

Vitáli

Gídes

Kalókeriní

Epáno Felós

Limanáki

Tower

Monastery

Gídes

Felós

Ágios Pétros

Gávrio

Zoodóhou Pigís

Ágios Nikólaos

Akr. Griá

Egéo Pélagos

Psilí Ámos

Kiprí

Arnás

Profítis Ilías

▲ 994

Bisti Mouvella

Apíkia

Steniés

Giália

Nimborió

Léondas

ÁNDROS

Strapouriés

Ménites

Messariá

Paleópoli

Batsí

Aladinoú Bridge

Sinetí

Ág. Taxiárhis

Fálika

Venetian Fortress

Panahrándou

Kohílou

Halkolimióna

Grlás

Pídima

Ormos Kórthi

Aïpátia

Kórthi

Amonakliós

Aïdónia

Moussiónas

Akr. Stenó

600 m

200

0

230

■ **Messariá** – This charming village also has a church dedicated to **Ágios Taxiárhis**★★ (sign), a masterpiece of Byzantine architecture dating from the 12C. Restored in the 18C, it has **sculpted marble decoration**★ and some very fine **frescoes**★. Built in a completely different style, the **Church of Ágios Nikólaos** (1734) is also worth visiting: below its blue dome, it has a remarkable carved wooden **iconostasis**★★.

Messariá also has several good tavernas, making it a pleasant place to stop for lunch, especially under the arbour at the Dionysos establishment (on the left on the way down).

■ Before reaching Hóra, make a small detour (to the right) to have a look at the **Aladinoú bridge**★, in its beautiful verdant setting.

■ Now you are only a few kilometres (via the village of Fálika) from the **Monastery of Panahrándou**★, a white fortress-like building clinging to the mountain (erratic opening hours, try going in the late morning). Built in the 10C, this vast complex – the largest on the island – comprises several **cloisters** and **churches** dating from different periods. The few monks who live there still use the cells and the communal facilities.

## ■ Ándros★★★ (Hóra)

*On entering the town, you can either turn left and go down towards the sea, the beach and the suburb of Nimborió, or turn right towards Hóra (our option). Leave your car in the streets nearby and continue on foot.*

Unlike its Cycladic sisters, Ándros and its capital have until recently been spared the onslaught of tourism, thanks to the influence of the local shipowners. The creation of Batsí and the development of the area around Gávrio offer no threat, being some way from the calm of Hóra and its surroundings. You will also be surprised to discover that the capital has a tranquil, cosy atmosphere, even in high season. There are at least two reasons for this: no modern buildings disturb the town's architectural harmony and visitors are made very welcome.

First you reach the **main square** of Hóra, dominated by the memorial to victims of the Balkan Wars, the town hall and a fine neo-Classical building which is now a home for the elderly. Follow the pedestrian street to the left; this is the town's main commercial thoroughfare, with a mixture of tiled roofs and white Cycladic terraces, and a few neo-Classical façades. The superb **Platía Théofilos Kaïris** lies below the shade of three large trees, its terraces of cafés beckoning to passers-by to stop for a drink and listen to the soothing murmur of the **fountain**. From here, a stone staircase leads down to **Paraporti beach**, fringed with tamarisks, a favourite meeting place for the flocks of ducks which inhabit the inland marshes.

Allow some time to visit the **Archaeological Museum**★ on the left of the square (8am-2.30pm; closed Monday; entrance fee), the first floor of which is devoted to the ancient site of **Zagora** (on the west coast of the island). The scale models and the reconstruction of a house, along with objects recovered from the site, vividly illustrate daily life in what was the largest city of the Geometric Period (900-700 BC) to have been found on the island. The museum also contains an unusual collection of finds made on the island: the famous **Hermes of Ándros**★, a marble copy of an original in bronze attributed to Praxiteles, some funerary steles and some early Christian, Venetian and Ottoman architectural features. Lovers of modern art may also visit the **Goulandris Museum**★ (10am-2pm and 6pm-8pm; closed Tuesday and Sunday afternoon; entrance fee). Not content with associating its name with the Museum of Cycladic Art in Athens, this shipowning dynasty from Ándros wanted to give their island a museum devoted to Greek and international expressions of modern and contemporary art. Among other things, you will find works by the neo-Classical sculptor **Mihalis Tobros** (1889-1974) and by the more controversial sculptor **Tákis** (who moved to France in the 1950s).

**Ándros**

## The Medieval District★

Built by the Venetians, **the town's old harbour** has since lost its two watchtowers. There remains only the **vaulted passageway** (*next to the bookshop*), beyond which lies the heart of medieval Hóra, reached by a pretty little street lined with **houses★** that are painted in delightful pastel shades, have tiled roofs and are further embellished with little balconies.

Dominating Paraporti beach, the **Church of Ágios Geórgios** (17C) stands in a charming little paved square, a pleasant place to linger under the shade of a palm tree and a eucalyptus.

You leave the medieval district by the vast **square** occupying the tip of the promontory. In the centre stands the bronze **statue** of an unknown sailor, cap over one ear and a bundle over his shoulder. Viewed against the backdrop of the ruins of a **Venetian fortress** built in 1207, he seems to be greeting the island. A hump-backed bridge used to connect the fortress to the island.

The large building on one side of the square houses the **Maritime Museum** (*10am-1pm / 6pm-8pm; closed Tuesday and Sunday afternoon; no entrance fee*), which contains scale models of boats, engravings, navigation instruments and numerous other exhibits evoking the maritime history of Ándros.

Finally, do take the time to look at the **lower part of the town**, which has retained its unusual charm, its houses embellished with **verandas** decorated with small columns.

# From village to village

For anyone interested in an excursion which is not too demanding, here are two short itineraries (*each one takes approximately half a day*), which take in the wonderful scenery in the area.

## From Ménites to the Ágios Nikólaos Monastery★★

■ Before entering Messariá, follow directions for **Ménites★** (*to the left*). Then turn right to get to the **springs★** gushing out of the beautiful marble lions' heads; it is a good chance to fill your water bottle. Then head for the terrace of the church where there is a superb **view★★** of the village, a veritable oasis – so green and cool, even in summer. A taverna (often very busy) overlooks the stream.

■ At **Strapouriés★** there is a beautiful **church★** and a number of **archontiká**, grand mansions which testify to the early fortunes of merchant shipping.

*Go back to the main road: left for Apíkia, right for Hóra. Turn right, then left and, before Steniés, left again, at the Pírgos sign.*

■ Lower down, the **Léondas bridge★** spans a river with its single arch. About 2km from the junction, on the left, a concrete road leads up towards the **Bisti Mouvella tower★**, one of the **fortified houses** which are a particular feature of Ándros. From its small terrace, there is a **view★★** over Hóra and the hills covered with a mixture of cypresses, olive trees, pines, almond and oak trees. Here and there, houses with red-tiled roofs have **dovecotes**, making it rather reminiscent of Tuscany.

■ Leave your vehicle and follow the steps leading to the village of **Steniés★★**, the white houses forming a sort of amphitheatre overlooking the sea. Walking through the streets, look out for the remarkable **neo-Classical residences★**, which have been restored and are used in the summer by Athenians who originate from Ándros.

■ The road that climbs up towards Apíkia has a splendid **view★★** of Hóra and the surrounding area. After the col, it drops down again between tall trees. When you arrive in **Apíkia★**, climb up towards the **Sáriza spring★** (excellent drinking water), which gushes out of a marble lion's head between small columns (18C). Note also the pretty **church**.

■ Beyond Apíkia, the woodland gives way to a drier, more open landscape. This rather austere but beautiful place was chosen as the site for the imposing **Ágios Nikólaos Monastery\*** (16C). It overlooks a steep gorge which runs down towards the sea, the low garrigue alternating with cultivated terraces. There is a large square in front of the monastery (superb **view\*\***). Behind its impressive enclosure wall, the courtyard reveals an unusual multicoloured **chapel**, with a blue dome and red and yellow walls. The silence, the fountain and an enormous chestnut tree make this a very restful spot.

■ Come back via **Nimborió beach**, where there is an interesting **view\*** over Hóra, emphasising its defensive layout, created by linking together the walls of the outer-most houses.

### Kórthi and the south of the island

■ From Hóra, a wiggly road winds its way towards Sinetí through splendid scenery, the wild setting for the pretty village of **Kohílou\*** and a few **watermills** (*before and after Exo Vouni, on the left*). Not far away, **Sinetí beach** nestles in a narrow bay while, from above Kohílou, a track climbs up towards the ruins of a **Venetian fortress**, known as the "castle of the old lady" (beautiful **view\*\***).

■ The road then drops down in a series of wide bends to the **valley of Kórthi**, dotted with the occasional **dovecote**. It eventually arrives at **Órmos Kórthi**, an uninspiring seaside resort. If you want to swim, carry on to **Griás Pídima beach**, beyond the lighthouse to the north. South of the beach, set on the hillside, the village of **Ano Kórthi\*** is worth visiting to look at its **old houses**.

*Leaving the main road on your right and Ano Kórthi on your left, leave the bay and head in the direction of Aïdónia. Be warned that the road has many twists and turns, which considerably lengthen the journey.*

■ Following the contours of the hillside, the road passes through some of the most picturesque villages on the island: **Aïdónia\***, **Moussiónas\*** and **Amonakliós\***, the traditional architecture of which blends in perfectly with the magical mountain landscape.
Where you rejoin the main road at **Aïpátia**, the scenery is equally beautiful, dotted with **traditional villages** and **dovecotes**.

**Ándros**

The turquoise shores of the south coast of Ándros

M. Pizzocaro/ON LOCATION

## COMING AND GOING

**By boat** – From Rafína, the usual port of departure for Ándros, there are between 3 and 5 ferries a day (a 3hr30min journey), generally divided between the morning (about 8am) and the late afternoon (about 6pm). There are other connections by catamaran. Buses for Rafína (leaving from Aréos park) from 5.40am, then every 20min until 8am, and every 30min until 10.30pm (allow 1hr to reach the port). From Piraeus (4hr journey), there are 4 departures a week, at about 4.30pm and 6.30pm.

On Ándros, all the boats arrive at and depart from Gávrio.

*Harbourmaster's office at Gávrio*, ☎ (0282) 71 213.

## GETTING AROUND

**By bus** – The bus for Hóra (bus stop on the outskirts of town) and Kórthi via Batsí will be waiting when you get off the boat. From Hóra, there are bus services to Batsí, Gávrio, Apíkia, Strapouriés, Steniés and Kórthi: bus station outside the town, ☎ (0282) 22 316.

**Roads** – Be aware of the distances involved and of the terrain which can considerably lengthen any journey. For example, it takes 30min to cover the 35km between Hóra and Gávrio by scooter; it also takes 30min to cover the 26km of wiggly roads along the coast between Hóra and Órmos Kórthi.

**By rental vehicle** – Motorcycles and mopeds can be hired from **Rentabike**, in Gávrio (follow the harbour round to the left; the shop is in one of the last streets on the right). The shop may not look much, but the vehicles are reliable. Allow around €9 for a 50cc model.

**Dinos**, in Batsí, offers a wide range of new motorcycles, as well as car hire.

**Aris**, on the outskirts of Hóra, has motorcycles for hire, which are in good condition although a bit more expensive.

**By taxi** – In Gávrio, ☎ (0282) 71 561 / 71 171; in Batsí, ☎ (0282) 41 081; in Hóra, ☎ (0282) 22 171; in Kórthi, ☎ (0282) 62 171.

## ADDRESS BOOK

**Tourist information** – In Gávrio, a dovecote has been turned into a tourist information office, near the quay.

**Banks / Currency exchange** – There are four banks in Hóra, two in Batsí, one in Kórthi and one in Gávrio. Most of them have cash dispensers.

**Post office** – In Hóra, between the car park and the first square.

**Police** – In Gávrio, ☎ (0282) 71 220; in Hóra, ☎ (0282) 22 300; in Batsí, ☎ (0282); in Kórthi, ☎ (0282) 61 211.

**Medical service – *Medical centre*** in Hóra, ☎ (0282) 23 703 / 22 222. ***Doctors*** in Gávrio, ☎ (0282) 71 210; in Batsí, ☎ (0282) 41 326; in Kórthi, ☎ (0282) 61 211. ***Pharmacies***: four in Hóra, one in Gávrio, one in Kórthi.

## WHERE TO STAY

### • Gávrio

*Between €18 and €36*
**Galaxias**, at the harbour, to the left of the quay, ☎ (0282) 71 228 – 17rm. ⌂
✿ Clean, ideally placed and cheap, but without any particular charm. Ask for a room overlooking the harbour. Good taverna on the ground floor.

*Between €27 and €49*
**El-Do-So**, on the outskirts of Gávrio in the direction of Ágios Pétros, ☎ (0282) 71 196 / 71 296, (01) 82 39 418 – 10 studios. ⌂ ✿ ⌂ 30m from the sea, this complex built in the Cycladic style has attractive, well-equipped studios with terraces.

### • Ágios Pétros

*Between €27 and €49*
**Studio Irene**, 100m from the beach, ☎ (0282) 61 742 / 71 675 – 15rm. ⌂ ✿ [TV] ⌂ Studios with kitchenettes that are well kept. Pleasant setting.

*Between €33 and €60*
**Sophía**, 350m from the beach, ☎ (0282) 71 249, Fax (0282) 71 450 – 12 studios. ⌂ ✿ ✕ [TV] ⌂ Set in a garden, this attractive complex is built in the Cycladic style. Pleasantly decorated, the studios can accommodate up to 5 people. Friendly welcome.

### • Batsí

*Around €33*

🐌 **Ánna Mihaíl**, in the village of Batsí, in the street that runs above the church, ☎ (0282) 41 587 / 41 761 – 5rm. 🍴 🏠 Comfortable little studios with kitchenettes and sea views.

### • Ménites

*Around €38*

🐌 **Stamatoúla Ligídou**, an isolated house (look for the "Rooms" sign on the right, or contact the owner's daughter at the cake shop in the square in Hóra), ☎ (0282) 51 016 / 24 380 – 6rm. 🍴 Rooms with a kitchenette and veranda looking out onto the garden, with a magnificent view.

### • Órmos Kórthi

*Between €27 and €49*

**Villa Corfi**, on the right when you get close to the beach, ☎ (0282) 61 122, Fax (0282) 62 022. In an attractive blue and white building, studios furnished and well managed.

**Kórthion**, opposite the beach, ☎ (0282) 61 218, Fax (0282) 61 118 – 13rm. 🍴 ♿ ✗ Simple, clean, cheap and reasonably comfortable.

### • Apíkia

*Between €27 and €49*

Rooms to let, opposite the Sariza hotel, above the **O Tássos** restaurant, ☎ (0282) 22 303 / 23 525. 🍴 ✗ Pretty veranda facing the mountain. The restaurant is on the other side.

### • Nimborió

*Between €18 and €30*

**Stélla Réoukou**, opposite the beach, ☎ (0282) 22 471 / 24 419 – 5rm. A pretty terrace under a climbing vine houses a café. Rooms on the first floor, clean and comfortable.

### • Hóra

*Between €30 and €38*

🐌 **Aegli**, in the old town, opposite the big church standing on the right of the main street, before Platía Kaïris, ☎ (0282) 22 303, Fax (0282) 22 159 – 14rm. 🍴 ♿ 📋 📺 An old neo-classical hotel, full of charm, comfortable and very well-located. Book ahead.

### • Gávrio

**Karlos**, behind the church, in the direction of the campsite. A good, traditional taverna, with reasonable prices.
**Valma**, by the harbour, a good place for fresh fish.

### • Ágios Pétros

**Paralia**, fish, barbecued and cooked dishes.
**Yianoúlis**, good for meze: sea views.

### • Apíkia

*Around €15*

**O Tássos**, a terrace with a lovely view, good traditional cooking.
**Piyi Sáriza**, right opposite, the restaurant of the hotel of the same name. Recommended for the shady courtyard under the huge plane tree. Try the "froutaliá", an omelette made with potatoes, cubes of bacon and pork sausage, a traditional dish of Ándros and Tínos.

### • Strapouriés

🐌 **Pertésis**, famous for its "froutaliá", its chicken cooked with tomatoes and pilaff, and its "tiropitákia".

### • Batsí

**Stamátis**, with views over the harbour from the terrace, recommended for its fresh fish.
**Dolfins**, famous for its vegetable croquettes.

### • Hóra

**Paréa**, try its squid cooked in a wine sauce ("soupiès krassatès") and "yémista" (tomatoes or aubergines stuffed with rice).

### • Messariá

**Diónysos**, village atmosphere, under an arbour. Real traditional cooking.
At **Louis'**, the speciality is a variation of froutaliá with courgettes.

Ándros is not exactly an island for nightlife. The alternatives are: Hóra for a relaxing atmosphere; Batsí, if you are looking for something more exciting.

**Walking –** No other island offers walkers such a variety of landscape and tourist trails. Buy the **Touring Hiking Map** published by the Ministry for the Aegean.

**Making the most of Ándros**

# DELOS★★★
## (DÍLOS)

Aegean Sea – District of the Cyclades – Michelin map 980 fold 32
Regional map on the inside back cover – Map of the island page 276
3.6km² – Uninhabited island (excursions leave from Mýkonos)

**Not to be missed**
The whole site, and especially the area with the mosaics.
**And remember...**
At Mýkonos, purchase your ticket on the quay: the prices are higher at the agencies.
In order to make the most of the site, take the first boat to Delos
and catch the last boat back. Take food and water.

When you leave Mýkonos for its neighbouring island, you are transported into another dimension of time, far removed from the hustle and bustle of modern life. On Delos, the inhabitants are limited to the geckoes, those small lizard-like creatures, the goats grazing in the pastures (owned by farmers on Mýkonos) and the tourists who arrive by boat to explore the ancient site. Because, essentially, that's what Delos is: an immense marble city, sparkling in the sun, an open-air museum poised between the sky and the sea. Alone, emerging from a carpet of sunburnt grass, the ruins stand at the foot of Mt Kynthos, a small rounded hill 113m high, which is the only other feature on the island.

### The floating island

It is around the sacred island of Delos that the Cyclades revolve (see page 217). It is a sacred island because it was here that the nymph, Leto, having been seduced and abandoned by Zeus, chose to give birth to the divine twins, Artemis and Apollo. One version relates that the island itself was a metamorphosis of the libido of Zeus: after Leto, the insatiable seducer harassed another nymph called Asteria. To escape from the god, she transformed herself into an island, drifting aimlessly, until Leto, who was pregnant and pursued by the jealousy of Hera, asked her for hospitality. Asteria took in the poor goddess and would only agree to stop drifting on the condition that the island would become the sanctuary of the god that was about to be born.

### The cradle of Apollo

Reputedly the birthplace of Apollo, Delos prides itself on being the main sanctuary of Ancient Greece, along with Delphi, and was one of the richest trading centres in the Aegean. The first trading centre came into existence during the Mycenaean Period (2nd half of the 2nd millennium BC), but it did not last. The real expansion of Delos came about in the late 8C BC with the **Ionians**, who established a cult of Apollo here. The festivals held in honour of the god soon attracted not only a large number of pilgrims, but also merchants plying the routes between the coasts of Asia Minor and the shores of the Western Mediterranean. The island became the capital of an **"Amphictyony"**, a confederation of the islands of the archipelago.

Closely linked with the popularity of its cult, the growing prosperity of Delos soon began to interest Athens: in 478 BC, Athens united the Amphictyony and Attica, in the powerful **Delian League**, with the taxes contributed by members of the confederacy being bestowed on the island. Delos, which was by now a very wealthy place, developed fast and, from the Hellenistic Age onwards (1C BC), enjoyed unprecedented prosperity, heralding the first wave of urbanisation.

This golden age was followed by the Roman Period when, having been declared a free port, Delos attracted a large number of merchants and bankers from all over the Mediterranean, particularly Syria and Italy. As a dynamic, cosmopolitan city with a population of 25 000, Delos became the focus for the cult of several foreign gods. Its port, and the vast cereal and slave market were equipped with new warehouses and shops, while the rest of the city was embellished with grandiose monuments and villas.

In 88 BC, **Mithradates**, King of Pontus who was fighting against the Romans, sacked the island and massacred all its inhabitants. Delos was never to recover: despite the efforts of the philhellenic Emperor Hadrian, and subsequently of the Christians who made it a bishopric in the 4C AD, the city fell slowly into an irreversible decline. Targeted by pirates, it saw its monuments plundered by looters in search of antiquities. It wasn't until 1873 that Delos began to surface again when the French School of Archaeology in Athens began to excavate the area.

**Death forbidden**
In 550 BC, in an effort to preserve the sacred status of Delos, the Athenian tyrant Peisistratus decreed that the sanctuary must be purified and all traces of death on the island were to be removed. From then on, anyone who died was buried on the nearby island of Rínia, and the old graves and their contents were also transferred. Two centuries later, a second purification programme resulted in the radical move of prohibiting births and deaths on Delos! This decree meant that pregnant women and elderly citizens nearing their time were relegated to the same island... now uninhabited.

## Tour of the site

*8.30am-3pm; closed Monday. Entrance fee. Allow 3hr minimum. When you disembark, with the old port area on your right, continue straight on towards the sanctuary, which lies further on to the left (north). Allow at least 30min to visit the museum. If you have time, carry on as far as the stadium (north-east; again allow 30min). Otherwise, go straight to the Terrace of the Foreign Gods, then up to the top of Mt Kynthos. On the way down, you will have a chance to look at the villas in the theatre district, completing your tour with the ancient harbour. Guides are available: the tour is conducted in English and is quite expensive (€15).*

### On the way to the sanctuary

The first attraction is the **Agora of the Competialists**, a vast square paved with marble dating from the Hellenistic Age. It owes its name to a corporation of Italian merchants who came to honour the Lares Compitales, the Roman gods of the crossroads. Then, on the left, lies the **Processional Way★**, a magnificent avenue *(drómos)* 13m wide leading to the sanctuary of Apollo. There was a portico on either side, dotted with honorary statues and monuments, traces of which can still be seen at ground level: on the left stands the **Stoa of Philip**, which Philip V of Macedon had built in about 210 BC, and, on the right, the **Pergamon Stoa**, which was built 30 years later by the kings of Pergamon. At the end of the avenue, a **statue of Hermes (7)** from the 4C BC *(a copy)* seems to be inviting visitors to come through the **propylaea** marking the entrance to the sanctuary.

The sacred felines of Delos: lions or lionesses?

G. de Benoist/MICHELIN

**Delos**

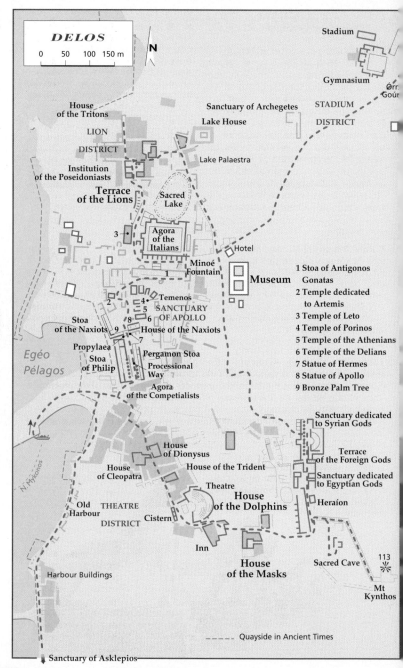

**DELOS**

0   50   100  150 m

N

Stadium

Gymnasium

Órr.
Goú...

House
of the Tritons

LION
DISTRICT

Sanctuary of Archegetes

Lake House

STADIUM

DISTRICT

Institution
of the Poseidoniasts

Lake Palaestra

Terrace
of the Lions

Sacred
Lake

3

Agora
of the
Italians

Hotel

Minoé
Fountain

Museum

1

2

Temenos

4

SANCTUARY
OF APOLLO

5

Stoa
of the Naxiots

8

6

9

House of the Naxiots

7

Propylaea

Stoa
of Philip

Pergamon Stoa

Processional
Way

Agora
of the Competialists

Egéo
Pélagos

1 Stoa of Antigonos
   Gonatas
2 Temple dedicated
   to Artemis
3 Temple of Leto
4 Temple of Porinos
5 Temple of the Athenians
6 Temple of the Delians
7 Statue of Hermes
8 Statue of Apollo
9 Bronze Palm Tree

Sanctuary dedicated
to Syrian Gods

Terrace
of the Foreign Gods

House
of Dionysus

House of the Trident

Sanctuary dedicated
to Egyptian Gods

House
of Cleopatra

Theatre

House
of the Dolphins

Heraíon

N. Mýkonos

Old
Harbour

THEATRE
DISTRICT

Cistern

Inn

113

House
of the Masks

Sacred Cave

Mt
Kynthos

Harbour Buildings

- - - - - Quayside in Ancient Times

Sanctuary of Asklepios

238

## The sanctuary of Apollo★★ (Hierón)

As you enter the hierón, the first thing to look out for on the right are the eroded walls of the **House of the Naxiots★**, which is in fact a temple commissioned by the inhabitants of Náxos in the second half of the 7C BC. Against the back wall (*to the north*) stands an enormous marble plinth which used to support a colossal **statue of Apollo (8)**.

To the left of the propylaea lie the ruins of the **Stoa of the Naxiots** (6C BC) in front of which stood a **bronze palm tree (9)**, an offering from the Greek strategist, Nikias, representing the tree under which Leto gave birth to the divine twins. Only the pedestal remains (when it collapsed, this statue broke the statue of Apollo!).

Beyond the portico, on the right, lies the heart of the sanctuary, the **temenos**. There were once three temples dedicated to Apollo, the remains of which can still be seen lying next to each other. The **Delians** were duty bound to build the largest: constructed in stages between the 5C and 3C BC, their **Doric temple (6)** replaced the one built by the **Athenians (5)**, which was smaller. The smallest temple is also the oldest (6C BC), and is known as the **Temple of Porinos (4)** because of the limestone tufa of which it is built. Completing the complex, five **treasuries** are arranged in an arc behind the temples, where the cities belonging to the Delian League laid their offerings.

Continue along the Sacred Way to get to the **temple dedicated to Artemis (2)** (*on the left*). In the naos, you will find two of the remaining pieces of the **statue of Apollo** (6C BC), the pedestal of which can be seen in the House of the Naxiots.

Leave the sanctuary by the **Stoa of Antigonos Gonatas (1)**, a votive building 120m long, commissioned by a king of Macedon. Of the numerous statues and votive figures which once stood in front of the colonnade, only the statue of a Roman magistrate remains (*at the far end of the stoa*). Look out for the splendid **friezes** of bulls' heads which archaeologists have reconstructed on the ground. Finally, just behind the portico, the **Minoé fountain** has an elegant square basin.

## The Lion District★

Beyond the sanctuary lies the Lion District, the urban centre built in the Hellenistic Age. You enter it by the **Agora of the Italians** (*on the right*) where each merchant had his own cell decorated with **mosaics★**. On the left, are the foundations of the **Temple of Leto (3)** (6C BC).

Next comes the famous **Terrace of the Lions** – five hieratic animals, sitting on their haunches. The originals have been removed to the museum to protect them from erosion, and copies put in their place. Sculpted in the late 7C BC, at the request of the Naxiots, they used to guard the Temple of Leto. Originally there were nine of them (or sixteen according to some sources). Since the end of the 17C, one of them has stood at the entrance to the Arsenal in Venice, with a different head.

They all overlooked the **Sacred Lake**, the birthplace of Apollo and Artemis. In the 20C, the lake was filled in because it was a breeding ground for mosquitoes which were spreading malaria. A wall marks its position and a palm tree stands in the centre, paying modest homage to Leto and her two divine offspring.

### The Delian festivals

Under Athenian domination, Delos would come alive every four years for the sumptuous Delian festivals: in February, the Apollonia took place, and in May, the Delian festival attracted numerous leaders from the Greek cities and states. From the harbour, the pilgrims went along the Processional Way chanting hymns to the god, as far as the Temple of Apollo, where sacred dances welcomed them. Then the procession walked around the sanctuary to watch various animal sacrifices, and the ceremonies ended with more dancing, accompanied by gymnastic and musical competitions.

**Delos**

Continuing along the Sacred Way, a little further on, you reach the four tall columns of the **Institution of the Poseidoniasts** where, under the aegis of Poseidon, the merchants and shipowners of Berytos (modern Beirut) once congregated. They stand in front of an area of grandiose villas with patios. For example the **House of the Tritons★** (fine **mosaic**), and, further on, to the right, the **Lake House★**.

## The Stadium District

*Take the path to the left in front of the museum.* The first ruins, on the left, are those of the **Sanctuary of Archegetes**, the precinct dedicated to Anius, the son of Apollo, the legendary founder of the city and its first king. Further on, the impressive remains of the **gymnasium** (3C BC) lie scattered in the grass. Beyond it, the **stadium** has a sandy track 182m long, the starting line of which is still clearly visible.

Below lie the ruins of the houses that used to stand next to the stadium, on a street running parallel to it, and the foundations of a **synagogue** erected in the 1C BC *(right next to the sea)*.

## The museum★★★

*Same opening hours as the site, and access with same ticket.* Its magnificent collections – complete with a **scale model★** of the city – are an excellent illustration of the island's wealth over the centuries. The first three rooms *(opposite the entrance)* contain a remarkable collection of **works from the Archaic Period★★**: in particular, a **sphynx★** dating from the 6C BC *(central hall, no 1)*, which used to grace the top of a column, a **kouros★**, and numerous fragments of decoration from the temples.

The famous **lions of Delos★★★** are hidden away behind the large central room, in the corner on the right. Despite the dullness of the blue wall in the background, they are still astonishingly graceful. Room 5 contains large-scale works and Room 6 houses some very realistic sculptures of the inhabitants of Delos of the late 2C BC. Room 7 displays all the luxury of the Hellenistic Age: superb **mosaics** and **wall paintings★★** from the wealthiest villas in the city. Various tools evoking everyday life are displayed next to a case of erotica. The tour of the museum ends with artefacts from the 8C, 7C and 6C BC *(Room 8, to the right of the entrance)* including sculptures and vases showing traces of oriental influence found in the Heraíon *(see below)*.

*From the museum, follow the track leading to Mt Kynthos.*

## The Terrace of the Foreign Gods★★

After the ruins and before reaching the terrace of the foreign gods, make a slight detour down to the right to look at the **House of Hermes★** (2C BC). It is named after the sculpture that was discovered there: a beautiful head of the god dating from the 5C BC *(now in the museum)*.

A few metres further on, you emerge onto a long platform overlooking the villa. Hera was worshipped from the 6C BC, then, during the Hellenistic Age, the foreign peoples living on Delos added several sanctuaries dedicated to their own respective divinities. The first sanctuary you come to – the largest – was dedicated to the **Syrian gods** Hadad and Atargatis. A Sacred Way leads through it, lined by two porticoes and a small **theatre** where mysterious orgiastic rituals associated with the cult of Atargatis were performed. On the right of the semi-circle, there were rooms with benches where ritual feasts were held, while, on the left, there was a cistern where the statue of the goddess was submerged.

The next sanctuary along was dedicated to the **Egyptian gods**. Behind the remains of the **Temple of Serapis**, which is surrounded by a courtyard, stands the reconstruction of the façade of the **Temple of Isis**: behind the two Doric columns is a headless statue of the goddess. Directly opposite is an altar where the faithful used to place their offerings.

Finally, next to it, stands the primitive sanctuary of the **Heraíon** which was built in the late 6C BC in honour of Hera. The marble foundations and three truncated columns are all that remain of this temple.

*A little further on, on the left, steps lead up to the top of Mt Kynthos.*

## Mt Kynthos★★

*Allow about 30min to go up and down.* It is worth climbing to the top not so much for the ruins but for the **panorama★★** over Delos and the circle of the Cyclades, which is superb. On the way to the top, you will pass the ruins of the sanctuary of Agathé Týche, just before the **Sacred Cave** of Heracles, a simple fissure in the rock where a statue of the hero (no longer extant) was kept, sheltered by a roof composed of slabs of granite.

*Retrace your steps to the Heraíon, then turn left and walk down towards the harbour.*

## The Theatre District★★★

Opulent Hellenistic villas *(marked by signs)* stand on either side of the street, many of them concealing mosaics in an exceptionally good state of preservation. Two of the villas, in particular, are worth a detour: the **House of the Dolphins★★★** *(only visible from the outside)*, where the central courtyard contains a magnificent **mosaic★★** depicting dolphins, and, almost opposite it, the **House of the Masks★★★** whose **mosaics★★★** are mostly still in situ: from east to west, they depict Dionysus surrounded by centaurs, theatrical masks which gave the house its name, a flautist and a dancing Silenus figure, a bird, and, on the threshold, a pair of dolphins.

Further along, there is a huge **inn** *(on the left)* with an enormous **cistern**. Excellently situated, it stands opposite the **theatre★** on the other side of the street, which is built into the hollow of the hillside. Erected in the 3C BC, it could accommodate 5 500 spectators.

Below the theatre, two fine houses stand opposite each other: on the right, the **House of Dionysus★**, where a **mosaic★** depicts Apollo riding a leopard, and, on the left, the **House of Cleopatra★**, where visitors are welcomed by elegant statues of Cleopatra and her husband Discourides *(copies)*.

*Go back to the Agora of the Competialists, then walk along the shore, the sea on your left.*

## The harbour

The **harbour district** is less interesting than the parts of the site already described. Beyond *(about 1km away)*, stood the **Sanctuary of Asklepios**: the remains of three of the buildings associated with the sanctuary lie in the **Bay of Fourní**.

--- Making the most of Delos ---

### COMING AND GOING

Delos is a 30min boat ride from Mýkonos.

**By cruise boat** – In addition to those from Mýkonos, cruise boats also depart from nearby islands (Tínos, Ándros, Páros or Náxos, in particular) and stop at Delos. But the joint ticket for visiting Mýkonos and Delos will leave you little time for exploring Delos.

**By the Mýkonos-Delos shuttle service** – The best way to reach Delos is to catch a launch at the small fishing harbour in the centre of Mýkonos, not the ferry port. Three companies share the services to Delos (a 25 to 35min boat ride): **Héra**, **Niki**, and **Delos Express**. The last mentioned allows you most time on Delos with a departure at 8.30am and the last boat back at 3pm. All three companies provide visitors with a plan of the site and offer guided tours (additional fee). However, remember that whatever the time of your boat back, you must take boats belonging to the same company for both the outward and return journey (each boat runs a shuttle service several times a day).

**By pleasure boat** – These boats can moor at the harbour of Delos, every day except Monday, between 8am and 3pm.

### WHERE TO STAY, HAVING A DRINK

There is nowhere to stay on Delos; the nearest hotels are situated on Mýkonos *(see page 279)*. As far as refreshment is concerned, the *cafeteria* is the only place on the island, and offers basic dishes at a price.

# FOLÉGANDROS

Western Aegean – District of the Cyclades – Michelin map 980 fold 44
Regional map on the inside back cover – 32km²
Pop 558 – Allow 2 days

**Not to be missed**
Strolling around Hóra and discovering the delights of távli in one of it s shady squares.
Diving into the crystal-clear waters at Kátergo or Firá after a long walk.
Sailing around the island in a caique.

**And remember...**
Avoid the month of August: it is very windy and there are too many people
for such a small island.

Isolated, bare and wild, the southernmost island of the Cyclades (and one of the smallest) has a special charm. Perhaps because, despite the changes brought about by tourism, the traditional way of life is still in evidence here. The villages are rather rudimentary and the landscape is austere, often buffeted by the wind. It is perhaps for this reason that Hóra seems like a refuge: it resembles a large warm house that imbues visitors with a desire to explore all its rooms and follow all its corridors, the kástro being its most mysterious corner. After walking and swimming in solitude – solitude may be harder to find in August – you can choose between enjoying the lively night-life of the squares of Hóra, or having a peaceful dinner on the water's edge, at Karavostássis or Angáli.

## A deserted island

Because most of Folégandros is arid and mountainous, the island could only offer the most rudimentary and precarious base in terms of human occupation; but, even more significantly, it was because of pirates and raids by the Turks that the island was abandoned on several occasions. In 1715, a Turkish admiral sacked the island and made slaves of almost all its inhabitants, many of whom either perished during the return voyage or were executed on Chios. Having been imprisoned in Istanbul, the few survivors benefited from the intervention of the French Ambassador and returned to the island in 1718. Despite this, this rural society did not emerge from its isolation until the 19C, thanks to the arrival of the telegraph (in 1885) and visits from passing steam-ships, then, later on, the building of a lighthouse (1921) and, more particularly, gifts from islanders who had emigrated to Alexandria, Athens and Istanbul, which made it possible to establish two schools. However, this period of relative prosperity was brief since, from 1920 until 1969, Folégandros was to be a land of exile for political prisoners who, for 50 years, shared the simple way of life of its inhabitants. A situation that did nothing to encourage tourism, until the last twenty years when it slowly began to flourish.

## Karavostássis and the south★

Nestling in a bay of beautifully clear water, next to a pebble **beach** fringed with tamarisks, the island's harbour – which formerly consisted of a few fishermen's huts – has become a holiday resort which comes alive in the summer season, its houses clustered around the only small church, **Ágios Artémios**.

■ There are two beaches to the north of Karavostássis, **Várdia** and **Deméneou** (*can only be reached by boat*). Opt for the former, which is larger and easier to reach. However, be aware that the sea floor shelves steeply, the sun goes down fairly early and the north wind can blow very hard there.

■ You can always venture a little further, beyond the small beaches of **Latináki**, **Vitséntzou** and **Poundáki**, to Livádi★ beach *(a 30min walk from the harbour; taverna)*, a long strip of sand dotted with tamarisks, which is also the starting-point for a walk in one of the few fertile parts of the island.

■ But the best beach on Folégandros is **Kátergo** beach, which lies tucked away behind the village of the same name *(at the end of the road, the road on the left leads to the campsite)*; on the way, look out for the **Church of Ágios Módestos** *(5km before the end of the asphalt road, the second church on the right)*, painted white, dedicated to the patron saint of livestock. In the 1930s, some of the **abandoned houses** nearby used to be occupied by political exiles. From here, a path leads down to the beach.

## Hóra★★★
*3.3km from the harbour. Allow 3hr.*

Built around its kástro, on the edge of a steep **cliff★★** poised directly above the sea (at least 210m high), the town of Hóra on Folégandros is, without any doubt, one of the prettiest in the Cyclades. Even the buildings erected to accommodate tourists have not detracted from its harmonious architecture. The main attraction is its setting, the cliff on which it is built forming an imposing wall from which there is a spectacular **view★** over the sea *(especially from Platía Pounda and along the road leading to Panagía)*.

### The kástro★★★
Built by the Venetians in the years that followed the Fourth Crusade (1204), the kástro forms a triangle against the cliff, of which Platía Pounda is the base and the Church of Panagía Pantánassa the tip. As at Sífnos, several lines of houses constituted the defences of this

Alleyways in the kástro, Folégandros

G. de Benoist/MICHELIN

**Folégandros**

fortified town, a succession of continuous façades without any access points, facing outward and linked together at each end by narrow passageways, forming concentric enclosure walls. With the passing of time, the fear of pirates diminished and the inhabitants modified this crude form of medieval architecture by building staircases and balconies here and there which, today, constitute part of the charm of the place. Be sure to take some time to explore it, both during the day and at night.

Worth a visit is the **Church of Panagía Pantánassa** (late 17C), which stands right on the cliff edge (splendid **view\*\***). In the fresco by the door on the right, the church's benefactor, Giórgos Staís, is the figure depicted at the feet of St George. The interior is decorated with some fine post-Byzantine **icons.**

### A walk through the village\*\* (Hório)

The actual village is just as attractive. You could easily get tired exploring its pleasant cobbled streets if Folégandros did not have such an irresistible series of little **squares**, each with its own church, in which to stop and rest. This complex is unique in the Cyclades, and has an almost theatrical charm. Starting from **Platía Pounda**, which is the largest, you then pass through a succession of squares named **Doúnavi**, **Kontaríni**, **Piátsa** (the oldest square), then, on the right, **Platía Maráki** and **Platía Tachidromíou** (literally post-office square, although the post office is now located at the edge of the village). Planted with flowers or trees, each one has a character of its own, and is the place to come for a game of távli until the time for aperitifs. And if you are not inclined to play backgammon or drink ouzo, you can set off to explore the village's 16 post-Byzantine **churches**, built in the 17C and 18C (and almost all altered in the 19C).

Continue along **Kalderími,** the street that connects Platía Maráki to the bus stop for Páno Meriá, looking out for the fine late-19C **houses**.

From Platía Pounda, follow the street on the left that goes off between the **war memorial** (Iróon) and the small neo-Classical building housing the island's cultural centre. It zigzags uphill to the square in front of the brilliant white **Panagía Kímissis Church\*\*** (Dormition) in complete contrast to the ochre-brown of the rocks all around. This, the finest church on the island, with its remarkable **bell-tower**, once formed the centre of a convent, and was almost certainly built on the site of an earlier building, as the **throne\*\*** inside suggests. You will also notice a few **ancient remains** (at the bottom of the bell-tower, at the entrance to the church) which possibly come from the ancient acropolis, **Paleókastro** (*lower down, on the edge of the cliff, can be reached by a path*). Although the site is in ruins, it has a magnificent **view\*** over Hóra and the sea.

Nearby is **Hrissospiliá**, the "golden cave", a site of worship in Antiquity (*closed to the public while archaeological excavations are in progress*).

### Country walks

Make time to explore the tracks and paths around Hóra, a pleasant walk through the island's agricultural past (*for the first two walks, leave Hóra following the little street that leads off from Platía Tachidromíou, and, for the last walk, follow the walls of the kástro*). This is your opportunity to visit the pretty little churches of **Ágios Vassílios\***, **Ágios Sávas\*** and **Panagía Plakianí\***, all three of which were built on the hill overlooking the town. A few clumps of olive trees and vines vie with the garrigue in the abandoned fields which slope down towards the sea.

But one of the best walks is the one to the **Ágios Nikólaos Monastery\*\*** (*west of Petoússis*), built in the hills where flocks of sheep and goats once grazed. In ruins in parts, but splendidly located.

## The north cape\*\*

*From Hóra, follow the Páno Meriá road. After about 1.5km, take the lane on the left opposite the road with the three windmills; surfaced sections of road alternate with more difficult stretches; allow 1hr in all.*

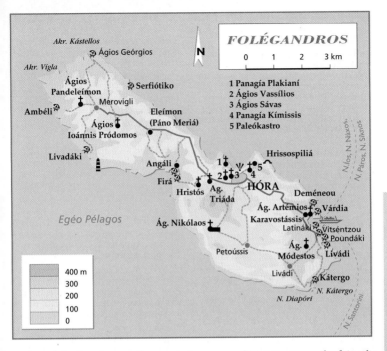

**FOLÉGANDROS**

0  1  2  3 km

1 Panagía Plakianí
2 Ágios Vassílios
3 Ágios Sávas
4 Panagía Kímissis
5 Paleókastro

Akr. Kástellos
Ágios Geórgios
Akr. Vígla
Ágios Pandeleímon
Serfiótiko
Merovigli
Ambéli
Eleímon (Páno Meriá)
Ágios Ioánnis Pródomos
Livadáki
Angáli
Firá
Hristós
Ag. Triáda
HÓRA
Hrissospiliá
Deméneou
Egéo Pélagos
Ag. Nikólaos
Ág. Artémios
Várdia
Karavostássis
Latináki
Vitséntzou
Poundáki
Petoússis
Ág. Módestos
Livádi
Livádi
Kátergo
N. Kátergo
N. Diapóri
N. Santoríni
N. íos, N. Náxos
N. Páros, N. Síkinos

400 m
300
200
100
0

■ The path leading down to the crystal-clear waters of **Firá Bay★★**, south of Angáli Bay, passes through some beautiful **countryside★★**, dotted with little churches, such as **Agía Triáda** and **Hristós** (*both on the left*).

**Angáli beach** is only a 15min walk from the bay. The water is clear, the sand is lovely and warm and the wind hardly ever blows. A tiny paradise (with tavernas)... but one which you will have to share with a fair number of other pleasure-seekers.

■ Rejoin the road heading north and continue to the village of **Páno Meriá** (or Áno Meriá), a curious collection of farms, either scattered or in groups forming hamlets on the plateau. They are dotted along the ridge road that runs the length of the island, the most important one being **Eleímon** (*on the right before the first windmill*). In this part of the island, where even the smallest patch of arable land has been made into terraces, the early inhabitants of Hóra built small huts in which to keep their tools. But when piracy ceased to be a threat, the local farmers gradually moved into the area, hence this somewhat surprising scattering of farmsteads.
If you want to know more about the local way of life, visit the **Folklore Museum** (*sign*) which is housed in an old farm (with a fine **view★** over Hóra and Síkinos).

■ Continue on to **Ágios Ioánnis Pródomos★** (*about 100m lower down, on the left*), one of the oldest churches on the island. At the end of the road, the left fork leads down to **Livadáki beach** (*remember to take your snorkel and flippers*), whilst the road on the right leads through some of the finest **scenery★★** on Folégandros, to the **Church of Ágios Pandeleímon★**, a good viewing point for the most magnificent sunsets.

■ The path to the delightful **Ambéli beach★** (*to the left after Merovigli*), takes you through an area that is still surprisingly green and unspoilt. Even further on, under the shade of the tamarisk trees, the sandy beach of **Serfiótiko** (*can be reached in 45min along a path leading off to the right before Ágios Andréas*) is worth the walk (unless it is very windy): the water is an exquisite shade of turquoise.

**245**

**The Cyclades**

### COMING AND GOING

**By boat** – In summer, a ferry departs daily from Piraeus. The length of the journey (between 7hr and 11hr) varies according to the boat's itinerary: the lines serving Páros-Náxos-Íos-Santoríni-Folégandros or the western Cyclades (Kíthnos-Sérifos; Sífnos-Mílos-Folégandros-Síkinos-Íos-Santoríni), are the fastest.

### FINDING YOUR WAY

The guide to the island (available in Greek or English) is still the best of its kind (plenty of photographs, very precise itineraries). Small maps show the networks of roads and footpaths for each sector of the island.

### GETTING AROUND

**By bus** – A bus awaits the arrival of every boat (night and day), and leaves Hóra 1hr before each ferry departure. From Hóra, the bus continues to Páno Meriá (sometimes you have to change). There are bus timetables at the three bus shelters in Karavostássis, Hóra and Páno Meriá. On the road from Páno Meriá, you can ask the driver to stop at the beginning of a footpath in addition to the scheduled stops.

**Roads** – A single asphalt road runs across the island and another one runs a few kilometres towards Angáli beach. There are also a few driveable tracks leading to isolated farms.

**Footpaths** – Whether simple walks around Hóra or short day excursions, the ideal way to explore the island is on foot. Although some footpaths still have their original paving, others are in a very bad state of repair and are hard to follow at times. But the low walls on either side have withstood the vicissitudes of time much better and are a good guide. A tip for getting your bearings: all the churches and chapels face east. In any case, the island is small (5km by 13km), so you are never very far from the road. What's more, there are no poisonous snakes or wild animals other than rabbits, harmless lizards, partridges, numerous species of birds of prey, and seabirds along the coast. So there is nothing to stop you setting off to explore one of the more secluded bays. Just be sure to take water, food, and to wear proper walking shoes and a hat.

**By rental vehicle** – There is no car hire here, only motorcycle and moped hire. There are two agencies: one in Hóra, ☎ (0286) 41 316, the other at the harbour, ☎ (0286) 41 448.

**Fuel** – There is one fuel station on the road around Hóra.

**By taxi** – ☎ (0286) 41 048, mobile 094 693957.

**By caique** – Caiques from Karavostássis run services to most of the beaches on the island. If there is a strong wind, there may be alterations to the scheduled itineraries.

### ADDRESS BOOK

**Banks / Currency exchange** – Note that there are no banks or cash dispensers. The **post office** will change travellers' cheques and foreign currency, and travel agents will change only foreign currency.

**Post office / Telephone** – In Hóra: with your back to the cliff, take the road leading left out of Platía Pounda.

**Medical service** – **Health centre** in Hóra, Platía Pounda, ☎ (0286) 41 221. No pharmacy. The doctor on the island sells the drugs he prescribes.

**Police** – ☎ (0286) 41 249.

### WHERE TO STAY

Basically there is accommodation in Hóra and the harbour, and there are a few lodgings in Angáli and Páno Meriá, and at the Livádi campsite. In August, it is very difficult to find accommodation unless you book beforehand, even at the campsite. The island has many visitors, mainly from Athens, who come here every year and to whom hotel owners often give priority. If one of them tells you they are full, just ask them to suggest somewhere else: they are all related!

• **Livádi**

*Campsite (around €11)*
**Livádi campsite**, ☎ (0286) 41 204 – 50 pitches. Taverna, bar and washing machines.

• **Karavostássis**

*Between €18 and €30*
**Evangelía Divoli** (rooms to let), ☎ (41 269).

*Between €30 and €45*
**Hotel Aeolos**, 30m from the beach, ☎ (0286) 41 205 and ☎ (01) 92 23 819 – 18rm. A large white building, well situated, with a pleasant garden. The rooms are attractively decorated.

● **Hóra**
*Between €18 and €30*
For simple, clean rooms to let (with shower), contact **Pávlos Siderís**, ☎ (0286) 41 232, **María Véniou**, ☎ (0286) 41 265, or **Spiridoúla Agá**, ☎ (0286) 41 034.

*Between €30 and €60*
**Hotel Odysseos**, in Hóra, looks onto the cliff (follow the kástro wall), ☎ (0286) 41 276 – 13rm. ⁅ ℘ An attractive old house that has been renovated. Very well situated.

**Kástro**, in an old house in the kástro, ☎ (0286) 41 276 / 41 366 – 7rm. The ground-floor ceilings have enormous vaults; there's a roof-top garden with sea view, and home-made jam at breakfast. Charming.

**Folégandros**, on the left-hand side of Platía Pounda, ☎ (0286) 41 239, Fax (0286) 41 166, and Fax (01) 34 23 545 – 12 flats with fully equipped kitchens. ⁅ ℘ A very attractive, new building in the Cycladic style. Very well maintained, with a veranda facing the sea.

*Between €45 and €110*
**Anemó Mílos**, to the left of Platía Pounda near the cliff, (0286) 41 309, Fax (0286) 41 407, (01) 68 27 777, Fax (01) 68 23 962 – 18rm. ⁅ ℘ TV CC An attractive complex in the Cycladic style. Every room has a balcony with sea view, some overlooking the drop.

● **Angáli**
*Between €18 and €30*
For simple, clean rooms to let (with shower): **Iríni Véniou** ☎ (0286) 41 190, **Vangéli Lydís**, ☎ (0286) 41 318.

**EATING OUT**
The menu of local cuisine includes: "mátsata" (fresh pasta served with cockerel or rabbit cooked in tomato sauce), while salads feature capers and "souroutó" (a white creamy cheese). Try "liókafta" (dried fish) served with oil and vinegar, which goes perfectly with ouzo, and "kalasouna" (puff pastry with cheese and onion), an easy snack to take away. As a rule, unless you eat fish (expensive), meals cost under €15 per person.

● **Hóra**
**Pounda**, Platía Pounda, is an excellent place for local specialities, in a very pleasant setting (cobbled courtyard).

**Kritikós**, Platía Piátsa, the barbecue specialist; the meat comes from livestock reared on the island.

**Melissa**, Platía Doúnavi, serves real traditional Greek cooking.

**Folégandros**, Platía Pounda, for fish, local meze and many other dishes: it is a real institution.

**Piátsa**, Platía Piátsa, opposite Kritikós; serves meals from breakfast until dinner time.

● **Karavostássis**
**Kalí Kardiá** and **Kalymniós**, next to the beach, are the two best places at the harbour for eating fresh fish.

● **Páno Meriá**
**Iliovassílema** and **Mímis**, two tavernas (*near the museum*) if you want to sample traditional local dishes, especially mátsata, pasta dishes with meat (cockerel, veal or rabbit).

**HAVING A DRINK**
For a quiet evening, choose somewhere at the harbour, near the water. Hóra is much more lively; every evening a party atmosphere fills the nearby squares and streets as far as Kalderími (a favourite meeting-place for young people), between Platía Maráki and the bus stop for Páno Meriá.
The terrace of the **Rakentia** has a fantastic view. So does that of the **Anemó Mílos** hotel, for a coffee or breakfast. Also recommended: **Astárti** and **Kellári**, or, for a more lively ambience, **Laoúmi**, **Methexís** or **Patitíri**.

**OTHER THINGS TO DO**
**Excursions** – For a boat trip round the island, contact the **Sottovento** travel agency (Hóra), ☎ (0286) 41 444.

**Feasts & festivals** – The holy processions of Ágios Panteleímon, at Páno Meriá (27 July), and Panagía (15 August).

**SHOPPING GUIDE**
**Local delicacies** – Cheese, particularly "ladótiri", preserved in olive oil, or "anthótiri" (a soft paste) and thyme-flavoured honey.

**Making the most of Folégandros**

# Íos ★

District of the Cyclades – Michelin map 980 fold 44
Regional map on the inside back cover – 109km² – Pop 1 632

**Not to be missed**
The unspoilt beaches and crystal-clear waters of the southern tip.
For ravers, a drink in the small hours on the beach at Milopótas.

**And remember...**
People who hate noise in general and techno music in particular should stay away!
It can be very pleasant right at the very beginning or end of the season.
No need to hire a car.

As if intimidated by its more prestigious neighbours – Santoríni to the south, and Náxos and Páros to the north – Íos almost seems to be curling up in order to look smaller. However, it has the same landscape of hills burnt bare by the sun and of houses bathed in light so typical of the Cyclades. But in summer, it is true that it takes a great deal of imagination to remember that you are in Greece.

## A giant night-club

Like Mýkonos, Íos is famous for its frenetic night-life. The reality also exceeds its reputation, sometimes verging on a caricature. The summer population has the following characteristics: very young (around 20 or younger), well fed, with plenty of energy for dancing and chatting up the opposite sex. Most of them are from Northern Europe (Britain, Scandinavia, Germany) and come to Íos with only one thing in mind: clubbing.

If you have other ambitions (and bearing in mind that anyone over 30 has left it too late), there is scarcely any reason for stopping here, except perhaps fleeing to the south of the island. It is beautifully wild but has few facilities and very little in terms of accommodation.

Because all the activity on Íos is concentrated in its narrow western tip, the remaining 90% of the island remains virtually deserted. The harbour, the charming village of **Hóra**, and Milopótas beach form a long, almost continuous town with a population of just under 2 000, which in summer swells to 30 000! A veritable wave of people wearing shorts, caps and fluorescent swimsuits, who move in packs and dance in groups.

## Techno and biceps

On Íos, you are more likely to hear techno music (trance, trip-hop, jungle, hard-core, etc) than the noise of the surf. Here it is customary to surface at midday and recuperate with a large English breakfast. Afterwards, it is off to the beach and, once you've found a tiny rectangle of sand on which to lay your towel, settling down to perfect your tan – to see and be seen. The girls often go topless while the guys, their shades balanced on their nose, show off their glistening pectoral muscles. Later they spend hours preparing for their nocturnal activities. And when evening comes, loud music throbs from the village to the harbour, filling the night with pulsating bass notes.

## And apart from that?

Archaeology enthusiasts will be disappointed. Although the island has been inhabited since the pre-Cycladic Period, there is hardly anything left of its past to see (a few ancient crumbling walls, some temple ruins, fragments of Venetian fortifications...). Yet, over the centuries, many different peoples settled here, notably the Ionians who arrived in 1050 BC. Allied to the Athenian League during the Classical Period, the island passed through various hands: the Macedonians, Rhodians, Romans, Byzantines, Franks, Venetians and Turks, until it became part of Greece in 1829... and, since the 1970s, it has been taken over by night-clubbers.

**The Cyclades**

# Visiting the island

## The harbour and Hóra*

*One hour is enough to walk round the village, best done in the morning in order to avoid the crowds.* Well sheltered, the harbour has a myriad hotels, shops and tourist facilities. The place has no great charm, apart from the silhouette of the 17C **Church of Agía Iríni** (St Irene) to the east, and **Gialós beach★★**, a long crescent of sand stretching west of the quays, dotted with restaurants, bars and places with rooms to let.

From the harbour, stone steps shaded by eucalyptus trees lead up to the village of **Hóra★**. Built in the shape of an ancient amphitheatre on the hills overlooking the harbour, it conceals a charming labyrinth of **narrow cobbled streets** (designed to protect the inhabitants from the wind) which, every so often, pass through **arches** built to give protection from the sun (or the rain in winter). You can wander here at leisure, emerging in a small square bathed in sunshine, or by a church, in a tight tangle of small houses – a jumble of white, cube-shaped houses enhanced by the blue or pale green of the shutters, domes or bar tables. Climb to the top of the village, above the **windmills**: from the small modern open-air theatre, there's a **view★★** stretching as far as Santoríni.

West of the harbour, by the coast road (*20min on foot or 5min by bus*) lies the beautiful sandy beach of **Koumbára**. Just behind it other little, slightly more exposed beaches nestle among the rocks.

Finally, 2.5km beyond the town, is the long – and very popular – white sandy beach of **Milopótas**, a favourite place for all kinds of water sports and cool dudes.

## The northern cape

To the north-west, a good road crosses the fertile valley of **Páno Kámbos**, scattered with vineyards and olive groves. At the town of the same name, leave the tarmac road and take the relatively driveable track (*signs on the left; 8.2km*). It leads to some Hellenistic ruins which are supposed to be **Homer's tomb**.

Íos, the old town: blue domes and white houses

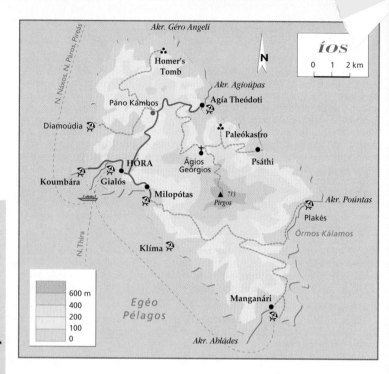

*Akr. Géro Angelí*

**Homer's Tomb**

**ÍOS**

0  1  2 km

N. Náxos, N. Páros, Pireás

*Akr. Agioúpas*

**Páno Kámbos**

**Agía Theódoti**

**Diamoúdia**

**Paleókastro**

**HÓRA**

**Ágios Geórgios**

**Psáthi**

**Koumbára**   **Gialós**

**Milopótas**

▲ 713
*Pirgos*

*Akr. Poúntas*

**Plakés**

*Órmos Kálamos*

N. Thíra

**Klíma**

600 m
400
200
100
0

*Egéo Pélagos*

**Manganári**

*Akr. Abládes*

■ Rejoin the tarmac road which leads to **Agía Theódoti beach** (overlooked by a 16C church), which is surprisingly quiet. From here, you can continue on foot *(by a 2km path starting at the right-hand side of the beach)* to the remains of the Byzantine fort of **Paleókastro**.

■ Further south lie the village of **Psáthi\*** and its small fertile valley, overlooking a beach of white sand lapped by deep-blue water. **Sea turtles** still come here to lay their eggs. To the left, there are more delightful beaches, hidden among the rocks.

### To the south\*

Because they are difficult to reach *(only accessible on foot or by boat)*, especially on the south-west coast, the island still has a few beautiful secluded beaches. **Klíma beach\***, especially *(6km south of Milopótas)*, is worth a detour, but, if you head due south, the beach at **Manganári Bay\*\*** is even better.

*The Milopótas-Manganári road has not yet been surfaced; the first 5km are laborious, the following twelve easier to negotiate; but it is feasible on a motorcycle. At the Kálamos-Manganári crossroads, turn left towards the beach (or get off the bus here and cover the remaining 3.6km on foot).*

The road forks as you approach Manganári, but they all lead to this delightful little bay with its beautiful beaches, clear water and lovely fine sand. Some take advantage of the fact that it is off the beaten track and has few facilities to use it as a nudist beach.

The Cyclades

### COMING AND GOING

**By boat –** Four ferries a week depart from Rafína (Athens). There are boat connections with Thessaloníki, Kavála, Lesbos, Chios, Sámos, Kálimnos, Kos and Rhodes.

Hydrofoils (Flying Dolphins) run services to Lesbos, Samothrace, Alexandroúpoli and Kavála.

### GETTING AROUND

**On foot –** Between Hóra and the harbour, it is possible to do almost everything on foot.

**By bus –** A very handy bus shuttle service runs (every 5min, from 8am until midnight) to and from Milopótas, the village, the harbour and Koumbára. So, unless you are looking for the solitude of a more remote beach, there is no point in hiring a car although the bus service to Manganári only operates in July and August.

**By boat –** All the main beaches can be reached by boat from the harbour.

**By motorcycle / moped –** Several places offer motorcycle and moped hire, but *Jacob's*, ☎ (0286) 91 047 / 92 097, is the best: plenty of choice and a high turnover of mopeds, motorcycles and cars. It has two offices: on the central quay at the harbour and at the beginning of Gialós beach.

### ADDRESS BOOK

**Tourist information – *Acteon Travel Agencies***, an excellent agency offering many services and good information: it has several offices, one at the harbour, two in Hóra (the one next to the church has Internet access) and one in Milopótas.

**Banks / Currency exchange – *National Bank*** and ***Commercial Bank***, in the pedestrian precinct in Hóra.

**Post office – *Central Post Office***, in the centre of the old village of Hóra.

**Other –** The customs and **port authority**, ☎ (0286) 91 264 are situated on the east side of the harbour.
**Police**, ☎ (0286) 91 222.

**Medical service – *Medical assistance***, ☎ (0286) 91 227. ***Pharmacy***, below the old village of Hóra.

### WHERE TO STAY

By force of circumstance, the island's inhabitants have turned to tourism to earn a living, abandoning most of their previous occupations (and with it their traditions). The season lasts from 2 to 4 months maximum, and the rates double or triple in July and August, when most of the hotels are full. People travelling on their own are therefore forced to pay the price of a double room.

• **The harbour and Gialós beach**

*Campsite (around €11)*
**Íos campsite**, to the right of the harbour as you arrive on Íos, at the end of the small beach, a 15min walk from the clubs of Hóra, ☎ (0286) 91 329 – tents and bungalows. A vast, recently restored campsite but tends to be full in summer. ✗ 🍴 🏊 🐾 💧 CC Bar, mini-market.

*Between €27 and €38*
🏠 **Galíni**, halfway along Gialós beach, ☎ (0286) 91 115 / 91 339, Fax (0286) 91 115 – 14rm. 🍴 🏠 A very well-run, comfortable hotel, set 150m back from the beach, in a peaceful location. Pleasant shady terrace with flowers. The rooms have fridges.

**Irene**, about 50m behind the central quay at the harbour, ☎ and Fax (0286) 91 023 – 17rm. A relatively quiet location, without any great charm, but practical. Breakfast is served on the terrace outside.

• **Hóra**

There are myriad hotels in Hóra. The simplest thing is to ask for information at the **Acteon Agency**.

*Between €27 and €38*
**Ártemis**, on the right coming uphill from the Acteon Agency, at the bottom of Hóra, on the Milopótas road, ☎ (0286) 91 202 – 18rm. 🍴 🏠 Central location, set among several others, with a friendly lady owner. Clean rooms.

*Around €45*
**Hotel Hermes**, on the road between Hóra and Milopótas, on the right, built

on a rocky overhang, ☎ (0286) 91 471, Fax (0286) 91 608 – 25rm. *❄☂☖* ☖ Hotel with standard comforts, a very well-designed swimming pool and a stunning view. Value for money but busy.

**Hotel Far Out**, on the road between Hóra and Milopótas, on the left going downhill, ☎ (0286) 91 446 / 91 702, Fax (0286) 91 701 – 45rm. *❄ ♪ ▤ TV* ☖ ☖ ☖ CC A luxury establishment, very well situated, with the advantage of being fairly near Hóra, yet sufficiently far from the noise, with Milopótas below. All modern comforts, with a beautiful pool and tasteful decor. Very good value for money.

*Over €60*

**Sun Club**, two-thirds of the way between Gialós and Hóra, on the right, ☎ (0286) 92 140 / 92 150, Fax (0286) 91 088 – 13rm. *❄ ♪ ▤ TV ☖* ☖ ☖ CC Comfortable and peaceful, but the place lacks open space, greenery and shade. Lovely pool and jacuzzi, however, and a clear view of the harbour. Professional service.

• **Milopótas**

The beach, which attracts large numbers of people in summer, is within earshot of several noisy establishments.

*Campsite (around €12)*

**Far-Out Camping Club**, right at the south end of the beach, ☎ (0286) 91 468 / 91 301, Fax (0286) 92 303. ✕ ☖ ☖ ☖ ※ ☖ CC A very large, well-equipped campsite (200 campers in summer!) offering many sporting activities and musical attractions: two pools with slides, terraces, bungalows, various water sports (deep-sea diving), basketball, volleyball, etc. Very good facilities and a pleasant atmosphere. Obviously it attracts a large number of people.

*Around €45*

**Marcos Beach Hotel**, set back from Milopótas beach, in the centre, on high ground, ☎ (0286) 91 571, Fax (0286) 91 671- 35rm. *❄ ♪ ☖ ☖ ☖* CC A fairly quiet hotel with a lovely pool. It is slightly cramped and is often full. Quite expensive, but very practical if you want to stay near the beach.

• **Manganári**

*Over €60*

**Manganári Club Hotel**, ☎ (0286) 91 200, Fax (0286) 91 204, contact in Athens ☎ (01) 68 53 250, Fax (01) 68 10 690 – 40 bungalows. *❄* ♪ ✕ ☖ CC Difficult to reach by land: a boat will come and fetch you at Manganári beach. Hidden in the corner of a little bay with a tiny beach, this hotel has a delightful setting with views out to the island of Santoríni. An ideal retreat for people wanting to get away from it all, but stylish. Guests stay in simple, tastefully decorated bungalows. No special activities, nothing flashy, just peace and quiet and lots of it. The quality is reflected in the prices (around €110 half board – good buffets – in high season).

EATING OUT

• **Harbour**

*Around €9*

**The Octopus Tree**, east of the fishing harbour. ☖ This tiny taverna on the quay offers a limited choice of very good dishes: mega-fresh salads, fish from the latest catch (the owner is a deep-sea fisherman). Simple, but well run, with reasonable prices.

• **Hóra**

*Under €9*

**Moonlight café**, below Hóra on the east side of the town. Going uphill after the church, take the 1st street on the left. ☖ The ideal place for people who get up late and want brunch: full English breakfasts, large sandwiches, beer and coffee, can be consumed on the small terrace.

*Between €9 and €15*

**Pithari**, below the village, at the northern corner of the large church. ☖ A small, family-run taverna, one of the few offering traditional Greek cuisine.

**The Nest**, opposite the 2nd street on the left after the main village square, ☎ (0286) 91 778. Varied menu, fast service and reasonable prices. There isn't much room as there's no terrace, but the restaurant has air conditioning.

**Cosmopolitain**, right next door to **The Nest** (same owner), ☎ (0286) 91 129. No terrace here either. Try its specialities: "kefliko", lamb cooked with four types of cheese, "goulash Bekri", unless you prefer meze or a pizza. Good value for money.

## • Koumbára

*Between €9 and €15*

**Polydoros Pouseos**, Koumbára has three restaurants; this one is just before the beach, and is the only restaurant on the right, ☎ (0286) 91 132. Without any doubt the best restaurant on the island: a varied menu (fish, dishes served with various sauces, barbecued dishes, salads), wide selection of wines and cocktails, and you can try real specialities here. Be sure to try the local cheeses: "Welalonini" from Íos, "Saganáki" (grilled), etc. The setting is nothing special, but the large covered terrace is very pleasant.

## • Manganári

*Around €9*

**Christos Tavern**, south of the beach, ☎ (0286) 92 286. Situated on the water's edge, the oldest taverna in Manganári has a terrace with a wonderful view. It also has 10 rooms – the idyllic setting compensates for the rather basic facilities.

### HAVING A DRINK

Despite the crowds that descend on Íos at night, the atmosphere remains pleasant and light-hearted: security problems are rare, apart from the occasional pickpocket. Beware of cheap, local cocktails – they are sometimes laced with low-quality local alcohol; these "bombas", as the Greeks call them, are lethal and to be avoided...

### Cafés, bars

## • Harbour

**Frog's Club**, on the eastern quay of the harbour, ☎ (0286) 91 688. Good cocktails, beers, meze.

## • Koumbára

**La Luna**, at the beginning of the beach, ☎ (0286) 91 532. Spacious covered terrace. Sitting in a comfortable armchair with a "margarita sunrise", gently caressed by the evening breeze, with the sunset reflected in the sea, it is easy to get carried away. The ideal place for a drink in the evening, soothed by good music. This place also serves breakfasts and has a limited menu of other dishes.

## • Hóra

Almost always jam-packed, the most reputable bars are clustered around the pedestrian precinct in the old village.

**Red Bull Bar**, in the central square of Hóra, ☎ (0286) 91 019. A very trendy bar with a video-wall.

**Slammer Bar**, Hóra, ☎ (0286) 92 119. Lots of people here too; a good atmosphere.

### Night-clubs

## • Hóra

The night-clubs are concentrated in Hóra or at the beginning of the road to Milopótas. Fashions come and go to the sound of the latest music. The simplest thing is to relax and be guided by the music.

**Dubliner**, ☎ (0286) 92 072, a night-club with an Irish flavour, comfortable, with tables inside and out. Numerous DJs.

**Sweet Irish Dream**, roomy, with broad tables to dance on...

**Scorpion**, on the Milopótas road. One of the largest clubs in the Cyclades, with numerous DJs.

**Lemon**, next to the Commercial Bank. Like many other night-clubs, but possibly less littered with beer bottles...

**Íos Club**, higher up, on the right-hand side of the road, ☎ (0286) 91419. The dance-floor is outside, taking advantage of the fantastic view. But it is a place to avoid on very windy days.

**Ellinádiko**, next to the town hall, ☎ (0286) 91 539: Greek music, and a young Greek clientele.

# KÉA★★
## (TZIÁ)

Western Aegean – District of the Cyclades – Michelin map 980 fold 31
Regional map on the inside back cover – 131km²
Pop 1 245 – Allow 3 days

**Not to be missed**
Visiting the ancient site of Karthéa.
Exploring the centre of the island,
with its traditional villages and Byzantine monasteries.
Strolling through the streets of Ioulís.

**And remember...**
Avoid weekends at all costs, often there is not a single room to be found.
Come here in early summer, when the island still has its mantle of spring colours.

Situated only a few miles from Cape Soúnion on the Greek mainland, the most westerly of the Cyclades has three characteristics, each of which has shaped its history. The first is the position of the island: because it is close to the mainland, it has become a favourite destination for Athenians and yachting enthusiasts in particular. They are usually well off and either own a villa there or rent one of the many flats to let on the west coast.

Another feature of Kéa, in complete contrast to the first, is that it is an island with a strong farming tradition. What was once a flourishing rural society is now reduced to a few hillside villages, a small farming community which meets in Ioulís on Sundays and on the days of the *panigíri* festival. With a higher rainfall than its neighbours, the amount of greenery on Kéa will surprise you. **Almond trees**, and especially **oaks** carpet its valleys and ravines, while terraces have been built on the steep hillsides for growing vines and cereals.

The third feature of this little world, its past, is frozen in majestic silence. Inhabited since Neolithic times, ancient Kéos was a brilliant ancient civilisation, and its major cities – Korissía, Ioulís, and especially Karthéa – left numerous remains, some of them in magnificent settings.

## From the Nymphs to the son of Apollo

The mythological and historical destiny of the island seems to be linked to a succession of names. Luxuriant, cool and with an abundance of water, legend has it that it was called **Hydroussa**, the island of the nymphs, until they were chased away by a **lion** which had come down from the mountains. With the name of **Siri**, a period of drought ensued under the sign of Sirius, the brightest star in the night sky and one of the pre-Olympian gods of the local pantheon. Its next name, **Efxántis**, emphasises the close links that existed between the towns of the Cycladic Period and Crete, since Efxántios, founder of the local tribe of the Exfanditès, was descended from King Minos. The arrival of **Kéos**, son of Apollo and leader of the Locrians (a people originally from Naupaktos), is also associated with the prehistoric population of the island and the emergence of new divinities. The story, half myth, half fact, which certainly dates from the Archaic Period, refers to the period when, from the 12C BC onwards, Ionian colonists from Attica settled here. After the 7C BC the Kéos confederation was also known as the **Tetrápolis**, the "Four Cities". The change of its name from Kéos to **Kéa**, finally came about in the 7C under the administration of Justinian, and "Zéa" (or "Zia") appeared with the arrival of the Venetians in the 12C. It is a corruption of this term which gave rise to the modern name **Tziá**, the name by which all Greeks continue to refer to the island, even though the Government decided to restore "Kéa" as its official name.

# On the north-west coast

■ **Korissía**★ (Livádi) – Built at the foot of a hill, the small harbour of Korissía is charming. Originally arranged along a single quay, it was extended at the time of the arrival of hordes of refugees from Asia Minor in 1922, beside the road leading up towards Ioulís. Tourism has also extended it in the direction of Vourkári. The few remains of **ancient Korissía**, the ruins of walls belonging to a temple dedicated to Apollo, are not very inspiring, but it is worth making a small detour via the **hill of Agía Triáda** (*directly above the church of the harbour and accessed by a path*), if only to appreciate the majesty of the site and the **view**★ over the Bay of Ágios Nikólaos. The **beach near the harbour** is handy but not as attractive as **Gialiskári beach**★ (*5min on foot in the direction of Vourkári*) which is much more pleasant. It is fringed by a wood of tamarisks, pines and eucalyptus. The only drawback is that it is very popular (*slightly less so in the morning and late afternoon*), and loud music emanates from the café at the end of the beach.

■ If it's peace and quiet you're looking for, allow a good hour's walk by the coast road to get to the delightful **Xíla beach**★ (*about 7km; take the necessary provisions if you intend to spend the whole day there*).

■ Nestling in the Bay of Ágios Nikólaos, **Vourkári,** an old fishing village, has evolved into a **marina** providing berths for numerous sailing boats, including some magnificent yachts. The atmosphere is more "jet-set" than anything else, but this is a pleasant enough place to come and enjoy the fish and meze in the tavernas lining the quay (*more expensive than others*).

■ At the far end of the bay, the archaeological site of **Agía Iríni**★ (*9am-2pm; closed Monday and Wednesday*) invites you to take a step back in time. A thousand years of human occupation are here waiting to be discovered, starting in the early Cycladic Period (about 2800 BC). This maze of crumbling walls reveals the extent of this old city, including a defensive wall and a palace dating from the Mycenaean Period. If you go there on a very windy day, you will soon understand why the ancients chose to build the city there: the site provides exceptional protection from the elements.

■ Largely in ruins, the **warehouses** (where coal for steamships used to be stored) on the **Kóka Peninsula** (*15min on foot*) are not very interesting, but from the top of the rocks which stretch out as far as the **Ágios Nikólaos lighthouse**, there are some wonderful **views**★, especially at sunset. Make time to explore the garrigue-covered peninsula – the lowest-lying land on the island – bearing in mind that it was once the site of the earliest human settlements of the archipelago, in the late Neolithic Period (about 3300 BC). The tiny **beach** nearby has a charm all of its own.

■ The road from Vourkári to Otziás passes through the broadest valley on the island, a perfect area for walking (*halfway along the valley, a wooden signboard shows the footpaths and tracks, with the timings of the walks, which crisscross the area as far as Ioulís*). Olive and almond trees grow on either side of the road all the way to the large beach of **Otziás**★. Holiday villas pepper the hills, and houses are clustered on the rock around the **Church of Ágios Sóstis**. Fringed by a thick hedge of tamarisks, the beach is very pleasant but usually crowded.

*After Ágios Sóstis, the asphalt road gives way to a track for 7km leading to the Monastery of Kastrianí (see below).*

# Hóra and its environs★★

Leaving Korissía, on the left you pass the disused chimney of what was the island's only **factory** (where they used to make enamelled metal tools). Further on, the road passes through the heart of a veritable oasis of cypresses, citrus fruit trees and almond trees, planted here and there. There are also a few vegetable gardens and tall houses with tiled roofs. The landscape is so green that it is easy to forget that you are in the Cyclades.

■ The hamlet of **Milopótamos** (literally "river at a mill") is situated in a green depression into which all the water from the neighbouring hills flows. Opposite the fuel station, the track *(on the right)* leads to the charmingly named hamlet of **Fléa**\*, following the river of the same name. The river used to feed a series of **watermills**, set one behind the other.

■ Beyond Milopótamos, the road zigzags upwards to emerge unexpectedly in an arid landscape, from which terraces have been carved and are dotted with almond and oak trees. After 300m, it crosses the **old paved roadway** which once linked Livádi to Ioulís, a track which (30min) leads to the **fountain of Ágios Konstandínos**\*, where time seems to have stopped.

■ **Ioulís**\*\*\* (Hóra) – In its majestic setting of hills and aromatic scrubland, Ioulís is undoubtedly one of the most beautiful villages in Greece. Set against the mountain, it is arranged in the shape of an amphitheatre, below a ridge crowned with old windmills. Lower down, the houses are surrounded by orchards and gardens. It is impossible not to succumb to the charm of this town, its architecture combining mainland (the tiled roofs of Attica), Cycladic (small whitewashed houses) and local influences. Strolling through its maze of little streets and steps will be one of the lasting memories of your stay on Kéa.

From the **Rokoménos fountain** *(below the village, where the bus stops and where you have to leave your vehicle)*, climb up to the square situated on the edge of the village, and walk through the *stégadi* (vaulted passageway) to explore the village's medieval charm. On the left, **Odós Harálambos** (the patron saint of the island) leads up towards the first hill, site of the **ancient acropolis** and the scattered ruins of a

The guardian of Hóra: the Lion of Kéa

**Venetian citadel** (kástro). The climb is particularly worthwhile for the magnificent **view\*\*** at the top.

On the right of the square, follow the main road; it crosses **Katohóri**, the "lower village", which was the district inhabited by the local dignitaries. You will pass the **Archaeological Museum\*** *(8.30am-3pm; closed Monday; no entrance fee)* which has just been restored. It houses objects from the island's prehistoric and ancient sites.

The street leads to the **main square** of the village, where there is a neo-Classical façade (1902) next to the

### The lion's enigmatic smile

Carved out of the rock on the top of a hill, the Lion of Kéa watches over Hóra. 3m wide and 9m long, this enormous stone feline guards its secrets, and its smile, borrowed from kouroi of the Archaic Period is not the least of them. This strange sculpture, which is thought to date from the 7C BC, very probably portrays the legendary lion which forced the nymphs to flee, unleashing a catastrophic drought. Once peace had been restored between the human inhabitants and their gods, and the island had regained its mild climate and fertile soil, the lion undoubtedly changed from being a symbol of death to one of alliance and fertility.

**town hall**, and there are shops and terraces belonging to cafés and tavernas. Above the central street, take a walk along **Odós Ieromnímonos\***, where there are a number of attractive houses which once belonged to the local merchants, then head back towards the edge of the village via the **cathedral**.

This main square used to constitute the southern limit of the historical centre of Ioulís. More recently, the other side of the village has expanded sideways over successive folds of the hillside, along the ancient cobbled lanes that once connected Hóra to the rest of the island. At the small O Arghýris kafenío, two streets ending in paths create a fork. The left-hand fork leads down towards more houses before reaching

L. Hapsis/ON LOCATION

**Kéa (Tziá)**

the **Kanáli fountain**. The right-hand fork splits again a little further on: here the left-hand fork passes the **Church of Ágios Spirídon**, before continuing to the **Lion of Kéa**★ (Léondas), an astonishing monumental sculpture carved out of the rock.
Both directions offer marvellous **walks**★★ around Hóra. One path, in particular, climbs up to the 26 abandoned **windmills**★ which crown the top of the hill, like the ramparts of a fortress.

## The north-east★
*All these tours start at Hóra. Allow half a day for each.*

### In the Spathí valley★★
*Turn off the road around Ioulís (heading east) and take the road on the left about 500m after the paved street that leads down towards Hóra. Be careful, the track is generally good, but there are some difficult stony sections in places.* This tree-lined track soon gives wonderful **views**★ over Hóra. Further on, the **Pírgos fountain** and the **Chapel of Ágios Dimítrios** mark the beginning of the splendid Spathí valley, along which the road winds until it meets the sea. The bottom of this gorge opens out into a wild landscape, with luxuriant vegetation in places. It is not unusual to see a bird of prey soaring high above the gorge.

■ After 5km, the road forks as it approaches the sea and the landscape becomes more arid. Now (on the left) the **Monastery of Kastrianí**★ *(8.4km from Hóra)* comes into sight, a veritable eyrie poised directly above the sea. Behind its enclosing wall, where blue alternates with white, the scent of pines fills the air. From the tip of the garden, a splendid **panorama**★ of Kéa and the Aegean awaits you. The monastery was built on the site where, in 1700, some shepherds discovered an icon of the Virgin which proved to have miraculous powers (there is an important festival on 15 August). The **original church**★, which lies below the modern building, has been an important place of pilgrimage since it was built in 1708.

■ Back on the road, the road that goes off to the right leads downhill in broad curves to the narrow **Bay of Spathí**★★ (Órmos Spathí) *(1.3km)* where a broad **sandy beach**★★ stretches out below an impressive rocky landscape *(road bad in places)*. A few scattered houses, a taverna set back from the beach and a few patches of cultivated land fringe the beach and some of the clearest water in the Aegean.

### Messariá and its Byzantine monasteries★

■ From Hóra head east. The second road on the left *(ending in a path)* climbs towards the **Byzantine monastery of Agía Ána**★ (16C), the romantic ruins of which are scattered around the beautiful white church (wonderful view).

■ Back on the road, you enter **Messariá**, a region of fertile plateaux grooved with green terraces. The centre of life on the island in the Byzantine Era, it conceals the remains of what was once the largest monastery on the island. Crowned with ramparts, it looks like a medieval fortress watching over the fields. The dazzling white **Church of Panagía Episcopí**★★ stands like a jewel, surrounded by the ruins.

■ Then you come to the foot of **Mt Profítis Ilías**, crowned by a windmill and the inevitable television mast. A stone staircase leads up to the summit, from where there is a magnificent **view**★★ over the terraces of Messariá (to the north), the wooded valleys of the centre of the island and the dry hillsides of ancient Karthéa.

### Péra Meriá and the road to the beaches★★
*From Kastaniés, a good track leads down towards Sikamniá (9.6km). For the last 2km of the road which forks towards Kalidoníhi (8.4km), the surface is poor.*

■ The gentle, unspoiled landscapes of Péra Meriá are the stronghold of the venerable oak. For a long time, **acorns**, which were used as a dye in the tanning process, were the island's main export. Today, the few inhabitants devote themselves to rearing

N. Spanopoúla

Kéfala

Ágios Sóstis

*KÓKA*

Ágios Nikólaos

Agía Iríni    Otziás

Vourkári

Gialiskári

Kastrianí

Korissía
(Livádi)

Spathí    Spathí

Milopótamos    IOULÍS
(HÓRA)    Ag. Dimítrios

Agía
Triáda    Kalidoníhi

Xíla    Fléa

Fountain
of Ágios Konstandínos    *PÉRA MERIÁ*

Agía Ána    Péra Meriá    Psilí
Ámos

*MESSARIÁ*    Panagía Episcopí

Sklavonikólas    Profítis Ilías    560    Sikamniá

Kastaniés

Agía Marína    Panagía Loutrianí    Psathí

Ágios Pandeleímon    545    Orkós

Písses    Ágii Apóstoli    Eliniká

*KÁTO MERIÁ*

Koúndouros    Ágios Simeón    Ágios Fílipos

Ág. Emilianós    Stavroudáki    Egéo Pélagos

Kambí    Karthéa

Havouná

Panagía
Mirtidiótissa    Órm. Póles

Liparós    Kaliskiá

400 m
200
0

**KÉA (TZIÁ)**

0    1    2    3 km

N

Akr. Támelos

---

livestock. As you pass through the village of **Péra Meriá**, you will notice some traditional rural dwellings or **katikíes★**.

*At the next crossroads, turn right, then immediately left.*

■ Leaving the wooded slopes of the hill of **Agía Triáda**, crowned with its little white church and red bell-tower, the road winds down towards the sea, which sparkles in the distance at the end of a stretch of arid landscape. On the left are the two little beaches of **Kalidoníhi★★** and **Psilí Ámos★★**, where the white sand and the turquoise water will delight anyone in search of solitude and unspoilt beauty. The beach at

Sikamniá**, which is just as beautiful, also offers the shade of a few tamarisks and a taverna.

■ Situated in a beautiful coastal valley, the beach and small holiday resort of Orkós are charming, but they are more exposed to the meltem. **Psathí beach**, which you can see from the road, is even more pleasant.

## The south**

From the road coming out of Hóra, take in the **view*** over Korissía and its valley. In the distance you can see the **island of Makrónissos**, its reputation tarnished by the colonels' decision to deport more than 6 000 political opponents of the regime to this island.

**The katikíes, or house of the mountains**
Typical of the rural parts of the island, katikíes are usually built on hillsides, away from the dangers of the sea. Facing south-west, they turn their backs on the winds from the north. An unusual feature of this architecture is the habit of using a single stone slab to roof each room. Since the width of these slabs had to be limited, the walls were built with a slight slope in order to make it possible to gain a little space at ground level. This technique, which dates back to very early times, ensured that the dwellings were warm in winter and cool in summer. Next to the living quarters, the farm buildings – the cistern, stable and grain store – looked onto a central paved courtyard that was often shaded by a bower.

■ In the centre of **Sklavonikólas** (consisting of a few houses on either side of the road), a path leads off on the left (*500m after the fuel station*) and follows a narrow pass between two massifs. For 2km, a rough road winds through thickly wooded **landscape****. The **Church of Panagía Loutrianí*** is tucked away near a spring, at the far end of a ravine, surrounded by the ruins of the ramparts.

■ On the right-hand side of the road, a very good track (*after just over 1km*) leads to the **Monastery of Agía Marína**** (festival 17 July), nestling in the bottom of a pretty wooded valley. Founded during the time of Ottoman occupation, rebuilt in the early 19C and abandoned in 1837 (but very well maintained), its austere white walls and charming red dome stand in the shade of an impressive **Hellenistic tower**** with massive drystone walls. The tower, which once had three storeys, is a rare example of a defensive building of this size.

### The south-west coast*
Today, as in Antiquity, the **Písses valley**, patterned with orchards and vegetable gardens, is the most fertile on the island. It opens out onto the small seaside resort of **Písses**, with a beach that is pleasant but not exceptional.

■ Approaching the **Bay of Koúndouros** by the coast road, the landscape is dry and rocky, so typical of the Cyclades. As you drive along, you will be surprised by the large number of residences under construction – all being built in the local style with drystone walls – proof that tourism is booming. Many of the windmills have also been converted.
Well sheltered from the meltem, the bay provides moorings for myriad boats and has a series of pleasant **beaches***, **Ágios Emilianós beach*** (festival on 18 July) being the largest. This part of the coast, which tends to be very busy at weekends and in high season, has plenty of bars and restaurants, rivalling Vourkári.

■ At the end of a beautiful road lined with large oak trees lies the charming village of **Kambí** and its **beach***. Old warehouses, now converted into guest rooms, are a reminder that, in days gone by, large quantities of acorns were shipped from here.

■ Far removed from everything (3km from Kambí), with only a few houses and a chapel nearby, **Liparós beach***(*from the Havouná road, a track on the right leads down to it*) awaits those in search of peace and quiet.

## The Káto Meriá region*

*Beyond Kambí, the road follows the coast, before turning inland again. Turn left, and follow a fairly good but very steep track for 3km before rejoining the asphalt road at the Koúndouros intersection.*

The region of Káto Meriá, where the vegetation is less dense and the contours more gentle, is given over to cattle (*drive carefully*) and is also the most populated part of the island. The surrounding area is dotted with **farms** and old **katikíes**.

■ 2.5km along the tarmac road, a track on the left leads to the **Byzantine church of Ágii Apóstoli*** (*at the end of a track*). With its white walls, red-tiled roofs and blue dome, this is one of the island's most beautiful monuments (12C).

*Back on the tarmac road, take the next track on the right (after 3.6km).*

■ Further along (*2.5km*), the road climbs up again between some houses towards the post-Byzantine church of **Ágios Simeón**, the doorway of which incorporates some **columns** from the temple dedicated to Aphrodite which once stood on the site.

*If you retrace your steps, near the first house you pass, a path leads off on the right in the direction of the sea (30min walk).* It passes through a magnificent landscape of **orchards**, where the trees are planted in beautiful lines.

■ The vegetation becomes less dense, and the path eventually emerges at **Ágios Fílipos beach***. Buffeted by the wind, it is hardly suitable for people who want to lie around on the beach, but the chapel perched on a rock in the shade of a large tree provides some of the finest images of the Cyclades to be had on postcards. The stone benches and tables are perfect for picnics.

■ Back on the road again (after 4.6km), among the scattered houses of the village of **Eliniká**, you will find a dirt track which climbs up through an oak forest to **Mt Ágios Pandeleímon** (545m). Perched on the summit, the **monastery*** offers a marvellous **view**** over the whole of the southern half of Kéa, something quite unforgettable at sunset. Its post-Byzantine **church** stands next to the foundations of a **Venetian tower**.

## Along the south-east coast: Karthéa and the Bay of Póles**

*After Kambí, turn right in the direction of Stavroudáki and Havouná. The track (good) leads up through a valley to the hamlet of Stavroudáki, where a section of concrete road begins. At the crossroads, follow the road on the right that leads down to the sea. From here, a path leads to the site of Karthéa, about 3km away.*

Hidden away in the wildest part of the island, the Bay of Póles and its two beaches, **Mikrès Póles*** (*to the south, with the chapel*) and **Megáles Póles**** (*to the north*), will make a deep impression: just getting there along bumpy tracks makes it seem quite an adventure, and the landscape on this forgotten part of the coast is breathtaking. On the way to the site, an **ancient tower** (in ruins), circular this time, stands next to the track. Now only 2m high (though obviously higher in Antiquity), it used to defend the entrance to the territory of the city of Karthéa. Beyond it lies the sea. The rocky spur separating the two beaches was once the site of the ancient city of **Karthéa****. The remains of two temples are still visible (*access via Megáles Póles beach*). As you continue your ascent, you will pass the **Chapel of Panagía Mirtidiótissa**, poised like a sentinel watching over the eternal sleep of the pagan gods. From the chapel there is a good **view*** over the sea and the rocky hills of Kíthnos.

A **path** scales the promontory dominating Mikrès Póles and continues to the nearby beach at **Kaliskiá***, lying in splendid isolation at the tip of the island.

**Kéa (Tziá)**

**The Cyclades**

## COMING AND GOING

**By boat** – Kéa is served from the port of Lávrio, in Attica (55km from Athens). In summer, two **ferries** (the Myrina Express and the Express Karistos) ply the route between 4 and 6 times a day (crossing: 1hr20min).

**Lávrio port authority**, ☎ (0292) 25 249. From Athens, to reach Lávrio: buses leave every 30min between 5.45am and 5.45pm from Aéros Park in Odós Mavromáteon (journey: 1hr30min). On your return, be sure to catch a ferry that arrives in Lávrio before 9pm, the departure time of the last bus back to Athens.

In summer, and wind permitting, the **Flying Dolphins** run a service 4 or 5 times a week between Zéa Marina (Piraeus) and Kéa (crossing: 1hr25min), before continuing to Kíthnos. If it is very windy, the Flying Dolphins do not venture out of port; if in doubt, enquire. In Kéa, the Minoan Flying Dolphins agency is situated opposite the quay, ☎ (0288) 21 435; they reimburse without any fuss. In Piraeus, ☎ (01) 42 80 001.

A ferry service runs to Kéa and Kíthnos twice a week, and a service to Kéa and Síros once or twice a week.

**Harbourmaster's office at Korissía**, ☎ (0288) 21 344.

## GETTING AROUND

**By bus** – Bus timetables and itineraries are displayed on the door of the small **tourist information office**, opposite the quay where you alight from the boat. The bus makes it quite easy to travel between Ioulís, Korissía, Vourkári and Otziás, and between Ioulís and Písses. However, a scooter or motorcycle is still the best way of visiting Kéa's treasures.

**By motorcycle / moped** – A machine with an 80cc engine and good suspension should enable you to cover all the roads and tracks on the island. A small all-terrain motorcycle (125cc) is ideal.

**Moto Center**, on the outskirts of Korissía in the direction of Ioulís, ☎ (0288) 21 884. It costs around €11-

12 a day to hire a 50cc motorcycle, and around €17 a day for a 200cc.

**Antonis Rent a Bike**, at the harbour (signposted), ☎ (0288) 32 104. Same prices.

**By taxi** – ☎ (0288) 22 171 / 22 217.

## ADDRESS BOOK (IOULÍS)

**Tourist information** – Opposite the quay.

**Banks / Currency exchange** – There is a branch of the **National Bank** (in a bookshop) in the street on the right after the fork. Foreign currency and travellers' cheques accepted. You can also change money at the post office.

**Post office / Telephone** – **Main post office**, in Odós Harálambos, after the museum. 7.30am-2pm, Monday to Friday. Changes money. **OTE** (telephone), in Korissía on the outskirts of the village.

**Medical service** – **Health centre**, ☎ (0288) 22 200. **Pharmacy**, on the right when entering the town, ☎ (0288) 22 277.

**Police** – ☎ (0288) 21 100.

## WHERE TO STAY

This is the main problem on Kéa, and becomes virtually impossible during summer weekends. There are few hotels on the island but many rooms to let (very often furnished studios).

• **Korissía**

*Between €30 and €40*
**Hotel Tziá**, on the beach, on the Vourkári road, ☎ (0288) 21 305, Fax (0288) 21 140 – 21rm. ⁆🍳 ✗ 🆑 Small, simple, clean rooms with a balcony or terrace overlooking the beach.

*Between €38 and €45*
**Hotel Karthaia**, in the harbour, ☎ (0288) 21 204 – 30rm. ⁆🍳 ✗ 🆑 The building is by no means elegant, but the rooms are comfortable.

• **Vourkári**

*Between €38 and €44*
**I Léfkes**, on the edge of the village, on the left, at the end of a tree-lined lane, ☎ (0288) 21 443 / (01) 90 29 081 – 9 furnished studios (well-equipped kitchens). ⁆

• **Otziás**

*Around €37*
Two delightful houses each surrounded by a garden with trees, 20m from the road coming from Otziás ("Rooms to Let" signs on both sides of the road): **María Tzouvarás**, ☎ (0288) 21 151 / (01) 97 52 736 – 5rm. ⌁
**Ioánnis Stefas**, ☎ (0288) 21 316 – 6rm. ⌁

• **Ioulís**

*Between €30 and €40*
**Hotel Ioulís**, at the tip of the kástro, ☎ (0288) 22 177 – 11rm. ⌁ ℘ The building is rather unattractive and the rooms are in need of renovation; but the view is the most beautiful on the island, and there is the added charm of being right next to the Venetian fortress.
**Hotel Filoxénia**, follow the street on the right before the fork, ☎ (0288) 22 057 – 6rm. Its small rooms are charming.

• **Písses**

**Campsite**, 30m from the beach, but the setting and the quality could be better. Contact the O Giannis hotel, just below it. Around €11 per person.

*Around €30*
**O Márkos**, rooms to let, on the edge of Písses, in a drystone building on the left, ☎ (0288) 31 317 – 4 studios. ⌁ ⌂ Small flats with well-equipped kitchens for 2 or 3 people. A bit gloomy but cool.

*Between €38 and €44*
**O Giánnis**, the owner's house on the left after O Márkos, ☎ (0288) 31 332 / 31 335, Fax (0288) 31 303 – 18 studios. ⌁ ⌂ Simple but pleasant furnished accommodation (for 3 people) with fully equipped kitchens. The owner also runs the Písses campsite.

• **Koúndouros**

*Around €43*
**Saint-Georges** (Ágios Geórgos), on the left on the hill (sign on road), ☎ (0288) 31 277 / 31 275 / (01) 60 08 282 – 18rm. ⌁ 天 ⌂ ✕ Buildings and rooms (with fridge) decorated in Cycladic style. The restaurant has a magnificent view over the bay and a gastronomic reputation.

• **Korissía**
**Akri**, the classic taverna serving fish, meze and cooked dishes. The best place to eat at the harbour.
**Lagouderá**, a pleasant alternative to Akri. The meze are very good here.
**Apothíki**, upmarket cuisine, but more expensive than Akri.

• **Vourkári**
**Aristos** and **Níkos**: two good places for eating fish and lobster, but quite pricey.
**Strofí tou Mími**, on the edge of the village, at the beginning of the road to Otziás. Serves fish and excellent barbecued dishes in pretty surroundings.

• **Otziás**
**Yánnis**, on the beach, a good place for fish and meze.
**Cyclades**, on your right as you come into the village, the best place for home cooking.

• **Ioulís**
In the square, **Yánnis Podóyiros** serves good food, but be prepared to wait.
**Stéki**, near the Ágios Spiridonos Church. Barbecues and excellent cooked dishes with fine views of the valley.

**Vinillion**, set in a large house on the edge of the village of Vourkári. The best bar on the island, with eclectic music and a great atmosphere.
In Ioulís, you could try **Art Café**, or **Léon**, the stronghold of techno music, and for a more traditional atmosphere, **Kouíz** and **Kamíni**.

A number of shops sell local craft products in Hóra's little back streets. **Tziá honey**, delicately flavoured with thyme, is a local delicacy and is used to make the excellent local **pastéli**, a sort of nougat made with sesame seeds. The wine made on the island, **mávro** (red) or "mavroúdi", is not bad either. Kéa also produces large quantities of **almonds**.

**Making the most of Kéa (Tziá)**

# KÍTHNOS *

Western Aegean – District of the Cyclades – Michelin map 980 fold 31
Regional map on the inside back cover – 99.2km²
Pop 1 632

**Not to be missed**
A stroll around the alleys of Hóra.
The beautiful mountain village of Driopída.
Léfkes and the surrounding beaches.

**And remember...**
Spend at least a day exploring the beaches on the east coast.
Try the grilled lobster in one of the tavernas at the water's edge at Mérihas or Loutrá.

Kíthnos stretches from north to south forming a modest crest of sun-baked hills (Mt Profítis Ilías peaks at just 337m!) carpeted with *phrygana* (low scrublands), the scent of rosemary, sage, oregano and thyme filling the air. After years of over-pasturing (also known as "the appetite of goats") only the occasional olive or fig tree breaks up this sparse vegetation. And beyond the pockets of greenery which punctuate the coastline, the only hint of green in an otherwise burnt-out landscape is the sinuous valley which stretches from Mérihas to Loutrá. The island attracts few visitors apart from the hydrotherapy devotees who arrive each summer, usually in August, heading for the thermal waters at Loutrá and Kíthnos, and a number of Athenian families: originally from the island, they often have a second home here. It has to be said that the island has little in the way of night-life. But travellers wanting to stay off the beaten track, in search of a deserted stretch of sand, will not be disappointed. For here lies the real wealth of Kíthnos: countless sandy beaches line the east coast, often just ribbons of sand which can only be reached by boat. Unless you are an experienced walker, make sure you set off with a good map. The island has a good network of small roads and it is relatively easy to find accommodation and somewhere good to eat (*see "Making the most of Kíthnos"*); in short, Kíthnos is a great place to spend some time away from the crowds.

## The island of the Driopides
Although inhabited since the end of the Mesolithic Era (7500-6500 BC), Kíthnos has few vestiges of its past apart from the ruins of the ancient city of Vriókastro and of the medieval fortress at Kefalókastro. The local toponymy also reveals traces of the island's first inhabitants, the Driopides, a pre-Hellenic tribe originating from Euboea whose legendary chief, Kíthnos, gave his name to the island. Apart from these mysterious ancestors, the only reference the history books make is to the *Kythniaká*, the clashes of February 1862 which, several months prior to the discharge of Otto, set government troops against rebels from Síros and Tínos who had come to liberate well-known opponents of the regime held on the island. Kíthnos is still often referred to as **Therma**, thanks to the hot springs at Loutrá. These volcanic springs have been used since Otto's reign, with Otto himself making several trips to the island.

## From Mérihas to Loutrá
*11km*

■ **Mérihas** – *located halfway between the north and south points of the island and with plenty of restaurants and rooms to rent, Mérihas is the best starting point to explore Kíthnos*. Mérihas has preserved the peaceful atmosphere of the modest fishing village it still was twenty years ago. Although it lacks any particular charm, it is a pleasant place with its sandy beach, tamarisks and ducks. Far from damaging its fishing trade, the recent introduction of tourism to the island, which began in 1974 with the construction of a jetty for ferries to dock, has, on the contrary, breathed life into it.

The Cyclades

As fine connoisseurs, the amateur sailors who frequent Kíthnos come to Mérihas to enjoy grilled fish and lobster. In the mornings (*between 8am and 9am*), don't miss the **return of the caiques**, then watch the keen negotiations which determine the fate of the catch.

New buildings have sprung up at both ends of the bay, along the rocks and behind the row of houses opposite the harbour which used to form the heart of the village and which is now brightened up by shops and restaurants. To the right stands the rather unattractive concrete block of the **Posidonion** hotel, happily the only example of seaside architecture peculiar to the colonels' junta.

Five minutes from the jetty, a flight of steps leads to **Martinákia beach**, usually besieged by the families staying in Mérihas. You might prefer the beach at **Episkopí**\* (*2km from the village, take the concrete path on the left*), shaded by tamarisks and much quieter. Flanked by two hills, it is the perfect spot to watch a splendid **sunset**.

But the two most beautiful **beaches** on the west coast are still unquestionably **Fikiáda**\* and **Kolóna**\*\*, separated from each other by a ribbon of sand which gives its name to the latter. *You can get there by the caique moored opposite the Ostria*

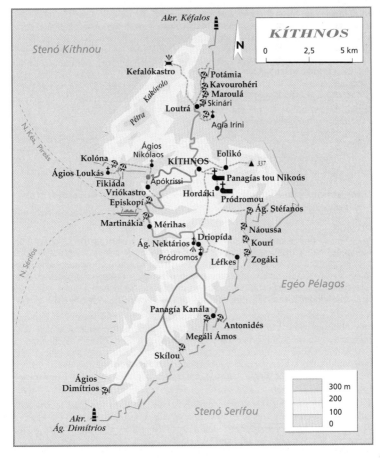

*restaurant (shuttle service from 10am-4pm) or by road to Apókrissi (3km): take the left-hand fork shortly before arriving at Kíthnos. From there, follow the route north. After about 500m, pass the Ágios Nikólaos Chapel on your right and go west along the coast (about 2km from Ágios Nikólaos to Kolóna).*

■ **Vriókastro★** – *From Apókrissi, the ruins of Vriókastro are only a 30min walk along the path, heading south this time.*

Probably inhabited since the end of the 5C BC, the ancient capital of the island occupies a vast site stretching as far as the islet of **Ágios Loukás★**, seat of the agora (occupied until Roman times). There you can still see three **water tanks** dug out of the rock, while the foundations of a tower and the **defensive wall** of the fortified city, now partially submerged, are preserved.

*Rejoin the Kíthnos road which crosses an increasingly arid landscape as you leave the coastal valley behind.*

■ **Kíthnos★★** – *7.5km from Mérihas.* Completely hidden from the road *(which leaves the town on the right heading towards Loutrá)*, the **Hóra** of Kíthnos appears at the last minute. Less spectacular than the one at Kéa – which some of the houses with their tiled roofs resemble – Kíthnos is no less authentic and typical of the Cyclades with its quiet, paved alleyways just inviting you to take a stroll, decorated here and there with motifs painted in coloured whitewash (sirens, fish, flowers, boats or geometric designs). Built on top of a hill, the island's capital (since the 18C) also reveals a succession of lively, small squares with a collection of restaurants, cafés and souvenir shops, home to the island's night-life. Of all the beautiful churches in Hóra, two, above all, are worth a visit: the **Basilica of Agía Triáda★** (Holy Trinity), recognisable by the ancient architectural remains on the ground beside it, is the oldest church on the island. But it owes its present-day appearance – a single nave topped by a dome – to numerous modifications undertaken over the centuries.

A rare vestige of 17C Kíthnos, the **Church of Ágios Sávas★** (1613; the date of the building can be seen on the lintel above the great door) also stands with its cupola above a single nave, marked with the arms of **Antonio Cozzadini** (Gozadhinou, in Greek), the governor of Kíthnos under Venetian rule. Like other Frankish churches, Ágios Sávas embraces both Orthodox (right-hand pews) and Catholic (left-hand pews) worship. Also on display is a remarkable carved, wooden **iconostasis★** (17C).

*To the south-west of the town, a small section of the tarmac road opens into a three-way fork:*

■ To the north-east, a concrete road leads to **Eolikó★**, a **wind farm** *(1.5km from the turning)*. Along with the neighbouring **solar energy park**, a huge collection of solar panels arranged along the dirt track which joins the road to Loutrá, the Eolikó produces all the island's energy. In response to its new needs, Kíthnos has put everything into sustainable energy sources and has set up two electric power stations: one – the first of its kind in Greece – entirely fuelled by wind power, the other by solar energy.

■ Following the middle road, you climb towards the ancient **monastery of Panagía tou Nikoús★** (Our Lady of Victory), the **long white outer wall** of which, surmounted by two cupolas, can be seen from afar. Under Turkish occupation, a clandestine school was hidden in its cellar. Further north, a path then leads to the **Hordáki** locality where the ancient **monastery of Pródromou** (the "Precursor", in other words, John the Baptist) stands, containing a carved, wooden **iconostasis★** from the 16C.

■ Finally, the right-hand fork goes directly south and joins the road to Driopída *(about 5km further on)*. This is an invitation to take a beautiful stroll to the heart of the island and its wild **scenery★** *(allow at least 90min; some signs and arrows painted in red will help you negotiate the many paths)*.

■ **Loutrá** – *4.5km from Kíthnos*. A small seaside spa with modern architecture, Loutrá extends from the Ágía Iríni Bay to the beach at Skinári. Dominating the bay, the **Hotel Xénia Anagénissis** houses the very first spa, integrated into the present-day building, built in an elegant neo-Classical style by a German architect.

Exposed to the meltem wind, this stretch of the coast is not really suitable for swimming, but when it is very calm, the beaches at **Kavourohéri***  (*frequented mainly by nudists*) and **Potámia*** can provide a pleasant outing (*about 1hr on foot; take food and drink*).

On your return, stop at **Andréas**, a taverna situated opposite **Maroulá beach**, in a hamlet of two or three houses which overlook the path. Absolutely everything you eat here comes from the owners' garden, poultry yards or stables. Loutrá is also a pleasant place to dine at the water's edge, but after 10pm the atmosphere is rather dead.

*As you leave the town, there is a sign to Kefalókastro (also called Kástro Orias). Follow a dirt track for 3km, then a path for another 2km (allow about 90min on foot).*

■ **Kefalókastro*** – the island's capital during Byzantine and Frankish rule, this medieval citadel was captured and destroyed by the Turks in 1537 before being completely abandoned by its inhabitants a century later. From the top of a promontory overlooking the sea, you can see the ruins of its **great wall**, along with the remains of a few houses and two ruined churches. But it is worth the walk especially for the beautiful, **panoramic view*** of the northern tip of the island.

Kíthnos, a mountain chapel (near Driopída)

Th. Labropoulos/ON LOCATION

**Kíthnos**

# From Mérihas to Panagía Kanála

■ **Driopída**★★ (Syllaca) – 5km from Mérihas. Overlooked by the recent development in tourism, Driopída is, nevertheless, the most beautiful village on the island. Its little houses, almost all of which are one-storey with **tiled roofs**, are huddled up the side of a hill, climbing both banks of a dried-up torrent. Once one of the main trades of the town, the **ceramics** tradition is continued by just one family, the **Milas**. Their **workshop**★ (not to be confused with the recently opened shop Vitalis), located near the **Katafíki grotto** (currently closed to the public), is worth a quick look.

Like its inhabitants, the village is ageing and growing smaller, allowing the houses furthest from the centre to fall into decay. But this slightly nostalgic atmosphere adds to the charm of the place and it is not unusual to come across a donkey at the corner of a side street.

Behind **Agía Ánna**, the large parish church recognisable by its blue dome and two bell-towers, lurks **Ágios Minás**★ (on the left, a little further down the village), home to a precious, carved wooden **iconostasis**★ and a remarkable **episcopal throne**. Nearby (just after the statues of F Dhélogramatis and E Arealis), is the **Byzantine Museum**★ (its opening times are still unpredictable and the key is held by the Orthodox priest at St Anna's), which houses some of the most precious icons from the island's churches. When leaving Driopída, do not miss the magnificent **view**★★ which unfolds from the terrace of **Ágios Nektários** (on the right, 300m from the village towards Panagía Kanála).

*After the deserted windmills which cover the hill, follow the dirt road which goes to the left. At the first chapel you come to, go left again. A little further on, an asphalt road forks: to the left, it goes to Ágios Stéfanos, to the right, it descends towards Léfkes (2km).*

■ **Léfkes**★★ – Nestling at the edge of a delightful beach planted with old tamarisks, this village consists of barely thirty houses. With its pretty chapel built near a narrow landing-stage and its taverna set on the terrace, Léfkes will enchant you with its simplicity and gentleness.

On your return, on the dirt road which goes towards Ágios Stéfanos, you will find on the right a sign to the **beaches of Zogáki**★★, **Kourí**★★ **and Náoussa**★★, the best of the beaches on the east coast (steps descend to the first, about a hundred metres further on). Sheltered from the winds and bathed by crystal clear waters, each of these coves has its own charm... and a taverna where you can spend the hottest hours of the day. From there, you can get to Kourí, Náoussa and the superb beach at **Ágios Stéfanos**★★ on foot (much more easily than following the track).

*Take the main road again and follow it south.*

■ **Panagía Kanála** – 7km from Driopída. The village takes its name from the 19C **basilica**★ which stands in the middle of the only pine wood on the island. Dedicated to the Virgin Mary, patron saint of Kíthnos, it preserves an **icon**★ miraculously found, it is said, at the bottom of a water channel ("canal"). Post-Byzantine in style, the 17C piece is attributed to Adonis Skordhilis.

Nearby, you can enjoy some of the prettiest beaches of the region: **Megáli Ámos**★ to the west or **Antonidés**★, to the east. If they are crowded (the beaches are busier these days), you can always go to the beach at **Skílou**★. It's fine for lazing around and swimming, and there are fewer people there.

*Take the main road and head south.*

The road follows the line of the crest before descending again towards the southern tip of the island, providing splendid **viewpoints**★ all the way there.
There is a walk that will take you along the beach at **Ágios Dimítrios**★ (10km from Driopída), a bay which feels as if it is at the ends of the earth.

### COMING AND GOING

**By boat** – From the port at Lávrio, ☎ (0292) 25 249, two daily return trips to Kíthnos, via Kéa. From Piraeus, at least 1 daily ferry, in the morning between 7am-8am, except for Friday and Tuesday (departs in the afternoon, between 3pm-4pm). About a 2hr15min boat ride.

From Lávrio, **KTEL** buses run (90min journey) to Athens (arrival and departure Platía Eghíptou). Make sure that the boat in question arrives at Lávrio before 9.30am, when the last bus for Athens leaves. Finally, Kíthnos is also linked to Kéa and Síros (3hr15min) by the Aegean Line.

The hydroplane and **Minoan Flying Dolphins** Highspeed Ferries timetables are relatively reliable. Two boats a day, except Friday (4.15pm) and Sunday (7.45am). Wednesday and Saturday: 7.45am and 8.15am; Monday: 7.30am and 3pm; Tuesday: 7.45am and 3pm; Thursday: 8am and 8.15am.

**Information**: ☎ (01) 42 80 001. Boats leave from Zéa Marina in Piraeus and go directly to Kíthnos, without stopping at Kéa. Take note that these boats are often cancelled, sometimes at the last minute, due to weather conditions. If it is windy, go by ferry. Tickets are on sale in many of the offices at the harbour in Mérihas.

### GETTING AROUND

**By bus** – Two bus services, which run until around 11pm, link Mérihas to Loutrá (via Kíthnos) and Mérihas to Panagía Kanála (via Driopída). Departures and arrivals at Mérihas take place at the crossroads at the end of the jetty. In summer, there are about ten round-trips a day.

**By taxi** – If you need a taxi for a particular time, it is best to book ahead by phone. Mérihas: ☎ (0281) 32 128; Kíthnos: ☎ (0281) 31 272; Loutrá: ☎ (0281) 31 212; Driopída: ☎ (0281) 31 290.

**By motorcycle** – The best way of exploring the island is still on two wheels (50cc). **Antonis Rent a Bike**, right at the beginning of the road that climbs towards Kíthnos, ☎ (0281) 32 104 /

32 248. Around €12 a day. The same agent also hires out cars (around €45 a day).

**Fuel** – Kíthnos only has one **Elinoil fuel station**, situated at the entrance to Hóra.

### ADDRESS BOOK

**Tourist information** – A modest stall on the jetty, ☎ (0281) 32 250. You can find a very rough map of the island there, brochures in English and Italian listing addresses of rooms to rent and restaurants.

**Post office** – At Kíthnos. Monday-Friday, 8am-12 noon.

**Banks / Currency exchange** – There are no banks on the island (and thus no cash dispensers), but in Mérihas, the cellarman (next to the bus stop), **Cava Kíthnos**, also serves as a maritime office and a branch of the National Bank of Greece. In this role, he exchanges currency and accepts travellers' cheques.

**Medical service** – **Municipal clinics**, in Driopída: ☎ (0281) 31 202; in Kíthnos: ☎ (0281) 32 234.

**Tourist police** – In Hóra, ☎ (0281) 31 201.

**Port authority** – In Mérihas, ☎ (0281) 32 290.

### WHERE TO STAY

Like Kéa, Kíthnos mainly enjoys a clientele of Greek holidaymakers there for a long stay. The hotels therefore essentially consist of studios or apartments with kitchens (with at least a fridge, 2 electric hobs, a sink and cooking equipment), and there are no campsites on the island. No rooms in Kíthnos or Driopída. Out of season, the rates are between €6 and €12 cheaper. In most cases, the owners only speak a few words of English and a telephone reservation is only good for a few days.

• **Mérihas**

*Around €24*

**Kíthnos**, at the end of the jetty, at the top of the flight of steps to the left, ☎ (0281) 32 247, Fax (0281) 32 092 – 12rm. ⁅ ✆ ✈ Fridges. A small, simple hotel, recognisable by its broad blue-

and white-striped awnings, occupying two floors above a café-cum-cake shop. Modest-sized rooms with basic comforts, but with a pretty view over the harbour. A one- or two-night resting stop while you look for something better.

*Between €27 and €37*
Mérihas has studios that sleep 2 or 3 people, with a balcony or a veranda. Clean, convenient and in general newly-built, this kind of accommodation is rarely decorated with the same care as those on islands where tourism is more developed. On the other hand, they are much more reasonably priced. The usual decor consists of white walls and pale wooden furniture, almost always the same, consisting of two beds, a table, a few armchairs and a wardrobe.

**Panorama**, behind the Kíthnos hotel, ☎ (0281) 32 184 / 32 808 – 7 well-equipped studios. Dominating the whole bay, this very well-located white building in the Cycladic style gets the sun all day long. The rooms overlook a terrace covered with a blue wooden arbour. The studios have the bare necessities, but at an attractive price.

**Fínikas**, ☎ (0281) 32 203 – 10 well-equipped studios. In the village behind the Byzantino Bar. The studios, which each have a balcony, overlook a pleasant shady garden planted with pines and palm trees.

**Giórgos Martínos**, on the other side of the bay, behind the Kadouni Taverna, ☎ (0281) 32 469 / (01) 57 70 614 – 10 well-equipped studios (which can sleep up to 4 people). Tastefully decorated and cleaned every three days, the rooms overlook a lovely paved terrace where you can have breakfast looking down on the harbour.

**Chrístos Liakópoulos**, at the beginning of Martinákia beach, ☎ (0281) 32 371 – 5 well-equipped studios. Small, one-storey houses, built side by side facing the beach. Each room has its own balcony, shaded by an arbour. Ideal for those who enjoy an early morning dip in the sea.

• **Loutrá**
*Between €33 for a room and €43 for a bedsit*
**Porto Klaras**, 15m from the jetty, up a little alleyway, ☎ (0281) 31 276 / 31 600 / (01) 48 36 904 – 20rm (rooms,

studios and furnished flats). 🍴 ♒ TV CC A beautiful 2-storey building in the Cycladic style, with flowers everywhere. White, blue and rough stone alternate in the sombre, elegant interior design.

• **Panagía Kanála**
*Around €27*
**Níkos Bourítis**, a stone's throw from the bus stop, ☎ (0281) 32 350 / 32 298 – 11 well-equipped studios. Each one has its own balcony and sun-blind, which can be regulated according to your desire for sunshine. On the ground floor, a bougainvillaea grows against the Cycladic whiteness of its whitewashed walls. From the balconies, you can see the bell-tower of the basilica.

*Around €40*
**Margarita**, ☎ (0281) 32 265 / (01) 53 20 103 – 7 well-equipped studios. Near the beach, a pretty white 1-storey building, with a veranda opening onto the beach for each bedsit, sheltered by a tiled canopy at first-floor level, with a vaulted portico on the ground floor. Even the furniture is slightly more elegant than elsewhere.

**EATING OUT**
It is the good fortune of the less touristy islands that they are mainly visited by Greeks, who are demanding customers. You eat well at reasonable rates almost everywhere: from €7.50, with the exception of fish and lobster. Since these resources are dwindling, fish such as "barboúni", "sargós", "lithríni", "fagrí" and "skorpína" are sold at about €35 a kilo. The first four varieties of fish are delicious cooked on a charcoal grill, whereas the last is a choice cut often used to make soup. But it would be a pity to stay on Kíthnos without tasting some braised "barboúnia" washed down with a local white wine and some meze.

• **Mérihas**
**Ostria**, on the jetty, with all the atmosphere of the harbour. Don't be put off by the rather ordinary decor: this taverna serves the best Kamarès fish. The menu, which is very varied, offers barbecued meats and numerous cooked dishes. Don't miss the "astako-makaronádha", spaghetti cooked with lobster, one of the specialities of the house.

**Yialós**, at the beginning of the beach, with tables on the terrace or on the beach, among tamarisk trees. A good place to taste the local "maghirevtá", literally the "cooked" (especially meat with sauces) with a large selection of appetising meze.

**Sailors**, roughly in the centre of the seafront. A taverna with checked tablecloths, Cycladic blue chairs, with tables on the terrace or on the beach. An excellent all-round restaurant, it serves fish, octopus, lobster or meat, lovingly barbecued on the charcoal grill.

**Kantouni**, just beyond the bridge. Tables on the terrace or on the beach. THE place to taste barbecued meat: "kontosoúvli" (kebabs), "biftéki", "kokorétsi" (brochettes of sheep's tripe), "païdhákïa" (lamb chops), all accompanied by "sfougáto", little balls of cheese.

### • Hóra

**To Steki** and **To Kentro**. Here you will find the coolness of Hóra, a large selection of meze and excellent grilled meat, and, the island's rarest commodity, a lively atmosphere! The house wine, "dópio krassí", is a must.

### • Loutrá

**Xerolithia**, a few metres from the jetty. This taverna (which is also a café in the morning and an ouzo bar in the late afternoon) is run by an elderly architect (but it's his mother slaving away in the kitchen). This place offers high-quality cuisine in a tasteful atmosphere. Not to mention the lovely view which can be enjoyed as much from the rooftop terrace in the evening as from the ground-floor terrace in the morning.

**Trechantiri**, follow the road on the right, when you arrive at Loutrá, for about 1km. The terrace of this excellent taverna (fish and meat) overlooks the pretty Bay of Agía Iríni.

### OTHER THINGS TO DO

**Feasts & festivals** – On this austere-looking island, the **panigíri** are exuberant. An enormous meal, music and traditional dancing usually animate the villages. The most important festivals: Panagía Kanála (15 August and 8 September), Panagía tou Nikoús (15 August), Panagía tis Flambourias (24 August), Agía Triáda (end of June), and Aï Lia (in the mountains, 20 July).

# MÝKONOS★★

Western Aegean – District of the Cyclades – Michelin map 980 fold 32
Regional map on the inside back cover – 86km² – Pop 6 000

**Not to be missed**
Strolling through Hóra during the day for its beauty and at night
for its electric atmosphere.
Chilling out on its golden beaches bathed with crystalline waters.

**And remember...**
Avoid the first 20 days of August and weekends, when accommodation,
eating out and travelling are a headache.

Mýkonos, queen of the Aegean Sea, has, like St Tropez, a natural chic which it has acquired through a half century of patronage by the Greek and international jet set. It is true that fashions change and the island regularly goes through purgatory; but it invariably returns to favour probably due to the extreme simplicity of the ingredients of its success: a magnificent Hóra and beaches.

## A belated notoriety

Mýkonos has taken dazzling revenge on a destiny long hidden. Archaeology has had much difficulty in finding any traces of Cycladic civilization here, and begrudgingly allows for the presence of two ancient cities. For this small, arid, granite island initially lived in the shadow of its glowing neighbour **Delos**, then under Latin rule, under the sphere of influence of **Tínos**.

Life changed even less on the island during its time under Ottoman rule and it became a hideaway for pirates. In the 18C, privateering gave way to a thriving economy based on trade. Some of the shipowners' families made their fortunes, but the arrival of steamships returned Mýkonos to its sad fate. Growing archaeological interest in Delos heralded a merited, if timid, beginning to tourism between the wars, which would gain momentum in the 1950s.

Mýkonos harbour: dining at the water's edge.

B. Pérousse/MICHELIN

# Mýkonos Town*** (Hóra)
*Allow half a day*

From Platía Mandó Mavrogénous (named after a heroine of the Greek Revolution) you arrive at **Agía Kiriakí Church** (Holy Sunday) which contains the most beautiful **icons** in Hóra. From here, follow Odós Andrónikou, better known by the name **Matogiáni***, Mýkonos' most chic shopping street. The ground floors of the traditional houses are home to the most famous Greek **jewellers** and the top names in luxury watch making, alternating with various shops and other shopping arcades. On the first floor, cafés and bars wait until late afternoon to take over the street, which metamorphoses into a huge discotheque at night.

To the right on **Odós Énoplon Dinámeon**, another stronghold of luxury boutiques, you can take a look at the **Lénas House** *(on the right, 7pm-9pm; no entrance fee)*, a typical 19C noble residence. Converted into an annexe for the Museum of Folk Art, it displays the interior design and furniture of the period.

A little further on, the **Aegean Maritime Museum** *(10.30am-1pm, 5.30pm-8.30pm; no entrance fee)* occupies another beautiful former home, a gift, like its neighbour of the shipowner G Drakópoulos (originally from Mýkonos). There you can see an eclectic collection evoking the world of the sea from Antiquity to the 19C: there are models of boats, engravings, maps and nautical instruments. The pleasant garden is embellished with marbles (replicas and originals) from Delos, anchors and other nautical objects.

Beyond the two **chapels**, you come across the arcades in the charming **Three Wells Square** (Platía Tría Pigádia), where it is said that the young girls of the island have to drink water from the three wells if they wish to find a husband. From there, turn into **Odós Mitropóleos** *(on the right)*, which takes you on foot to the **Metropolitan Church** (Mitrópoli) *(on the left beside the white chapels)*, an imposing building topped by a dome and red roofs (really splendid interior decoration), matched by the blue dome of the **Catholic church***, located just behind. Note the coat of arms of the Ghizzi family above the great door and the **Venetian frescoes** inside.

On the left, the equally famous **Káto Míli windmills*** ("Lower Windmills") stand in a row on a mound above the harbour. They used to take in imported grain which, once milled, was returned to its place of origin. It was sometimes used on site in the manufacture of dry biscuits, the staple food for seafarers, which the passing boats would stock up on. The third windmill is open to visitors, and is still working with its small, triangular, canvas sails.

## The Alefkándra District**

Enjoy the pretty **view*** from the windmills across the houses of the Alefkándra district, known as **Little Venice**. It is one of the most sought out parts of Hóra in the late afternoon and at sunset. A row of **tall houses***, some dating from the 18C, stand at the water's edge, with balconies or corbelled wooden **loggias** overlooking the waves. This unusual architecture was probably linked to the shady dealings of their rich owners, captains involved in piracy. This was in fact the main pursuit of the island's sailors in the 16C and 17C and Mýkonos' initial wealth was built on it. It is presumed that direct access to the sea enabled the easy and discreet transit of booty. The Alefkándra district forms one side of the **kástro** – which is why it is called the Venetian town, with the outer-lying houses forming the defence system. As its name suggests, the **Church of the Panagía Paraportianí**** stands between the sea and one of the kástro's gates, while five others are hidden inside, all built in the 16C and 17C except **Ágii Anargiri** (15C), which takes pride of place in the heart of the district. Late in the evening, it becomes the focus for the wild night-life.

Next to it, the long building parallel to the sea – an old, stone house belonging to a sea captain – is home to the **Museum of Folk Art**★ (*5.30pm-8.30pm, Sunday 6.30pm-8.30pm; no entrance fee*). Fabrics, embroidery, scenes of the island, furniture and objects from Mýkonos homes evoke daily life. It faces **Agía Eléni**★, one of the island's largest churches which houses ancient **Byzantine icons**.

Afterwards, go back to the **old harbour**, the **marble quays** forming a harmonious curve in front of the **town hall** arcades (18C). They also border the neo-Classical façade of the small **church**, dedicated to St Nicholas – patron saint of sailors – in common with half of Hóra's chapels. At the end of the beach, where a number of caiques wait to be repainted, are the last vestiges of the old **naval shipyards**. Behind are a number of large **houses**, some lined with arcades, which tell of the timid beginnings of Mýkonos as a seaside resort in the 1930s.

Then leave the seafront to venture into **old Mýkonos**★★, a small district bordered by Odós Matogiáni and Odós Mitropóleos and the **municipal gardens**. You will rarely see as many **churches** and **chapels** per square metre. Particularly at the end of **Odós Agíou Dimitríou**, where no less than **four churches** are lined up side by side, earning the nickname the "Four Gossips"!

Leave the medieval Hóra for the modern harbour, at the entrance to which stands the **Archaeological Museum**★ (*9am-3.30pm, Sunday 10am-3.00pm; closed Tuesday; entrance fee*). Apart from a beautiful **amphora**★★ found on Mýkonos, depicting scenes from the Trojan War, the objects on display – funeral offerings, some very beautiful red-figure vases, ceramics and jewels dating from various periods – came from

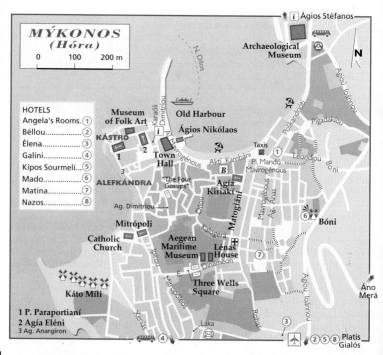

excavations of the purification grave on **Rínia**: during a fatal epidemic, Athens demanded that the inhabitants of Delos bury their dead with their treasure so as not to contaminate the Sanctuary of Apollo *(see page 239)*.

Complete your stroll in Mýkonos with a visit to the **Bóni windmill\***, restored and in working order, situated on an esplanade with a magnificent **view\*\*** of the town.

## On the west coast

### Towards Cape Armenistís

*From the jetty, follow the road to the left or take a bus near the Archaeological Museum.*

■ Nestling on the edge of the **bay** of the same name – the most sheltered anchorage for cruise boats when the meltem wind lets loose – **Toúrlos** *(3km to the north of Hóra)* is a small seaside resort currently being developed, the sandy **beach** now lined with luxury hotels, although it is still relatively quiet.

■ **Ágios Stéfanos** *(4.5km, last bus stop)* offers the same scene but the crowds which invade its small **beach\*** have spoilt its charm. A good track follows the long **Houlákia beach**, which is lovely in calm weather.

■ As you approach Cape **Armenistís** *(about 4km from Ágios Stéfanos)*, the landscape, dominated on the left by **Mt Profítis Ilías** (372m), becomes wilder and the beaches give way to rocky slopes. At the very end of the cape, a gigantic **lighthouse** (1885), almost 100m tall, watches over the strait between Tínos and Mýkonos where the loud wind whistles by.

### Towards Ágios Ioánnis beach\*

*After the windmills (Káto Míli), take the coast road. By bus, departures for Ornós, Kórfos and Ágios Ioánnis near the Olympic Airways office.*

■ On the outskirts of Hóra, the **Megáli Ámos beach** is a delight to both day-trippers to Mýkonos and resident morning-swim enthusiasts. With its white sand and limpid water, it marks the beginning of the south coast beaches, but also the urbanisation which is encroaching on the neighbouring hills...

■ A little further on is the rather surprising sight of the **Diakóftis Peninsula**, linked to the island by a narrow, sandy **isthmus** fringed by the **beaches of Ornós\*** *(to the south)* and **Kórfos** *(to the north)*. The place is overrun with luxury villas and tourist facilities, attracting the crowds to the neighbouring beaches. But the beach at Ornós, protected from the wind, is quieter again towards the end of the day and its little **harbour** is a charming place to dine.

■ The road continues towards **Ágios Ioánnis\*** *(reached by a well-signposted road to the left; 10min by bus)*, a very popular beach with **sunset** and beach volleyball enthusiasts, two passions which, luckily, take place at different times of day. Despite the beach umbrellas and deckchairs, this sandy, pebble cove looking across to Delos is visited by relatively few people.

## The beaches of the south coast

*Head towards the airport, then take the right fork to Psaroú and Platís Gialós (4.5km from Hóra). Same bus route (leaving from the Olympic Airways office) for Psaroú and Platís Gialós (15min by bus).*

The most beautiful beaches with golden sand and crystalline waters are to be found along the island's southern coast; but obviously most of them are very crowded, such as those at **Psaroú\*** and **Platís Gialós**, curled up at the back of a bay closed in by arid hills. The developers are not mistaken in establishing the island's **main seaside resort** here, with hotels, studios, tavernas, cafés and bars within easy reach of the beach umbrellas. Platís Gialós even offers its own boat trips to the other beaches and to Delos, whilst Psaroú has a water-sports school.

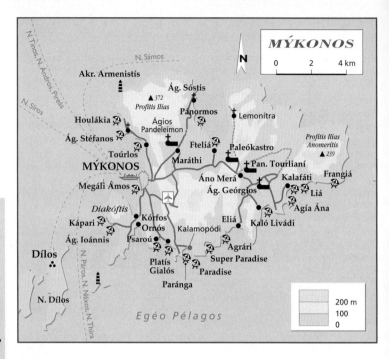

Less fashionable than in the past, **Paradise**\* *(6km from Hóra; bus leaves from the Olympic Airways office, or take the campsites' minibuses which are parked on the harbour by the ferry arrivals; you can also reach it by caique from Hóra or Platís Gialós)* is still a sight in itself: an immense, open-air (techno) bar with a lot of nudity. The (very noisy) campsite ensures that many people visit this 'beach', mainly young Greeks and Germans.

Even though its neighbour **Paránga**\* is a little quieter, the campsite attracts many people and the DJs are also in evidence. With fewer decibels, however, than at **Super Paradise**\* (Plindri), the other legendary Mýkonos 'beach bar', a favourite rendezvous (along with Paradise and Eliá) of the island's homosexual community *(at the end of a dirt track which you find by going straight on after the turnings for Platís Gialós and the airport; no bus service, but caiques from Hóra and Platís Gialós).*

You can take refuge one hill further along at **Agrári**\*\*.

Popular with celebrities, this beach is much more peaceful than the others, even if it seems very organised (beach umbrellas, deckchairs, water sports and 'beach bar'). At least the surrounding hills remain unspoilt.

## On Pánormos Bay\*

*Leave Hóra towards the north-east (Áno Merá), then follow the first left-hand fork to Maráthi (4.5km from Hóra), Pánormos (6.5km) and Ágios Sóstis (8km). No bus service.*

Those in search of solitude will be much happier on **Pánormos beach**\*\*, which extends beyond the charming hamlet of **Maráthi**. Its sand is less golden than that of the south coast, but here you will find neither beach umbrellas nor water sports. The meltem makes itself felt but does not interfere with swimming.

You can also opt for **Ágios Sóstis beach★★**, well sheltered from the wind at the back of a little cove and one of the prettiest and quietest on the island.

Nestling at the back of the very steep-sided Pánormos Bay is **Fteliá beach★** *(on the Áno Merá road, on the left after 7km)*. This is paradise for **windsurfers**, as the meltem is very strong.

## From Pánormos Bay to the south-east coast

A little before Áno Merá, a road *(signposted to the left)* climbs towards the hill where the 18C **Paleókastro Monastery★** perches, a church of beautifully pure lines. From up here, where the remains of a **Venetian fortress★**, including a massive defence tower can be found, you have a **panoramic view★★** across the centre of the island.

■ The second-largest town on Mýkonos (after Hóra), **Áno Merá★** *(10km from Hóra; bus leaves from near the Archaeological Museum)* was once a mere hamlet, but with the explosion of tourism, it has devoured the surrounding arid plateau. It is worth stopping off, all the same. Head for the cafés in the **village square** where you can eat good, grilled food.

■ Built in the mid-16C and modified in 1767, the **Panagía Tourlianí Monastery★** *(1km out of the village, signposted)* houses the icon of the island's patron saint. A splendid bell-tower covered in marble carvings, a carved wooden **iconostasis** and some very fine **icons★★** (in the little museum) are just some of the jewels of this fine collection. The enclosed courtyard is cooled by a marble fountain.

■ 3km from Áno Merá towards Kalafáti, the hamlet of **Abelókipous** is home to the delightful **Ágios Geórgios Monastery★** (17C), a remarkable geometric composition in three colours (red, white and blue) which is worth a detour.

### Along the beaches
It is best to avoid **Eliá**, disfigured for good by concrete and the dreadful neighbouring aquatic theme park, **Watermania** *(14km from Hóra; served by one bus, leaves from the Archaeological Museum; caiques from Hóra and Platís Gialós)*.

Push on as far as **Kalafáti★**, a long, pale, sandy bay frequented by families from the surrounding hotels, windsurfers and water-sports enthusiasts (diving school). Right at the end, a **fishing hamlet** supplies fresh fish to the local tavernas, one of which is located in a **grotto** (Spillia).

You could also head for the beach at **Kaló Livádi★★** *(15km; by bus, leaves from the Archaeological Museum; allow 15-20min on foot from the Eliá crossroads)*, which also boasts its own hamlet and chapel, and very few beach-umbrellas. The sea is so transparent and calm, it looks like a swimming pool.

**Liá★★** is not to be outdone with its turquoise water *(2km from Kalafáti following the track)*. It can get quite busy but never crowded and boasts two excellent fish tavernas (La Luna and, even better, Liá).

The remaining "must see" is **Frangiá★★**, accessible by boat *(you can also go down to the sea from the path which climbs towards Mt Profítis Ilías Anomerítis)*. It is, for now, the last refuge for those in search of solitude.

**Mýkonos**

**The Cyclades**

## COMING AND GOING

**By air** – In the summer, several daily flights from Athens (less than 1hr) with Olympic Airways. **Reservations**, ☎ (01) 96 66 666. In July and August, the flights are often fully booked; so for a return with specific dates, book very far in advance. Several weekly flights to Thessaloníki, Santoríni, Rhodes and Herakleion (Crete).

**Mýkonos Airport**, ☎ (0289) 22 327.
**Olympic Airways**, Platía Fabrika, ☎ (0289) 22 490 / 22 495.

**By boat** – From Piraeus, three daily ferries (in the morning) on the Síros, Tínos, Mýkonos line (5hr45min), and a daily Highspeed (Minoan Flying Dolphins, ☎ (01) 42 80 001.) About a 3hr boat ride.

From Rafína, three ferries (two in the morning and one in the afternoon) on the Ándros, Tínos, Mýkonos line (4hr15min); two daily departures on a Sea Jet (Strintzis company, ☎ (0294) 23 561), on the Tínos-Mýkonos (2hr30min)-Páros line. Two daily departures on a Flying Cat (Minoan Flying Dolphins, ☎ (0294) 25 100), serving Tínos and Mýkonos (2hr45min).

In Mýkonos, the **Delia office** (on the harbour, ☎ (0289) 22 322 / 22 422) is the exclusive agent for the Minoan Flying Dolphins company.

Many daily crossings to Ándros, Síros, Tínos, Páros and Náxos and less frequently to Sífnos, Ikaría, Sámos, Íos and Santoríni. Summer crossings to Crete (Herakleion), Skiáthos and Thessaloníki. Watch out for the small boats which go to Páros, Náxos, the Lesser Cyclades, Amorgós, Íos and Santoríni: the journey is often very long (over 10hr to Santoríni), and if the wind is strong (often in summer), you risk being tossed about. In strong winds, take a ferry run by the large companies.

**Harbourmaster's office**, at the harbour, next to the National Bank, ☎ (0289) 22 218.

## GETTING AROUND

**By bus** – Hóra has two bus stations. The buses parked near the Olympic Airways office **(Platía Fabrika)** are for Ornós, Ágios Ioánnis, Platís Gialós, Psaroú, the airport and Paradise (Kalamopódi, its original name).

Buses parked next to the **Archaeological Museum** go to Ágios Stéfanos, Toúrlos, Áno Merá, Eliá, Kalafáti and Kaló Livádi. The network leaves out a good number of beaches, giving you the chance of finding fewer people there. Timetables vary according to destinations: find out when you arrive.

**KTEL bus company**, ☎ (0289) 23 360. Some hotels and the Paradise campsite also offer their clients shuttle buses to Hóra. The **Hard Rock Café** has even put on a free link (a pink minibus) to the harbour, every 30min between midnight and 5am.

**By car / motorcycle** – There are few things to visit on Mýkonos, but looking for a peaceful beach justifies hiring a two- or four-wheeled vehicle. Given the island's small size and its fairly even landscape a two-wheeler might be better.

Many people drive on the narrow Mýkonos roads late at night and they are not always sober, so be careful.

**Vehicle rental** – As with everything else: Mýkonos is more expensive than other places. Several motorcycle / moped rental firms as you come off the jetty between the church and the OTE office. They also have some cars; or you can go to the agencies (the two-wheelers are more expensive there), almost all of which are located to the south-west of Hóra (except **Avis** which is at the harbour).

**Auto Rene**, Maouna, ☎ (0289) 24 552, **Euro Club**, Fabrika, ☎ (0289) 23 791, **Apollon**, Maouna, ☎ (0289) 24 136 (branches at the airport and in Ornós). Travel agencies and some hotels (and the Paradise campsite which is cheaper) also offer their clients a vehicle hire service.

**Fuel** – Two fuel stations on the way out of Hóra towards Áno Merá, another beyond Vríssi, a little before Platís Gialós.

**By taxi** – Taxi rank at the harbour, Platía Mandó Mavrogénous, ☎ (0289) 22 400 / 23 700.

**By caique** – Caiques leave every morning from Hóra for the beaches at Super Paradise, Agrári and Eliá. From Platís Gialós, caiques for Paradise, Super Paradise, Agrári and Eliá. These small boats do not take to sea in bad weather (strong meltem). Around €3 for a return ticket.

## ADDRESS BOOK

**Tourist information** – In front of the town hall (general information), ☎ (0289) 23 990. The **Association of Mýkonos Hoteliers**, ☎ (0289) 24 540, and the **Association of Rental Propritors**, ☎ (0289) 24 860 are housed in the same buildings as the tourist police. Or, you can get hold of **Mýkonos Summertime** (free, in English) which contains a lot of practical information (shopping, excursions, etc).

**Travel agents** – Many in Hóra, taking care of transport, lodging and all your leisure activities.
**Windmills**, Fabrika, ☎ (0289) 26 555-7, Fax (0289) 22 066.

**Mýkonos Accommodation Center**, ☎ (0289) 24 137, mac@mac.myk. forthnet.gr. Also try the website: www.mykonos-accommodation.com
**Delia**, at the harbour, ☎ (0289) 22 322.

**Banks / Currency exchange** – Bureaux de change, travel agents and the five banks in Hóra (closing time around 1pm; the National Bank reopens in the late afternoon in the summer) change money at variable rates. You will be spoilt for choice. They all have cash dispensers.

**Post office / Telephone** – The post office is in the southern part of the town, near Odós Artakinoú; OTE office at the harbour.

**Medical service** – There are many doctors in Hóra, four pharmacies, two vets and a public hospital with relatively good facilities, ☎ (0289) 23 998 / 23 994. In emergencies, you can also contact the tourist police, ☎ (0289) 22 482.

**Police – Tourist police**, at the end of the jetty, ☎ (0289) 22 482; **Municipal police**, Odós Láka, ☎ (0289) 22 716 / 22 235.

**Laundry** – Two launderettes, one on Odós Agh Anáryiron (next to Paraportianí), the other near the Olympic Airways office.

### WHERE TO STAY

Accommodation is much more expensive in Mýkonos than elsewhere and very hard to come by, especially during the summer (it costs half the price out of season). As charming as Hóra is, it is more expensive, and make sure you avoid the group of bars and busy roads. Accommodation on the hills and near the town is cheaper and quieter. Prices are lower if you stay for more than two days.

• **Mýkonos (Hóra)**
*Campsites (around €12)*
**Paradise campsite**, Paradise beach, ☎ (0289) 22 852 / 22 129, Fax (0289) 24 350 – 68 pitches. ✗ ⟦cc⟧ (rooms and bungalows to rent). Many facilities (cafeteria, bar, left-luggage, shops), but lots of people, not much space and quite noisy.

**Mýkonos campsite**, Paránga beach, ☎ (0289) 245 78 – 100 pitches. More family-oriented, quieter, with good facilities, (mini-market, launderette, telephones, etc) quite crowded, go and check out the toilet block before settling in.

*Around €23*
**Angela's Rooms**, Platía Mandó Mavrogénous, ☎ (0289) 22 967. Very close to the centre without being too noisy. The owner is friendly and the rooms adequate. Good value for money.

*Between €38 and €55*
**Kípos Sourmelí**, Vríssi hamlet (1.5km from Hóra on the Platís Gialós bus route), ☎ (0289) 22 905 – 10rm. A Cycladic style hotel with a nice garden.
**Béllou**, Megáli Ámos, 30m from the beach, ☎ (0289) 22 589, Fax (0289) 27 093 – 8rm. Right by the harbour, a small, quiet and clean hotel.

**Galíni**, Odós Láka, ☎ (0289) 22 065 – 7rm. ♪ 🏠 Same standard as the previous hotel and in the same quarter.

**Between €55 and €75**

🍴 **Matina**, Odós Fournákia 3, ☎ (0289) 22 387, Fax (0289) 245 01 – 20rm. A delightful hotel in Cycladic colours surrounded by vegetation and flowers. Comfortable and not too expensive.

**Mado**, Odós Evangelístrias 1, ☎ (0289) 22 330 – 15rm. ♪ 🏠 📺 Comfortable establishment with friendly owners.

🍴 **Nazos**, near the School of Fine Arts, ☎ (0289) 22 626 / 22 604 – 14rm. ♪ 🏠 🚕 Very well located with a panoramic view of Hóra and the harbour, a beautiful, Cycladic-style hotel, comfortable and well kept.

**Élena**, Odós Rohar, behind the theatre, ☎ (0289) 23 457 – 26rm. ♪ 🏠 A garden, a little building with traditional, blue balconies and a pretty view of the town. Comfortable.

### • Toúrlos

**Around €30**

**Pension Maria's**, behind the Toúrlos taverna, ☎ (0289) 230 09. 🏠 Rustic comfort but the rooms (with shower) are clean and the owner friendly.

**Around €55**

**Iliovassílema**, 20m from the beach, ☎ (0289) 230 13, Fax (0289) 23 931 – 17rm. ♪ 🏠 🚕 A very elegant little hotel with a pretty view overlooking the beach. Choose a room that looks out on this side.

### • Ágios Stéfanos

**Between €38 and €56**

**Mina**, 50m from the beach, ☎ (0289) 23 024 – 15rm. ♪ 🏠 The rooms are quite decent and the hotel runs a watersports centre.

🍴 **Vangéllis**, on the Houlákia beach, 15min from the last bus stop, ☎ (0289) 22 458 – 8rm. ♪ 🏠 ✕ 🚕 A simple, clean and friendly place. The owner will collect you from the harbour, serves Greek cuisine and even allows animals. At these prices, book ahead.

**Ártemis**, opposite the bus stop, 20m from the beach, ☎ (0289) 22 345 – 23rm. ♪ 🏠 ✕ 🚕 A comfortable Cycladic-style, seaside hotel, carefully thought-out.

### • Agrári

**Around €55**

**Agrári Beach**, on the beach, ☎ (0289) 71 295, Fax (0289) 72 202 – 33rm. ♪ 🏠 📋 📺 🚕 Quite new, this hotel offers good value for money by Mýkonos standards. Free transport to Hóra at night.

## EATING OUT

On Mýkonos, you can eat Italian, Tex-Mex, Chinese, French, international, vegetarian and every combination in between. It is usually good quality (some of the best in the country), served with care, but often quite expensive, so that good places with reasonable prices are besieged.

### • Mýkonos (Hóra)

**Between €9 and €12**

**Antoninis**, Platía Mandó Mavrogénous. This taverna serves good, simple, inexpensive Greek cuisine. The prawn salad and casseroled lobster come recommended.

🍴 **O Níkos**, behind the town hall, good, traditional Greek cuisine, fresh fish and very reasonable prices despite the cosmopolitan clientele. You have to fight for a table.

**Around €17**

**Chez Maria**, Odós Kalogerá 27, in a delightful garden, serves Greek and international specialities: "cremidópita" (savoury pastry with onions), "ahinosaláta" (sea-urchin salad), "róka" salad and fish.

**Illiovassílema**, Skarpa near Little Venice, set in an old residential building. Twelve tables at the edge of the sea with a view of Delos, and on the menu, fresh fish, seafood, "cremidópita", all at quite reasonable prices for Mýkonos.

**Cavo Tagoo**, the restaurant of the luxury hotel of the same name, beyond the harbour, ☎ (0289) 23 692. Good for getting away from the bustle of Hóra. You eat beside the swimming pool with a view of the sea. Fillet of beef in "mavrodáfni" sauce (a sweet wine), lamb with rosemary, seven fish paté... A touch of luxury at a very reasonable price. Book.

- **Toúrlos**

*Between €9 and €12*

🐌 **Mathios**, lovely view of the bay, wide range of traditional Greek dishes, very appetizing and inexpensive. An ideal cafeteria for dinner.

- **Pánormos**

*Between €9 and €12*

**Adonis**, on the beach. A stylish café. You can also taste small dishes to (quiet!) background music.

*Around €17*

**Pánormos**, on the left as you arrive. A very good taverna (which also serves breakfast) with a beautiful view across the beach. Cooked dishes, fresh fish, good service and value for money.

- **Fteliá**

*Between €12 and €18*

🐌 **Chríssanthos**, the owner is Greek and the chef Italian. Among the specialities: tomatoes stuffed with capers, cuttlefish risotto, or potatoes sautéed in olive oil. It is delicious and worth paying a little more for than the average taverna.

- **Áno Merá**

*Between €9 and €12*

**Stavros**, at the town's entrance, his meat kebabs and traditional dishes meet with great success. Go early if you want a table without too long a wait.

**Vangelis**, in the village square. Grilled meat, cooked dishes and local produce ("tyrovoliá" and "kopanistí" cheeses and "loúza", smoked pork sausage with aromatic herbs, etc) at very reasonable prices.

**Pitharhio**, a little beyond Stavros. Good Greek family cooking prepared with local produce.

- **Kalafáti**

*Around €17*

**Spilia**, in a grotto which is submerged in winter, a unique and magical place reached from the beach or by boat. Choose your lobster or your "sargós" (caught by the owner) and while waiting for it to be prepared, try the mussels, pastries, prawns and squid.

**HAVING A DRINK**

There is something for everyone and at night the town becomes a veritable night-club. Here are some 'glamorous' spots, the thing that Mýkonos does best: the evening starts quite early in the Little Venice quarter, at the **Caprice**, a good place to admire the sunset, at **Diva**, at the **Kástro Bar** (classical music), or **Celebrities**, in Matogiáni. After dinner, unless you want a quiet evening overlooking the (packed) harbour, the usual routine consists of a bar crawl, beginning with the least noisy (which is all relative) and most spacious bar, and finishing up with the most "happening" (crowded, with high noise levels). The first category includes the **Cinéma** (at Tría Pigádia), a huge bar in the shape of a serpent with a giant poster of Gilda, very popular with top models, the **7 Sins** (behind Platía Mandó Mavrogénous) and **Argo** (Odós Enópion Dinámeon) for fans of 1960s and 1970s music, and **Mercedes Remezzo** (at the harbour), for current hits. In the second category are **Madd** (at the harbour) and **Factory**, which becomes **Loft-Loft** at the weekends (next to Paraportianí). Good reputation and techno music guaranteed.

**OTHER THINGS TO DO**

**Hiking –** With the Road Edition map in hand, a radical way of getting off the beaten track on an island where no one goes in for hiking.

**Boat trip to Delos –** Departures between 8.30am and 11am, return trips until 3pm when the site closes. About a 30min boat ride. Tickets for sale at travel agents or directly at the old harbour.

**Horse riding –** Contact an agency, particularly **Windmills**.

**Water sports –** On many beaches (see above); water-skiing, jet-skiing, windsurfing and diving. **Paradise diving club**, ☎ (0289) 26 539.

**SHOPPING GUIDE**

**Hóra** has a lot of upmarket boutiques (jewellery, watchmakers, ceramics, accessories, etc) as well as art galleries, clothes and souvenir shops, and all the other services befitting a little metropolis in the summertime.

**Making the most of Mýkonos**

# MÍLOS★★

District of the Cyclades – Michelin map 980 fold 43
Regional map on the inside back cover
151km² – Pop 4 390 – Allow 2 days

**Not to be missed**
A cocktail up in Pláka at sunset.
The pleasures of swimming on the northern coast.
A boat trip around the island.

**And remember...**
Avoid staying in the noisy centre of Adámas.
To get to the more isolated beaches and the fishing villages, hire a vehicle.

Almost as well known as the haunting gaze of the Mona Lisa, the sensual curves of the *Vénus de Milo* (in the Louvre Museum in Paris) have made the name of this pearl of the Cyclades, situated in the south-west of the archipelago, a familiar one. Here, nature herself rivals the beauty of the immaculate whiteness of the old Cycladic villages, displaying a diversity of landscapes unequalled in the whole of the Aegean, with infinite variations in the colours and rock formations. The island of Mílos has an unusual combination of geological outcrops, mainly resulting from volcanic activity. And it is to its volcanic origins that the island owes the jagged nature of its coastline, indented with marine grottoes, rocky bays, and inlets fringed by ribbons of sand.

## An impressive diversity of minerals

Mílos is shaped like a large horseshoe, protectively encircling the extensive Bay of Mílos (or Adámandas Bay); its physiognomy, with its distorted lines, is not dissimilar to – although rather less spectacular than – that of its sister island, Santoríni, also created by a **volcano** with a crater now flooded by the sea. This volcanic activity, now much less violent, today takes the form of gaseous emissions and hot water springs, scattered all over the island, and is also evident in the great richness of mineral resources. For several thousands of years, the main source of wealth on the island of Mílos came from beneath the surface of the ground. **Agía Kiriakí** (southeast), in particular, a Roman town destroyed by an earthquake in about 1650, was built on a geothermal site, and for a long time flourished as a major centre for mining and trading the island's minerals.

## Around the Bay of Mílos★★ (Órmos Miloú)

The eight principal villages of the island are dotted on the hills around the Bay of Mílos. To the west, the countryside is wilder, with steep mountains where asphalted roads and coastal paths are few and far between.

### Adámas (Adámandas)

*Allow 1hr.* The principal port of the island, Adámandas, more commonly known as Adámas, was founded at the beginning of the 19C by refugees from Crete. The town is not particularly charming, but commerce and other essential services have brought the quayside to life, and you will find plenty of accommodation here.

High above the town, the **Cathedral of Ágios Harálambos** looks down over the bay, making it a good **viewpoint★**. But the jewel of Adámas is situated lower down: the Byzantine church of **Agía Triáda★★★**, dating from the13C, acts as an **Ecclesiastical Museum★★** *(from the bus stop, go back up about 100m to the right and follow the signs; open 9am-2pm / 6pm-9pm; no entrance fee).* Its main attraction is a magnificent **icon★★** of St John the Baptist, painted in 1639, as well as a rich **iconostasis★**. There are also interesting temporary exhibitions of sacred art (modern icons).

The **Mining Museum**\*\*, situated 300m south-east of the centre of Adámas, oppo-site **Papikinoú beach** *(open every day 9am-2pm / 6pm-9pm; no entrance fee)*, has an inspired display of all the minerals, rocks, ores and other materials concealed within the volcanic interior of Mílos, such as obsidian, kaolin, perlite, lead, manganese, poz-zolana and gypsum, as well as all kinds of instruments used in the mining industry and the various extraction processes; clear information panels throughout explain the geological history of the island.

## Choose your beach

*If the prows of the boats in the harbour at Adámas point towards land, it means that the wind is coming from the north, in which case, swimming will be better from the more shel-tered beaches to the south, or to the east of the bay. But if they are pointing out to sea, opt for the northern coast.*

The main road which runs around the Bay of Mílos (on two levels) gives access to myriad beaches, all well sheltered. The choice is yours, from **Lagáda** and **Papikinoú**, both very clean despite being situated in the town, to the long **Ahivadolímni beach**, further south, excellent for sailing and water-skiing.

That is, unless you venture further west, on the other side of the bay, opposite Adámas. Go past Ahivadolímni beach, then carry on for about 7km as far as the old abandoned convent, **Moní Agía Marína**. The road comes to an end, giving way to a stony path. This leads down through the middle of an old pinewood to **Fatoúrena beach**\*\*, an enchanting bay with a saltwater lagoon *(on the left)*.

From here, continue to the west along the coastal path. After a few kilometres you will come across **Empouriós**\*\*, a picturesque hamlet, home to half-a-dozen fam-ilies. Head for the taverna terrace (with its irresistibly kitschy decor) to sip an ouzo and enjoy the **view**\*\*. Try to be there as the sun sets and the whole bay, with Adámas and the whiteness of Pláka up above, is bathed in a fiery glow.

## Pláka\*\*\*

*Allow 3hr.* Adámas is not the capital of the island; the true heart of Mílos is to be found here in Pláka among the immaculately whitewashed houses. Less busy and bustling than the port, Pláka is nonetheless still a thriving town, stretching as far as the neighbouring villages of **Tripití**, **Plákes** and **Triovássalos**.

To the west of the village the **Church of Korfiátissa** occupies a lofty site, its marble esplanade overhanging the abyss.

From here, take a journey back into the history of Mílos by visiting the **Folklore Museum**\*\* *(signposted; open 10am-2pm / 6pm-9pm, Sunday 10am-2pm; closed Monday; entrance fee)*. Lo-cated in a traditional house in old Pláka, various 19C interiors and scenes from the life of that time have been re-constructed in an attractive jumble of objects, old photographs, embroidery, portraits, furniture, strange fishing im-plements, old maps, etc.

If you have time, go for a wander around the maze of alleyways in the lower town, hemmed in by countless tiny houses, all lovingly cared for. Climb up through this labyrinth to the rocky peak of the **kástro**\*\*, above the village, crowned by a church. From the top, the **view**\*\* stretches endlessly over the entire bay.

### From obsidian to copper

On Mílos, the Neolithic Period coincides with the use of obsidian, a volcanic stone found in abundance on the island. A vitreous stone, black or grey in colour, sharp and easy to cut, it proved ideally suited for making blades and points for weapons or tools. The success of these obsidian implements, which the inhabitants of Mílos were the first to de-velop, made the island a main trading centre until the 3rd millennium BC, which wit-nessed the discovery of copper and advances in the art of making implements. The inhab-itants of Filakopí also proved to be expert at this, developing weapons and tools that were easier to handle and more effective, which they sold throughout the Aegean re-gion, as far as the Egyptian coast. Because of this, their capital became one of the out-standing centres of Cycladic civilisation.

**Mílos**

On the left, on the way back down, is the attractive **Ipapánti Church**★★ (Thalassitra), which contains some remarkable 17C **icons**★.

Do not leave Pláka without a stop at the **Archaeological Museum**★★ *(on the way into the village, to the left of the main road; 8.30am-3pm; entrance fee)*. In addition to various ancient works of art – sculptures and bas-reliefs – including a copy of the **Venus** (Aphrodite) kept in Paris, are a number of remarkable pieces dating from the Neolithic and Mycenaean Periods: tools, weapons, pottery and some delicate **Cycladian statuettes**★ (3rd millennium BC) which were unearthed in different places all over the island. We must not forget the jewel of the museum: the **Lady of Filakopí**★★ (1200 BC), a clay figurine possibly representing a female divinity, scarcely 20cm high, with astonishingly modern lines. She bears the name of the Neolithic site where she was discovered in 1977 *(see later)*.

### Around Pláka

■ To the south of Pláka, nestling behind the village of Tripití, are some **catacombs**★★, an astonishing labyrinth of tunnels and rooms hollowed out of the mountain 150m above sea level. A section of this network is open to the public *(8.30am-1pm; closed Monday; no entrance fee)*. 185m long, it contains three **rooms** linked by five **corridors**. Concealed from sight, the first Christians (2C AD) organised their ceremonies and buried their dead here, in tombs built into the walls or even in the tunnel floors.

■ Nearby, lower down, lie the ruins of the ancient city of **Klíma**★, destroyed in the 5C or 6C AD. You can still see a beautiful **Roman theatre**★★ there, its terraced steps facing the sea. Further west, a path climbs up to a **chapel**★, on a rocky escarpment overhanging the gulf.

■ 500m below the ruins, stop for a while and savour the colours of the attractive hamlet of **Klíma**★★★, where you can see a number of **sirmata**, the charming fishermen's huts so characteristic of Mílos, just like dolls' houses built along the water's edge.

■ To the north-west of Pláka, **Plathiená beach**★★ is one of the loveliest on the island. It has no facilities to offer, apart from the shade of its few trees and the fact that it faces due west, making it perfect for relaxing in the late afternoon (in calm weather).

## The north coast★★★

In this part of the island, geology and erosion have sculpted a very unusual landscape: there are rocky platforms gently shelving down to the sea, ideal for swimming, sentinel rocks and waterfalls, sheltered bays and tiny beaches, grottoes and marine caves hollowed out in the volcanic tufa. This northern coast offers a number of unusual places for bathing and whilst some have been developed, others remain unspoilt.

*From Pláka, take the road to Polónia to the east, then turn left to Triovássalos.*

■ Head towards the point of the peninsula enclosing the Bay of Mílos, to the north-west of Pláka, to get to **Firopótamos★**, a pretty harbour dotted with fishermen's huts alongside a sandy beach.

■ Further east, on the way to Triovássalos, stop off at the harbour of **Mantrákia★★**, where the locals have done up the traditional **sirmata** to house their caiques during the winter, and have a look at the **troglodytic dwellings**, modest caves hollowed out from the rock, in which they live during the summer.

■ Continuing along the north coast, you will soon reach the magnificent natural site of **Sarakinikó★★★**, an amazing lunar landscape of white pumice, carved by the wind into cones, domes and terraces, and lapped by a deep blue sea. Tucked away among the rocks are countless little places where you can take a dip (*if it is at all rough, be careful as you come back out of the sea, as the waves can throw you against the rocks*).

■ A bit further east, the picturesque Bay of **Mítakas★★** opens up, with its colourful **sirmata**. Further on, beyond the little church, lies the hamlet of **Ágios Konstandínos★**, its few houses nestling in a minuscule, rock-encircled bay. Pozzolana stacks are interspersed with solidified flows of lava, forming a rough, chaotic landscape marbled with greys and browns.

Out to sea, you can see the small **volcanic island of Glaroníssia★★** (*accessible during the boat trip around the island*), which has become a haven for seagulls. The **lava** has been sculpted into hexagonal pillars, like organ pipes dropping down into the sea.

Mílos, the "sirmata" (boat houses) of Mantrákia

J. Soury/MICHELIN

**Mílos**

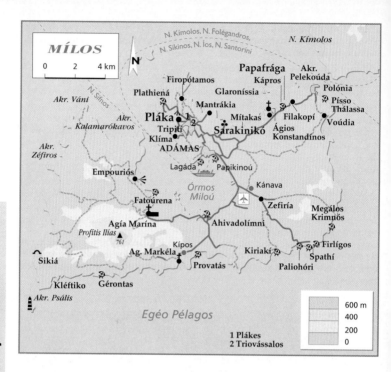

■ Further on are two more beautiful beaches before you come to the village of **Kápros\*** which heralds the spectacular bay of **Papafrága\*\*\***, a narrow rocky inlet guarded by a stone **arch**, with its turquoise waters enclosed by walls of lava riddled with caves.

■ The coastal road then leads on to **Filakopí**, a bay where traces of Neolithic Mílos lie partly submerged. Consisting of a group of small settlements, the island's first capital flourished as long ago as the middle of the 3rd millennium BC. It bears witness to an already highly developed organisation evident in the structure of the settlements, as well as in advanced systems of agriculture, animal husbandry and trade. It prospered for 3 500 years, before being destroyed by the Dorians and abandoned in the 11C BC. Excavations, begun over a hundred years ago, are still in progress, and unfortunately the site is not open to the public.

■ Further on, you come to **Polónia\*\***, a look-out point situated on the north-east tip of the island, watching over the narrow strait which separates it from the island of Kímolos. This old fishing village has developed into an attractive seaside resort. Popular with Greek holidaymakers, it is now the second most visited summer resort on the island, and rooms to let, hotels and various other buildings are springing up like mushrooms. In spite of all this, the atmosphere remains tranquil, cradled by the sea breeze which blows more strongly here than elsewhere and is very welcome in summer. To the left of the harbour is a pleasant **beach**, relatively sheltered and shaded by tamarisks.

Go round the bay as far as the **chapel** which faces Kímolos. Further on, you come to the hamlet of **Pelekoúda**, where the north wind blows straight onto the rocks and the few, rather squat, buildings which can withstand it.

■ To the east of Polónia, the coast has yet more **sandy beaches**, including **Písso Thálassa**. Finally, further south, along from the industrial zone which processes the mineral deposits, is the bay of **Voúdia**, with a beach of pale sand, a good place to unwind.

## The beaches of the south**

From Adámas, before you get to the salt-pans which flank the airport, turn left towards the fertile plain which lies around **Zefiría**, a small town which prospered from the end of the Middle Ages up to the 19C, thanks to the presence of pirates, who made it their base. From here, carry on down to the south coast, which is well sheltered from the westerly winds; as this part of the island has few roads, the beaches are very quiet.

To the south-east, you can choose between the wide bays at **Paliohóri** or **Kiriakí**, or else the sandy beach at **Provatás**.

A bit further west, just before the **Agía Markéla Chapel**, a road goes down towards another rarely visited sand and pebble beach with limpid water.

Even further west, the beach of **Gérontas\*** lies tucked away, only accessible by boat. The only way to get there is to take a **tour of the island\*\*** (*starts out from Adámas; see "Excursions" section, page 289*), which will give you a chance to see the superb scenery of the south-west point, including the **marine grotto of Sikiá\*\*** and the majestic **white cliffs of Kléftiko\*\***, unusual sugar-loaf mounds riddled with caves, nicknamed "marine meteors" by the locals.

To the east of the (popular) **Spathí** beach (*at the end of the Bay of Paliohóri*), you can get to the lesser known beaches of **Firlígos** and **Megálos Krimnos** on foot. There are other, even more isolated beaches along the east coast, but access by land is difficult.

The east of the island is lined with quarries which have eaten into the rocky landscape, revealing a myriad colours. The **sulphur mines** still have a few pieces of equipment dating from the 19C. Today, however, the quarries are worked by convoys of trucks and bulldozers of Cyclopean proportions.

## Making the most of Mílos

### COMING AND GOING

**By boat** – Several ferries per day to Piraeus, either direct or via Kíthnos, Sérifos, Sífnos. 2 ferries per week to Santoríni, Folégandros and Páros. 3 per week to Crete.
**Harbourmaster's office**, ☎ (0287) 22 100, on the central quay in Adámas harbour.

**By air** – The airport is 4km south of Adámas. You have to take a taxi to get there (taxi rank in the central square in Adámas). **Olympic Airways**, in Adámas, 25 Martíou 11, ☎ (0287) 22 380. At least one flight per day to Athens.

### GETTING AROUND

**By bus** – Adámas-Tripití-Pláka (every hour), Adámas-Polónia (4 daily), Adá-mas-Paliohóri (3 daily), Adámas-Provatás (2 daily). Bus stop on the central square in Adámas.

**By rental car** – Scooter and car hire offices are nearly all concentrated in Adámas, mainly on the quayside.

### ADDRESS BOOK (ADÁMAS)

**Tourist information** – *Municipal tourist information office*, opposite the ferry dock. Several travel agencies on the quays: *Vichos Tours*, *Mílos Travel*, *Terry's Travel*, etc.

**Bank / Currency exchange** – You will find numerous banks along the east quay and in the town centre.

**Post office / Telephone** – *Main post office*, on the quays.

**Medical service – *Medical emergency service*** in Adámas, ☎ (0287) 21 755. To the west of the harbour, before Lagáda beach, are the medicinal baths (thermal springs), chlorine and sodium based, with various curative properties.

## WHERE TO STAY

### • Adámas

The town has numerous hotels and rooms to let, situated in the centre, behind the harbour, but they are fairly noisy. Here is a selection of the quietest locations:

*Around €27*

🦐*Delfini*, 200m west of the landing-stage, at the start of Lagáda beach, set back 50m, ☎ 0287) 22 001, Fax (0287) 22 688 – 24rm. ⁜¶ � John and Katherina, a very friendly retired couple, take care in the running of this hotel, which is well situated near the beach, quiet, and not expensive. The rooms are clean, and a (generous) breakfast is served on the terrace.

***Hotel Seminaris***, ☎ (0287) 22 117 / 22 118, Fax (0287) 22 118 – 15rm and 7 studios. ⁜¶ 🖉 🚞 One of the only hotels with a quiet location in the town centre, with a small terrace reached through a tunnel. Clean rooms and well-equipped studios (situated in an annexe). The manager is a good source of advice. Book in advance.

*Between €27 and €38*

***Lagáda Beach Hotel***, just behind Lagáda beach, west of the harbour, ☎ (0287) 42 27 192, Fax (0301) 41 3136 – 100rm. ⁜¶ 🖉 ✗ 🚞 🏊 🦤 A large complex with a garden, quiet and well situated a short distance from the harbour. Price includes breakfast.

*Over €60*

***Hotel Capetan Georgantas***, in the central street running from the quay, on the right, ☎ (0287) 23 215 to 23 218, Fax (0287) 23 219 – 20rm. ⁜¶ 🖉 🖽 ✗ 🖳 🚞 🏊 🦤 A beautiful pool, all modern comforts and services, and a good location, in the town centre, 300m from the beach. Reductions for children.

### • Klíma

*Over €38*

🦐*Panorama*, 100m above the little harbour, ☎ (0287) 21 623, Fax (0287) 22 112 – 8rm. ⁜¶ 🖉 🖽 ✗ 🚞 Comfortable rooms with balcony, enjoying a wonderful view over the village. Very attractive terrace.

### • Polónia

*Over €38*

🦐*Apollon*, on the north-east point, in the residential quarter of Polónia, ☎ (0287) 41 347, Fax (0287) 41 240 – 11rm. ⁜¶ 🖉 🖽 🖳 ✗ 🚞 🆑 Very clean and comfortable rooms and studios, well ventilated, with a family atmosphere and a particularly good setting, offering a view of the small island of Kímolos. Rather expensive, because the hotel is very popular in summer. Booking recommended.

### • Ahivadolímni

*Campsite (around €12)*

🦐 *Mílos campsite*, 7km from Adámas, 3km after the airport, ☎ (0287) 31 410, Fax (0287) 31 412 – 80 pitches. ⁜¶ ✗ 🚞 🏊 🦤 🆑 Clean, quiet and spacious, this campsite has lots of shade and about thirty well-equipped chalets. Direct access to the vast Ahivadolímni beach down below, and its sheltered bay, ideal for swimming or water sports. A wide range of facilities: laundry, mini-market, bicycle hire, transfers to and from the harbour, etc.

## EATING OUT

### • Adámas

***Bakery***, level with the crossroads. Very good range on offer, with various kinds of bread, cakes, snacks and local specialities.

*Around €9*

🦐*Astakós*, to the west, at the end of Lagáda beach. 🚞 🆑 A restaurant offering very good value, with lively and friendly service. Meals are served on the spacious terrace, in a beautiful setting, on the beach and yet quiet. The menu, which changes, has various dishes (generous portions), meals for 2 people, fish and shellfish (crayfish).

*Around €9*

**Flísvos**, on the central quayside, to the east of the landing-stage, ☎ (0287) 22 275. 🍴 A large restaurant-ouzo bar, with an extensive menu and quick service. A good choice for an evening meal, with the benefit of the terrace and the view of the boats. Numerous other ouzo bars along the quayside.

**Trapatsélis**, 50m east of the quays (on the road to the airport), at the start of Papikinoú beach, ☎ (0287) 22 010. 🍴 Fresh fish depending on the catch. Reliable.

● **Pláka**

Most of the restaurants in the village are of a good quality, but not usually very cheap.

*Between €9 and €15*

**Archondoúla**, in the main alleyway of the upper village, ☎ (0287) 21 384. 🍴 Pleasant setting. Cold appetizers. A bit expensive.

● **Triovássalos**

*Around €9*

**Ritsos**, on the road to Pláka, as you come in to Triovássalos, on the left. 🍴 An ouzo bar where the old folk gather to relax quietly in the evenings. Simple, cool and not expensive: an ideal spot to have a drink, a few meze, or the dish of the day. It's a pity that the terrace, alongside the main road, is rather noisy.

● **Tripití**

*Between €9 and €15*

🐟 **Methisméni Politía**, on the left as you come back up from the catacombs, ☎ (0287) 23 100. 🍴 Probably the best restaurant on the island! Meals are served on the terrace, which is large, secluded, and has the benefit of a very attractive setting, away from the village. The menu offers various dishes of the day, specialities of the island and quite an assortment of original salads. Sample one of the specialities: shrimp souvláki, pasta with clams, octopus in red sauce, not forgetting the cheeses and wines. Excellent value for money.

● **Klíma**

**Panórama**, 100m higher up from the little harbour (see "Where to stay"), ☎ (0287) 21 623. 🍴 The cuisine is always good and the setting is lovely, with fine views over Klíma and the sea. Very peaceful.

● **Polónia**

🐟 **Apanemía**, on the right as you come into town on the main road, ☎ (0287) 41 248. 🍴 Quiet taverna with terrace. Fresh fish depending on catch. Limited menu, but food is simple and tasty.

● **Mantrákia**

*Around €9*

**Médousa**, ☎ (0287) 23 670. 🍴 The only taverna in Mantrákia, serves fresh and tasty dishes. Only open at midday.

**HAVING A DRINK**

● **Tripití**

**Konaki**, ☎ (0287) 23 451, a café-bar with a beautiful view. Attractive location.

● **Pláka**

**Utopia**, in the centre of the village, ☎ (0287) 23 678. Very beautiful surroundings, especially so at sunset. Good easy-listening music which you can enjoy as you sink back into the comfortable armchairs sipping your cocktail or one of their many milkshakes.

● **Adámas**

**Fuego**, on Lagáda beach, next to the Astakas restaurant, ☎ 0944 392049. A rather trendy night-club.

**OTHER THINGS TO DO**

**Excursions –** From Polónia, 4 boats daily to **Kímolos**.

And remember to go on the superb boat trip around the island (1 day): there are 3 boats in Adámas harbour. Departure 9am, with many stops on the beaches, off the cliffs and the marine grottoes. A late lunch on Kímolos.

# NÁXOS★★

Aegean Sea – Capital of the Cyclades – Michelin map 980 folds 32-44
Regional map on the inside back cover – 428km²
Pop 14 840 – Allow 3-4 days

**Not to be missed**
Hóra and its medieval kástro, one of the best preserved in the Cyclades.
A stroll through the streets of the village of Apíranthos.
The Panagía Drossianí Monastery and the region of Tragéa.

**And remember...**
If you do not have much time, concentrate on the east of the island.
The condition of the roads is not always good, so take care,
especially on motorcycles.

The largest island of the Cyclades has long been appreciated for its endless sandy beaches and the exceptionally well-preserved medieval citadel which overlooks Hóra. However, many of the island's treasures remain to be discovered, such as the marble city of Apíranthos and dozens of Byzantine monasteries and fortified residences erected long ago by the occupying Venetians and the wealthy inhabitants of Náxos. When these monuments are opened to visitors, Náxos will doubtless become established as one of the jewels of tourism in the Aegean.

## A green island in the heart of the Cyclades

Numerous **springs** have made Náxos a fertile island, entrusted by the Ancients to the protection of Demeter, the goddess of the earth, and of Dionysus, who instructed the inhabitants in the art of viticulture. To judge by the **vines** which flourish on the terraced hillsides, and the sweet-smelling pastures of Tragéa in the centre, this is a tradition to which the islanders remain faithful.

Because of its size, agricultural richness, and central situation, Náxos has played a major role in the Aegean region since ancient times. The island's golden age was around 3200-2200 BC, a bountiful period marked by the substantial production of

Náxos: on the islet of Palátia, the high door of the Temple of Apollo

L. Hapsis/ON LOCATION

The Cyclades

290

vases, tools and **idols** (*see page 218*); works of art sculpted from the white marble of the mountains and polished with emery, two materials which the islanders have exploited for centuries. The economic power of the island permitted Náxos to extend its influence over the neighbouring islands and to found the first Greek settlement on Sicily. Furthermore, when the Franks became a power in the Aegean, in the early 13C, Náxos was where the Duke of the Archipelago, **Marco Sanudo**, chose to establish his base. Finally, after four centuries of

**The Venetian Duchy of Náxos**

After the fall of Constantinople (1453), the Greek lands were shared out among the crusaders. While the Franks took over the mainland, the Genoese and Venetians became the established rulers in the islands. But Náxos had been Venetian since 1204, when Marco Sanudo made it the capital of the islands in his duchy. He had the fortress built at Hóra, with the intention of making this a place where his family and Catholic compatriots could live, leaving the Bourgos quarter for the Orthodox Greeks, and Evraïkí (further east), for the Jews. He divided land up among his vassal noblemen, which they continued to exploit for centuries, even after the Turks invaded the island in 1537. As symbols of their power, these lords built fortified towers, emblazoned with their emblem, capable of withstanding raids from Arab pirates. Some of these constructions still house the descendants of these first colonists – still some 200 in number.

Turkish rule (16C-19C), when the island was reunited with liberated Greece, it became the administrative centre of the Cyclades.

## Hóra★★★ (Náxos Town)
*Allow 1 day to visit the citadel, the Temple of Apollo and two museums*

The three main stages of the history of Náxos can be seen immediately on arrival in the harbour of Hóra, its capital: the door of the Temple of Apollo recalls the splendours of Ancient Greece, the Venetian citadel which dominates the town evokes the Middle Ages, with an abrupt return to modern times with the busy harbour. To the right of this stretch the **beaches of Ágios Geórgios**, **Ágios Prokópios** and **Agía Ánna**, long ribbons of fine sand lined with hotels, some more attractive than others. Begin the tour of the town with the **Mitrópolis Museum** (*8am-2.30pm; closed Monday; no entrance fee*), which is in the cathedral square, situated between the landing-stage and the Grotta district. Opened in 1999, it preserves the remnants of this ancient town's strange history: it prospered between the 13C-11C BC, then was transformed into a **cemetery for dignitaries** before being brought back to life when numerous Roman villas were built.

As you head back to the harbour, cross the narrow strip of land which leads to the **islet of Palátia** where the **door of the Temple of Apollo★** (Portara) stands, an Archaic sanctuary dedicated to Apollo of Delos. Commissioned to be built in the 6C BC, it was never completed, leaving this strange, wind-swept, stone structure (beautiful **view★** down over the kástro).

## The kástro★★★
*In the harbour, head off up the alleyway to the right of the Old Captain's café.* With its maze of medieval vaulted lanes and the sombre residences of the Venetian nobles which take the place of town walls, the unspoilt old town of Náxos can pride itself on being one of the most beautiful medieval places in the Cyclades.

Continuing up past the **vaulted passageways** of the old market, you come out at the top of the hill, on the square where the **Roman Catholic Cathedral** stands (*only open during Mass, 5pm-6.20pm during the week, 9.30am on Sunday*), behind which, hidden away, is a very beautiful **Archaeological Museum★★** (*8am-2.30pm, except Monday; entrance fee*). This is housed in a 17C former Jesuit school where **Níkos Kazantzákis** studied. The first room is mostly given over to a collection of objects dating from the 3rd millennium BC during the Mycenaean Period, some **Cycladic**

**idols★** discovered on Náxos and the neighbouring islands, some **zoomorphic pottery★** (hedgehog, birds, pigs, etc) and a collection of **Mycenaean pottery** combining geometrical figures with vegetable or animal motifs.

On leaving the museum, take a stroll through the **Venetian alleyways** of the citadel accompanied by the gentle strains of Vivaldi coming from the antique shops.

## To the east of Hóra: the Tragéa region★★

*Leave Náxos in the direction of the airport. 50km circuit. Allow one day. This is the best tour if you only have one day available to spend on the island. Depending on your mood, take either your swimsuit or some good walking shoes.*

### The mining of emery

Where does it come from, this abrasive powder with its crystalline reflections which can sand walls, saucepans and other everyday utensils? Emery is a rock made up of corundum, an extremely hard crystalline stone which can be used to make jewellery, depending on its colour. Occurring in the mountains around Apíranthos and Kóronos, Náxos' deposits of emery were widely exploited for industrial purposes during the 19C. Mule caravans were soon to be replaced by a cableway, which brought the mineral down from the hills for many years. The discovery of artificial corundum, however, put paid to the mining industry on Náxos. The cableway still remains, stationary nowadays, with its rusty skeleton of pylons and cables.

To the east, the region of Tragéa reveals a landscape of contrasts, green plains alternating with rocky mountains. In the Middle Ages, the local inhabitants would retreat to this region to escape from pirates. They built a great number of churches and monasteries, which earned the island the nickname of "little Mistra", after the church-studded hilltop town which was the last provincial capital of Byzantium. Then, during the 16C and 17C, the hills bristled with **"towers"**, the fortified dwellings of the Venetian nobles and rich Greeks who shared these lands... not always willingly.

■ **Halkí** – Past the village of **Áno Potamiá**, with its tumbledown buildings beneath the fruit trees, is the island's former capital (up to the Second World War). Built between the 10C-12C, the **Panagía Protothrónos Church** has some interesting **frescoes** (if the door is shut, ask at the café opposite and they will get the priest to open it up for you). The **Barozzi Tower★** (17C) which stands behind it is impressive for its size and its **marble door** emblazoned with an emblem.

■ A little further on, in **Akádimi**, stands the 18C **Papadákis Tower**. On your way in to **Kerámi** take the road to the right, in front of the taverna. Fifty metres further on, the Byzantine church of **Agioi Apostoli** *(usually closed)*, is hidden away, a sombre piece of architecture lost amid the olive trees.

■ **Filóti**, marks the beginning of the mountains. On the right, as you leave the village, is a track which climbs the slopes of **Mt Zeus**, the highest peak in the Cyclades (1 004m). In takes less than an hour to walk to **Zeus' Grotto**, an ancient sanctuary dedicated to Zeus, who, legend has it, was born there. During the period of Turkish rule, the cave was used by Christians as a refuge.

■ **Apíranthos★★★** – Dominated by two towers with the sculpted emblem of the Venetian lion, Apíranthos is unquestionably the most beautiful town on Náxos. Despite the increasing numbers of tourist boutiques, you will be captivated by the peaceful charm of this little marble town, founded by refugees from Crete. Take a walk through the little streets, covered alleyways and small shady squares.

The town has several museums *(one ticket gives admission to three of them, but they are of limited interest: the Natural History Museum, the Geology Museum and the Museum of Folklore, to the right of the central square)*. Devote more time to the **Archaeology Museum** *(8.30am-2.30pm; no entrance fee; if the door is shut, ask for the curator in the* neighbouring *café*) where the objects excavated on Náxos are on display in one room, among them a **tripod** from the Geometric Period, some **Cycladic idols**, and, above all, some **engraved marble plaques★** from the 3rd millennium BC. Unique in Greece, these pieces represent familiar scenes: hunting, dancing, sailing boats, etc. As you leave, treat yourself to a swim by going to **Mountsoúna** (*12km further east*), the old port from which the island's emery was exported.

■ If you are a good walker and can stand the heat, you could hike to the austere **Church of Agía Kiráki★★** (*allow 4hr on a fairly easy 5km path, which starts out to the right as you leave the village heading east; ask for the key in the Archaeology Museum in Apíranthos*). Its 9C **frescoes★** are beautiful examples of iconoclastic art.

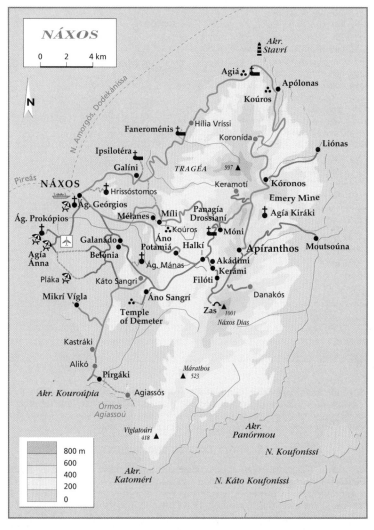

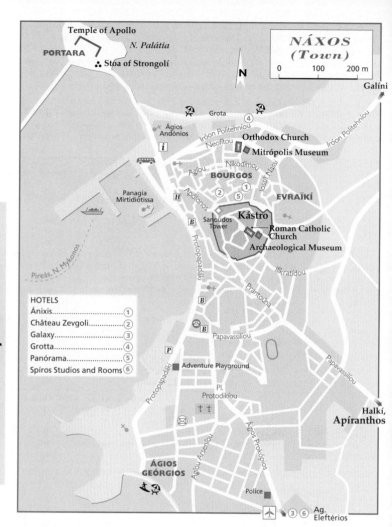

Temple of Apollo
N. Palátia
PORTARA
Stóa of Strongolí
N
Galíni

**NÁXOS (Town)**
0    100    200 m

Grota
Ágios Andónios
Iróon Politehníou
Neofítou
Iróon Politehníou

Orthodox Church
Mitrópolis Museum

Agíou
Nikodímou
Iosíf Níassi
BOURGOS

Panagía Mirtidiótissa
Apóllonos
EVRAÏKÍ

Kástro
Sanoudos Tower
Roman Catholic Church
Archaeological Museum

Pireás, N. Mykonos

Protopapadáki
Ifíkratídou

Prantoúna

Papavassílou

HOTELS
Ánixis........................①
Château Zevgoli..............②
Galaxy.........................③
Grotta..........................④
Panórama.....................⑤
Spíros Studios and Rooms ⑥

Protopapadáki

Adventure Playground

Pl. Protodikíou

Halkí, Apíranthos

Ágios Arseníou
Ágios Prokópios

ÁGIOS GEÓRGIOS

Police

Ag. Eleftérios

*Rejoin the main road and retrace your steps back to Halkí. From here, if you are only spending one day on the island, you can make your way back north to Hóra, stopping off on the way to visit the Panagía Drossianí Monastery and the Míli kouros (see below). For visitors with more time, complete your tour with a trip to the south.*

## A short trip to the south

Beyond the village of **Sangrí**, which is dominated by a Frankish castle, and the **Ágios Eleftérios Monastery**, one of the oldest on the island (*both closed*), follow the signs to the **Temple of Demeter\***. Standing on a small rocky outcrop in the middle of the fields, this sober (much restored) Doric structure was the place of worship of a cult comparable to that of Eleusis.

*On your return to Sangrí, take the road to the left which rejoins the main road running north-south.* Even at the end of the day, it is worth taking advantage of the beaches which stretch endlessly from **Mikrí Vígla** to **Pirgáki**. Far from the crowds, you can swim in peace, in unspoilt surroundings where cedars, myrtle and heather grow. On the way back, make one last stop at **Galanádo** to visit the **Tower of Belónia**, the best preserved on Náxos, and the **Ágios Ioánnis Church** with its two separate chapels, one Roman Catholic, one Greek Orthodox.

*Leave Hóra in the direction of Grotta and follow the coast road before heading into the mountains.*

## The north of Náxos★
From Hóra to Apólonas
*Allow one day for this tour, 80km there and back.*
*Take your swimsuit so that you can have a swim in a little bay or in Apólonas, where you stop for lunch.*

■ The first section of the tour takes you to **Galíni** (*turn right along the road which eventually becomes a track, then 2km further on, turn left at the sign which says "private"*). At the end of the path, austere and majestic, stands the **fortified monastery of Ipsilotéra★** (*not open to visitors*). Built in the 17C by the rich Greek, Iákobos Kokkós, this building, dedicated to the Holy Virgin, was fortified when the Kokkós family came into conflict with the Venetians. The rebelling peasants took refuge there, arming its walls with loopholes, machicolations and crenelles, making it into the strongest fortress on the island.

■ *Rejoin the main road and continue east for 6km.* On your left, the **Monastery of Faneroménis★** (17C) stands overlooking the sea. Linger a while to fully appreciate this isolated fortress before you go into the chapel (iconostasis).

■ About 12km further on, on the left, you get a view of the ruins of the **Tower of Agiá**, which overlooks the whole north-west coast. On the other side of the road, the white **monastery of Agiá** stands out starkly against its green background.

■ Finally, before returning to the coastal town of **Apólonas**, go up to the right of the main road as far as the quarry of the **Archaic kouros★** (*unrestricted access*), a colossal figure, 10m long, which lies among the blocks of stone from which it was sculpted. Rejected due to faulty workmanship, it has lain abandoned since the 6C BC. You can also have lunch there. You can have a swim as well, if you continue on to **Kóronos**, where there is a road on the left leading down to **Liónas beach**.

*On rejoining the main road, continue south through the beautiful mountainous countryside.*

■ 2km beyond **Moní**, make sure you do not miss the delightful **Panagía Drossianí Monastery★★**, sheltered among the olive trees, on a bend in the road (*to the left of the road; badly signposted. 10am-1pm / 4pm-7pm*). Built in the 9C and 10C, the stunningly simple church contains some very ancient **frescoes★**, some dating from the 7C: most notably, on the left, a very appealing Virgin Mary, holding the portrait of her son in her hands.

*Retrace your steps to Moní and take the road to Hóra, to the left.*

■ Beyond the **quarries** – still in operation – which provided the white marble for the island's temples and some of the major works of art of Greek Antiquity, you reach **Míli**, where the second unfinished statue on Náxos lies, the **kouros of Flério** or **Mélanes★** (*follow the arrows; free admission, through a private garden; there is a café hidden among the trees*). Sculpted in the 6C BC, the stone figure of a young man strives to take a step... in vain.

**The Cyclades**

## COMING AND GOING

**By boat** – Náxos is a 6hr journey from Athens by ferry. At least two ferries a day provide a connection to Piraeus via the islands in between. One of these goes to Mýkonos, Síros, Tínos, Páros, Íos and Sífnos. Several connections a week to Amorgós, the Lesser Cyclades, Santoríni and Herakleion. A good network of hydrofoils to Piraeus or Rafína (1 daily), Páros, Sífnos, Síros, Tínos and Amorgós.

**By air** – The only flights into the island's airport are with **Olympic Airways** from Athens. For transfers to Hóra, either take the bus, or a taxi from the rank opposite the entrance.

## GETTING AROUND

**By bus** – Numerous buses travel around the island. The **KTEL bus station** is at the harbour, opposite the landing-stage. ☎ (0285) 22 291.

**By taxi** – Taxi rank at the harbour, opposite the landing-stage, ☎ (0285) 22 444.

**By rental car** – Various rental agencies at the harbour. As the roads on Náxos are not always in a good state of repair, a car is preferable to any two-wheeled vehicle. Good network of fuel stations.

## ADDRESS BOOK

**Tourist information** – At the harbour you will find several travel agencies, including **Náxos Tourist Information**, just on the right of the landing-stage, ☎ (0285) 25 201 and, in case of emergencies: 24 525 – [cc] 8.30am-12 midnight. You can make reservations for hotels, vehicle hire, excursions and plane tickets. They also provide a fax service, left-luggage, and message boards.

**Post office / Telephone** – At the end of the jetty, along the play area just to the left.

**OTE** (telephone), at the end of the harbour, to the right of the landing-stage.

**Internet** – The **Café Náxos Computer** is inside a vehicle rental office, in Platía Protodikíou. 9am-11.30pm.

**Bank / Currency exchange** – Most establishments are in the harbour area and have cash dispensers.

**Police** – In Odós Ágios Prokópios, ☎ (0285) 22 100 (from Odós Papavas-

silíou, take the second turning on the right, about 200m further on).

**Medical service** – There is a **health centre**, but it does not have a very good reputation (from the harbour take Odós Papavassilíou; the centre is 500m further back), ☎ (0285) 23 333). There are two pharmacies on the jetty.

**Dry cleaning – Holiday Laundry**, behind the bus station, ☎ (0285) 23 988. 9am-2pm and 6pm-8pm, Sunday 10am-2pm.

## WHERE TO STAY

### • Hóra

*Between €23 and €38*

**Ánixis**, in the old town, north of the kástro, ☎ (0285) 22 932, Fax (0285) 22 112. ✱⬆ An attractive small hotel which opens onto a terraced garden. Nearly all the rooms have a bathroom and a balcony.

*Between €45 and €55*

**Grotta**, 700m from the harbour, in the continuation of Odós Iróon Politehníou, to the north of town, ☎ (0285) 22 215, Fax (0285) 22 000, grotta@naxos-island.com – 10rm. ✱⬆ 𝒫 ⌘ [cc] Very welcoming, with pleasant rooms, each with a fridge. The rooms facing the sea have an unrestricted view over Portara and the kástro.

**Panorama**, at the lower end of the kástro (follow the arrows in the old town), ☎ and Fax (0285) 24 404 / 22 330. ✱⬆ ⤬ ✗ Fridge in every room. A simple hotel, but clean and comfortable.

*Around €75*

⌂**Château Zevgoli**, at the lower end of the kástro, in the old town (follow the arrows), ☎ (0285) 22 993 / 26 123 / 26 131, mobile 094 306099, Fax (0285) 25 200 – 10rm. ✱⬆ 𝒫 ⤬ [tv] [cc] A charming hotel with a patio. Every room is different: canopied bed in no 8, romantic balcony in no 12 and harbour view in no 10. Open all year. Booking essential.

### • Ágios Geórgios

*Between €30 and €60*

**Spiros Studios and Rooms**, 10min walk from the harbour, ☎ (0285) 24 854, Fax (0285) 25 003 – 21rm and 14 studios. 𝒫 ✱⬆ ⌘ ⌘ A modern, quiet and comfortable establishment. Well equipped kitchens in the studios.

*Between €60 and €90*
**Galaxy**, near Ágios Geórgios beach, ☎ (0285) 22 422 / 423, Fax (0285) 22889 – 54rm / studios. A modern bungalow complex which is a tasteful reproduction of Cycladic style: vaulted exterior passageways, marble floors, and exposed beams.

• **Mikrí Vígla**
*Between €45 and €75*
**Mikrí Vígla Hotel**, on the west coast, ☎ (0285) 75 241 / 42 / 43, Fax (0285) 75 240 – 86rm. A complex of comfortable bungalows, with sports equipment provided, for children and adults: volleyball, waterskiing, surfing club.

EATING OUT
• **Hóra, around the harbour**
**Al Metro**, a popular bakery to the right of the "Zoom" bookshop, in a shopping gallery.
*Around €7.50*
**Rendévou**, to the right of the National Bank, the best breakfasts in town and excellent pastries.
**Meltémi**, at the end of the harbour, on the right, a long-established restaurant serving traditional Greek cuisine. Seafront terrace and large dining room.
**O Apostólis**, at the harbour, a good restaurant for fresh fish and grilled octopus.
**Kellári**, to the right of O Apostólis. Moussaká and "pastíccios" served in addition to good oven-cooked pizzas and the restaurant's own fresh pasta.

• **In the old town**
*Between €7.50 and €11*
**Mezopoleíon Melodia**, under the arcades, in the lower part of the kástro, a typical ouzo bar. Good menu for meze, octopus and Náxos potatoes.

• **Agía Ánna**
*Around €18*
**Gorgóna**, a large family-run cafeteria, very popular with locals.

• **Mélanes**
*Around €7.50*
**O Giórghis**, ☎ (0285) 62 180, a taverna with a terrace overlooking a valley. Specialities chicken and rabbit.

• **Apíranthos**
*Around €13*
**Leftéris**, ☎ (0285) 61 333, in the main street. One of the best places to eat on Náxos, with homemade tarama, creamy desserts and attentive service.

• **Áno Potamiá**
*Around €7.50*
**I Pigí**, on the road into the village, a taverna with a garden shaded by lemon trees, hibiscus and jasmine. Generous servings of meze including a melted "mintzíthra" (soft white goat cheese); local white wine and a friendly welcome.

HAVING A DRINK
• **Hóra**
**Ellis bar**, in the street to the left of the Náxos tourist information office. Rembétiko concerts.
**Bar Veggéra**, at the southern end of the harbour. On Saturdays, disco with DJ from 8.30pm.

OTHER THINGS TO DO
**Outdoor pursuits – Flisvos Sport Club**, (surfing), on Ágios Geórgios beach, ☎ (0285) 24 308. Also hires out mountain bikes. **Maragas water sports**, on Plaka beach, ☎ 0945 722404.

**Excursions –** In Hóra, there are many organised bus tours, and, departing Agía Ánna, daily boat trips around the island aboard the **Nectarius**.

**English newspapers – Zoom bookshop**, in Hóra, to the right of the harbour.

**Feasts & Festivals –** 14 July, in Hóra, feast of St Nicodemus, patron saint of the town. The first week in August: **Dionisía**, festival in honour of the god of wine, with concerts and free meals in the main square in Hóra.
15 August, celebrations for the Assumption in Sangrí, Apíranthos and especially in Filóti.

SHOPPING GUIDE
**Local delicacies –** Náxos is famed for its liqueurs made from lemons or *kitro* (Vallindras distilleries in Hóra and Halkí), its wines and its cheeses. These local products can be bought from **Tirokomiká proïónda**, in Hóra, Odós Papavassilíou, ☎ (0285) 22 230 / 22 096.

**Embroidery –** A traditional craft still practised in Moní and Apíranthos.

# PÁROS★★

Central Aegean – District of the Cyclades
Michelin map 980 folds 32-44 – Regional map on the inside back cover
196km$^2$ – Pop 10 410 – Allow 3 days (including Andíparos)

### Not to be missed

A walk around Parikía, Náoussa and Léfkes followed by a simple meal of fish and octopus.
A visit to Panagía Ekatondapilianí (in Parikía),
the Longovárdas Monastery and the caves on Andíparos.

### And remember...

If the hotels on Páros are full, stay on Andíparos: the island is cheaper, there is a frequent ferry service, and there are just as many beautiful beaches.

Geared up to tourists, but retaining its Greek character, popular for its beaches, but also rich in natural attractions and historic curiosities, Páros is an eclectic destination where everyone can find something to suit them. Hence the island's popularity with foreign tourists, as well as with Greeks from the mainland, who visit the island in large numbers during the summer. But Páros is a very large island, where you can still find places to swim and walk in peace, and it accommodates the seasonal influx with a certain nonchalance, leaving its capital, Parikía, to suffer from the upheaval. As further proof that the island can still inspire contemplation: if you go off to explore the hills that look down over the coastline, you will find the largest number of active monasteries in existence in the Aegean.

## Wine and marble

Water in sufficient quantities, good land for the cultivation of grain, and hillsides ideally suited for ripening the grapes to make a fruity wine: the inhabitants of Páros have never lacked anything. But nature gave them a further resource by endowing the island with the finest **marble**. With these great blessings, Páros was to become, under the firm rule of its Dorian oligarchy, one of the great powers in the region from the 1st millennium BC onwards. Four centuries later, only Náxos could contest this supremacy, which had been partly acquired through the lucrative slave trade. Outdone by its rival, Páros was to get its revenge; at the Battle of Marathon, a trireme of its soldiers sided with the Persians against their fellow-countrymen. Then, at the Battle of Salamis, Páros remained prudently neutral. Finally, **Themistocles** forced the traitress back into the fold of Athens and the Delian League. Thereafter, the island earned its living from the riches of its soil, as well as from the activities of its pirates and the wealth of those born on the island, who went off to distant Constantinople to make their fortunes, the great **Mavrogénis** family being a good example.

## Parikía★★ (Hóra)
*Allow a good half-day*

At first sight, Parikía is a bit deceptive with its continuous succession of cafés, bars and tavernas packed together along a seafront which is not in the least picturesque. But, as soon as you leave this chaos behind and venture into the old town (*to the right of the quay*), the atmosphere changes radically, and a superb, typically Cycladic little town is revealed, especially in the early morning. Bougainvillaea, churches with blue domes, white houses and vaulted passageways: the winding alleyways here have got it all. Look out for the beautiful marble **fountains** (*in the main street*) and some **18C residences** with their façades embellished with marble.

Built in 1592, the **Panagía Septemvrianí Church** (*go up the alley next to the Commercial Bank*) is one of the oldest in the town, where most of the religious buildings are post-Byzantine. These can be found, amid some charming dwellings, by climbing up to the **Venetian kástro\***. Built in the 13C on the foundations of an ancient **Temple of Demeter**, it incorporates entire sections of the temple walls and many elements of its decor.

## A Byzantine stroll

Try not to miss out on the **Panagía Ekatondapilianí\*\*\***, one of the rare early Christian basilicas (rebuilt in the 10C) still to be seen in Greece. Its name means "a hundred doors", but you will only be able to count 99, tradition requiring the one hundredth to appear only when Constantinople is retaken. The church is also known by the name of **Panagía Katapolianí**: literally "towards the lower town". Preceded by a

### A promise kept

In the 4C, St Helen, the mother of the first Byzantine emperor – Constantine the Great (324-337) – set sail for Palestine in the hope of bringing the Holy Cross back to the shores of the Bosphorus, where her son had just established the Christian capital. But a storm forced the boat to drop anchor in the Bay of Parikía. When she reached land, the queen took refuge in a chapel and made a vow to erect a great basilica there when she had succeeded in her quest. Unfortunately, she died shortly after returning with the sacred relic in her possession. Two centuries later, it was Justinian who fulfilled her promise by building a majestic sanctuary. The discovery by archaeologists of remains belonging to a 4C church seems to give some credence to the legend.

white cloister with cells set into it, it has a curious perpendicular **narthex**, with the church itself being a combination of the basilical style and the Greek-cross formation, crowned by a high central dome. Inside, stone contrasts with the whiteness of the marble. The **iconostasis\*\***, raised up on four 6C columns (worshippers could see mass in the choir), is adorned with three remarkable 17C **icons\***. Behind this, a **synthronon** occupies the apse, a small amphitheatre constructed from stones from the ancient theatre. The prelates sat here, on the marble seats. Beneath the altar flows

In the white streets of Parikía

F. Guiziou/HEMISPHERES

Páros

299

the spring where St Teóktisti, the patron saint of the island, quenched her thirst, and a chapel is dedicated to her (on the left). Also on this side is the oldest part of the church, the **Ágios Nikólaos Chapel**, possibly 4C, with its Doric colonnade. In the right aisle, there is a **baptistry★★** from the 4C, one of the best preserved of its kind, its baptismal foundations in the form of a Greek cross. The **frescoes**, however, the oldest on the island, have suffered great damage.

The small adjacent **Byzantine Museum** (on the left as you come out, 9am-1pm and 5pm-9pm; entrance fee) has a display of 15C-18C icons and some religious artefacts. End your tour with a visit to the **Archaeological Museum★** (go left as you come out, further down to the right, 8.30am-2.30pm; closed Monday; entrance fee), where the discoveries made on the island have been gathered together, in particular a **callipygian goddess**, a small marble statue of an obese woman personifying fecundity. This exhibit dates back to the Neolithic Period which marked the earliest human life on the island (4th millennium BC). Surrounding it is a fan-shaped display of marble pieces illustrating the richness of works produced by Parian artists from Ancient times to the 5C. The museum also has a beautiful collection of pottery and figurines on display, as well as some inscriptions, including a fragment of the famous **Parian Chronicle**, a chronicle of Greek history from 1581 BC up to 265 BC, the year it was written (you will have to make a trip to the Ashmolean Museum in Oxford to read the rest).

The **ancient relics** of Parikía – which was first inhabited in the second half of the 3rd millennium BC – are of little interest. Parikía largely owes its survival to its **beaches★**, which can be reached on foot (and are therefore always popular with visitors, even at night). First, to the right of the landing-stage, is **Zoodóhou Pigís**, fringed with tamarisks, then **Delfíni** (about 1km further on as you head out of town), then the very lively **Parásporos** (1km further on; beach-bar), where you go to see and be seen. To the left of the landing-stage lie more beaches, first **Livádia**, then **Kriós★** in the next bay, which is the best of them all, with fine sand and crystal-clear water.

## Náoussa and the north

*From Parikía, take the Náoussa road; after 4km, a track leads up to the right towards the Longovárdas Monastery which is 2km further on.*

■ More of a fortress, the **Longovárdas Monastery★** is home to a community of several dozen monks (Open 9am-12noon; no women allowed inside – they have to make do with the superb panorama). Built in 1638 and restored in various stages, the buildings are laid out around a courtyard in the shade of a large cypress tree, with rows of cells and communal rooms, as well as **artists' studios** and a remarkable **library** (open to the public). Note the typically Cycladic façade of the **church★**, as well as its 17C **frescoes**.

■ **Náoussa★★** – A little further along the coast, this little harbour seems to have leapt straight off a picture post-card. Byzantine churches, a partly-submerged Venetian **kástro**, dazzlingly white lanes, it is all here. Not forgetting the fishing harbour where the colourful caiques bob about, and the lively tavernas and ouzo bars where the octopus catch is hung out to dry. This is a good opportunity to try some fresh fish or *octapódi*, grilled, marinated, or in a sauce. And if you come here on 6 July, you will be able to see the **wine and fish festival**, which attracts people from all over the region. On the night of 23 August, a hundred illuminated boats anchor in the bay while folk dancers perform on the quays to commemorate the heroic resistance that the inhabitants put up to the terrible raid in 1537 by the redoubtable Barbarossa (see page 170). A victim of its own popularity, Náoussa has recently undergone a wave of tourist development. The village has become the focal point for trendy bars, and there has been much building work, not all of it tasteful. Untouched by this upheaval, the **Venetian fortress★** (14C-15C), although in ruins, still dominates the far end of the harbour.

In the village is the large parish church, **Ágios Nikólaos Mostrátos**, which houses a small **Byzantine Museum** which has a wealth of icons. It is worth a look.

Not far away, a very new **Archaeological Museum** (*next to the post office*) houses relics which have been discovered in the area, particularly at **Koukounariés**, a Mycenaean and Archaic site located to the south-west of Náoussa.

## Beaches

■ To the east is **Kolibíthres**★★ with its numerous little sandy bays. With their rocks wrinkled like papier mâché, they are stunning to look at, and consequently very popular. All the more so because the neighbouring beaches have been taken over by the large seaside complex of **Porto Páros** and its hideous aqua-park.

■ Further into the **Bay of Ágios Ioánnis**, you come to **Monastíri beach**, where there is water-skiing, beach-volleyball, badminton, music, a bar and a restaurant. A little higher up, hollowed out of the rock, there is an **amphitheatre** which can seat 600 and is used for performances during the summer.

■ On the other side of the bay lies **Náoussa beach**★, attractive although rather busy, just like the beach at **Lángeri**★ (*accessible by caique from Náoussa*). The smaller neighbouring beach is a lot quieter (*by caique or by road, followed by a 10min walk*).

■ Beyond the gulf, the **Bay of Alikí** (*not to be confused with Alikí beach, on the south coast*), is much favoured by **windsurfers**. The most experienced head for the very windy beach of **Santa María**★★, to the south of the bay (*near the campsite*), leaving the smaller one to the north for those who just like to chill out.

■ But the atmosphere is much more relaxed at **Ambelás**★, a fishing harbour popular with local people who come for the fresh fish. From there, you can take a pleasant stroll along the coast, as far as the beach at **Filitzi** (*4km walk*).

## Towards Alikí and the south★
*As you leave Parikía, turn left off the main road*

■ As its name indicates, the **Hristoú Dássous Monastery** ("Christ's forest") is situated on a hill in the midst of the trees, and from here, you can see the whole coastline. This women-only convent contains the **tomb of St Arsénios** (feast days, 6 and 18 August), the patron saint of the island who died there in 1877. It is open to everyone (*cover arms and legs*), but only female visitors are allowed to visit the corridors and the cells.

The priest takes time out

■ Further on (*1km*) you come to the beginning of the **Valley of the Butterflies** (Petaloúdes) (*9am-8pm; entrance fee*), a lush valley with a delicious freshness emanating from it. The valley is filled with cypresses, planes, bay trees and carobs, as well as with fruit trees, and attracts millions of butterflies which come here to reproduce every summer. During the day, these nocturnal insects hide away in the vegetation without moving and it is forbidden to leave the paths, in order not to disturb them. From time to time, they react to sound, and will delight you with an aerial ballet, which can prove fatal to them if done too often.

G. de Benoist/MICHELIN

**Páros**

301

■ Back on the coast road again, you will soon come to **Agía Iríni beach\***, very exotic with its palm trees and tamarisks, then to the pretty **Voutákou beach\*** *(5km further south)*, a short distance from the little village of the same name.

■ The fishing village of **Alikí** is an ideal spot for a lunch break, followed by a swim at the very pleasant sandy **beach** which is next to the village *(accessible via a dirt track)*.

■ If this is crowded, continue on to **Fáranga beach\*\*** *(go back to the track and follow it for about 2km further south, signposted)*, where you will find just one cafeteria *(on the right)* and a few straw parasols set among tamarisks and arid hillocks.

■ The road goes through **Angeriá\***, a traditional, Cycladic-style village, relatively untouched by tourism. Then it continues on to the **Monastery of Ágii Theódori\* (view\*\*)**. From here, if you are on a motorcycle or in a four-wheel-drive vehicle, the track which climbs up towards the centre of the island *(and meets up with an asphalt road after 4km)* has views over some of the most beautiful scenery on Páros.

## The centre of the island and the east coast**
*From Parikía, head towards Maráthi and Léfkes*

■ After Maráthi, another traditional village, a track that is suitable for motor vehicles *(to the right of the main road)* follows a valley which leads to the famous **marble quarries\*** (Latomía Marmárou), which have been worked since Antiquity *(the approach to it is marked by abandoned buildings; leave your car by the chapel and continue on foot for 100m before climbing over the low wall on the left; then follow the path which leads to the site)*. You come to three quarries, where you can visit the **tunnels** *(slippery in places)*. Quite steep, they penetrate a long way into the earth in places, as the whitest marble is extracted from deep down. A sculpted bas-relief stands at the entrance to the **Nymphs' Grotto** *(entrance forbidden)*, a work of art from the 3C BC which depicts gods and mythological heroes. The second entrance has been called the **Entrance of the French** ever since a Franco-Belgian team came and took some marble for Napoleon's tomb.

■ The road then takes you on to the **Monastery of Ágios Minás**, an impressive 17C fortified building. Then comes **Kóstos**, a charming village with old houses, churches and a small shady square.

■ **Léfkes\*\*** — Clinging to the side of a hill, amid pines, cypresses, fruit trees and a few palms, this stunningly beautiful mountain village was once surrounded by myriad windmills. Take time to wander through its **alleyways\***, which are punctu-

### The material of "Beauty"
The "Venus de Milo", the "Victory of Samothrace", the "Hermes of Praxiteles", the Parthenon frieze, and many other jewels of Antiquity have in common the fact that they were carved from Parian marble. This is of an exceptional purity and whiteness: crystalline and translucent, "lychnitis" (its name comes from "lychnaria", the miners' oil lamps) allows light to pass through it to a depth of 3.5cm (compared with 2.5cm for Italian Carrara marble and 1.5cm for Pentelic marble). However, with such remarkable qualities it is particularly difficult to work, and sculptors, who are aware of its capacity to shatter at the slightest chisel cut which is not perfectly executed, hold it in great respect. Under the Romans, large numbers of slaves would labour night and day to extract this precious mineral.

ated with doorframes, benches, arcades and wells carved in marble. Going back up the central street, Odós Ramnos, you will see the distant silhouette of the **Agía Tríada Church\*** (1835), with its two finely carved marble **steeples\***. Marble also features in the interior (pulpit, iconostasis and bishop's throne). The village also has traditional pottery workshops, and the **Folk Museum**, in the **Léfkes Village Hotel**, is devoted to the crafts and craftspeople of the Aegean.

**The Cyclades**

**PÁROS ANDÍPAROS**

0    3    6 km

Akr. Kórakas
Monastíri    Lángeri
Kolibíthres
Koukounariés    S. María
Longovárdas    Náoussa
Kriós    Livádia
Delfíni    Maráthi    Latomía    Ambelás
Parásporos    PARIKÍA    Marmárou
Ág. Minás    Kóstos    Filitzi
Agía Iríni    Léfkes    Mármara
Sifnéiko    Kástro    Pródromos    Mólos
Psarolikés    Petaloúdes    Vígla
Livádi    Panagía    Pounda    Márpissa    Písso Livádi
Glífa    Ágii    Logarás
N. Andíparos    Theódori    Messáda
Spíleo    Voutákou    Driós    Hrissí Aktí
Ág. Geórgios    Angeriá
Alikí    Lolandóni
Sorós    Fáranga    Glífa
Tripití

Egéo Pélagos
Piréas
N. Síros, N. Mýkonos
† Hristoú Dássous
N. Despotikó
Akr. Petalída
N. Íos

600 m
200
0

*Páros*

■ **Pródromos** (Dragoula) – You enter this fortified village through an elegant **arcade** formed by the towers of two churches. The 17C cathedral, **Ágios Ioánnis Pródromos** (St John "the precursor", ie John the Baptist), contains some old icons and a wooden iconostasis.

■ Beyond the village of **Mármara** ("marble"), the road runs along the coast to the magnificent **Bay of Mólos**★★. Next to its long beach *(to the left)*, hidden behind the promontory *(to the right)*, is the little **Bay of Vígla.**

■ **Márpissa**★ – A short distance south of Mármara, the beautiful white houses of Márpissa are set out in the form of an amphitheatre at the foot of the mound upon which once stood the **kástro of Kéfalos** (now in ruins), the last bastion of the Venetian rulers. The **Ágios Antonios Monastery** (11am-7pm) still looks down over it, affording a magnificent **view**★★. This beautiful white building has some 17C **frescoes**★, in particular a large depiction of the *Last Judgement*. Go for a stroll through the village as well, where there are churches and old houses, without forgetting the very pleasant kafenía.

### Along the coast
Between the seaside resort of Písso Livádi and the village of Driós lies the third stretch of the island dedicated to tourism, with a wide range of accommodation and beaches. Some of these beaches are fairly quiet and popular with families, such as **Písso Livádi**★ *(next to the little harbour and its tavernas; some bars)*, **Logarás**★★ or **Driós**★,

while others are frequented by a younger more trendy set, such as the very lively **Poúnda** (*club*), **Messáda**★★ (popular with nudists) and the famous **Hrissí Aktí**★★ (Golden Beach), one of the largest on the island, with golden sand and turquoise waters. Hrissí Aktí is the other favourite beach for windsurfing, and international competitions are held there.

Between Driós and **Cape Mávros**, the south coast reveals countryside of a slightly wilder nature, where some little sandy bays and the more secluded beaches of **Lolandóni**★, **Glífa**★ and **Tripití**★★ are hidden away.

## Andíparos (Antiparos)

*From Parikía, small boats provide a ferry service (30min). If you want to go by car, take the ferry from Poúnda (every 30min; 15min crossing). Allow 1 day.*

### Kástro★ (Andíparos)

With the advent of tourism, this former hideout of Maltese and French pirates (around 1 700 of them) has become a typical small Cycladic town, decked in flowers. As on many of the islands in the Cyclades, *kástro* (dating from around 1400) does not signify a fortress, but a fortified village, with the strengthened external walls of the houses constituting the defences.

Opposite the first jetty (*where the boats from Parikía dock*) is the start of the **Kabiara**★, the liveliest street on Andíparos. Lined with tavernas and cafés, this long paved street opens out into **Platía Ágios Nikólaos** before continuing on towards the **beach of Sifnéiko**★, on the other side of the island, famed for its sunsets.

Near the village, the two beaches at **Psarolikés** (*south of the kástro*) are very busy. You would do better to head for **Panagía**★, **Glífa**, or **Sorós**★, or even better, **Ágios Geórgios**★★ (*tavernas and bars*), lapped by the clearest waters. If there is no wind blowing, **Livádi**★★ is the best choice.

No fewer than 410 steps lead down into the heart of the **Cave of the Stalactites**★★ (Spíleo Stalaktíkon) (*10.30am 3.45pm; entrance fee*), 160m underground. Here, in an enormous room, 216m long by 203m wide and 18m high, a forest of stalactites and stalagmites is revealed. This underground cathedral which was known to the Ancients, has received various visitors over the ages, including fugitives and other notable guests, sometimes unscrupulous, like the Russians who took away a large number of engraved stalactites in 1774. A mass was even celebrated here in 1673.

---

## Making the most of Páros

---

### COMING AND GOING

**By air** – In summer, there are several flights per day to Athens (50min), and connecting flights to Rhodes and Herakleion (Crete).

*Alikí* Airport, 9km from Parikía, ☎ (0284) 91 257.

*Olympic Airways Office*, in Parikía (on the main square), ☎ (0284) 21 900.

**By boat** – From Piraeus, 4 to 6 ferries per day (5-6hr crossing), and one connection per day on the Highspeed 1, a fast boat (3hr15min) which carries on to Náxos. From Rafína, one ferry daily (5hr), and one fast connection per day on Sea Jet 1 (2hr50min), which carries on to Náxos and Amorgós.

From Páros, there are frequent ferries to Náxos, Íos and Santoríni, and a less frequent service to Síkinos, Folégandros, Anáfi, Amorgós, the Lesser Cyclades, Ikaría, Sámos, Fourní, Herakleion and the Dodecanese Islands. Méga Dolphins boats go to Kímolos, Mýkonos, Náxos, Sérifos, Sífnos and Síros, services vary in frequency.

*Harbourmaster's office in Parikía*, ☎ (0284) 21 240.

### GETTING AROUND

Note: the directions below all refer to a common starting point, ie where the visitor gets off the boat.

**By bus** – In Parikía, the bus stop is to the left of the landing-stage. *KTEL company*, ☎ (0284) 21 395. Timetables are displayed opposite the Budget office. Four routes: Náoussa-Parikía (30min) and return service; Náoussa-Léfkes-Písso Livádi (40min); Parikía-Poúnda (Andíparos), in 15min (at 8am, 10am, 12noon, 2pm, 4pm and 7pm); Parikía-Alikí-Angeriá in 20min (at 7.30am, 9am, 11am, 1pm, 2pm, 4pm, 6pm and 8pm). In summer, there is an extra route, Náoussa-Driós. Buses run during the night in the summer. On Andíparos, one bus every 30min does the harbour-cave-Sorós-Ágios Geórgios route.

**Road network** – A good road goes round the island, while there is another going across it, from Parikía to Márpissa via Léfkes. Along the coast, minor roads connect the coastal road to the resorts and most of the beaches. There are also several good tracks (indicated in the text), but few paths (not many villages). The roads are very busy; take care.

**By rental car** – On Páros, vehicle rental is quite expensive. In Parikía, *Motorplan* (for two-wheelers), opposite the landing-stage, ☎ (0284) 24678: well-maintained machines at a reasonable price. Also see the *Cyclades* (cars and motorcycles) and *Polos* travel agents listed below ("Address book").

**Fuel** – Many filling stations on the main Parikía-Náoussa-Golden Beach road, but there are just two (by the airport) between Golden Beach and Parikía, via Driós and Alikí.

**By taxi** – In Parikía, ☎ (0284) 21 261; in Náoussa, ☎ (0284) 51 240.

**By boat** – Boats for Andíparos dock next to the landing-stage. Approximately one departure every 2hr. Some companies include a visit to the cave, but this does not really justify the supplement charged.

**ADDRESS BOOK (PARIKÍA)**

**Tourist information** – Next to the landing-stage. They issue free copies of *Skymap* (street maps of Parikía, Livádia and Náoussa and a small map of Páros), and a selection of addresses (insufficient information if you are looking for accommodation).

**Travel agencies** – The *Cyclades* agency, left of the landing-stage, ☎ (0284) 21 738, Fax (0284) 22 146, provides a good service, including vehicle hire, tourist accommodation and ticket sales.
The *Polos* agency (vehicle hire, ticket sales), right of the landing-stage, ☎ (0284) 22 092-3, provides an equally good service.

**Banking / Currency exchange** – Five banks, four of which have cash dispensers, all located close to the landing-stage.

**Post office / Telephone** – The post office is on the left of the landing-stage. *OTE*, to the right of the landing-stage, next to the Polos agency.

**Medical service** – *Medical centre* (privately run), left of the landing-stage, at the near end of the street that runs parallel to the quayside, ☎ (0284) 24 410 / 22 477, modern, reliable, but expensive. *Health centre* (public), left of the landing-stage, a short distance before the private centre, ☎ (0284) 22 500-3.
Two *pharmacies* in Parikía, one in Náoussa and one in Márpissa.

**Tourist police** – Opposite the landing-stage, next to the Commercial Bank, ☎ (0284) 21 673.

**Other** – *Left luggage office*, on 1st floor of travel agency next to the windmill.
*English newspapers*, in the bookshop just before the Ekatondapilianí Church. Another at the beginning of the main street.
*Launderette*, 100m left of the landing-stage.

**WHERE TO STAY**

Although there are plenty of places to stay on Páros, it is never enough in the summer, and prices rise steeply. Remember that Andíparos is less expensive.

• **Parikía**
*Campsites (around €12)*
There are three campsites near Parikía: *Koula*, *Kriós* and *Parásporos*. The first two are right on the beach, the third is 700m from the sea. A minibus will meet you off the ferry. All three sites are busy and offer virtually the same facilities.

Parásporos is probably the best, with lots of greenery, a brand new swimming pool and decent washing facilities.

*Between €30 and €49*

**Dina**, to the right of the landing-stage, in a street that goes off at a right-angle (next to Odós Velentza), ☎ (0284) 21 325 – 8rm. ⌁ ✎ A charming hotel in the old town, with pretty rooms and a small garden, 100m from the sea.

**Kontès**, opposite the jetty, ☎ (0284) 21 096 – 26rm. ⌁ ✎ Clean, comfortable and very central. A good option if you arrive late.

☺ **Stergiá**, turn left at the landing-stage, in a narrow street that goes off at a right-angle, 50m from the sea, ☎ (0284) 21 745 – 16rm. ⌁ Attractive hotel with lots of flowers, rooms are comfortable. Warm welcome.

**Vayia**, taking the Náoussa road on the left at the far side of the square, 300m from the harbour, ☎ (0284) 21 068 – 17rm. ⌁ ✎ A hotel with a family atmosphere, surrounded by olive trees, a short way out of the town, quiet and comfortable.

**Kapetan Manólis**, straight ahead as you leave the landing-stage, at the top of the steps, on the left, ☎ (0284) 21 144 – 13rm. ⌁ ✎ Ask for one of the rooms which overlooks the garden.

☺ **Anthippi**, on the right, a short way out of town, ☎ (0284) 21 601, in Athens (01) 27 56 382 – 7rm and studios. ⌁ With kitchen. Recently restored, the rooms in this old house have been decorated with great care: antique furniture, stone and marble, and a pretty view over Parikía Bay. Accommodation unlike anywhere else on the island, and rare in the Cyclades: booking strongly recommended.

● **Andíparos**

*Between €24 and €45*

**Ártemis**, 400m from the harbour to the right, ☎ (0284) 61 460, Fax (0284) 61 472 – 30rm. ⌁ Fridge. A new establishment, 10m from the sea, with garden. Comfortable rooms, balconies with sea view.

**Madaléna**, at the harbour, ☎ (0284) 61 206. ⌁ Recently renovated, this seafront hotel (10m from the harbour) is right by the beach. Well-kept rooms (with balcony)

**Chrissoúla**, on the left, towards Psara beach, ☎ (0284) 61 224. ⌁ A quiet hotel, with comfortable rooms.

**Antíparos**, at the harbour, ☎ (0284) 61 358. ⌁ ✗ Fridge. A simple hotel, with standard facilities. During the day, the manageress can be found in the kitchens in the small taverna.

● **Náoussa**

*Around €45*

**Kalypso**, Náoussa, 10min from the centre, next to the beach, ☎ (0284) 51 488, Fax (0284) 51 607 – 23rm. ⌁ ✎ ⌂ **CC** A comfortable, well-situated establishment overlooking the sea, with lots of charm. A very generous buffet breakfast is provided.

*Between €23 and €38*

**Ambelás**, 100m from Ambelás beach, ☎ (0284) 51 324 – 16rm. ⌁ ✗ A small hotel-restaurant serving very good food. View over Náxos from your balcony.

**Mado**, in the centre of Náoussa, ☎ (0284) 51 590 – 14rm. Comfortable, with a very attractive garden where you can have breakfast.

● **Písso Livádi**

*Between €27 and €38*

**Magia**, 80m up from the beach, ☎ (0284) 41 390 – 13rm. ⌁ Modest accommodation, but very clean and well situated. Lovely view.

*Between €30 and €45*

☺ **Aktaion**, Logarás, ☎ (0284) 41 098 – 25rm and studios. ⌁ ✎ A very pleasant establishment, attractively decorated, set in a large garden with a view of the sea at the end. Comfortable rooms.

**Afendákis**, in Márpissa, on the Písso Livádi road, ☎ (0284) 41 141 – 12rm and studios. ⌁ ✎ ⌂ A lovely Cycladic-style building in a verdant setting. Comfortable rooms, some with sea view. Attractive terrace for breakfast.

**WHERE TO EAT**
● **Parikía**

*Under €12*

**Trelós Kókoras** ("the mad rooster"), near Tamarisco. Specialises in pancakes, in a pleasant location.

**Tamarisco**, not far from the branch of the National Bank, in a garden. Good Greek cooking, and some international cuisine.

**Magaya**, on Delfíni beach, beyond Parikía. A pleasant setting and varied cuisine (excellent seafood macaroni).

*Between €12 and €15*

🐟 **Porfirá**, on the Náoussa road, left of Panagía. A taverna which has excellent seafood and delicious fish meze, in an attractive setting. Try the sea-urchin salad. Evenings only.

**Boudaráki**, south of Hóra, near the windmill. An excellent taverna serving fish, hot dishes and meats.

### • Náoussa

*Around €9*

🐟 **Barbarossa**, ouzo bar, at the harbour. Serves seafood of every kind, including delicious lobster, with meze. The locals drink "saouma", the local rakí. It is very popular and always busy here; be prepared to wait.

**Mastrostáthis**, ouzo bar at the harbour. The fish meze are very good.

*Around €15*

**Chrístos**, Near the bus stop, in the town centre, not far from the square. In a cool courtyard, tastefully decorated, serving Greek and Mediterranean dishes, complemented by a fine wine list. Expensive.

### • Léfkes

*Around €12*

**O Klarinos**, in the village square, this hotel-restaurant has a wide-ranging menu and a very attractive setting.

*Around €15*

**Léfkes Village**, undeniably the finest hotel on the island (around €125 for a double room in high season). Even if you are not staying here, you can come for breakfast, lunch or dinner on the terrace with its sweeping view over the surrounding area. An enchanting setting, very stylish decor, and the restaurant serves delicious food including local specialities, complemented by wines from all over Greece.

### • West coast

*Between €11 and €13*

🐟 **Katsounas**, Santa María beach. A good taverna specialising in fish dishes. The lady-owner makes her own cheeses while her husband is out fishing; a perfect combination resulting in simple but tasty food.

🐟 **Théa**, on Messáda beach with a sea view and traditional music. Greek cuisine with flavours borrowed from Asia Minor. Meat dishes with delicious sauces, and very sweet oriental desserts ("ekmek-kataifi").

**Driós Beach**, follow the road to the beach. An excellent taverna for fish, where the owner prides himself on serving the freshest of the catch.

### HAVING A DRINK

### • Parikía

During the day, most of the activity is centred around the main street and the old market. For a pancake or a fruit juice (delicious), try **Karpousi**, or **The Balcony** bar, also in the main street, with its charming terrace.

**Evinos**, to the right of the landing-stage. Perched on top of a large rock, this café offers fine views.

In the evening (and into the night):

**Mílos**, inside a real windmill with great views of the sunset; also at **Kialoa** and **Splash**.

### • Náoussa

For some years, night-life on Páros (especially Greek) has centred on Náoussa. There are two bars at the harbour: **Sofrano** and **Agosta**, both quite smart, as well as the more traditional **Linardot**, at the far end of the harbour.

**Maístro**, a bit further back, up in the alleys; Greek music.

### OTHER THINGS TO DO

**Open-air cinemas** – Parikía has two cinemas. The **Rex**, to the south of town, on the outer road, showings start at 8.30pm and 10.30pm. The **Páros**, at Livádia, in the road that runs at a right-angle to the Aeoli restaurant; showings start at 9pm. Films shown are generally American with Greek subtitles.

**Diving** – **Santa María Diving Club**, on Alikí beach, ☎ (0284) 53 007; **Aegean Diving College**, Poúnda Beach Club, ☎ (0284) 41 717. All levels catered for; equipment provided.

**Windsurfing** – The best places are: **Agía María** Bay (Santa María and Alikí beaches), **Hrissí Aktí** (Golden Beach), **Néa Hrissí Aktí** (up from Golden Beach) and **Mólos**. Equipment for hire.

**Excursions** – You are only 1hr by ferry from Hóra on Náxos, one of the most beautiful locations for medieval architecture in the whole of the Aegean. You should take advantage of this (see "Making the most of Náxos", page 296).

# SANTORÍNI ★★★
## (THÍRA)
Eastern Aegean – District of the Cyclades – Michelin map 980 fold 44
Regional map on the inside back cover – 83km²
Pop 11 481 – Allow 3-4 days

### Not to be missed
A stroll around Firá and along the cliffs to Ía for sunset.
Akrotíri, Thíra and the Profítis Ilías Monastery.
Taking a boat trip in the caldera.

### And remember...
Visit Santoríni out of season: prices are more than halved.

With its violently eroded silhouette and its beaches of black sand, Santoríni affords a spectacle like nowhere else on earth. This is apocalyptic terrain, which the vineyards and white splashes of the villages have fought hard to soften with their typically Cycladic charm. As if strangely fascinated, your eye is continually drawn back to the cliff, this formidable wall of rock surging up out of the water, which every evening is set aglow by the fiery rays of the setting sun, a reminder of the cataclysm which wreaked havoc on the landscape. But there is a corresponding downside to this phenomenon: more than half a million visitors descend on Santoríni every summer – an amazing feat for an island with no water – and there are tourists everywhere.

## Into the mouth of the volcano
Arriving by ferry in **Athiniós**, the island's harbour, is an unforgettable experience. Below you, the sea is more than 400m deep and you are surrounded by an enormous natural harbour 10km in diameter and almost fully enclosed. The cliff slices

Firá, a town on the edge of an abyss

into the bottomless blue waters of the sea, the jagged rock face standing 150-300m high, displaying all the colours of its volcanic components with layers of black lava, reddish scoria, grey-violet cinders and pozzolana, all underscored by a pale band of pumice stone.

## In search of Atlantis

35 centuries ago, this huge, sea-filled cauldron was a volcanic mountain, the ravaged summit of which is still visible today, forming what is now the little islet of Néa Kaméni. During the Quaternary Period, the intense volcanic activity in the region had created a circular island, which its early inhabitants called **Strongilí**, the "Round One". The great civilisation that blossomed here was to survive unchallenged – maybe this was the famous Atlantis that inspired **Plato**? Whatever it was, from the 5C BC this fertile land was settled by farming and trading folk. The golden era was around the late Bronze Age (c 1500 BC), the inhabitants maintaining close links with the Minoan civilisation (Crete) which dominated the Aegean at that time. During the 16C BC, however, a series of earthquakes shook the area, stirring the volcano back into life. It seems that its threatening noises soon persuaded the inhabitants to abandon the island, (the absence of precious objects and human remains on the site at Akrotíri would seem to bear this out). They made the right decision: a year later, the island was no more. An extraordinarily violent explosion literally pulverised the volcano, leaving in its place an immense caldera encircled by breathtakingly high cliffs.

In the aftermath of this disaster, the first people to come back to the island were the **Phoenicians**, followed by the Dorians of Spartan origin at the end of the 12C BC. These were led by King **Thíras**, who gave his name to the town built on the fortified settlement of Messa Vouno. But being neither merchants nor seafaring folk, these settlers for a long time missed out on the trade carried on in the Aegean. Thíra only emerged from the shadows under the Ptolemaic dynasty (300-145 BC), but retreated into them once more under the Romans. Nevertheless, the existence of three early Christian basilicas (ancient Thíra, Messa Vouno andAeríssa) demonstrates a certain

B. Pérousse/MICHELIN

**Santoríni**

degree of prosperity, which lasted into the Byzantine Period. A modest community of Catholic Greeks survives from the period of Latin rule (1204-1566), and there are also the remains of five **fortified villages** or *kastelli* (Skáros, Ía, Pírgos, Niborio and Akrotíri), as well as a church called **Santa Irena**, from where "Santoríni" would get its name. For a period of one hundred years, until the mid-19C, the island was wealthy thanks to its maritime trade. But it was to be sorely tested by the 1956 earthquake, and only evolved into a tourist destination in the 1970s.

**The greatest cataclysm of Antiquity**
Compressed inside the crater, the accumulated gases exploded violently, throwing out enormous quantities of volcanic cinders which burnt and covered the area all around. The entire centre of the island collapsed (83km$^2$), hollowing out a gigantic abyss nearly 800m deep in the place of the mountain. Then a crack opened up in the ridge of this caldera and the sea flooded in. A thick cloud of ash and pumice stone (traces of which have been found as far away as Crete) polluted the atmosphere for several days while a colossal tidal wave engulfed the whole Aegean coastline. The wave has been estimated as over 200m high at source, and some 70m high when it hit the Cretan coast less than half an hour later. This gives further fuel to the theory, though a rather controversial one, that the disappearance of the Minoan civilisation was largely a result of this cataclysm (see also page 18).

## Firá★★★ (Thíra)

*If you don't mind steps, set out on foot and head for the settlements of Firá and beyond to the northern tip of the island by way of the narrow lanes which meander along the caldera. From any one of these, between Imerovígli and Finikiá (about 7km), the road offers spectacular views.*

From the harbour of **Méssa Gialós★** (Skala) where the water is so deep that it is impossible to drop anchor – your eyes will be fixed on the white ridge of the houses of Firá, perched on the edge of the cliff 260m above the water. A vertiginous **set of steps** scales the cliff wall, with fantastic plunging **views★★** back down over the harbour. Making slow progress, a procession of **mules** climbs to the top, transporting tourists in the welcoming but chaotic fashion which is part of the traditional culture of Santoríni. Visitors in a hurry travel by **cable car** (*every 15min, from 6.45am-8.15pm; fee*).

**Discreet, but always present**
After Strongilí was swallowed up, there are historical records of 14 eruptions in the swirling waters of the caldera. With some long periods of inactivity (731 years between the 4th and 5th eruptions), these phenomena formed the two islets of Paleá and Néa Kaméni. Since 1950, the only signs of volcanic activity have been the sulphurous gases coming from Néa Kaméni. Detectors placed at various points around the islet are set to signal the slightest hint of activity.

The **capital of the island** was founded at the end of the 18C, when the coastline was no longer as vulnerable and the inhabitants could leave the fortress of Skáros in search of flatter ground where it was easier to build and they had better access to the sea. Nowadays, the cafés, discotheques, restaurants, boutiques and other facilities in Firá make it the focus of summer life on the island. Whether you are staying in Kamári, Períssa or elsewhere, Firá is the place to go if you are looking for some atmosphere and a good taverna. Not forgetting the lure of the caldera.

**A town on the edge of the abyss**
Following the contours of the cliff, Firá is a long, straggling town, cut in two by Odós 25 Martíou, from where the island's main north-south road starts out. At the heart of the town, **Platía Theotokopoúlou**, where the bus terminal and the taxi ranks are located, is always busy. On the eastern side of town, the houses look down over the

great expanse of vine-covered lava sloping down to the sea. With construction and development work everywhere, this district has little of interest. To the west, however, there is a picturesque maze of old paved alleyways, terraces and steps, which run between the little houses painted white, pale yellow or ochre.

You should also allow some time for a visit to the **New Museum\*\*\***, which has managed to retrieve the famous **Akrotíri frescoes\*\*\*** from Athens, where they were previously on display in the National Archaeological Museum.

A short distance from the museum, the **Orthodox Cathedral of Santoríni\*** (1970) sits enthroned like a great white cake, on the site of the old church destroyed by the tremor of 1956. Splendid **views\*\*** over the caldera open up from the adjoining terrace.

Down below is the old quarter of **Káto Firá\*** (the low town), a silent maze of little streets bathed in light which seems ready to topple into the void. From this terraced cascade of houses, two domes rear up: the white one belongs to the **Ágios Ioánnis Church**, and the other, with its typical lantern, to the **Church of Ágios Minás\***. Then the street heads back up to the left towards Odós Ipapandís.

### The Catholic Quarter\*\* (Katholica)

You can then choose between two alternatives. You can either follow **Odós Agíou Miná\*** along the precipice: lined with cafés and restaurants, it is very popular at **sunset\*\***. Or you can explore old Firá along **Odós Ipapandís\*** from the corner of Odós Danézi. Today, as in previous times, its wide steps form the commercial centre of the town. There are also some rare examples of **archontiká**, beautiful houses built for the gentry (look out for *no 76*, **Nomikoú House**). Not far from here and worth a visit is the old **market of Firá**, a lively centre of activity.

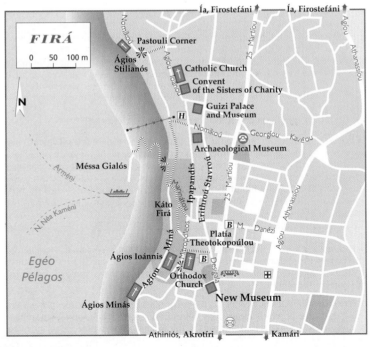

At the corner of Odós Ipapandís and Odós Nomikoú, the **Archaeological Museum**★★ (8.30am-3pm; closed Monday; entrance fee) has a display of objects discovered on the site of ancient Thíra (Messa Vouno), which was excavated between 1896 and 1900, as well as some objects unearthed on the site at Akrotíri. Displayed in chronological order, the exhibition starts in the foyer, with **Cycladic idols** and **vases** dating from the 3rd millennium, and pottery from Akrotíri. It continues into Room 1, where there are ceramic works from the 8C-6C BC, including a very beautiful **amphora**★ (Archaic Period) decorated with reliefs, as well as a number of marble statuettes and fragments of Archaic kouroi. Room 2 has a display of ceramics from the 6C-4C BC, some terracotta figurines, as well as some statues and reliefs dating from the Hellenistic and Roman Periods.

With its groined vaults, **Odós Erithroú Stavroú**★ is typical of Santoríni. Also note the decorated marble entrance to **Koutsoyannópoulos House** (1882) at no 182. This stands opposite the **Guizi Palace**★ (Mégaro Guizi) (10.30am-1.30pm / 5pm-8pm, Sunday 10.30am-4.30pm; entrance fee), a patrician villa completed in 1700, its beautiful windows and doors embellished with dark stone. Restored after the tremor of 1956, it has been converted into a **Cultural Centre** to preserve manuscripts, old publications, costumes and traditional objects from the 16C-19C, as well as some etchings and photographs of Santoríni prior to the tremor of 1956.

Beyond the Guizi Palace, on the right, a small paved area gives access (to the left) to the former **Convent of the Sisters of Charity**★. Completely restored, the building has been converted into a carpet-making workshop (open to the public).

The Dominican convent to the side of it is a closed community, but a nun will still admit visitors to the **Abbey Church**★ (Rosaria), an astonishing mixture of Baroque and Cycladic architecture. Nearby stands the **Catholic cathedral**★ (Ágios Ioánnis), renovated after the 1956 earthquake, with its remarkable, eclectic **tower**.

Then some steps lead down towards Odós Nomikoú, where you can have a quick look at the **Ágios Stilianós Chapel**, clinging to the edge of the precipice, with its amazing four-coloured tower.

In front of you is the beginning of the **Frangika**★ (the name, coined from "franc", refers to the Catholics), the northern quarter of Firá, linking Firá to Firostefáni. The majority of the Catholics on Santoríni live grouped together in this community. Retracing your steps, go as far as **Pastouli Corner** (on the right angle bend just before the junction with Agíou Miná): it is one of the most famous **viewpoints**★★ on Santoríni – the view is the one reproduced on all the postcards of the island.

## From Firá to Ía: on the caldera★★★

■ **Firostefáni**★ – Also built on the edge of the cliff, nowadays this village runs into the town of Firá, forming its northern quarter. Stretching along the caldera, it affords breathtaking **views**★★ over the enormous cirque. To get to it, go past Ágios Stilianós, through the Frangika as far as the Catholic church of Agíon Theodóron which marks its starting point. **Platía Firostefáni** (less than 1km from Platía Theotokopoúlou) is no more than 50m away, with the great **Ágios Iérassimos Church**, encircled by cypress trees.

*As you come out of Firostefáni, follow the cliff path.*

■ Nestling in a hollow, the **Monastery of St Nicholas**★ (Ágios Nikólaos) was founded in 1651 by the Ghizzis. Around its great square courtyard stands the abbey church (very beautiful carved wooden **iconostasis**★) as well as the communal rooms and 40 cells for the monks.

■ **Imerovígli**★ – *2.4km from Platía Theotokopoúlou.* Before there was a village at this spot, the name of which means "day observatory", there was a **lookout post** here which alerted the locals to any pirates in the vicinity, allowing the inhabitants time to take refuge in the neighbouring citadel of **Skáros\***, which was destroyed by the Turks *(as you walk along the caldera, you will come to the path that leads to it).* Steps go down towards this abrupt rocky outcrop, an impregnable rock overhang on which the dukes' palace once stood. A path to the side of the cliff goes around the mound of Skáros, before bringing you, at the end of a very impressive **walk\*\***, to the **Théosképasti Chapel** which overhangs the abyss.

■ **Ía\*\*\*** (Oia) – *9km from Imerovígli.* Even more so than Firá, Ía (the Greek name Oia is pronounced "ia") is unquestionably the most beautiful village of the west coast, simultaneously offering the picturesque spectacle of the pastel-coloured **troglodytic dwellings**, clinging to the cliff, and the nostalgic charm of the **patrician villas**, as well as the very chic atmosphere of the more stylish tourist establishments. Quieter than the capital, it also radiates a more typically Cycladic atmosphere, inviting long, leisurely, walks. And this is the place to come for an unforgettable view of the **sunset**.

Also known by the name of **Apáno Méria** ("the place high up"), Ía is in fact made up of five settlements, from east to west as follows: **Finikiá**, Ía itself, **Thólos** (a short distance to the north) and, at the base of the cliff, **Arméni** and **Amoúdi**, Ía's anchorage *(which can also be reached by an asphalt road)*, with two flights of steps – and more than 200 steps – providing access.

Ía's late 19C prosperity was due to Amoúdi. In about 1890, 130 ships (for a population of 2 500!) traded throughout the eastern Mediterranean. The sailors lived in the troglodytic dwellings, while the captains lived in the opulent houses of the high town in the Sidéras district. This prosperous period is testified to by the number and opulence of the churches, and by the marble paving of the squares and alleyways. Inside an attractive, neo-Classical, building *(on the left, at the beginning of the main road that goes down to Amoúdi)*, the **Maritime Museum** *(10am-1pm / 5pm-8pm; closed Tuesday; entrance fee)* retraces the life of the island's sailors and shipowners: there are models of boats, figureheads, navigational instruments, pictures, etchings, etc.

Nothing much remains of the **kastelli**, the citadel on top of the rocky overhang up above the bay, and it has now become a favourite rendezvous for lovers at **sunset**. The black pebbles of **Amoúdi beach\*** and the nearby rocks can get fairly crowded, but the setting and the walk to it are worth a look. Then, for an evening meal, head for the tavernas that line the quay.

## "Volcanic" architecture

Not satisfied with having obliterated Atlantis, the volcano of Santoríni continues to threaten the island. The architecture of the villages has therefore been designed with the aim of withstanding any untimely stirrings of the sleeping giant. As there are no traditional building materials present on the island – no wood for carpentry work, nor clay for tiles – it was necessary to use the materials provided by the volcano, such as scoria, pumice, cinders and pozzolana, the last of these making a very good cement. The scarcity of wood meant that conventional ceilings and roofs had to be replaced by domes and vaults. Another option was troglodytic dwellings ("scafta"), as the volcanic tufa, being both soft and stable, lends itself perfectly to the hollowing out of rooms large enough to live in. A masonry section can extend the "scafta", always longer than it is wide, with a vaulted roof and a façade with three openings let into it. Nowadays, these traditional houses with their unrestricted view over the caldera sell for huge amounts of money.

## A tour around the centre of the island

This itinerary connects two of the three great sites of the island (with Akrotíri). If you enjoy hiking through wonderful landscapes, the Kamári-Thíra-Políssa or Kamári-Thíra-Profítis Ilías-Políssa **walks\*\*** are undoubtedly the best that Santoríni has to offer, and are within the capabilities of just about everyone.

**Santorini**

■ **Ancient Thíra★★★** (Arhéa Thíra) – *8am-2pm; closed Monday; no entrance fee. You can get there by bus (3km from Kamári to the Seralla pass). Don't go by moped, as the road is cobbled, winding and very steep. From Períssa, take the path which starts level with the Mariana Hotel, along the last street to the north of the resort, at the base of Messa Vouno. Allow 90min for the walk, through magnificent countryside, but under a remorseless sun (cover up, take water, and make your visit in the morning if possible).*

If ancient Thíra is now no more than a ruin, this town with its Hellenistic embellishments will still seduce you with the majesty of its setting. The ancient town stands on a narrow chalk ridge which connects Mt Profítis Ilías with Messa Vouno, at 369m above sea level. Founded in the 9C BC by the Dorians, this natural fortress reached its apogee under the Macedonian Ptolemaic dynasty (300-150 BC) from Egypt, who had established a naval base here (boats were moored at Kamári and at Períssa). It fell into decline under the Romans, however, before being abandoned in the 13C. The tour starts with the **Byzantine quarter** (fortifications, churches), which precedes the **Sanctuary of Artemídoros**, dedicated to a Ptolemaic admiral. This sacred enclosed area has retained its altar and some **reliefs** engraved in the rock.

Back once more on the main thoroughfare, go up towards the **guardhouse**, with its **gymnasium** which stands on the left. As you come back down, go left towards the **northern agora**. This marks the point where the town was at its widest... some 150m! To the right, you will see the **Temple of Dionysus** and then the **House of the Phallus** (given this name because of an unambiguous inscription), and finally the columns of the **royal portico**, while the **southern agora** is situated to the left. Following the sacred path, you then pass in front of the **theatre** and, nearer to the cliff, the remains of the **Sanctuary of the Egyptian Gods**. Concealed behind the theatre are some more thermal baths and, further on, as you come down, the Chapel

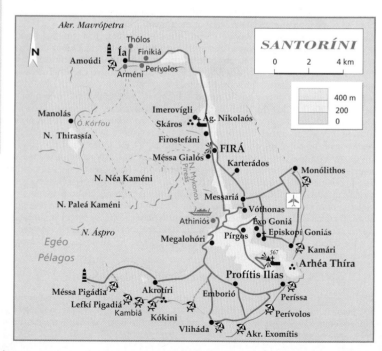

of the Annunciation. Reduced to nothing more than a modest path, the Sacred Way then leads to the sacred quarter, which linked up to the **Archaic town**, where Apollo's Temple sat on high *(on the right)*.

*Finally, return via the path that runs along the cliff.*

### From Kamári to Pírgos★

■ For 2km, the seafront of **Kamári** is lined with hotels, rental offices, cafés and discotheques: a pedestrian area, it is shaded by eucalyptus and tamarisk trees. As services and entertainment are concentrated here, the island's great resort attracts large numbers of people, but in spite of everything, a certain calm reigns, and the area is not without charm. Bristling with parasols *(fee charged)*, the extensive **beach** of sand and black shingle is lapped by a limpid sea *(do not venture too far out and look out for the currents, which can be strong at times)*. Water-sports fanatics should head for the northern end of the beach (15min on foot).

*Go through the village of Méssa Goniá (1.5km from Kamári), then take the track to the left.*

■ After a pretty walk *(700m)*, you come to the foot of Mt Profítis Ilías, surrounded by vineyards, where you will find the **Panagía Episkopí Church★** (Episkopí Goniás) *(9am-5pm)*, built on the ruins of the Bishop of Santoríni's see, founded in the 11C by Emperor Alexius I. The new church, itself very beautiful, has retained the magnificent **iconostasis★★** from the original building, sculpted wholly from marble, as well as a few of its remarkable **frescoes★★** (12C) on the arches *(to the right)*.

■ A small village clinging to the hillside, *(2.8km from Kamári; to the left of the road)*, **Exo Goniá★** nestles around the base of the impressive church of **Ágios Harálambos** (pretty frescoes), which, with its red-tiled roof, can be seen from all four corners of the island.

■ Atop a mound at the foot of Mt Profítis Ilías, **Pírgos★** *(5km from Kamári)* has everything that an important Cycladic village should have, with its white houses built on the terraces of a natural amphitheatre. Fortified during the Byzantine Period (*"pírgos"* means "fortress"), it is the only *kastelli* on the island to have retained its medieval character, with remains of its **fortifications★** in the upper part of the village. In addition to the many 17C **churches★** is **Kímissi tis Theotókou** which dates from the 11C.

■ **Mt Profítis Ilías★★** – *4km from Pírgos. 8am-1pm / 2.30pm-7pm; no fee; respectable clothing required.* From Pírgos to the highest point on the island (567m), the winding road offers any number of superb **viewpoints★**. Crowning the mountain's summit is the fortress-like **monastery★** (18C-19C) of the same name. Its former wealth (it possessed an important estate) is revealed in the magnificence of its **katholikón**, which contains a sumptuous **iconostasis★★** in carved gilded wood, as well as a number of icons. Do not omit a visit to the **museum**, where the monastery's heritage is stored, and where there is also a section dedicated to the daily life of the island.

To conclude this tour, if the 2km of rough tracks that lead there – through magnificent **countryside★** - don't put you off, you could choose to visit one of the three small **sandy beaches★** between Vliháda and Akrotíri, the last ones on the island to remain undeveloped *(past Megalohóri, go to the left towards Emborió. Then, after 500m, go right towards Vliháda. 600m further on, a track goes off to the right; after another 300m, you come to a path at right angles, from which four tracks go off towards the sea. Take the one facing you; the beach is 1.7km away.*

## The wine circuit

■ The starting point for this wine tour, **Karterádos★** *(south of Firá)* is a curiosity of the island's landscape: this village is situated in a ravine the sides of which are riddled with **troglodytic caves** (scafta); as for the houses built in the middle of the depression, their roofs are on a level with the road.

■ Surrounded by vines and vegetable gardens, **Messariá** is one of the main wine-producing centres of the island. Take the opportunity to sample a glass of **assirtiko** in the taverna in the village square. In a beautiful neo-Classical building (1860), near the church, the ground floor has been converted into the **Archontiko Argirou Museum** *(guided tour, 11am-12am-1pm-5pm-6pm-7pm; entrance fee)*, which is a reconstruction of a 19C middle-class interior. On the first floor, there are rooms and flats to rent, with period furnishings.

■ Exposed to the wind (and therefore popular with windsurfers), the coastal resort of **Monólithos** *(3.7km east of Messariá in the direction of the airport)* has one advantage over all its rivals on the east coast: edged with a wide stretch of shallow, sandy sea, the black sand beach is an ideal place for children to swim. For this reason, there are always plenty of people under the parasols here.

■ Back once more on the main road, by the right fork leading to Pírgos, you will see a **wine-making cooperative** where you can taste and buy the various wines of the island. Then make a short detour through **Megalohóri**✶, a small village with white houses. The **Boutaris cellars**, one of the main producers of wine in Greece, are situated at the end of a road on the right, as you leave Megalohóri. As well as **wine-tastings**, there is a **film show** telling the story of the origins of the island's vineyards *(1pm-6pm; fee charged for entrance and wine-tasting)*.

**"Santoríni vini!"**

Santoríni is the leading producer of white wine in Greece, and its vine-type is one of the country's best. Indeed, the richness of its volcanic soil gives its wines an inimitable bouquet, as well as protecting the vines against disease. While the average age of the assirtiko vine, the most widely grown on the island, is approaching 70 years, the oldest plants, near Akrotíri, are nearly 150 years old and have come unharmed through the dark years of the phylloxera which devastated French vineyards. The assirtiko vine produces a fairly fruity, medium dry white wine, while vinsando (made by leaving the grapes to super-maturation), aidani (known for its jasmine bouquet) or even the rare nyhtari, are sweet, fragrant wines. Look closely at the vine-stocks, and you will be surprised to see that, instead of growing straight, they are forced to grow in a spiral, forming a kind of basket. It is the strong and ever-present winds which have led the wine-growers to develop this unusual technique. All that is left to do now is sample these wines in the island's tavernas, or in the cellars which offer tastings (see text).

■ **Emborió**✶ (Niborio), the biggest village of the south, dominates a fertile plain at the foot of Mt Profítis Ilías. Take some time to stroll around the picturesque lanes between the old houses. To the north, you can take a look at the only **goulas**✶✶ on the island to remain virtually intact, an impressive fortress of pale stone built under Turkish rule.

■ **Toeríssa** – The harbour of Emborió is another large resort on the east coast, stretching along an immense **beach of black sand**✶ *(7km)* which is sheltered from the wind by the rocky mass of **Messa Vouno** but scorching in summer. Although smaller than Kamári, it is just as popular, and, at the height of the season, the beach is not always the cleanest. You can get away from the crowds by walking a short distance, as the beaches of **Perívolos**✶ (cafés and tavernas) and **Exomítis**✶ extend for kilometres right to the very northernmost tip of the island *(a road runs alongside the beach)*. But don't forget that the sea gets deep very quickly and that the waves can be fierce when the meltem is blowing.

■ At **Vliháda**✶ *(3.8km after the Akrotíri-Emborió fork)*, on the other side of the promontory, there is a change of scenery. A sudden reminder of the volcano, note the strange dark rocks that break through the surface of the water, rather like statues. The sea, which is calmer here than on the east coast, is also clearer: this is the time to put your snorkelling mask and flippers on.

## Southernmost Santoríni★★

*After exploring Akrotíri, indulge yourself with a swim
in the little bays of the south coast.
Finally, do not leave Santoríni without taking a trip
around the caldera in a caique.*

■ **Akrotíri★★** — *About 1km beyond the village. 8.30am-7pm; closed Monday; car-park
and entrance fees are charged. Avoid the first two hours after opening, which are allotted
to groups. Be prepared – it gets very hot under the corrugated iron which protects the site.
To the right of the entrance there is a map and explanations of how the tour is organised
in relation to the excavation work. A very cursory plan (in Greek and English) is provided
with your ticket.*

A century separates the first work done by the French School of Archaeology in
Athens and the excavations of Professor **S Marinátos**, between 1967-74, who, from
under a thick layer of volcanic ash, unearthed the first traces of the best preserved
prehistoric town in all of the Aegean. You can now walk the streets of a town which
is 3 500 years old and is believed to be the **city of Atlantis**. And although Akrotíri
dates from the early Minoan Period (or late Bronze Age, 1650-1500 BC), some discoveries dating back to the Neolithic Period indicate that this site was continuously
inhabited for 3 000 years, from the middle of the 5th millennium BC – a site which
is unique, and very emotive.

But there is no religious architecture here: it is thought that each house had its own
place of worship; there are not even any monuments (a clerical class probably exer-
cised some form of government), no gods or heroes immortalised in marble, but, on
the contrary, everything that generally would not survive the passage of time: the
familiar, daily, domestic items. Made of wood, freestone or beaten earth, the **houses**
of Akrotíri had two or three spacious storeys, covered by a roof terrace, with shops
or workshops occupying the ground floor. Alleyways, interspersed with small
squares, meandered around the town, while below the flagged road surface, there
were terracotta **pipes** to channel waste water away. Thus Akrotíri displays evidence
of having been a prosperous and highly structured society, enjoying a level of comfort
and sophistication comparable to that of the Minoans, whose influence is manifest.
As well as buildings, the site has yielded thousands of pots, and the frescoes that
decorated the houses (in the museum) provide an incomparable testament to how
daily life was organised. The excavations have also shown that the inhabitants of
Akrotíri used **a written script** known as Linear B (*see page 19*).

■ As you head back along the road, you could go for a further stroll around **Akrotíri
village★**, built around a small hill. At the top of the hill, some **bastions★** of a
**Venetian fortress** can still be seen.

### The beaches of the south coast★

Further on, dotted along the south coast, there are some beautiful shingle or sand
beaches. They are sheltered from the wind and with the sea being more shallow here
than elsewhere, they are obviously packed with people. One of these is **Kókini★**,
tucked away at the end of a track (*on the right a short distance past Akrotíri*), with
lines of parasols along the base of a spectacular cliff of red rock.

You would do better to try **Lefkí Pigadiá★**, an enchanting cove which you can get
to by caique from Skala (*or on foot for the more adventurous, via the path from Kambiá
which runs 200m higher up*). Unless you opt for **Méssa Pigádia★**, which is larger and
better for snorkelling (*access via a track*).

### In the caldera: a stroll around Néa Kaméni★★

*Wear stout shoes, take water and a swimsuit.* Finally: one of the "musts" of Santoríni.
All the caique tours follow more or less the same itinerary: the boat lands at the
northern end of the islet of Néa Kaméni, from where a path of hot cinders leads right

up to the **crater of the volcano**. Every so often, sulphurous vapours emanate from the ground, creating a strange atmosphere. You will then call at a bay on the neighbouring islet of **Paleá Kaméni**, which is called **Zestá Nerá** (Hot Springs), where you will be encouraged to swim – in water which is green, warm and sulphurous – a most unusual experience. After this, the boat ties up on the island of **Thirassía**, leaving you the choice of a swim in the **Bay of Kórfou**, next to the moored boats (of no great interest) or a visit to the island's principal village, **Manolás***, perched at the top of a flight of 145 steps *(can be scaled on foot or on the back of a mule)*. If you want to explore Thirassía at a more leisurely pace, you can get to the island directly on one of the caiques which sail from Amoúdi-Thirassía.

## Making the most of Santoríni

### COMING AND GOING

**By air –** Several flights daily with Olympic Airways from Athens; flight takes 50min. Connecting flights to Mýkonos, Rhodes, Herakleion. On arrival, there is an Olympic bus service to Firá. Reservations in Athens, ☎ (01) 96 66 666. Olympic Airways Office on Santoríni: in Firá, ☎ (0286) 22 493. There are also some charter flights from European cities.

**By boat –** From Rafína, one ferry daily (via Síros, Páros, Náxos; crossing takes about 10hr). Five Sea Jets weekly (via Síros, Páros, Íos; 6hr), but they depart at about 8am, which means that you have to get the bus from Athens at about 6.30am to get to the port.

From Piraeus: between 4-8 ferries daily, with departure times spread throughout the day. The most frequent route stops at Páros, Náxos and Íos (about 12hr). You would do best to time your departure for late afternoon (one boat sails around 5pm, another at about 6.30pm) or in the evening (one boat, which sails at about 10pm), so that you can arrive in the morning, especially if you have no accommodation booked. As the crossing is a long one, get to the port with enough time to get a good seat in the cabin.

From Santoríni, there are many ferry and hydrofoil services connecting with the other islands of the Cyclades. Unless absolutely necessary (to get to the Lesser Cyclades), avoid the small boats: the crossing is long (more than 10hr to get to Mýkonos), and frequently windy.

Boats arrive at the harbour of **Athiniós**, 10km south of Firá. By day and night alike, there is a bus to Firá (terminus just before Platía Theotokopoúlou). For Períssa, get off at the top of the road from the harbour and wait for the connection. Information: **harbourmaster's office**, in Firá, just past Platía Theotokopoúlou (on the left), ☎ (0286) 22 239, or from travel agencies.

### GETTING AROUND

**By bus –** There is a very good bus service, which runs 24 hours a day, every 30min during the day (until about 11pm), then every hour during the night (the most frequent are to Kamári and Períssa). Five routes: Firá-Imerovígli-Vourvoulo-Ía, Firá-Messariá-Pírgos-Akrotíri, Firá-Messariá-Pírgos-Megalohóri-Emborió-Períssa, Firá-Kamári, Firá-Monólithos.

From Firá, one bus departs for Athiniós 1hr before each sailing. It is best to leave 2hrs before your sailing in case there is a traffic jam, as the ferries don't wait. As bus timetables vary, check at the station in Firá. You pay the driver.

**Road network –** There is a lot of traffic on the roads so take care. The roads are good, and there are just a few beaches which can only be reached via dirt tracks.

**By rental vehicle –** It is best to hire in the village where you are staying. In case of technical hitches, that avoids the problem of transfers. For mopeds and motorcycles, carry out an on-the-spot check of the fuel tank (gauges are unreliable), the lights and the tyres. Whatever the type of vehicle hired (car or two-wheeler), a driving licence is obligatory.

**Fuel –** There are nine fuel stations across the island.

**By taxi** – ☎ (0286) 22 555.

**By caique** – Caiques to Thirassía, Paleá Kaméni and Néa Kaméni sail from the harbour in Firá (Skala). Organised excursions generally depart from Athiniós.

## ADDRESS BOOK

There is no tourist information office, but the many travel agencies in Firá, Kamári, Ía and Períssa offer all necessary tourist services.

**Bank / Currency exchange** – Many banks (with cash dispensers) in Firá and Kamári.

**Post office** – In Firá, Odós 25 Martíou. Kamári also has a post office. 8.30am-1.30pm.

**Police** – In Firá, Odós 25 Martíou (opposite the post office), ☎ (0286) 22 649.

**Medical service – *Medical emergencies*** (Firá hospital), ☎ (0286) 22 232.

## WHERE TO STAY

Along with Mýkonos, Santoríni is the most expensive island in the Cyclades. On top of which, if you are only staying for one night, you will pay a tax of 10%! Book in advance, and remember that the longer your stay, the better the rate. Firá, Firostefáni, Imerovígli or Ía (less expensive than Firá) offer a beautiful setting and a lively atmosphere. However, it takes about 30min to get to the beach. By way of compensation, the hotels have pools, but their prices reflect this. The eastern part of Firá, where there is no view, is less expensive. If you like swimming, opt for Kamári or Períssa. There is also a wider range of accommodation, in terms of both prices and facilities, available here.

The *Kamári Tours agency* has contacts with many hotels and places with accommodation to let on Santoríni. In Kamári, ☎ (0286) 31 390 / 31 455, Fax (0286) 31 497 / 32 758, kamaritours@santonet.gr

In Athens, Odós Filelínon 26, ☎ (01) 33 10 680, Fax (01) 33 10 684. Note: the hotels listed below are not on the plan.

• **Firá**

*Campsite*, 350m from the town centre, ☎ (0286) 22 944 / 25 062-4, Fax (0286) 25 065. ✘ ⊿ Good facilities, trees provide shade. Tents for hire, bar, mini-market, laundry. Around €12.

*Between €27 and €49*

***Hotel Mylos***, Firostefáni, ☎ (0286) 23 884 – 8rm. ✺ A small, traditional hotel with simple, clean rooms, some with view over cliff.

***Iliovassílema***, Firostefáni, ☎ (0286) 23 046 – 7rm. A small white building, clean and simple rooms with view over the caldera.

*Between €33 and €60*

***Hotel Galíni***, Katholica, ☎ (0286) 22 095, Fax (0286) 23 097- 13rm. ✺ ℰ 📺 ⇪ Clinging to the cliff, this hotel is comfortable, rooms are attractive with view over the caldera.

***Kafiéris***, Firostefáni, ☎ (0286) 22 189 – 10rm. ✺ Attractive rooms, decor typical of the island, with view.

*Over €100*

🏵 ***Eftérpi Villas***, Firostefáni, ☎ (0286) 22 541, Fax (0286) 22 542 – 10 studios (2-5 people). ✺ ℰ 📺 ⇪ Well-equipped traditional-style maisonettes with superb terraces overlooking the caldera.

• **Ía**

*Between €30 and €60*

🏵 ***Hotel Gallíni***, as you come in to Ía on the right, ☎ (0286) 71 396. ✺ ⊿ ⇪ This traditional-style establishment is full of atmosphere. Rooms and studios are simple and comfortable.

🏵 ***Hotel Flower***, after the Gallíni, on the right, under the bougainvillaea, ☎ (0286) 71 130 – 14rm. ✺ ⊿ ⇪ A cosy little hotel, looking out towards the plain and the east coast.

***Hotel Delfini***, after the fork, at the start of the pedestrian street, steps on the left, ☎ (0286) 71 600, Fax (0286) 71 601 – 23rm. Pretty rooms with or without view of the caldera (price varies accordingly). Excellent value for money.

***Anemónes***, after the Fregata hotel, on the left, in the pedestrian street, ☎ (0286) 71 220 – 9rm. A house in local style, with simple but comfortable rooms, with a view.

*Over €100*

🏵 ***Hotel Katikiès***, at the entrance to the pedestrian street, after the church, steps on the left, ☎ (0286) 71 401, Fax (0286) 71 129, or contact Kamári Tours – 15rm. ✺ ℰ 📺 ⊿ ⇪ 🆑 A very attractive establishment, decor typical of Santoríni. Terraces with magnificent view over the caldera, excellent breakfast, and a spectacular cliff-edge swimming pool.

● **Veríssa**

*Between €27 and €49*

**Pension Ánemos**, 100m from the beach, in front of Hotel Klio (to book, contact Kamári Tours) – 9rm. 🍴 A small guesthouse (no breakfast) with modest levels of comfort, but with a certain charm.

*Between €38 and €52*

**Hotel Klio**, 100m from the beach, at the end of the road perpendicular to the Kazamiaki hotel, ☎ (0286) 81 596 – 15rm. 🍴 A small hotel, simple and clean, in a quiet corner of Veríssa.

⚐ **Hotel Zorzis**, 150m from the beach, after the Kamári Tours agency, ☎ (0286) 81 104 – 15rm. 🍴 A most attractive building, enhanced by the floral displays. Clean and comfortable rooms.

*Between €45 and €60*

**Hotel Thíra Mare**, 500m from the beach, via the street running alongside Hotel Klio, ☎ (0286) 81 114 – 31rm. 🍴 🏊 cc A lovely hotel benefiting from a tranquil location. Pretty swimming pool and modern facilities.

● **Kamári**

*Between €30 and €45*

**Hotel Areti**, 200m from the beach, not far from the church in the town centre; to book, contact Kamári Tours – 20rm. 🍴 🌿 🛖 Rooms are attractive and comfortable (with radio), all with balcony, in a quiet and pleasant setting.

**Pension Tarélis**, 50m from the beach, next to the tennis club, 300m before the road to the airport, ☎ (0286) 31 773 – 20rm. 🍴 🌿 Simple and comfortable rooms.

**Pension Nina**, 80m from the beach, behind the Maria taverna, ☎ (0286) 31 697 – 14rm. 🍴 🛖 A very simple guesthouse, with clean and sunny rooms.

**Pension Kapelos Ianis**, 50m from the beach, behind the Tropical Beach hotel, ☎ (0286) 31 166 – 13rm. 🍴 🛖 An unpretentious family guesthouse, building typical of the Cyclades, clean, with a garden. No breakfast.

**Hotel Kafouros**, 100m from the beach, behind Pension Tarélis; book through

Kamári Tours – 22rm and studios. 🍴 In an elegant white building complete with blue arches, surrounded by a beautiful garden. A quiet spot, and the rooms have a pretty balcony.

**Pension Saliveros**, 200m from the beach, half way between there and the church in the centre; book through Kamári Tours – 14rm. 🍴 A Cycladic-style building, with an attractive garden. Comfortable rooms. No breakfast, but there is a taverna nearby.

*Between €45 and €60*

⚐ **Captain Elias**, 30m from the beach, opposite Pension Tarélis; book through Kamári Tours – 6 studios. 🍴 Pleasant accommodation and decor. Kitchenettes.

⚐ **Elisabeth Studios**, 50m from the beach, next to last entry; book through Kamári Tours – 12 studios. 🍴 Similar in style to above. Clean and comfortable.

*Between €45 and €60*

**Hotel Anastasia**, 400m from the beach, at the end of the street perpendicular to the campsite; book through Kamári Tours – 26rm. 🍴 🌿 🏊 🛖 cc A comfortable hotel, well situated with mountain and sea views, a shady terrace beside a pretty swimming pool, and a garden.

## Where to eat

There is no shortage of tavernas and restaurants, not forgetting the island's own gastronomic specialities waiting to be discovered: "kounéli tirávgoulo" (rabbit with onion and cheese), "fáva" (puréed broad-beans), "domatokeftédes" and "pseftokeftédes" (vegetable fritters), "skordomakaronáda" (little garlic pastries), or "moshári tis panegíris" (literally festive beef, a stew cooked in wine).

● **Ía**

*Around €15*

⚐ **Skala**, in the main street, has the finest terrace in town. Well-established taverna with traditional as well as more adventurous fare.

*Around €45*

**800**, in the former captain's residence, one of the smartest (and most expensive) restaurants on the island. Very original cuisine, a mouth-watering blend of Greek and other exotic flavours: "sfougáto", (courgettes, onion, cheese, eggs), stuffed "piperiés", (squid stuffed with grapes and rice), "tirópita anatolís" pastries stuffed with five cheeses, etc.

- **Firá**

*Around €12*

🖉 **Aktaion**, Firostefáni. This taverna, complete with courtyard, serves some excellent dishes and desserts, accompanied by a local wine which is equally palatable. All at a very good price.

🖉 **Nikolas**, a traditional restaurant with home cooking, which is always very popular (arrive early or late).

*Over €30*

**Célini**, at the far end of Firá. Serves a kind of nouvelle cuisine, Santoríni-style. Extensive wine list.

**Sphinx**, excellent cuisine and service (Italian, French and Greek dishes), on the more expensive side (no doubt you pay for the view of the caldera).

- **Monólithos**

*Around €18*

**Domata**, Agía Paraskevi near the airport. Greek cuisine, using local produce in a very imaginative way.

- **Pírgos**

**Kafenío Kandoúni**, as you go into the village, on the left, under the pine trees. Serves delicious home-made desserts.

**Taverna Kallisti**, up from the square, an equally good choice.

- **Períssa**

*Around €18*

🖉 **O Perívolos**, Perívolos, Emborió beach. Fresh fish, lobster and meze.

**Parádisos**, Exomítis. Try the "laderá" (dishes of vegetables with olive oil), the grilled sausages, or the fish, which is excellent.

- **Kamári**

*Between €12 and €18*

**Ouzéria Póntios**, near the sports stadium. Good wines and a large choice of meze.

**Taverna Andréas**, on the right before the second bus stop. A very simple taverna which serves Greek food (generous servings) and much else besides.

### HAVING A DRINK

Firá remains THE centre for night-life on the island.

- **Firá**

The trendy district is not far from Platía Theotokopoúlou, around Odós Desigala:

🖉 **Franco's**, famed throughout the world. You go there to watch the sunset, lounging on a comfortable chaise longue turned to face the caldera, with opera music in the background. An experience to try at least once... budget permitting.

**Kira Thira**, known for its sangria. Jazz music, relaxing atmosphere.

**Enigma**, a discotheque with a very Greek ambience.

**Koo Club**, an outdoor discotheque and bar, mainstream house, and Greek "dance" music. **Casablanca**, funk, acid jazz, hip hop.

🖉 **Santorinia**, Firostefáni, beyond the King Thiras hotel. A cabaret venue built into the rock, where musicians play "rembétika". Starts at midnight, with drinks and meze.

- **Monólithos**

**Action Folie**, on the beach, open at midday, sometimes has live music in the evening.

- **Períssa**

**Beach Club Jazz** (Períssa) and **Isla** (Perívolos).

- **Kamári**

**Hook**, a friendly bar at the end of the beach, near the sands.

**Avis**, another good "beach bar".

**Mango**, in front of the beach, for breakfast.

### OTHER THINGS TO DO

As with all top tourist destinations, Santoríni (Monólithos, Kamári, Períssa) offers just about every kind of leisure activity: water sports, horse riding, excursions, etc. Some travel agencies even offer one-day trips to the other islands.

**Tour of the caldera** – For a full tour of the caldera, allow between €14-18.

### SHOPPING GUIDE

Look out for the pumice stone, wine, traditional island cheese ("Hloro") or tiny little tomatoes (Santoríni's other traditional crop).

**Making the most of Santoríni**

# SÉRIFOS★

Western Aegean – District of the Cyclades – Michelin map 980 fold 31
Regional map on the inside back cover
75km² – Pop 1 095 – Allow one day

**Not to be missed**
Hóra (Sérifos Town), a jewel of the Cyclades.
The numerous beaches and little bays all along the coast.

**And remember...**
Sheltered from the meltem and easier to get to, the south coast has the best beaches,
but these are also the most popular.
In calm weather, take advantage of the north coast beaches, but remember that the
water gets deep quickly and is a bit colder here than around the neighbouring islands.

An English traveller in the 19C wrote that there was no more magical view in the
Cyclades than the sight of Hóra on Sérifos, crowning a rocky spur overhanging the
sea. A century earlier, on discovering the island in spring, the French botanist Piton
de Tournefort also marvelled at the spectacle of its bare hills, dotted with a rare
species of wild pink. Since then, apart from a century of mining operations (of which
there is little trace), and the tourist facilities which have grown up in the harbour
and surrounding area, Sérifos has scarcely changed. Steep and rocky, the land of
Perseus, the hero who cut off Medusa's head *(see page 49)*, still presents this typically Cycladic image, where beauty is synonymous with poverty.

Although, inland, there are some small green valleys which break up the arid coastal
hills, the island has neither the varied countryside nor the architectural treasures
which Sífnos offers, and the locals themselves seem rather less hospitable than their
neighbours. But the coastline, indented by myriad bays, inlets and creeks, will afford
you the rare pleasure of swimming on secluded beaches. Not to mention the journey
there, often an adventure in itself...

## Mineral ores and sand

The destiny of Sérifos was sealed by its geography: for the pirates who often came
to the island, the jagged outline of its coast provided natural refuges – sometimes
to shelter and other times to raid its underground riches. Known of since earliest
Antiquity, the iron deposits in its south-west hills were systematically mined from
the mid-14C onwards. Under Venetian rule during this period, the Serenissima's
envoy, **Ermolao Minotto**, brought a large number of slaves to the island. The Greek
concession owners received a percentage of the profit, and some even made their
fortune. Even more importantly, in spite of heavy duties levied by Venice and then
by the Ottoman Empire, Sérifos soon became known as one of the richest islands
of the archipelago; a reputation which aroused the envy of its rivals, as attested to
by the high walls around the Taxiárhes Monastery. Revived in 1865, the mining
industry declined between the two World Wars with many islanders forced into
leaving the island, while others went back to a modest rural existence. The last ten
years or so have seen immense change and the explosion of tourism has changed
everything.

## A tour of the south★

### Livádi★
Nestling at the end of a deep bay, sheltered from the wind, the coastal resort of Livádi
stretches from **Poundi**, a kind of village huddled around the quay where the ferries
come in, as far as **Avlomónas beach**, a long ribbon of sand and shingle (and ducks)
edged with tamarisks, where the island's tourist facilities are mostly concentrated. In
spite of a handful of hotels built during the 1960s and 1970s which mar its seafront,

*The Cyclades*

the modern architecture, which is in Cycladic style, integrates fairly well with the landscape of arid hills. A little way back from the shoreline, there is a small green plain, a pretty patchwork of vegetable gardens and orange groves.

To the south, Livadákia beach *(15min on foot from the harbour)* offers the shade of its many tamarisks and beautiful pale sands. Obviously you will not be alone to enjoy these attractions, as everyone staying at the campsite, hotels and chalets situated along the beach comes here.

Because of this, you might do better to opt for Karávi beach, which is hidden behind the hill *(go back to the main road and head towards Ramos, then follow the first path to the left)*: the beach is equally beautiful, but quieter. Only a few nudists and campers come here. Out to sea, **underwater excavations** have yielded a multitude of amphorae from a boat shipwrecked in the 1C BC.

There is also the delightful Avlomónas beach *(5min from the harbour)*, where the sea is beautifully clear.

### The peninsula of the beaches★

To the east of Livádi, the coast takes the shape of a peninsula, prolonged by three points. The path going round it *(a short distance before Avlomónas beach, on the left)* makes for a very pleasant **stroll★** *(allow 1-2hr, depending on your pace)* through a land-scape of rocks, imbued with the fragrance from the sparse vegetation of aromatic plants.

■ The path passes Tsilipáki Bay, coiled among the rocks like a lagoon, then goes on to Liá beach *(via the path from Livádi to Psili Ámos, or the one which goes from Avlomónas to Liá)* and its turquoise sea (which gets deep very quickly!). Tucked away between two hills, it is backed by a grove of tamarisks and reeds. Like nearly all the island's coastline, the shore here has little clumps of greenery irrigated by **springs**.

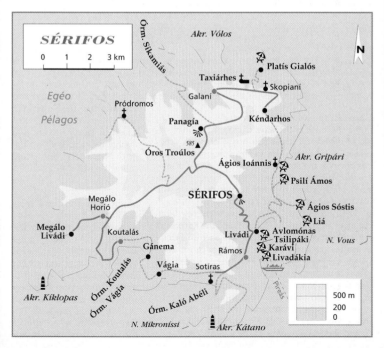

■ Just as attractive, Ágios Sóstis beach lies hidden away at the end of a deep and narrow bay (*there are no tavernas on these two beaches, so take some provisions with you*).

■ An unmissable part of your tour (although it can get quite crowded): the superb **Psilí Ámos beach**★★ (*directions given by a sign as you leave Livádi; 10min by motorcycle and 25min on foot; two tavernas*). Shallow, limpid water lapping a stretch of fine white sand planted with tamarisks. But if this really is too crowded, continue on as far as **Ágios Ioánnis beach**★.

■ After **Cape Gripári** at the end of a very steep path, is the final section of cliff path which leads to the village of **Kéndarhos** (also called Kállitso). Built like an amphitheatre at the top of a hill overlooking the sea, and a small agricultural **valley**, it is a delightful haven of greenery which runs down to the coast. On its slopes, which border a riverbed (dry in summer), grow vines, olive trees, fig trees, almond trees and other types of fruit tree, which give shade to the vegetable gardens.

## Hóra★★★ (Sérifos Town)

*15min by bus via the winding main road, or on foot via the wide stone steps hewn out of the chalk. The ascent, which is not as difficult as it looks, affords magnificent views of the countryside.*

In spite of the tourists who have invaded the island, the town of Hóra on Sérifos has remained as it was: a medieval village, typically Cycladic, a shimmering cascade of white houses clinging to the brown rock contrasting with the azure sky and sea. And quite often you will find it deserted, with its maze of steps and narrow alleyways, nearly all on a slope, lined by houses built from the stones of the old Venetian citadel. Many of these tall and narrow one-storey houses have been bought by Athenians and foreigners who have had great difficulty in trying to bring some modern comforts into them. Such are the building restrictions which scrupulously respect the local architectural style, aimed at conserving the harmony of the place.

### Kató Hóra★, the low village

*By bus or on foot. The first thing you come to in the lower part of the village is the summit of a small mound.* Nearby, the **Folklore Museum** (*5pm-8pm; closed Monday*) displays a collection of objects from daily life during the 19C and early 20C, donated by inhabitants of Sérifos. Opposite, there are steps up towards the top of the town, to **Páno Piátsa**, where the **Town Hall** (late 19C) stands with its neo-Classical façade. Its ground floor houses the **Archaeological Museum** (*9am-1pm; closed Monday*) which has a collection of pieces found on the island, notably some sculpted marble items from the Roman Period.

As you come out into the square, find a shady corner and take a break (*two tavernas there serve meze and cooked dishes*). To one side, the white mass of the **Ágios Athanássios** (18C) is dazzling when the sun is at its brightest. You can go inside to admire its carved wooden **iconostasis**.

**Benefactor and cashier wanted**

In the aftermath of the wave of emigration which depleted the island's population, not all of the churches on Sérifos have been able to find a proprietor – as is customary in the archipelago – to take charge of their upkeep. This led to the institution of *ktítor* ("possessor") which gathers together a group of people who make a vow to take care of a church for a given length of time (2 or 3 years). This is how, with their financial input and donations from visitors, the ktítores of Ágios Constantínos and Heléni have been able to lay a new marble floor, install a new wooden iconostasis and renovate the stairs. However, a further and rather unusual consequence of the shortage of manpower which afflicts Sérifos, is the notice that you will see in the old bakery in Hóra (on the wood-fired oven), which reads "tó psomí plirónetai stó supermarket"; in other words: because there is no cashier, "bread should be paid for at the supermarket".

Sérifos, recreation time in Hóra

At the top of the village are a few stones dotted here and there, remnants of the **kástro**, the Venetian citadel which was built on the remains of a Roman fort. In its place stands the **Church of Ágios Constantínos and Heléni**★ from where there is a spectacular **panorama**★★ over the southern point of the island.

## Tour of the island★
*Past the village of Rámos, a good dirt road leads
to the village of Gánema*

Cut into by deep bays which are sheltered from the meltem, the south coast is the perfect place for chancing upon your favourite beach or little bay. With this in mind, you could head for the crystalline waters of **Kaló Abéli** *(take the first dirt track on the left after Rámos, a short distance before the end of the asphalt road).*

■ Reached via the track, the three great beaches of the **Bay of Koutalás**★ are also very attractive: you can choose between **Vágia**★★, where the whiteness of the rocks gives it a lunar atmosphere – the best of the three for watching the sunset – **Gánema**★, sand and shingle, with a good taverna, or **Koutalás**★, at the far end of the bay in the shade of its tamarisks.

■ **Megálo Livádi**★ – Loading port for the mineral ores, and headquarters of the Sérifos-Spiliazéza mining company, the village was founded with the opening of the mine in 1880, and once had as many as 700 inhabitants. Still remaining from its former activities are the two **loading hoppers**, a few relics on the brow of the hill, and a beautiful **neo-Classical building**★ (the old offices); rather out of place it stands on the edge of the shore fanned by palm trees and tamarisks. A slight atmosphere of melancholy pervades the tranquillity of the port and its **beach**, nestling in a bay which is so enclosed that the sea is more like a lake.

■ **Panagía**★ – Clinging to the foothills of **Mt Troúlos** (585m), the highest point of the island, this pretty village with its white houses enjoys a fine **view**★ over the island's interior. Look out for the **Church of Panagía**★★, the oldest on Sérifos (10C-11C), with its distinctive deep red roof tiles. Concealed inside it are some remarkable **frescoes**★★ *(right-hand aisle)* dating from the 13C.

**325**

■ Beyond Panagía, a little track on the left leads to the **Bay of Sikamiás\*\***, a magnificent inlet edged with a large sandy beach, one of the most beautiful on Sérifos (*taverna nearby*).

■ **The Taxiárhes Monastery** – *By bus, get off after Galaní, then continue on foot. 9.30am-2pm / 5.30pm-7.30pm. One solitary monk in attendance;* ☎ *(0281) 51 027.* More of a fortress, this monastery built in about 1600 endured numerous assaults by pirates who were drawn there by its reputation for rich treasures. In fact, there are still a few gems conserved in the **katholikón\*\***, including **Byzantine manuscripts** (in the library), a carved marble and gilded wood **iconostasis\***, gleaming **lustres**, and on the walls, some **frescoes** attributed to one of the Skordilis brothers. Outside, the marble-paved courtyard is scented with the perfume of jasmine and pine. From the monastery, a path goes down towards the **Bay of Platís Gialós\*** and its beautiful sandy beach.

## Making the most of Sérifos

### COMING AND GOING

**By boat** – From Piraeus, one or two ferries daily (5 days a week) sail to Sérifos (3hr15min), (the Kíthnos-Sérifos-Sífnos-Mílos line). Information: (01) 42 26 000-4. One Minoan Flying Dolphins catamaran daily does the crossing from Piraeus in 2hr. Office in Piraeus: (01) 42 80 001. Office in Athens: ☎ (01) 32 44 600. Connections with Kímolos, Kíthnos, Mílos, Mýkonos, Sérifos and Tínos. *Sérifos harbourmaster's office*, ☎ (0281) 51 470.

### GETTING AROUND

**By bus** – There is a frequent bus service between Livádi and Hóra, less frequently extended to Galaní and Kéndarhos. The bus stop and the yellow notice board with timetables are at the end of the asphalt street where the paved pedestrian street begins, 200m from the boat. But do check times as they are subject to slight daily variations.

**By rental vehicle** – *Blue Bird*, a good agency for two-wheelers, as you get off the boat, ☎ (0281) 51 511. *Corali*, ☎ (0281) 51 488. Both agencies take credit cards.

### ADDRESS BOOK

**Tourist information** – Information office 100m from where you get off the boat, on the left as you come up the steps, next to the Captain Hook bar. The map of the island that is issued has very little detail, and no map of the paths is available. However, 100m from the jetty, there is a large map of the harbour which provides all practical information.

**Bank / Currency exchange** – Banks and cash dispensers in Livádi.

**Post office** – In Hóra.

**Medical service** – There is a doctor in Hóra, (0281) 51 202. One pharmacy in Livádi, (0281) 51 205.

**Other** – *Police*, ☎ (0281) 51 300.

### WHERE TO STAY

Most of the accommodation available on the island is centred around Livádi harbour and along Livadákia beach.

● **Livádi**

*Between €30 and €45*

**Hotel Aretí**, ☎ (0281) 51 479 – 12rm. 🍴 🚿 An unpretentious hotel in a central position on the harbour front, with comfortable rooms and balcony, and a peaceful garden.

**Hotel Naias**, at the harbour, 100m from the sea, ☎ (0281) 51 749, Fax (0281) 51 587 – 20rm. 🍴 🚿 🏧 CC Cycladic in style, although rather uninspiring, but comfortable and clean.

● **Livadákia**

*Campsite (around €12)*

🏕 **Corali Camping**, ☎ (0281) 51 500/ 51 073, (01) 69 11 062 / 69 84 470. ✗ CC This resort includes a 300-pitch campsite and all necessary facilities (laundry rooms, etc), chalets with kitchen and flower-filled terraces, a taverna, bar, phone booths and a grocery store, all very well maintained, only 10m from the sea, amid pines, tamarisks and oleanders. Information 50m from the jetty, at the Krinas Travel agency.

*Around €38*

**Hotel Alexándros-Vassilía**, next to the campsite, (0281) 51 119, Fax (0281) 51 903, (01) 98 88 766, Fax (01) 56 15 456 – 20rm. ⌷ ✕ 🚗 ⚡ CC Fridges. Comfortable rooms leading onto terraces shaded by a large blue pergola.

EATING OUT

Sérifos, unlike its neighbour Sífnos, has no particular gastronomic tradition. However, try the chick-pea soup, or "revíthia". The island has some problems with water supply in summer; it is therefore best to drink bottled water.

● **Hóra**

**Pétros**, in the only street running from the bus stop. The taverna is further up, on the left. The best restaurant on the island has on its menu a large selection of cooked dishes and grilled meats. Try the "lemonáto", veal served with a delicately flavoured lemon sauce.

**Manoulis**, in the town hall square. Good selection of meze.

**Para**, an ouzo bar which is also a snackbar. Ordinary food, but the setting is pleasant and the view magnificent.

● **Livádi**

**Margarítta**, at the end of the road along the seafront, along the dirt path on the left. This taverna serves excellent cooked dishes. Try and get there fairly early, as service is rather slow.

**Cycládes**, a good place to go for cooked dishes and grills.

● **Gánema**

The beach-side taverna has simple, good quality food, in a very pleasant setting.

● **Psilí Ámos**

Two very good tavernas here, the Adonis is perhaps marginally the better of the two.

HAVING A DRINK

● **Livádi**

Along the beach in Livádi, you are spoilt for choice. Choose according to your tastes in music: **Alter Ego** and **Mousès** for lovers of Greek folk music.

**Bar Karnágio**, good rock music, with tables on the beach.

**Naftikós Ómilos**, a café-bar located on a hillock, where you can have breakfast while contemplating the view of the bay. In the evening, the music is less intrusive than elsewhere.

OTHER THINGS TO DO

**Feasts & Festivals –** There are various processions in honour of the saints: 5 May, **Agía Iríni** in Koutalás; 27 July, **Ágios Penteleímon** in Pendé Pigadiá; 6 August, **Ágios Sotíros** in Kaló Abéli, 14 August in Panagía Ramou, 15 August in Pírgos and 16 August in Panagía, and 7 September, **Ágios Sóstis** in Livádi.

Making the most of Sérifos

# SÍFNOS ★★

Western Aegean – District of the Cyclades – Michelin map 980 fold 43
Regional map on the inside back cover - 74km²
Pop 1 960 – Allow 3 days

**Not to be missed**
Strolling through the flower-decked streets in Artemónas
and in the alleys of Kástro.
A walk along the monastery paths and around the island's defence towers.
Relaxing on the white sands of Vathí and tasting the local cuisine.

**And remember...**
If you are planning to stay in Apolonía or the surrounding area,
ask the hotelier to come and meet you as you get off the bus,
rather than wandering the hilly streets for hours laden with luggage.

Sífnos is a microcosm of the Cyclades, where everything seems to have been fashioned with great care and style – even the landscape itself, with its contours enhanced by attractive low drystone walls. A landscape of arid mountains, where all that can flourish is a scrubby growth of sage and juniper – the domain of goats and bees – of long sandy beaches and of hillsides with verdant terraces carved into them, dotted here and there with windmills, dovecotes and chapels. History has strewn the island with fascinating reminders of its past, among them ancient towers, a medieval town and noble monasteries. Sífnos is to be discovered at a leisurely pace – strolling through the flower-decked alleyways of its villages, travelling along the mule-paths which meander over valleys and hills, and watching the potters fashioning their wares just as their ancestors did. The kindness of the locals and a well-earned gastronomic reputation are the final touches. In essence, this is an island which charms you with its harmonious combination of modern leisure and ancient tradition.

## Of gold and learning

Exploited since the most ancient times by the island's successive occupants – the Phoenicians, the Minoans, then the Ionians – the gold and silver mines of Sífnos brought considerable prosperity to its inhabitants. But the deposits

**Sífnos: a generous host**
On Sífnos, spiritual and physical nourishment are equally appreciated. Indeed, the island is famous for its gastronomic cuisine, reputedly among the best in Greece. On the menu are: "kaparosaláta" (a salad with spicy capers), "mastélo" (lamb marinated in red wine), "xinomintzíthra" (soft cheese made from ewe's milk), "revitháda" (chick peas with onion and bay-leaf), "mansirá" (soft white cheese preserved in wine-must), "bourékia" (a cake originally from Constantinople, with a filling of honey, sesame and almond paste), "kalasoúna" (a sweet dish with a base of red courgettes). Even the classic Greek dishes are more tasty here given the quality of the local produce: "soupiés me kremídia" (cuttlefish with onions), "piperiés" (peppers), "octapódi me macarónia" (spaghetti with octopus), "tirópita" (flaky pastries with cheese). Not forgetting the very drinkable local wine.

were quickly exhausted and, as early as the 5C BC, the decline began, accelerated by wars that Sífnos entered into with Athens, its protector. This decline became even more pronounced when the coastline came under attack, first from pirates from the Barbary coast in Venetian times, then from Maltese raiders during the period of Turkish rule. Such a turbulent past left permanent marks on the life of Sífnos, as witnessed by the concentration of its population in the centre of the island.

During the 17C, however, the threat diminished and Sífnos experienced an astonishing surge of intellectual activity, not totally unconnected to the prosperity of its merchants. Catholic monks taught here from 1625 to 1634, succeeded by monks from the monasteries of Pátmos and Mt Athos. Then the famous fraternity of the Holy Sepulchre founded a theological school, which was to remain open until 1835. In short, the island was a centre for spiritual and patriotic life, which could only have predisposed its inhabitants to participate actively in the Greek revolution; this they did, under the leadership of **Nikólaos Hrissolegoú**, a schoolmaster who was later to become Minister for Education under King Otto.

## From Kamáres to the Apolonía area

■ **Kamáres\*** – As you approach Sífnos, the ruggedness of the west coast, an arid, rocky mass silhouetted against the sky, may come as a surprise. Hemmed in between two high mountains, the Bay of Kamáres appears right at the last minute. Exposed to winds from the north and west, this harbour never used to receive many visitors, as the caiques favoured the more sheltered Bay of Vathí and the trading boats preferred the small harbour of Fáros. Kamáres owes its development at the end of the 19C to

Sífnos, a monastery on the sea: Panagía Hrissopigí

G. de Benoist/MICHELIN

**A watchful island**

The development of piracy in the Aegean during the course of the 2C BC – a menace that was to remain a constant threat to life on the island until the beginning of the 19C – explains the very large number of towers ("pírgos") on Sífnos. Remains of 55 of these buildings, more than in the rest of the Cyclades, can be found all over the island. Of circular construction, most of these towers had a diameter of between 7m and 10m, and were used by those living in the vicinity as a lookout post and refuge.

the export of iron and lead extracted by a French company. Marks on the landscape point to where the metals were mined until 1918. The jetty was added in 1907.

But the major attraction of this coastal resort with its friendly, family atmosphere remains its **beach★**. Very flat and clean, it is one of the longest on the island.

This band of sand stretches from the tiny village of **Agía Marína** (on the left), where there are still two **pottery workshops**, to the **harbour** itself, where all commercial activity is concentrated. Tavernas, cafés and bars line the length of the jetty and the alleyways of the original village. For a good view of the **sunset**, head for the steps which lead up to the Church of Agía Marína.

As you leave Kamáres for Apolonía, the road follows a dry riverbed which winds through the countryside, scented by wild flowers and aromatic plants. At intervals along the way are some austere **white chapels**, a few **dovecotes** with their elegant geometrical patterning as well as the ruins of a Hellenistic tower, **Kabanarió** (about 4km from Kamáres, on the left, opposite the Church of Ágii-Anárgiri, 100m from the road), which is one of the best preserved on the island.

As you approach Apolonía, the scrubland gives way to **fields with espaliers** of olive trees, fruit trees and vines. The locals refer to these narrow terraces as louriá ("belts"), their function being to stop the land from slipping with the winter rains and to retain water in the drier months.

■ **Apolonía★** – As you enter the village, you come to **Platía Iróon**, the main square, where there is a small **museum★** (open every day, 10am-2pm / 7pm-11pm; entrance fee) with displays of traditional clothes, embroidery, fabrics, pottery, weapons, and agricultural and domestic implements.

But it is not until the next crossroads that you will discover why this town is the capital (since 1836), as you come out onto a magnificent **viewpoint★★** with a panorama which takes in the town and the surrounding area: built in the form of an amphitheatre upon three verdant hills which are carved into terraces as regular as flights of steps, the town extends in all directions with the neighbouring villages of **Páno Petáli** and **Artemónas** to the north, **Katavatí** to the south, and **Káto Petáli**, **Ágios Loukás** and **Exámbela**, which can be seen a little further east. Together, they form a continuous network of houses, in the shape of a long snake of an immaculate whiteness, with the blue domes of their churches dotted here and there.

Allow yourself some time for a walk around the town. Cafés, tavernas and boutiques are nearly all concentrated along the narrow cobbled alleyway of **Stilianoú Prokou★** which, starting from Platía Iróon, on the right, goes as far as the foot of the **Cathedral of Ágios Spirídonos★**, a vast building restored in 1901, which contains the very beautiful **Hrissopigí icon★★**, said to have miraculous powers.

**Every day has its "panigíri"**

Every church has its patron saint. With 208 officially listed churches and chapels, Sífnos has no shortage of saints to be celebrated ("panigíri")! In family homes, banquets are held in the courtyard, in the shade of a vine-clad trellis. That is unless the whole village has come together in one of those long, narrow rooms that some of the churches have, which has been specially decked out for the occasion. The lead-up to the event is invariably the same: copious tsoukalia of "revitháda" (chick peas, the traditional local dish) are taken to the baker for cooking. The festivities go on until late into the night, to the sound of the violin and to the rhythm of the bálo and the nissiótika, the traditional dances of the islands.

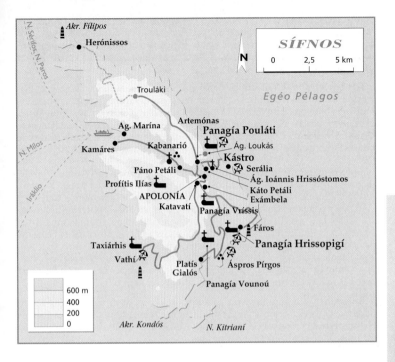

Nearby, in the small square dedicated to the writer **Cléanthis Triandáfilos** – possibly on the site of a temple to Apollo – is the **Church of Stávros** (also called Ágios Athanássios) and its treasures: some remarkable **frescoes** and a **carved wooden iconostasis.**

But the most beautiful church in Apolonía remains the **Panagía Ouranofóra**★★ (or Ghieraniofóra) (in the high part of the town, near Páno Petáli). Built in the 18C, it contains **columns** which came from a much older church, possibly a pre-Christian sanctuary. Note also the sculpted **marble plaque**★ above the entrance, featuring St George and the Virgin Mary.

*Past Platía Iróon, on the left, you will find a small kafenío, Lákis, situated at the corner of two alleyways. Pass Odós Barou on your left and take the street which heads up towards Páno Petáli and then on to Artemónas.*

■ About 150m further on *(signposted)*, a **church** in the shade of a pine tree adjoins the old building of the **Monídrio Ágios Artémios**★, the "little monastery" founded in 1629 by the Sifniot monk **Ieremía Orfanó** (Jeremiah the Orphan). There is a **plaque** recalling the fact that five schools were accommodated here between 1829 and 1988.

■ **Páno Petáli**★★ – Almost without being aware of it, you leave Apolonía and enter the lanes of the neighbouring village, dominated by the **Ágios Ioánnis Church,** Italianate in style. Soon after, you reach the foot of the **Panagía Ta Gourniá**★★, a church notable for some **mural frescoes**★★ and a **wooden iconostasis**★★ decorated with beautiful icons.

Further on, you come to **Platía Nikólaos Hrissolegoú**, where the **bust** of the school-master who became King Otto's Minister for Education stands imposingly. The alleyway off to the right then takes you to the enchanting district of Ágios Loukás, the fiefdom of the **Church of Ágios Antípas⋆**, which is worth a detour for the **marble engravings**, dated 1636.

■ **Artemónas⋆⋆** – You will probably enter the village without realising it. It is thought that Artemónas owes its name to the goddess Artemis, Apollo's twin sister. A **temple** once occupied the site where the **Church of Kohis⋆⋆** now stands. In this old quarter, where the important people of the island used to live, beautiful **neo-Classical residences** built in the 18C-19C alternate with small **traditional-style houses**, with gardens of flowering bougainvillaea and jasmine hemmed in between them.

Worth a detour is the marvellous **iconostasis⋆⋆** in the **Panagía tis Ámou Church⋆** (*in the centre of the village*), a veritable piece of lace-work in gilded wood.

At the end of the asphalt road, look out for the **Ágios Konstandínos Church⋆⋆** (1462), a magnificent example of Cycladic architecture. Possibly because a theological school was based here in the 17C, this venerable church has the privilege of ringing the bells for liturgies on Saturdays, Sundays and feast days, and of being the point from which all the village processions start out.

Next, climb to the top of the hill, above the **Church of Ágios Merkoúrios**, where two **windmills⋆** are still in operation. From the top, a spectacular **panoramic view⋆** over Kástro and the neighbouring islands unfolds before you.

■ **Kástro⋆⋆⋆** – If you decide to go down on foot as far as the village of Kástro (*about 30min*), make a stop along the way at the enchanting **Church of Ágios Ioánnis Hrissóstomos⋆⋆** (*reached via a path which goes off to the right*), built in the 17C on the walls of a Venetian defensive structure.

Inhabited since Antiquity, Kástro was the capital of the island under Venetian rule (1207-1537), and continued as such until 1836. Today, it is content to be a fashionable village: cafés, tavernas, artists' studios and craftsmen's workshops exploit its medieval atmosphere and its exceptional natural setting. Indeed, Kástro is a remarkable example of a **Venetian fortified town**, combining a rocky site – perfect natural protection – with a defensive wall formed by the external walls of the houses and penetrated by three gateways. These houses are generally made up of three storeys, with the ground floor opening towards the exterior, while the two other floors can only be reached from inside the town.

While strolling through this maze of steps, alleyways and narrow passageways, take time to admire the Italian-style balconies, the columns and the marble blazons on the lintels of the **patrician houses⋆⋆**.

Kástro also has numerous **churches⋆⋆** built in the 16C-17C, nearly all worthy of a visit. And from the wall there are superb **views⋆** down over the sea and the surrounding area.

If you have the time, you should also pay a visit to the **Archaeological Museum** (*open every day, 9am-2pm*), where Archaic and Classical statues, and pottery from the Ancient and Byzantine Periods are on display.

A wide flight of steps leads towards the rock and the **Church of the Seven Martyrs⋆⋆**, whose names are displayed on a plaque. There is a spectacular view of the **sunrise⋆** from this promontory.

■ **Serália⋆⋆** – Kástro's old harbour, Serália, is no more than a modest little bay with a few square metres of sand, inviting you to take a short (but pleasant) **swim**, before going on to sample the local cuisine at the nearby taverna (Sifaki). Higher up are the quaint churches of **Ágios Stefános⋆** and **Ágios Ioánnis⋆** which look down over the *cemetery of Kástro*, amid the remains of the school of the Holy Sepulchre.

*Leave Kástro on the Artemónas road, then head in the direction of Herónissos, before following the dirt track on the right (suitable for motor vehicles), for about 3km, which leads to the Panagía Poulátí Monastery. There is also a path which leads to it along the coast.*

■ **The Panagía Poulátí Monastery**★★ – Built on the edge of the cliff, this abandoned monastery of 1871 occupies an enchanting **setting**★★★: above the brown-ochre of the rocks and the green-grey carpet of olive trees, the dark spears of the cypress trees emphasise even more strongly the whiteness of the church, the dome vanishing into the blue sky. Down below, hollowed out in the indented coast, is a **little bay**★★ where the water is crystal clear.

## The south
*From Apolonía, return to Katavatí either by road
or by the steps that lead to the village.*

■ As you pass through the village of **Katavatí**★ with its typically Cycladic vernacular architecture, note the care that its inhabitants take to deck their houses and terraces with flowers, using all kinds of pots of an infinite variety of shapes and sizes.

*At the end of the village's narrow main street, a sign indicates the way to the Profítis Ilías tou Psiloú Monastery. The path begins at the back of the Panagía Evangelistría Church, and takes you (90min on foot) to the highest point of the island (685m), from which the monastery gets its description, "tou Psiloú", literally "of the heights".*

■ **The Profítis Ilías Monastery**★★ – First a church, then a monastery from 1650 onwards, Profítis Ilías is the most important Byzantine building on Sífnos, with some sections dating from the 12C. The high wall of bleached stone, dotted with turrets, above which juts the white dome of the katholikón, makes a very striking visual composition. This medieval tone is continued throughout the tour (conducted by an accompanying monk) which includes the galleries, cells and underground passageways, all this great weight of architecture supported on old marble columns. All this and the unforgettable **panoramic view**★★ over the eastern Cyclades. On 19 July, the islanders go up to the monastery for its celebrations. The ascent begins at about 6pm in the evening, and the descent takes place by torchlight, after nightfall.

■ **Vathí beach**★★ – *Can be reached from Katavatí along the road, or by a path.* The best beach on the island curves around a magnificent bay, encircled by hills on which olive trees alternate with scrub. An unexpected sight here is the **Taxiárhis Monastery**★★ (16C); the building is completely white, topped with two domes, and stands on a mole along the shoreline. At one time there were a lot of potters' workshops along the beach; the few that remain are on the left.

*Take the road heading in the direction of Fáros.*

■ **The Panagía Vríssis Monastery**★ – As you leave Apolonía, you go through the village of **Exámbela**, which marks the start of the most agricultural region of the island. 500m further on are the fortified walls of the monastery, built around 1600. A ring of cells and various rooms make up the defensive perimeter wall, around a courtyard with the **abbey church**★ standing in its centre. One of the rooms contains a small **Byzantine museum**.

■ **Fáros**★ – The principal harbour of the island until 1883, nowadays Fáros has a flotilla of fishing boats and is just beginning to cater for tourists. If you follow the path which goes to the **lighthouse**, you could have a swim at **Fassolou beach**★. At the other end of the bay, **Cape Petálos** is crowned by the **Panagía Hrissopigí Monastery**★★★ (1650), dedicated to the patron saint of Sífnos. This is the most visited pilgrimage destination on the island and boasts a **miraculous icon** of the Virgin Mary. To the left stretches the sandy beach of **Apokofto**★, fringed with tamarisks *(take care as you wade into the sea, the rocky bed is very slippery)*, while the rocks sheltered by the **Saourès**\* on the right are recommended for windy days and for the very clear sea there.

■ To the left 100m from the road, *(just before the hairpin bend which goes sharply down towards Platís Gialós)*, are the ruins of **Áspros Pírgos**\*, a Hellenistic town. Of its defensive wall, the **white tower**\*\* is still standing, and is one of the easiest to get to on the island, with a view down over the coastline.

■ **Platís Gialós**\* – The vast Platís Gialós beach has become the island's main resort. Once a great centre for pottery, there are still some workshops in production (to the far left of the beach) which are open to the public. To the north of the bay, at the summit of the hill, look out for the white walls of the **Panagía Vounoú Monastery**\* (Our Lady of the Mountain). Built in 1813, it contains the **Panagía Eléoussa** or **Mahéroussa icon** (1756). The ascent offers a fine **panorama**\*.

## Making the most of Sífnos

**COMING AND GOING**

From Piraeus, one ferry daily to Mílos via Kíthnos, Sérifos and Sífnos (5hr crossing). *Information*, ☎ (01) 422 60 00-4.

The Minoan Flying Dolphins company has hydrofoils and catamarans which make the crossing from Piraeus every day in 2hr30min. Office in Piraeus, ☎ (01) 42 80 001; *Athens office*, ☎ (01) 32 44 600. Connections to Kímolos, Kíthnos, Mílos, Mýkonos, Páros, Sérifos, Tínos and Káristos.

**GETTING AROUND**

**By bus** – Four bus routes link the twelve villages on the island. More frequent services on the Kamáres-Apolonía-Artemónas-Platís Gialós route than in the direction of Fáros, Káto Petáli, Kástro and Vathí. Timetables are posted on the notice boards at every bus stop and in the tourist information office.

**By rental vehicle** – The island is well suited to two-wheeled vehicles, as there are only short distances to be covered (Vathí is only 10km from Apolonía). In Kamáres, cars can be hired at the *Stavros hotel*.

Motorcycles etc from *Dionysos*, 200m past the previous entry.

In Apolonía: *Apollo* and *Sun's Moto*, on the Platís Gialós road after the crossroads. Less expensive than in Kamáres, ☎ (0284) 32 237. To hire a 50cc machine, budget for around €7.50 per day and around €30 per day for a car.

**Fuel** – There are three fuel stations on the island, near Apolonía.

**By taxi** – There are around ten taxis in service, ☎ (0284) 31 656 / 31 719 / 31 626.

**ADDRESS BOOK**

**Tourist information** – In Apolonía, on the quay, 50m to the right, and Fax (0284) 31 997. Friendly service, with all the essential information available, including a map of the island with ten tours marked on it, and a map of the paths drawn up by John Birkett-Smith. They also have guidebooks along with bus timetables and routes. You can also book accommodation anywhere on the island, through the *association of proprietors* of accommodation to let, ☎ (0284) 31 333.

**Bank / Currency exchange** – Apolonía, in Platía Iróon.

**Post office / Telephone** – Apolonía, in Platía Iróon.

**Medical service – *Pharmacy*** in Apolonía, Platía Iróon, ☎ (0284) 33 033. *Medical Centre*, in Apolonía, ☎ (0284) 31 315.

**Police** – In Apolonía, ☎ (0284) 31 210.

**Harbourmaster's office** – In Kamáres, ☎ (0284) 33 617.

**Bookshop** – The bookshop in Apolonía (on the left past Platía Iróon) has a large selection of books and brochures on Sífnos.

**WHERE TO STAY**

Hotel accommodation is often good quality, and the Sifniots are very welcoming. However, avoid the period from 20 July to the end of August. All establishments provide breakfast.

- **Kamáres**
*Between €24 and €38*

**Hotel Boulis**, 50m from the sea, ☎ (0284) 32 122 / 31 640, Fax (0284) 32 381 – 45rm. 🔌 🖉 ⛰ ✕ 🏠
Slightly gaudy interior decoration, but clean and comfortable throughout, with a friendly atmosphere. The best rooms (all with their own veranda) have a sea view.

*Between €60 and €120*
**Alkyonis Villas**, 100m from the beach, (0284) 33 101-2 / 32 225 – 10 apartments for 3 to 5 people. Sea view, traditional Cycladic style, with kitchens, and large verandas.

- **Apolonía**
*Between €24 and €36*

🙂**Mrs Yérondi** (rooms to let), opposite the Hotel Pétali, ☎(0284) 32 316 – 8rm. 🔌 Fridge. A very friendly welcome and quiet, comfortable rooms, simply furnished in traditional style. Also a fantastic view and a pretty courtyard.

🙂**Dina** (rooms to let), ☎(0284) 31 125, ☎(01) 93 47 279 – 8rm. 🔌 Fridge. A charming establishment, with a very beautiful flower-filled courtyard and a warm welcome from Mrs Constantína Lazarídou, who speaks English.

**Villa Setos** (rooms to let), ☎(0284) 31 145 – 5rm. 🔌 An old building dating from 1920, carefully refurbished in local style, with all modern comforts.

**Margaríta Mánou-Karídi** (rooms to let), as you go out of Katavatí, ☎ (0284) 32 013 – 8rm. 🔌 Fridge. Village atmosphere, with view of Mt Profítis Ilías. Simple but comfortable.

*Around €45*
**Hotel Anthoússa**, Apolonía, ☎(0284) 31 431 / 32 330 – 10rm. 🔌 📖 ✕ 🏠
Above a café-cum-bakery, central location (a bit noisy). Excellent breakfast, all modern comforts, simple decor and a friendly welcome.

*Between €43 and €90*
🙂**Hotel Pétali**, on the pedestrian street between Apolonía and Artemónas, ☎ and Fax (0284) 33 024 – 10rm. 🔌 🖉 ✕ 🏠 **CC** The most attractive hotel on Sífnos, with one of its best restaurants (fairly expensive, however). This traditional-style building combines beauty and comfort. Magnificent view.

**EATING OUT**
See the sidebar on local gastronomy at the beginning of the chapter.

- **Kamáres**
*Around €15*

🙂**Kapetán Andréas**. The owner himself catches the squid, lobster, "barboúnia" and "baládes". Meals served on the beach, under the shade of the tamarisks. And if you do not like fish, there is also braised side of beef. All moderately priced.

- **Apolonía**
*Around €11*

🙂**Liotrivi**, Platía Artemónas. Small wooden tables in a charming setting: this is THE taverna for discovering the local cuisine (thirty or so cooked dishes), at moderate prices.

**The Star**, Kástro. Traditional cuisine made from produce grown in the proprietor's garden.

- **Vathí**
*Around €11*

🙂**To Tsikali**, on the beach to the right. Fish and local cuisine, simple and delicious food at moderate prices.

- **Platís Gialós**
*Around €11*

**Sofia** and **Fonis**, two good places for traditional cuisine, both on the beach.

- **Hrissopigí beach**
*Around €11*

Two good tavernas: **Hrissopigí**, and **O Tapsis**.

**HAVING A DRINK**

🙂**Folie**, in Kamáres, 🙂**Remezzo** in Kástro and some of the bars (**Isidora**, **Botzi**, **Argo** and **Delfini**) along Odós Stylianou Prokopou, in Apolonía.

**OTHER THINGS TO DO**

**Feasts & Festivals** – These are the main ones: Taxiárhis Church in Vathí (12 June), Profítis Ilías Monastery (19 July), Panagía Ta Ghournia Church (15 August), and Ágios Simeon Church (31 August).

**SHOPPING GUIDE**

**Crafts** – Pottery (particularly the "tsoukália" and the "fláros" which crown the roofs of the houses), traditional textiles and jewellery.

**Making the most of Sífnos**

# SÍROS★★

Aegean Sea – District of the Cyclades – Michelin map 980 fold 32
Regional map on the inside back cover – 86km² – Pop 19 870

**Not to be missed**
Ermoúpoli and its neo-Classical architecture.
Meandering through the alleyways of Áno Síros.
A hike in the hills at Áno Meriá, to the north of the island.

**And remember...**
Two days are enough to visit the island, but to immerse yourself in the cultural
atmosphere of Ermoúpoli, a further day would not go amiss.

Síros is an unexpected jewel for anyone wanting to get away from the tourist crowds
and enjoy more of the natural charms of the Cyclades. Today, as in years gone by,
a small number of the Athenian elite have also found a refuge here, just a few hours
by ferry from Athens. Ignored for a long time, its image tarnished by its industrial
past, the island is still slightly off the main tourist routes and as such, has retained
its true spirit. A spirit, moreover, which is very rich, displaying many faces: Catholic
and Orthodox influences for example, with their cathedrals which, planted like
banners atop the hills of the capital, almost seem to taunt one another; its rural and
urban divide, which splits the island into two, leaving the highlands to the north to
traditional farms and to hikers, while the south, with its gentler landscape and coastline indented with little bays, boasts a number of elegant coastal resorts, overlooked
by the neo-Classical villas of the more prosperous inhabitants of Ermoúpoli.

## The island of the Pope
While prehistoric times gave rise to a remarkable Cycladic culture (2800-2300 BC)
with a prolific number of artefacts (as seen in Athens), this island does not feature
historically until the 13C, when it was taken over by Venetians from Náxos. It was

The neo-Classical elegance of the port of Ermoúpoli, Síros

subsequently used as a refuge by Frankish Catholics driven out from the other islands of the Cyclades by the Turks. The exiles settled on the hill of Áno Síros, where they built their fortified town, which they placed under the protection of Rome, giving Síros its nickname of "the island of the Pope". When the Ottomans laid siege to this area in the 16C, France resumed its role as protector, signing a statute of extraterritoriality with Istanbul. With the Turkish dignitaries' role reduced to a very minor one, French monks took charge of administration, law and education. From that time on, the island began to prosper, its trading port becoming in-

### Two hills, two religions

When the French botanist, Piton de Tournefort, visited Síros in 1700, the island only had about 2 Orthodox households compared to 6 000 Catholic ones. Although strong in numbers, the latter remained rather wary when Orthodox Greeks arrived on the island in their thousands during the War of Independence. In refusing to integrate the two communities, they were responsible for the establishment of two separate societies, kept apart by religion as much as by geographical area (each having its own hill) and commercial activities. Happily these differences have since disappeared and their integration is best symbolised by the Good Friday celebrations: Catholic and Orthodox *epitáphios* are paraded together in Platía Miaoúli in Ermoúpoli, marking communal prayers.

creasingly important in the Cyclades. During the Greek War of Independence, Síros retained its neutrality, and was used as a place of refuge by the many Greeks who fled from the Turks and brought the island into its golden age.

### The cultural capital of Greece

The skills of these craftsmen and traders were soon to produce amazing results. It was these refugees who started up workshops, factories, cotton mills, tanneries and shipyards, creating a prosperous new town, which they called Ermoúpoli, the "town of Hermes", the patron saint of trade. Elegant neo-Classical buildings flourished and the town grew bigger. Influenced by the ideas of the Age of Enlightenment and of the French Revolution, these new inhabitants of the island also founded schools, literary circles and printing houses. The really wealthy, dressed in Parisian fashion, also enjoyed a dazzling whirl of parties and balls. Thus, from being an island lost in the Aegean, Síros soon asserted itself as the commercial and intellectual capital of Greece. This period of good fortune would last for almost all of the 19C, but was brought to an end by the opening of the Corinth Canal (1893), when commercial and political power was once more focused on Athens and Piraeus.

## Ermoúpoli★★★ (Síros)

*Capital of Síros. Keep the morning for exploring the town,*
*which is the best place to have lunch.*
*End the day in Áno Síros, where the little lanes come to life as the sun goes down.*

Even at night, the twin hills of Síros are clearly profiled against the sky, dark rocky masses dotted with lights which recall the duality of the two religious communities of the island. They are crowned by two cathedrals, one for each bastion: on the right, the tall white façade of the Orthodox church of Ágios Nikólaos stands on Anástasi ("resurrection") hill, while on the left, the cathedral of Ágios Geórgios marks the Catholic fiefdom of **Áno Síros**, "high Síros". Built on the slopes of these two hills is the town, furrowed by endless flights of steps, its white and yellow-ochre houses clinging to the hillside like mountain goats.

It is at the **port**, however, that the spirit of Síros can be best appreciated, with its different faces revealing the history of its prosperity. To the east on the Nissaki Peninsula, stand the old transit **warehouses** and the imposing marble façade of the **customs house**, sober neo-Classical buildings lining the quaysides. To the west (*on the left*) is what used to be the red-light district of the port, home to the brothels and bars where sailors would come to smoke hashish imported from Asia Minor.

*At the centre of the port, turn into Odós Híos, where there is a small but lively market every morning (except Sunday). This street comes to an end in Platía Miaoúli.*

## Platía Miaoúli★★★

Built between 1876-80 by the German architect **Ernst Ziller** on the model of an Italian piazza, Platía Miaoúli is where Ermoúpoli's heart beats most strongly. With elegant **patrician residences** shaded by palm trees and arcaded galleries sheltering restaurants and cafés, it makes for a remarkable (listed) neo-Classical setting, unique in Greece. The principal building on the square is the enormous edifice of the **town hall**★★ – one of the largest in the whole country – which is preceded by a no less monumental stairway of 40 steps. At the top of these propylaea stands the pedimented porch, punctuated by two series of three arches. Spanning the width of the central hall – which is used as an exhibition hall for old fire-engines – are two high glass-roofed galleries, one of which houses a pleasant **café**.

The town hall is framed on either side by two buildings: on the left, the building known as the **house of Ladópoulos**, which serves as the central archive office for the Cyclades, while, on the right, the house designed by the Italian architect **Pietro Sampo** has been converted into a cultural centre commonly referred to as the **Hellas circle**. Wealthy tradesmen used to meet here in colonial-style clubs and society events were also held here. In the centre of the square is an imposing statue of the Hydriot admiral, **Andréas Miaoúlis** (*see page 177*), flanked by two cannons.

Behind the town hall, you could take a quick look at the **Museum of Archaeology** of Síros (*Odós Benáki, 8am-3pm; closed Monday; no entrance fee*). Opened in 1834, this is one of the oldest museums of its kind in Greece. Its three rooms contain a small collection of artefacts found on Síros, among them funeral steles and Cycladic idols (*Room 1*), marble sculptures and pottery from the 3rd millennium BC from the Chalandrianí necropolis (*Room 2*). Also note the beautiful black granite **Egyptian statuette** of a priest (730 BC).

*As you leave the museum, turn left into Odós Karaolí & Dimitríou.*

On the way, you pass the **Church of the Metamórfossis**. It was built in 1824 on the model of the Panagía of Tínos with the aid of funds raised by the survivors of the Turkish massacres. Almost all of the precinct is paved with stones brought from Rhodes, while the interior, which is richly decorated, features various **icons** donated by local guilds.

*Continue along Odós Karaolí & Dimitríou as far as Platía Vardáka.*

Another reference to Italian architecture, the **Apollon Theatre**★★ (*10.30am-1pm / 6pm-8pm; no entrance fee*) which dominates **Platía Vardáka** was

### A neo-Classical town

From 1837 onwards, it took just twenty years for the lower part of Ermoúpoli – under the influence of various architects, first Bavarian, then Italian, and finally Greek, but all inspired by classical models – to acquire its present-day physiognomy. Strongly influenced by the Italian Renaissance and the Romantic Movement, the grandiose houses, several storeys high, combined stucco with marble, their façades adorned with large bay windows and wrought-iron balconies supported by sculpted consoles. The interior decor was often a riot of painted mouldings, trompe-l'œil effects and frescoes depicting mythological scenes.

### Síros, a never-ending festival

After its decline in the early 20C, the island has seen a revival of its strong cultural heritage. From 15 July to the end of August, and to a lesser extent during the winter, the streets of Áno Síros and Ermoúpoli are brought alive with concerts, exhibitions, folk festivals and other local events. Galleries of art and design are also proliferating and there is even talk of opening a Museum of Siriot Industry. Similarly, Platía Miaoúli is the perfect setting for the many nocturnal shows that take place there.

designed in 1864 by the French architect, Chabeau, on the model (in miniature!) of La Scala in Milan. In the 19C, all Síros' jet set flocked there to see performances by the most famous European troupes. The painted ceiling is a veritable portrait gallery of famous musicians: Rossini, Mozart and Donizetti.

In Odós Vardáka stands the **Ágios Nikólaos Church**, financed by the Greek diaspora from Russia and Chios. The Corinthian columns, the carved lintels and the gold-embellished **iconostasis**★ are sculpted from Parian marble.

Further on is the more exclusive neighbourhood of **Vapória**, where the shipowners had their sumptuous **villas**★ built, now undergoing restoration.

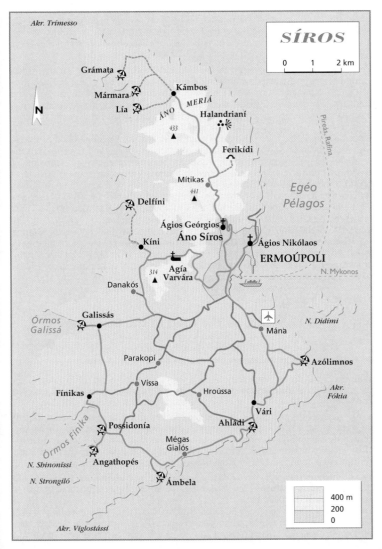

On returning to the quayside, head in the direction of the landing-stage and turn right into Odós Kitínou.

Make for the **Church of the Kímissis** (*7.30am-12noon / 4pm-7pm from April to August, 4.30pm-5.30pm from September to March*). There you will find an **icon by El Greco★** depicting the *Dormition of the Virgin*, a work by the young painter who, at that time, was still known as Doménikos Theotokópoulos.

## Áno Síros★★★
*Allow 2hr*

*From Ermoúpoli, you can get to Áno Síros by bus or taxi (as far as Portara, one of the gates to the town), or even on foot, which is the best way: from the upper part of Ermoúpoli, you can either go via the "Bridge of the French" which connects the two towns, or head along the main road (quite steep – 30min walk) which passes alongside the Orthodox ceme-tery (with its ostentatious steles) and the Catholic one (more restrained).*

The urbanisation of Síros began in the 13C, developing initially up on the higher ground before graduating down towards the sea in circles of increasing size, as waves of Catholic immigrants arrived. Hence it is to history as much as to the lie of the land that this typically Cycladic medieval town – where no vehicles are allowed – owes its charm and its physiognomy, with small white houses and *steádia* (covered passageways), narrow alleys and little squares.

Once through Portara, you rejoin the main street and the neighbourhood of **Pláka**, the vibrant heart of Áno Síros, where the commercial services and tavernas are con-centrated, as well as a few small museums. Among these are an exhibition of **traditional crafts** and an area dedicated to **Márkos Vamvakáris**, the famous rem-bétiko composer, born on Síros in 1905.

As you wander through this labyrinth, continue up as far as the **Ágios Geórgios Cathedral**, at the summit of the hill. Built in 1598, it was destroyed by the Turks on several occasions (the last time was in 1830) and rebuilt each time.

To the left of the church, what was the first Greek seminary now houses the **Centre for Historical Studies of the Catholic Diocese of Síros** (*11am-2pm / 6.30pm-9pm in July and August; short guided tour for which a fee is charged*). This contains, among other things, a library of 3 500 antique books – the oldest of which dates from 1524 – some legal documents, as well as a letter from Andréas Miaoúlis demanding 500 casks of wine from the Siriots... to keep up the morale of his troops during the struggle against the invading Turks.

## The south, or the road of the beaches
*40km circuit there and back, starting out from Ermoúpoli
(as you come out of Ermoúpoli, head in the direction of the airport).
Allow one day, to include stops for lunch and swims.*

With good bus connections, the coastal resorts to the south-east of Ermoúpoli are the most popular: **Azólimnos** and **Vári**, with their shallow water, **Ahládi**, or even **Ámbela** (*first road on the left after Mégas Gialós*), which is the most sheltered.

■ You might, however, prefer the smarter beaches of the west coast, even though they are busier. Notably, **Possidonía★** (*12km away*), also known as Dellagrazia, chosen by the Catholic bourgeoisie of Ermoúpoli as their holiday resort in the 19C. Now virtually deserted, their imposing **villas★** still look down over the pine forest and the neighbouring beach of **Angathopés**, very popular with the jet set.

■ Continuing northwards, you cross the yachting harbour of **Fínikas**, just before the beautiful beach at **Galissás** (*3km further on*), the former hippy stronghold (which is absolutely packed in summer).

You would do better to spend more time in **Kíni★**, a pretty fishing harbour which lies coiled around the hollow of a horseshoe-shaped bay (*first road on the right, then left towards Danakós*), a very pleasant spot to sit and gaze at the sunset. And if you fancy a swim, head for the beautiful beach at **Delfíni** nearby *(20min walk via a path which goes off to the right as you look at the sea)*, as long as you don't mind nudists.

■ Heading back towards Ermoúpoli, you could stop at Agía Varvára, a modern Orthodox convent covered in **frescoes** in the manner of Puvis de Chavannes, where the nuns sell *(fairly expensive)* items produced in their weaving workshop.

## Áno Meriá★, the "high country"

*From Áno Síros, take the only road which heads north. Circuit of approximately 20km (allow 2hr by car or half a day if you are planning an excursion on foot). If you intend to head through the scrubland to find a secluded beach, make sure you are wearing good strong shoes and take water with you.*

To the north of Áno Síros, the countryside is more mountainous; a landscape of bare hillsides, with little isolated villages dotted here and there. Both serene and wild, this region has some very pleasant walks to offer. Here are two of them:

■ First, the walk which goes up to the **Ferikídi grotto** *(a short distance past Mítikas, via a track on the right)*, a rocky cave said to have been lived in by **Pherecydes**, who taught Pythagoras. A native of Síros, he was also possibly the inventor of the sundial.

■ Continue to the prehistoric site of **Halandrianí** *(back on the main road, a short distance further on via a road which is not very good, but is signposted)*, its ruins lost on the hillside in a barren landscape of rocks and scorched grass. There is practically nothing left of this ancient Cycladic settlement (c 2400-2100 BC), nor of its necropolis, from where 600 tombs were unearthed by Professor **Tsoundas** at the end of the 19C. But more than anything else, these walks are worth doing for the **scenery★** – hills sculpted into terraces, ridged with low stone walls, sheltering virtually nothing other than flocks of sheep – and the **viewpoint★** over the neighbouring islands.

*Back on the main road, turn right.*

■ The road ends at **Kámbos**, the starting point for several excursions to the finest beaches on the island: **Lía** *(30min walk)*, **Mármara** *(30min)* or **Grámata** *(90min)*.

---

## Making the most of Síros

Making the most of Síros

COMING AND GOING

**By boat** – Daily ferry connections with Piraeus (crossing takes 3hr45min), and by hydrofoil with Piraeus and Rafína. Frequent crossings to Mýkonos (1hr20min). Several connections weekly to Amorgós, the Lesser Cyclades, Santoríni, Herakleion (Crete), Íos, Mílos, Pátmos, Rhodes, Sámos, and one weekly to Thessaloníki. Ticket offices on the quayside. **Harbourmaster's office**, ☎ (0281) 88 888 / 82 690.

**By air** – One flight daily in winter, two in summer to Athens (flight takes 30min). From the airport, get to Ermoúpoli by taxi, ☎ (0281) 87 025. In town, there is an **Olympic Airways** office, to the right of the landing-stage, ☎ (0281) 88 018 / 82 634.

GETTING AROUND

**By bus** – There is a good bus network, and the terminal is to the right of the landing-stage. There are about 20 buses to Galissás, Fínikas, Possidonía, Mégas Gialós, Vári, Azólimnos. Ten or so to Kíni, 6 daily to Áno Síros (from 10.30am-8pm), 5 to Vrontado (from 9.30am-1.30pm), and 2 to Dili, mornings only.

**By taxi** – Taxi rank in Platía Miaoúli, to the right of the town hall, ☎ (0281) 86 222.

**By rental car** – Several car rental agencies in the port area in Ermoúpoli. One of the cheapest is **Vassilikós**, opposite the bus station, ☎ (0281) 84 444. Motorcycles and mopeds can also be hired in Galissás. Avoid driving in Ermoúpoli, which gets congested in summer.

## ADDRESS BOOK

**Tourist information** – This takes the form of a kiosk which issues leaflets on accommodation on the island (at the centre of the quayside). Open in summer, 9am-10pm.

**Bank / Currency exchange** – Most of the banks, eg **Ioníkí** in Platía Miaoúli, have cash dispensers.

**Post office** – Odós Protopapadáki, ☎ (0281) 82 590.

**Telephone** – **OTE**, to the right of the town hall, Platía Miaoúli, ☎ (0281) 86 099 (telephone), and 88 499 (telegrams).

**Internet** – **Net Café**, on the quayside in Ermoúpoli, just before the Hermes hotel, ☎ (0281) 87 068. Has 5 computers.

**Police** – On the corner of Odós Náxou and Odós Eptaníssou, ☎ (0281) 82 612 / 82 616.

**Left luggage** – **Luggage Deposit** on the quayside, to the right of the landing-stage (9am-11pm) or in Platía Miaoúli, opposite the town hall.

**Medical service** – **Hospital** in Ermoúpoli, ☎ (0281) 22 222, also various pharmacies, including one in Odós Venizélou, near Platía Miaoúli. Dispensary in Fínikas, ☎ (0281) 42 655.

### WHERE TO STAY

• **Ermoúpoli**

*Between €27 and €45*

**Sylvia**, Odós Omírou 42, ☎ (0281) 81 081 / 87 189 – 9rm. ⌑ ✆ 🛏 🏠 🆑 The rooms are rather uninspiring, but the 19C neo-Classical house is quiet and has been renovated with some style. Breakfast on the roof-garden.

*Between €60 and €90*

**Hermes**, Platía Kanári, at the end of the quay to the right of the landing-stage, ☎ (0281) 83 011 / 12, Fax (0281) 87 412 – 52rm. ⌑ ✆ 🖥 📺 ✗ 🏠 🆑 THE grand hotel of Ermoúpoli, with elegant lounge areas. Ask for one of the rooms in the new wing, where the balconies overlook the garden. Health club. Very close to the beach. Open all year.

**Espérance**, Odós Folégandrou 1 and Aktí Papágou, ☎ (0281) 81 671, mobile 0932 929282, Fax (0281) 85 707 – 8rm. ⌑ ✆ 🖥 📺 ✗ Two neo-Classical houses offering attractive rooms and studios.

🛏 **Villa Maria**, Odós Ídras 42, behind Platía Miaoúli, (10min walk), ☎ (0281) 81 561, Fax (0281) 86 536 – 8rm. ⌑ ✆ 🖥 ✗ 📺 🏠 🆑 A 19C family house which has been converted into an attractive hotel, where each room has its own style. One has a kitchenette, the others share two communal kitchens. When you book, tell them your time of arrival so that the door will be open (no reception) and take a taxi (difficult to find). A very warm welcome. Open all year.

**Diogénis**, Odós Papágou, ☎ (0281) 86 301-5, Fax (0281) 83 334 – 43rm. ⌑ ✆ 🖥 📺 🆑 Near the harbour, this former brothel has recently been attractively renovated. The small rooms have double-glazing. Has a certain charm, despite a rather rustic reception. Open all year.

**Arhontikó Vourli**, Odós Mavrokordátou 5, in the Vaporia district, ☎ and Fax (0281) 88 440 – 8rm, one of which is a suite. ⌑ ✆ 🖥 🖈 Very stylish, in the house of a 19C Greek minister, good location. Restored in the style of the original, the yellow-ochre façade opens out onto a small garden, and the rooms are furnished with authentic neo-Classical items (canopied beds).

• **Galissás**

*Between €68 and €100*

**Dolphin Bay Hotel**, ☎ (0281) 42 924, Fax (0281) 42 843 – 152rm. ⌑ ✆ 📺 ✗ ⟡ 🖈 🗼 🆑 7km from Ermoúpoli, a modern complex very close to the beach. The very well-equipped rooms all have a terrace. Two restaurants and two swimming pools, one of which is for children, as well as a bar.

### EATING OUT

• **Ermoúpoli**

*Around €7.50*

🛏 **Kokoliás**, in the Kamínia district, in the heights of Ermoúpoli (go by taxi, as it is a difficult place to find). With its stunning view of the harbour, this taverna is popular with the local people. Delicious meze and other dishes. Tables here are in great demand on Saturday evenings.

*Between €9 and €14*

**Ioánnina**, at the port to the left of the Hermès hotel, has a large traditional dining room extending onto a seafront terrace, where they serve delicious grilled lamb (their speciality). Prompt service and good value for money.

**Restaurant in the Hermes hotel**, very popular at tea time with ladies of Siriot high society. Good food, served in the dining room or on the terrace (with sea view).

**Ambyx**, at the harbour, to the left of the landing-stage, ☎ (0281) 83 989. This is the best Italian restaurant on Síros, occupying a former distillery. Good starters, thin-crust pizzas with various toppings (seafood, vegetables, etc), and dishes of the day. Generous portions.

● **Áno Síros**

*Around €15*

**Kamára**, to the right of the entrance gate into Áno Síros (Kamára), steps lead up to the terrace of the trendiest restaurant on the island: a marvellous view over the harbour and authentic French cuisine. Slightly overpriced, but worth it for the ambience and the friendliness of the Franco-German proprietors. Open from March to October.

### HAVING A DRINK

● **Ermoúpoli**

Lined with lively cafés and restaurants, **Platía Miaoúli** is a very pleasant place to relax, with a children's play area, and open-air exhibitions.

**Agorá**, in Odós Hiou, to the left of the town hall, ☎ (0281) 88 329. A very trendy bar-restaurant. Frescoed walls and flower-decked patios. Ideal spot for a drink, beneath the bougainvillaea. Also serves good Greek food.

**Daidadi ice-cream parlour**, near the Diogenis hotel, ☎ (0281) 85 959. This little shop on Platía Papágou, to the left of the landing-stage, serves the best ice creams on Síros. Open summer only.

**Zacharoplasteío Márkos Athimarítis cake shop**, in Odós Kéas, which runs from the harbour by the Psarapoúla Ouzerí, ☎ (0281) 82 261. This is the best cake shop in town.

**Kritzinis Wines**, in Odós Ágios Proíou, second turning on the right in Odós Kéas. Open until 11pm.

**Síros Casino**, in a central position on the seafront, ☎ (0281) 84 400. Roulette, black-jack, poker and slot machines, a large dining room and a night-club.

● **Galissás**

**Argo**, on the road out of Galissás, heading north. An attractive road-side taverna with a good reputation. At the weekend, jazz or rembétiko concerts.

### OTHER THINGS TO DO

**Outdoor pursuits** – In the village of Hroússa, between Vári and Possidonía, there are stables for keen horse riders. Two go-kart tracks in Hroússa and Kíni.

**Excursions** – The **Esperos** sailing boat does an island tour (book with the agencies in Ermoúpoli).

**English newspapers** – In Ermoúpoli, on the quay to the right of the landing-stage, in the bookshop to the left of the Net Café. In Galissás, at the harbour.

**Cinema** – Open-air cinema at the **Palace**, Odós Hiou, to the left of the town hall. Foreign films with Greek subtitles, with a bar selling souvlákia. One show daily at 9pm in summer. In winter, everyone retreats to the **Pallas** cinema, between the town hall and the Apollon Theatre.

**Feasts & Festivals** – The two biggest festivals on Síros are the carnival and the Good Friday ceremony. From mid-July to mid-August, the **Ermoupólia** festival of culture takes place, with concerts of Greek and classical music, theatrical performances, exhibitions, etc.

### SHOPPING GUIDE

**Local delicacies** – Sample the local Turkish delight and "halvadópita", a nougat speciality. The best are at **Korrès**, Odós Hiou, left of the town hall.

**Prekas**, on the right in Odós Hiou. A good traditional Greek grocery store.

# TÍNOS

Northern Aegean  District of the Cyclades – Michelin map 980 fold 32
Regional map on the inside back cover – 195km² Pop 7 747
Allow 3-4 days

**Not to be missed**
Experiencing the fervour surrounding the Panagía Church and its miraculous icon.
Exploring the island's ancient villages and glorious countryside by road or on foot.
Sampling a goat's meat dish in one of the country inns.

**And remember...**
The evenings can get quite cold up in the hills, so take some warm clothing
(especially if you are travelling by motorcycle).

The first thing you will notice about Tínos is the captain's dexterity in manoeuvring his ship into a harbour which is only marginally wider than the ferry (in rough weather, boats anchor alongside a quay outside the harbour). You are also likely to be greeted by the meltem. Then the scene on the quayside is not quite what you might expect. As well as the double line of hoteliers waiting to greet their guests there is a seemingly frenzied crowd ready to take the ferry by storm and only restrained by metal barriers. Hardly have they got off the boat than some of the female passengers drop to their knees and begin their climb up the main street to the basilica. You will have realised by now that Tínos is no ordinary island; the intense activity engulfing the little town of Hóra is because it is the most important place of pilgrimage for Marian worship in Greece.

## The island of the Virgin Mary

Over the years, Tínos has successfully adapted to its semi-religious, semi-touristic vocation, so much so that there is no shortage of hotels, restaurants or souvenir shops. Pilgrims come to the island all year round, but things get truly frenetic on the day of the great festival in honour of the Virgin Mary (Assumption) on 15 August. This celebration attracts hundreds of **Gypsies**, traditionally devoted to the worship of Mary. With the shrilling of their clarinets and the clash of their tambourines, they add a racy note to the festive atmosphere.

While this is happening, a **nautical parade** takes place out at sea, commemorating – in the very same waters where the tragedy occurred – the torpedoing of the Greek steamer *Elli* by an Italian submarine on 15 August 1940; an event which preceded the declaration of war between the two countries by just a few weeks. Because, as is often the case in Greece, religious celebrations go hand-in-hand with national holidays, all this activity culminates in the procession of the **miraculous icon** when a tidal wave of people push frantically to pass under the reliquary borne aloft by a team of sailors.

But don't be put off, the pilgrims' zealous activities focus on a few streets in Hóra and the beaches nearest to it. Leave town and harbour behind you and head towards the hinterland or along the coast,

### The meltem, a kindly wind

From May to early September, winds known by the name of "meltemiá" blow from the north and north-east throughout the central and eastern Aegean. On coming into contact with higher ground, local currents develop, doubling the speed of these air streams which can reach Force 8 or 9 on the Beaufort scale. Situated at the centre of one of these areas of turbulence, Tínos is frequently subjected to fairly strong winds which, although they freshen the summer torpor, also whip up the sand on the beaches and this can be unpleasant. It is also said that if Aeolus (the god of the winds) keeps the inhabitants of Tínos safe from many diseases, the local character has taken on his capricious qualities, sometimes exuberant, sometimes sombre...

and you will discover some of the most beautiful villages in the Cyclades. Tínos is one of the few remaining islands of the archipelago to have retained its ancestral agricultural and pastoral way of life. Of course, the farming methods have changed slightly and many of the terraced fields are no longer cultivated; but they continue to enhance the beauty of the landscape, its mountains dotted with churches, chapels and dovecotes, crisscrossed by paths which are still trodden by donkeys and mules. Finally, Tínos also has a number of beaches which, if not deserted, are at least less busy than elsewhere.

## Tínos, the "Latin" island

Tínos is home to an important community of Catholics (about 40% of the population) although in no way can they be distinguished from their Orthodox compatriots. This "minority" came about as a result of the lengthy presence of Venetians on the island. During the course of the 16C, while the archipelago of the Cyclades Islands passed into Turkish hands, the citadel of Xóvourgo and its network of fortified villages repulsed their attacks. The outcome of this was that the island remained continuously under Venetian rule from 1207 to 1715. In addition to the agricultural produce necessary for their own subsistence, the islanders cultivated and exported large quantities of **silk** (mulberry trees are still found all over the island). But things were to change as the island was settled by people fleeing here from the troubles at the time of the Greek Revolution and Tínos became incorporated into the new Greek nation. Mixed marriages became commonplace (mostly favouring the eastern religion) and the Orthodox community progressively grew in size until it became the majority. This new community was based around the harbour and the villages of the neighbouring hills (Pano Méri), while the Catholics withdrew to the old villages in the centre of the island (Kato Méri).

## Tínos Town★ (Hóra)
### Allow 2hr

Formerly the port and centre of the trading activities of the merchants of the medieval town of **Xóvourgo**, Hóra is now a small town, its development largely boosted by tourism, as witnessed by the three- or four-storey hotels which protrude rather unattractively above the tiled roofs of the old houses. However, many of the narrow streets have retained their traditional charm, with their cobblestones, wrought-iron balconies and the flower-decked courtyards of the houses which line them.

Go up the wide Leofóros Megalocháris which climbs the 200m from the harbour to the church. On the left, you will find the **Archaeological Museum★** *(open every day except Monday, 8.30am-3pm; entrance fee)* which contains a colossal **pithos**, a storage jar from the 7C BC discovered on the site at Exómvourgo *(see below)*, as well as artefacts unearthed during excavations of the sanctuary of Poseidon and Amphitrite.

**Odós Evangelístria**, the town's oldest commercial street, is a veritable souk, a collection of many stalls selling everything you can imagine, from religious artefacts to the most unusual pieces of ironmongery.

From here, continue on to the **Panagía Evangelístria Church★★** *(7am-8pm; cover up, ie trousers and long skirts)*, a beautiful neo-Classical building built from 1820-30 – the first major building to be constructed in the newly-established kingdom of Greece – on the site of a Byzantine church. Its pale yellow façade stands at the centre of a rectangle of white buildings, which consist of the cells intended for the pilgrims, an **art gallery★** and the **Museum of the Artists of Tínos★** *(open every day, 8.30am-3pm)*. There you can see works of art by 19C Tinian artists (Lytrás, Gýsis, Iakovídes, Chalépas, **Filippótis**, etc), some of whom attained international fame. There are two other buildings which house the **Antónios Sóchos Museum**, devoted to a sculptor born in Istérnia (1888-1975), and a small **Museum of Religious Art★**, where the icons (some of which date from the 16C and 17C) are worth a quick look.

From the pebble-paved square in front of the church, a porch which extends into the precinct opens out onto a **courtyard** paved with marble, where two lateral flights of steps lead to the **basilica**★. There you will find, surrounded by the countless ex-voto offerings left by the pilgrims, the famous **icon of the Virgin Mary**★ *(on the left)*. In her case of silver, pearls and precious stones, she receives the homage of the faithful. After each kiss on the protective glass, it is wiped clean with a cloth by an attendant. This icon was discovered – as a result of a dream – by the future **St Pelagía**, then a young nun at the neighbouring abbey, in what is now a vaulted **chapel** situated under the shrine. Another fine basilica with three naves, the old Orthodox cathedral of the island, the **Church of the Taxiárhis**★ *(behind the cafés which line the very western end of the seafront)* was restored in 1759.

After this, immerse yourself in the lively atmosphere of the **market**★ which is held every day until 1pm in front of Platía Palládas *(near the second jetty)*. Among the fruit and vegetables grown in the market gardens in the centre of the island, look out for some of the local specialities, such as **capers**, **rakí** (an alcoholic drink distilled from wine-must and flavoured with aromatic plants), as well as strings of **dried tomatoes**, the **graviéra**, (Tinian goat cheese), not forgetting the **loúza** (a smoked pork sausage), which is the main ingredient of **froutaliá** (Tinian omelette).

### The beaches nearby

On either side of the harbour, the shore is lined by two large **beaches**: **Ágios Márkos** *(to the west)* – the more attractive of the two – and **Ágios Fokás** *(to the east)*, both lined with tamarisk trees and popular with families. But better than either of these are the small sandy **bays**★★ hidden away behind the Tínos Beach Hotel and the large **beach of Kiónia**★ *(4km west of the harbour)*.

Also worth trying is the **small rocky Bay of Stavrós** *(at the halfway point, on the left; taverna)*, overlooked by a chapel. With its jetty, it offers some shelter which is very welcome when the wind is strong.

Being rather built-up in an uninspiring sprawl, the south-east point of the island is of little interest apart from its two very beautiful beaches: **Ágios Ioánnis Porto**★, a small sandy bay which is easy to get to *(turn left after the large church of Agía Varvára)* and, particularly, **Pahiá Ámos**★★ *(reached via a track)*, a superb crescent of pale sand backed by dunes and protected by two rocky promontories.

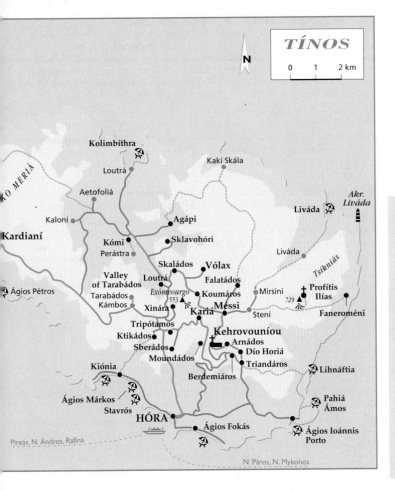

## In the hills of Hóra★★

*Allow a whole day for this itinerary towards Méssi.*
*As you head out of Tínos (Hóra), take the road which goes to Pánormos.*

■ After 4km, you come to the first junction: to the right, skirting the side of a hill, one of the prettiest roads on the island follows the contours of the valley before meeting up again with the road to Falatádos. It goes to Tripótamos★★, a charming village surrounded by trees and fields. Head down through its silent alleyways to the **Isodíon tis Theotókou Church★★** (the Church of the Presentation of the Virgin Mary) with its rich marble decor and its **terrace** paved with pebbles, from where there is a lovely **view★** down over the valley and the distant sea. For a long time, the village prided itself on its most distinguished resident, the philosopher **Cornelius Castoriádis**, who died in 1998.

*Continue along the road, leaving the village of Sberádos, nestling deep in the valley to the right.*

■ Beyond the hamlet of **Kariá** is the village of **Moundádos**★★ (*on the left; leave your vehicle and go down on foot*), tucked away above a ravine and scarcely visible amid the trees. Walk through its whitewashed cobbled **alleyways**, and indulge in a languorous stroll among the abandoned houses, the air sweetly perfumed by the fig and mulberry trees... Top up the oil in the lamp which watches over the **fountain** icon, and go up the staircase onto the roof of the **Ágios Ioánnis tou Prodrómou Church** (St John the Baptist) to savour the beautiful **panorama**★ that awaits you.

*At the first fork, turn left, and then right after the Ágios Nikólaos Church, which at one time stood on watch at the side of the path but is now in the middle of the road!*

On the left, a few hundred metres higher up, there is a wonderful **viewpoint**★★ over the whole of the eastern side of the island. When the meltem has been blowing for a few days, the air up here is so pure that you can see as far as the coast of Mýkonos and, in the distance, the dark landmass of Náxos.

■ Often reproduced on postcards, the restored **houses** of **Berdemiáros**★ alternate bare drystone walls with whitewashed façades, interspersed with old **dovecotes**.

■ Clinging to the south-eastern slope of the mountain (*to the left-hand side of the road*), **Triandáros**★ stands in a patch of greenery, a sign that there is water present. As you enter the village, look out for **Ágii Apostóli**★ (1887).

From here, a track approximately 4.5km long leads to the **pebble beach of Lihnáftia**★, where you are guaranteed a quiet swim. There is only the odd house dotted here and there among the lush vegetation of reeds and pine trees, which gives the place a special atmosphere.

■ **Dío Horiá**★★ – Just up from Triandáros lies one of those very quaint villages with a **communal fountain** (pigádia), so typical of Tínos. Allow yourself the luxury of getting lost for a while in the lanes, overlooked by the **Kímissis tis Theotókou Church**★ (Dormition of the Virgin Mary).

■ Even higher up, **Arnádos** holds the title of the highest village on the island. Not far from the parish church, there is a small **religious museum** (*open every day except Monday, 8.30am-3pm*) with a display of icons brought here from churches on the island, as well as liturgical books, religious artefacts and priests' robes.

■ **The Kehrovouníou Convent**★★★ – (*Open every day, 7am-1pm / 2.30pm-7pm; trousers and long skirts must be worn*). This vast monastery, constructed in the 10C-11C, constitutes a veritable village, with little houses, alleyways and small squares arranged around the **Kímissis tis Theotókou Church**★★. This has a remarkable carved wooden **iconostasis**★ and some mural **frescoes**. Also pay a visit to the **cell of St Pelagía**, who was canonised in 1970, the shrine dedicated to the vision that she had on 23 July 1822, and the small **museum**★ (18C and 19C icons and religious artefacts). The nuns also offer their **craftwork** for sale to visitors: sachets of aromatic herbs (the vervain, louiza, is excellent), candles, honey and icons.

*Beyond the convent, you come to a junction.*

■ Go straight on to get to **Méssi**, with its amazing **church**★ which is not unlike the religious architecture of central America, then on to the charming little farming town of **Falatádos**★, a starting point for the many paths and dirt-tracks which are ideal for superb **walks**★ in the surrounding countryside.

*Return on the road to Mirsíni. Beyond the village, take the dirt track (poor in places, but driveable), which leads down to the Bay of Liváda.*

■ Before returning to Hóra, you might want to enjoy the two pebble **beaches**★ of the **Bay of Liváda**★ (*taverna*). If the weather is calm, this is an ideal location for observing the **marine fauna** (with snorkel).

# In the heart of the island: the Catholic villages★★

*Allow a good half-day.*
*From Méssi, take the road to Kómi (the final destination of this tour) and Kolimbíthra.*

■ From the Méssi crossroads, the road wends its way to the foot of **Mt Exómvourgo** (553m) in a landscape of arid hills, dotted here and there with white chapels, dove-cotes, clumps of olive and fig-trees, and the occasional goat. A Venetian-built **citadel** once stood at the summit of the mountain. Destroyed by the Turks, nothing remains of it but a few stones, although the **view★** justifies the climb *(not difficult)*.

■ As proudly announced by a sign on the way in, **Koumáros★** is a traditional village. Clinging to the side of Mt Exómvourgo, it offers a fine **panorama★**.

■ A fork off to the right goes to **Vólax★★**, another spectacular village, hidden among its fields. Here and there, among the houses, you will notice some large **rock spheres** of volcanic origin. The "main" alleyway leads to a pretty **church**, then wends its way to the **wash-houses**. Along the way, there are signs to a small **museum** which displays all kinds of tools connected with the local craft of **basket weaving**.

*Head back to the main road.*

■ As you pass through **Skaládos**, have a quick look at the **clock tower**, a beautiful example of the imaginative architectural synthesis which is typical of the island. On the way out of the village, go and have an ice cream at the café-cum-grocery store just past the last hairpin bend. From the terrace, you will have a superb **view-point★★★** – one of the most beautiful on the island – down over the valley which stretches as far as the Bay of Kolimbíthra. Lined up on the ridge of the far slope, the villages of Kámbos, Tarabádos and Smardákitos sparkle in the sun, like small white dots embroidered on the backcloth formed by the green of the terraced fields and olive groves. The hillside descends to the bottom of a ravine; note along the way, a series of **dovecotes** carefully sheltered from the wind. Even lower down, you will see Kómi at the edge of a verdant plain crisscrossed by hedges of reeds and bull-rushes.

■ In the village of **Loutrá★**, look out for the **college★**, an imposing building which was home to a seminary of Jesuits (mainly French) – a constant presence on the island dating back to the mid-17C. Now converted into the **Folklore Museum★**, its exhibits are modest, but some of the rooms have retained their original furniture.

## Quarrelling clock towers

With 750 churches and chapels (70% Orthodox and 30% Catholic), Tínos is a delight for lovers of religious architecture. This is due both to the strength of religious feeling – on this island of many pilgrimages – and also to a certain rivalry between the two Christian faiths. Not to mention certain local traditions, such as honouring the saints by passing their names on from generation to generation. Or the tradition of safeguarding the ownership of a field or building by erecting an adjoining private chapel. Hence the blossoming of an imaginative popular art form, bringing about an original synthesis of Venetian and Byzantine influences. By observing the clock towers, sometimes topped by a sky-blue pyramid, sometimes by a crown of stone, you can usually distinguish a Catholic church from an Orthodox one.

■ Go back up towards the Pánormos road, to get to **Xinára★** *(on the left)*, the see of the **Catholic bishop** of Tínos. The vast **Episcopal church★** dedicated to the Rodariou Virgin is worth the detour.

■ Back on the road to Kómi again, push on as far as **Sklavohóri★★** *(little road on the right)*, the village where the painter **Nikifóros Gýsis** (1842-1900) was born. In spite of its Orthodox majority, Sklavohóri has a **Catholic church**, at the entrance to the village, and a remarkable communal **wash-house★** from the early 19C.

**Tínos**

**349**

Dovecotes of Tínos: the chapels of the birds

■ When you get to Kómi, turn right and head further into the depths of a valley dotted with old **dovecotes★**. **Agápi★★★** has retained the medieval atmosphere which is characteristic of all the fortified villages in the centre of the island, with a defensive wall made up of the external walls of the peripheral houses.

## The north cape: Éxo Meriá★★
*From Hóra to Pánormos. Allow half a day.*

■ 4km from Hóra, past Tripótamos, turn left along the small road which leads to **Ktikádos★** *(1.5km)*. Looking down over a ravine, the village extends in a thin line either side of a narrow central street. The **Catholic church**, with a clock tower claimed to be the oldest on the island, watches over the entrance to the town, with the **wash-houses** and the **Orthodox church** at the other end.
From the edge of the village, a path goes down towards **Kiónia** *(about a 90min walk)* through magnificent **countryside★** punctuated at intervals by a few **dovecotes**.

■ You will find some authentic examples of this vernacular building type in the **valley of Tarabádos★★★** *(to the right of the road beyond Kámbos, on the way out of the village of the same name)*. Here, on the side of the hill, in the midst of mulberry, fig, cherry and olive trees, stand the most beautiful **dovecotes★★★** on the island.

*Return to the main road to the north.*

■ A short distance before Kardianí, an asphalt road (on the left) goes down to the tiny village of **Gianáki** *(taverna)*, which skirts the edge of the **beach of Kalívia★★** (pebbles), reached via a dirt track *(second left; the first goes to the beach of Ágios Pétros)*.

■ **Kardianí★★★** – Hidden among olives, cypresses, holm oaks and fig trees, Kardianí looks down over the sea, its white houses clinging to the hillside. Spend some time wandering through its lanes and vaulted passageways, a delightful labyrinth of light and shade. The village has two churches, **Genéthliou tis Theotókou★★**, which is set behind a fountain and a square hedged by cypresses, and **Agía Triáda★★**, which are both considered to be among the jewels of the island; as are also its marble **wash-houses★**, supplied with water by a stone channel.

■ The village where many of the island's artists were born – this artistic tradition is depicted in the Museum of the Artists of Istérnia *(8.30am-3pm; closed Monday)* – Istérnia** is arranged in the shape of an amphitheatre around an imposing **church*** which has ceramic-tiled domes. On the façades of most of the houses, you will notice a marble plate bearing the name of the proprietor and the date of construction.

Beyond Istérnia, you will see, on the right, the **Katapolianís Monastery** (1786), built on a rise. The road then follows the contours of a kind of col, where the ruins of three old **windmills** stand. It then heads back down again through a dry, rocky landscape on the other side of the mountain.

**Flying high**

Tínos has some 800 dovecotes, the oldest of which date from the 18C. After the departure of the Venetian nobles, for whom the breeding of pigeons constituted a feudal privilege, the islanders built these amazing structures in great numbers. Sheltered from the wind, they were erected on the side of a hill or in valley bottoms and generally near cultivated land. The lower floor was used as a store for agricultural equipment and the upper floor was where the birds lived. Varying in size, but nearly always to the same design, these dovecotes are usually richly decorated with a pattern of geometric motifs, worked in relief in local slate: the rows of diamonds, stars or cypresses form a wonderful contrast against the whitewashed walls.

■ **Pírgos**★★★ – Down below, Pírgos comes into view, a small town of dazzling whiteness, which owes its brilliance – and its fortune – to the nearby marble quarries. Stroll through the **alleyways** where the sun beats down: above the doors and windows, around the fountains, in the churches and in the cemetery *(follow the alley that starts from behind the fountain)*, **marble** reigns supreme, and is used to decorate the most modest houses as well as the neo-Classical mansions. In addition to this traditional decorative craft, two sculptors have elevated the reputation of their village to a national level: **Ianoúlis Halépas** (1854-1938), whose **house*** is open to visitors *(on the way into the village)*, and **Dimítris Filippótis** (1839-1919).
The **Museum of Local Artists**★★ *(open every day 10.30am-1.30pm / 5.30pm-7pm)* will give you some insight into the style and work of the local artists, both ancient and contemporary (there has been a School of Fine Arts in the village since 1955). Along the street leading to the main square, there are **small shops** selling their work. In the shade of a two-hundred-year-old plane tree, the **village square**★★ – obviously also known as the "square of the artists" – is the ideal spot to sample a portion of *galaktoboúriko*, a kind of creamy flan.

■ As you come out of Pírgos, the road goes down towards **Pánormos*** *(4km further on)*, the prettiest of the island's harbours. Sheltered from the wind by its two rocky hills, this little bay was where ships used to come to be loaded with marble. Nowadays, it is a pretty little seaside resort, with some beautiful **beaches**. The best ones are the two furthest from the harbour. You can get there by caique *(fee charged)*, or on foot along a dirt path which goes around the north of the bay.

## Making the most of Tínos

COMING AND GOING

**By boat** – In summer, 3 ferries leave Piraeus every morning (between 7-8am) on the Síros-Tínos-Mýkonos route. Information from agencies in Piraeus or from the **harbourmaster's office**, ☎ (01) 42 26 000-4. The crossing takes around 5hr. The same boats come back 2hr later and return to Piraeus via Síros. Do remember that the boats are crammed to overflowing around 15 August and every weekend. When the sea is calm and the wind not too strong, hydrofoils (Flying Dolphins) go between Tínos and Piraeus.

From the port of Rafína on the east coast of Attica (the Ándros-Tínos-Mýkonos-Síros line), 2 boats daily (4hr crossing): one in the morning, the other in the afternoon. A catamaran also does the crossing. Information from the agencies at the harbour or from the **harbourmaster's office**, ☎ (0294) 22 487 / 22 300 / 28 888. From Rafína, there is a bus service to the centre of Athens (Platía Éghiptou); the last bus leaves at 10.30pm. From Tínos, you can get to the other islands of the Cyclades via Páros (one ferry daily).

### GETTING AROUND

**By bus** – The local **KTEL** bus network, ☎ (0283) 22 440, runs a daily service to all the villages on the island. As their frequency is subject to seasonal variations, enquire at the tourist information office (see below), or ask the bus drivers themselves (buses park in front of the landing-stage). Also be aware that bus stops are not always clearly marked. If in doubt (and there is no one else waiting), ask the locals for confirmation. The simplest form of question ("Leoforío edhó?" "Bus here?") will do the trick.

**By car** – All the villages of the island are served by a good-quality network of roads. As for the tracks, some can be driven by ordinary cars at slow speed, while others require a four-wheel drive.

**By motorcycle / moped** – Some of the hills may well present too great a challenge for two on a 50cc machine! Take care in the wind, which becomes stronger the higher you climb. But two-wheelers (preferably 80 or 100cc) are still a good way of getting around.

**Vehicle hire** – In Hóra: **Vidalis**, on the right, at the top of Odós Alavánou (which leads out of town), and one more agency past Platía Palládas, ☎ (0283) 23 400, Fax (0283) 25 995. Very wide choice of cars in good condition. Charges discounted for longer periods of hire and depending on season. Expect to pay around €38 per day for a Fiat Panda, and between €11 and €15 for a small moped (50cc).

**Jason Rent-a-Car**, just past Vidalis, ☎ (0283) 22 583. Same prices as previous entry.

**Takis Wheels**, Odós Trion Ierarchnon 13, where taxis are based, ☎ (0283) 22 834. Mainly hires two-wheelers. Well maintained, at attractive prices.

**Fuel** – 3 fuel stations on the road out of Hóra towards Triandáros, 1 along the road to Tripótamos; 1 just before Stení. Remember that are no fuel stations between Tripótamos and Pánormos, and that most are closed on Sunday.

**By taxi** – Taxis park opposite the landing-stage. Taxi ranks in **Hóra**, ☎ (0283) 22 470, and in **Pírgos**, ☎ (0283) 31 250.

### ADDRESS BOOK

It is worth bearing in mind that the port of Síros, **Ermoúpoli**, the administrative centre of the Aegean and the only real city in the archipelago, is less than 1hr away by boat.

**Tourist information** – On the ground floor of the town hall (on the right, at the start of the main street leading up towards the church), ☎ (0283) 23 780. Maps, list of hotels, information, but no booking services.

**Travel agencies** – **Lagouros Travel** (Mrs Loukía Fónsou), opposite the landing-stage, next door to the Serano Café, ☎ (0283) 24 289, Fax (0283) 23 900. Friendly reception. All services provided are of course charged for.

**Post office** – To the east of the harbour, past the Hotel Tinion. 8.30am-1.30pm. Try to get there early; after 10am, you will have to wait.

**Telephone** – **OTE** Agency, on the right in Leofóros Megalocháris.

**Bank / Currency exchange** – Most of the banks are located along the seafront. Nearly all have cash dispensers which take international credit cards.

**Tourist police** – In **Hóra**, opposite the second landing-stage, as you go out of town to the west, ☎ (0283) 23 670; during summer months, alternatively: ☎ (0283) 22 255.
In **Pírgos**, ☎ (0283) 31 371.

**Harbourmaster's office** – At the start of Odós Iearchón (the street where the taxis are), ☎ (0283) 22 348.

**Medical service** – Medical centre, at the eastern end of town (go up towards Platía Vidali, pass two streets on the right, then go straight on; the centre is about 500m further on), ☎ (0283) 22 210. Open in summer.

**Other** – English newspapers are available from the newsagent opposite the roundabout, where Megalocháris begins. You will also be able to get a copy of **Toubi's map** (the only one sold on the island), which shows the road network and some of the dirt tracks.

WHERE TO STAY

A well-established place of pilgrimage, Hóra has a large number of hotels and rooms to let. But, to meet the needs of the pilgrims - a clientele of Greeks, often middle-aged - a good number of these establishments are not at all suited to foreign visitors. Moreover, they are usually full up around 15 August and at weekends during the summer.

Away from the harbour, along the beaches of Ágios Fokás, Ágios Sóstis and Ágios Ioánnis Porto, are some very attractive establishments, some with a swimming pool. But unless you have a vehicle at your disposal, these hotels are a bit isolated from the rest of the island; most even have their own restaurant. Ideal if you are looking for somewhere quiet, comfortable, and near the sea.

The remaining option is to stay in a village, possibly with a family, which has a charm all of its own. There are increasing numbers of rooms to let, and you can always rent accommodation in a temporarily unoccupied family dwelling.

• **Tínos**

*Around €2*

**Tínos campsite**, 400m from Platía Vidali and less than 200m from the beach of Ágios Fokás (signposted from the Hotel Tinion), ☎ (0283) 22 344 / 23 548, Fax (0283) 24 373. ⟨cc⟩ Also has rooms and simple chalets, with or without private shower, some with kitchen, at reasonable prices. Cotton rugs and slate slabs used as trays go some way towards making you forget the concrete benches in the shaded restaurant. Clean toilet blocks.

*Between €5 and €23*

**Gianis Rooms**, next to the Oceanis hotel, to the east of the harbour, ☎ (0283) 22 515 - 11rm. This family-run establishment has lovely rooms, with high ceilings. Showers (clean) at the bottom of the garden.

*Between €38 and €75*

**Hotel Leandros**, Lamera 4, ☎ (0283) 23 545, Fax (0283) 24 390 - 11rm. For 2 or 3 persons (small supplement). ⟨cc⟩ 5min west of the harbour, past Platía Palládas. Clean rooms, comfortable and very quiet, without a view, but opening onto a flower-filled patio with tables, which acts as a garden lounge.

**Hotel Tinion**, east of the harbour, past Odós Alavánou, ☎ (0283) 22 261, Fax (0283) 24 754 - 20rm. ⟨cc⟩ This completely white hotel has a rather colonial charm. The rooms have very high ceilings and old tiling, and, if you can, choose one that opens onto the large terrace overlooking the harbour. Comfortable, despite the old-fashioned fittings. Ideal for a short stay out of season (before 15 July and after 1 September).

**Boreádhes** (Mrs Máro Sterióti), past the Ágios Antónios Church, Platía Palládas, ☎ (0283) 23 845 - 2 studios, 1 apartment, 7 double + 1 single rm. A fine building in traditional style, very tastefully decorated (canopied beds). Library.

• **Kiónia**

*Around €38*

**Studio Vidali**, 100m from Kiónia beach (3km from Hóra), ☎ (01) 66 67 419, ☎ (0283) 22 686 - 10 studios and 11rm with kitchen. ⟨cc⟩ All have a veranda, and are well, but simply, equipped. Good location, too, next to several beautiful beaches, and easy to get to Hóra.

• **Ágios Fokás**

*Around €38*

**Golden Beach**, 30m from the beach of the same name and 1.5km from Hóra, ☎ (0283) 22 579 / 24 579 / 24 139, ☎ (01) 42 24 35, Fax (0284) 23 385 - 9 studios with kitchen (for 2 to 5

**Making the most of Tínos**

people). ⌐❩ ℰ ✕ 🏠 🌊 CC A very attractive complex in typical Cycladic style, situated in a pleasant flower-filled garden. Very acceptable taverna.

### • Ágios Ioánnis Porto
*Around €38*
**Aktí Aegéou**, 30m from the beach of the same name, ☎ (0283) 24 248 / 25 523, Fax (0283) 23 523 - 11 studios with kitchen (for 2 to 5 people). ⌐❩ ℰ ✕ 🏠 🌊 CC Same standard as the previous entry, with a swimming pool.

### • Falatádos
*Between €21 and €30*
**Léfkes Taverna**, the first one you come to on the way into the village, 2rm.
**Apergi Taverna**, on the left on the road which skirts the village. Contact Roula Aperghi at the taverna.

### • Tripótamos
*Around €38*
**Studio Halari**, information from the confectionary shop of the same name, at the start of Odós Evangelístria, on the left, ☎ (0283) 23 274 / 41 152. ⌐❩ 🏠 Apartments and studios with kitchen in a pretty building in the middle of the countryside. Well situated - you can get to the villages of Ktikádos, Hatzi,rádhos, Sberádos and Xinára on foot, and Hóra is only 4km away (frequent buses). A paved path (near the bus stop) goes down towards Kiónia. Comfortable accommodation with good facilities. It is cool here in the evening; if you can, choose a room with a south-facing balcony. The proprietors are friendly. An ideal place for a longer stay.

### • Kardianí
*Between €21 and €30*
You will find several rooms to let in the very pretty village of Kardianí. Enquire at the **Mariléna** kafenío, past the Kioura Church square.
*Between €37 and €43*
**Gianáki Beach**, enquire at the taverna. Rooms open straight onto the beach.
**Kalívia Beach**, on the left just before the beach - 3rm. ⌐❩ 🏠 On one of the quietest and most attractive beaches on the island. Self-sufficient, with two electric plates and a fridge, and the proprietor is generous with the produce from his vegetable garden.

### • Pírgos
*Between €67 and €85*
**Antónis Tzès**, ☎ (01) 53 13 313, ☎ (0283) 31 681 - 4 studios with kitchen, lounge and one or two bedrooms. ⌐❩ 🏠 In a very beautiful, Cycladic-style building which has a panoramic view over the surrounding area. Tastefully furnished.

The tavernas of Hóra are not particularly inspiring and are crowded at weekends. If you have transport, head for the nearby villages (but wear some warm clothing as it gets quite cool in the hills in the evenings). The local gastronomy is rustic in style, but delicious. You will have the choice of veal ("moshári"), the best in Greece, rabbit ("kounéli"), lamb ("arnáki") or goat ("katsíki"), cooked either in the oven, or in a lemon ("lemonáto") or tomato sauce ("kókini sálsa"). You could also opt for "froutaliá", an omelette with a potato and pork sausage filling. Apart from the delicious cod fritters ("bakaliára"), these tavernas do not usually have fish on the menu. With the exception of this dish, which is always expensive, you can eat anywhere for less than €11.

### • Tínos
**To Koutoúki tis Hellénis**, Odós Gagou 5, first street on the right off Évangelístria. One of the best places by the harbour. A vaulted stone building. Specialities: mushrooms in garlic ("manitária"), shellfish with rice ("yalisterés"), spaghetti with lobster sauce ("astoko-makaronádha").
**Xébarko**, the second establishment you come to starting from the western extremity of the harbour. Very tastefully restored and decorated, this old kafenío is THE café for those in the know, both Greek and international. It is just about the only restaurant on the seafront where, in high season, you can have breakfast, eat a sandwich or a pasta dish (large portions), or have a drink in the evening, without being crammed in among noisy family groups.

### • Kiónia
**Bourou**, before the Tínos Beach Hotel. A great place to go if you are hungry after your swim, with something to satisfy all tastes: savoury aubergine pastries

("kolokithópita"), moussaká, broad bean purée ("fáva"), squid.

● **Porto**
**Adónis**, before the Ágios Ioánnis Church, in the direction of the beach. This taverna, which looks very ordinary, is one of the oldest on Tínos. You will not taste a better "kakaviá", (Greek seafood stew) anywhere else. Equally recommended for its fried fish and its "ladherá", plates of vegetables (lentils, haricot beans, potatoes, tomatoes, peppers, etc) cooked in olive oil. Not to be missed: the "yemistá", tomatoes and peppers stuffed with rice. Very good value for money.

● **Ktikádos**
**Drossiá**, on the right in the main street of the village. A large paved terrace which overhangs a ravine. Try to get here before 9pm, both for the view and to avoid a long wait. Meats in sauce or oven-baked, a wide choice of starters. Superb setting.

● **Falatádos**
**Aperghi**, the second taverna on the left on the road which goes around the village. A terrace in the shade of large trees, where it is not unusual to hear owls hooting at night. Family cooking prepared using own produce.

● **Stení**
The only taverna in the village. For those who like their meat. Order mutton chops ("païdhákïa"), served with salads, chips and local red wine. And to complete this feast, try a drop of rakí with a portion of baklava.

● **Kardianí**
**Ánemos**, on Gianáki beach. Fish, fried food, meze, family cooking.

● **Pánormos**
**Agía Thálassa**, one of the first tavernas in the harbour. Certainly the best restaurant on the island (more expensive than the previous entries). Traditional recipes with an imaginative twist. Try the "kouloúra saláta" (large biscuits made with chick-pea flour, a Cretan speciality, topped with tomatoes, olive oil, oregano, capers and feta cheese), the stuffed squid ("soupiès yemistés"), the octopus in wine sauce, or a kebab. The menu also features fresh fish.

### HAVING A DRINK

**Bars, night-clubs** – Tínos is not exactly an island for night-owls, and there are not many good bars. Just next to the **Xébarko** café, ideal for after-dinner drinking and entertainment, is **Koursaros**: rock music with a saloon-bar atmosphere.
Anyone wanting to dance through the night should go to **Veguera**, perched up on high above Hóra (large terrace, techno music, with Greek music just before closing), or to **Mílos** (rock); with tables outside, this is the nicest place to go for a drink on the island. There is a bar on Kiónia beach (take your sleeping bag).

### OTHER THINGS TO DO

**Exploring Delos** – A boat leaves Tínos daily at 9am, drops you on Delos at around 9.30am, comes back to pick you up when the site closes at 3pm, and then stops off for 2hr on Mýkonos. Returns to Tínos at about 6pm. Take care, however, as on some days when the meltem wind is very strong, maritime traffic can be subject to disruption. It is best to enquire in advance.

**Feasts & festivals** – Tínos has no shortage of "panigíri", village feasts with accompanying traditional music (information from the town hall): **Kardianí**, 50 days after Easter (mid-June), Agía Paraskeví in **Istérnia** (26 July), Agía Marína in **Pírgos** (17 July), Ágios Ioánnis in **Kómi** (29 August).

### SHOPPING GUIDE

**Local delicacies** – In the confectionery shops in Hóra: "tiropitákia", delicious little sweet pastries with soft white cheese, Turkish delight and "amigdalotá" (almond cakes; also sold on the boat from Síros).

**Crafts** – Basket weaving in **Vollax**, and marble sculptures in **Pírgos**.

**Making the most of Tínos**

Cretan lights: the old harbour at Réthimnon

# CRETE

The first impression you have of this great island, the last stop in the Mediterranean before the coast of Africa, is of an immense natural fortress. 100km south of the Peloponnese, Crete (Kríti) is the largest Greek island (8 300km²) and the fifth largest in the Mediterranean after Sicily, Sardinia, Corsica and Cyprus. Since time began, its steep mountains firmly anchored in the sea have watched over a land of legend – the place where Rhea gave birth to her son Zeus. The many remains of the Minoan civilisation, mixing myth and historical reality, offer a unique opportunity to revisit some of the most fascinating stories of Antiquity, among them those of Theseus and the Minotaur, Icarus and his dream, and Daedalus and the labyrinth.

Everything about the island makes one feel that it was indeed chosen by the gods as the scene for their exploits, great and small. The olive plantations stretching as far as the eye can see, the orange groves in the valleys, and the vineyards jealously tended for thousands of years, all bear witness to a fertile land. The relief, which only the wild goats seem to have fathomed, is extraordinarily capricious, as is borne out by the vast Lassíthi Plateau, a strange circular plain high among the mountains.

The Cretans themselves only joined the Greek State in 1913, a decision they took of their own free will. Still Cretan rather than Greek, they exude a kind of unostentatious pride, as if they were in possession of some ancient secret known only to themselves. In view of their history, this would seem more than justified, since for centuries, they have astonished the world by their ability to preserve their identity and to control their fate. Even today, in the face of a worrying tourist invasion, they remain unshakeable, seeming to take control of the situation with complete peace of mind and no concessions – but with a smile.

The island is dominated by three chains of mountains between which huddle fertile plateaux. In the west the **Lefká Óri** mountains culminate at 2 453m, enclosing the Omalós Plateau at an altitude of 900m. In the middle of the island is **Mt Ida** (2 456m), while in the east is **Mt Díkti**, rising to a height of 2 148m. In the north of the island the mountains give way to wide fertile **plains**, suitable for growing olives – Crete's main source of wealth since the Minoan Era – and also bananas.

## The Minoan civilisation, fifteen centuries of peace

The proximity to great civilisations, such as those of Egypt and Asia Minor, favoured cultural and commercial exchanges, while the mildness of the island climate, the fertility of the soil and the peaceful atmosphere that reigned over the Mediterranean in the second millennium BC enabled Europe's oldest civilisation to prosper for almost fifteen centuries. The civilisation in question is the legendary one of **King Minos**, drifting between myth and reality.

It is customary to divide the history of the Minoans into four periods. The **Pre-Palace Period** (2500-2000 BC), which laid the foundations for the culture, was succeeded by the **Old Palace Period** (2000-1700 BC). This saw the construction of the **early palaces**; real cities with places of worship, trade guilds, and houses. Little remains of the period, as a natural disaster devastated the coast of Crete in 1700 BC (*see page 18*). However, the Minoans recovered from the disaster, rebuilt their palaces, and entered the richest years in their history, the **New Palace Period** (1700-1400 BC), marked by intense artistic, cultural and commercial activity.

But in 1400 BC, **Mycenaean invasions** heralded its decline. The palaces were destroyed or abandoned during the **Post-Palace Period** (1400-1100 BC). This was marked by the birth of a new civilisation with a more warlike disposition, whose population retired to the mountains to build its first fortified cities. Through internal

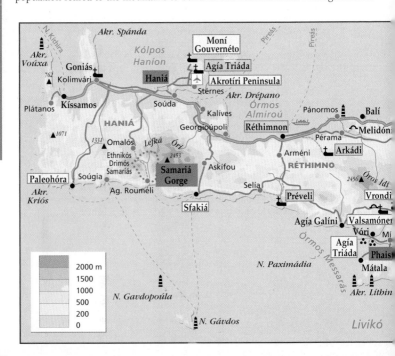

warfare, these cities led Crete into a dark age that the Romans took advantage of in the 2C BC. After several abortive attempts, the latter managed to gain control of the island in 67 BC, setting up their Cretan capital in **Gortyn**.

## From Byzantium to Venice

In 330 AD, the island came under Byzantine control, but in 824, it fell into the hands of the **Arabs** who turned it into an independent State, ousting Gortyn in favour of El Khandaq, the Candia of the Venetians (Herakleion). However, in 960 AD **Nicephorus Phocas**, a general and future Byzantine emperor, managed to win back the city at the end of a bloody siege. Crete became Byzantine once again, but only for a short while. After the Fourth Crusade (1204), the island was assigned to the Venetians. A new administration was put in place, which favoured trade, the arts and the literary world, offering the island a new golden age.

## A nation of resistance fighters

However, the Turkish threat was growing ever stronger, and in less than two years the island fell into Ottoman hands (1645). Only the **great siege** of Candia brought glory to the combined forces of the Cretans and their Venetian allies, when their resistance to the Turkish onslaught enabled them to hold out for no less than 21 years. Crete was first declared an autonomous State in 1898, and became part of Greece in 1913, when the **Treaty of Bucharest** was signed (*see page 29*). During and after the German invasion of May 1941, the Cretans had plenty of opportunities to display their courage and tenacity. The **Battle of Crete** was one of the most bitterly contested of the Second World War and the Cretan resistance to the subsequent occupation was fierce and unrelenting.

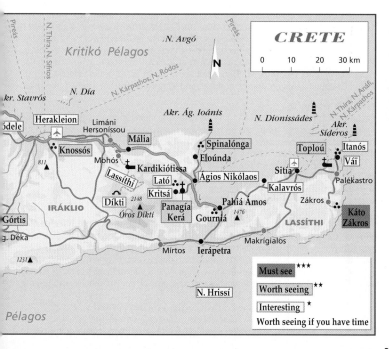

# HERAKLEION★
## (IRÁKLIO)

Administrative capital of the island – Capital of the district of Iráklio
Michelin map 980 fold 39 – Map of the island pages 358-359
Pop 106 000 (160 000 in built-up area)

**Not to be missed**
The Archaeological Museum.
A walk in the square round the Morosini Fountain
and through the market in Odós 1866.
The old harbour, Fort Koúles and the Venetian arsenals.
The collection of icons in St Catherine's Church.

**And remember...**
Leave your car in one of the car parks at the entrance to the town.

The island's main international airport is at Herakleion. For many people, the town is the gateway to Crete, an obligatory stopover before dispersing to the various resorts on the coast. The first contact with Herakleion may surprise visitors or even put them off, as the noisy, modern, densely populated city has none of the classical charms of either Haniá or Réthimnon. There is little of outstanding architectural interest because the town was almost entirely destroyed during the Second World War and then revived, perhaps too hastily, with a huge amount of concrete. The only historical features are the massive ramparts, the Venetian fort and arsenals and some elegant Venetian buildings in the heart of the town. However, there are places to enjoy in Herakleion if you take the time to explore. You will be amazed to find that although the town looks like a large capital, it is in fact laid out on a reassuringly small scale: everything a modern city has to offer is grouped together in an area no bigger than a pocket handkerchief. Recent buildings contrast with the medieval layout of the streets, but barely will you have left the hectic thoroughfares than you will discover a host of peaceful little squares where people come at all times to relax and enjoy iced coffee and cake. Behind its ramparts, Herakleion pays no heed to critics. Herein lies its charm. Cretan life goes on unpretentiously, and tourism is far from dictating the rules.

## A hero's name

As the port for the neighbouring city of Knossós, Herakleion was given its name in honour of Heracles who, according to legend, accomplished one of his famous Twelve Labours here. But while the town already existed at the time of the Minoans, its history only really began in 826 AD with the arrival of the **Arabs**, who seized the island from the Byzantines. They surrounded the city with solid walls protected by a deep ditch, which gave the city its new name, **Rabdh El Khandaq** or the Fortress with a Ditch. The Arabs remained masters of Crete for almost 140 years, and the growing El Khandaq established itself as a base of great strategic value on the doorstep of the Aegean.

However, in 961, after an eight-month siege by the troops of General **Nicephorus Phocas** (the future emperor), the Byzantines at last managed to take back the city. Byzantium very soon began to restore its supremacy in Crete: the Muslims were converted to Christianity and the land was shared out between the Byzantine Empire's noble families. Its position as capital now confirmed, El Khandaq had its fortifications rebuilt and the town became the official seat of the Byzantine governor, up until the early 13C.

But in 1204, the Fourth Crusade, in which the Venetians played a large part, got the better of Constantinople. There began a sharing out of the remains of the Empire. The **Venetian Republic** obtained Crete and in its turn took over El

Herakleion, Fort Koúles guards the Venetian harbour

Khandaq, changing its name to **Candia**. This was the beginning of a great period of economic and cultural prosperity that was to last for more than four centuries. The town was adorned with squares, fountains, palaces and churches. The fortifications were extended once again, and completed by a harbour and large arsenals. 1669 marked the end of this auspicious period. After an incredible 21-year-long siege, and in spite of help sent (rather late) by the great European powers, Crete fell into the hands of the Turks. Candia, the last stronghold to resist, fell to the **Ottomans,** who gave it a new name, **Megálo Kástro** (Great Fortress). The town then began to decline, with **Haniá** taking over as the main town on Crete.

Until the late 19C, Candia – like the rest of the island – was the scene of many bloody tragedies, which stemmed from the fierce Cretan resistance to the Turks. When the island became part of Greece in 1913, the town took back its original name, Herakleion. Showing heroic tenacity during the Second World War, it was greatly damaged once again, and it was only in 1971 that the modern Herakleion, now rebuilt, was restored to its status as island capital.

## Tour of the town

*See Plan page 366. Allow at least a whole day, beginning with Platía Eleftherías, at the main entrance to the town.*

There is no better place than **Platía Eleftherías** to illustrate the many sides to Herakleion's character. Here the ramparts seem to have abandoned all vigilance, and open widely to welcome in visitors. The square is a huge, bright, well laid out area where tall metal pylons, futuristic sculptures set in an arc, lend the place an air of modernity.

*To reach Platía Eleftheríou Venizélou in the centre of town, take Odós Dedálou, a small pedestrian street, rather than the noisy, bustling Leofóros Dikeossínis, a major thoroughfare that runs parallel to it.*

## Around Platía Eleftheríou Venizélou (or Platía Krínis)

Since the time of the Venetians, life in the city has concentrated round this small square, which brings to mind – in a more modest version – the Piazza San Marco in Venice. Tourist restaurants rub shoulders with snack bars and stalls where locals come to get a bite to eat before returning to their offices. This is also where young people meet in the evening before heading off to the countless trendy places in the adjoining streets.

In the middle of the square stands the majestic **Morosini Fountain\*\***, which bears the name of the city notable who financed it in 1628. It was originally called the Giant's Fountain on account of the statue that once stood on top – an imposing Poseidon armed with his trident (probably destroyed in an earthquake). Four lions support the upper basin, while bas-reliefs of mythological scenes adorn the eight sections of the main basin. The water is brought in by the fountain's own aqueduct.

A stone's throw from the square in the direction of the harbour is the **Loggia**, a basilica-like structure also built by Morosini in 1628. Today it houses the town hall, while in the past it was the produce exchange, where city notables gathered to relax and discuss business. The Duke used to appear on one of the balconies to address the people or attend the official ceremonies that took place in the square.

Just behind the Loggia is a peaceful little square on which stands the **Church of Ágios Títos**, a small 16C edifice noteworthy for its restrained elegance.

*Continue along Leofóros 25 Avgoústou, which is lined with the handsome façades of neo-Classical buildings, the few remains of 19C Herakleion.*

## The Venetian Harbour and Fort Koúles\* (Kástro Koúles)

As you come out onto the waterfront, you will see the three high arches of the enormous **arsenals\*** on the right at the end of the quay. They give you an idea of the naval activity – mainly military – that reigned here in the 14C. Today the old harbour is given over to a handful of peaceful fishermen, and despite the heavy traffic in the area around it, it is one of the most pleasant places in town.

The modern harbour stretches out immediately to the east, receiving its daily share of ferries from Piraeus and the islands in the Aegean.

The bright walls of **Fort Koúles\*** stand out against the sea right at the end of the jetty *(9am-2.30pm; closed Monday; entrance fee, student reduction; allow 30min)*. This fine work, the mainstay of the town's fortifications, bears the coat of arms of the **Lion of St Mark**. It was built by the Venetians between 1523 and 1540 to reinforce the town against the warlike ambitions of **Süleyman the Magnificent**. The echo and the shadowy light in the huge **vaulted storerooms\*** - powder magazines, armouries, stores for cannonballs, etc – create a solemn atmosphere. A paved ramp leads to the **inner courtyard** terrace above the storerooms. This has been converted into an open-air theatre and affords a superb **view\*\*** of the sea. Don't miss the climb up the **watchtower** *(be careful, there is no parapet)* for a fine bird's-eye view of the fort itself.

*Continue westwards from the fort along the rather basic concrete promenade.*

## Historical and Ethnographical Museum\*

*Odós Kalokairinou 7. 9am-5pm Monday to Friday, and 9am-2pm Saturday; closed Sunday. Entrance fee. Allow about 45min.* The museum is housed on three floors of an elegant neo-Classical mansion flanked by a modern building, and provides a good opportunity to learn something about the history and culture of Crete. Ancient frescoes, Byzantine icons, historical relics and traditional costumes, along with typically Cretan arts and crafts are laid out in chronological order in the twelve rooms. The ground floor has an interesting **model\*** of the town, illustrating the different eras in its development. The **Kazantzákis Room** on the first floor pays tribute to the famous writer who was born in Herakleion. Manuscripts, letters and personal items make up a reconstruction of his study, together with a collection of his complete works. Take a look also at Room X on the second floor, which displays the interior of a traditional rural dwelling.

*From the museum, the narrow Odós Hortátson leads from the waterfront to the town centre. At the end of the street, take Odós Koronéou, which leads to El Greco Park.*

## Around the market★ (Odós 1866)

Several busy streets radiate out from the junction formed by Platía Eleftheríou Venizélou and the hectic Leofóros Dikeossínis. One of them is **Odós 1866**, and it is here that the town's daily market is located. The increasing presence of tourists – for whom several easily avoided stalls are intended – does not seem to distract from the commercial fever of the place. This is at its height between 10am and midday, and then again in the late afternoon, until closing time *(around 7pm)*. Grocery and hardware stores of all kinds fill the first part of the market, spilling out into the street. Oil, saffron, olives, pistachio nuts and a wide range of household goods are carefully inspected by housewives on their daily trip to the market. Butchers and dairymen come next, and, of course, street vendors, whose haranguing is soon drowned out by the women shoppers. At the end of the street, on the right, is an alley of fishmongers, who display the day's catch – octopus, mullet, squid, etc – in a less rowdy fashion.

The market opens onto **Platía Kornárou★**, a pleasant square adorned with a **Turkish fountain** in the shape of a kiosk. It is now an outdoor café, with tables shaded by olive trees. An ideal place (in spite of noisy scooters) for coffee, freshly squeezed orange juice, or a light meal. Just beside the Turkish fountain stands the **Bembo fountain** (1588), named after the Venetian who commissioned it. The fountain is a rather odd combination of Venetian coats of arms and a Roman statue of a headless man.

*Head west from the square along Odós Vikéla, then bear right into Odós Agía Miná, which leads to the Cathedral.*

Platía Kornárou, in the shade of the Turkish fountain

G. de Benoist/MICHELIN

## St Catherine's Church★ (Agía Ekateríni)

*On the square named after the church, near the Cathedral. 8.30am-1.30pm Monday and Saturday, and 5pm-7pm Tuesday, Thursday and Friday. Entrance fee. Allow 30min.* The church with its simple plan was built by the Venetians in 1555 and then converted into a mosque by the Ottomans in the 17C. It is dwarfed by the imposing mass of the **Ágios Minas Cathedral★** – the largest in Greece – a huge piece of wedding-cake architecture that was built near the church in the 19C. However, to pay tribute to the church's illustrious past – it was both the headquarters and study centre of the famous **Monastery of St Catherine of Sinai** in the 16C and 17C – an outstanding **Museum of Religious Art** has been set up inside. Among the many 13C and 14C paintings, relics, liturgical manuscripts and carvings are some splendid **Byzantine icons★★**. The museum is particularly proud of six of them, attributed to **Mihális Damaskinós** (16C), a Cretan painter who was born in Herakleion, and also worked in the Ionian Islands and in Venice.

*Make your way to Platía Elefthérias, at the eastern entrance to the town.*

## Archaeological Museum★★★ (Arheologikó Moussío)

*Daily, 8am-7pm. Entrance fee (expensive), except for the under 18s, students and journalists. Allow a good 3hr. If you can, go in the late afternoon when there are fewer tourists and you have more of a chance of seeing the finest exhibits.*

The austerity of the 20 rooms in this rather timeworn museum contrasts with the staggering wealth of the collections. All the ancient exhibits come from excavations on the island, bearing witness to five millennia of Cretan history, from the Neolithic Period (5000-2000 BC) to the Greco-Roman Era (500 BC-300 AD). While we may regret the absence of explanations – the objects in the display cases are given only a short text at best – the museum remains an essential place to visit before exploring the major sites of the Minoan civilisation. These are **Knossós, Mália, Phaistos, Agía Triáda** and **Káto Zákros** (*see Minoan history page 18 and the chapters on the respective sites*).

**Room I**, devoted to the Neolithic Period (5000-2500 BC) and the Pre-Palace Minoan civilisation (2500-2000 BC), displays objects found in the **tomb of Messara** in the middle of the island. In addition to pottery and votive statuettes made of ivory, marble and alabaster, the site also contained a fine collection of seals and gold jewellery (*cases 16, 17 and 18*). Don't miss what are known as the **Vassilikí** vases in case 6, whose characteristic colouring is believed to result from a special type of firing.

Most of the finds in **Rooms II** and **III** come from the palaces at **Knossós** and **Mália**, and also from mountain shrines (Old Palace Period, 2000-1700 BC). Case 29 contains **Kamáres ceramics★** with attractive motifs of flowers and octopi, as well as jars and votive objects. Try and find a way through the crowds around case 41 in Room III, which contains one of Antiquity's most famous enigmas: the **Phaistos Disk★★**. The extraordinary hieroglyphs inscribed in a spiral on both sides of the clay tablet remain undeciphered to this day.

**Rooms IV** and **V** take you into the golden age of Minoan culture: the New Palace Period (1700-1400 BC). The **snake goddesses★**, delicate statuettes of bare-breasted women (*case 50*), suggest the matriarchal nature of the civilisation. In the same case, take a look at the strange **flying fish** carved out of stone. Opposite (*case 51*) is the famous rhyton (drinking vessel) made of black soapstone in the shape of a **bull's head★★**. You will already have seen thousands of copies of this in the souvenir shops in town. With its rock-crystal eye and its muzzle superbly outlined in mother-of-pearl, it was reserved for very grand ceremonies. Case 56 close by presents an extraordinary **ivory acrobat★** engaged in ritual bull-leaping.

**Rooms VI** to **IX** contain other choice pieces whose delicacy and originality testify to the high level of artistic activity during the Minoan Era. Note, particularly, the **warrior's helmet★** adorned with the teeth of a wild boar (*Room VI, case 78*) and the magnificent gold jewellery that has inspired so many 20C creations. One such piece is the **bee pendant★★**, a masterpiece by goldsmiths from Mália *(Room VII, case 101)*. Note also the enormous **copper ingots** (30 kilos) in case 99, which strangely enough were used as currency in the New Palace Period. Don't leave the room without seeing the most beautiful finds from Agía Triáda, three remarkably delicate vessels used for ritual libations: the **Harvester Vase★** *(case 94)*, the **Chieftain Cup★** *(case 95)* and a fine **conical rhyton★** decorated with scenes of acrobatics and bull-leaping *(case 96)*. In Room VIII, take a look at the very delicate **rock-crystal vase★★** *(case 109)* discovered at Káto Zákros.

The historical context changes with **Room X**, devoted to the Post-Palace Period (1400-1100 BC). Minoan civilisation was then on the decline and produced a great many **figurines** (female idols) and cult objects.
Go quickly through **Rooms XI** and **XII** (Sub-Minoan and Geometric Periods, 1100-650 BC), to spend time looking at the amazing terracotta

A Minoan gem: rhyton in the shape of a bull's head

**sarcophagi** shaped like small baths, in **Room XIII**. One of them still contains the bones of the deceased. The dead were laid with arms folded and knees drawn up to the torso, hence the small size of the coffins.

Rooms upstairs display the **frescoes★★** that decorated the palace walls at Knossós: they include dolphins, a bull-leaping scene, and a procession. The works have been superbly restored and illustrate the extreme sophistication of the palaces during the New Palace Period (1700-1400 BC). A **wooden model★** of Knossós gives a good idea of the place's complex architecture – a real maze.
In the middle of **Room XIV** is one of the chief exhibits in the museum: the **Agía Triáda sarcophagus★★★** *(case 171)*, the only stone sarcophagus discovered on Crete (the others are terracotta). It is completely covered in painted scenes of an important funeral – including the sacrifice of a bull, priestesses pouring libations and people bearing offerings – and is probably the final resting-place of a distinguished member of the royal family.

The famous **Parisienne★★** in **Room XV** is in fact a very small fragment of a fresco depicting a priestess. She was so named by the man who discovered her, Sir Arthur Evans *(see page 373)*, on account of her mischievous expression. It is pleasant to stroll through the room that follows to see more outstanding frescoes. Among them are some amusing scenes, such as the **Monkey picking Crocuses**.

**Rooms XVII** and **XVIII** are closed for an indefinite period and contain, respectively, the **Giamalákis collection** (diverse objects ranging from the Neolithic to the Venetian Periods) and minor arts from the Archaic, Classical, Hellenistic and Roman Periods (7C-4C BC).
The tour ends with **Rooms XIX** and **XX**, on the ground floor, where sculptures and examples of Greek and Greco-Roman architecture (5C and 4C BC) are rather poorly displayed. Nevertheless, take a look at the amazing **votive shields★** in cases 208 and 209.

*When you leave the museum, there's a terrace on the right with a cafeteria where you can regain your strength in the shade with cool drinks and cakes.*

You may like to end the day by walking along the **Venetian ramparts** to the **tomb of Níkos Kazantzákis**, a small monument on the Martinéngo Bastion in the south of the town.

*To get to places to the east of Herakleion, take the avenue that runs along the waterfront. The way to Ágios Nikólaos is well signposted. The road follows the coast as far as Mália. It is a 30km strip of villages converted by mass tourism into soulless resorts.*

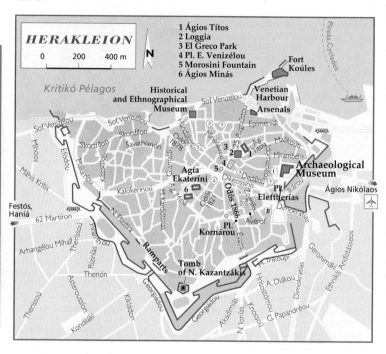

HERAKLEION

0    200    400 m    N

1 Ágios Títos
2 Loggia
3 El Greco Park
4 Pl. E. Venizélou
5 Morosini Fountain
6 Ágios Minás

Crete

## COMING AND GOING

**By air** – The **international airport** is only 4km from the town. In high season (June to the end of September), there are daily charter flights direct from Northern Europe. In the low season, however, you have to take a regular flight and change at Athens. The bus link between the airport and Platía Eleftherías on the edge of the town centre takes a few minutes and is inexpensive (bus station opposite the departures hall).

**Olympic Airways** and **Cronus Air** have several daily flights between Athens and Herakleion (50min). There are two flights a week from Thessaloníki (about 75min).

**Airport information**, ☎ (081) 24 56 44.

**By bus** – The **KTEL** bus company provides daily links with the four corners of the island, from the two bus stations (tickets sold on the spot).

As bus times are always subject to change, get hold of a timetable from one of the bus stations or from the tourist office. This gives full details (including charges and journey times) of services operated by all the island's bus companies. Buses are comfortable and are by far the cheapest means of transport on the island: about 6 cents per km. Speeds are about 35kph.

**Bus Station A**, Platía Koudourióti, ☎ (081) 24 50 17 / 24 50 19 / 24 50 20. In the north-east of the town, 300m from the ferry dock. 10 to 15 daily departures to Mália, Ágios Nikólaos, Ierápetra, Sitía, Haniá and Réthimnon.

**Bus Station B**, 50m outside Haniá Gate, in the west of the town. ☎ (081) 25 59 65. Regular connections with the main towns in the south of the island (10 to 15 buses a day): Míres, Festós (Phaistos), Mátala and Agía Galíni.

**By boat** – The ferry companies **Minoan Lines** and **Anek Lines** operate regular services between Herakleion and the following destinations:
Piraeus: 2 boats a day, at 7.45pm and 8pm. Extra boat on Wednesday at 8am. The crossing takes about 12hr (174 nautical miles).

Santoríni: daily departure at 7am. A second boat on Tuesday (8pm), Wednesday (8am) and Friday (8pm).
Thessaloníki: two boats a week, on Tuesday and Friday at 8pm.
Íos: departures on Tuesday, Thursday, Saturday and Sunday at 7am.
Amorgós: Monday, Wednesday and Friday at 7am.
Páros: daily departure at 7am. Second boat on Tuesday at 8pm and on Wednesday at 6am.
Náxos: daily departure at 7am. Second boat on Wednesday at 8am and Friday at 8pm.
Tínos: daily departure at 7am. Second boat on Friday at 8pm.
Síros: daily departure at 7am. Second boat on Tuesday at 8pm.
Mýkonos: daily departure at 7am.
Tickets are on sale at all the travel agents in Leofóros 25 Avgoústou.

**Harbourmaster's office** (for pleasure boats), ☎ (081) 22 60 73.

## FINDING YOUR WAY

Despite its status as island capital, Herakleion is built on a human scale. You will quickly become familiar with its layout, and will sometimes be surprised at just how short the distances are. Radiating out from Platía Eleftheríou Venizélou, the heart of the city, are the main thoroughfares leading to the four corners of the town.

## GETTING AROUND

**By car** – Don't even think about using a car here. It would just be a waste of time, not to mention the very expensive parking fines you are likely to incur. There is very little on-street parking, and the police are by no means conciliatory. So, leave your car in one of the car parks at the main entrances to the town, where prices are very reasonable (even for one or two days). One of the car parks is by Platía Eleftherías, outside the ramparts. There's another in the moat, accessible through Kenouria Gate (south-west of Platía Eleftherías), and a third near the ferry dock.

**By taxi** – There are plenty of affordable taxis, but you don't really need them for getting around town. However, they are useful for destinations outside Herakleion. They are obviously more expensive than buses but give you much more flexibility.

**By rental car** – Most of the international car hire companies have a desk in the arrivals hall at the airport. In town, the companies are concentrated along Leofóros 25 Avgoústou, which leads to the harbour. Local firms rent out cars in excellent condition, generally at lower rates than the big names. Don't hesitate to negotiate: reductions of 10 to 20% are often granted, even more at the beginning or end of the season.

*Hasstel*, Leofóros 25 Avgoústou 86 (on the left heading towards the harbour), ☎ (081) 28 54 39, Fax (081) 28 59 87. *Alamo*, Leofóros 25 Avgoústou 3, ☎ (081) 24 38 22 / 24 38 32, Fax (081) 24 35 15. Also at the airport, ☎ (081) 22 60 02, Fax (081) 22 24 46. This firm has branches in Anissara, Haniá, Réthimnon and Ágios Nikólaos, as well as in other main towns in Greece, which could come in handy if you have a problem.

**By rental motorcycle or scooter** – The hot climate and relatively small size of the island make two-wheelers a very popular means of transport with tourists. Nonetheless, you should still remember the dangers: car driving is often eccentric, and many roads are in a dubious condition (potholes, falling rocks round bends), taking drivers by surprise. So be careful, and wear a helmet even if no one else does (not mandatory on Crete).

*Motor Club Bike Rentals*, Platía Ágglon (facing the Venetian harbour), ☎ (081) 22 24 08 / 28 60 12 / 28 60 31, Fax (081) 22 28 62. At the airport (arrivals hall), ☎ (081) 22 33 10. This reliable firm rents out 50 to 600cc vehicles for between €9 and €38 a day. Branches at Mália, Haniá and Réthimnon.

### ADDRESS BOOK

**Tourist information** – Odós Xanthoudídou, directly opposite the entrance to the Archaeological Museum. 8am-2.30pm / 3pm-5pm (variable times). Free town plans, maps of the island, and also bus and ferry timetables. There is also an office at the airport, but it is totally useless.

**Bank / Currency exchange** – Banks are only open mornings, 8am to 1.30 or 2pm, and are closed Saturday and Sunday. On the other hand, plenty of cash dispensers for the main international cards (Visa, Eurocard, MasterCard, etc) are available 24hr a day almost everywhere in town. In the airport, the only dispenser, strangely, is in the departures section. If you are stuck, you can change money (cash, travellers' cheques) at all the travel agencies along Leofóros 25 Avgoústou, but at a less advantageous rate than at the banks.

**Post office / Telephone** – *Main post office*, Platía Daskaloyánni, just behind Platía Eleftherías. Monday-Friday, 7.30am-8pm, and Saturday 7.30am to 2pm. Stamps are also sold in souvenir shops, usually at 10% extra. There is another mobile post office in Platía El Greco. Phone booths all over the town operate with cards (€3) that you can buy in tobacconists' kiosks and souvenir shops. In the airport, some of the phones take credit cards.

**Internet** – *Surfing Cyber Café*, Odós Minótavrou 1, beside the El Greco Park. Open from 10am to 2-3am. Half a dozen recent machines (€1.50 for 30min), in a rather frenzied musical atmosphere. An access point is also available at the airport, between the arrivals and departures halls.

**Medical service** – The main hospital is inside the ramparts, in the south-west of the town. ☎ (081) 39 21 11. Dial 166 for emergencies.

**Airline companies** – *Olympic Airways*, Platía Eleftherías, ☎ (081) 22 91 91.

**Other** – *Wash Salon Launderette*, Odós Hándakos 18 (in a small shady square, on the right when coming from the Morosini Fountain). This is a central location and the place also has a convenient *left luggage* service.
*Emergency services*, ☎ 100.
*Police*, ☎ (081) 28 99 00.

## WHERE TO STAY

As Herakleion is not very tourist-oriented (most people only stay a day or two, to visit Knossós and the Archaeological Museum), it does not have many hotels. You should therefore book at least a week in advance, especially in summer. Remember too, that given the proximity of the airport, planes fly over the town day and night. So choose a room with double glazing (more and more hotels are including this in their renovation programmes).

### Under €30

**Hotel Mirabello**, Odós Theotokopoúlou 20, ☎ (081) 28 50 52 / 22 58 52 – 25rm. TV A modest but well-located hotel right near the centre, offering good value for money. All the windows have recently been changed and double glazing installed. Only 7 rooms have private bathrooms, but the shared amenities are new. Two weak points: the cleanliness, which is not always perfect, and the bedding, which could do with some brightening up. Closed in winter.

**Hellas Rent Rooms**, Odós Hándakos 24, ☎ (081) 28 88 51, Fax (081) 28 44 42 – 13rm. An attractive, modest little guesthouse with a lot going for it. Run by a young couple. Friendly atmosphere. A delightful terrace on the top floor, for breakfast and drinks in the evening. Simple though spacious rooms with good-quality bedding. Very clean shared showers and toilets on the landing. If you get up late, remember that there is only hot water from 8am-10am, and in the evening from 6.30pm-10.30pm.

### Between €30 and €45

**Hotel Dedalos**, Odós Dedálou 15, ☎ (081) 24 48 12, Fax (081) 2243 91 – 38rm. Don't be taken in by the luxurious reception area, as the rooms are not of the same standard and could do with a good brightening up (green flowery wallpaper, neon lights). However, the place is clean and well located, though the area is popular with young people in the evening (so it can get noisy). Some rooms have air conditioning.

### Between €45 and €75

**El Greco Hotel**, Odós 1821 4, ☎ and Fax (081) 28 10 71 to 75 – 75rm. TV CC Right in the centre. The hotel dates from the 1970s and has regularly been renovated, offering a good standard of comfort at reasonable rates. All the rooms on the four floors have little balconies. The more expensive ones have air conditioning. Ask for the quieter rooms at the back. The hotel is often full, so you should book.

**Hotel Atrion**, Odós Chronaki 9, ☎ (081) 22 92 25, Fax (081) 22 32 92 – 65rm. TV CC A modern hotel with good standard comfort, specialising in tour groups. The rooms are not particularly charming but are fairly quiet. They could, however, do with a little brightening up (worn carpets). To pay the "normal" price, you should book through a travel agent. The rates at reception are prohibitive, as the place prefers to work with tour operators. Copious, varied buffet breakfast with Viennese bread, pastries, ham, cheese, eggs, etc.

**Mediterranean Hotel**, Platía Daskaloyánni, ☎ (081) 28 93 31 to 34, Fax (081) 28 93 35 – 55rm. TV CC A concrete cube in the heart of town, built in 1974. It has kept its period decor and furniture. People who like that style will love it. Roof terrace with a fine view of the town. Questionable reception manner, and prices are high for the comfort provided. Several rooms for families with 3 or 4 beds.

### Over €75

**Hotel Astoria**, Platía Eleftherías, ☎ (081) 34 30 80, Fax (081) 22 90 78, astoria@her.forthnet.gr – 131rm. TV CC The only luxury international hotel in town. Spacious, impeccable rooms, no more, no less. Minibars, hairdryers in the bathrooms, and large bathtubs. Each room has a small balcony. The roof terrace with a tiny swimming pool and a bar looks over the town and its surroundings.

## EATING OUT

Here, you can eat anything at any time of the day. From the local fast-food places, where hurried managers come to lunch on the famous *gíros pita* (grilled lamb in pita bread, with tomatoes, onions, lettuce and dressing), to the trendy restaurants frequented by intellectuals in the evening – you will be spoilt for choice. Avoid the tourist restaurants concentrated around the Morosini Fountain and in Odós Dedálou, which are very easy to identify: glowing photos of the dishes in the window, touting waiters and plates overflowing with French fries. They are expensive and mostly serve hurriedly thrown together dishes. The exception is breakfast, which is generous and cheap.

*Around €7.50*

**Iona**, Odós Evans 3, a stone's throw from Platía Eleftheríou Venizélou. A simple popular restaurant for everybody. Choose from among the varied stews, pasta, goulash dishes, stuffed or grilled vegetables, or fish from the day's catch. People come here to eat inexpensively, without any airs and graces.

**Ikaros**, Platía Daskaloyánni (beside the post office), ☎ (081) 22 42 48. 🍴 The same type of place as the one above with the added advantage of being in a pleasant little shaded square, where the atmosphere is peaceful and there are cafés and an ouzo bar. Pity about the overhasty service.

*Around €15*

🐚 **Pagopion (Ice Factory)**, Platía Ágios Títos, just behind the town hall. 🍴 This ultra-trendy bar-restaurant serves varied and copious portions of elaborate international fare in a very effective decor (don't leave without a look at the washrooms!). Steak with shredded red cabbage, beans and Dijon mustard, spaghetti with spinach and feta. Mainly frequented by well-heeled locals. An excellent place if you want a change from kebabs and moussaká.

**Pantheon**, Odós Fotíou (a passageway hidden in the middle of the market, linking Odós 1866 and Odós Evans). 🍴 The restaurant is on both sides of the alley and serves traditional local fare at reasonable prices. By traditional we mean lots of olive oil. Forget about the menu, just go inside and choose from the day's specials, which may include a variety of stews, pork with yoghurt, and freshly caught fish.

**Pizzeria Adria**, Odós Androgéo 5, ☎ (081) 33 03 71. 🍴 A few metres from the liveliest streets in the evening. You concoct your own topping or choose from among the dozen or so delicious pizzas on the menu. But be warned: in Herakleion, pizza is a real luxury.

*Around €18*

**Giovanni**, Odós Koráïs 12, in a pedestrian street near the Archaeological Museum, ☎ (081) 34 63 38. Old-style decor, with candles in the evening. Very friendly service and excellent Italian (pasta) or (less tasty) Greek food. Alternatively, you could just have a selection of good meze. To begin with, you are handed a hot table napkin with delicious garlic bread.

**La Belle Époque**, Leofóros Giórgos Papandréou 113, in Amoudára (west of Herakleion, on the old Réthimnon road, a short distance beyond the Carrefour supermarket), ☎ and Fax (081) 25 25 31. A restaurant with a 1930s-style decor that is as trim as the carefully prepared food put together by a young Cretan chef. Here you can try the most refined examples of local cuisine.

**HAVING A DRINK**

Fashionable bars compete with each other for the most creative style, with jazz, techno or Latino flavours – the young people of Herakleion are spoilt for choice. They prefer iced coffee to alcohol and backgammon to video games, so a healthy, appealing atmosphere emanates from the town's night-clubs. From Platía Eleftheríou Venizélou, take Odós Dedálou and then turn left into Odós Predikári, and here, depending on whether you like acid jazz or rock, you'll find somewhere suitable, with tables overflowing into the street until the early hours.

**Bars – Café Capo**, Odós Dedálou, on the left beyond the Virgin store going up from Platía Eleftheríou Venizélou. A huge bar with a deafening electronic medley of techno music, with giant video screens and dim dot lighting. This is the place to try an iced coffee with the habitual blob of vanilla ice cream. A must for local young people.

**Pagopion (Ice Factory)**, Platía Ágios Títos (see *"Eating out"*). ⛱ We hope that this bar keeps its excellent DJ, who plays amazing musical finds. If drinks were a little less expensive you would happily stay longer.

🍴 **Fix**, Odós Pardiari, on the left coming from Odós Dedálou. ⛱ A peaceful atmosphere with gentle jazz in the background and a subdued pre-1940s decor. If there were less of a crowd, the place could almost be described as relaxing. Enquire about the concerts put on in winter.

**Cafés –** The **ouzo bar** in Platía Daskaloyánni, just behind Platía Eleftherías, is probably the pleasantest place in town to try an ouzo and titbits. Come here at sunset when the trees in the square are alive with birdsong.

**Cubes**, Platía Kornárou, at the Turkish fountain. ⛱ This is not really a restaurant but a pleasant refreshment stall where you can take a break with a salad or a thick sandwich. A favourite spot with locals, who come for a quick snack after the market in the late morning. A little expensive all the same.

### OTHER THINGS TO DO

**Excursions –** Agents along Leofóros 25 Avgoústou offer a variety of boat trips. **Arabatzoglou Bros**, Leofóros 25 Avgoústou 52, ☎ (081) 34 17 01 to 04, Fax (081) 34 17 06. Excursions to Santoríni on Monday, Wednesday, Thursday and Friday. Departure at 6.15am, return trip at 9pm. Crossing time about 4hr30min. Breakfast and dinner served on board.

**Feasts & festivals – Herakleion Summer Festival**, enquiries ☎ (081) 24 66 63. From I July to 15 September the town organises concerts, exhibitions, plays (particularly in Fort Koúles), singing and dancing.

### SHOPPING GUIDE

**Market –** The town's main market has been named after the street in which it is located, **Odós 866**. Before leaving the island, you can stock up on goods that are often so expensive in other parts of the world, such as olive oil, pistachio nuts (delicious), thyme honey and Mediterranean flavourings. This is also where you will find the attractive ring-shaped loaves of bread with delicate motifs carved into the dough, prepared for purely ornamental purposes on important family occasions.

**Bookshop –** Odós Hándakos, on the right of the square when coming from the Morosini Fountain. A large bookshop, where the works are classified according to language.

**Other – George Mamouzelos' shop**, Leofóros 25 Avgoústou 20, on the left as you go down to the harbour, ☎ (081) 28 11 26. Sponges and nothing but sponges! A little more expensive than those at the market, but a lot more beautiful. Open only in summer.

# KNOSSÓS ★★

District of Iráklio – 5km south-east of Herakleion
Michelin map 980 fold 39 – Map of the island pages 358-359

**Not to be missed**
A preliminary visit to the Archaeological Museum in Herakleion.

**And remember...**
Tour the site at the end of the day, when the tourist coaches are
beginning to leave and it is less crowded.
Bring a hat: in summer the sun beats down hard.

The oldest city in Greece is set among dry hills in the south-east of the Herakleion plain. With its chequerboard of courtyards, corridors, stairways, upper floors, chambers, royal apartments and shrines, the mythical lair of the terrible Minotaur is well and truly a labyrinth. So follow our own version of Ariadne's thread to understand the layout of the huge palace complex... and to find your way out! The excavation of the site in the early 20C marked a major step in our understanding of the Minoan civilisation *(see page 18)*. A civilisation steeped in legend, which still seems to haunt the site, in spite of the impressive crowds of visitors and the fact that there is no definitive proof that Knossós was indeed the palace of King Minos. As Knossós is one of the main attractions on Crete, you will have to pick your way between tour groups, unless you arrive the moment the place opens or at the end of the day.

### From legend...

According to tradition, the architect who designed Knossós, the cunning **Daedalus**, was inspired by a very complicated edifice, the **Labyrinth** or Palace of the Axe – the double-headed axe being the main ritual symbol of the Minoan religion. King Minos is believed to have commissioned the building to confine the **Minotaur**, a monster with a man's body and a bull's head, born of the unnatural union of Queen Pasiphae and a bull. The ruthless Minos used to feed his enemies to the Minotaur. Aegeus, King of Athens, learnt this to his cost: having had Minos' son killed, he had to give in to the vengeful demands of the Cretan, who, every nine years required the Athenians to send seven youths and seven maidens to be sacrificed to the Minotaur. To put an end to this, the Athenians sent as part of the tribute **Theseus**, the son of Aegeus, who entered the palace and slew the beast. **Ariadne**, Minos' daughter, was seduced by the hero and gave him a plan of the palace that she had secretly obtained from Daedalus. She also gave him a thread to unwind and so find his way out of the labyrinth.

A sensual Minoan goddess
(Archaeological Museum, Herakleion)

### ...to archaeology

The hill at Knossós was already inhabited in the Neolithic Period. In about 2000 BC, a palace was built and then destroyed in

1700 BC, probably by an earthquake. It was replaced by a new palace in the heart of a city with about 50 000 inhabitants; it is the remains of this palace that can be seen today. The gigantic complex of buildings on the site had no fortifications, and originally consisted of no less than 1 300 rooms. However, in around 1530 BC (possibly 1630 BC) the palace was once again devastated, probably as a result of a tidal wave provoked by the eruption of the volcano on Santoríni. Then the

**Icarus' fateful flight**

The other great myth attached to Knossós is that of Icarus. To punish Daedalus for his betrayal, King Minos imprisoned him in the palace. But the ingenious architect managed to escape. He used wax and feathers to make wings for himself and his son Icarus, and they flew away. Icarus, alas, flew too close to the sun, which melted the wax, and the unfortunate young man fell into the sea near the present island of Ikaría, while his father succeeded in reaching Cumae in Italy.

palace was sacked and occupied for a short period by the Mycenaeans before finally being destroyed by fire – in unknown circumstances – between 1375 and 1250 BC. Nonetheless, a more modest settlement survived in the neighbourhood and in the 4C BC Knossós was still of some importance politically. Eventually in the late 3C BC it was supplanted by Gortyn.

The existence of Knossós as the palace of the Minotaur had been suggested by the German explorer Heinrich Schliemann (*see page 19*) interpreting the Homeric epic as if it were history, as he had done for Troy and Mycenae. He was followed by the Cretan **Kalokairinós** who had been the first to identify the site, and had done research in 1878. But it was the eminent British archaeologist, **Sir Arthur Evans** (1851-1941), who gained credit for excavating the palace. From 1900 to 1931 he endeavoured to make the place live again, investing his life and his fortune... and much concrete. This he used to serve his imagination, which, if the truth must be told, occasionally departed from historical fact. So, mixed in with the remains are a number of false ruins – skilfully eroded cement wall fragments of questionable historical and aesthetic value. Here the debate on whether or not one should reconstruct, and to what extent, takes on its full meaning.

## Tour of the site

*Daily, 8am-7pm. Entrance fee. Plenty of buses travel here daily from Herakleion (leaving from Platía Eleftheríou Venizélou). By car, leave town south of Platía Eleftherías, taking Leofóros Dimokratías. The site is then clearly signposted all along the route. The car park is free, but often crowded with tourist coaches. However, on the left of the road leading to the site there are several other parking areas where you will be asked to leave your car. They are supposedly free but you should give a tip, and you will find they are really practical when the place gets crowded (June to September). Allow 2hr.*

Beyond the entrance, you go through a tree-lined lane to the West Court, a paved area that was probably an **agora**. Note, on the left, the **Offerings Pits** where, it is believed, discarded sacred objects were disposed of (unless the pits were in fact silos). Opposite is the base of the outer palace wall, about 1m high.

Take the walkway on the right to the **West Entrance**, the propylaeum (monumental gateway) which gave access to the **Corridor of the Procession**. One of the columns in the gallery has been reconstructed, and the remains of the wall **frescoes** showing people bearing offerings are in the Archaeological Museum in Herakleion.

### South Palace

The walkway turns left, leading to the **Grand Propylaeum**, a pillared porch that precedes a wide staircase leading to the upper floor. On the wall you can see a copy of one of the frescoes that once adorned it (bearers of offerings) The **Upper Floor** (*closed for an indefinite period*) comprised a number of pillared rooms (possibly reception rooms), some of which have been restored and decorated with copies of frescoes.

**Knossós**

It was in this section that the Parisienne, one of the gems of the Archaeological Museum in Herakleion, was discovered.

Below and to the west is a corridor leading to storerooms once used for stocking large provision jars, or **pithoi**, some of which are still in place.

*To the east, another staircase leads down to the central courtyard.*

The **central courtyard**, a vast sandy area (60m x 29m) is surrounded by the main buildings – shrines, royal apartments, etc. It was probably the site of the perilous ritual **bull-leaping** performed by acrobats.

### Shrines

On the south side of the courtyard, in the passage that forms the end of the Corridor of the Procession, is a copy of the fresco of the **Prince of the Lilies** (*the original is exhibited in the Archaeological Museum in Herakleion*).

Along the west side of the courtyard (*left*), on either side of a staircase lie the rooms devoted to religious use. On the left of the staircase, a **vestibule** leads into the "pillar crypts" (*opposite, no access but visible from the courtyard*) where ritual cere-monies took place. On the right is the **Treasury**, a small shrine where religious objects were found, in particular the famous **snake goddesses** that can be seen in the Archaeological Museum in Herakleion. The sacred serpents may have been kept here.

A little further on, still on the right of the staircase is the **Sanctuary**. A **vestibule**, in the middle of which Evans placed a porphyry basin, leads into the **Throne Room** which contains a bench and the alabaster throne on which the High Priestess of the Labyrinth may have sat. The griffin frescoes are reconstructions. Opposite the throne, steps beneath arches descend to a **lustral basin**, used for purificatory ablutions.

### Royal Apartments

The royal apartments, both public and private, are on the east side of the courtyard. They are closed for repairs but you can see part of them from the **grand staircase\*** leading to them (*as well as from below the courtyard, on the south ramp*). The apart-ments are linked by a network of corridors and passages, and occupy four floors: two above the level of the courtyard and two below. They were built into the slope of the hill above the river with a fine view over the countryside. As in other parts of the palace, the staircase goes around a **light well**, which would also have provided for the circulation of air in the rooms.

Once you have gone round the lower section, look through the glass into the **Queen's Chamber\***, which is lit by another light well and adorned with a copy of the **Dolphin Fresco\*\***. In the small adjoining **bathroom** (*inaccessible*) is a bath made of terracotta. This material was also used to make the piping that carried the palace's supply of fresh water under pressure (you will see parts of this system all over the site).

Nearby, on the right, is the **King's Chamber\***, with a wooden throne (copy). An openwork screen separates it from the **Hall of the Double Axes\***, which served as a Guard Room.

### Outbuildings

From the royal apartments, take the covered portico, which served as a promenade and which leads to the outbuildings on the north side of the palace. There were **workshops for craftsmen**, stonecutters, gold- and silversmiths, potters (remains of kilns), and also some storerooms. One of them, the **pithoi storeroom**, has a series of enormous terracotta **jars\*** (partially reconstructed), which were used for storing wine, oil, grain, honey, etc. This room dates from the first palace.

A little further on, you pass the **School for Scribes**, before getting lost among the ruins of other **storerooms**, one of which still contains its impressive *pithoi* jars.

## Around the North Entrance

To finish the tour, return to the central courtyard and take a narrow passage to the right. This runs alongside a **portico** partially reconstructed by Evans, showing a **relief fresco** of a bull. The lane then leads to what Evans called the **Customs House**, recognisable by the pillars with wide square bases thought to have supported a banqueting hall on the floor above. Nearby is the North Entrance to the palace. Beyond, on the left, you can go down to another small **lustral basin⋆**.

The Royal Road, a lovely paved avenue 4m wide, may have led to Katsámbas and Amnisós, the two harbours east of Herakleion that served Knossós. To the right it passes by a set of well-preserved terraces, which are thought to belong to the **theatre** mentioned by Homer, the setting for ritual dances.

*From here return to the West Entrance.*

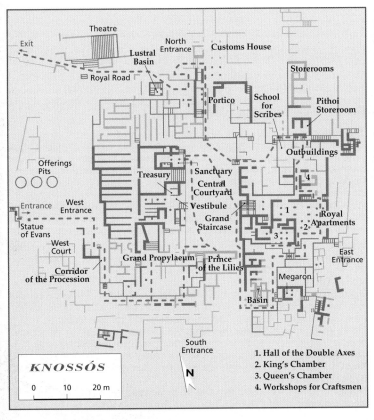

KNOSSÓS

0   10   20 m

N

1. Hall of the Double Axes
2. King's Chamber
3. Queen's Chamber
4. Workshops for Craftsmen

# MÁLIA★★

District of Iráklio – 39km east of Herakleion, 32km west of Ágios Nikólaos
Michelin map 980 fold 39 – Map of the island pages 358-359

**Not to be missed**
The ruins of the residential quarter and,
just beside them, an unspoiled beach.
**And remember...**
Use Ágios Nikólaos, the most attractive town on the coast,
as a base for visiting Mália.

Mália, another great Minoan city, is just as worthwhile as the prestigious Knossós, but nonetheless remains little known. Here you can escape the crowds. Furthermore, the place has none of Sir Evans' false concrete ruins, so the city appears as it was. An impressive maze of levelled walls not only marks out the plan of a palace but a whole city of craftsmen. Another important point is that Mália ceased to be inhabited at the end of the second millennium BC, after the natural disaster that struck all of northern Crete (*see page 372*), and so the original layout of the city is not cluttered by later constructions. Mália appears to the visitor like a line drawing of ochre-red stone.

## Tour of the site

*A signpost on the main road to Ágios Nikólaos indicates the site on the left (on the right if you are coming from Ágios Nikólaos). 8.30am-3pm, 7 days a week in high season (May-October), from Tuesday to Sunday in the low season. Entrance fee. Allow 45min.*

Mália stretches out over a wide rocky platform facing the sea. There are two distinct areas, the Royal Palace and the craftsmen's living quarters. The site was identified by the archaeologist **Joseph Hatzidákis** and since 1921 has been excavated by the French School of Archaeology in Athens.

### The Palace★

The Mália palace, a contemporary of the one at Knossós, follows a similar though more modest layout, built around a central courtyard. A wide paved **agora** (outer courtyard) leads to the palace complex. Facing it are the foundations of the western façade, a series of storerooms linked to the interior by a long corridor that leads to the royal apartments.

Walk up the **Minoan Road★** on the far left, a paved lane leading to the North Entrance to the palace. It goes past an enormous **pithos★**, a 1.75m-high jar that could hold more than 1 000 litres of wine or oil.

You enter the palace itself through a **vestibule** and a portico supported by columns (*the bases remain*). On the left, another **pithos** marks the site of a second row of storerooms, while on the right the small **North Court** (also known as the Keep) gives access to the royal apartments.

Opposite, once past what is known as the **Oblique Building**, follow the corridor into the **central courtyard**. The north and east sides are bordered by porticoes, and the west side is occupied, as at Knossós, by official and religious buildings.

On the north side you can see the **Hypostyle Room**, recognisable by its two rows of pillars. It is flanked on the left by a **vestibule**, probably used for banquets.

The north-west corner is taken up by the **Sanctuary** area, comprising notably the **Royal Loggia**, which gives onto the courtyard (just opposite lies a half-buried **Byzantine cannonball**).

Beyond are the steps of a **staircase** that led to the upper floor, and then a room for worship, known as the **Pillared Crypt**, with two square pillars.

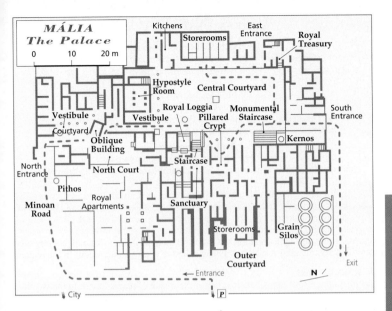

MÁLIA
The Palace

0    10    20 m

Kitchens
East Entrance
Royal Treasury
Storerooms
Hypostyle Room
Central Courtyard
Royal Loggia
Vestibule
Vestibule
Monumental Staircase
Pillared Crypt
South Entrance
Courtyard
Kernos
Oblique Building
Staircase
North Entrance
North Court
Pithos
Royal Apartments
Sanctuary
Minoan Road
Storerooms
Grain Silos
Outer Courtyard
Exit
← Entrance
N
City
P

Further on, you come to the four steps of a **monumental staircase**. Just beside it is an unusual round stone table, indented in the centre, with little cavities round the edge. The function of this **kernos** (or cupped table) remains a mystery: was it a gaming table or an altar for offerings? The debate is still open.

Lastly, the buildings on the eastern side of the courtyard include the **Royal Treasury** (right), which is separated from the **storerooms** by the East Entrance. The storerooms are protected by a roof and have kept their **wall benches**, on which stood jars of oil and wine. Further on, you come to what have been identified by the archaeologists as kitchens. On leaving (via the South Entrance), you pass eight large grain **silos** dug into the ground (right).

## The city*

*Take the Minoan Road westwards.* On leaving the palace complex it is well worth walking through the craftsmen's district. This makes up a whole village dating from the Old Palace Period, with bright ochre-red walls now protected by a huge modern roof. The walkway installed above the remains enables you to go from alleyway to alleyway and overlook the entire excavation area where the layout of each house is clearly visible. Beyond the agora (right), the road leads first to the **Hypostyle Crypt**. The steps at the end gave access to **meeting rooms**, still partially furnished with benches, which were probably part of the **Prytaneion**, where the city magistrates met. It is flanked by **storerooms**.

Beyond here was the town itself, a tight network of religious buildings and **houses***, most of which have kept their basement and ground floor. Everything was here, from the tanner's to the potter's, not forgetting the baker's.

Lastly, you can cool off at the **beach** nearby. Untouched compared with the one at the Mália resort, it is one of the most attractive along the coast. You can also have a snack or a drink under the arbour at the adjoining taverna.

*Beyond Mália, the road leaves the coast to disappear inland through some lovely countryside with olive groves and Byzantine churches perched on hills. You then reach the Gulf of Mirambélo, where Ágios Nikólaos nestles in the curve of the bay.*

# ÁGIOS NIKÓLAOS★
## THE MT DÍKTI REGION★
Capital of the district of Lassíthi – 69km east of Herakleion
Michelin map 980 fold 39 – Map of the island pages 358-359 – Pop 8 000

### Not to be missed
A trip inland.
An excursion to the Spinalónga Peninsula (see following chapter).
Golden Bay (Istro beach) and the village of Kalavrós, for its panorama.

### And remember...
Stay at Ágios Nikólaos for at least two days.
It's very pleasant in the evening and is an ideal base for exploring the region.

The lively resort of Ágios Nikólaos is often compared to St Tropez in France. Its white houses cover the hillsides overlooking the blue waters of the Gulf of Mirambélo, rising above a sheltered bay and a deep lake that is steeped in legend. A mellow, typically Mediterranean atmosphere emanates from the smart little pedestrian streets and the restaurant tables spilling out onto the quayside. The town exploits this successfully, inviting the traveller to stay a few days to enjoy the attractions in the region.

## A sketchy past
The main interest of Ágios Nikólaos lies in the wealth of places to visit in the vicinity. It owes its charm to the harmony of its small white buildings, its parasols, its flowers and the boats in the harbour. The town has preserved nothing of its past, apart from some levelled walls being excavated by archaeologists in an area up from the harbour, plus a few 19C houses that you will come across as you wander around. Ágios Nikólaos was built over the ruins of the ancient harbour that served **Lató**, a Roman city inland (see below), which prospered in the 3C BC. It acquired its name at the beginning of the Byzantine Period (6C) when it became the seat of a bishopric. From a modest fishing village, the town only began to grow during the last years of Turkish occupation, and has mainly developed since the advent of tourism in Crete.

## Short tour of the town

Take time off from exploring the surrounding area (see below and the following chapter) and stroll through the streets, along the quayside and around **Lake Voulisméni★**. It is around this expanse of brackish water that the town's tourist activity is centred. Dominated by a steep cliff on which stand houses and outdoor restaurants (fine **panorama★**), the lake is 64m deep, which is rather surprising given its modest diameter. An ancient legend holds that the lake is bottomless, its dark waters leading to the unfathomable abyss of the world beyond. It is in fact fed by an underground river that reappears here, and it has been linked to the sea by a narrow **canal** since 1870.

Go south by climbing the steps at the side of the lake. Once you have passed **Platía Elfeftheríou Venizélou**, a large square, continue up to **Kefalí hill** (near the Prefecture) through steep alleyways that look over the sea. Here, a stone's throw from the tourist bustle, the atmosphere changes and you find yourself in a quiet, wholly different world. From here, you can go down to **Kitroplatía beach** in the south-easternmost part of town, a peaceful little pebble bay with tavernas.

## Archaeological Museum
Towards the edge of town, in Odós Konstandínou Paleológou, about 400m on the right as you come up from the lake. Tuesday to Sunday, 8.30am-3pm. Entrance fee. Archaeology enthusiasts will be impressed by this small, very well-laid-out museum, whose seven rooms retrace the ancient history of the region. Most of the objects displayed date

Crete

Ágios Nikólaos, a typically Mediterranean harbour

from the **Early Minoan Period** (3000-2300 BC), particularly the large collection of **vases**, **bronze daggers**, jewellery and various pieces from **Agía Fotía** *(near Sitía)*, the largest ancient necropolis unearthed on Crete. More than 260 tombs excavated there contained a wealth of objects providing information on the daily life and religious practices of the time. The museum's showpiece is the **Goddess of Mírto\***, an extraordinary libations vase in the shape of a woman that came from excavations in **Fournou Korifi**, near the village of **Mírtos Ierápetra**. This Minoan goddess of fertility has a very large body, slim arms and a small head.

## West of Ágios Nikólaos

*Head south-west towards Kritsá. Several buses a day.*

■ **Church of Panagía Kerá\*\*** – *8km from Ágios Nikólaos, on the right, just before you get to Kritsá. Daily, 8.30am-3pm. Entrance fee.* If you are travelling by car, stop at a place called **Logari**. Standing behind an olive grove in a charming rural setting is a modest Byzantine church with whitewashed walls, barely 10m x 10m, that you would never dream contained a treasure. It was built in several stages by the Venetians in the 13C and 14C and consists of a nave and two aisles – narrow and vaulted – entirely covered in exquisitely beautiful **frescoes\*\*** that have been very well preserved. The fourteen panels of frescoes illustrate the **apocryphal Gospels** – rare in Byzantine art – with the Life of the Virgin Mary (nave), St Anne (south aisle) and St Antony (north aisle). Among the oldest, note the eight large panels in the **west vault\*\*** of the nave showing the Massacre of the Innocents, Rachel mourning for her Children, Elizabeth rescuing St John the Baptist (hiding him in the hollow of a rock), and the **Nativity\*\***, where the Virgin Mary's face has been portrayed with great nobility. Take the time to admire the contrasting colours and the finely drawn expressions, which make these frescoes one of the great masterpieces of Byzantine art on Crete.

■ **Kritsá\*** – A kilometre further on, you come to the picturesque village of Kritsá, whose white and ochre-coloured houses cling to a steep slope in the foothills of the Díkti massif (2 148m). The "authentic" charm of the village has unfortunately made it one of the great local tourist attractions – and the nearby Church of Panagía Kerá and the Lató ruins also draw a large crowd. But don't be put off by your first impressions. Once you have passed the lines of tourist coaches in the car park, go quickly across the busy main street with its souvenir shops and villagers selling lace, pottery and honey, and keep climbing. You will at last reach deserted streets frequented only by those who live there.

*Head back towards Ágios Nikólaos and take the road immediately on your left after leaving Kritsá. Be warned: to simplify the traffic, there are two separate one-way roads for entering and leaving the village. The Lató road is well signposted when you come into Kritsá, but not so easy to find in the other direction. If you miss it, turn back before reaching the Church of Panagía Kerá.*

■ **Lató*** – *Open Tuesday to Sunday, 8.30am-3pm. Free entry (but no interpretation).* The ruins of this large **Dorian city** spread across the hillside in a superb site between two crags, melting into a wild jumble of grey rock. The **view**★★ over the gulf and the sea testifies to its choice strategic position. Lató was a powerful, prosperous city, minting coins and holding sway over the whole region from the 7C to the 3C BC. A large stone inscription indicating the boundaries of the State shows that its influence could be felt as far as **Mt Anginara** in the east.

The little-visited site has the added attraction of being peaceful, so it is a pleasure to walk among the ruins. Excavated by archaeologists from the French School in Athens, Lató still exercises something of the appeal it must once have had. Once through the **three successive entrances** that controlled access to the town, you walk along the main street, a steep pathway of 80 steps leading to the **agora**★. On the right *(south)* were the **storerooms**, while a powerful **wall** reinforced by towers ran along the left side. The agora is an immense pentagon, closed off to the north by the terraces of the **Prytaneion**. In the middle, there was a large covered **cistern** and a **small temple** in which numerous 6C BC figurines were discovered. You can continue south-east to the **theatre**, and then walk among the rocks to enjoy the beauty of the site and the fine panorama.

## Lassíthi Plateau★

*It is best to have your own transport. Take the Herakleion road from Ágios Nikólaos and after about 15km, head left up a little road that winds up the mountain in a series of hairpin bends (well signposted). You can also go on one of the coach tours offered by companies in Ágios Nikólaos (a lot less pleasant), or use the local bus service.*

As you climb, there are bird's-eye **views**★★ of the surrounding valleys. The temperature drops, and the wind rises. Heralded by the ruins of old **windmills** once used for grinding wheat, the plateau finally appears beyond the pass. It is a huge oval plain covering 72km² (12km x 6km) suspended at an altitude of 800m, completely hemmed in by mountains. Snow-covered in winter and green in summer, the fertile land is cultivated by the population of 17 villages, producing cereals, fruit, potatoes, etc. Olives do not grow here. The unusual climate and difficult access made the plateau a refuge for the Cretans during the many periods of oppression in the past. When the Venetians arrived, it was here that the island resistance was organised. The Venetians ended up by expelling the rebels in 1253 and declaring the area forbidden territory. It was only 200 years later, in 1463, that the occupying force had to reopen the plateau to the population because of a shortage of grain.

Today, Lassíthi Plateau has lost some of its traditional life. Don't go by the photographs showing a plateau bristling with picturesque **windmills**. Once intended for pumping water for irrigation, these have now been replaced by modern equipment, with just a few rusty skeletons remaining. Furthermore, much of the land is left fallow as farming has given way to arts and crafts – embroidery, pottery and honey – for tourists. The melancholy scenery, however, is captivating. You can go round the plateau, from village to village, along the **one and only road** that surrounds it.

Crete

■ A little 1km-long road leads from the village of **Psychró** to the **Díktean Cave** perched at an altitude of 1 025m *(daily, 8.30am-4pm; expensive car park and entrance fee)*. This is the region's main archaeological, natural (and lucrative) attraction, with coachloads of tourists arriving from morning to evening. The cave is at the top of a steep path that you climb on foot, or ride up on one of the donkeys for hire. The cave consists of a large area that divides further down into four small sections with stalactites and stalagmites, before continuing to a tiny **underground lake** 60m below ground. This is where **Rhea**, fleeing her husband, is believed to have sought refuge to give birth to Zeus. As the many archaeological finds suggest, the cave was an important place of worship in the Middle Minoan Period.

■ If you have the time, take the Herakleion road on the north side of the plateau for several kilometres to the **Monastery of Kardikiótissa** (or Panagía Kerá) *(8am-1pm; modest clothing required)*. The church is devoted to the Virgin Mary and contains some outstanding 14C **frescoes★**.

## On the Sitía road

*74km. Allow 4hr, taking your time. The bus takes about 90min, making detours into coastal villages. By car, head southwards out of Ágios Nikólaos in the direction of Sitía or Ierápetra. The scenery is best seen in the light of late afternoon or early evening. However, you should avoid travelling at night because nasty surprises can await you around corners (such as falling rocks).*

The Sitía road runs alongside the **Gulf of Mirambélo★★**, passing either beside rough waves, or high above the water. On the right, you have the steep mountainside, on the left the sea of Crete, punctuated by deserted islets glinting in the sun.

■ About ten kilometres beyond Ágios Nikólaos, **tavernas** and tourist shops (right) line the approach to the beach at **Golden Bay★** (Istro). With its white sand and turquoise water, the beach nestles some 50m below the road, in a little bay surrounded by rocks, which you reach along a **path**.

*Continue for about ten kilometres. A signpost on the right shows the way to Gourniá, an archaeological site on the hillside, on the right facing the sea.*

■ **Gourniá** – *19km from Ágios Nikólaos. Tuesday to Sunday, 8.30am-3pm. Entrance fee.* This ancient Minoan city was remarkably well excavated by the archaeological team led by the American **Harriet Boyd-Hawes** in the early 20C. The town plan is clearly visible owing to the low walls that mark out the main streets, the network of steep alleyways punctuated by flights of steps, the public buildings, the modest craftsmen's dwellings and the shops. With its coastal location, Gourniá was an important trading port. It was destroyed in 1450 BC, and, like most Minoan cities, lay deserted for a while, before being occupied for the last time in the Mycenaean Era from 1400-1200 BC.

The ruins date for the most part from the **New Palace Period** (1500-1450 BC). In the centre, crowning the hill, stood the **Governor's Palace**, modelled on the palaces at Knossós, Mália and Phaistos, but on a smaller scale. On the north side, a small rectangular building contained a **shrine** dedicated to the **snake goddess**. Many objects were found here and are now in the Ágios Nikólaos museum, including **figurines** of the deity, and **vases** for the reptiles.

*Continue eastwards for 4km.*

■ Though it first seems rather desolate, the fishing village of **Pahía Ámos** is actually quite charming with its attractive and unspoiled **beach**. There are tavernas for refreshment before continuing your journey beside the roaring sea.

The road gradually begins to wind up to Sitía, with the countryside becoming less arid.

■ Just before **Messa Mouliana**, a practicable track (*though best taken on foot*) heads left towards the sea. After 3km it ends at **Kalavrós\***, a hamlet clinging to a steep hillside in a wonderful setting. The houses look as though they're on the point of falling into the abyss, defying the laws of gravity. If you've made the effort to come here, you will not be disappointed: the **panorama\*\*\*** is staggering.

*Go back to the main road and continue east through mountain villages. As you approach Sitia Bay you will see windmills on the hills.*

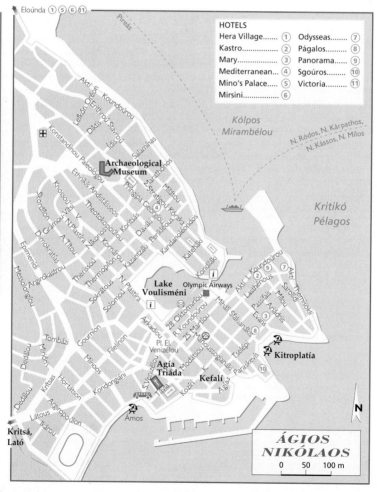

HOTELS

| | | | |
|---|---|---|---|
| Hera Village...... | ① | Odysseas........ | ⑦ |
| Kastro............... | ② | Págalos.......... | ⑧ |
| Mary................. | ③ | Panorama...... | ⑨ |
| Mediterranean... | ④ | Sgoúros......... | ⑩ |
| Mino's Palace..... | ⑤ | Victoria......... | ⑪ |
| Mirsini.............. | ⑥ | | |

Eloúnda ① ⑤ ⑥ ⑪

Piréas

Kólpos Mirambélou

N. Ródos, N. Kárpathos, N. Kássos, N. Mílos

Kritikó Pélagos

Archaeological Museum

Lake Voulisméni    Olympic Airways

Kitroplatía

Agía Triáda    Kefalí

Ámos

Kritsá, Lató

**ÁGIOS NIKÓLAOS**

0    50    100 m

N

COMING AND GOING

**By bus** – The **bus station** is in the southern part of the town, near Ámos beach and the marina. Plenty of daily buses run to most of the towns in the east and to the tourist sights in the environs (return trips), ☎ (0841) 22 234 / 28 284.
**Herakleion** (90min travelling time): 24 buses a day, from 6am to 10.30pm. **Ierápetra** (1hr): 9 buses a day, from 6.30am to 9pm. **Sitía** (90min): 6 buses a day, from 6.15am to 6pm. **Eloúnda** (15min): 20 buses a day, from 6.15am (7.10am on weekends) to 9pm. **Pláka** (20min): 7 buses a day, from 6.15am (9am on weekends) to 7pm. **Kritsá** and the **Church of Panagía Kerá** (15min): 12 buses a day, from 6am to 7.30pm. **Lassíthi Plateau**: a bus on Monday, Wednesday and Friday (ask about times at the bus station). **Mália** archaeological site and beach: 2 buses a day (9.15am and 10.15am). **Síssi**: 2 buses a day, from Monday to Saturday, at 9.15am and 5.30pm. **Gortyn**, **Phaistos**, **Mátala**: (about 2hr30min): from Monday to Saturday, 1 bus at 8.30am, return from Mátala at 5.15pm.

**By boat** – **Harbourmaster's office**, ☎ (0841) 22 312. **Nostos Tours** ferries connect with Piraeus, the Dodecanese, the Cyclades and Sitía town:
**Piraeus**: Monday, Tuesday, Thursday, Saturday and Sunday, 1 boat at 6pm, and on Thursday an extra boat at 7am.
**Rhodes**: Wednesday at 6.45am, Friday at 9am, Saturday at 8am.
**Diafáni**: Wednesday at 6.45am and Friday at 9am. **Kárpathos**: Wednesday at 6.45am, Friday at 9am and Saturday at 8am. **Mílos**: a boat at 6pm on Monday, Tuesday, Thursday, Saturday and Sunday. **Sitía**: a boat on Monday, Tuesday, Thursday and Saturday at 8am, Wednesday at 6.45am and Friday at 10am.

FINDING YOUR WAY

Although it is small, the town has a fairly complex layout because of its hilly site. Take **Platía Eleftheríou Venizélou** as the central landmark, rather than the lake. The main streets radiate out from here to the four corners of the town. Watch out for streets and quays with similar names: Aktí Koundoúrou runs alongside the shore in the direction of Eloúnda, Odós Roussou Koundoúrou links the harbour to Platía Eleftheríou Venizélou, while Aktí Iossif Koundoúrou borders the south-east part of the harbour.

GETTING AROUND

**By car** – Ideally, you should park your car and go round on foot. In summer, the area round the lake is often closed to traffic.

**By taxi** – A convenient way of exploring the surrounding area. Taxis can be found near the lake, near the canal and in Odós Kondiláki, ☎ (841) 24 000.

ADDRESS BOOK

**Tourist information** – Right in the centre, a few metres from the canal, ☎ (0841) 22 357. Here you will find brochures of the main hotels in town and round about, as well as a very useful town plan (free). Unfortunately the staff are not very friendly.

**Bank / Currency exchange** – Banks are open Monday to Friday from 8am to 2pm (1.30pm on Friday). There are several cash dispensers in Odós 28 Oktomvríou. You can also change money at the tourist office, or in the travel agents in the same street.

**Post office / Telephone** – **Main post office**, Odós 28 Oktomvríou, on the right as you come up from the harbour, ☎ (0841) 22 276. Monday-Friday, 7.30am-8pm.

**Internet** – **Internet Café Peripou**, Odós 28 Oktomvríou 25. Open all year, seven days a week, 9.30am-2am. You often have to wait a while to use a machine but the place is really very pleasant: attractive decor, music, books and discs to borrow, and a terrace overlooking the lake.

**Medical service** – **Hospital**, 500m from the centre, Odós Konstandínou Paleológou, towards Herakleion. ☎ (0841) 25 221.

**Dentist**: Dr K Vardavas, Odós 28 Ok-tomvríou (at the very beginning of the street as you come from the harbour, on the left), ☎ (0841) 28 884.

**Car rental** – All the travel agents concentrated on Odós 28 Oktomvríou have cars for hire.

**Motorcycle and scooter rental** – There are several outfits along Aktí Koundoúrou (the long quay in the north-west heading towards Eloúnda). Don't hesitate to negotiate rates.

**Airline company** – *Olympic Airways*, ☎ (0841) 22 033 / 28 929.

**Other** – *Police*, ☎ (0841) 22 321. *Tourist police*, ☎ (0841) 26 900.

### WHERE TO STAY

As a very tourist-oriented resort, Ágios Nikólaos has a wide choice of hotels and guesthouses. Be warned, however, that the place is packed in summer, including the up-market hotels, so booking is advisable. The Lake Hotel, the town's most prominent establishment (impossible to miss with its sign dominating the lake) has been closed for some time. It is expected to reopen, but people have been waiting year after year!

*Under €30*

🏠 **Mary Pension**, Odós Evans 13, ☎ (0841) 23 760 / 24 384 / 26 361 – 9rm. ⌁ Ring at the second floor to get the charming lady owner, who takes great personal care of her guests. Visitors have access to a kitchen and a roof terrace (bare concrete, but with a sea view).

**Odysseas**, Odós Sarolídi 7 (on the corner of Aktí Themisoklí), ☎ (0841) 28 440 – 25rm. ⌁ ℘ ✗ A very new hotel, done up in white and blue, with a cool sea atmosphere. The spacious rooms (some with 3 or 4 beds suitable for families) and very reasonable rates make this one of the most pleasant places in town.

**Mediterranean Pension**, Odós Daváki 27, ☎ (0841) 23 611, 8rm. ⌁ ✗ Often full, frequented by regular visitors who come back year after year. Run by Emmanuél Kentrianákis, an American of Greek origin. The rooms are very spacious with large balconies, a double bed and two singles. Suitable for families and friends. Nothing remarkable, but clean, and you are given a friendly welcome.

*Between €30 and €45*

🏠 **Hotel Panorama**, Odós Sarolídi 2, (on the corner of Aktí Iossif Koundoúrou), ☎ (0841) 28 890, Fax (0841) 27 268 – 29rm. ⌁ 🖼 ℘ You feel really at home here. Although it is very simple, this little hotel is so charming and has such a warm family atmosphere that you almost feel like sitting down comfortably in front of the television in the large reception area. Ask for a room with a view of the harbour. Breakfast not included.

**Hotel Sgoúros**, Kiroplatía beach, ☎ (0841) 28 931 / 23 931, Fax (0841) 25 568 – 29rm. ⌁ ℘ ✗ cc Very modern, comfortable, and in an extremely good position on the pebble beach on the far side of the hill that closes off the harbour which is one of the most attractive parts of the town. No special charm but very reasonable rates. One of the rare hotels to stay open in winter.

**Hotel Págalos**, Odós Tselépi 17, ☎ (0841) 23 860 / 22 936 – 23rm. ⌁ ℘ TV Adjoining a mini-market. A reasonable place, no more: good to fall back on when everything is full (which is often the case in Ágios Nikólaos).

**Victoria Hotel**, Aktí Koundoúrou 34, ☎ (0841) 22 731, Fax (0841) 22 266 – 18rm. ⌁ ✗ ℘ You will either be welcomed by the mother or by the daughter (English-speaking), both of whom are called Victoria and both of whom are charming, as is the hotel. This is the only place in town with refined, tasteful decor. There are traditional hangings on the walls, together with sofas, wrought iron, pottery, and a pleasant mezzanine overlooking the reception. The rooms are plain, with dried flowers and ceiling fans. Disadvantages: rather casual service and the place is sometimes noisy in the evening. Advantages: as it is a little out-of-the-way, prices are reasonable.

**Hotel Mirsini**, Aktí Koundoúrou 35, ☎ (0841) 28 590 / 23 170, Fax (0841) 23 171 – 31rm. ⌁ ✗ ℘ cc Just beside the Victoria Hotel. A tall modern building with standard rooms, mainly for groups. Impeccable service. A little soulless, though this may change with the renovations.

Crete

*Between €45 and €75*

**Hotel Kastro**, Odós Lasthénous 23, ☎ (0841) 24 918 / 25 526, Fax (0841) 25 827 – 12 studios. 🛏 🏖 ✐ ✗ All white, with old beams, carpets, and traditional fabrics for bedcovers and curtains: very effective decor. The hotel is well located, in a delightful quiet street behind the harbour. Rather high prices, but the rooms are really studios with kitchenettes and comfortable balconies. Mainly used by clients sent by tour operators. Booking essential.

*Over €75*

**Hera Village**, on the Eloúnda road (4km out of town), ☎ (0841) 28 971 / 28 973, Fax (0841) 22 270 – 90rm. 🛏 📋 ✐ ✗ 🛎 cc This vast guesthouse (almost a holiday village), which is only open in summer, opened about fifteen years ago and has already acquired something of a patina of age, with both positive and negative results. The enormous, comfortable studios all have kitchenettes as well as pleasant terraces where a profusion of plants provides privacy. The decor is both restrained and picturesque, in the style of a troglodyte dwelling (whitewashed walls and built-up bed bases). There's a saltwater swimming pool and an unrestricted view of the sea, which justifies the price.

**Minos Palace**, on the Eloúnda road (running on from Aktí Koundoúrou), ☎ (0841) 23 801 / 9, Fax (0841) 23 816 – 151rm. 🛏 📋 ✐ TV ✗ 🛎 ⚘ ⚗ ✗ cc A huge extravagance! We should tell you straight out that it is very, very expensive, and prices are not negotiable. But everything is up to par: antique furniture, large reception area with flagstone flooring, magnificent terrace shaded by olive trees overlooking the sea. As for the rooms, they offer refined, classical luxury. There's nothing mediocre about the place, and the staff are hand-picked to respond readily to the demands of a (somewhat elderly) well-heeled clientele.

**EATING OUT**

You are spoilt for choice, with places to eat ranging from sandwich stalls in the street to chic French-style restaurants. The obvious tourist-oriented open-air places round the lake all look similar, although, contrary to expectations, some are thoroughly worthwhile. However, watch out for prices, which are not always clearly posted. The seemingly deserted small streets round about also have good restaurants, often with imaginative menus at very reasonable prices – something rare in Crete.

*Around €7.50*

☺ **Avli**, Odós Príngipa Georgíou 12, ☎ (0841) 82 479. 🛎 Hard to resist this charming little taverna-cum-ouzo-bar. Behind a bougainvillaea hedge is a gigantic fig tree that shades a gravel courtyard in which stand a few welcoming tables that look onto an attractive old L-shaped house. Good food, and very friendly service.

**Embassy**, on the corner of Odós Kondiláki and Odós Príngipa Georgíou. 🛎 This is another shaded terrace with flagstones, set back a little from the lake. You will be welcomed in English and served simple though excellent Greek food.

**The Pine Tree**, Odós Konstandínou Paleológou 18. 🛎 The last of the terraces on the lakeside. While it is true that the service is a touch perfunctory, an effort is made with the food: a little bit of dill in a Greek salad changes everything! This is also one of the rare restaurants where you can lunch on delicious octopus marinated in white wine, at a reasonable price.

*Around €15*

☺ **Pelagos**, Odós Kateháki 10, set back from the lake, ☎ (0841) 25 737. 🛎 cc The place lives up to its name, with excellent fish, including swordfish fillets, crayfish, sea-urchin soup and mussels with cheese. The setting is delightful: the interior decor of the attractive old house immediately gives an idea of what is to come. There is a choice of seating, and when booking (essential for dinner) you may opt for a table in the garden beneath the trees. Watch out for the wine list: good, but not cheap.

**Faros**, on Kitroplatía beach, ☎ (0841) 23 141. 🛎 Let your nose guide you to the enormous barbecue tended by the owner. Choose a place beside the pebble beach and enjoy an ouzo. Don't worry if there's no more lamb with cheese, you will not regret ordering fresh fish cooked on a skewer over the wood fire.

**Neon**, Odós Nikoláou Plastíra, ☎ (0841) 28 842. 🍴 CC You cannot miss this establishment dominating the lake, its sign proudly in evidence. Take the steps at the end of the quay, and the restaurant is halfway up, on the right. While the place is very tourist-oriented, it is hard to resist its exceptional terrace site. And you won't be disappointed, as the food is prepared with great care. The adventurous could try the pork olive with cheese and garlic, and others the excellent brochettes or seafood.

**Hollands Restaurant**, Odós Dion Solomoú 10, ☎ (0841) 25 582. 🍴 CC This unexpected restaurant is run by a lady from Holland, much to the delight of her many compatriots holidaying here. You may find it a bit odd to be eating 100% Dutch in Crete, but there's nothing better if you feel like a change from Mediterranean fare.

*Around €30*

**Cretan Stars**, Aktí Iossif Koundoúrou 8, ☎ (0841) 25 517, Fax (0841) 24 556. 🍴 CC You must come to this elegant old mansion properly dressed. Then you will escape the rather condescending look by the *maître d'hôtel* who will greet you at the top of the stairs, asking if you have booked. The decor of the reception area is in a refined, traditional style, with varnished panelling, a grand piano, an antique statue, etc. Beyond is a magnificent patio where your table awaits beneath an enormous palm tree. Try the swordfish flambé with ouzo.

### HAVING A DRINK

Ágios Nikólaos is a paradise for nightowls. The bars here are legion, and even if you're exhausted after a day's walking, you will find it difficult to resist going to listen to the music (mostly good) that begins as soon as night falls.

**Bars** – **Café du Lac**, Odós 28 Oktomvríou 17, ☎ (0841) 26 837. Open very late in the evening, 7 days a week, even in winter. One of the major hangouts for the local young people. Quietly trendy atmosphere. Subdued lighting,

light-coloured wood and red panelling. Excellent choice of international music. People either come here to play backgammon for hours while drinking iced coffee, or just spend 10min or so in the night air on the terrace, facing the lake.

**Armida Boat**, Aktí Koundoúrou (in the harbour), ☎ (0841) 28 350. The large pirate boat in full swing in the harbour lets you know what's coming before you venture aboard: rock music, beers and cocktails. Warm reception. Worth a look, just for the boat itself.

☕ **Café Candia**, Aktí Iossif Koundoúrou 12, ☎ (0841) 26 355. While there is a terrace, it's quite a feat just finding a table, especially in summer. It's even difficult to get standing room at the bar. This is because everybody, from 7 to 77, comes here to listen to Latino music in a lively relaxed atmosphere. Luckily, the friendly, efficient service always makes you want to stay a while.

**Cafés** – **Café Migomis**, Odós Nikoláou Plastíra 22, ☎ (0841) 23 904. A large comfortable terrace with a decor of exotic wood and varnished cane, built around a gigantic tree that is growing through the roof. The place overlooks the lake, and is very pleasant to relax in with a cool drink or an aperitif in the early evening. People come here to enjoy the quiet easygoing atmosphere and the panoramic view.

☕ **Internet Café Peripou**, Odós 28 Oktomvríou 25. Unlike other places of the kind, you don't just come here for the Internet access. Books and CDs are available for people who want a peaceful time listening to New Age music, reading, chatting, playing games, or surfing the Web. Carefully thought-out decor, a shade intellectual, very pleasant indeed. Opens in the morning for coffee on the terrace and stays open until very late in the evening.

### OTHER THINGS TO DO

The area is full of things to do and see: there are boat trips to Spinalónga Island (see the following chapter), excursions to Lassíthi Plateau, mountain-bike tours and scuba diving. Several very obliging agencies in Odós 28 Oktomvríou will be happy to explain all the possible activities.

**Boat trips** – You would do best just to go directly to the harbour, where you will find the boats. **Nostos Tours**, Odós Roussou Koundoúrou, ☎ (0841) 22 819, Fax (0841) 25 336, has several large boats that operate daily, taking a good hundred holidaymakers on trips to Spinalónga Island. It is better to go from Eloúnda, on more modest vessels, but if you prefer to set out from Ágios Nikólaos, you have a choice between a half-day trip (leaving at 12.30pm, returning at 5pm) and a full-day one (leaving at 10am, returning at 5pm, Wednesday, Thursday, Saturday and Sunday). The full-day option includes a barbecue prepared on the island by the crew.

**Blue Star**, another boat company run along the same lines as the one above, offering similar services and prices. Also in the harbour.

**Boat George**, ☎ (0841) 22 109 / 24 156 / 25 539, Fax (0841) 22 753. This traditional fishing vessel is a good deal more charming than the ones above because it is much smaller (26 people maximum), and will take you where you want in Mirambélo Bay. George organises short tailor-made cruises for groups who've made bookings. Otherwise, you can go on a day trip. The boat is moored opposite the tourist office, and sets out at 9.30am on Monday, Wednesday or Friday. Comfort on board is a lot more spartan than on the large tourist boats, but you won't regret your choice.

**Walking – Mountain Biking & Hiking**, ☎ (0841) 28 098. The agency's experienced guides take small groups out on foot or on mountain bikes to explore the area's wealth of fascinating landscapes. Everything is laid on: gear, minibus transfers and picnics. Ideal for a breath of fresh air off the beaten track.

**Scuba diving** – There are about thirty inviting diving spots along Mirambélo Bay. Monastiri, Explose, Kremastá Nerá ("hanging waters")... the names alone are enough to make your mouth water! Beautiful silent explorations await you among giant sponges, as you look for groupers, octopi and moray eels.

**Creta's Happy Divers**, Aktí Koundoúrou (opposite the Coral Hotel), ☎ (0841) 82 546. This aptly named club has friendly staff and very reasonable rates, given the quality of the equipment and supervisors. Quiet Níkos with his dry sense of humour will take you out in the club's ultra-fast boat to a different spot every day. It is possible to try for the Open Water PADI certificate.

**Beaches** – There are no really good beaches around Ágios Nikólaos, and don't expect to be alone. If you don't mind pebbles, head for the beach at Kiroplatía. Not many cars, a few tavernas... a few hundred metres from the town centre. If you really must have sand, there's Ammos beach, just beside the bus station, which is naturally noisier. Otherwise, head for the rather more unspoilt beach at Golden Bay (plenty of buses daily).

**Feasts & festivals** – In 1999, the town inaugurated its first **Nationalities Festival**. Every day a different European nationality is honoured through its dances and culinary specialities. The festivities, like a sort of village fair, are held at the open-air theatre near the lake in early October.

### SHOPPING GUIDE

**Market** – Wednesday morning, in Odós Ethnikís Andistásseos.

**Bookshop** – Odós 28 Oktomvríou, up on the right: books, stationery, island and regional maps.

**Other** – For **icon** enthusiasts, several shops selling them compete for business along Odós 28 Oktomvríou. In the same street you will also find a **delicatessen** with a vast and appetising range of typical island products, including honey, oil, fine spirits and preserves.

**Kera**, Aktí Koundoúrou 8. CC Jewellery, carpets, local arts and crafts, icons and lace for sale in a beautiful giftshop.

# SPINALÓNGA ISLAND★★

## ELOÚNDA

District of Lassíthi – 10km from Ágios Nikólaos
Michelin map 980 fold 39 – Map of the island pages 358-359

**Not to be missed**
A tour of Spinalónga Island, exploring its ruins.
A walk and a picnic on Spinalónga Peninsula.
**And remember...**
To reach the island, leave from Eloúnda rather than Ágios Nikólaos:
the boats are smaller (10 people), and the crossing more enjoyable.

A beautiful corniche road leads north from Ágios Nikólaos for about ten kilometres to the resort of Eloúnda. This is a pleasant fishing port with a lively, colourful waterfront that faces the **Póros Isthmus**, a flat, narrow, spray-swept passage connecting the Spinalónga Peninsula to the mainland. The peninsula stretches out alongside the coast forming a ridge of wild arid hills, like the rough back of an animal, protecting Eloúnda Bay from the wind.

Beyond the tip of the peninsula lies a strange isolated rock: an islet dotted with ruins and defended by a fortress looking like the prow of a ship. Spinalónga – island and peninsula – awaits you in a bright setting of stone, blue waves and wind. A superb trip.

## Spinalónga Peninsula★

As you enter Eloúnda, take the street on the right that heads off in a hairpin bend towards the bay. This brings you to a tarmac track beside the waves (watch out for the spray when there's a strong wind), which leads to the isthmus that crosses the bay to the peninsula. In Venetian times there were extensive salt pans here. At the end you come to two stone **windmills**. These guard the **canal** built by the French army in 1897 to link the bay with the Gulf of Mirambélo. Here and there you will see partly submerged **ruins**, the remains of the ancient city of **Olonte**. This was a forerunner to Eloúnda, and vied for power with **Lató** (see page 380). Beyond, in the hills, there are just rocks and deserted heaths, ideal for walks and picnics, and perhaps a swim in one of the creeks on the windward side of the peninsula (be warned, however, the sea is rough).

## Spinalónga citadel★★

Allow half a day. There's a ferry (fee) from Eloúnda harbour to the island. Daily departures every 30min, from 9.30am to 4.30pm. The tour of the citadel (free) will take you between 1hr and 90min. For the return journey, your ticket is valid for any boat, but make sure it is indeed going to Eloúnda (especially if you have left your car there), as some go all the way to Ágios Nikólaos. You can also take a fishing boat from Pláka village, a few kilometres north of Eloúnda. The crossing is shorter, but can only be done when the sea is calm.

High up on its rock, the fortress seems lost in time, almost like something from the pages of a child's storybook. In Antiquity, Spinalónga Island was of major strategic importance: as an advance post at the northern entrance to the bay, it was here that the city of Olonte could scan the horizon, giving warning of any intrusion into its waters. In 1579, the Venitians built a **fortress★** to protect their fleet in Eloúnda harbour. The fortress had **35 cannons**, and resisted numerous attacks until 1715 when it was besieged by the Turkish admiral, **Kapoudan Pasha**. In 1903, after the last Turkish residents had left, the islet was used as a **leper colony**, a truly isolated spot that was only abandoned in the 1950s. Today the powerful walls still rise above the waves but only protect the wild vegetation of pines and scrub dotted with the remains of the **ghost town\*\*** of the leper colony. A strange atmosphere reigns over the roofless houses with their gaping windows and doors open to the silence.

Back on land, if you have the energy, continue to the attractive village of **Pláka**, and beyond. The road climbs once again, affording a magnificent **view\*\*\*** of the peninsula and the bay. Go up into the mountain, where you will come across small stone villages that feel very remote from the mass tourism a few kilometres away. In **Seles**, take the road to **Káto Seles**, which leads through superb scenery down to the coast where isolated dwellings look out onto a raging sea. The wind blows hard, and you have the exhilarating feeling of being at the end of the world.

## Making the most of Eloúnda

### COMING AND GOING

**By bus** – From Ágios Nikólaos numerous buses (one an hour until 9pm) run daily to Eloúnda. You can catch them from the bus station or at the bus stops along Aktí Koundoúrou.

### ADDRESS BOOK

Everything is concentrated around the harbour, where the bus drops you off.

**Tourist information** – At the foot of the church, in the curve of the fishing harbour.

**Bank / Currency exchange** – Cash dispenser opposite the fishing boats, 30m from the tourist office.

**Post office / Telephone** – Telephone booth just beside the tourist office.

**Supermarket** – Opposite the fishing harbour.

### WHERE TO STAY

Eloúnda is not ideal for accommodation. Mass tourism has turned it into a centre for hotel-clubs and other leisure complexes, and prices are high.

*Between €30 and €45*

**Hotel Kalypso**, in the harbour, ☎ (0841) 41 367, Fax (0841) 41 424 – 16rm. ⁂ 🖹 ℓ ✗ [cc] A very professional place in a good location, with comfortable rooms, but pretty steep prices. Blue furniture, small balconies, very seaside-style decor. You enter through the restaurant. Ask for a room with a view of the fishing harbour.

*Between €45 and €75*

**Spinalónga Village**, on the Pláka road, ☎ (0841) 41 494 / 41 496, Fax (0841) 41 285 – 17rm. ⁂ 🖹 ℓ ✗ [cc] An elegant group of large studios to let beside the sea at a short distance from the village, opposite Spinalónga citadel. The stone buildings blend in harmoniously with the natural landscape, which is not often the case in Crete. The place was opened in 1978, remained closed for a long time and then reopened in 1998. Altogether an attractive, intelligently run complex.

### EATING OUT

*Around €11*

**Vritomartes**, right at the centre of the harbour, with its terrace jutting out into the sea. This modest restaurant is nothing extraordinary: like everything here, it is intended for tourists (and many come here on their return from the citadel). But the location, set back from the street, is pleasant, and smiling waiters serve standard though very fresh fare (the dining room, however, could be cleaner).

# SITÍA

## KÁTO ZÁKROS★★★ AND THE EAST COAST★★

District of Lassíthi – 74km from Ágios Nikólaos
Michelin map 980 fold 40 – Map of the island pages 358-359 - Pop 7 400

**Not to be missed**
A walk through the steep alleyways up from the harbour.
Toploú Monastery. The wild setting of Itanós.
The Minoan palace at Káto Zákros and the Valley of the Dead.

**And remember...**
Have a drink at dusk at the Platía Brasserie on the main square.
To reach the palace at Zákros, forget about the road
and walk through the Valley of the Dead.

The quiet town of Sitía, with its harmonious shades of white and ochre, gives off a fragrance of sand and dust, like some distant place in the Orient, off the tourist trail. On going into the dazzlingly bright silent town, the traveller may feel a little forlorn and disappointed. In fact, Sitía does not reveal its charms as quickly as Ágios Nikólaos; it is more discreet and more authentic, and well worth a visit. Here, as in Ierápetra in the south of the island, tourism is not (yet) the main economic activity. People make a living from farming, particularly bananas, and especially from vineyards that produce **Sitía**, one of Crete's best white wines, which the whole town celebrates with local festivities in mid-August.

So, even if you only come to eastern Crete for the beaches and the scenery, why not enjoy the easygoing atmosphere of the town and stay a while after your trip along the coast. This will give you an opportunity to discover the great kindness of the inhabitants, who won't think of you as a tourist, more as a visitor, and will find countless ways of thanking you for your stay.

### Grandeur and revival

In Antiquity, the Minoans did not fail to take an interest in the sheltered bay, which was strategically located on the doorstep of the Dodecanese. There they founded the port of **Eteia**, attached to the neighbouring town of Pressos. Vying with powerful Ierápetra, the town prospered throughout Antiquity, up until the Byzantine Era. Its present name was given to it by the Venetians, who built a fort and ramparts in 1631. In vain, however, as in the mid-17C Sitía succumbed to attacks by the **Ottomans** who, curiously, were little interested in its position, and abandoned the town once they had sacked it. For two centuries, the name of Sitía merely evoked the ruins of a prestigious past. It was only in 1870 that the town rose from its ashes and took on its present appearance. The lively modern town is built on a hillside stretching down to the sea. At the top is the kástro, the last bastion of a glorious past.

### Tour of the town
*Allow 2hr*

The heart of the town is the area around **Platía Iróon Politehníou**, near the harbour. From here, take **Odós Kapetán Sífi** up the hill, and wander through the quiet streets in the northern district. Early in the morning, as you head away from the bustle in the centre and pass the white façades of the houses, you can hear the sounds of people quietly going about their business through open kitchen windows or in little vegetable gardens full of pumpkins. Children on their way to school, women chatting in doorways... Between the concrete houses that owe their charm only to the flowers in their window boxes, the ruins of old buildings appear, like

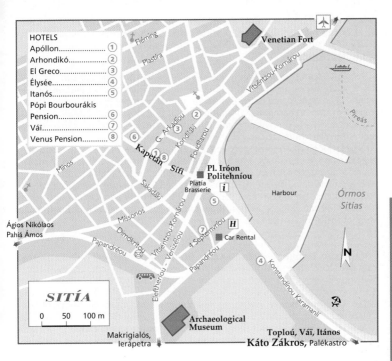

**HOTELS**

| | |
|---|---|
| Apóllon | ① |
| Arhondikó | ② |
| El Greco | ③ |
| Élysée | ④ |
| Itanós | ⑤ |
| Pópi Bourbourákis Pension | ⑥ |
| Váï | ⑦ |
| Venus Pension | ⑧ |

**Venetian Fort**

Órmos Sitías

Harbour

Pl. Iróon Politehníou

Platía Brasserie

Car Rental

**Archaeological Museum**

*SITÍA*

0   50   100 m

Makrigialós, Ierápetra

Toploú, Váï, Itános
**Káto Zákros,** Palékastro

the one opposite the El Greco Hotel in Odós G Arkadíou. Its walls have survived the latest earthquakes and still proudly remind us that the town has many old stories to tell.

In the north-east, Sitía's steepest streets lead to the **Venetian fort**\* (Kasarma), a small, square, well-preserved structure dominating the town (*Tuesday-Sunday, 8.30am-2pm; free*). Apart from its majestic **keep**, nothing remains inside, but the climb is mainly worthwhile for the bird's-eye **view**\* of the harbour. All summer, plays are staged within its walls as part of the town's annual festival.

In the south, you can also visit the **Archaeological Museum** (*Leofóros Eleftheríou Venizélou, on the left in the direction of Ierápetra, Tuesday-Sunday, 8.30am-3pm*). This rather cheerless building was built in the 1970s and contains the archaeological finds of the region, dating mainly from the Minoan Era. In addition to an impressive collection of **vases** (pithoi), there is a fine **ivory bust** (*Room 1*), a fragment of a statuette unearthed at Palékastro, and also Linear A **tablets** from various sites, including Káto Zákros. There's one very unusual item, a **winepress**\* with its original accessories, discovered in Zákros palace. You can also see some Greco-Roman objects including lamps and vases.

## Wide-open spaces\*\*
*A tour to the east of Sitía. Around 40km one way. Allow a day.*

One wonders how this part of the island has managed to avoid the tourist invasion. There are no concrete buildings or large hotels, just the mountains, a few roads burnt white by the sun, and the ever-present sea. With its wild majestic beauty, this part of the coast not only has the finest beaches in Crete, it also has some unspoilt, grandiose scenery, which gives all who travel this way a pleasant sense of well-being.

*From Sitía, head eastwards along the Väï road, which hugs the coast. After about 15km, the main road continues to Palékastro, while another winds left up the mountain affording beautiful bird's-eye views of the sea below. 3.5km and several flocks of goats further on, you come to a monastery.*

■ **Toploú Monastery**★★ (Moní Toploú) – *9am-1pm / 2pm-6pm. Entrance fee. Allow 30min. Bring modest clothing (long trousers for men, something to cover the shoulders for women).* The small square fortress, known as the Monastery with the Cannons is protected by powerful **ramparts**★ 10m high. It was probably founded in the 14C, but was almost entirely destroyed by an earthquake in 1612. The complex that you see today only dates from the late 17C, when the place was rebuilt and fortified to stave off attacks by **pirates** prowling around the coast. An atmosphere of deep spirituality reigns among the buildings, which are carefully maintained by a handful of monks *(many of the private buildings are not open to the public)*. Apart from the plain **church** with a double nave, the monastery has a wonderful **museum**★ containing various liturgical items, paintings – note the delightful 15C **Virgin and Child** – icons from the 17C, 18C and 19C, as well as an outstanding collection of **ancient books**★ and maps of the Mediterranean area.

*As you leave the monastery, take a few minutes to admire the panorama, then head north.*

■ **Väï Palm Grove**★ – *Open from dawn to dusk. Free, but the car park is expensive.* Väï's stretch of white sand fringed with palm trees is thought to be the most beautiful beach on Crete. Or rather, was. Unfortunately, over-intensive tourist development has got the better of it, and it is now difficult to find just a few square inches to lay your sandals. Everything has been organised for the thousands of holidaymakers who crowd here every year: a large, busy, noisy car park, a tourist office *(that changes money)*, souvenir shops, a restaurant, a **water-sports club**, sun loungers and umbrellas *(fee)*. In other words, nothing like the postcards and tourist brochures showing pictures of bygone days.

Toploú Monastery,
a bastion in the hills

G. de Benoist/MICHELIN

Sitía: sewing session before putting out to sea

If you want to swim, you would do a lot better in other nearby areas *(see below)*. As for the palm trees, legend has it that the **natural palm grove**\* – unique in Europe – originated in Antiquity, springing from the date pips left by Phoenician traders (or Egyptian soldiers) who moored in the bay! Whatever the case, we know today that the palm existed on Crete under the Minoans, who went as far as making the tree sacred. To the right of the beach, facing the sea, a path leads off to a **viewpoint**\* where you have a panorama of the bay and the north of the island.

*Continue northwards along the road to Itanós.*

■ **Itanós**\* – Not much remains of this ancient Minoan city state. As an important port, Itanós prospered until it was sacked in the 15C by pirates who forced the inhabitants to take refuge in the hinterland. You come here, therefore, more for the beauty of the **site**\*\*. The road stops at the ruins. If you follow the footpath overlooking the sea for 5min, you come to the next bay on, where there is an extensive white sandy **beach**\*\* that is clean and little frequented (everyone is at Váï). Blue sea, fine sand, and silence: one of the loveliest beaches in the area.

Refreshed by a swim, you will be in fine form to explore the north-east tip of the island. The area is one of wild arid beauty, where the hillsides are crisscrossed by a multitude of **rambling tracks** never far from the sea.

*Head back and, if you have a vehicle, bear right immediately after leaving Itanós.* The road climbs in hairpin bends, affording magnificent panoramas. Take a second road left, which leads to a viewpoint where you have an unrestricted **view**\*\*\* of the sea. Beyond, there stretches a military zone, which is closed to civilians.

## ■ Káto Zákros\*\*\*

*From Sitía, head east to Palékastro. There, fork left, heading south. Zákros village is well signposted. The site is 3km from the village, on the left. Bring water.*

Beside the road is a gorge covered in scrub and dotted here and there with caves where a series of **Minoan burial places** have been discovered, giving the place its name: **Valley of the Dead**\*. From here you have a choice between the **road**\*\* down

393

to Káto Zákros – a splendid run, with a bird's-eye view of the sea – or a ramble through the valley. This is an easy **walk★★★** (*about 90min there and back*) in a superb mountain setting, which brings you to the gates of Zákros palace. As you emerge, you are rewarded with the sight of Zákros beach.

## The fourth largest Minoan palace

At the exit from the Valley of the Dead, occupying an area of about 10 000m², is the fourth largest Minoan palace on Crete. Its exceptional geographical position made it the main political and commercial gateway to the Middle East. A first palace had been built beside the sea in 1900 BC, but the ruins that you see today belong to the second complex, rebuilt in 1600 BC. Káto Zákros was not only the permanent residence of the royal family, but also the administrative, commercial and religious centre of the whole region. As with most Minoan palaces, it disappeared abruptly in 1450 BC, probably as a result of a volcanic eruption.

The same layout applies here as at Knossós, Mália and Phaistos: a central courtyard around which are arranged the royal apartments (almost nothing remains), the reception rooms, places of worship and the workshops. More modest living quarters extended over the whole north part of the site.

### Tour of the palace

*Tuesday-Sunday, 8am-7pm. Entrance fee.* Start your tour on the opposite side from the entrance (*towards the exit*). **Harbour Street** is a wide paved avenue that was once the main entrance to the town. Steps lead down to the **North-east Court**, adjoining which is the palace's main **water supply**, a circular well still filled with water.

A little further on, a short staircase goes down to the **Tykté Kréne** (the "well-built fountain"), a lustral basin with a square shape, probably used for worship. The remains of offerings were found here, notably a jar of amazingly well-preserved olives. Beyond, to the right, are the ruins of the **Royal Apartments**, which open onto the vast **central courtyard** (30m x 12m). Opposite, along the north-west wing, were the **Royal Megaron**, a kind of reception room, and the **Banqueting Hall**.

Behind, a **staircase** leads to the **Sanctuary**, which is divided into two small rooms: the **treasury** and the **lustral bath**. Many items of worship unearthed here can be seen at the museum in Sitía.

The north side of the courtyard is taken up by the **kitchens**, a large pillared room, and the **storerooms**. Behind rises the hill where dwellings (now thoroughly ruined) were arranged in blocks.

Cross over the central courtyard to the south-east corner to see the ruins of an **altar** together with another **lustral basin**. Lastly, near the site entrance there once stood the city's workshops and **stores**.

*Return to the site exit in the north-east and go for a drink in one of the outdoor cafés in Zákros harbour. Then take the road to Sitía.*

## COMING AND GOING

**By air** – The town has a small recently opened airport, 1km to the north. Two flights a week to Athens, Wednesday and Sunday. Flights also to Kárpathos and Kássos, on Wednesday. Be warned: there are no buses to the airport.

**Olympic Airways**, Odós Vitséntzou Kornárou 146, ☎ (0843) 25 080 / 25 090.

**By sea** – 3 days a week, ferries connect Sitía with Piraeus, via Ágios Nikólaos and Milos: departures on Sunday and Tuesday at 3.30pm and Thursday at 5.50pm. One boat a week to Kássos, Kárpathos, Diafáni, Halkída and Rhodes, Saturday at 3.30pm.
Enquiries and tickets at travel agents in Odós Kornárou, in the centre.
**Deputy harbourmaster's office**, ☎ (0843) 22 310.

**By bus** – The bus station, ☎ (0843) 22 272, is in the southern part of the town on the corner of Odós A Papandréou and Odós Eleftheríou Venizélou. Buses from here serve all the sites and villages in the eastern half of the island. Don't hesitate to ask the very friendly staff for information.
– For Herakleion, via Ágios Nikólaos (3hr15min travelling time): 6 buses a day, between 6.15am and 8pm.
– For Ierápetra (90min): 6 buses a day, between 6.15am and 8pm.
– For Káto Zákros: 2 buses a day, at 11am and 2.30pm. Return at 12.45pm and 4pm.
– Váï Palm Grove: 4 buses a day, between 9.30am and 4pm. Last bus for the return journey at 6pm.

## FINDING YOUR WAY

Sitía is not very large. Everything is concentrated around Platía Iróon Politehníou in the curve of the harbour: shops, banks, restaurants and hotels.

## GETTING AROUND

**By car** – You will easily find room to park a little away from the centre. Leave your car and visit the town on foot.

**By rental vehicle** – Odós Papandréou, 50m from the seafront, two agencies side by side hire out cars and two-wheel vehicles.

## ADDRESS BOOK

**Tourist information** – On the seafront promenade alongside Leofóros Konstandínou Karamanlí. In theory, open daily except Sunday, 9am-2.30pm, but the times tend to be variable, especially at the beginning and the end of the tourist season. ☎ (0843) 24 955.

**Bank / Currency exchange** – You will find several banks around Platía Iróon Politehníou. Monday-Thursday, 8am-2pm, 1.30pm on Friday. Cash dispensers take international bank cards.
**National Bank**, Odós Eleftheríou Venizélou, in the curve of the harbour.

**Post office / Telephone** – **Main post office**, Odós Dimókritou. Monday-Friday, 7.30am-2pm.

**Internet** – There's no Internet centre in Sitía, but several bars are planning a connection.

**Medical service** – **Hospital**, outside the town, ☎ (0843) 24 311 to 24 314.
**Emergencies**, dial 166.
**Pharmacy**, Odós Eleftheríou Venizélou, just to the left coming from Platía Iróon Politehníou.

**Other** – **Police**, ☎ (0843) 22 259 / 22 266.

## WHERE TO STAY

About ten rather impersonal hotels compete for business between the harbour, the seafront and the town centre. These concrete cubes dating from the 1970s could do with some serious freshening up. There are few charming places to stay in Sitía.

*Under €30*

*Hotel Arhondikó*, Odós I Kondiláki 16, ☎ (0843) 28 172 / 22 993 – 9rm. Just two streets up from the harbour. A delightful guesthouse in a good position well away from the downtown bustle. Go through the little courtyard shaded by an orange tree to the elegant old house where you will be given a friendly welcome. The old tiling on the floor, plenty of light, and the carefully thought-out decor create a warm atmosphere. Like the rest, the rooms (upstairs) are spacious and comfortable. However, only 4 of them have private bathrooms. Remember to book. No breakfast.

**Venus Pension**, Odós I Kondiláki 60, ☎ (0843) 24 307 – 6rm. 🕯 A traditional guesthouse with rather over-elaborate decor but otherwise impeccable. The new rooms, freshly tiled in white, exude cleanliness. The lady owner lavishes attention on her guests and, if you ask, will even bring breakfast up to the rooms!

**Popi Bourbourakis Pension**, Odós Ioannídou 2 ☎ (0843) 23 868 – 6rm. Nothing extraordinary, but it can be useful for those on a tight budget. The rooms are fairly good overall, though they could do with some freshening up. Two have private bathrooms. No breakfast.

### Between €30 and €45

**Hotel El Greco**, Odós Arkadíou 13, ☎ (0843) 23 133, Fax (0843) 26 391 – 20rm. 🕯 ⤫ ℰ A simple friendly little hotel, fairly rare in Sitía. Traditional decor, warm welcome, and clean comfortable rooms with enormous private balconies (some give onto the sea). Generous breakfasts are served in the pinewood mezzanine over the reception. This is probably the best hotel in the price range.

**Hotel Apollon**, Odós Kapetán Sífi 28, ☎ (0843) 22 733, Fax (0843) 28 155 – 37rm. 🕯 ▤ ℰ TV CC The hotel is in a peaceful district and has been completely renovated in a restrained modern style. It mainly caters to groups and is run professionally by the manager. The rooms could be a little bigger but, all in all, everything is comfortable. 3 rooms have small bathtubs.

**Hotel Élysée**, Leofóros Konstandínou Karamanlí 14, ☎ (0843) 22 312, Fax (0843) 23 427, 26rm. 🕯 ▤ ℰ TV CC On the seafront. A modern, soulless, rather austere place. And yet it is one of the less dismal of its category in Sitía. The rooms are clean and spacious, and there's a car park behind the hotel.

**Váï Hotel**, on the corner of Odós 4 Septemvríou and Odós Itanou Dimókritou, ☎ (0843) 22 528, Fax (0843) 22 288 – 44rm. 🕯 ℰ Behind the antiquated reception area are austere though clean and fairly comfortable rooms. The bathrooms, all with tubs, are in good condition. The hotel mainly caters to a local clientele: no English spoken.

### Between €45 and €75

**Hotel Itanós**, Leofóros Konstandínou Karamanlí 4, ☎ (0843) 22 900 / 901 / 146, Fax (0843) 22 915 – 72rm. 🕯 ▤ ℰ TV ⤫ CC Yet another place dating from the 1970s, and originally on a par with its peers. Except that the manager had the good idea of renovating it completely in 1998 and – not such a good idea – of increasing the prices. Overall, the result is quite successful, though a bit flashy. Marble in the bathrooms, very pleasant roof terrace. In a word, every modern comfort and the decor of an international hotel. There is a bar-cafeteria on the first floor with a good view of the harbour.

### EATING OUT

Most of the tourist restaurants are naturally along the seafront in the harbour. Although touting, which is tiresome, is current practice, you eat fairly well. In any case, with the exception of one or two places elsewhere, you have no choice but to eat here. And there's a pleasant atmosphere at the harbour in the evening.

### Around €7.50

**Kali Kardia**, Odós Foudilarou 22, ☎ (0843) 22 249. 🍽 A small, simple, working-class restaurant frequented by local people. Basic fare (taramosaláta, moussaká, etc), but good quality and generous helpings, served with a smile.

**Mitsakalis Snack-Cafeteria**, on the corner of Odós 4 Septemvríou and Leofóros Konstandínou Karamanlí. 🍽 A simple, modern place ideal for breakfast or a snack on the hoof. Pleasant service, local clientele.

### Around €15

**Sitía Tavern**, Odós Eleftheríou Venizélou 161, ☎ (0843) 28 758. 🍽 CC One of the many tourist restaurants in the harbour area. The waiter will happily explain the different fish specialities on the menu. Go for the delicious swordfish au gratin with garlic.

Crete

**Remezzo**, Odós Eleftheríou Venizélou 167, ☎ (0843) 28 607. 🍽 CC The same kind of place as the one above, 3 terraces along. This is one of the oldest restaurants in the harbour. Feel free to ask the waiters' advice on dishes not on the menu and fix the price directly with them. They will be only too delighted, and will lovingly concoct a generous assortment of meze guaranteed to stir the envy of neighbouring diners.

**Kretan House**, Leofóros Konstandínou Karamanlí, 30m from the Hotel Élysée. 🍽 A good place with friendly service though you have to put up with a bit of touting. This is where you can try real island specialities: *omatiés* (little sausages made with rice, liver, onions and almonds), *kochlis boumbouristi* (fried snails with olive oil, vinegar and tomatoes). Pleasant atmosphere in spite of the noise.

*Around €30*

**The Balcony**, on the corner of Odós Kazantzáki and Odós Foudilarou, ☎ (0843) 25 084. 🍽 This rather chic restaurant on the top floor of an old house prides itself on its creative Cretan cooking. Carefully thought-out decor (exposed stone and glass panels) with a menu to match: vegetarian moussaká for a change, or *kléftiko* (a lamb dish with potatoes, cheese and herbs).

## HAVING A DRINK

Night owls will have difficulty finding a lively place in Sitía in the evening. However, there are several fairly trendy bars in the harbour area frequented by local young people.

**Bars – En Plo**, Leofóros Konstandínou Karamanlí 2, ☎ (0843) 23 761. Open very late in the evening, 7 days a week, even in winter. A very new bar with original decor, all in wood. People come here during the day to read the paper and drink espresso (excellent). Lively atmosphere in the evening, with a big crowd especially on Friday and Saturday.

**Albatros**, Odós Eleftheríou Venizélou 187 (at the harbour). 🍽 A large bar that plays local and international rock music. Subdued lighting much appreciated by young people from the area who meet here in the evening and drink iced coffee. Friendly and relaxed.

**Cafés – Platía Brasserie**, Platía Iróon Politehníou. 🍽 This large central café, the oldest in town, is an institution. Men come here at the end of the day to discuss local business. A good place to take the temperature of Sitía with an ouzo and pistachios in the evening when the birds gather in the enormous palm tree that dominates the square.

## OTHER THINGS TO DO

**Walking – La Chlorophylle**, 72057 Sfaka (Sitía), ☎ and Fax (0843) 94 725. Anne Lebrun takes out small groups of ramblers along the most beautiful paths in Crete to discover the local flora and fauna. She is an experienced botanist and will share her passion for the outdoors, showing you another side to the island.

**Beaches** – The town beach is in the south-east, at the end of Leofóros Konstandínou Karamanlí, on the Vaï road. It is large and clean, but there are so many other less crowded beaches in the area.

**Wine festival** – Every year in mid-August the whole town simmers with excitement to welcome the new vintage of the local wine.

## SHOPPING GUIDE

**Local delicacies** – You will find everything you want at reasonable prices in the shop on the corner of Odós Papandréou and Leofóros Konstandínou Karamanlí – wines and liqueurs, olive oil, ouzo, etc.

**Supermarket** – Leofóros Konstandínou Karamanlí, just beside the Kangaroo snack bar. This sells a bit of everything, including international newspapers.

**Arts and crafts – Onap Ethnic Shop**, Odós Kapetán Sífi, on the left going uphill. Nothing Greek here, let alone Cretan, but a lot of beautiful items from Africa and Indonesia.

# IERÁPETRA

District of Lassíthi – 63km from Sitía
Michelin map 980 fold 39 – Map of the island pages 358-359 – Pop 9 500

**Not to be missed**
A walk through the old town.
A day on the beach at Hrissí Island.

**And remember...**
Stay a day at the most, for Hrissí Island, then head west.

Coming from Sitía, you cross the island from north to south, going through mountains, valleys and lost villages. When you reach the coast, the scene becomes a lot less picturesque: there's a 24km concrete strip of hotels, apartments, souvenir shops and the like, which continues to grow and is gradually transforming the whole of the coastline. Then the traffic becomes denser and the tourist facilities give way to buildings that look more like real life: you have arrived in Ierápetra, a large agricultural centre that seems to have other occupations than tourism. Here, greenhouse-produced tomatoes, bananas and cucumbers have made the town one of the richest in Crete.

## Short tour of the town

*Plan page 401. Allow 2-3hr for a walk. The town's main thoroughfares meet in the centre at Platía Kanouráki, set slightly back from the seafront.*

As a bustling modern commercial centre, where a large middle class busies itself from morning till night, Ierápetra pays little attention to its visitors and, at first glance, hardly seems to merit a stroll.

Nevertheless, you should take a look at the small **Archaeological Museum** (*Tuesday-Sunday, 8.30am-3pm; entrance fee*), which displays a jumble of objects discovered in the region (vases, oil lamps, sarcophagi and statues) from a whole range of periods.

There's more to see in the **old town★★**, which is separated from the modern district by **Leofóros Hoúta**. This avenue heads off south-west, marking the border between two worlds. On the left is a quiet maze of cobblestone alleyways with low houses, which soon makes you forget the hectic pace of the rest of the town. **Odós Anagnostáki** leads to the **mosque** and its minaret built by the Turks, near which stands a public **fountain**.

Now continue east towards the sea and try and find the place known as **Napoleon's House** (*about 30m from the beach, along an alley just opposite Babi's restaurant. It's no use asking your way, the district is such a maze that even the locals will have trouble helping you!*). The modest abandoned building just beside a house with blue shutters is one of the oldest in the town. **Bonaparte** is believed to have stayed here one night on his way back from his campaign in Egypt. There's not much evidence to back this up, but don't upset the inhabitants by looking doubtful – they are very proud of the fact.

Make your way back to the seafront and go along **Odós Samouíl** to the **Venetian fort**, which guards the entrance to the harbour (*free access, no fixed times. Watch out for the slippery steps that lead to the first floor, where, by the way, the view is nothing special*). Just opposite, take a look inside the delightful Byzantine-style **church**, all spick and span.

To finish off, you have a choice between the **beach**, which is quite pretty and clean and stretches along the whole of the southern part of the town, and the long **promenade** on the seafront, a pleasant place to stroll with its benches looking out over the ocean.

## Hrissí Island*

*Plenty of daily return trips from Ierápetra (crossing about 1hr). Allow 1 day (see also "Other things to do").* If there's one thing in Ierápetra of interest to tourists, it's this small uninhabited paradise. Obviously, the hordes of holidaymakers scrambling onto its shores every day spoil the pleasure somewhat, but the island has enough **beaches*** for you to enjoy the trip. So pack your sunscreen and swimsuit, and get ready to enjoy the pink sand and the crystal waters of the Libyan Sea, stretching between Europe and Africa. If after a while you feel like a walk, you can go to the **forest of hundred-year-old cedars** that covers the middle of the island.

*The only way to continue along the south coast without going through Herakleion again is to hire a car. No bus does the direct trip to Mátala (about 120km). To get the most out of the drive, leave Ierápetra early in the morning (towards Mírtos).*

---
## Making the most of Ierápetra
---

### COMING AND GOING

**By bus –** The bus station is in the north of the town, in Leofóros Koundouriótou, ☎ (0842) 28 237. Daily connections with the main towns in the east.
Herakleion: 10 buses a day, between 6.30am and 8pm (2hr30min travelling time). Sitía: 6 buses a day, between 6.15am and 8pm (1hr30min). Mírtos: 6 buses a day, between 6.30am and 8pm (30min). Ágios Nikólaos: 9 buses a day, between 6.30am and 8pm (1hr).

### FINDING YOUR WAY

The town stretches along the seafront on a north-south axis. In the centre, slightly set back from the shore, is Platía Kanouráki, which forms a hub from which the main thoroughfares radiate. The south is given over to the old town and the harbour, and the north to the modern shopping districts of the city centre.

### GETTING AROUND

**By car –** The traffic generally flows smoothly, except in Odós Samouíl, which is often jammed. It is sometimes difficult to park, especially in the southern part of the old town. You should leave your car and then walk, as the town is a reasonable size to tour on foot.
**By taxi –** Platía Kanouráki, ☎ (0842) 27 350 / 26 600.
**Vehicle rental – *Europlan Car Rental***, Odós M Kothri 39. Hires out cars, motorcycles and scooters. Another agent in the same street, on the corner of Odós Gianákou, rents out two-wheel vehicles.

### ADDRESS BOOK

There is no official tourist information centre, but the travel agents all have tourist office signs and provide an equivalent service.

**Bank / Currency exchange –** There are cash dispensers in the town centre. ***Commercial Bank***, Leofóros Adrianoú 10. Monday-Friday, 8am-2pm.
***National Bank***, Odós M Kothri. Monday-Thursday, 8am-2pm, 1.30pm on Friday.

**Post office / Telephone – *Main post office***, Odós Kornárou, beside a large domestic appliance shop. Not easy to find, especially as travel agents hand out old maps showing it at its former address. Monday-Friday, 8am-2pm. Changes money.

**Internet – *Orpheas***, Leofóros Koundouriótou 25. A rather cosy bar that makes you pay twice as much for Internet access as anywhere else on Crete.

**Medical service – *Hospital***, ☎ (0842) 26 766, in the northern part of the town, slightly above the bus station.
***Pharmacies***, all over the town centre, with two in Leofóros Koundouriótou.

**Emergencies – *Police***, ☎ (0842) 22 560.

### WHERE TO STAY

Because of its size, Ierápetra has a limited range of accommodation. Most of the hotels are along the waterfront and in the streets parallel.

#### Campsite (around €11)

**Koutsounari**, 9km from Ierápetra on the coast road heading east, ☎ (0842) 61 213 / 186 / 512. Open from May to October. Olives, palms and tamarisks provide good shade. Large clean bathrooms in good condition.

#### Under €30

**Katarina Rooms**, beside the Ástron Hotel, on the seafront promenade, ☎ (0842) 28 345, Fax (0842) 28 591-15rm. ⚐▤ ℘ The entrance is through the souvenir shop. Because it does not provide the services of a standard hotel (no real reception), it charges unbeatable prices for the location and type of accommodation, which is on a par with that of the other hotels on the seafront. Tiles, white walls, bathrooms in good condition, little balconies. Ask for a room with a sea view.

**Hotel Kástro**, Odós Samouíl 54, ☎ (0842) 23 853 – 4rm. ⚐ Enquire at the souvenir shop on the ground floor. Simple though clean and spacious rooms. Proximity to the beach increases the price a little, but the hotel is still a good place for budget travellers. No breakfast (but there are tavernas opposite). Friendly welcome.

#### Between €30 and €45

**Hotel El Greco**, Odós M Kothri 42, ☎ (0842) 28 471, Fax (0842) 24 515 – 30rm. ⚐ ℘ ✕ CC Good value for money. Clean well-kept rooms, half of them with a sea view. Flagstone flooring in the reception area. Rather eccentric though friendly and professional service. You can have breakfast (extra, and a bit expensive) on the terrace in the sunshine, facing the sea.

**Hotel Zakrós**, Odós Adrianoú 12, ☎ (0842) 24 101 / 2, Fax (0842) 24 103 – 49rm. ⚐▤ ℘ TV CC Similar comfort to the Hotel El Greco (with larger bathrooms), but in a less attractive district. To reach the recently renovated but somewhat flashy reception (white marble, gold decorations), you have to go through the alleyway in Odós Adrianoú.

**Cámiros Hotel**, Odós M Kothri 15, ☎ (0842) 28 704, Fax (0842) 24 104 – 30rm. ⚐ Only as a backup: in terms of reception, it is difficult to imagine worse. Clean standard rooms, at rather steep prices.

#### Between €45 and €75

**Ástron Hotel**, Odós M Kothri 56, ☎ (0842) 25 114 / 117 / 191 / 728, Fax (0842) 25 917 – 66rm. ⚐▤ ℘ TV ✕ ♨ CC Average international-standard luxury. Very professional service. Good classical style rooms with white furniture, mini-bars and balconies, for a fairly reasonable price. Business clientele. One of the rare hotels in town to stay open all year round. A bit soulless.

### EATING OUT

At all costs, avoid the restaurants at the foot of the hotels on the seafront promenade. They are expensive, the food is not good and the service is rushed. Go instead to the harbour, along Odós Samouíl and near the fort. There are many places there, and it is hard to choose.

#### Around €7.50

**Tonia**, Odós Samouíl, 30m from the Hotel Kástro heading towards the centre. ▥ A friendly snack bar serving the classic dishes: Greek salad, *gíros pita*, and some Cretan specialities (*tiropitákias*, cheese turnovers) to eat on the hoof.

#### Around €15

**Babi's**, Odós M Kothri 68, ☎ (0842) 24 048. ▥ Mainly frequented by local people, even though the menu appears in different languages and includes a few intruders intended for tourists (pizza, frankfurters!). Go rather for the fish and seafood specialities: swordfish fillet, cuttlefish in wine, and grilled fish on skewers.

### HAVING A DRINK

Nights are very quiet in Ierápetra. There are a few bars on the seafront promenade where the local young people gather in the evening (and which close early), but not much else.

**Cafés – Cafeteria Betepano**, on the corner of Odós M Kothri and Leofóros Koundouriótou. ▥ This small square in the heart of town sees people coming from morning till night to spend a few minutes eating delicious cakes before hurrying off about their business.

🕮 **Ouzerí**, Platía Kanouráki, the second café at the beginning of Leofóros Hoúta. This is where you should come before the evening meal to mix in with the local population, drink an ouzo and try the meze: croutons, cheese, olives, tomatoes and prawns.

### OTHER THINGS TO DO

**Beaches** – There's a good, relatively clean pebble beach south of the town beyond the harbour. But it is worth going a short distance out of Ierápetra to a much nicer, less busy one a few kilometres away in the direction of Sitía.

**Excursions** – All the travel agents, notably those on the seafront, sell tickets for **Hrissí Island**. Fairly expensive. Daily departures with several boats at 10.30am and 12.30pm, return trip at 4pm. The crossing takes about 1hr.

### SHOPPING GUIDE

If you like spirits and liqueurs, you will find what you need at Leofóros Hoúta 6. A shop at Odós Adrianoú 9 sells a range of local arts and crafts (lace, icons) and antiques.

**Other** – There's a simple little **cake shop** at Leofóros Hoúta 53.

**English newspapers** next to the bus station and at the beginning of Leofóros Koundouriótou, near Platía Kanouráki.

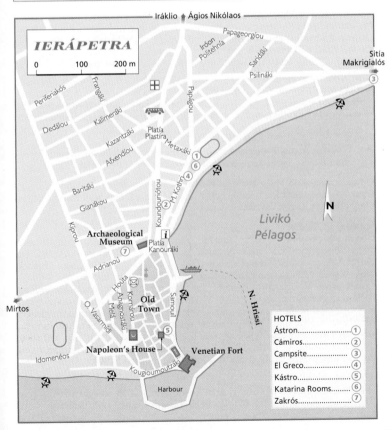

*IERÁPETRA*

0    100    200 m

Iráklio ● Ágios Nikólaos

Sitía
Makrigialós

Livíkó
Pélagos

**HOTELS**

| Ástron | ① |
| Cámiros | ② |
| Campsite | ③ |
| El Greco | ④ |
| Kástro | ⑤ |
| Katarina Rooms | ⑥ |
| Zakrós | ⑦ |

# THE MESSARÁ PLAIN★★
## GORTYN★★ AND PHAISTOS★★★

District of Iráklio – 75km from Herakleion – Michelin map 980 fold 38
Map of the island pages 358-359 - Tour of about 80km – Allow 2 days
Accommodation in Mátala (see page 411) then in Agía Galíni (see page 415)

### Not to be missed
The Roman ruins at Gortyn and the Minoan palace at Phaistos.
The Minoan villa at Agía Triáda.
The Byzantine monastery at Vrondissí.

### And remember...
You must have a car to do this itinerary.
Spend the first night in Mátala, and the second in Agía Galíni –
the most convenient way to enjoy the area,
its cultural heritage and scenery, not forgetting a few swims.

With its monasteries, caves and Minoan remains, the fertile plain of Messará – the largest on the island – abounds in historical treasures, and also has lovely scenery. The area stretches northwards to the foothills of **Mt Psilorítis** – the legendary **Mt Ida** – offering a variety of excursions. You may like to follow the itinerary we propose, taking the time to wander here and there off the beaten track, discovering the real Crete and its legends. And however fascinated you are by archaeology, you will find it hard to resist the beautiful sand beaches along the coast.

*Leave Ierápetra in the early morning, tour Gortyn and Phaistos, then end the day on the beach at Mátala, which is also a good place to stay overnight.*
*Early the next morning, tour Agía Triáda, then go walking in the Kamáres heights to see two monasteries. In the evening, make your way to Agía Galíni, where good tavernas await you.*

## ■ Gortyn★★ (Górtis)
*28km west of Pírgos, and about 8km east of Míres. Daily, 8am-7pm.*
*Entrance fee for the basilica and the odeon (the rest is free). Allow 45min.*

On the approach to Míres, the road suddenly crosses a vast area of jumbled stones scattered among the olive trees on either side of the road. This is all that remains of the prestigious Roman city where Zeus once loved the beautiful Europa.

### Capital of Crete
Gortyn was occupied from the Neolithic Period onwards, as is borne out by many archaeological finds, but only experienced its first hours of glory in the Archaic Era (7C BC). In the 3C BC, it had already taken over its powerful neighbour Phaistos, robbing it of its status as capital of Messará, and brilliantly stood up to its rival Knossós, against which it waged a ruthless war. Far from reducing its influence, the Romans decided as soon as they arrived (69-67 BC) to make Gortyn their administrative centre and the capital of the island, covering it with monuments and statues to the glory of the Empire. Gortyn pursued its prestigious destiny in the Byzantine Era, thanks to the **Apostle Titus**, a disciple of St Paul, who became the island's first bishop, and chose the city as the seat of Christianity in Crete. However, in 828, Gortyn began a slow decline, was ravaged by the Arabs, and foundered for good in 961.

### Tour of the site
Once through the entrance *(car park on the left)*, you will see straight away on your left the majestic ruins of the **Basilica of St Titus**★★ (Ágios Títos), dedicated to the martyred bishop. It was probably built in the 7C, and consisted of a nave and two

parallel aisles. The layout is still clearly visible on the ground, lined by the bases of the columns that separated each aisle. The only parts still standing, the **apse** and its two **chapels**, still serve as a modest place of worship, with candles and liturgical objects.

Go across the **agora** to the **Odeon\***, a small theatre built in the early 2C AD on the foundations of an Archaic building. Much of the material taken from the first edifice (5C BC) is visible, including the famous **Laws of Gortyn\*\***, engraved on the abutments of the entrance arch. When the citizens went to musical performances, they could read them at leisure. The laws make up the most complete legal text in the Greek world, dealing with individual liberty, property rights, inheritance, etc. They are written in a Dorian Cretan dialect and should be read in the *boustrophedon manner*, "as an ox turns in ploughing" (*from left to right and from right to left in alternate lines*).

Close by is a **plane tree**, the descendant of the tree beneath which, according to legend, Zeus and Europa consummated their love.

*As you leave the site, several other remains are visible on the other side of the road, lost among the olive trees. Most of them are being excavated and you will only see them behind wire netting. Carry on eastwards beside the main road for about 300m, and then bear right on to the path that leads to the principal ruins.*

### The love of a bull

Always yearning for female conquests, Zeus surprised the young Europa as she was playing in her garden. On seeing such grace and beauty, the god was seized with desire and decided to abduct the young girl. To do this, he turned into a magnificent white bull "with horns like the crescent of the moon" and, gently approaching Europa, lay down at her feet. Frightened at first, she soon began to stroke his shiny coat before sitting on his back. The bull immediately got up, leapt into the sea and swam out all the way to the coast of Crete. There, Zeus chose a convenient spot, setting his mistress down beside a spring in Gortyn, in the shade of a plane tree, which ever since has had the characteristic of never losing its leaves. From this love three sons were born, including Minos, the future king of Knossós, and Rhadamanthys, who founded powerful Phaistos.

Gortyn: the Basilica of St Titus

Gortyn

B. Kaufmann/MICHELIN

**403**

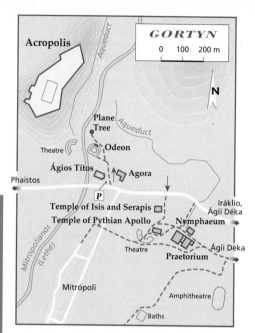

You first come to the **Temple of Isis and Serapis**, two Egyptian gods who were very popular with the Romans. The edifice was built in the 2C BC and has kept the remains of its **cella** and a **purification basin**.

Further on there once stood the temple dedicated to **Pythian Apollo** (of Delphi), together with a theatre. The sanctuary was built over Minoan walls and dates from the Archaic Era, but was modified several times up until the Roman Period.

Continue eastwards along the path for about 200m to the imposing ruins of the recently excavated **Praetorium★**, which served as the seat of the provincial administration and the official residence of the Governor. The building, which was constructed under Trajan in the 2C AD, was rebuilt and modified after an earthquake in 374. Beside it, you can see the low walls of the **baths** and an impressive **basilica chamber** erected during the reconstruction. Just opposite, on the other side of the path, you will see the remains of a nymphaeum, which was supplied with water by an aqueduct and converted into a fountain in the Byzantine Era.

*For archaeology enthusiasts, or simply for the pleasure of a walk, there are other ruins to see (far less well preserved) in the south: the amphitheatre, the baths and further on, the stadium.*

*Then take the Míres road. Go through the town and after 7km bear left, into the road to Phaistos and Mátala.*

## ■ Phaistos★★★ (Festós)

*8km west of Míres. Daily, 8am-7pm (5pm in winter). Entrance fee (expensive). Free car park at the entrance to the site. Allow 45min, without counting the time to contemplate the view (best at the end of the day with the setting sun).*

The majestic promontory on which the ruined terraces of the city rise is bathed in an almost blinding white light. With pines dotted here and there, the city with its light-coloured stone walls faces the **Gheropótamos Valley** and the Messará Plain, which stretches as far as the eye can see to the blue barrier of the mountains in the north. The setting is spectacular, in keeping with one of the most powerful Minoan cities, the second largest after Knossós. In fact, there is no comparison between Phaistos and the older palace. More authentic and more moving, it has not been turned into a kind of stage set by wilful reconstruction and over-generous use of concrete. The stones have been left to speak for themselves, and the **panorama★★★** is unforgettable.

## 17 centuries of influence

The area was first inhabited in Neolithic times (around 3000 BC), and saw its first palace built in 1900 BC. According to legend, this was founded by **Rhadamanthys**, the second son of Zeus and Europa, and the brother of Minos, King of Knossós. Held in high esteem for his justice and wisdom, the demigod made sure that his dynasty reigned until the end of the Minoan Period. In 1700 BC, the complex was destroyed by the earthquake that ravaged most of the palaces in Crete (there are some Old Palace Period remains in the south-west part). A new, larger and more luxurious centre was then built, making up most of the ruins that you see today. A second earthquake is thought to have caused the southern slope of the hill to subside, thus damaging the palace and taking the southern section with it. But thanks to its **two ports**, Mátala and Kommos, the prosperous city state – called by **Homer** "the town with many inhabitants" – lived a life of splendour down through the centuries to the Hellenistic Era.

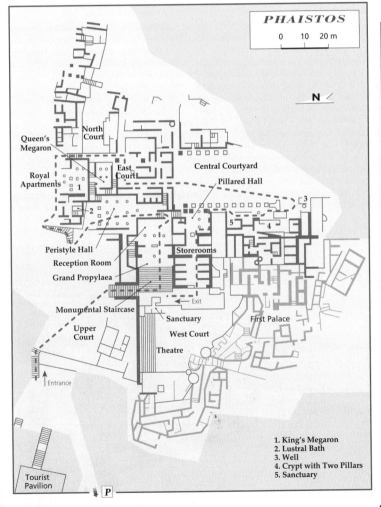

PHAISTOS

0   10   20 m

N

Queen's Megaron
North Court
Royal Apartments
East Court
Central Courtyard
Pillared Hall
Peristyle Hall
Reception Room
Grand Propylaea
Storerooms
Monumental Staircase
Sanctuary
First Palace
Upper Court
West Court
Theatre
Entrance
Exit

1. King's Megaron
2. Lustral Bath
3. Well
4. Crypt with Two Pillars
5. Sanctuary

Tourist Pavilion
P

It was its long-standing rival Gortyn that finally got the better of it in 200 BC, robbing it of its status as regional capital. Life in the city went on timidly for a while and then died out completely under Roman domination. Excavations begun by the Italians **Halbherr** and **Pernier** in 1900 were continued 50 years later under the direction of the **Italian School of Athens**. The resulting finds have proved essential for the understanding of Minoan culture: among them were **jewellery**, Kamáres vases and cult objects, not forgetting the famous clay **disk**, known as the Phaistos Disk, engraved with hieroglyphs that still remain a mystery *(Archaeological Museum in Herakleion)*.

## Tour of the site

Once past the site office at the entrance, you walk along a shaded lane to the **Upper Court**. In addition to the magnificent **view★★** over the surrounding area, the place enables you to take in all the ruins at a glance. Take the time to get your bearings and pick out a few landmarks before beginning your exploration.

The first staircase leads down to the **West Court**, a vast paved esplanade crossed diagonally by the narrow **Processions Corridor** *(outline clearly marked on the ground)*. It is closed to the north by the eight rectilinear terraces of the **Theatre**, where the inhabitants attended ceremonies and rituals. In the south-east, behind a series of round **silos**, there once stood the **propylaea** of the former palace *(the area is closed to the public but can be seen through the wire fencing)*.

On the right side of the theatre *(facing it)*, four **adjoining rooms** form a small **Sanctuary** (belonging to the old palace) with benches. This once contained tables for offerings, vases and various religious utensils.

Beyond, opposite the staircase down which you arrived, take the **monumental staircase★**, which leads to the **Grand Propylaea**, the porch of the new palace. Imagine how people felt almost three millennia ago, walking up the wide steps to enter the palace and appear before the king.

Go through the first reception room, where you can see the bases of several columns, then continue left into the **Peristyle Hall**, a square court surrounded by a portico, off which led the **Royal Apartments**. These consisted of the **King's**

Caves and parasols: Mátala beach

P. Frilet/HEMISPHERES

**Megaron**, a small **lustral bath** for purification purposes, a **reception room**, and the **Queen's Megaron**, of which one of the rooms has retained its **alabaster paving★**.

You leave the royal residence through the **North Court**, off which lead two corridors. The first goes to the **East Court**, in the middle of which is an **oven** that is dug into the ground. Potter's wheels found on the spot suggest that it was used for firing pottery. The second corridor, which is lined with **channels** to catch rainwater, leads into the vast **central courtyard★** that has kept all its paving. As in all Minoan palaces, this was the heart of the city, where the official ceremonies, sacrifices and bull-leaping took place.

Go to the south-west end of the courtyard where you will see a **well**, and then turn right to head all the way back along the courtyard in the opposite direction. You will pass a narrow **crypt with two pillars** and then another room surrounded by benches, believed to be a **Sanctuary**.

Beyond, you go through a wider **Pillared Hall**, also known as the Main Room, and then left into a corridor of **storerooms**. The eight cells, down both sides of the corridor, were used for storing palace provisions including cereals, oil and wine, which were kept in **pithoi**, the enormous terracotta jars that you can see in the Archaeological Museum in Herakleion and at Knossós. Lastly, at the end of the corridor you come back to the theatre area, the starting point for the tour.

*You may like to have a drink on the pleasant panoramic terrace at the entrance to the site. Then, either continue to Agía Triáda (2.5km away), or end the day on the beach at Mátala, where there is plenty of accommodation.*

## ■ Mátala

*25km south-west of Míres.*
*See also "Making the most of Mátala" at the end of the chapter, page 410.*

It is hard to believe that this is where Zeus swam ashore after having abducted Europa, bringing his beloved to the plane trees of Gortyn. Forget about the town's status as the former port of Phaistos, and the so-called "attractive fishing harbour" whose remains are meticulously maintained like a picturesque stage set for the benefit of holidaymakers...

Be that as it may, Mátala is still a very pleasant place, unlike the concrete complexes you find too often in Crete. It is also very small, its only thoroughfare ending at the harbour, with the side streets full of decent hotels and guesthouses. Furthermore, the setting is green, affording some refreshing shade, and there's an immense **beach★** of white sand *(on the right heading towards the harbour, along a dead end leading to some steps)*. Altogether a convenient place to eat and sleep before continuing a tour of the area.

### On the Kathmandu trail

Every year, young handsome tanned tourists, mainly German, get together in Mátala for a week in the sun, on a kind of cultural pilgrimage. They want to get a taste of what it was like for those who, at the height of the hippie era, would come to the Mátala caves before heading off to Kathmandu. Naturally, if you ask, you will be told that the older inhabitants were once part of the scene...

More than being an attraction in themselves, the **caves** are mainly worthwhile for the fine **viewpoint★** they offer. Dug out of the **cliff★** overlooking the beach *(on the right when facing the sea)*, they were once home to the defenders of flower power. Not realising at all the commercial interest their stay would one day bring, the hippies left traces of their psychedelic ceremonies in the form of **frescoes** and **graffiti**. To keep the myth going, the caves are now protected by grilles, and are cleared of visitors in the evening. From a more historical point of view, it is also believed that they were used as tombs or places of worship in ancient times.

# ■ Agía Triáda villa*

*From Mátala, take the Míres road (north-east), then, after 9km, turn left at the sign-post (in Greek). The ruins are 3.5km further on, along a small road left, opposite the one leading to Phaistos.*

Although Agía Triáda is much more modest than the other Minoan sites on the island, it by no means lacks interest. Firstly, on account of its green **setting**\*\* – just as good as that of Phaistos – surrounded by mountains, overlooking the plain from a vantage point among the pines and olives. Secondly, because the place is little visited. On the other hand, you need a lot of imagination to make sense of the ruins themselves, which have been thoroughly levelled.

## Summer quarters

The small palace built in 1600 BC was termed a villa by the Italian archaeologists who discovered it in the early 20C. The archaeologists believed that it was perhaps a summer residence for the king, or for an important dignitary from Phaistos. Today, this seems to be the most likely assumption, as the palace is only a few kilometres away, and a long **paved road** linking the two sites has been uncovered.

After being destroyed in 1450 BC, the luxurious residence was partially rebuilt but very soon changed its purpose, becoming mainly a place of worship, as is borne out by the incredible amount of liturgical objects found on the site. Other outstanding works, masterpieces of Minoan art, also come from here, including the delicate conical **Harvester Vase** made of soapstone, exhibited in the Archaeological Museum in Herakleion.

## Tour of the site

*Daily, 8.30am-3pm. Entrance fee. Allow 45min.* It is easy to get your bearings from the pavilion that juts out slightly above the ruins at the entrance to the site. On the right are the houses of a **village** dating from the late Minoan Period (1350 BC). Further north, on the hillside, are the remains of a large **necropolis**, whose many tombs in the two mausoleums (once covered by a dome) contained rich offerings. Among them was the extraordinary **Agía Triáda sarcophagus**, covered in painted scenes of a funeral, another gem in the Archaeological Museum in Herakleion.

Facing you is the main part of the palace: apartments, places of worship, reception rooms, storerooms and working quarters. This stretched right to the southern end of the site, watched over by a charming Byzantine chapel, Ágios Geórgios.

A long paved **ramp leading to the sea** crosses the whole of the site. On either side of it were the main buildings, including the **palace** itself (ruined), which stretched along the whole of the left side, linking up with the village.

Steps lead to the foot of the ruins. On the left, a majestic **staircase** goes up to the **Altar Court**, extended on the side by the **paved road**.

Opposite, if you take the ramp right to the end, you will find steps on the left that lead to a small court that marked the middle of the **west wing** of the palace. In the area around you can see the walls of small rooms in which were discovered some amazingly well-preserved **frescoes** depicting light, bucolic themes, including wild cats, and a young woman in a garden (*displayed in the Archaeological Museum in Herakleion*).

Further south, another series of rooms once housed the villa's **kitchens**. They had no windows, but were lit by a light well.

Retrace your steps eastwards to see the remains of what must have been the palace's **living quarters** (megaron), then, beyond the Altar Court and the paved road, the area with the **storerooms**.

End your visit with a three-thousand-year leap to see the **Ágios Geórgios Chapel**, built in the 14C. Note the finely carved motifs that decorate the façade. You can ask the site warden for the key to have a look inside.

# Into the hills★

*On leaving Agía Triáda, turn left to reach the main Míres-Timbáki road, to the north. Then turn right (1km further on, signposted Vóri-Kamáres).*

The **Psilorítis massif**, a long grey-blue ridge, lies to the north of the Messará Plain. Dominating this harsh rocky area dotted with meagre scrubland is the legendary **Mt Ida** (Psilorítis) and its snow-capped peak, rising to a height of 2 456m. On its sides are a host of caves that the ancients converted into shrines.

■ **Vóri** – Stop off in this quiet little town on the **Kamáres** road, which would be of little interest if it were not for the fascinating **Ethnographic Museum of Crete**★★ (*10am-6pm; entrance fee*). The museum was founded by the Messará Cultural Association and was given a special mention by the Council of Europe in 1992 in the context of the prize for the Best Museum in Europe. Before entering the museum enclosure (*near the church*), note the fine **lancet arch** at the entrance, which was taken from a former building. Inside is an outstanding collection of well-presented objects illustrating daily life on Crete in the 18C and 19C, when the island was still mainly rural. Fishing tackle, farm tools, weaving looms, locks, **door knockers**★ and **musical instruments**★ are shown in thematic display cases with plenty of descriptions. Note among the items the amazing **ploughs** that seem to date back to the very beginnings of time. They look a little like sledges, bristling on the lower part with small metallic saws or sharp flint spikes for turning the soil.

On leaving, walk out onto the square in front of the **church** (19C), to see the beautiful **sundial** decorating the façade.

### Ida, Zeus' cradle

Long before he set up court on the top of Mt Olympus, Zeus was born in Crete, in a cave on Mt Ida. Since then, legend and history have come together, and the sacred site has been found. When the first excavations were carried out in the 19C, it was thought that the Kamáres cave, where religious objects were found, was the place. But we now know that Zeus' childhood home was in fact what is known as the Idaian Cave, hollowed out of the western slope and giving onto the Nída Plateau. In it were found a great many objects, the oldest dating from the Minoan Era, bearing witness to a cult of the highest importance.

*Continue northwards from Vóri in the direction of Kamáres, through the villages of Margarikári and Grigoría.*

■ **The Kamáres Cave** – *For energetic walkers. You should be in good physical condition, and should take a guide (enquire at the village). Allow 5hr on foot there and back.* The natural cave above Kamáres village, hidden away on Mt Psilorítis at a height of 1 525m, is thought to be an important Minoan place of worship, probably dedicated to **Eileithyia**, the goddess of childbirth. It was discovered by chance in 1890 by a farmer, and soon interested Italian archaeologists who found the famous **Kamáres vases** here, now exhibited in the Archaeological Museum in Herakleion. The cave itself is of no great interest but it provides hikers with a good mountain walk.

*3.5km east of Kamáres you come to Vorízia. A track on the right at the entrance to the village leads to the monastery.*

■ **Moní Valsamónero**★ – *8.30am-3pm; entrance fee.* It is difficult not to succumb to the charm of this abandoned monastery high up in a superb setting among the greenery in the mountains. It was founded in the 14C, its delicate architecture drawing on the Italian style. The church, **Ágios Fanoúrios**, contains some wonderfully well-preserved **frescoes**★★ from the same period, illustrating in sparkling colours scenes from the Life of the Virgin Mary and the saints (*left aisle*). Other frescoes dating from the 15C decorate the right-hand aisle and the narthex.

*Return to the main road and head east.*

## Olive oil, elixir of youth

Lots of fruit and vegetables, little meat, a good deal of fish, milk products (yoghurt, goat cheese) and, of course, olive oil in abundance. In Crete, the oil is measured in cups and it is not unusual for an average family to consume a litre a day. This is the secret that gives Cretans a statistically higher longevity than people living in colder climes. Whether you enjoy the local cuisine or not, all dieticians confirm that it is a model for a balanced diet. Rich in fibres, minerals and vitamins, the Cretan diet gives the body proteins and lipids, while sparing it the excess animal fat to which other bodies are too often subjected.

■ **Moní Vrondissí**★ – *4km beyond Vorízia; free*. Yet another delightful monastery nestling in the foothills of Mt Psilorítis, with a splendid **panorama**★★ of the Messará Plain. Moní Vrondissí was an important cultural centre under the Venetians, and saw some talented artists, including the painter **Mihális Damaskinós**. Later, in the dark moments of the struggle against the Turks, it became a focus for Cretan resistance.

Near the entrance, beneath the plane trees, stands a **Venetian fountain** made of marble. It is decorated with a 15C **bas-relief** of Adam and Eve in the Garden of Eden, God, and four figures symbolising the rivers in the garden, from whose mouths the water flows. Inside the **church**, which contains two aisles (one for the Orthodox rite, dedicated to St Thomas, and the other for the Catholic rite, dedicated to St Antony), you can see some beautiful **frescoes**★ on the ceiling (*right-hand aisle*). There are also some outstanding **wood paintings**★.

*Make your way to Agía Galíni, where you can spend the night (32km, see the following chapter).*

## Making the most of Mátala

### COMING AND GOING

**By bus** – No direct link with Ierápetra, though you can do the trip in stages, hopping from bus to bus (rather long and complicated). For Herakleion (2hr travelling time): 8 buses a day, between 7.30am and 6pm. For Míres (30min): 8 buses a day, between 8.40am and 7.10pm. For Phaistos (30min): 7 buses a day, between 9.30am and 8pm. For Agía Galíni (45min): 6 buses a day, between 7am and 5.15pm.

### FINDING YOUR WAY

This is easy: the main street, lined with shops, bars and restaurants, leads from the entrance of the village to the harbour. The beach is on the right, and the hotels and guesthouses on the left.

### GETTING AROUND

**By car** – There's a car park (often full in summer) at the end of the street on the left, beyond the entrance to the village. Otherwise, you will have to park in the vicinity.

**By rental vehicle** – There are several agents in the village. Motorcycles can be hired at the entrance to the village, on the right, opposite the Zafiria Hotel.

**Monza Travel**, in the middle of the junction at the end of the main street, cutting it in two.

### ADDRESS BOOK

**Bank / Currency exchange** – There are several places where you can change money. However, make sure you have cash on you, as there are no cash dispensers (some are being planned).

**Post office / Telephone** – **Main post office**, in the centre. Monday-Saturday, 9am-1pm.

### WHERE TO STAY

Mátala is organised to accommodate tourists by the thousand.

*Under €30*

**Angela Rooms**, in the street leading left off the main street, heading towards the harbour, ☎ and Fax (0892) 45 191 – 6rm. ⚐ Angela's clean spacious rooms are in a very neat garden setting, away from the bustle (but not from the mosquitoes). No breakfast.

*Between €30 and €45*

🏷 **Hotel Níkos**, just beyond Angela Rooms, in the same street on the right, ☎ (0892) 45 375, Fax (0892) 45 120 – 20rm. ⚐ ⚱ An attractive low building with terraces and small gardens. Tropical plants, natural colours, baked clay flooring... altogether very effective. The welcome is just as good, and the clean spacious rooms all have big showers. Barely more expensive than the place above, but with breakfast (excellent, with freshly squeezed fruit juice).

**Zafíria Hotel**, at the entrance to the village, on the left ☎ (0892) 45 366 / 112 / 747, Fax (0892) 45 725 – 59rm. ⚐ 🖉 ✗ CC A recent, fairly standard hotel that is clean and comfortable (floor tiling, balconies in every room), but lacks charm. And you are not that much more protected from mosquitoes. Worth noting: some rooms have double beds.

### EATING OUT

*Around €7.50*

**Nasos**, to the right of the main street, in the dead end that leads to the beach. ⛺

This small friendly snack bar has a sign proudly claiming that it makes "The best *gíros pita* in Mátala". That may or may not be true, but there's no denying that it really is good!

**Giannis Restaurant**, beyond the market in the main street, on the right. ⛺ Less flashy than others and it doesn't tout as much for custom, but don't expect a fabulous menu: good classic local fare at affordable prices.

*Around €15*

**Mythos Restaurant**, on the cliff above the harbour. ⛺ Probably the only restaurant with a good view of Mátala creek and its famous caves. Naturally, the place considers itself chic and you pay for the surroundings. Apart from the eternal standard menu, there are also pizzas and some German dishes in an effort to adapt to tourist tastes.

### HAVING A DRINK

The bars are legion and change all the time, making it impossible to recommend any names. Choose the decor that pleases you most...

### SHOPPING GUIDE

There's a small covered **market** at the end of the main street, to the right of the junction. It is tourist-oriented but very friendly. You will find all sorts of local arts and crafts (lace, jewellery and leather goods).

**Making the most of Mátala**

# FROM AGÍA GALÍNI TO SFAKIÁ★
## PRÉVELI MONASTERY★★
District of Réthimnon – Tour of 80km
Michelin map 980 fold 37-38 – Map of the island pages 358-359

### And remember...
Leave Agía Galíni in the morning to make the most of the road and
arrive in Sfakiá in the afternoon.
Spend the night there if it is too late to reach Haniá, otherwise head north.

Crete

Once you have passed the crowded beaches lined with hotels all along Messará Bay, a new Crete appears, happily recalling the wild beauty of the east of the island. The **road**★ stretching west from Agía Galíni towards Sfakiá runs through peaceful villages, rocky landscapes and olive groves, taking you into typically Mediterranean country-side smelling sweetly of thyme. Further on, the mountains begin to close in and the scenery becomes dramatic, with monasteries clinging to the sides of deep gorges.

■ **Agía Galíni** – *32km north-west of Mátala, at the far end of the bay.* Agía Galíni is a small resort largely designed to accommodate the many tourists who come for the beach and the sites of cultural interest in the region. Like its neighbour Mátala, it is a good base for exploring the Messará Plain. The approach from Mátala is a long descent towards the sea, with the road twisting for several kilo-metres past hastily built hotels. Fortunately, the village huddling at the foot of a promontory facing the sea is hemmed in by the hills and cannot extend indefi-nitely. It has therefore preserved some of its charm, with a **harbour**, and pedestrian streets and tavernas that exude a family atmosphere in sharp contrast with those in Mátala.

*About 30km north-west of Agía Galíni you come to Spíli, a large country village. Continue along the main road for 10km then bear left to Moní Préveli.*

### ■ Moní Préveli★★

*48.5km from Agía Galíni. Large car park at the viewpoint near the entrance to the monastery. 8am-7pm from 25 March to 31 May. 8am-1.30pm / 3.30pm-8pm from 1 June to 31 October. Closed November to March. Entrance fee. Try to come before the service at 5pm when the sun begins to go down and the monks go to church.*

Before reaching the monastery, the road enters the moun-tains, making its way between the steep sides of the **Kurtalioti gorge**★. Stop to admire the **panorama**★★ – perhaps one of the most beautiful on the island – and you may see one of the **eagles** that often hover overhead.

### From bottom...
Originally, the monastery was divided into two centres. The remains of the **first complex**, which was ravaged during the Second World War and then abandoned, can be seen below the road leading to the main monastery higher up. Although the **ruins**★ are fenced off and inaccessible, there's something moving about them in their harsh setting of rock and scrub. Stay a few minutes before continuing to the top.

### ...to top

High up in this wild and rocky landscape several hundred metres above the sea, the isolated monastery seems to be watching over the world. It consists of small white-washed buildings set on terraces. A deep sense of serenity and spirituality pervades the site. And yet the monastery has gone through four centuries of hard times, a history that has earned it universal respect. Préveli was an important stronghold of resistance against the Turks, and proved its valour again under German occupation, providing shelter to Greek fighters as well as to New Zealand and British troops during the **Battle of Crete** (1941).

You are free to walk along the lanes serving the main buildings, but otherwise only the church* may be visited, when mass is not in progress. Inside, among the gems of religious art are many **icons**, as well as an impressive **silver candelabra\*\***, a **gold cross\*** set in diamonds and a sumptuous **episcopal throne\***.

The monastery museum displays a small collection of liturgical objects (vestments, manuscripts and old books), and mainly sells products made by the monks, including icons, honey, candles and herbs.

As you leave, on the road just before the viewpoint at the entrance to the monastery, a steep path leads down (*30min*) to **Préveli beach\*\***, one of the loveliest on the island. (*However, give yourself enough time to climb back up again, as you still have a drive of about 2hr to Sfakiá.*)

■ **Sfakiá\*** (Hóra Sfakión) − *District of Haniá. 80km south of Haniá.* Nestling in a creek at the foot of a mountain, this tiny resort is one of the most attractive places to stay on this part of the coast. It caters to some of the tourists who trek through

Préveli Monastery, a mountain refuge

G. de Benoist/MICHELIN

the **Samariá Gorge** *(see page 428)*, and has two distinct faces: Sfakiá before the walkers arrive, and Sfakiá after. Every day, an hour or two before the boat puts in, the place simmers with activity: ovens are heated, beds made, and taverna tables laid. Consisting of a few stepped streets, a little harbour and a modest pebble **beach**, Sfakiá has no other charm than its restful atmosphere, which is particularly pleasant in the évening.

Sfakiá harbour in its remote setting

G. Simeone/CIAF

Crete

## Making the most of Agía Galíni

### COMING AND GOING

**By bus** – The *bus station* is in the main street by a little square to the right, a short distance before the harbour. Every 2hr there are buses to Herakleion, Réthimnon, Haniá, Spíli, Plakiás, Moní Préveli, Omalós (Samariá Gorge), Frangokástello, Sfakiá (Hóra Sfakión), Mátala, Timbáki, Phaistos and Míres.

### GETTING AROUND

**By car** – The *car park* (fee) in the harbour is often full in summer. It's better to leave your car at the top of the village and walk down.

**By rental vehicle** – Several places in the main street hire out cars, motorcycles and scooters.

**By taxi** – On the main street. Convenient for excursions in the surrounding area if you don't want to hire a car.

### ADDRESS BOOK

**Bank / Currency exchange** – *Cretan Holidays*, on the left as you go down the main street, changes money. Make sure you have cash, as there are no cash dispensers.

**Post office** – *Main post office*, in the main street. Monday-Saturday, 9am-2pm / 5pm-6pm.

**Medical service** – *Doctor*, Dr Ioánnis Georgantákis, in the main street, on the left as you go down, near the harbour, ☎ (0832) 91 056. Surgery open even on Sunday, 10am-2pm / 5pm-9pm.

## WHERE TO STAY

As in Mátala, you are spoilt for choice. However, Agía Galíni takes advantage of its position and is relatively expensive. And don't hope to negotiate prices in summer – everywhere is full.

### Campsite (around €12)

**Agía Galíni Camping**, 2km before you arrive in the village (clearly signposted on the left), ☎ (0832) 91 384 / 141, Fax (0832) 91 239 – 25 caravan pitches. ⌇ Several shady spots but overall there's not much shelter from the sun. The rather rundown washrooms are being renovated. There's a restaurant and a supermarket – convenient when you consider the distance to the village – and a brand new swimming pool.

### Under €30

**Manos Rooms**, in the main street on the right, a short distance before the harbour, ☎ (0832) 91 394 – 12rm. ⌇ Just a simple house run with an iron hand by an amiable female proprietor. Its great advantage is its proximity to the centre, at a modest price. Clean spacious rooms (9 with private bathrooms). Ask for one at the back where you are guaranteed peace and quiet. Don't hesitate to negotiate prices at the beginning or the end of the season, when there are fewer tourists.

### Between €30 and €45

**Astir Hotel**, first street on the right as you arrive in Agía Galíni, before going down into the village, ☎ and Fax (0832) 91 174 – 15rm. ⌇ A recent establishment, hence its position a little away from the centre. Run by a charming young owner who is also a good businesswoman. She is planning to add another floor, and takes many bookings in advance for groups sent by tour operators. Standard, comfortable rooms, with good views of the sea.

**Hotel Rea**, at the bottom of the main street, on the right, 50m beyond Manos Rooms, ☎ (0832) 91 390, Fax (0832) 91 196 – 18rm. ⌇ Be warned, only Greek and German spoken. Nothing outstanding about the hotel, but everything is impeccable. A good place, in a good position and not too expensive. You should reserve. The hotel is very popular, even at the end of the season.

**Hotel Petra**, at the entrance to the village, on a bend to the right as you go down, ☎ (0832) 91 155, Fax (0832) 91 175 – 30rm. ⌇ ⤫ ✗ ⅽⅽ This comfortable family hotel has an attractive, easily recognisable façade covered in climbing plants. Friendly professional service. The rooms are well looked after (some have large baths), all in white and furnished simply. Prices similar to those at Hotel Rea, for slightly more comfort, but the place is a little far from the harbour.

**Rooms Stelios**, at the top of the village, on the left as you go down, ☎ (0832) 91 383 Fax (0832) 91 030 – 19rm. ⌇ ⤫ ⅽⅽ Definitely a business venture. Unfortunately, the welcome is not always up to par. But the rates are reasonable for the good-quality comfort provided. Clean rooms. Good views of the sea below.

### Over €45

**Fevro Hotel**, on the right as you go down, on the last bend before the harbour, ☎ (0832) 91 275, Fax (0832) 91 475 – 50rm. This large hotel, run by two young sisters, clings to the hillside and – by some miracle – does not disfigure the landscape. The spotless, spacious rooms are attractively decorated and have superb tiled bathrooms. The place is something of a luxury, but why not give yourself a treat.

**El Greco Hotel**, at the top of the village, on the left as you go down, ☎ (0832) 91 187, Fax (0832) 91 491 – 25rm. ⌇ ▤ Everything here is new and exudes freshness. You are welcomed by two friendly young women who make you feel that they love their job. Impeccable rooms with mini-bars and lovely tiled bathrooms in perfect condition. Small balconies with a view of the sea.

## EATING OUT

The pedestrian streets above the harbour are full of tourist restaurants that are fairly good (especially for the setting), and all offer similar value. However, it is difficult to find anything, other than the usual Greek specialities and international dishes.

### Around €7.50

**The Corner**, on a corner as its name suggests, in the street on the left before you reach the harbour. ☕ The service is cordial and straightforward, and the prices much lower than in the adjoining restaurants, which offer similar quality. Obviously, the decor is not as good (neon lights), but if you sit out on the terrace, there's no difference. All in all, a good place to fall back on if you are on a budget. Generous helpings of grilled meat, with *tzatzíki* and raw vegetables, washed down with a decent local white wine.

*Around €15*

**King Minos**, in the main street, just beyond the last bend on the right before you reach the harbour. 🍴 The restaurant serves mixed grill specialities with lamb chops, meatballs, etc, making a pleasant change from moussaká.

**Madame Ordans**, near the harbour. A smart restaurant in an elegant setting, with very tasty original cooking. One of the best places to eat in the area.

### HAVING A DRINK

Even though everything stays open late in the evening (in the daytime people are at the beach or on excursions in the surrounding area), you won't party much at Agía Galíni. The atmosphere is more geared towards families. You'll find one or two bars in the streets above the harbour where you can have a drink in the evening before going back to your hotel, but that's it.

### OTHER THINGS TO DO

Every day, boats take people out on cruises in **Messará Bay**, to caves, isolated beaches or on fishing trips. Departure at 10.30am, return trip at 5pm. Barbecue included. If the weather is good, you can go as far as Paximádia Island. Enquire at the harbour.

**Beach** – To the left of the harbour as you look out to sea, behind the rocks. Pleasant, clean, but packed in summer.

### SHOPPING GUIDE

**Supermarket**, in the main street, as you go down, 100m from the Flavros Hotel.

There are several souvenir shops in the village, including one specialising in **articles made of olive wood**, which are quite attractive. In the main street, on the left before you reach the harbour.

## Making the most of Sfakiá

### COMING AND GOING

**By bus** – The **bus station** is at the entrance to the village, on the main square, to the right of the post office. 4 services a day to Haniá, Réthimnon, Herakleion and Plakías, at 7am, 11am, 5.30pm and 7.30pm.

**By boat** – 4 boats a day to Loutró and Agía Rouméli, at 10.30am, 12.30pm, 4.45pm and 7pm.
5 ferries a week to Gávdos Island (only in summer).

### ADDRESS BOOK

**Bank / Currency exchange** – There are no banks, but you will find 3 or 4 shops that change money in the main street and by the harbour.

**Post office / Telephone** – **Main post office**, at the entrance to the village. Monday-Friday, 7.30am-2pm. There's a telephone booth just beside it.

### WHERE TO STAY

*Under €30*

**Hotel Stavris**, at the end of the street behind the seafront, ☎ (0825) 91 220 / 201, Fax (0825) 91 152 – 34rm. 🍴 Two houses built to accommodate the many hikers who come here in the summer. Very simple and plain, but comfortable. 3 larger rooms have kitchenettes. The enterprising owner also has apartments to let in Frangokástello close by. Breakfast at the bar.

Crete

**Pension Sofia**, in the street behind the seafront, ☎ (0825) 91 259 / 265 – 14rm. ⌂ Rather antiquated... The blue and purple paint tries in vain to cheer up the rooms that are a little too small and rather dismal. Half of them have private showers. Not much in the way of hot water. No breakfast.

**Lefka Ori**, on the waterfront, ☎ (0825) 91 209, Fax (0825) 91 350 – 10rm. ⌂ ✗ Standard, comfortable rooms above the restaurant. 3 have kitchens, 8 balconies.

*Between €30 and €45*

**Xenia Hotel**, right at the end of the seafront, ☎ (0825) 91 490 / 202, Fax (0825) 91 491 – 11rm. ⌂ ✗ A very attractive place that makes a little more effort than the others with passing tourists. Spacious reception area with pleasant decor (fine furniture, exposed beams). Large cool rooms with blue doors and imitation marble flooring. All have fridges and balconies. Breakfast is served at the snack bar adjoining the hotel, looking onto the sea. Everything considered, the rates are fairly reasonable.

**Alkion Hotel**, on the seafront, ☎ (0825) 91 180 / 279, Fax (0825) 91 330 – 15rm. ⌂ ✗ Run by a large, rather gruff owner who keeps an eye on the staff... with good results: not only does the restaurant serve the best food in the village, but the rooms upstairs are impeccable: spotless, with new bedding, marble flooring and mostly a view of the sea.

**Hotel Samariás and Livicon**, on the seafront beside the Alkion Hotel, ☎ (0825) 91 211 / 223, Fax (0825) 91 222 – 25rm. ⌂ ✗ The same type of place as the one above but a little more expensive. Large, clean, attractive rooms with white furniture and flagstone flooring.

**EATING OUT**

All the restaurants are in a row along the waterfront. The further you go, the more tourist-oriented they become. So choose the more intimate first ones.

*Around €15*

**Alkion** ⌂ Here at last is a restaurant that offers a change from the usual tourist fare. You are given really good Greek food with several local dishes, and a very friendly welcome especially when there are not too many people. The waiters take the time to explain exactly what the dishes presented on the counter contain. The choice is difficult because everything is so appetising. Try tender lamb in aubergines, with melted cheese and olives cooked in oil, washed down with *Kourtaki*, the local wine.

**OTHER THINGS TO DO**

**Boat trips – Captain Giannis**, in the harbour, ☎ (0825) 91 261. His boat takes people out on trips for a day or half a day to nearby bays: Loutró, Agía Rouméli, etc.

**Walking –** There's a path between Sfakiá and Frangokástello, through the Imbros Gorge. Enquire at the village.

**Beaches –** The village beach with sun beds and umbrellas is behind the rocks that close off the seafront. Accessible by path. However, you will have no problem finding other beaches nearby with far fewer people.

Making the most of Sfakiá

# HANIÁ ★★★
## (CANEA)
Capital of the district of Haniá – 142km from Herakleion
Michelin map 980 fold 37 – Map of the island pages 358-359 – Pop 85 000

### Not to be missed
A walk in the old town.
The Venetian harbour.
The church-museum of Ágios Frangíscos.

### And remember...
Stay in Haniá for 3 days, making it your base for touring the area
and exploring the Samariá Gorge (see page 428).

Barely do you reach the outskirts of Haniá when you get a big surprise, thinking that you have come to the wrong place: a hectic, noisy, industrial town. When you arrive by car, you immediately have to deal with the pollution and noise of the truly infernal traffic. By bus, you have the same impression: far from being an advertisement for the town, the stifling terminal makes you feel dizzy and you just want to get out and head for the harbour, hoping to find a more welcoming spot.

Then you have a second surprise – pleasant this time: you discover an immensely attractive town with Venetian façades, an Ottoman mosque and a quiet harbour. Then you may feel that you never want to leave. However, you'll find that you return to modern Haniá – even if it is just to mingle in the market or wander around Platía 1866, the working-class heart of town – and you will realise that one cannot exist without the other.

Haniá, on the waterfront

### The first capital of Crete
Haniá Bay has been inhabited since the Neolithic Period, and during the Minoan Period saw the flourishing of the huge palace complex of **Kydonia**, the most powerful city state in western Crete. The town proved to be a fierce rival to Knossós and Gortyn, especially in the 2C BC. It kept its name, prospering for more than two thousand years until the end of the first Byzantine Period in the early 9C, when it was probably destroyed by the **Arabs**. The many finds from excavations carried out in the **Kastéli** district between 1965 and 1970 bear witness to an eventful past; they include fragments of Minoan frescoes, tablets of Linear B script, a Hellenic mosaic and Roman statues. However, during the second Byzantine Period, Kydonia lost its influence, shrinking gradually to the size of a village. It wasn't until the arrival of the **Venetians** in 1252 that it began to look like the place we see today. Renamed **Canea**, the city was redesigned in the Italian manner and adorned with beautiful buildings, while Kastéli hill was surrounded by fortifications. Between 1336 and 1356, it was taken over by palaces, dignitaries' mansions and churches,

## The Battle of Crete

In May 1941, the Canea area was the scene of the heaviest fighting of the Battle of Crete. Driven from the mainland, some 40 000 British, Australian and New Zealand soldiers as well as many Greeks and Cypriots stood ready to save the island from the Germans. On 20 May, the enemy launched Operation Mercury, focusing on towns along the north-west coast, including Réthimnon, Soúda and Herakleion. Resistance was fierce, backed up by the courage of the inhabitants and losses among the German parachute troops were severe. But in the end the British had to sound the retreat and those who did not die in action fled to Egypt. Now occupied, Crete suffered heavy reprisals. Among the worst-hit places was Haniá, one of the main centres of resistance. Terrible damage was done by bombing, the effects of which can still be seen throughout the town, in the roofless houses with beams burnt to a cinder.

and distinct working-class districts began to develop.

200 years later, the Italian engineer **Michele Sanmicheli** was called upon to reconsider plans for protecting the town, which had just been subjected to humiliating attacks by the pirate **Barbarossa**. But like the rest of the island, Canea fell into the hands of the **Turks** in 1645, succumbing after a siege that lasted nearly two months. Now masters of the town, the Turks began restoring the ramparts, but in the end abandoned the stones to the inhabitants, who collected them for new buildings, only leaving meagre remains for posterity.

In 1851, the Turks set up the Cretan headquarters for their Ottoman administration in Canea. The town kept its status as capital of Crete well beyond the declaration of independence and the date on which Crete became part of the Hellenic State. It was not until 1971 that Herakleion took over as capital.

L. Hapsis/ON LOCATION

# Tour of the town
*Allow two full days*

You'll never tire of wandering through the streets of old Haniá from early in the morning when the town wakes up and a thousand little sounds of daily life escape through the windows, through the afternoon when everyone has a siesta, to dusk when the golden light falls on the façades of the old Venetian and Ottoman houses.

## The Venetian harbour★★
It is from this superb crescent-shaped quayside that the old districts of Haniá radiate. The harbour, the town's main source of pride, has been laid out as a wide promenade lined with bars and restaurants. The slightly excessive care taken over the renovation – immaculately laid paving, old-style soft lighting, and the fact that fishermen have been asked to move their boats to the eastern part of the harbour – makes the place feel a little artificial. But in spite of this it is still charming, and the noble Venetian façades are always a pleasure to look at (even if the restaurant frontages too often hide their elegant staircases).

Opposite, at the end of the jetty that closes off the harbour, the **lighthouse** gives a final touch to the picture. It was built in the 16C by the Venetians, and modified in the mid-18C by the **Egyptians**, who made it look like a minaret.

*On the north-west tip of the harbour is the Topanas district, your starting-point for a stroll through the old town.*

## The Topanas District★★★
On the way, you can visit the **Naval Museum of Crete**, laid out within the old walls of **Fort Firkas** (*at the end of the harbour, on the corner of Odós Agélou. 10am-2pm from 1 November to 31 March, 10am-4pm from 1 April to 31 October; entrance fee, student reductions*). The Venetian bastion built in 1629 had the privilege of seeing the first Greek flag hoisted on Cretan soil on 1 December 1913, during the official ceremony when the island became part of the Hellenic State. The museum relates the naval history of the island from Antiquity to the present day through a fine collection of **model ships**. For enthusiasts of great naval battles... otherwise take Odós Agélou and head back into the old town.

The district occupies the whole of the western part of the harbour south of the fort and takes its name from the cannons (*topia* in Turkish) that the Turks installed in the **San Salvatore Bastion** (Gritti) designed by the engineer Sanmicheli (in part still standing). Topanas, the aristocratic stronghold of the town, was also home to the main consulates of the Great Powers, and at the end of Turkish domination was inhabited by rich Christian families. Today, the district is peppered with charming little hotels that live side by side with working-class houses. Take the time to lose yourself among the alleyways leading from the harbour. You will see some outstanding **Venetian mansions★**, spared by the ravages of time and the Battle of Crete, and some old **Ottoman houses**, full of melancholy charm with their upper floors made of wood.

*Make your way eastwards along Odós Zambelíou, which runs parallel to the harbour promenade, to Platía Venizélou.*

## The Hevraïkí District★
Wedged between the buildings in the heart of the old Jewish quarter (which is now only so in name) is the Venetian church of **Ágios Frangíscos★**, a majestic basilica built by the Franciscans in the 14C. It was carefully restored in 1963 and now houses a fine **Archaeological Museum★★** (*Odós Halídon 30. Tuesday-Sunday 8am-7pm, Monday 12.30pm-7pm; entrance fee; allow about 20min*). Superbly set off by the solemn atmosphere in the three aisles, each object with its accompanying explana-

F. Guiziou/HEMISPHERES

A taste of Venice or the Orient: the discreet charm of old Haniá

tions seems to have been restored, its soul intact. Most of the items, including painted stone sarcophagi, coins and everyday utensils, come from excavations in **Kydonia** on **Kastéli** hill.

On the right beyond the entrance, you can go into the well-tree'd **gardens**★ around the church, the only place where you can admire the outside of the building. Note also, at the end and to the right, an attractive octagonal **Turkish fountain**.

On leaving the museum, go up the street a few paces to the **Cathedral**, which is dedicated to the Virgin Mary, St Nicholas and the Three Martyrs (the boys the saint is believed to have restored to life). A little disappointing, it was built in 1857, then ravaged by fire before being renovated in the late 19C.

More interesting is the **Catholic church** opposite with its attractive pink interior. Not far away is the **Museum of Cretan Folklore**★ (*9am-3pm / 6pm-9pm; closed Sunday; entrance fee*), where you can see lovely **embroideries** dating from the 18C and 19C, as well as reconstructions of scenes from daily life on Crete.

*By continuing up Odós Halídon, you gradually move into the modern town. Odós Skridlóf or "Leather Street" on the left is full of stalls selling all kinds of leather goods. Unless you want to change your sandals, the street offers little of interest other than to lead you towards the town's main market.*

### Around the covered market★★

The market was built in the early 20C and opened in 1913 during the major festivities the capital put on to celebrate Crete's union with Greece. You will see all kinds of foodstuffs in the vast cruciform hall, including fish, seafood, meat, local delicatessen products, cheese, spices and cakes. The activity reaches its height in the late morning. Different smells waft over you, especially those emanating from the little restaurants lining the passageways.

*On leaving the market, go for a breath of fresh air beneath the trees in the public gardens.*

Make your way back to **Platía Elefthéríou Venizélou** near the harbour, and walk along the quayside towards the **Janissaries' Mosque** – the oldest in Crete (1645) – whose white dome looks out across the harbour to the lighthouse.

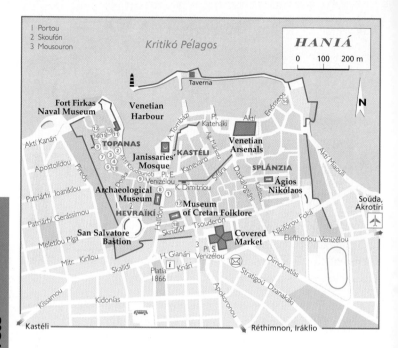

1 Portou
2 Skoufón
3 Mousouron

*Kritikó Pélagos*

**HANIÁ**

0    100    200 m

Taverna

**Fort Firkas Naval Museum**

**Venetian Harbour**

Aktí Kanári

Apostolídou

Pireós

Patriárhi Ioaníkíou

Patriárhi Gerássimou

Meletíou Píga

Mitr. Kiríllou

Kíssamou

Kidonías

**Kastéli**

TOPANAS

**Janissaries' Mosque**

Doúka

Arholeóndoú

Pl. E. Venizélou

**Archaeological Museum**

HEVRAÍKÍ

Halídon

Skalídi

Platía 1866

Knári

**San Salvatore Bastion**

**KASTÉLI**

Kanevaro

K. Dimitríou

A. Tombázi

Pl. Katehakí

Ag. Márkou

Sífaka

**Venetian Arsenals**

Dáskalogiánni

**SPLÁNZIA**

**Ágios Nikólaos**

Aktí

Enósseos

Aktí Miaoúli

Soúda,
Akrotíri

**Museum of Cretan Folklore**

Tsouderón

Skridlóf

3  Pl. S. Venizélou

H. Gianári

Nikifórou Foká

Eleftheríou Venizélou

Dimokratías

Stratigoú Dzanakáki

Apokorónou

**Covered Market**

N

Kastéli

Réthimnon, Iráklio

Just behind it rises **Kastéli**\* hill, the site of ancient **Kydonia** where the Venetians first chose to settle in 1252. The oldest district in the town was heavily damaged during the Second World War but is nevertheless full of charm with its scattered ruins dating from every period in history. As you wander through the streets, you will come across the ruins mixed together in an unusual architectural jumble, lending the district a strange melancholy atmosphere.

### The Splánzia District\*

Lastly, by continuing eastwards, you come to the most enclosed part of the harbour, a working area where the quayside is lined with the impressive arches of the **Venetian arsenals**, built between 1526 and 1599. Of the 17 that once stood in a row, only seven remain, some still used for navigational purposes, others for exhibitions.

On the way, you can take a look at the 14C **Church of Ágios Nikólaos**, which is interestingly flanked by a campanile... as well as by a minaret, added by the Turks.

## COMING AND GOING

**By air** – The airport is about fifteen kilometres from the town on the Akrotíri Peninsula. There's a shuttle bus connecting it with Haniá. In summer, plenty of charter flights come in from the main towns in Europe. During the rest of the year, there are several daily flights from Athens (travelling time: 45min). One flight a week to Thessaloníki (75min).

**By bus** – The **bus station** is in the southern part of the town, behind the Samariás Hotel. For Réthimnon and Herakleion: 20 buses a day, between 5.30am and 8.30pm. For Omalós (Samariá Gorge): 4 buses a day, between 6.15am and 4.30pm. Paleohóra: 5 buses a day, between 7.30am and 5pm. Sfakiá: 3 buses a day, between 8.30am and 2pm. Soúgia: one bus a day at 1.30pm. Kíssamos (Kastéli): 13 buses a day, between 6am and 8.30pm. Also plenty of buses to villages and tourist attractions in the area. **Enquiries**, ☎ (0821) 93 306.

**By boat** – Haniá only has services to and from Piraeus. The ferries arrive at the port in Soúda, 7km east of the town (bus connections). Timetables are subject to change (enquire at one of the travel agencies in town), but you can count on at least one departure a day, at 8.30pm. In summer, there are two boats a day, one in the morning and one in the evening.
**Harbourmaster's office**, ☎ (0821) 89 240.

## FINDING YOUR WAY

Take the tourist harbour as your main landmark. All around it are the districts of the old town. Leading off from Platía Eleftheríou Venizélou at the eastern end of the harbour is Odós Halídon, the main thoroughfare, which links it to Platía 1866, the centre of the modern town.

## GETTING AROUND

**By car** – The traffic is impossible, and in any case you cannot get to the old centre by car. The best thing to do is to park as soon as you arrive, either around

Platía 1866 (fee), or behind the San Salvatore Bastion, which closes off the harbour district to the west.

**By taxi** – The main taxi rank is on Platía 1866, opposite Odós Kriári. There's another rank on Platía M Krítis, not far from the market.

**By rental car, motorcycle or scooter** – Most of the agencies are grouped together in Odós Halídon and Odós S Dzanakáki, south of the market. **Reisen**, Odós Halídon 75, ☎ (0821) 54 100 / 56 249, Fax (0821) 56 249. **Avis**, Odós S Dzanakáki 58, ☎ (0821) 50 510. **Interrent**, Odós S Dzanakáki 62b, ☎ (0821) 60 571.

## ADDRESS BOOK

**Tourist information** – Odós Kriári 40. Monday-Friday, 7.30am-3pm; closed weekends. No currency exchange.

**Bank / Currency exchange** – Nearly all the travel agents in Odós Halídon change money. You will also find plenty of banks with cash dispensers in the modern town, particularly north of Platía 1866 and near the market. Open Monday to Friday, 8.30am-1.30pm. On the other hand, there's nothing in the old town.

**Alpha Credit Bank**, Odós Halídon 106, ☎ (0821) 73 703. **National Bank**, Platía Eleftheríou Venizélou, ☎ (0821) 28 800.

**Post office / Telephone** – **Main post office**, Odós S Dzanakáki, on the left as you come from the market. Monday-Friday, 7.30am-8pm. Open on Saturday morning. Currency exchange: 7.30am-1.30pm.

**Internet** – **Vranas**, on the corner of Odós Agíon Déka and Odós Kalinákou Sarpáki. A quiet café with 6 brand new machines. €3 an hour.
There's another Internet café in the harbour, on your right when you face inland. The card you buy is for 2hr, which is not very economical if you only have two e-mails to send, and especially considering that the terminals (only two) are often out of order.

**Medical service – *Hospital***, Odós Dragoúmi 6-8, ☎ (0821) 27 000. In case of *emergency*, dial 166.

**Airline companies – *Olympic Airways***, Odós S Dzanakáki 88, ☎ (0821) 58 005 / 57 701 to 703. **Air Greece**, Odós Kidonías 164. *Cronus Airlines*, Odós Eleftheríou Venizélou. *Aegean*, at the airport.

**Other – *Laundry***, Odós Karaolí Dimitríou. Monday-Saturday, 9am-2.30pm / 6pm-9pm.
***Tourist police***, ☎ (0821) 94 477.

## WHERE TO STAY

You are spoilt for choice (which does not mean you shouldn't book in summer), and what a choice! Most of the hotels and guesthouses in the old town are in old Venetian or Turkish houses that are extremely charming, even the most modest. Obviously, the level of comfort has been somewhat affected by age (creaking floorboards, non-existent soundproofing).

*Under €30*

*Kydonia*, Odós Halídon 20, ☎ (0821) 74 650 / 64 926 – 6rm. ⌘ To find it, look for the Chinese restaurant sign in the alleyway on the right as you come from the harbour. This attractive old house is very clean and has a cool, restful atmosphere (plants, light-grey walls, a few paintings), and a slightly rickety feel, which only adds to the charm. Large spotless rooms, some with mezzanines (no 3, for instance). Excellent "charm for money" value.

**Hotel Manos**, Odós Zambelíou 24, ☎ (0821) 94 156 – 11rm. ⌘ 🍴 🏊 A cool, pleasant house, decorated very simply in blue and white, creating a seaside atmosphere. Parquet floors in some rooms, otherwise tiles or linoleum (to be avoided). Fridges in rooms and, if you're lucky, a view of the sea, for a very reasonable price indeed.

**Maria Rooms**, Odós Agélou 4, adjoining the Meltemi Hotel (see below), ☎ (0821) 71 052, Fax (0821) 76 922 – 8rm. ⌘ 🍴 A rather dilapidated old house, but full of charm, with a family atmosphere. The whole family is involved in running the place: the daughter, who is at reception in the late after-

noon, the grandmother who does her embroidery by the entrance until late into the night, and Maria, who takes over in the morning. The rooms are not exactly stylish but they are spacious. Grey paint, parquet floors. 5 of the rooms have private bathrooms. There's a telephone that takes cards. Convenient access for cars.

**Stella Rooms**, Odós Agélou 10, ☎ (0821) 73 756 / 87 662 / 71 200 – 8rm. ⌘ A good place with affordable rates. Enquire at the craft shop just next door. Very clean medium-size rooms with new bathrooms. 4 rooms have little balconies giving onto the street. Simple and pleasant.

**Irini Pension**, Odós Theotokopoúlou 9, ☎ (0821) 93 909 – 3rm. ⌘ Three floors with three large rooms that feel more like small apartments: kitchenette, fridge, and an enormous bedroom. Non-existent decor, with furniture salvaged from all over the place. But there are not that many low-price places in Haniá.

**Altis Pension**, Odós Halídon 5, ☎ (0821) 28 688 – 6rm. ⌘ Just to get a good night's sleep. The building and rooms have no special character, but the place is clean, inexpensive and in a very good position.

**Xenia**, Odós Betólo 41, ☎ (0821) 54 298 – 22rm. ⌘ Enquire at the shop on the ground floor. Fairly reasonable rooms. The place could be a backup for a night if your budget is running low and everywhere else is full.

*Between €30 and €45*

*Pension Eva*, on the corner of Odós Theofánous and Odós Zambelíou, ☎ and Fax (0821) 76 706 – 4rm. ⌘ 📋 🆑 The entrance is through a jeweller's shop on the ground floor, where you will be welcomed by a friendly young woman. Upstairs, the 4 enormous peaceful rooms are attractively decorated with old furnishings in a rather pre-1940s style.

**Thereza Rooms**, Odós Agélou 8, ☎ and Fax (0821) 92 798 – 8rm. ⌘ 🏊 Another long narrow old house, very near the harbour. Bright, carefully decorated old rooms with high ceilings (attractive black and white photos), although they seem a bit dusty. Pity about the carpeting that covers the parquet

*Crete*

floors. Small roof terrace where you can prepare breakfast. Best to book in summer.

**Meltemi**, Odós Agélou 2, very near the harbour, ☎ (0821) 92 802 – 10rm. 📶 Rather expensive, explained by the fact that the hotel is just a few metres from the harbour promenade. An old house with clean plain rooms, without any special charm. Breakfast is served on the ground floor terrace giving onto the harbour.

**Vranas Studios**, on the corner of Odós Agíon Déka and Odós Kalinákou Sarpáki, ☎ and Fax (0821) 58 618 / 43 788 – 12rm. 📶 🗎 🄿 🆃🅅 Clean, functional, fully renovated studios in the heart of the old town. Kitchenettes, large bathtubs, simple beige decor with wood. The friendly owner also runs the Internet café on the ground floor.

*Between €45 and €75*

**Palazzo Hotel**, Odós Theotokopoúlou 54, ☎ (0821) 93 227, Fax (0821) 93 229 – 11rm. 📶 🗎 🄿 🆃🅅 🆑🅲 You are given a warm welcome at this hotel with its wonderful old façade and antique furnishings. All the rooms are spacious (with safes and fridges) and are named after Greek gods and goddesses (Athena, Apollo, etc), so much more elegant than plain numbers. Six of the rooms have balconies and some have baths. For breakfast, you go up to the roof garden where there is a lovely view of the town and the sea. Closed between 1 November and 31 March.

**El Greco**, Odós Theotokopoúlou 47-49, ☎ (0821) 94 030 / 90 432 / 91 818, Fax (0821) 91 829, hotel@elgreco.gr – 26rm. 📶 🗎 🄿 🆃🅅 🆑🅲 This old house has been entirely renovated in a very contemporary style, with standard luxury and very professional reception and service. The rooms are not very large but they are clean with pleasant decor (beech-wood furniture, soft colours). Every one has a balcony. You can have a relaxing drink on the superb terrace, listening to the sounds floating up from the old town.

**Porto Del Colombo**, on the corner of Odós Theofánous and Odós Moshón, ☎ and Fax (0821) 70 945 – 10rm. 📶 🗎 🄿 🆃🅅 🆑🅲 One of the oldest Turkish houses in town. The place is enormous, and probably served as a prison, hence its many small windows. However, don't be put off: the rooms may be a little dark but are nonetheless charming. Ask for no 1 or no 2, which have very high ceilings (the equivalent of two floors). Open in winter.

**Contessa**, Odós Theofánous 15, ☎ and Fax (0821) 98 565 / 6 – 6rm. 📶 🍽 🄿 🆑🅲 An establishment very much in the style of the one above, but less austere. No doubt the larger windows have something to do with it. Refined traditional Cretan decor. Very friendly, unaffected welcome. You feel like staying on to enjoy the snug atmosphere. The rooms are nearly all different. Some very popular ones reserved year after year by regular visitors are positively delightful, with their old-fashioned ceiling paintings. Can be noisy on account of a café nearby. Closed in winter.

*Over €75*

**Casa Delfino Suites**, Odós Theofánous 9, ☎ (0821) 87 400 / 93 098, Fax (0821) 96 500, e-mail : casadel@cha.forthnet.gr 📶 🗎 🄿 🆃🅅 🆑🅲 Quite simply magnificent! Enormous elegant luxury suites (perhaps a little cold), for what may seem like extravagance but in the end is a reasonable price. Marble bathrooms, large mezzanines, sumptuous floor tiles... and those are just the standard suites. If you want more and your budget stretches that far, there's always the spacious royal suite on 4 different levels. Wood, copper finishings, immaculate bathrooms – this old Venetian mansion has been superbly renovated. Book.

**Amphora**, at no 20 in the second passageway off Odós Theotokopoúlou, on the right as you go towards the harbour, ☎ and Fax (0821) 93 224 / 226 – 20rm. 📶 🍽 🄿 🆃🅅 ✕ 🆑🅲 The large building dates from the 14C. Old-fashioned luxury, with decor that mixes the Cretan rustic style with the neo-Classical, a rather questionable combination. But the service is professional and the rooms very comfortable. Some rooms give directly onto the harbour, hence the price. However, choose one at the back if you prefer less noise. Good buffet breakfast with everything homemade. Open all year.

**Porto Veneziano Hotel**, in the eastern part of the harbour, beyond the Venetian arsenals, ☎ (0821) 27 100, Fax (0821) 27 105, portoven @otenet.gr – 57rm. 🍴 📺 📶 📺 CC A recent though quite attractive building. Modern, slightly flashy decor, for those who like contemporary luxury. Everything is spotless. Large standard rooms with balconies (some with a view of the sea). The exceptional position of the hotel partly justifies the price. There's a pleasant garden behind, where you have breakfast.

### EATING OUT

Avoid the overcrowded restaurants on the harbour promenade and head for the ones in the alleyways just behind. These are not really less tourist oriented but the atmosphere is more intimate. Some superb ones are open to the sky, installed in the ruins of houses destroyed during the Battle of Crete. However, though the setting is pleasant, the food is rarely up to par. For good fresh fish, walk to the end of the harbour, beyond the Venetian arsenals.

*Around €7.50*

**Restaurant Vasilis**, Aktí Enósseos, in the eastern part of the harbour. 🍴 A good unpretentious place where local people come at lunch and supper to tackle healthy portions of fish, sea urchin soup and traditional dishes, washed down with the local white wine.

**Apostolis**, Aktí Enósseos 3. 🍴 Same type as the one above. If you stay a day or two in Haniá, you'll find you come back to this part of town away from the tourist bustle, to enjoy these simple places and their harbour atmosphere.

*Around €15*

**Taverna Fortezza**, in the fortress in the middle of the jetty that closes off the harbour. 🍴 Better for its exceptional location than its food (classic fare, perhaps a little too international). If you are too tired to walk all the way round, you can go across the water in the restaurant's own water-taxi.

🍴 **Taverna Dinos**, Porto Veneziano, beyond the Venetian arsenals, ☎ (0821) 41 865 / 57 448. 🍴 Another very good place in the quieter part of the harbour.

Perfect service (the waiter worked in London). Aubergine salads, fresh sea urchins and grilled fish... delicious in every way.

**Les Vagabonds**, Odós Portou 48, ☎ (0821) 91 089. 🍴 The owner ran a restaurant in the Latin Quarter in Paris for a long time before returning to his native land. He has given his Haniá restaurant a little Parisian touch, with prints of jazz scenes, music to match, and a cellar atmosphere, even on the terrace, which gives onto a pleasant alleyway. As for the menu, no great surprises, unfortunately. Closed in winter.

**Taverna Semiramis**, passageway to the right of Odós Skoufón, as you come from the harbour, ☎ (0821) 98 650. 🍴 A small taverna frequented mainly by tourists, but tourists who've gone slightly off the beaten track. Live traditional music (a bit much after a while), but diligent service and good traditional fare. Try the succulent Cretan lamb slow-cooked in olive oil and white wine.

**Hippopotamus**, Aktí Enósseos 2n Par (second small street to the right beyond the Venetian arsenals). 🍴 Don't expect to be served a piece of steak weighing 350g, rather, some typically Mexican dishes including burritos, enchiladas, tacos and guacamole. For a change from *souvláki*. Not cheap, unfortunately.

*Between €15 and €30*

🍴 **Tholos Restaurant**, Odós Agíon Déka 36, just opposite the Vranas Internet café, ☎ (0821) 46 725. 🍴 CC Installed on two floors in the ruins of an old Venetian mansion. A smart restaurant that deserves its good reputation: the service is perfect, the tables are attractive and the menu carefully chosen, brilliantly mixing traditional Cretan dishes with house creations. Ask for a table on the upper floor, and enjoy the Oriental-style music that adds a final touch to the atmosphere.

**Monasteri**, Aktí Tombázi 12, ☎ (0821) 55 527 / 51 250. 🍴 CC Perhaps the only really good place in the liveliest part of the harbour, though obviously the prices reflect this. The waiters go a bit over the top with their "catering school" style, but you'll get along fine if you joke with them. Try "the nun's mistake", grilled pork with a variety of fried vegetables (tomatoes, courgettes, aubergines).

### Having a drink

The trendiest bars are in the harbour area, on your right when you face inland, attracting local young people in the evening. It won't take you long to notice this if you are trying to sleep in the area.

**Bars – Santé** (Internet café), in the harbour, on the corner of Odós Agélou. Noisy post-modern atmosphere, with wild trip hop and rock music. Far from restful, but if you want a lively evening, this is the place to come.

**Konstantinoypolis**, Odós Episkópou Dorothéou, behind the Cathedral. Traditional Greek café décor: two terraces upstairs and a lot of old furniture creating a cosy atmosphere that you can enjoy for hours with a coffee. The parrot that greets you on the ground floor only speaks Greek.

**Ariadne**, Aktí Tombázi 2, behind the mosque. It is amazing that they have managed to create an intimate atmosphere in such a gigantic bar. The place is almost like a night-club with subdued lighting, a bit of colour here and there, but the music is fairly quiet jazz or rock. Dozens of teak chairs and tables spill out onto the quayside.

**Cafés – Café Ouzerí Limani**, Aktí Tombázi, 30m before you reach the mosque. A traditional old café, which is nonetheless quite chic, where Greek couples come at dusk to enjoy the harbour air and a drink. As in all ouzo bars, ouzo is less expensive than elsewhere and is served with little snacks of olives, tomatoes, feta and prawns.

**Tearoom – Kronos**, Odós Mousouron 23, behind the market. A smart place in the heart of the shopping area. A little expensive, but the cakes are delicious.

### Other things to do

**Excursions** – All the travel agents in town offer excursions to the **Samariá Gorge**. Daily departures (three times a week at the end of the summer) at 7am, return trip at 7pm. There are obviously boat trips too: cruises to **Gramvoússa Island** (off the far west of the island, departure at 8am, return trip at 5pm) as well as more local excursions.

**Zorbas Travel**, Plataniás, ☎ (0821) 60 445 / 38 068, Fax (0821) 60 945, zorbas@otenet.gr, www.zorbastravel.gr Car rental, hotel bookings, currency exchange, excursions, etc. A small travel agent with very obliging staff who sort out all your problems without overcharging.

**Evangelos Boat**, in the harbour. This glass-bottomed boat takes people to Théodori Island west of Haniá. The trip lasts about 3hr. On the way, you will see the wreck of a German plane that sank to a depth of 6m during the Second World War. Departures at 10.30am and 2pm.

**Scuba diving – Blue Adventure Diving**, Aktí Enósseos, ☎ (0821) 28 678 / 74 860, Fax (0821) 40 608. As this is the only diving club in town, the rates are quite high and the service is sometimes a bit casual. But you will find it hard to leave Haniá without going to look at the underwater caves close by. As for the amphorae, they are indeed old, but were put there by the Ministry of Tourism for the benefit of divers! PADI / CMAS. You can get your Open Water PADI certificate in 4 days.

**Beach** – To the west, just outside the old town. Lovely big beach with facilities, but very popular in summer. However, you will be pushed to find a deserted beach on this part of the coast.

### Shopping guide

**Market** – You will find all sorts of local goods here, including oil, confectionery, spices, liqueurs and cheese.

**Bookshop** – A large bookshop and stationer's at the top of Odós Halídon, on the right, a short distance before you reach Platía 1866: literature, travel guides and maps.

**Leather – Odós Skridlóf**, known as "Leather Street" is the centre for leather goods. But be warned, not all the items are local and in the end you can find more original things in Réthimnon.

# Around Haniá★
## The Samariá Gorge★★★
District of Haniá – Michelin map 980 fold 37 – Map of the island pages 358-359

**Not to be missed**
The Agía Triáda and Gouvernéto monasteries on the Akrotíri Peninsula.
A walk through the Samariá Gorge.

**And remember...**
Relax on one of the Akrotíri beaches.

Pleasant as it is to wander through the old districts in Haniá, you should also take the time to explore its surrounding area. Between the Akrotíri Peninsula in the north, with its fine beaches, to the majestic Samariá Gorge in the south, one of the loveliest places to walk in Greece, there is much to see, and you can alternate between idleness, recreational activities and cultural trips as the feeling takes you.

## The Samariá Gorge★★★

*39km from Haniá. A full day's walk. To get there, either use the bus or join an organised tour. The bus from Haniá runs through the mountains and onto the Omalós Plateau to the village of the same name. 4km further on, a kiosk on the Xylóskalo pass marks the entrance to the gorge. Open daily from 1 May to 15 October (sometimes later, weather permitting, enquire), 6am-4pm. Fee. Ticket to be handed in at the mouth of the gorge. As the place is a National Park, it is forbidden to smoke, build fires, spend the night, hunt, pick anything, make any excessive noise, drink alcohol or, obviously, leave any litter. Wear stout shoes, and bring water (even though there are fountains en route) and a sun hat. Lastly, though the walk is not really strenuous, and it is downhill when approached from the Omalós end – allow 6 to 7hr – it requires a basic level of physical fitness.*

Looking as if it had been hacked out by a giant, a gap 18km long opens into the side of the White Mountains or **Lefká Óri**. The deep and narrow ravine, hollowed out by water over thousands of years, follows a winding course to the sea. The stream at the bottom, swollen in winter and almost dry in summer, runs between perpendicular rock walls before leaving the mountain and flowing into the sea.

The walk through the gorge – the longest in Europe – will certainly be one of the highlights of your trip to Crete. The site has been a National Park since 1966, and consists of a succession of breathtaking landscapes, with sheer rock faces so grandiose you feel Lilliputian. There's a rich plant life in the gorge as well as the famous **kri-kri**, a local wild goat that resembles a chamois. Perhaps the most dramatic moment of the descent is going through what are known as the Iron Gates. In summer, you will unfortunately not be alone, and will have to wait your turn patiently.

### Journey to the depths of the earth

From **Xylóskalo** you go down a wooden staircase and then a very steep path. For the first two kilometres, you enjoy the refreshing coolness of pines, and a superb mountain **panorama★★**, without realising that you have come down 1 000m from the top. Then you go past the **Chapel of Ágios Nikólaos**, in a green setting with springs nearby, and the **Church of Ágios Geórgios**, before reaching the bottom of the canyon where the stream flows.

The Lefká Óri or White Mountains, a land of gorges (here, the Arádena Gorge)

Crete

P. Frilet/HEMISPHERES

Halfway through the gorge, you come to the abandoned hamlet of **Samariás★**. The romantic ruins are of the houses that once belonged to woodcutters and their families, who had to leave when the gorge became a National Park. It is the 14C **Byzantine church★** in the village that gave its name to the gorge: *Ossa María*, Blessed Mary. Inside are several **frescoes** in the Byzantine Renaissance style.

Once you've forded the stream (*stepping stones*), follow the path to see the finest sight on the trip, the **Iron Gates★★★**. This is an impressively narrow passage where the sides, as smooth as walls, almost touch. Barely 3m apart, they rise skywards together to a height of 300m. Imperceptibly, the passage shrinks to a narrow corridor where the air becomes cooler. You cannot resist looking up repeatedly to see the band of blue sky above the fault.

Then the passage widens out again, into sudden brilliant sunshine. The riverbed dotted with oleanders spreads out into a peaceful valley that meets the sea at the little village of **Agía Rouméli★**. There you have a choice between a drink on one of the many taverna terraces, or a well-deserved swim from the pebble **beach**.

*There's a boat from Agía Rouméli to Sfakiá, where you can catch a bus. If you are on an organised tour, your transport back to Haniá will be taken care of.*

## On the Akrotíri Peninsula★

*A half-day trip from Haniá (not counting time on the beach). Head east out of town, following directions to the airport.*

From Haniá, you first climb **Profítis Ilías** hill, which affords a panoramic **view★** of the town and **Soúda Bay**, before reaching the Akrotíri Peninsula. The arid peninsula, a largely military zone (*many of the roads are closed to civilians*) nonetheless makes for a pleasant trip, dotted with traditional villages and lined with quiet **beaches** where families from Haniá come to relax on Sunday.

*Once through the hamlets of Korakíes and Aroní, take a narrow secondary road on the left and head north.*

■ **Agía Triáda Monastery★★** – *16km from Haniá, near the village of Koumarés. Open daily, 8am-2pm / 5pm-7pm. Entrance fee. Allow 20min.* You feel very small climbing the 19 steps of the large **staircase** leading to the monastery, and then going through the imposing **porch★** at the entrance, which is topped by a twin bell-tower and flanked by columns. You get the same impression standing in front of the **church★★** in the middle of the courtyard. Rising above the olive trees and cypresses, the church with its cruciform plan, **dome** and **campanile** with three bells proudly displays its pink façade in the Italian Renaissance style. Above the porch, an inscription in Greek dating from 1631 mentions that the church was founded by two brothers, Venetian noblemen, who converted to the Orthodox faith. The church has two chapels, one devoted to the Virgin Mary, the other to St John the Evangelist. The interior is unencumbered and soberly set off by a beautiful midnight blue **dome★** dotted with golden stars.

A small **museum** at the entrance to the monastery, on the left, has a collection of **Byzantine icons** and liturgical objects.

*On leaving Agía Triáda, continue along the road northwards for about 4km.*

■ **Moní Gouvernéto★** – *Open daily, 8am-12.30pm / 4.30pm-7.30pm. Entrance fee. Allow 20min.* This enormous monastery springs up in the middle of nowhere, looking more like a fortress than a peaceful holy place, with towers reinforcing each corner of the high enclosure. The imposing church of **Kyría ton Angélon** (Our Lady of the Angels) stands in the courtyard, its three small domes rising above a sober façade of pink stone. Built in the 16C by the Venetians, the church, like Agía Triáda, shows a strong Italian influence; it has a carved frieze and engaged

Crete

columns, on the bases of which are amusing **mascarons**, grotesque figures making faces. All around, in an atmosphere bathed in silence and serenity, are the 50 monks' **cells**, still partly occupied.

## West of Haniá
*From Haniá, take the coast road west*

For the first 20 kilometres, the whole coast is given over to mass tourism. Hotels, luxury holiday complexes, travel agents, car rental places and supermarkets have been built alongside the beaches that up to a few years ago were still the pride of the region. You have to go as far as the village of **Málerme** for a change of scenery, with the countryside becoming greener and wilder the further west you go towards the mountains.

■ Soon after **Rapanianá**, you can make a detour to see **Goniá Monastery** (*open daily, 8am-12.30pm / 4pm-7pm; free*), built by the Venetians beside the sea in the early 17C. There's an interesting collection of **icons**, several of which date from the 14C. The terrace behind the church affords a beautiful **panorama★** of the gulf.

■ **Kíssamos** (Kastéli) – Nestling in the curve of a gulf closed off by two **peninsulas**, the market town of Kíssamos owes its attraction to its simplicity and authenticity. Every year, a handful of holidaymakers put off by the major tourist centres comes here to melt into the quiet Cretan way of life for a few days. After a quick walk round the shopping streets, settle down on the main square for lunch.

The **harbour** is two kilometres west of the town. Boats take people from here on trips through the gulf to **Gramvoússa Island**, off the western end of the peninsula (*departure 9am, return trip 5.30pm, ☎ (0822) 24 344*).

Continuing south-west, you enter a forgotten land, where the **landscape★★** is a wild expanse of black rocks and spindly thornbushes. Dominated by mountains, the coast is thrashed by a roaring sea constantly subjected to violent winds.

## Heading south: Paleohóra★
*A 75min drive, about 70km south-west of Haniá, on the Libyan Sea.*
*In Málerme, bear left towards Paleohóra (signposted).*

The small town on a tiny south-facing peninsula well off the tourist trail is a paradise for people who just want to take it easy. Not only does it have one of the most beautiful beaches on the island, but it has also managed to keep its peaceful atmosphere, which you will appreciate when strolling along the white alleyways with their low houses and well-kept gardens.

In the east, the **harbour** has several tavernas looking onto a pleasant pebble beach. In the west, the vast **beach★★** of white sand fringed with tamarisks is the pride of the town and a delight to visitors. On the tip of the peninsula, a 13C **Venetian citadel** still watches over the town.

The main street crosses the town from north to south, only coming alive in the evening when cars are banned, and catering to a mix of locals and hungry holidaymakers. Shops open their metal shutters to display souvenirs and beachwear, bars and tavernas lay tables outdoors, and the strollers gradually move in.

**Crete**

## COMING AND GOING

**By bus** – The bus station is at the entrance to the town, on the left of the main street. For Haniá: 3 buses a day: 7.30am, 12noon and 3.30pm. For Omalós (Samariá Gorge): one bus a day at 6am.

**By boat** – For Soúgia and Agía Rouméli, daily departure at 9.30am, return trip at 4.45pm.

For Agía Rouméli, Loutró and Sfakiá, daily departure at 5pm, return trip at 10.30am.

For Gávdos Island, departure on Monday and Friday at 8.30am, return trip at 2.30pm.

## GETTING AROUND

**By car** – You can leave your car at the car park near the harbour, in the vicinity of the citadel.

**By rental vehicle** – Cars, motorcycles and scooters for hire in the main street, opposite the tourist office.

**By taxi** – There's a taxi rank right at the end of the main street, on the left when you face the church that closes off the street.

## ADDRESS BOOK

**Tourist information** – In the main street, on the right as you head south. Closed on Tuesday.

**Bank / Currency exchange** – There's a cash dispenser in the main street, on the right as you head south. Some shops also change money.

**Post office – Main post office**, in a mobile home in the street that runs alongside the sand beach. Monday to Friday, 7.30am-2pm.

**Internet** – Right at the top of the main street, opposite the taxi rank. Very expensive.

**Medical service – Dentist**, in a street running parallel to the beach, just behind the main street, ☎ (0823) 41 229.

**Laundry** – In the main street, 20m from the tourist office, on the other side of the street. 8am-2pm and 5pm-10pm.

## WHERE TO STAY

Paleohóra is full of guesthouses and rooms to let, which are all very similar: plain, clean and functional. Most of the bars and restaurants have rooms upstairs for the many holidaymakers that come here in summer. A lot of rooms have balconies, and kitchenettes suitable for families. You should book in summer.

*Under €30*

**Níkos Boubalís Rooms for Rent**, in the harbour, just before the Galaxy restaurant, ☎ (0823) 41 112 – 9rm. 🍴 Standard rooms, some of which have a view of the sea.

**Christos Koulierís**, in the harbour, beyond the supermarket, ☎ (0823) 41 359 – 5rm. 🍴 📺 Same type of place as the one above. Clean, quiet, comfortable rooms all in white.

**Manolis Restaurant**, in the harbour, a short way beyond Christos Koulieris, ☎ (0823) 41 521 – 12rm. 🍴 Balconies and fridges in all the rooms, 3 of which look onto the sea. Some have kitchenettes.

**Snack Bar Votsalo**, in the harbour, just before you get to the pebble beach, ☎ (0823) 41 526 – 12rm. 🍴 Simple rooms with the same level of comfort as the other places lining the harbour. All the rooms have balconies, some with a view of the sea. Friendly welcome.

**Eftihía**, in a little street on the harbour side of the main street, ☎ (0823) 41 432, Fax (0823) 41 765 – 10rm. 🍴 📺 Enormous clean rooms, all with kitchenettes. The owners do not speak English.

**Dionissos**, in the main street, on the right as you head south, ☎ (0823) 41 243 – 4rm. 🍴 This is a restaurant that serves Cretan specialities and has rooms to let upstairs. A little noisy in the evening.

**Hotel Oasis**, between the main street and the beach, ☎ (0823) 41 328 – 17rm. 🍴 Most of the rooms have a balcony and a view of the sea. 10 have kitchenettes. In view of the growing demand in summer, the hotel is planning to expand, adding 6 extra rooms and apartments.

### Between €30 and €45

**Hotel Rea**, in a street at right angles to the main street, heading towards the beach, ☎ (0823) 41 307 / 421, Fax (0823) 41 605 – 14rm. 🛏 ⅋ Hidden behind a wall of greenery, this snug little hotel is barely more expensive than the ones above. The kindly lady owner, who will greet you in English, is helped by her daughter in summer. The quiet rooms have attractive, simple decor. They all have balconies and safes. For a good start to the day, you are served a generous breakfast with freshly squeezed orange juice, on the terrace among the climbing plants.

### Over €45

**Palm Beach Hotel**, opposite the beach, on the south side, ☎ (0823) 41 512 / 556, Fax (0823) 41 578 – 54rm. 🛏 🖿 ⅋ ✕ 🆑 A modern hotel built in 1991, the only one of its kind in Paleohóra. Very professional, spotless and with no unpleasant surprises, but a little soulless.

### EATING OUT

Every evening, the main street is transformed into a gigantic open-air bar and restaurant, with tables and chairs spilling out onto the carriageway. This is where the locals prefer to come. The places on the waterfront, beside the beach or the harbour are almost exclusively intended for tourists.

### Around €7.50

**Acropolis**, right at the end of the main street, just before the taxi rank, on the other side of the street. 🥘 Cretans, holidaymakers, the young and the not-so-young all come here. The place is overrun as soon as night falls. And with reason: from a simple ouzo and delicious meze to the meal itself, everything is good, fresh and served in generous portions. Don't look at the menu but go straight inside and see what's on offer, like fresh fish, marinated peppers, and grilled octopus. Cheerful atmosphere guaranteed.

### Around €15

**Avegis Restaurant**, on the beach side of the street parallel to the main street, ☎ (0823) 41 228. 🥘 The restaurant is laid out among ruins open to the sky and has a rather magical atmosphere. In the front, the walls and some of the beams that held the roof remain. At the back, where there's no roof at all, large fig trees grow freely. Excellent traditional Cretan dishes.

**The Third Eye**, in a little street that starts from the beach, on the south side, ☎ (0823) 41 234. This rather sophisticated restaurant with a hippie-flavoured atmosphere serves good vegetarian food, barbecue specialities and dishes from such places as Indonesia and Nepal. A bit overrated, but it makes a change from Greek cuisine.

**Dionissos**, see the "Where to stay" section.

### OTHER THINGS TO DO

**Beach –** This is obviously the town's main attraction. It is superb and impeccably clean (proudly flying the blue flag, the emblem for the cleanest beaches in Greece).

**Excursions –** Some of the travel agencies near the harbour organise boat trips that last a day or half a day.

**E-motion Travel**, ☎ and Fax (0823) 41 755. The firm's two boats (carrying 100 or 135 passengers) take people out to Elafoníssi Island to enjoy the crystal-clear water and pink sandy beaches. This is also the opportunity to see dolphins, which are numerous in this part of Crete. On several occasions, passengers have even seen whales. Daily departure at 10am.

### SHOPPING GUIDE

**Supermarket**, facing the beach, and another on the waterfront on the harbour side.

There are several souvenir shops in town, but nothing really outstanding to buy.

# RÉTHIMNON★★
## (RÉTHIMNO)
Capital of the district of Réthimno – 71km from Haniá and from Herakleion
Michelin map 980 fold 38 – Map of the island pages 358-359 – Pop 23 000

**Not to be missed**
A stroll through the old town and around the Venetian harbour.
The panorama from the fortress.
Arkádi Monastery in the environs.
The refreshing atmosphere of the village of Fódele and the beach nearby.

**And remember...**
Come to Réthimnon on a Thursday to enjoy its open-air market.

Réthimnon, the third largest town in Crete after Herakleion and Haniá, is at first sight an odd mixture, with little appeal. The coast has been devoured by unsightly, disorderly tourist developments, with concrete invading the whole area around the town. Réthimnon itself has a hectic pace set by a hurried middle class that seems little inclined to take care of its cultural heritage. On the other hand, the old districts in the heart of the city, not so carefully maintained and therefore more authentic than those in Haniá, provide a few hours of worthwhile strolling. Here are old Venetian and Turkish houses, sometimes hastily restored but very charming,

The old harbour, Réthimnon

mosques and churches, peaceful alleyways echoing the low hum of the modern city, as well as the Venetian harbour dominated by its fortress, one of the rare districts spared the noise and pollution that suffocates the town. Lastly, Venizélou beach stretches eastwards from the town centre as far as the eye can see. Lined with bars, restaurants and shops, it attracts crowds from March to October who come to enjoy the ever restless sea.

## A Venetian and Ottoman city

The town that rose from the Minoan ashes of modest **Rithymna** experienced its first golden age under the Mycenaeans. Minting its own coins, it was one of the most powerful centres in Crete. However, it seems to have quickly lost influence, shrinking to a modest market town (albeit free) during the Roman and Byzantine Periods. The arrival of the Venetians on the island breathed new life into the city. They were interested in its position halfway between Herakleion and Canea, and made it the third largest administrative centre on Crete, a status it has kept to this day. Venetian domination changed the face of Réthimnon, with elegant edifices going up all over the town over a period of three centuries. Sumptuous mansions, a loggia (later a mosque and now a library), fountains (including the Rimóndi fountain), all make the town a gem of Italian architecture.

In the late 16C, the town was attacked by the pirate **Barbarossa**, who plundered and burnt it. The extent of the damage led the Venetians to strengthen the city's protective system by building ramparts and a fortress.

But all in vain: in 1645, after a short siege of 23 days during which the population took refuge in the fortress, Réthimnon succumbed to the Turkish attacks. The Ottoman regime then plunged the town into its darkest years, with reprisals, revolts, executions

of insurgents, and massive forced conversions to Islam. The only consolation was that the Turks left behind some wonderful examples of Ottoman architecture, particularly mosques, but also the mansions with wooden loggias which give the town all its charm. Lastly, during the Second World War, the inhabitants were to distinguish themselves by their bravery and resistance.

**A stone for the ramparts**
If you come across old George on one of his bicycle trips through the town, he may tell you how, in the 16C, to be allowed into the city visitors had to arrive at the gates of Réthimnon carrying a stone. As there was a lack of building material in the area, this tax "in kind" contributed in a modest way to the building of the ramparts that were so cruelly lacking during attacks by Barbarossa.

## Tour of the town
*The main interest of Réthimnon lies in the heart of its old town.*
*Allow one day.*

Take as your departure point the never ending **Leofóros Eleftheríou Venizélou**, which runs all the way along the beach. It is rather disappointing with its incessant traffic and the cafés, restaurants, tourist shops and hotels making it look like any old seafront thoroughfare. Just behind, however, on the south-west side of the town, the pedestrian alleyways in the **old quarter** are packed with interest. Go to the north-west end of the avenue and let your instinct guide you.

On the way, don't miss the **Venetian harbour★★**. Tucked away, it appears at the last moment, as you go round a building. The delightful pastel façades of the surrounding houses are reflected in the water on which float brightly coloured fishing craft, the whole forming a picturesque townscape. It would be nice to imagine the place a little more deserted, without the restaurant tables encumbering the entire waterfront.

*From the Venetian harbour, take Odós Neárhou into the old quarter. First, cross over Odós Arkadíou, a shopping street, and keep going straight ahead.*

### The old town★★
You first reach the **Loggia**, built by the Venetians in the late 16C before being converted into a mosque by the Turks. Admittedly less majestic than the one in Herakleion, it is nonetheless elegant with its **three arches**, beneath which the town's notables used to relax and discuss business.
However, you may like to spend more time on a square nearby, where, flanked by a strange shop built beneath a pointed arch, the **Rimóndi fountain★★** stands. This jewel of the Italian Renaissance was built in 1629 by Avise Rimondi, an administrator in Réthimnon, as part of his plan to embellish the town (in the middle, you can see the family **coat of arms**). Four slender Corinthian columns stand between the three lion heads spouting water.
By forking left, you come to the **Nerandzés Mosque** (*open daily until 8pm; free*), which was built within the walls of the former church of Santa Maria a short time after the arrival of the Turks, who gave it a gigantic **minaret★** (superb **viewpoint★★**). Today it is used as a concert hall.
Take the time to stroll through the alleyways round about where you will see some outstanding doorways and façades belonging to **Venetian houses★★**. As you continue south, the streets become increasingly working-class, with all sorts of stalls run by traders and craftspeople selling, among other things, embroidery and ironwork. One fascinating place only sells goat bells. Lastly, at the south end of **Odós Ethnikís Andistásseos**, you come to **Porta Guora**, a former Venetian gateway with rusticated stonework (16C) marking the boundary with the modern town.
On leaving the old quarter, try crossing noisy **Leofóros Igouménou Gavriíl** to cool off in the **public gardens**, an immense green space laid out in the former **Turkish cemetery**. There's a pleasant refreshment stall at the point where the eight lanes radiate out like a star.

## The Venetian fortress (Fortétza)*

*At the north-western end of the town. Once past the Venetian harbour, make your way to Platía Plastíra and then take Odós Makedonías, which leads to the fortress entrance. 8am-6.30pm; closed Monday. Entrance fee.* Following the contours of **Paleókastro Hill**, the fortress ramparts form a crown of stone with a diameter of 1 300m, dominating the entire town and surrounding area (splendid **panorama**** over the sea). Built between 1573 and 1580, the fortress sheltered all the inhabitants during the siege of Réthimnon before the town was taken by the Turks in 1645. It once consisted of a military hospital, munitions store-rooms, a barracks and various public buildings, but little remains. Today the walls with their four powerful **bastions** only enclose a desolate space where the sun beats down and a few palms and pines attempt to provide a little shade. The one thing that remains, in the middle, is a **mosque**, a former church dedicated to St Nicholas, with a refreshingly cool interior.

## Venetian houses Cretan style

Old Réthimnon has some jewels of Venetian architecture dating from the Renaissance to the 18C, which were modified to suit the Cretan style. Beneath their roof terraces, grand mansions abandoned the moulding that once adorned their façades for smoother walls, concentrating the decoration on the portal. Delicate reliefs, floral friezes or figurative motifs adorned the pediment or the abutments. As for houses, they were topped by a wide tiled roof, and wood was used to adorn the first floor with an elegant closed-in balcony, or "xóstego", a sort of suspended kiosk carved with geometric patterns. The Ottomans found this to be an attractive adaptation of their corbelled first floor, and often took on the "xóstego" for their own houses, thus preserving the architectural harmony of the streets.

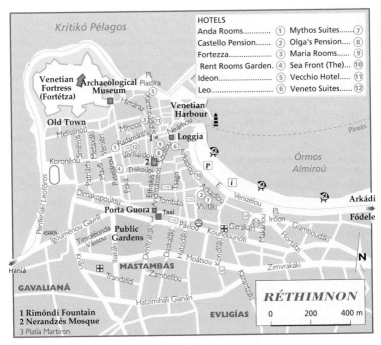

HOTELS

| | | | |
|---|---|---|---|
| Anda Rooms | ① | Mythos Suites | ⑦ |
| Castello Pension | ② | Olga's Pension | ⑧ |
| Fortezza | ③ | Maria Rooms | ⑨ |
| Rent Rooms Garden | ④ | Sea Front (The) | ⑩ |
| Ideon | ⑤ | Vecchio Hotel | ⑪ |
| Leo | ⑥ | Veneto Suites | ⑫ |

*Kritikó Pélagos*

Venetian Fortress (Fortétza)
Archaeological Museum
Pl. Plastíra
Old Town
Venetian Harbour
Loggia
*Órmos Almiroú*
Porta Guora
Taxi
Public Gardens
MASTAMBÁS
GAVALIANÁ
Haniá
Pireás
Arkádi
Fódele
Zimvrakáki
EVLIGÍAS

1 Rimóndi Fountain
2 Nerandzés Mosque
3 Platía Martíron

**RÉTHIMNON**

0    200    400 m

N

As you leave through the citadel's only gateway, take a look at the **Archaeological Museum** installed in the former prison, opposite the access ramp *(the entrance is on the stairs that go down to the street, 8am-6.30pm; closed Monday; entrance fee)*. The museum contains most of the finds from the town and its environs, bearing witness to Rithymna's prestigious Minoan past; there are ceramics, seals, jewellery and statuettes of goddesses. There is also a large **numismatic collection**, covering different eras.

**The Arkádi tragedy**

After the Greek uprising against the Turks in 1821, soldiers and Cretan civilian fighters (men and women) took refuge with the monks at Arkádi, to form with them one of the most active strongholds of resistance on the island. Secret meetings were held there regularly, and Arkádi managed to stand up to the occupying forces for more than 40 years. On 7 November 1866, the Turks decided to put an end to the situation, and with 15 000 men laid siege to the monastery. It took them two days. Preferring to die rather than surrender, the defenders set fire to the powder magazine, blowing up a great many of their own people but also all the Turks who had managed to enter the monastery. An ossuary outside the walls pays tribute to this heroic sacrifice, and every year on 8 November the whole of Greece remembers the martyrs of Arkádi.

## East of Réthimnon
*Tour of 90km, including detours (1 day)*

The Herakleion road runs straight along the coast. Leave it to make some interesting incursions inland.

■ **Arkádi Monastery★★** — *4km after leaving Réthimnon, you come to the village of Adelianos Kámbos. A sign on the right indicates the way to the monastery. You take the tarmac road for 18km. 8.30am-7pm; entrance fee.* Like many Cretan monasteries, Arkádi has surprisingly high outer walls that make it look like a fortress. While historians more or less agree that it dates from the 5C, they hesitate about the identity of its founder. Some say it was the Byzantine emperor **Arkádios**, others a simple monk with the same name. Be that as it may, the monastery was one of the most prosperous religious centres on the island from the 16C to the 18C. Centred around its **church** (1587), the 300 or so monks who lived there (far fewer today) made a comfortable income from copying manuscripts, working in the gold-thread embroidery workshop and making vestments. However, the monastery is mainly known on account of the tragic episode of the **Arkádi holocaust**, described by **Níkos Kazantzákis** in his book *Freedom or Death*, which made it a symbol of Cretan resistance to the Turks.

Perhaps it is the memory of these dark hours that lends Arkádi an austere, rather sad atmosphere, which even the almost Baroque architecture of the **church★**, with its outstanding **Renaissance façade★** set off by columns, cannot dissipate.

Just beyond the entrance, at the top of the staircase on the right, a **museum** displays some interesting **paintings on wood**, as well as a rich collection of liturgical objects.

■ On leaving Arkádi, you can take one of the mountain roads to see **Melidóni Cave** *(north-easterly direction, 8am-8pm; entrance fee)*, another stronghold of Cretan resistance. Three hundred and seventy people taking refuge in the cave were asphyxiated when the Turks made a fire at the entrance. The **Heroes' Room** in the middle of the cave contains the bones of the victims.

■ On a lighter note, you can then move on to **Balí** village and its harbour, to enjoy the beach and tavernas.

*From Balí, continue along the main coast road for about 25km.*

■ **Fódele★** — You shouldn't miss this delightful detour at the end of your trip. Nestling in a cool valley, this charming village could almost come from somewhere in the north of Europe, were it not for the **orange trees** bending under the weight of their fruit. The attractive 13C **Church of the Panagía\*** contains fragments of **Byzantine frescoes\***. You can walk along a dirt track through the countryside to **El Greco's house** (*9am-5pm; entrance fee*) where, it is said, the famous painter was born (though historians do not necessarily share this point of view).

Near the village, the fine sandy **beach\*\*** is one of the loveliest on the island.

## Making the most of Réthimnon

### COMING AND GOING

**By bus** – The *bus station* is in the south-western part of the town, near the ring road that runs alongside the seafront. For Herakleion: 21 buses a day, between 6.30am and 9.45pm. Express connections at 9am, 10am and 11am. Haniá: 20 buses a day, between 7am and 10pm, express connections at 12.30pm, 1.30pm and 2.30pm. *Agía Galíni*: departures at 7am, 10.30am, 12.45pm (except Saturday and Sunday) and 2.15pm. *Plakiás*: 5 buses a day, between 6.15am and 5pm. Sfakiá: one bus a day at 9am. Préveli Monastery: 2 buses a day, at 10.30am and 5pm. Arkádi Monastery: 3 buses a day, at 6am (except Saturday and Sunday), 10.30am and 2.30pm. *Enquiries*, ☎ (0831) 22 212.

**By boat** – One boat a day to Piraeus (crossing about 10hr). *Enquiries*, ☎ (0831) 29 221 / 26 876. *Harbourmaster's office*, ☎ (0831) 22 276.

### FINDING YOUR WAY

The old quarter forms a triangle bounded by the fortress in the west, the seafront in the north and Leofóros Pávlou Koudourióti in the south. The shopping street Odós Arkadíou runs parallel to the seafront, crossing the town from east to west.

### GETTING AROUND

**By car** – You will find a car park on the seafront in Leofóros Eleftheríou Venizélou, near the harbour. Leave your car there and explore the town on foot.

**By taxi** – Platía Martíron, near the south entrance to the old town and the public gardens, ☎ (0831) 25 000 / 28 316 / 29 316.

**By rental vehicle** – You will be spoilt for choice on the never-ending Leofóros Eleftheríou Venizélou, alongside the beach.

### ADDRESS BOOK

**Tourist information** – Facing the beach, on Leofóros Eleftheríou Venizélou. 9am-5pm Monday to Friday, 10am-4pm Saturday. Closed Sunday.

**Bank / Currency exchange** – You will find several banks in the modern town, notably along Leofóros Pávlou Koudourióti and around Platía Iróon. Monday-Friday, 8am-1.30pm. *Cash dispensers*, Leofóros Pávlou Koudourióti 98, and on the beach promenade.

**Post office / Telephone** – *Main post office*, in a yellow caravan on the beach, just beside the cash dispenser.

**Internet** – *Café Galero*, near the Rimóndi Fountain. *Netc@fé*, Odós T Veniéri 2-4 (near the beach, behind the Elina Hotel). Video games and Internet access, with colour printers and scanners.

**Medical service** – *Hospital*, in the south-west of the town, Odós Trandalídi, ☎ (0831) 27 814 / 926. *Emergencies*, ☎ 166. *Doctor*: Dr Andrew Papadákis, Odós Gerakári 170, ☎ (0831) 24 654 (surgery) and 25 141 (home number, in case of emergency). Surgery hours 9am-1pm and 6pm-7.30pm.

**Airline company** – *Olympic Airways*, at the eastern end of Leofóros Pávlou Koudourióti, ☎ (0831) 22 257.

**Other** – *Police*, ☎ (0831) 22 289.

**Laundry**, Odós Tombázi, near the Youth Hostel. Monday to Saturday, 8am-2pm / 5pm-8pm.

WHERE TO STAY

You can find every kind of accommodation in Réthimnon, from inexpensive guesthouses to luxury suites, not forgetting standard tourist hotels. Most of the latter – rather dull places – are concentrated along the beach. You can find much better in the town centre.

*Under €30*

**Olga's Pension**, Odós Soulíou 57, ☎ (0831) 28 665 / 53 206, Fax (0831) 29 851 – 15rm. ⚐ ✗ A budget place that is very pleasant and charming. You will be led through a maze of corridors and little courtyards thick with plants to the rooms. Sometimes small but always comfortable, they have attractive tiled bathrooms. Stella's Kitchen on the ground floor provides all sorts of home-made pastries for breakfast.

**Maria Rooms**, Odós Soulíou 22, ☎ (0831) 28 953 – 5rm. In a quiet street in the heart of the old town. The house is modest but very clean and cool, with plants brightening up a long passageway. Basins in rooms but no private bathrooms. Two rooms have 3 beds.

**Leo Hotel**, Odós Vafé 2, ☎ (0831) 26 197 – 11rm. ⚐ Installed in an old Turkish house, with a certain charm and reasonable rates. Dark parquet flooring, carpet on the stairs, plain decor. More of an effort regarding cleanliness would be welcome. Avoid rooms with added bathrooms, as these are prefabricated blocks. Be warned: the district is lively and a little noisy.

**Rent Rooms Garden**, Odós Nikifórou Foká 82, ☎ (0831) 28 586 – 5rm. ✗ Push open the door and go through the paved porch to the old house. With its antiquated atmosphere, its stonework and plants, this feels as if it is from a different era. Pleasant spacious rooms, each with its own outside bathroom.

*Between €30 and €45*

**Castello Pension**, Platía Karaolí Dimitríou 10, very near Odós Arkadíou and the Cathedral, ☎ (0831) 23 570, Fax (0831) 50 281 – 8rm. ⚐ ✗ An Olympian calm reigns in this superb, tastefully restored old house. Simple decor, all in white, a very cool garden with a little fountain, and quiet, impeccable rooms. If possible, ask for no 5: the bathroom is in the old hammam.

**The Sea Front**, Odós Arkadíou 159, ☎ (0831) 51 981 / 24 533, Fax (0831) 51 062 – 10rm. ⚐ ✗ ℰ CC Enquire at the travel agency on the ground floor. In a concrete building dating from the 1970s. Fairly large, very clean rooms with a view of the sea. Big bathrooms. Nothing extraordinary, but the place is comfortable and in a good position.

**Anda Rooms**, Odós Nikifórou Foká 33, ☎ (0831) 23 817 / 479 – 5rm. ⚐ ✗ Very new immaculate rooms with tiles. You are given a charming welcome by the lady owner who speaks English. The district is quiet in the evening.

*Between €45 and €75*

**Vecchio Hotel**, Odós Daliani 4, ☎ (0831) 54 985, Fax (0831) 54 986 – 27rm. ⚐ 🖬 ℰ 🛓 This attractive hotel in an old restored house verges on the luxurious, but at an affordable price. Some of the rooms are in a low, recently constructed building behind the swimming pool. All are very large and decorated in pastel colours.

**Hotel Ideon**, Platía Plastíra 10, ☎ (0831) 28 667 to 9, Fax (0831) 28 670 – 86rm. ⚐ 🖬 ℰ ✗ 🛓 CC A luxury hotel with a neo-Classical decor of old roses and marble. No surprises, nor any great charm. Elderly clientele.

**Hotel Fortezza**, Odós Melissinoú 16, ☎ (0831) 23 828 / 55 551 / 55, Fax (0831) 54 073 – 54rm. A modern hotel with stylish architecture and decor. Baked clay flooring, mezzanine in the reception. All the bathrooms have tubs. Impeccable rooms with every modern comfort. Upmarket package-tour type of place.

*Over €75*

**Mythos Suites Hotel**, Platía Karaolí Dimitríou 12, on the Cathedral square, ☎ (0831) 53 917, Fax (0831) 51 036 – 14rm. ⚐ 🖬 ℰ 🖵 🛓 CC Taste and luxury in suites and cottages of all sizes in the grounds of an old 16C manor house. Lovely renovated rooms that combine modern comfort with old world charm. Brick tiling on the floor, stylish furniture.

**Veneto Suites**, Odós Epimenídou 4, ☎ (0831) 56 634, Fax (0831) 56 635 – 9rm. ¶ 🗊 ✐ 📺 ✕ 🆑 In the heart of the old town. Suites decorated in extremely refined Baroque taste in a 700-year-old house. Wood, old stonework, arches and soft lighting. Very beautiful and very expensive. Somewhat presumptuous reception.

EATING OUT

*Around €7.50*

**Pontios**, Odós Melissinoú 34, near the fortress. ☂ A small terrace where the service is quick and you eat good, simple food. Ideal for a light lunch after going round the fortress. Try the *Paximadi*, a type of pizza with feta.

*Around €15*

**Kokkinos**, Platía Iróon. ☂ The traditional Cretan restaurant par excellence: you will be pushed to find tourists here. No great innovation on the menu, but you are guaranteed quality and a good atmosphere.

**Old Town**, Odós Vernádou 31, ☎ (0831) 26 436. ☂ Very tourist oriented like all the restaurants in the old town, but one of the best. And the food is good.

*Between €15 and €30*

**Veneto**, Odós Epimenídou 4, ☎ (0831) 56 634. In a magnificent setting in a courtyard garden, the restaurant adjoining the Veneto Suites hotel (see the "Where to stay" section) lives up to its reputation. Excellent Cretan and Greek fare, a little more creative than the average, and perfect service.

🍽 **Avli**, Odós Arkadíou. Superb decor, excellent service and refined, varied dishes: the best place to eat in town.

**HAVING A DRINK**

**Bars – Ouzerí**, Odós Vernádou. ☂ This café hidden behind a tobacco kiosk on the mosque corner holds its own in spite of the invasion of restaurants churning out food for tourists. Worth a look just for the contrast it offers. A good place for a drink in the evening to watch the world go by before looking for somewhere to eat.

**252**, just beyond the Venetian harbour, on the bend leading to Platía Plastíra. ☂ A very trendy bar that belts out deafening music for the young of the locality. Very effective decor, half ocean liner, half submarine.

**Café Galero**, on the square with the Rimóndi Fountain. ☂ A very large bar open late at night, where you come to finish off the evening with iced coffee or a margarita. Modern Latino music. Internet access upstairs.

**OTHER THINGS TO DO**

**Walking – The Happy Walker**, Odós Tombázi 56, ☎ and Fax (0831) 52 920. Sunday to Friday, 5pm-8.30pm. A specialised agency that organises daily nature walks that may include visits to villages and places of cultural interest.

**Boat trips – Dolphin Cruises**, in the Venetian harbour, ☎ (0831) 57 666. Excursions lasting 90min, 3hr or a whole day. Sea caves, fishing trips and visits to creeks and fishing villages.

**Scuba diving – Paradise Dive Center**, Leofóros Eleftheríou Venizélou, near the Venetian harbour, ☎ (0831) 26 317 / 53 258. The club, founded by a Frenchman, takes people to the south of the island, near Lefkogia. There are two other clubs outside the town, about ten kilometres east:

**Atlantis**, Grecotel, ☎ (0831) 71 640 / 71 002 / 29 491, Fax (0831) 71 668, atlantis@grecian.net

**Dolphin Diving Center**, Hotel Rethymno Mare-Scaleta, ☎ (0831) 71 703, Fax (0831) 71 734.

**Beach –** The beach is clean, vast and very popular in summer. Be careful when swimming, as the sea can be dangerous.

**SHOPPING GUIDE**

The streets in the old town are full of shops selling all sorts of local **arts and crafts**: leather goods, pottery, spices, honey, etc.

**Market –** A big food market is held in the car park beside the public gardens on Thursday, from early in the morning to 3pm.

**Bookshop –** Books and international newspapers may be found in Odós Petiháki, a small street on the left as you come up from the sea.

*Making the most of Réthimnon*

The painted houses of Pirgí (Chios)

# THE NORTH AEGEAN ISLANDS

Bordering Turkey a string of remarkable islands dot the Anatolian coast. They are both lush and arid, flat and mountainous, and they vacillate between two worlds. The Orient can already be felt; and four centuries of Ottoman rule have certainly left their mark on the villages. You will find stately pastel-coloured houses with wooden balconies hanging over the street in some parts or, in others, old grave markers in white marble, embellished with Persian calligraphy. Or perhaps the ruins of a hammam, re-conquered by a herd of goats...

But, as if to mark the imprint of the Greek soul for one last time, each of these islands exhibits its own character. Particularly **Límnos**, with its flat, dry land, situated a short distance from the Dardanelle Strait that connects with the nearby ruins of mythical Troy. Or indeed its neighbour **Lesbos** which resonates with the poems and songs of Sappho, or unusual **Chios** with its colourful black and white villages, or lastly the ruined altars at the Temple of Hera, bathed in the sunshine of **Sámos**.

And everywhere there are Byzantine churches with their noble red domes, narrow vaulted streets with balconies where vines of sun-ripened tomatoes hang, and blue-windowed kafenía blending the aromas of anise and coffee on the net-covered quays. In places, the countryside even has something of the Cyclades about it, with olive trees reigning over a seemingly barren landscape, where hills have been sculpted into terraces, forming rare circles of shade.

# CHIOS★★
## (HÍOS)

North Aegean – Capital of the district of Híos
8km from the Turkish coast – Michelin map 980 fold 45 – Regional map page 458
842km² – Pop 51 000 – Allow 5 days

**Not to be missed**
The black pebble beaches in Emboriós.
The Néa Moní Monastery, a UNESCO World Heritage Site.

**And remember...**
Chew the local mastic – it's good for your health!
If you're on the island on 15 August, celebrate Assumption with the locals in Pirgí.

The visitor passes from one country to another on Chios, a land of invisible borders. The devilishly tortured landscape adds to this impression. In the arid plains of the south lies the land of mastic, an aromatic resin whose harvest provides the economic livelihood of the villages where the locals lead a simple and pious life. The Kámbos, stronghold of the Genoese, who covered it with magnificent homes surrounded by luxurious orchards in the 15C, lies further north as you near the capital. Beyond, fertile volcanic mountains level out onto an immense plateau covered with red lichens. Finally, in the very northern part of the island, the private homes of rich Greek shipowners line the coast. Many of them are originally from the island and carry on the traditions of their ancestors who were tradesmen and sailors.

## At the crossroads of the seas

As long ago as Antiquity, Chios was a port of call on the trade route between Europe and Asia. This was a time of prosperity for the island, which was admired by its neighbours. Not only was it renowned for its figs, but also for the sophistication of its inhabitants, who were well versed in the arts. Indeed, the island is said to be the birthplace of **Homer** (8C BC) and is where the poet is believed to have written the Iliad and the Odyssey. Reputed throughout Greece, Chios' sculpture school developed the process of **bronze casting** in the 6C BC.

However, this golden age came to an end with the start of the invasions that troubled the entire Aegean Sea. The Persians ravaged Chios in 493 BC and, as it was often raided by pirates, the island regained some stability only with the presence of the Romans. Later, Chios passed into the hands of the Venetians (12C), then the Byzantines, before becoming the centre of a rich Genoese Empire in the

### Homer's stone

Four kilometres north of Chios, at the tip of the harbour of Vrondádos, the coast road passes by a small rocky platform standing on the shore which is known as Daskalópetra, or the "master's rock." Local people like to say that Homer had the habit of climbing them to declaim his works. The doubt remains but what does it matter when you have the picturesque harbour and the clear sea, and a little bit of imagination.

14C. Two centuries of prosperity ensued, thanks to the mastic trade, Genoese cloth and spices. But then the Turks captured the island in 1566.

## The massacres of Chios

In 1822, a wave of independence swept through Greece. A handful of Samiots in exile on Chios encouraged the island to rise up in arms. This revolt caused the Turks to carry out a massacre; of the 140 000 inhabitants on the island, only 1 800 remained. The rest were massacred or enslaved, or they fled to neighbouring islands. The event aroused intense emotion in Europe, inspiring the painter **Delacroix** to create his famous painting "The Massacre of Chios" and **Victor Hugo** to write a bitter poem entitled "The Greek Child." When Greece achieved sovereignty, the still scarred Chios didn't wait: it joined the Greek nation in 1912.

## Chios Town**
*Pop 25 000*

An intangible oriental atmosphere lingers over Chios, a humid city where fishy smells fight it out with the aroma of spices. The **port**\* opens out on the sea, its quays lined with a succession of bars and restaurants, where tourists and the local young crowd laze about.

Just behind, the small alleys unfurl like the arms of an octopus, hiding the **market**\*\* held each morning in the area around Odós Roïdou and Odós Rali. This is the time when the tiny stalls display freshly slaughtered meat and still quivering eels. Continuing along Odós Roïdou, you'll arrive in the merchants' district, which stretches to the foot of the popular **Platía Vounaki,** surrounded by cafés and ouzo bars.

*As you leave Odós Roïdou, go left at the south-east corner of the square.*

An ancient **mosque** dating from the 19C, whose dome merges harmoniously with the other rooftops, shelters the **Byzantine Museum**\* *(Open daily except Monday until 1pm; entrance fee. Only the entrance hall and the courtyard are open to the public).* Beautiful **icons**\* on wood adorn the interior, whilst the courtyard is cluttered with Byzantine, Genoese, Turkish and Jewish **steles.**

Outside, cars, trucks from the market and countless mopeds drive at full speed around the square. In the centre lie the **municipal gardens,** a vast enclave of greenery with paths lined with palm trees. Peacocks and pelicans live in an **aviary** *(in the middle of the north side).*

*Take the road between the town hall and the OTE office on the opposite side of the gardens from the museum at the north-east corner.*

### The Kástro District**

The thick wall of the kástro stands as a reminder of the island's turbulent past. A Genoese citadel in the 14C, it was taken by the Ottomans in the 16C and, during the insurrection in 1822, the Turks imprisoned 70 leading Greek citizens here before hanging them. The main entrance leads to a small peaceful square. In front of the door, the **palatáki**\* ("small palace") has a lovely **Genoese façade**\* covered with numerous windows. The interior houses a small collection of **Byzantine icons** *(same hours as the museum).*

Next door, the **Fort Museum** *(open daily except Monday until 1pm; entrance fee)* will be of interest to those who enjoy artillery, particularly the French **cannons.** At the same place *(in the corner on the left when leaving the museum),* a gate surrounds the **Turkish cemetery**\*, spiked with tapering steles. Next to it stands a small **mosque.**

*From here, go along Odós Georgiou Frouriou. A few metres away is the* **Ottoman Palace**\*\* *(closed to the public) dating from the 16C. With its faded blue façade and its wooden loggias, it encompasses an entire block of houses. The rear, ochre-coloured part of the building was the domain of the sultan's wives.*

Odós Frouriou runs through the entire kástro, which unveils its charms little by little. Here you'll find a small church, there a garden with lemon trees. At the very end, a bare hill offers superb **panoramic views**\*\* of the turquoise-coloured sea, the red and grey rooftops of the kástro and those of the **ancient Turkish baths**: four earthen-coloured domes pierced with small holes and overrun by reeds.

*If you have time, go back to the harbour and go along the quayside to the southern part of the town. Turn right into Odós Koraï about halfway along.*

**Chios**

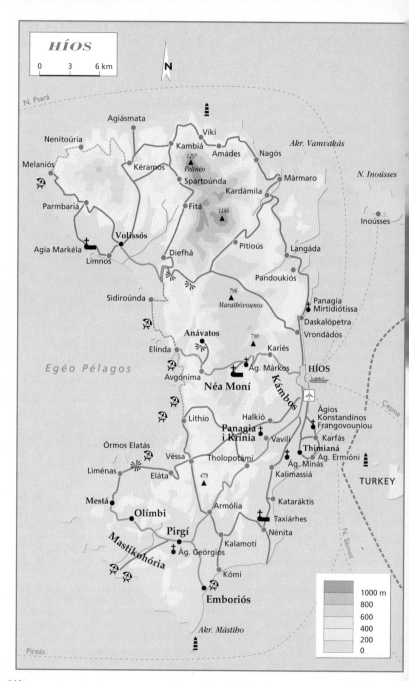

# HÍOS

0    3    6 km

N

N. Psará

Agiásmata
Víki
Nenitoúria
Kambiá
Amádes
Nagós
*Akr. Vamvakás*
Melaniós
Kéramos
1297
*Pelinéo*
Spartoúnda
Mármaro
N. Inoússes
Parmbariá
Kardámila
Fitá
1186
Langáda
Inoússes
Volissós
Diefhá
Pitioús
Agía Markéla
Limnos
Pandoukiós
Sidiroúnda
796
*Marathóvounos*
Panagía
Mirtidiótissa
Daskalópetra
Vrondádos
Anávatos
790
Kariés
Elínda
*Egéo Pélagos*
Avgónima
Ag. Márkos
HÍOS
Néa Moní
*Kámbos*
Lithío
Halkió
Ágios
Konstandínos
Frangovouníou
Karfás
Panagia
i Krinia
Vavíli
Thimianá
Órmos Elatás
Véssa
Tholopotámi
Ag. Ermióni
Liménas
479
Ag. Minás
Eláta
Kalimassiá
TURKEY
Mestá
Kataráktis
Olímbi
Armólia
Taxiárhes
Pirgí
Nénita
*Mastikohória*
Ag. Geórgios
Kalamotí
N. Sámos
Kómi
Emboriós
*Akr. Mástiho*
Pireás

1000 m
800
600
400
200
0

Çeşme

The **Koraïs library**\*\* owes its name to a Greek humanist, Adamántios Koraïs, who died in 1833. This lovely neo-Classical building was built in 1884, restored after the Second World War thanks to the patronage of the Argentis family and now contains Koraïs' works. Take a look at the glass cabinets; **old books**\*\*, such as *The History of Egypt*, printed at the time of Napoleon, can be found next to more recent works. Students and researchers alike occupy the reading tables in this peaceful haven surrounded by varnished wood and leather. The top floor has been transformed into a **museum**\*\* where you can view fine **portraits** of members of the Argentis family.

## The Kámbos\*\*\*

*From the city centre, take Odós Veriti towards the airport.*
*After leaving town, turn right on a lane after a 2km-long wall.*

South of the city you will find the Kámbos, meaning "the plain" in Greek, stretching out over a considerable area. In the 14C, the Genoese chose this area to build their homes, surrounded by luxuriant orange and lemon plantations. Here and there, in the midst of an orchard filled with acidic aromas, you will catch a glimpse of these simple residences whose refinement resides in their harmonious proportions, in the way they open out into the landscape with finely carved balconies, terraces, and elegant steps, and in the blend of **two-toned stonework** from the Thimianá quarries (*10km from Chios*).

### Concrete palaces

In order to build in the Kámbos today, one must reproduce the old Genoese-style architecture. This regulation is imposed by the town of Chios to preserve the harmony of the area. Prior to issuing a building permit, the design of the façade and the number of windows are subject to careful scrutiny. On the other hand, there are no restrictions on the materials used. It is therefore not uncommon to see a strange concrete structure rising from a little lawn (the orchards of yesteryear being long forgotten). Nothing is missing; from the high terrace, to the gracious overhang or climbing vine... except perhaps the rendering, thus leaving the bare concrete exposed in all its glory. So much for planning controls, which have produced blockhouses rather than a new generation of comely villas.

Don't miss one of these homes, the **Salvagos House**\*\*\*, which was purchased by the town to be restored and opened to the public (*at the end of the lane, take Odós Ralli Dim*). Accessible from the road, this noble villa opens onto a courtyard where the wild vegetation has invaded the immense wooden wheel of a **well**. The waters run into an open-air aqueduct before gushing forth into the main basin under the marble columns of the left wing of the building, through the mouths of the charming gargoyles. On the right stand the graceful arches of the stately **master's house**\* which has its own **chapel** (*the door on the far left on the ground floor*), still decorated with fragments of frescoes.

The road continues towards the heart of the Kámbos, a veritable maze of greenery where the high walls of each property frame the narrow country lanes. The monumental **gates**\* – through which the carts filled with oranges, lemons and mandarins must have entered – rival each other in elegance, each displaying the family's coat of arms, sculpted in marble. The ochre and pale yellow stonework mix with the foliage of the trees in the late afternoon sun to create a blend of delightful hues.

## The west coast

*From the centre of town, take Odós Demokratías that runs along*
*the north side of Platía Vounáki.*

A splendid **panoramic view**\*\* of the Bay of Chios and the sea with its icy wind can be enjoyed from the road that runs inland towards the west coast. Then after a long barren plain, wooded hills suddenly appear.

**Chios**

■ **Néa Moní Monastery**\*\*\* — *10km west of Chios. Road sign on the left. Daily, 8am-1pm / 4pm-8pm. Free.* A jewel of Byzantine art dating from the 11C, Néa Moní is beautifully set among pines and cypresses on the side of Mt Provatio. Legend has it that in the 11C, three hermits saw an icon of the Virgin glowing amongst a grove of trees there. Nikétas, John and Joseph immediately constructed a chapel around it and soon afterwards, the Byzantine emperor, Monomachus, ordered the construction of a prestigious monastery. However, a dark future lay ahead: in 1822, the Turks massacred the monks along with the women and children who had sought refuge there (it is a gruesome spectacle to see their bones in the little chapel to the left of the entrance), before setting the church on fire. Many of the mosaics were lost. And to conclude this sinister scenario, in 1881 a violent earthquake caused the church dome to collapse.

Rebuilt in 1900, the dome rises gracefully once again, crowning the **church**\*\*\*, which stands imposingly in the centre of the paved courtyard. Built of pink brick, it has a perfectly balanced octagonal plan. You enter through a passage added to the original structure that connects the church with the bell-tower on the right. Opposite is the exonarthex, decorated, like narthex and katholikón, with magnificent **restored mosaics**\*\*\*, masterpieces of vibrant colour and minuscule particles of gold, the pride and joy of Néa Moní.

A Byzantine jewel set among pines and cypresses, the Néa Moní Monastery (Chios)

The high walls of the monastery also house an **underground cistern**★★ *(on the right when entering the church)*, a **refectory**★★ *(behind the church)* and a handsome neo-Classical **guesthouse**★★. On the way, you may well meet one of the five nuns who still live here.

*Take the main road on the left towards Avgónima.*

■ **Anávatos**★★ *(12km from Néa Moní; follow the signs on the right from Avgónima)*, a village perched on a rocky peak, was deserted by its inhabitants following the Ottoman invasion in 1822. From afar, the **view**★★ of the village is striking, with little houses in soft yellow stone seeming to hang between heaven and earth. There is no noise other than the wind as you climb the steep streets. At the edge of the precipice, a ruined church has kept a fresco in lovely ochre and bluish shades.

*Return to Avgónima and turn right on the road towards the west coast. In Elínda, at the junction with the coast road, go right and head north.*

■ Another picturesque village, **Volissós**★ dates from the time of Homer *(46km from Chios. Note that buses operate only 3 days a week and the schedule changes frequently. Information available at the bus station in Chios)*. After crossing the rugged plains covered with red lichens, you will catch sight of the village's **medieval fortress★**, tumbling down a windswept peak that you must climb on foot via steep paths. At the top, adjoining the remains of a **Genoese fort**, stands a yellow **Byzantine church★** whose red dome is crowned with a gold cross, outlined against the blue sky.

**Chios**

P. de Wilde/HOA QUI

# The south – mastic country***
## (Mastikohóra)

The mastic country encompasses the entire southern part of the island. It is on this enormous plain exposed to the sun that the **lentisk** grows. This small bush yields an aromatic resin when its trunk is cut, which the locals believe to be endowed with numerous virtues (particularly for digestion).

■ At the top of a hill, **Pirgí***\*** (*24km south-west of Chios*) looks rather like a stage set with its grey and white houses, whose geometrical decoration is obtained by a process of scraping called *xista*. In the afternoons, elderly villagers bring their chairs out on their doorsteps to enjoy the fresh air. Some of them try to sell nuggets of mastic to the tourists. In the centre, the large 17C **Church of the Dormition** towers over the enormous main square surrounded by cool arcades.

■ With its honey-coloured houses that melt into the earth and the herds of goats that surround it, **Olímbi\*** (*5km from Pirgí along the same road*) resembles a country market town in central Asia. Here you'll discover lovely stone houses sculpted with friezes dating from the Middle Ages.

■ Another medieval village, **Mestá\*\*** (*5km from Olímbi, further down the road*) can be a bit of a trial if you suffer at all from claustrophobia. It's a real anthill, full of narrow passageways winding around the place and tunnelling beneath the houses.

*Turn right to get back to the sea on the return road after Pirgí.*

■ Complete your trip in style with a stop in **Emboriós***\*** (*6km south of Pirgí, 35km south of Chios. 3 buses daily depart from Pirgí*), the prettiest **harbour\*\*** in the south of the island, tucked away at the far end of an inlet. A small white square lined with several houses (including two restaurants and a grocery store) looks out onto a clear blue sea where the boats seem to float on air.

A road dips into the hills of pines on the right, leading to a number of **black pebble beaches***\*** – the second one is the best – nestling in the recesses of a volcanic cliff (*800m from the square*). The sight of the turquoise waters lapping the blue-black shore is worth a detour in itself.

## Making the most of Chios

### GETTING THERE

**By air** – The airport is 4km from town. Several flights depart daily for Athens and 2 flights weekly for Thessaloníki and Lesbos.

**By boat** – There are daily connections with Piraeus and several weekly departures for Sámos, Lesbos, Psará, Rhodes, and Límnos. One departure per week for Thessaloníki. Ferries for Çeşme in Turkey: daily, departure generally at 4pm except Tuesday and Thursday, departure at 9am. Tickets can be purchased the day before. Passports (or identity cards) are compulsory. The offices of the ferry companies (NEL and Miniotis) are near the pier.

### GETTING AROUND

**By bus** – Buses run infrequently and only operate certain days of the week to some towns (Volissós and Anávatos).

The bus station in Chios is set back a little from Platía Vounaki, near the first part of the gardens, on the left when going uphill.

**By taxi** – The yellow taxis are numerous and are meter-operated. *Radio Taxi Chios*, ☎ (0271) 41 111 / 43 312 / 43 313. The taxi rank is at the bottom of Platía Vounaki.

**By car** – This is a good option as the roads are in good condition.

### ADDRESS BOOK (CHIOS TOWN)

**Tourist information** – Odós Kanari, on the corner of Odós Roḯdou, ☎ (0271) 44 389, open daily until 2.30pm during the week, 1pm on Saturday and 9pm on Sunday. Many brochures are available and the staff speak English.

**Banks / Currency exchange** – The National Bank of Greece, on the north-east corner of Platía Vounaki, does currency exchange. Cash dispensers are available at the harbour and in the square behind the tourist information office.

**Post office – *Main post office***, Odós Psyhari, close to the quay in the middle of the harbour.

**Airline companies – *Olympic Airways***, in Leofóros Egeou, ☎ (0271) 20 359.

**Car rental –** At the harbour, ***Budget*** and ***Europcar***. English spoken.

Locals often rent rooms in their homes in many of the villages on the island, notably Pirgí, for the same price as a hotel room (around €23). Contact the organisation that manages the network, the ***Women's Agricultural Cooperative of Híos***, in Pirgí. The office is on the way into the village, ☎ (0271) 72 496, closed in the afternoon.

*Around €23*

🍴 ***Alex Rooms***, 29 Odós Livanou, Chios, in the centre, a stone's throw from the harbour, ☎ (0271) 26 054 – 7rm. Shared bathroom. Alex, a very cordial retired captain, is a real character. The rooms are soberly decorated and comfortable and the terrace is a good place to meet others.

***Olympos***, 25 Neorion, Prokimea, Chios, ☎ (0271) 20 629 / 27 425 – 16rm. 🕙 TV The ferries tie up at the foot of this small blue and white building where you will receive a warm welcome. The small rooms with their midnight blue carpets are clean and comfortable and excellent value. The ground floor houses a popular (and soundproof) bar / disco.

***Filoxenia***, between Roïdou and Voupalou, Chios, ☎ (0271) 22 813 – 21rm. 🕙 This quiet and old-fashioned hotel is also owned by a retired captain and bears witness to a glorious past. A lovely marble staircase leads to the upper levels with their mosaic floors. Unfortunately, the rooms are damp and the building is deteriorating.

*Around €45*

***Hotel Kyma***, on the southern point of the harbour, ☎ (0271) 44 500, Fax (0271) 44 600 – 14rm. 🕙 TV ▤ CC A small hotel that provides international-style rooms with a balcony overlooking the sea. The staff are very attentive and speak English.

***Hotel Agia Markella***, Vrondádos, in front of the sea just after the post office, 4km from the centre of Chios, ☎ (0271) 93 763 – 25rm. 🕙 TV This large establishment caters to its regular customers (for the most part Greek families on holiday) and resembles a turn-of-the-century hotel. The very spacious rooms are bright, modern and well kept.

*Over €75*

🍴 ***Mavrokordatiko***, Odós Mitaradis 1, Kámbos, 7km from the centre of Chios, ☎ (0271) 32 900 / 32 901 – 9rm. 🕙 ▤ ✒ TV ✗ CC An architectural gem in the heart of the Kámbos, this Genoese palace has been superbly restored and provides modern luxury with its warm and refined rooms. In the evening, tables are set out in the citrus garden under a trellis. A very smart and still reasonably priced place.

*Around €9*

***Ouzerí***, in the kástro in Chios, Odós Georgiou Frouriou 20. The stone courtyard where the tables are located is suffused with a medieval atmosphere. The varied menu offers Greek specialities at reasonable prices.

🍴 ***The Two Brothers***, on the street at the crossing with Alex Rooms, in Chios. This restaurant is often full and is open late. Good food (Smyrna meatballs, stuffed vine leaves, etc) in a warm and lively atmosphere.

***To Byzantio***, Odós Rali, Chios (on the corner, in the market district). This restaurant has several daily specials. The meals are always tasty and served in a characterful setting.

***Status***, at the far end of the quayside, Leofóros Egeou 108, Chios, ☎ (0271) 21 210. This large bar with its minimalist decor is the town's trendy club. Entrance around €3.

On Saturday evenings, you can go to the ***beach party*** just outside Chios on the road heading south.

**Cinema –** A pleasant open-air cinema in the municipal gardens. Two screenings per night. Films are in English with Greek subtitles.

Making the most of Chios

# LESBOS★★
## (LÉSVOS)
North Aegean – Capital of the district of Lésvos
Michelin map 980 fold 21 – Regional map page 458
1 633km² – Pop 105 000 – Allow 6 days

**Not to be missed**
The island's ouzo, reputed to be the best in Greece.
A visit to the fascinating Tériade Museum near Mitilíni.

**And remember...**
Rather than touring from a base in Mitilíni,
you will avoid long trips by changing your base according to your itinerary.

Like a giant three-fingered claw, Lesbos appears to be clutching at the sea which takes the shape of two great bays bounded by land of the utmost aridity. The island is made up of stone, sand, and sunburnt grass, which take on a flame-like crimson tint at day's end. Shade is rare. The rocky surface supports pines and olive trees, the latter bearing the black fruit from which the islanders extract an oil that is the most prized in all of Greece. The west, the driest part of the island, offers a lunar vision of a desert plain, battered by the winds. In the north and centre, on the other hand, little mountains (the highest peak is 1 000m in altitude) shelter several small fertile valleys.

A considerable distance separates the main ports of Lesbos, which is the third largest of the Greek islands. Mitilíni, Mólivos and Kaloní have grown independently and ex-

### Sappho, the muse of women
Artist and genius, woman and free spirit, Sappho is the most mythical figure of Lesbos. Her poetic works, which were highly reputed in Antiquity, rival those of Homer. Born in Eressós at the end of the 7C BC, the poetess is said to have run a "moisopolon domos" in Mitilíni, a school of art and poetry devoted to the praise of muses. Whether it was odes, hymns or songs, all of Sappho's verses, which she dedicated to Aphrodite or to her own students, spoke of love and beauty in a style that particularly touched female sensibilities. One effect of this was that the name of the island's female inhabitants became universally known... and took on certain connotations. Another effect is that homosexuals from the world over come in swarms to holiday in Eressós and the beach has been transformed into a veritable pilgrimage site, a unique meeting place for a still marginalized minority. They have their own campsite, as well as numerous hotels.

hibit very different characteristics. The lack of beautiful sandy beaches deters tourists, who only come here in relatively small numbers. Lesbos is not lacking in wealth, however. For example, its hospitable inhabitants, heirs to the ancient poets Alcaeus and Sappho as well as to a fascinating past where Byzantines, Genoese and Ottomans met and mingled. Traces of their past still mark the island, giving it the aura of an oriental pearl at the gateway to Europe.

### A race against death
Lesbos saw its golden age in the 7C and 6C BC. Powerful because of its fleet, it was welcomed with open arms into the Delian League. However, in 428 BC, it took advantage of the Peloponnesian War to proclaim its independence. Athens immediately sent a punitive expedition and the Assembly itself voted to massacre the inhabitants of Mitilíni. The next day, however, thanks to the intervention of the orator Diodotus, the decree was cancelled. A messenger was hastily despatched to catch up with the first one, just managing to save the population of the small capital. But the island didn't escape the sanctions imposed by Athens: with the

exception of present day Mólivos – the large port in the north which had always remained faithful to Athens – its lands were distributed to the cleruchies, Athenian colonisers (*see page 470*).

## Russia to the aid of the Christians

Annexed by Rome in 120 BC, Lesbos fell under Byzantine control after the collapse of the Roman Empire. As a result of the interplay of commercial treaties, it then passed into the hands of the Genoese, the **Gatteluzzi** dynasty, until the Turks conquered the island in 1462, marking the start of Christian oppression.

During the Russo-Turkish War (1768-74), Lesbos endured frontline battles for the control of the Sea of Marmara. At the end of the conflict, the peace treaty instituted religious freedom and authorised Russian intervention in the defence of the Orthodox Church. A network of resistance was thus created through the intermediary of the clergy. However, in Mitilíni, a first uprising against Constantinople resulted in bloodshed (1824). In 1912, Lesbos was finally freed from the Turkish yoke before officially becoming Greek in 1914. The last Turks left the island during an exchange of population in 1923.

# Mitilíni★★
*Allow a full morning*

The red roofs of the capital (pop 25 100) conceal an isthmus less than 1km wide, a narrow bridge between the land and a hill dropping to the sea, towards the Turkish coast. Two ports face each other, one in the south bay of the town where the ferries arrive, and the other in the north, which handles the ships carrying merchandise. Between the two nestles Mitilíni's popular old quarter. Around the 2C AD, the island's wealthy residents abandoned it for the western hill, a district known by the name of **Chorafa**. This is where you will find an impressive Hellenistic **theatre★** hidden in a pine forest (*in front of the castle hill, at the north port, take Odós Krinis and follow the brown and yellow sign indicating the site. 8.30am to 3pm; entrance fee*). A testimony to the cultural activity in Lesbos during Antiquity, the theatre could accommodate up to 15 000 spectators, thereby matching the theatre in Epidaurus. Restored by the Romans who were impressed with its size, today it displays no more than a few modest sections of its tiers.

*To return to the centre, go down the hill by Odós Zalogou Kydonion on the right. At the junction, go left onto Odós Vournazón to arrive at the southern port.*

## The southern port★

With its dense traffic, restaurant and café terraces, banks and hotels, the port is a never-ending bustle of activity. Running alongside the quays, the old **neo-Classical façades** blackened by exhaust fumes appear as ghosts from a forgotten past. Conversely, the **municipal theatre**, a stately white building dating from the 1960s, stands on the south corner of the port. Behind it runs **Odós Ermoú★**, a long shopping street that crosses the isthmus and connects the two ports. Fishmongers and market gardeners spread their wares at the beginning of the road during market days. A little further down on the left stands the enormous steel-grey **dome** of the **Ágios Therapon Church★★**, with its strange blend of Byzantine and Asiatic design, visible from the sea. The dome sits atop a neo-Renaissance-style basilica erected in 1860. The blue interior with its faux marble columns has an immense **iconostasis★★**. Opposite, the **Byzantine Museum★★** houses the richest collection of the island's **icons★★** (*Monday to Saturday, 10am-1pm; entrance fee*).

## Towards the north

Heading up Odós Ermoú, the road soon becomes too narrow to contain the commercial frenzy. In their shop windows, grocers stack **Kaloní sardines** packed in their characteristic blue and red tins. To the side, alleys plunge into Mitilíni's old district with its pastel-coloured façades, while Odós Ermoú emerges in the midst of the **north port***. Although more extensive and workaday in character than the southern port, it contains some authentic **ouzo bars*** and **tavernas*** which are good places to eat or just relax.

*If you want to climb up to the fortress, take Odós Mikras Asías that borders the east side of town at the foot of the hill.*

Beyond the **stately stone-built courthouse** *(on the right)*, a footpath on the left takes you on a 10min walk through the conifers to a **citadel*** *(8.30am-3pm; entrance fee)*. Its thick crenellated wall (packed with what appear to be secret tunnels) encircles the entire hill. Originally Byzantine, this fortress was rebuilt in the 14C by Francesco Gatteluzzi and resisted the Turks for five days before finally succumbing to them. Upon entering, you emerge onto a huge grassy expanse with the well-preserved remains of the **Gatteluzzi Palace***. Inside, the family's coat of arms – entwined horseshoes next to an eagle – stand guard over each door. Outside, elegant stone arches border the east side of the large square where you can enjoy a magnificent **view*** of the Mediterranean and the coast of Asia Minor.

*Return to Odós Mikras Asías, which further down changes its name to Odós 8 Noemvríou.*

On the left, set against a background of blue sea, stands the large and immaculate building of the **Archaeological Museum*** *(Tuesday-Sunday, 8.30am-2.30pm; entrance fee)*. The interior, a blend of neo-Classical design and modern materials, houses a large collection of busts and ancient statuettes found on the island. But the most interesting collection in the museum is in the second part where enormous **mosaics*** are displayed. These are said to come from the "House of Menander" (3C or 4C AD), a sumptuous villa in Chorafa, the ancient district. Veritable paintings, with their grimacing masks and declaiming choirs, they bring Greek theatre back to life. On the street outside, several stately private **villas** succeed one another close to the sea. Built in neo-Classical, Baroque or Renaissance style, they make a good excuse for a pleasant stroll at the end of the day.

### Leaving Mitilíni

*Follow the broad avenue of Leofóros E Venizélou leading south from the centre.* The finest Mitilinian homes were built in the 19C and line the seafront. Each has been renovated according to its owner's creativity. A Norman manor is therefore followed by an English cottage which itself adjoins an almond-coloured neo-Classical villa with a pediment and plaster garlands.

Soon after leaving town, after several twists and turns in the hills, you'll reach the village of **Variá** *(4km south of Mitilini. Local bus service all day departing from the bus terminal in the south port)* with its **Tériade Museum***, which is definitely worth a visit *(look for signs when entering the village. Tuesday-Sunday, 9am-1pm / 4.30pm-8pm; entrance fee)*. This museum is exceptional for its collections as well as for the beauty of its location – an extensive area covered with century-old olive trees. At the entrance, a white building houses the **Theófilos Museum***, dedicated to a painter of naïve art who was a native of Variá (1873-1934) and popular throughout Greece. His works, praised by the architect Le Corbusier among others, were often inspired by scenes that were sometimes rural and at other times dreamlike. Photographs and texts shed light on the ambiguity of the painter, vacillating between touching candour and harsh realism.

In the middle of the olive grove, a second much larger building houses the **Tériade Museum Library***, which exhibits the work of Stratis Eleftheriadis (Tériade), born in Mitilíni in 1897. First an art critic in Paris, then a publisher, he created the "great books" in which one of his painter friends (Picasso, Matisse, Giacometti, Chagall, etc) would make original illustrations to accompany a text of his choice. A copy of each book and the preparatory works are displayed in the cases.

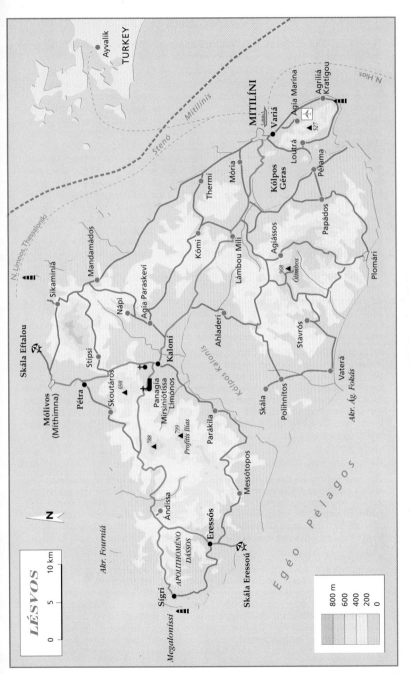

**LÉSVOS**

0  5  10 km

N

Megaloníssi
Akr. Fourniá
Akr. Fourniá

Skála Eftalou
Mólivos (Míthimna)
Pétra
Sikaminiá
Mandamádos
Stipsi
Skoutáros
Nápi
Agía Paraskeví
Kalóni
Panagía Mirsiniótissa Limónos
698
788
Profítis Ilías 799
Kólpos Kalonís
Ándissa
Parákila
Ahladeri
Eressós
Messótopos
Sígri
APOLITHOMÉNO DÁSSOS
Skála Eressoú

Kómi
Thermi
Móría
Lámbou Míli
Agiássos
Olímbos 968
Stavrós
Skála
Polihnítos
Vaterá
Akr. Ág. Fokás

MITILÍNI
Variá
Loutrá
Kólpos Géras
Péñama
Papádos
Plomári
Agía Marína
Agriliá
Kratígou
527

TURKEY
Ayvalík

N. Límnos, Thessaloníki
Steró
Mitilínis
Mitilínis
N. Híos

Egéo Pélagos
Egéo Pélagos

800 m
600
400
200
0

# Towards the west

Beyond the **Gulf of Géras**, an undulating and fertile plain, speckled with the grey and green of the olive groves, stretches alongside the road.

■ After the market gardening areas, you'll soon see the charming houses of **Kaloní**, the sardine capital. Since the turn of the twentieth century, fish have been caught in bulk in the gulf and then packaged in the town's canning factories.

Beyond Kaloní, Lesbos' image changes radically. There are no longer green hills but rather a volcanic plateau covered only by sparse, russet-coloured vegetation. Below, the village of **Eressós** (*9 km from Mitilíni*) is a small cheerful oasis with a shady square and flowers on the balconies.

■ **The beach at Eressós**★★ (Skála Eressoú) – *4km from the village of Eressós.* Visited primarily by Sappho's followers who come from all over to pay homage to the poetess, the beach in Eressós attracts more visitors than anywhere else on the island. Restaurants with outside terraces, bars with soft cushions overlooking the sea, and well-stocked grocery stores, everything combines to give the resort a relaxing holiday atmosphere, while its beautiful ribbon of grey sand runs for several kilometres and provides plenty of space to benefit from the limpid waves.

Rising out of the water, a large block of stone known as **Sappho's Rock** serves as a reminder that the poetess was born in Eressós. The **museum** (*set 800m back from the beach, take the second street on the left after the bridge on the main street. Open mornings until 2.30pm; free*) has a small collection of **statuettes** and **funerary stones** found in the area but is otherwise of little interest. Behind it lie the foundations of an ancient **temple** dedicated to Apollo, upon which a paleo-Christian church was later constructed, but which no longer exists. Each evening an orange light fills the narrow streets and paints the surrounding hills and, while the shadows dance on the sandy beach, a magnificent **sunset** captures the eye.

■ The **petrified forest of Sígri**★, a unique natural monument, is hidden in the hollows of a deep valley, which can be reached from the top of the hill (*14km by the road north of Eressós, 6km before reaching the village of Sígri. Signposted from Eressós. Entrance fee*). From above, the **view**★★★ is breathtaking: clinging to the bare russet slopes are tree trunks that were covered with lava and volcanic ash during a violent eruption 15 or 20 million years ago. The veins, bark and roots have taken on the metallic colour of the rock, forming strange sculptures that have been listed and protected.

# The north

The road returns via Kaloní, the island's nodal point. From here it turns north past market gardens and olive groves straight towards the village of **Pétra**. This is a popular stop for tour groups, although it offers little of interest with the exception of a high **rock**★ to which the village owes its name. Jutting 30m above the rooftops, it is crowned by the **Panagía Glykofiloússa Church** ("the Virgin of tender kisses"). If you want to kiss the attractive **icon of the Virgin** yourself, you'll need to climb 114 steps.

■ **Mólivos**★★ (Míthimna) – *62km from Mitilini, 6km north of Pétra.* After a series of sweeping bends along the seashore, a postcard image suddenly appears. However, Mólivos is also full of life and authentic charm, and poets and artists have come here to find harmony and beauty throughout the ages. A 14C **Genoese citadel**★ perches above the waves atop a pointed hill (*9am-4pm; entrance fee*), offering a grandiose **panoramic view**★★ of the olive trees blanketing the northern part of the island. The little Ottoman houses with their red-tiled roofs cling to the side of the hill, emphasising the bright, multi-coloured, graceful façades of their wooden loggias. The cobbled main street, narrow Odós 17 Noemvriou (*begins across from the tourist information office*), winds up between them to the heart of town.

Built in the late 18C, **Ianakos House**\*\* *(500m further on, to the right)* is a perfect example of a local building. It has wide windows in front of which slender columns rise to support an upper floor with a timber overhang painted red.

Returning to the main road, notice the lovely **Turkish fountains**\* which adorn nearly every street corner. A trellis protects the cobblestones from the heat of the sun, providing coolness and shade as the hill becomes increasingly steep.

*A second road joins the first one at the fork. Take the alleyway just beyond on the right.*

At the bend in the alleyway, behind a high sea-green wall, stands the **School of Fine Arts**\*\*, a splendid 19C neo-Classical building set against the hill *(visits are possible during the school year)*. In the summer, you'll have to be content merely to admire its decorative **façade**\*\* and its **monumental gate**\*.

*Return to the main road and at the intersection take the road on the left which leads down to the harbour.*

Hidden in a pretty courtyard surrounded by walls, the **museum**\*\* *(300m on the right at the end of the narrow alleyway)* occupies a lovely neo-Classical house with stones bronzed by the sun. The ground floor houses a small **library** with outdated titles, most of which are schoolbooks. In the basement, you'll find an **archaeological collection**\*\* which is much more interesting. The first room exhibits **religious objects**\* dating from the time when the residents of Míthimna worshipped Dionysus, Artemis and Athena. The inhabitants of the southern part of the island favoured the cult of Heracles. The second room retraces the events of the 20C, with touching black and white **photographs**\*\* of the island's freedom fighters.

For an example of Greek avant-garde, have a look at the town's **art gallery** lower down *(it's on the corner 100m away, just before the road connects with the paved road leading to the port. 9am-4pm; free)*, where the young artists from the School of Fine Arts exhibit their works. At the end of the road, the **port**\*\* of Mólivos appears *(300m away, continue down the road)*, an idyllic little inlet where coloured boats bob about on the water. Several restaurants *(which unfortunately are expensive given the quality of the food)* flaunt their tempting terraces while a small naval depot repairs boats at the end. The **view**\*\* of the façades of Mólivos is unparalleled from here.

Lesbos

The Genoese citadel of Mólivos, Lesbos

G. de Benoist/MICHELIN

■ **Skála Eftalou\***, a pebble beach at the foot of a steep cliff, is known for its **thermal springs\*\*** with healing virtues (*4km north of Mólivos. After passing several unappealing beaches on the side of the road, stop at the small car park on the seashore at the foot of a cliff on the left. The beach starts at the end of the car park*). The warm waters are collected in a small **pool** located in the middle of the beach under a pierced dome reminiscent of Turkish baths (*open until 4.30pm; free*). When you leave the baths, you will be as red as a lobster. The locals then run directly to the sea and dive into the waves, which seem icy after the heat. This provides an excellent thermal shock which is apparently good for the health!

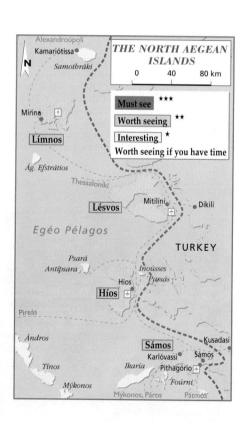

### GETTING THERE

**By air** – The airport is 8km south of Mitilíni. Domestic flights connect Lesbos with Athens four times a day, with one connection a day to Thessaloníki and Límnos, and twice a day to Chios.

**By boat** – In summer, several boats a week connect with Piraeus, 2 per week with Límnos, Kavála and Chios, 2 per week with Thessaloníki, and 1 per week with Sámos and Rhodes. Two boats weekly have morning departures for Ayvalik, in Turkey, and return in the afternoon. Note, however, that these connections are subject to alteration according to the state of Greco-Turkish relations. Information available at the **Dimakis Tours** agency, Odós P Koundouriótou 73, in Mitilíni (under the arcades at the port, near the tourist police station and customs), ☎ (0251) 20 716 / 27 865, Fax (0251) 43 603.

### GETTING AROUND

**By bus** – Buses depart from Mitilíni's bus terminal, located at the south port (central platform). Several departures daily for all the towns on the island. When there is no direct connection between towns, you need to go via Kaloní.

**By taxi** – Taxis are yellow and meter-operated.

**By car** – Car rental is possible in Mitilíni, Mólivos and Skála Eressoú through travel agencies.

### ADDRESS BOOK

**Tourist information** – At the Mitilíni harbourmaster's office, a tourist police office provides brochures and information. In Míthimna, a small kiosk at the foot of the hill when entering town houses the tourist information office.

**Banks / Currency exchange** – There are many cash dispensers and international banks on the quay of the south port in Mitilíni. There is a cash dispenser next to the tourist information kiosk in Mólivos, and on the main road in Skála Eressoú.

**Post office / Internet** – **Main post office** on Vournazón in Mitilíni, 500m above the gardens. Internet access in the **Playfield** game room, at the beginning of E Venizélou.

**Airline companies** – **Olympic Airways**, A Kavétsou 44, on the road to the airport in Mitilíni.

**Travel agencies** – **Dimakis Tours**, under the arcades of the port near the tourist police station and customs, Odós P Koundouriótou 73, in Mitilíni, ☎ (0253) 20 716 / 27 865, Fax (0251) 43 603. Many services, such as plane or boat tickets and car rental, are efficiently provided by friendly staff.

In Skála Eressoú, **Sappho Travel**, when entering the village, ☎ (0253) 53 077, Fax (0253) 52 140, managed by the charming Jo and Joanna, who have compiled a treasure chest of information and provide impeccable service (tickets, excursions, etc).

### WHERE TO STAY

**Míthimna campsite**, on the road from Skála Eftalou, signs on the left, 1.5km from Mólivos, ☎ (0253) 71 079 – 100 pitches. This campsite is located on a slight slope with trees that ensure shade at each of the pitches, which are surrounded by high hedges. Communal facilities which are dark but clean are found in the centre of the campsite. There is no shop but the place is pleasant and well located next to the beaches. Around €12 for two people.

• **Mitilíni**

*Between €15 and €30*

**Salina's and Thalia**, Odós Kinkíou, ☎ (0251) 42 073 / 24 640 – 8rm. ⌐] Follow the signs at the top of Odós Ermoú. Two guesthouses are located across from each other in a courtyard in old Mitilíni. The staff are attentive and the rooms are decent and clean.

**Pension Alkaíos**, Odós Alkaíou 16, ☎ (0251) 47 736 / 47 737 and Odós Alkaíou 32, ☎ (0251) 47 738 – 18rm. ⌐] Two lovely neighbouring buildings have been transformed into hotels on a quiet street a stone's throw from the port. The first, in a large garden and equipped with impressive steps, is the most pleasant. However, both have clean, simple rooms with high ceilings. Unfortunately most of them lack a proper bathroom but instead have a cubicle installed in the rooms. Good value.

**New Life Rooms**, between Odós Ermoú and Odós Olímpou, ☎ (0251) 42 650 – 7rm. ⌖ ⌔ The epitome of kitsch, this neo-Classical guesthouse, located in the heart of town, has a purple façade. Its rather stark rooms nevertheless have a certain charm. Good value.

*Over €30*

**Hotel Sappho**, Pávlou Koundouriótou 31, at the port, ☎ (0251) 22 888 – 29rm. ⌖ ⌔ ▤ TV ✕ A small modern establishment that has a good level of comfort and friendly staff.

*Around €60*

**Hotel Blue Sea**, Pávlou Koundouriótou 91, at the port, ☎ (0251) 23 994 – 100rm. ⌖ ⌔ TV ✕ CC A pretty building that resembles a steamship. The international-style rooms are spacious and impeccably clean but have no particular charm. Service is somewhat blasé.

*Over €105*

**Pyrgos Mytilini**, E Venizélou 49, ☎ (0251) 25 069 / 27 977 – 12rm. ⌖ ▤ TV ✕ CC This extravagant Baroque palace situated on the most stylish road in town was recently converted into a hotel. The rooms are all different and combine luxury with comfort, with enormous marble bathrooms.

• **Mólivos**

*Between €15 and €23*

**Nassos**, Odós Aríonos, near Yannakos House, ☎ (0253) 71 232 – 8rm. ⌖ This charming and tasteful old house in the heart of the city combines a family atmosphere with reasonable prices. Some rooms have a balcony overlooking the sea. It's advisable to book ahead in summer.

**Villa Ionna**, Odós Diikitiríou 24, ☎ (0253) 71 234 – 5rm. ⌖ Hidden in a beautiful garden in the heart of the old town, this magnificent Greco-Byzantine villa is furnished with memories. The aristocratic owners are descendants of the first residents. The atmosphere is unique and the rooms somewhat dusty but filled with charm.

**Paradise Rooms**, behind the car park at the foot of the hill, ☎ (0253) 71 063 / 71 778 – 3rm. ⌖ Impeccably managed by an elderly farming couple of great charm, this guesthouse has 3 brand-new studios that are large and clean and have small kitchens. They overlook a terrace sheltered by a vine-covered trellis in the heart of an enormous orchard. A genuine little paradise.

*Around €32*

**Hotel Adonis**, on the way into town at the foot of the hill, ☎ (0253) 71 866, Fax (0251) 71 636 – 22rm. ⌖ TV CC A superb stone mansion surrounded by a large garden with a fountain, this establishment benefits from an ideal location. Although the rooms are of modest size, they give the same impression of luxury with wainscoting, heavy curtains and lovely subdued light.

• **Skála Eressoú**

*Around €23*

**To Penelope**, on the 1st floor of Sofia Bar in the main square, ☎ (0253) 53 396 – 5rm. ⌖ Penelope reserves a warm welcome for travellers who are not too bothered about comfort and offers clean but basic rooms. These details are quickly forgotten as soon as you see the location of the rooms, overlooking a sun-filled terrace that faces the sea.

EATING OUT

• **Mitilíni**

*Around €7.50*

**Averof**, Pávlou Koundouriótou 37, at the port. Easy to spot because of its yellow awning and the date of its opening, 1841, inscribed above the door. This popular restaurant prepares delicious family-style cuisine. You can make your own selection from the large pots. The oilcloths and the dignified waiters with their large aprons create an old-fashioned and authentic ambience.

*Around €15*

**To Kastro** and **O Ermis**, at the far end of Odós Ermoú, a little before the north port. The two tavernas face each other on opposite sides of the street and both boast a terrace sheltered by a pretty trellis. The menu is similar: seafood, feta salad and moussaká, and the owners are friendly in both establishments, which makes it difficult to choose. The interior of **To Kastro** (on the left facing the port) is covered in wood and old framed photos and evokes the world of fishermen.

• **Mólivos**

*Between €7.50 and €15*

**Panorama**, across from the entrance to the citadel at the top of the hill, ☎ (0253) 71 848. Typically Greek dishes and pastries will delight those who enjoy simple and good meals, served in a dreamlike ambience where the view from the terrace takes in the surrounding countryside and the sea.

**Nassos**, managed by the owners of the guesthouse of the same name, further up the street, ☎ (0253) 71 022. Often full to bursting, this little restaurant serves fresh fish and lobster specialities as well as a wide choice of tasty dishes of the day.

**HAVING A DRINK**

The students and young people of Mitilíni frequent the numerous bars along the quays of the south port. The **Music Café**, on the corner of Odós Vernardáki and Odós M Komnináki is among the more original ones. This large airy pub with high ceilings is a venue for concerts on some evenings.

**OTHER THINGS TO DO**

**Festival** – The citadel in Mólivos is the ideal setting for the summer **drama** festival. Information available at the tourist information office.

**Cinema** – Mólivos also has a pleasant **open-air cinema**, showing English-language films with subtitles (around €5). The entrance is just before the tourist information kiosk facing the large car park and the bus stop.

**Making the most of Lesbos**

# LÍMNOS★★

North Aegean – District of Lésvos – Michelin map 980 fold 20 –
Regional map page 466
477km² – Pop 18 000 – Allow 3 days

**Not to be missed**
The archaeological sites at Polióhni, Ifestía and Kavírio.

**And remember...**
Although the sun shines brightly over Límnos, it can be very windy,
particularly in August; June and September are the best months.
Organise your own transport as buses run infrequently.

A sentry quietly keeping watch over the Dardanelles, the island of Límnos occupies an unparalleled strategic position at the crossing of maritime routes that cut through the north of the Aegean Sea, equidistant to Mt Athos in the west and the Turkish coast in the east. Moreover, the roar of Greek fighter planes and the extensive garrison stationed on the island serve as reminders of this geopolitical reality.

However, Límnos still gives the impression of a calm and serene island, endowed with lots of space; ideal for anyone looking for an authentic and refreshing atmosphere. Even in high season, you can go there without fear of the mass tourism common on Greek islands in the summer. In fact, Límnos has suffered from the presence of the military, which left it isolated from the tourist boom in the 1970s and 80s. But today, it uses the situation to its advantage, offering the visitor a well-preserved coastline, urban development that has been controlled, and a living environment where the tranquillity seems to have rubbed off on the gentle and friendly locals.

## A palette of varied landscapes

Two large bays squeeze the centre of the island, as if separating it into two pieces of crumpled paper. To the south, the **Gulf of Moúdros** forms an enormous natural harbour, while the smaller **Bay of Pourniás** lies to the north. From one part or another of these blue coves, Límnos reveals a surprising diversity of landscape. The 260km of jagged coastline is carved into by numerous unspoiled bays and rocky points that are often difficult to reach by land (particularly in the north). And the little fishing harbours, clear sandy beaches, and the moderately flat, pleasantly rustic interior, add up to a harmonious landscape composed of broad plains, scrub-mantled hills, and scattered clumps of pine trees.

Límnos also reveals several curious ecosystems, including lakes and wetland on the east coast, a miniature desert at the south-east point, and micro regions housing an unusual fauna of pink flamingos, migrating birds and deer.

And as if it were echoing nature, the **architecture** of the towns and villages (31 in all) exhibits the same variety of forms and decoration, particularly in their church towers which illustrate a thousand-year-old tradition of stone sculpture.

## The island of the blacksmith god

Because of its volcanic origins, Límnos was thought by the Ancients to be the home of Hephaestus, or Vulcan, the god of fire, who had his forge there. This protector of the island taught the first inhabitants the art of metalwork, a craft that is still practised today.

Real history however is more complex. It began in the 5th millennium BC, in the village of **Polióhni** (see below), which was founded by settlers from Asia Minor, followed soon after by other pre-Hellenic tribes. It was then passed from hand to hand by its many invaders. The island became the property of the **Athenians** in 512 BC. In the 4C BC, it had a Parliament, a Senate, and a dynamic political life similar to that of the great city in Attica, and until the accession of the Byzantines, its fate depended mainly on that of Athens. During the nine centuries of the Byzantine Empire, Límnos provided cotton, wheat, wine and honey for Constantinople, which also placed a lot of strategic importance on the island for control of the maritime routes. Because of its prosperity and relative safety, Límnos was also of interest to the monasteries of Mt Athos and Pátmos, both of which acquired large

properties there. Like the other islands in this part of the Aegean, Límnos was regularly fought over by the Saracens, the Venetians and the Genoese. The Turks finally took it from the Venetians in 1478 and maintained control until 1948.

## Mírina★★

Situated on the west coast, the island's capital (pop 5 000) is an agreeable seaside resort of manageable size that has preserved its lifestyle and charm of yesteryear. It's pleasant to meander down its cobbled streets lined with tavernas, old captains' homes and traditional houses with wooden balconies.

An urban centre since prehistoric times, the town has preserved a superb Byzantine **kástro★★** *(free)* from its past, a line of battlements crowning the imposing rocky ridge jutting out on the coast. Built at the end of the 12C, it was modified by the Venetians, the Genoese and the Ottomans. An incongruous sight: inside its walls wander a

**Límnos**

The Byzantine kástro watches over the harbour of Mírina, Límnos

M. Joana/La Photothèque SDP

number of remarkably tame deer. From the ramparts, there is a superb **view\*\*** of the town, divided into two parts by the ridge. On the south side, the small **fishing harbour** stretches along the picturesque quayside to the pleasant **Máditos beach**, while on the north are elegant neo-Classical houses belonging to rich shipowners or émigrés from Egypt who have returned to their native island. Further down, **Roméïkos Gialós and Richá Nerá beaches\*\*** succeed each other, with calm, clear and shallow water making them ideal for children. Everything faces west so you can enjoy the unforgettable **sunsets\*\***.

If the weather is clear, you will even be able to see the northern point of the peninsula of Halkidikí (Chalcidice) and Mt Athos on the horizon.

Don't miss out on the **Archaeological Museum\*\*** (*on the road facing the sea, near Roméïkos beach. 8.30am-3pm, closed Monday; entrance fee*), which has educational displays of artefacts from the numerous sites on the island (such as Mírina, Polióhni, Ifestía, Kavírio) which have been excavated by Italian archaeologists. Even though the best pieces are in Athens, it's worth a visit to this museum to view the funerary steles, statues, religious objects from the Sanctuary of the Kabeiroi (*see further on*), pottery, and terracotta figurines. Notice in particular the **votive lamps\*** in the shape of Sirens (8C-6C BC), those hybrid creatures with human heads and the bodies of birds feared by all sailors.

Next door, the **Ecclesiastical Museum** (*unspecified hours; free*) will only be of interest if you are passionate about religious art. The museum contains Byzantine icons, liturgical clothing, books and sacred objects.

## Around Mírina

The ruins of the **Sanctuary of Artemis Selene\*** are reached by taking the coastal road to the north (*at least 2km*). Built in the 7C BC for the patron saint of Mírina, the sanctuary is currently hidden inside the **Portomyrina Palace**. This is a good opportunity to enjoy a drink at the bar of this luxurious hotel.

Carry on a bit further north to the village of **Káspakas\*\***, a beautiful maze of narrow streets set on the mountainside. From here there is a precipitous descent to the **Bay of Ágios Ioánnis\***, an attractive cove lined with several pretty **beaches**.

South-east of Mírina, other beaches are dotted along the coast, providing plenty of opportunities for simply lounging around. First, the beach at **Platí\***, with several tavernas, hotels and water sports facilities, is popular for its shade. The small beach of **Thános\*** is hidden on the other side of **Cape Tigáni**. Next comes the Bay of Pávlos and its popular **Nevgátis beach\***, a magnificent crescent-shaped expanse of sand 2km long.

## Excursion to the island of Ágios Efstrátios\*\*

*Approximately 33.5km south of Limnos. Connection twice a week on the small ferry "Aiolis", departing from Mírina, travel time 2hr30min or 3hr via caique. The regular ferry of the Kavála-Rafína line also serves Ágios Efstrátios (every 2-3 days). Information available at the Myrina Tourist & Travel Agency, in Mírina.* This little island, a large part of which belongs to Mt Athos, carries the name of the missionary saint who prayed there. Nature is intact here and the island has no asphalt roads. Access to most of the splendid **sandy beaches\*\*** with their transparent waters is by boat. This is the perfect setting for some enjoyable swimming and lovely **walks**. A violent earthquake in 1968 left this island virtually uninhabited; scarcely 300 people live on it today. You will find a number of rooms available to rent during the summer months.

# On the Gulf of Moúdros\*\*

On the south coast, the road winds between the hills and the sea in a lovely setting of curves and plains sown with barley and wheat.

■ Upon arriving in **Kondías,** a village of typical shipowners' houses, a small road on the right leads to lovely **Diapóri beach\*** at the far end of a small bay.

■ Not far from the abandoned village of **Palió Pedinó** is the little port of **Néa Koútali\*,** specialising in sponge fishing, with several almost deserted beaches.

Beyond, the road opens onto the Gulf of Moúdros, embracing its enormous expanse of blue water. The **panoramic view\*\*** from the village of **Kalithéa** is spectacular. Dur-

In 1915, Churchill, First Lord of the Admiralty, promoted the idea of a Franco-British naval expedition in the Dardanelles in order to open a communication route to Russia. After a successful landing on 25 February, nearly a third of the fleet was destroyed by underwater mines during the naval attack on 18 March. From April to August the Allies attempted a series of land operations in vain on the Gallipoli peninsula and on the coast of Asia Minor. They were driven back by the Turks who were commanded by the German general, Liman von Sanders and by Mustafa Kemal, the future Atatürk. At the end of August, the Allies abandoned the operations and, in December, they retreated without having established any ties with Russia. They left behind more than 100 000 dead (British, French, Indians, Australians and New Zealanders) all for nothing.

ing the First World War, the Gulf of Moúdros played an important role during the Allied operations in the Dardanelles (1914-16). Because of its excellent location for moorings, the Gulf was transformed into a giant naval base, housing up to 500 ships and 30 000 soldiers. The many victims of the tragic Battle of the Dardanelles are buried in the **Allied Cemetery,** slightly east of town *(signposted).*

■ An economic centre for the western part of the island, the small town of Moúdros is also a base for **sponge fishermen.** You can also enjoy some of the pleasant sandy beaches in the vicinity, particularly **Fanaráki beach.**

## Heading east

■ **Polióhni\*\*** — *9am-3.30pm. Closed Monday. Free. Allow 30min.* Nestling at the water's edge in a lovely natural setting, this **prehistoric city** was unearthed by Italian archaeologists. Polióhni is in fact considered to be among the oldest of the organised communities in Europe. It is even older than the legendary Troy whose ruins can be seen across from Límnos on the Turkish coast, a short distance across the Dardanelles Strait. Moreover, the history of Polióhni is similar to its neighbour in Asia Minor and, like Schliemann *(see page 19)* in **Troy,** archaeologists have discovered a fabulous treasure of gold jewellery of similar design. Founded during the Neolithic Period (5000-4000 BC), the city originally consisted of a group of sizeable huts. Then it was organised into a proper urban centre, flourishing in the Bronze Age (4000-2000 BC) thanks to its copper industry and its control of trade on the Aegean. The fortified city was then abandoned around 1200 BC following an earthquake, which brutally destroyed it.

The ruins may not be very impressive even though the site has been well restored, but nevertheless, whether or not you're an archaeology buff, you can't help but be moved by the ancient remains. For they reveal that a democratic social organisation already existed in prehistoric times. In addition to the many stone houses scattered along a street and a square endowed with a well, you can clearly distinguish the rectangle of the council building, or **bouleuterion.** Also be sure to note the large **granary** and the eroded walls of the mighty **fortifications.**

If you continue towards the south point of the island from Polióhni in the direction of the **Ágios Sózon Monastery** (patron saint's holiday on 7 September), you will enter a unique landscape of desert-like sand dunes. Its nickname, the **"Sahara of Límnos"\*,** seems very appropriate.

**Límnos**

# Bay of Pourniás

■ **Ifestía★** (Hephaïstéia) – *In the north-east part of the island, 42km from Mírina. Take the 5km long trail (suitable for vehicles) through the blue thistles (signposted) just after Kondopoúli. 9.30am-3pm. Closed Monday. Free. Allow 45min.* Perched on a little headland cape almost surrounded by the sea, this ancient city was named after Hephaestus, to whom it was dedicated. It was founded by the **Pelasgi** (ancestors of the Achaeans, *see page 56*) and prospered during the 1st millennium BC, reaching its peak between the 6C and 4C BC. Destroyed by the Persians in 511 BC, it was rebuilt by the Athenians and remained the economic centre of the island until the 11C.

The site is quite extensive and gives an idea of the importance of the city. And since many areas still remain unexcavated, you have the satisfying impression of being the discoverer yourself, particularly as visitors are somewhat rare. The ruins of a **theatre** dating from the Hellenistic Period stand against the side of a hill facing the sea, well sheltered from the wind. Take the time to admire the **panoramic view★★** from its steps. You will also see the modest remains of a **temple** dedicated to Artemis, as well as a **necropolis** in the south-west.

1. Roméïkos Gialós
2. Richá Nerá
3. Máditos
4. Thános
5. Nevgátis

N. Ágios Efstrátios

*Back on the road to Kondopoúli, turn left towards Ágios Aléxandros (5km). At the village, a trail on the left goes towards Kavírio and the sea (3km).*

■ **Kavírio, the Sanctuary of the Kabeiroi**★★ – *9.30am-3pm. Closed Monday. Free. Allow 30min.* Like the Temple of Artemis, erected outside Mírina, the Sanctuary of the Kabeiroi is located several kilometres outside Ifestía *(to the north-east).* This was undoubtedly in order to provide it with one of the most beautiful sites on the island, as the

**The mystery of the Kabeiroi**
Until the dawn of the Christian Era, the sanctuary of the Kabeiroi – rustic deities who protected peasants and sailors – housed the secret rites related to fertility and the cult of Hephaestus. Nocturnal celebrations took place in a forest near the temple where the initiated met, each adorned with a crown of olive branches and a red ribbon, the guarantor of courage. Once a year, the residents of Límnos extinguished all fires on the island and sent a ship to Delos, to the source of sacred light. While the priests sat in Philoctetes' Cave and invoked the gods in an esoteric language, all activity on the island had to stop until the boat returned carrying the divine flame, symbol of the rebirth of terrestrial life. This "spring" day gave rise to a great celebration.

Ancients knew so well how to choose. Isolated at the end of **Cape Chloé**★★, the ruins occupy a rocky promontory that dominates the waves and provides a superb **viewpoint**★★ over the Aegean. This is, however, the only interesting aspect of the site. The remains themselves are rather sparse, apart from the lovely esplanade belonging to the temple, a large rectangle marked off by the shafts of columns facing the sea. This Hellenistic sanctuary was founded by Seleucus, one of Alexander the Great's lieutenants. A wall that has since disappeared stood facing inland, closing off the sanctuary to the uninitiated. Beneath it is **Philoctetes' Cave**. The cave owes its name to the Greek archer who was bitten by a sacred serpent. His companions, who were en route to besiege Troy, had to abandon him there in the hopes that he would recover. In fact, an oracle had predicted that Troy would fall if Philoctetes fought with Heracles' weapons. He did this successfully once he had recovered, and went on to kill Paris, son of King Priam.

■ Below Kavírio, the road veers towards **Pláka,** a charming fishing village isolated at the far end of the north-east point of the island.

*Take the road back to Kondopoúli, heading west along the Bay of Pourniás.*

■ On the way back to Mírina, you can stop for a swim at **Kótsinas beach,** where the water is rather shallow. The bay adjoins the village of Kótsinas, which preserves the important remains of a **Byzantine city**. According to the Ancients, the famous "Límnos earth," a heavy clay endowed with numerous medicinal virtues (for intestinal problems, ulcers, various infections, poisoning, etc) – used to heal Philoctetes – comes from a neighbouring hill.

Another alternative is to go to **Kéros beach**★, which is favoured by windsurfers. It borders a watery plain interspersed with lakes and bogs, where the strange waters of **Lake Hortarolímni**★★ flow in rose and brown colours. A little further on, **Lake Alikí** attracts a number of rare birds, including **pink flamingos** which migrate here for the winter.

## GETTING THERE

**By air** – The airport is located in the centre of the island, 22km from Mírina, north of the Gulf of Moúdros. Flights available on **Olympic Airways** to / from Mírina for Athens (3 flights daily in the summer), Thessaloníki, and Lesbos.

**By boat** – 4 ferries a week in the summer from Rafína (Athens). Connections from Mírina to Thessaloníki, Kavála, Lesbos, Chios, Sámos, Kalímnos, Kos, and Rhodes. Ferry quay located south of town, at the foot of the castle.

Hydrofoils (Flying Dolphins) for Lesbos, Samothrace, Alexandroúpoli, and Kavála. Note that schedules vary. Information available at **Myrina Tourist & Travel Agency**, near the fishing harbour, ☎ (0254) 22 460.

## GETTING AROUND

**By bus** – Bus **terminal** at Platía E Venizélou, in Mírina. There is only one departure in the afternoons for the main destinations, except Kondiás and Moúdros, which have a slightly better service. It's better to hire a car.

**By rental car** – There are a number of rental agencies for cars, jeeps or two-wheel vehicles in Mírina: **Myrina Rent a Car**, ☎ (0254) 24 476, **Auto Europe**, ☎ (0254) 23 777, **Petrides**, ☎ (0254) 22 039, **Holiday**, ☎ (0254) 23 280, etc. If you choose to hire a motor scooter, be careful of the frequently windy days and long distances.

## ADDRESS BOOK

**Banks / Currency exchange** – The two banks on Odós N Garoufalídhou have cash dispensers.

**Post office / Telephone** – **Main post office**, N Garoufalídhou. **OTE**, Ipsipílis.

**Internet** – **Internet Café**, N Garoufalídhou.

**Airline companies** – **Olympic Airways**, N Garoufalídhou, ☎ (0254) 22 214.

**Harbourmaster's office** – ☎ (0254) 22 225 / 22 2284.

**Police** – ☎ (0254) 22 200.

**Medical service** – **Hospital**, ☎ (0254) 22 222 / 22 345.

**Laundry** – **Self-service Laundromat**, N Garoufalídhou.

**Bookshop** – **Karaatzadeios**, on Mírina's main street near the market.

## WHERE TO STAY

• **Mírina**

*Under €27*
**Apollo Pavilion**, N Garoufalídhou, ☎ (0254) 23 712 / 24 315, Fax (0254) 23 712 – 11rm. ⁜🍴 ♒ 🏝 🏠 A practical and cheap place to stay for backpackers (around €12 without shower). Communal fridge. The owner speaks English. Open all year.

*Around €27*
📧**Poseidon**, at the end of Roméïkos Gialós beach, set 50m back, ☎ (0254) 24 821 / 23 982, Fax (0254) 24 856 – 20rm. ⁜🍴 ♒ 📧 📺 🏠 ♒ 💳 A comfortable and well-kept hotel, located in a quiet setting at the edge of town (beyond the Archaeological Museum). The airy rooms have fridge and balcony, some overlooking the sea. Friendly staff.

📧**Filoktítis**, set 200m back from the Richá Nerá beach, ☎ (0254) 23 344 / 24 063 – 16rm. ⁜🍴 ♒ 📧 📺 ✗ 🏠 ♒ 💳 A new establishment that is comfortable, clean and spacious with very professional staff. A ramp is available for disabled guests. The owner is also the chef of an excellent restaurant and will welcome you warmly. Very good value.

*Between €27 and €38*
**Kosmos**, on Roméïkos Gialós quay, ☎ (0254) 22 050 – 8rm. ⁜🍴 ♒ 📧 📺 This is perhaps the most charming of the many hotels of a similar standard that line the quays. Unfortunately it's rather noisy in the evening.

*Over €75*
📧**Portomyrína Palace**, under 2km north of Mírina on the road to Káspakas, ☎ (0254) 24 805 / 24 806, Fax (0254) 24 858 – 70rm and 80 bungalows. ⁜🍴 ♒ 📧 🏝 📺 ✗ 🏠 ♒ 🌸 💿 💳 A brand new palace, built in a superb setting at the heart of Arlon Bay, with a view of Mt Athos and the sunset over the sea. The hotel contains the modest remains of the Sanctuary of Artemis (see above). A magnificent pool at the sea's edge, private beach, indoor pool, games room, gym, water sports, 2 tennis courts,

*The North Aegean*

massage, entertainment, everything is available here. The bungalows are well designed and perfect for families.

### • Ágios Ioánnis

**Between €38 and €45**
**Sunset**, north of the beach near the hill-top chapel. Walk back up on the right side, ☎ (0254) 61 555 / 61 593 – 14rm. ⚐ 🍴 A lovely hotel in quiet surroundings that provides a splendid view of the sea and the beach, 50m away. Although there is no air conditioning, the hotel is airy. Family-sized rooms, ideal for groups or families. Breakfast is extra.

### • Platí

This is a pleasant resort. Apart from the large complex located south of the beach, the area has several rooms to rent as well as guesthouses facing the sea. Even in the old village, 600m higher up, you will find rooms to rent if you inquire in the tavernas, notably at "Zimbabwe".

**Between €27 and €38**
**Plati Beach Hotel**, in the middle of the beach, ☎ (0254) 23 583 – 14rm. ⚐ 🍴 🎋 ✕ 🍴 The only hotel at the water's edge. An acceptable establishment even if the service is not always up to scratch.

**Over €60**
**Afrodíti**, set 200m back from the beach (on the left when arriving from Mírina), ☎ (0254) 23 141 / 25 032, Fax (0254) 25 031 – 14rm and 1 suite. ⚐ 🍴 🎋 📺 ✕ 🍴 ⛱ ☂ 🆑 Expensive and a bit flashy but the pool is superb and very welcome. Groups are not accepted. Rooms are comfortable and breakfast is copious. You can have a drink at the bar, overlooking the pool and the flower garden. Staff speak English. Open only in summer.

### • Moúdros

**Between €27 and €38**
**Kyma,** on the seafront, ☎ (0254) 71 066 / 71 166, Fax (0254) 71 484 – 25rm. ⚐ 🍴 ✕ 🍴 🆑 A good place to stay with rooms with balconies, despite antiquated decor. Good quality restaurant with a pleasant terrace.

EATING OUT

### • Mírina

Mírina has many restaurants around the fishing harbour or at the beginning of the quays at Roméïkos beach.

**Around €9**
**Plátanos**, on the main street (Karatza), ☎ (0254) 22 070. 🍴 This typical and popular restaurant is shaded by plane trees. You can make your choice directly in the kitchen. No fish, but tasty and copious dishes of meat in sauces, pasta, and stuffed vegetables.

**Between €9 and €15**
**Filoktítis**, set 200m back from Richá Nerá beach (see "Where to stay" above), ☎ (0254) 23 344 / 24 063. 🍴 🆑 A pleasant terrace with attentive service. The usual Greek specialities but tasty.

**Kósmos**, on the quay at Roméïkos, by the hotel of the same name, ☎ (0254) 22 050. 🍴 A café-restaurant serving good Greek food.

**Over €15**
**Gláros**, on the quay at the fishing harbour, ☎ (0254) 22 220. 🍴 🆑 A reputable seafood restaurant in a very attractive setting in the middle of the harbour. Rather expensive however.

### • Platí

You'll find a number of average quality tavernas at the edge of the beach. In the upper part of the village itself, there are 3 pleasant and shady tavernas.

**Around €9**
**Taverna Zimbabwe**, ☎ (0254) 25 490. 🍴 The friendly owner lived in Zimbabwe for a long time before opening this modest but charming taverna, with a shady terrace where you can enjoy tasty family-style cuisine. Reasonable prices. Open all year.

HAVING A DRINK

### • Mírina

**Kapatkíos**, on the quayside at the beginning of Roméïkos beach, ☎ (0254) 24 855. Café, bar and pub. An ideal place to enjoy a cocktail while watching an unforgettable sunset over Mt Athos and listening to good music. Lovely terrace at the water's edge. Next door, the restaurant offers seafood and good Greek specialities on its menu.

SHOPPING GUIDE

**Local delicacies** – Retsína, fig jam, thyme honey (from the village of Skandáli), cheese (Kalthaki and Melihoro), and wine (Kalmbáki, white wine).

# SÁMOS★

North Aegean – Capital of the district of Sámos
2km from the Turkish coast – Michelin map 980 fold 34 – Regional map page 458
477km² – Pop 33 000 – Allow 4 days

**Not to be missed**
The Heraíon, one of the most ancient temples in Greece.
The wine of Sámos, a muscat with a resin taste.

**And remember...**
If you're looking for peace and quiet, stay at the
fishing village of Ágios Konstandínos.

Although modest in size, the easternmost island of the Greek archipelago is proud of its great variety of landscapes. Inland to the north, the high hills hide stone hamlets surrounded by vines, while the nearby pines and scrublands give off an amber fragrance which you can find in the island's popular wine, the **muscat of Sámos**. In the south, the wind sweeps the tall grasses on the plains, a setting that would be more reminiscent of the steppes of Anatolia were it not for the Aegean's salty breeze. For the sea is never far away. Chalk cliffs and pebbly inlets wind around the coast between the island's three ports and main towns: busy Karlovássi, lovely and languid Vathí, and Pithagório where bars and discos celebrate summer and the holiday season, just a step away from a sanctuary buried in silence. This is the Temple of Hera, whose enormous blocks of immaculate marble remind us of its importance as one of the oldest and largest buildings of Ancient Greece, constructed 2 700 years ago.

## A coveted island

Populated by Ionians from the mainland, the island had its golden age in the middle of the 6C BC under the enlightened tyrant **Polycrates**. A friend of the poets Anacreon and Ibycus, the monarch encouraged intellectual and artistic creativity, and it is thanks to him that the audacious Temple of Hera and the surprising tunnel of Eupalinus were built, two works which were models of their kind. Between East and West, Sámos also ranked as an important naval and trade power.

However, its choice strategic position quickly placed it at the heart of conflict. The island passed from one hand to another until it attempted to proclaim its autonomy in 440 during the "Sámos Revolt". This act was not particularly appreciated by Pericles, who travelled in person to subjugate the island after a terrible siege. Henceforth, each new occupying force imposed its identity. In the 4C BC, Greece sent Athenian settlers, the **cleruchies** who in the 15C were driven away by the Ottomans who wished to settle in Sámos. This led some of the island's inhabitants to go into exile in Lesbos or Chios. In 1821, however, the Samiots joined the national independence movement led by **Likoúrgos Logothétis**, who is remembered in history as a hero. In 1824, the Turkish flotilla was conquered at Pithagório and in 1913, the island joined the Greek nation.

## The north coast

### Vathí★ (Sámos Town)

*Capital of Sámos. Pop 6 000.* The best views of the town and its brightly coloured Greek and Ottoman-style houses are from the ferry as it makes its approach. From the **upper part★** of town (Áno Vathí) there are splendid **panoramic views★** of the houses on the opposite slope, which slowly turn a crimson colour as the sun sets. From here, **alleyways** descend steeply towards "the stage": the harbour and its little expanse of water. It's very pleasant to stroll along the **quayside★**. At the northern end, the harbourmaster's office (*where the ferries tie up*) is next to a **taverna** that is very popular with older Greeks.

A little further away stands the **Roman Catholic Church** *(300m south)*, a large ochre-coloured Baroque gem, visible from afar. The walk then continues along **Platía Pithagóra**, which is guarded by a **marble lion**, the symbol of Samiot courage. A hundred metres further on are the **municipal gardens\*\*** *(set back from the quays, turn left three streets after the National Bank of Greece)*. Mornings find the locals sitting under the palm trees, enjoying the cool of the fountain and watching the activity in the market *(at the foot of the Orthodox church)* and people leaving Mass.

The neo-Classical white façade of the **town hall** stands on the opposite side of the gardens *(on the north-east corner)*. To its left on the square, don't miss the remarkable **Archaeological Museum\*\*\*** *(Tuesday-Sunday, 8.30am-3pm; entrance fee)*, which houses the finest relics from the Temple of Hera. A visit to the museum serves as an excellent introduction to the site located in the southern part of the island. Begin with the modern building, where several marble **korai\*** from the 6C BC are displayed. In the second room, the **group of three figures\*** attributed to the Samiot sculptor **Geneleos** originally stood at the entrance to the Sacred Way in the Heraíon. From the next room you climb a small mound from which you can admire a gigantic marble **kouros\*\*\***, 4.75 m high. Historians remain divided about what it represents: Apollo, a demigod or perhaps an ideal human, a servant of the goddess?

## From the village to the beach

*Head west towards Karlovássi when leaving Vathí.*

■ The road borders a breathtakingly high cliff overhanging the sea all the way to **Kokári** *(10km from Vathí)*, a fishing village that has kept some of its charming **stone houses**. Does its long pebble beach, lined with restaurants, souvenir shops and motorcycle rental shops justify its being so popular with the tourists?

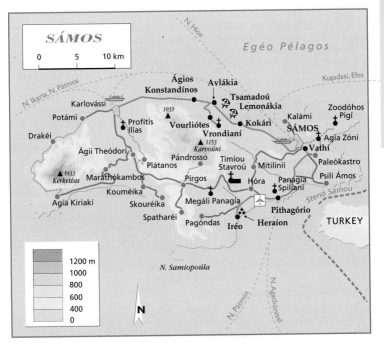

■ A better choice is **Avlákia beach**★ *(3km further along the same road, signposted)*, in the idyllic setting of two steep-sided rocky inlets, **Tsamadoú**★ and **Lemonákia**.

*Go left at the junction immediately after Avlákia.* As you drive further inland, the road climbs in sharp bends and the air becomes cooler under the shade of the pine trees.

■ High up in the hills, **Vourliótes**★ *(4km from Avlákia)* resembles an eagle's nest. This village, with its long wine-producing tradition, is one of the most picturesque on the island. The main street goes up and down like a roller coaster, and the half-open wooden shutters occasionally reveal a cramped interior. Even the walls of the houses, with their Ottoman **corbelling**★, are lopsided. It's something of a relief to get to the central square *(follow the main street)*; quite apart from the four restaurants shaded by leafy plane trees, it is the only level surface in the village!

■ Taking the same ascending road, enjoy yet another lovely drive by visiting the **Moní Vrondianí Monastery**★ *(signposted from Vourliótes, 3km away. Stop at the car park, 100m before reaching the monastery)*, the oldest in Sámos (1476). Its white walls stand between two hills mantled with fragrant fig and mulberry trees. An antique wooden portal opens under the **bell-tower**, and old homespun robes hang under the cool porch. In the centre of the sun-filled courtyard stands the main **chapel**★, while a strange collection of rusted tools rest on whitewashed wooden blocks.

*Head back to the coast and turn left towards Karlovássi.*

■ The well-preserved fishing village of **Ágios Konstandínos**★★ *(2km from Avlákia, 15km from Vathí)* hides its single row of houses between the sea and a dense pine forest. Their coloured shutters open directly onto the pebble beach and the **harbour**★★ with its clutch of little fishing boats. Fresh fish is prepared in the kitchens every evening. Even the postman delivers only once a week.

## On the south coast

### Pithagório★

*14km from Vathí. Pop 1 500.* Built over the ruins of the ancient town of Sámos, Pithagório attracts many more tourists than Vathí. The **harbour** is in the southern part of the town, with a **pier** still resting on a jetty built by Polycrates, while an unbroken string of bars, lit by violet lights in the evenings, occupies the quayside. The main street, **Odós Logothétis**, leads to the tiny town centre, with its array of souvenir shops and car rental agencies.

$a^2+b^2=c^2$
Pithagório owes its name to Pythagoras, who was born here around 580 BC. A distinguished mathematician to whom we owe the famous theory that the square on the hypotenuse of a right-angled triangle is equal to the sum of the squares on the other two sides. Easy, isn't it? The man himself appears to have been more obscure, having dedicated part of his life to mysticism. He believed in reincarnation and in "metempsychosis", or the transmigration of souls.

*Return to Odós Logothétis and continue to climb towards the centre. Go left onto Metamórfosis Sotiros.* In the middle of an elevated esplanade you'll see the rounded blue and white forms of the stately **Church of the Transfiguration**★ (Metamórfosis). It adjoins the **Likoúrgos Logothétis Fort**★★, built from great blocks of ochre-coloured stone perched on a hill and overlooking the eastern coast. You can just imagine the proud patriot contemplating his victory over the Turks in 1824 from the top of the fort's elegant tower, which overlooks the pleasant tamarisk-shaded **beach**★ below.

*At the junction when leaving Pithagório, head towards, Vathí ("Sámos-Town"). The road climbs. Stop at the car park on the left after three bends.*

### The Tunnel of Eupalinus★★

*1.5km north-east of Pithagório. Open 9am-2pm. Closed Monday. Entrance fee. Bring warm clothing.* According to Herodotus, the work was a "marvel of its day." Built by Polycrates, this 1 350m-long aqueduct *(only a small section of approximately 50m can be visited)* supplied the ancient town of Sámos with fresh water, by diverting an important watercourse from the north of the island. Its construction was completed in 524 BC. Construction proceeded simultaneously from either end, and such was the accuracy of the plans drawn up by the architect, **Eupalinus of Megara**, that the meeting of the two bores was only out by a matter of a few feet.

You enter through a small white house clinging to the side of **Mt Kástri**. A steep staircase plunges into the narrow passageway dug into the rock. Through the grille which runs the entire length, you will be able to see a dark channel down below. This is the tunnel, or to give it its proper name, the aqueduct. The tunnel served as a refuge for local people in the event of an attack.

*Go back down towards Pithagório, and at the junction take the road heading west towards the airport and Iréo.*

### The Heraíon★★

*8km west of Pithagório on the coast. 1km before reaching the village of Iréo look out for a yellow sign indicating the site. Turn left at this junction, which is where the buses stop. You then have to walk 800m. Open every day except Monday, 8.30am-2.30pm. Entrance fee.* A rusty gate opens onto a plain backed by barren mountains in the distance. On the left after entering, marble blocks mark out an enormous rectangle on the ground. These are the only remains of the last Temple of Hera, dedicated to the goddess of fertility who, according to mythology, was born in Sámos. Several sanctuaries succeeded one another at the same site. The first dates from the 7C BC and is the oldest known Greek temple. The last, built by Polycrates at the end of the 6C, easily supersedes its predecessors by its size: it is 108.6m long and 55.1m wide (twice the size of the Parthenon). Surrounded by three rows of columns (a total of 155, of which only one still stands), it contained a tall statue of the goddess *(now in the Louvre in Paris)*. The Ionian order, which originated on the island (as well as at Ephesus on the Turkish coast), reached its peak here – and its limits. Construction continued until the 3C BC but the work was apparently never roofed.

The three korai at the Heraíon of Sámos

T. Saint-Criq/MICHELIN

**Sámos**

At the other end of the temple, on the left, **three korai**\*\* without heads are lined up against a background of reeds (*the originals are kept at the museum in Vathí*). They stood at the beginning of the **Sacred Way**\*\*, which connected the sanctuary to the ancient town of Sámos.

## Making the most of Sámos

### GETTING THERE

**By air** – 4km from Pithagório, the airport has flights on Olympic Airways to Athens several times a day and to Thessaloníki twice a week.

**By boat** – Most of the arrivals and departures take place in Vathí, but there are also some in Pithagório. There are connections from the island to nearly everywhere in the Aegean. Daily departures for Piraeus, as well as for Ikaría, Fourní, Náxos and Páros. There are fewer departures for the other islands: 3 ferries a week for Chios, one weekly for Lesbos and Rhodes. Departure days may change so be sure to ask for information at the travel agencies. Daily service to Kusadasi on the Turkish coast (in general, you need to leave your passport at the agency the day before departure).

### GETTING AROUND

**By car** – Rental agencies (such as **Hertz** and **Budget**) are found in every town along the coast. This is a practical means of transport given the small amount of distance to cover, the number of service stations and the good condition of the roads. Avoid the small mountain roads inland.

**By bus** – The excellent bus network serves the entire island all day.
In Vathí, the bus terminal is opposite the ferry landing-stage, at the southern end of the harbour on Odós Lekáti. In Pithagório, the bus stop is located at the junction between Odós Logothétis and Odós Polykrátous.

**By taxi** – Yellow in colour. In Vathí, the taxi rank is on Platía Pithagóra, and in Pithagório it's at the harbour, at the top of Odós Likoúrgos Logothétis.

## Making the most of Vathí

### ADDRESS BOOK

**Tourist information** – In the alleyway behind Platía Pithagóra, to the north of the square, ☏ (0273) 28 530. Friendly service.

**Bank / Currency exchange** – National Bank of Greece and several cash dispensers at the harbour.

**Post office** – *Main post office*, Odós Smírnis, four streets south of the municipal gardens on the road that leaves from the quayside.

**Airline companies** – *Olympic Airways*, Odós Smírnis before reaching the post office, ☏ (0273) 27 237.

### WHERE TO STAY

*Under €30*
*Pension Avli*, Odós Areós, ☏ (0273) 22 939 – 11rm. ⚐ This former convent with stone vaults, a courtyard decorated with flowers, and wainscoting in the

rooms, has unparalleled charm. Try to book ahead.

*Hotel Acropolis*, Kalistrátou 1, on the seafront, north of the harbour, ☏ (0273) 27 604 – 11rm. ⚐ ✕ This modern, clean, and comfortable establishment has a family atmosphere. The rooms overlooking the sea have pretty balconies, and there is a small supermarket next door.

*Pension Ionna*, Menemenéica, Poíkou 15, ☏ (0273) 28 411 – 4rm. Shared bathroom. The view of the town from this small green and white house in the heights of Vathí is magnificent, especially from the roof terrace, which is shaded by a vine-covered trellis.

*Around €60*
*Aeolis Hotel*, at the harbour, Themistokléous Sofoúli 30, ☏ (0273) 28 904 – 31rm. ⚐ 🖩 ✐ TV ✕ ☖ CC The best hotel in town in this category, well maintained and stylish.

- **Ágios Konstandínos**

On the north coast, approximately 15km west of Vathí.

*Around €23*

The Four Seasons, in the upper part of the village, ☎ (0273) 94 247 – 6rm. Shared bathroom. A family-run guesthouse with a warm atmosphere. Clean rooms with old-fashioned charm. The view of the sea is spectacular.

### EATING OUT

*Around €15*

To dili, Ano Vathí, at the end of Odós Smírnis (in the same road as the post office), ☎ (0273) 24 902. The name means "sunset", and whether seated in the garden or under the trellis, you will have a grandstand view of the evening light on the houses on the opposite slope, while your charming hostess serves delicious family-style meals.

Taverna Gregori, Odós Smírnis, ☎ (0273) 22 718. Another good place to dine, without the view but with a lovely trellis. Dishes are simple but copious and the prices reasonable.

### HAVING A DRINK

Traditional music and dance performances are organised at weekends on the square by the town hall as soon as it gets dark. The crowd is mostly Greek.

---

## Making the most of Pithagório

### ADDRESS BOOK

**Tourist information** – In the middle of Odós Logothétis, ☎ (0273) 61 389. The helpful staff speak English. You'll find good information here, including bus and inter-island boat schedules.

**Banks / Currency exchange** – The National Bank of Greece and several cash dispensers are located in Odós Logothétis.

**Post office** – *Main post office*, right at the top of Odós Logothétis, at the opposite end from the harbour.

**Airline companies** – *Olympic Airways*, in Odós Logothétis, after the post office, ☎ (0273) 61 300.

### WHERE TO STAY

*€30*

Pension Hélena, in Odós Polykrátous, 500m to the right when coming from Odós Logothétis, ☎ (0273) 61 322 – 3rm. Hélena and Plutarch, a charming elderly couple, provide well-kept rooms in their beautiful home.

Pension Déspina, museum square, ☎ (0273) 61 677, Fax (0273) 61472 – 16rm. A good place to stay if you're travelling in a group, being one of the rare establishments of its size in the village. Rooms lack charm but are clean and quiet, and only 5min from the harbour.

### EATING OUT

Avoid the restaurants at the harbour, which are expensive and mediocre.

*Around €45*

Riva Restaurant, between the harbour and the castle, ☎ (0273) 62 395. Facing the sea in a pebble garden. This is an opportunity to sample the wines of Sámos. The menu offers a wide choice of drinks and meals. Fabulous service.

### HAVING A DRINK

There is an infinite choice of bars. If you enjoy dancing to electronic rhythms, visit Totem, 2km before Pithagório, on the road to Sámos.

### SHOPPING GUIDE

**Sámos wines** – Wine in every price category is sold at the grocery stores in Odós Logothétis.

**Embroidered linen** – At the end of the quays, on the right facing the sea, you'll find a modest shop that supplies lovely handmade items.

Rhodes, the last gateway to the West

# THE DODECANESE

A string of bright islands in the far south-east of the Aegean Sea – at the outermost bounds of Greece and the European Union – lies close to the Turkish coast, almost touching it. The group of "twelve islands" – *Dódeka Nisia* in Greek – accompanied by myriad islets and reefs stretches between Crete in the south-west and Sámos in the north. Each has its own distinctive character, and the group, also known as the Southern Sporades, is united only by their common destiny. The attraction of **Pátmos** lies in the harmony of its landscapes and the human scale of its dwellings, which lend it a comforting note of serenity. The atmosphere changes on the two largest islands, **Rhodes** and **Kos**, which are by far the most popular with visitors, with an abundance both of archaeological remains and tourist amenities. Different again are **Kálimnos**, with its sponge fishermen, wild **Kárpathos**, proud of its traditions, and aristocratic **Sími**, with an outstanding architectural heritage.

What they all have in common, however, is the light. Islands in the sun, the *Dódeka Nisia* have one of the best climates in the Mediterranean, suitable for interests of every kind – swimming, scuba diving, country walks and cultural tours. Just leave the beaten track and avoid the peak summer season and you will find peace and quiet on deserted beaches and a daily life punctuated by undying traditions. One of them is hospitality: while the World Wars brought about massive emigration, some nationals have come back to the islands of their childhood and, open to the world, are extremely welcoming.

## Between two worlds

The islands of the Dodecanese, some of which have been inhabited since the Neolithic Period, saw brilliant civilisations flourish at an early date. Indeed, as the islands lie close to one another, they favour coastal navigation, which is suitable for trade. They thus became the centre of a great intermixing of peoples that was to last three millennia, and continues to this day. While the Dodecanese now mainly look towards the West, they are nonetheless geographically connected to Asia Minor, to which they remain very attached through a thousand years of Byzantine culture. On the dividing line between East and West, the islands have always formed a frontier zone. In spite of their fierce desire for self-government, the city states have always been coveted, and often besieged and invaded. The Dodecanese did not join Greece until 1948, and the geopolitical stakes remain high, as is borne out by the omnipresence of the Greek army and Turkish demands to renegotiate the borders.

## Rhodes, the foremost island in the Dodecanese

The island the furthest away from Athens is paradoxically the best known of the Dodecanese. Admittedly, Rhodes is the largest island (1 400km$^2$) in the group, and is a major economic and cultural centre. Rhodes Town is the regional capital and the only large urban centre in the Dodecanese, drawing the rest of the island to it like a magnet. Above all it has an **exceptional historic heritage**. The walls of the medieval city speak for themselves, forming the largest ensemble of fortifications in Europe. This prestigious past has left a series of strong, often intimately linked imprints: a mixture of races and civilisations that Rhodes Town embodies to perfection, softening them with a pleasant Mediterranean art of living.

Rhodes combines all the attractions of the Dodecanese and Cyclades Islands: a cosmopolitan tourist capital with an intense cultural life, lovely **beaches**, good forests for walking in and beautiful villages hidden among the mountains.

## Under the sign of the sun god

Rhodes is dedicated to the sun, which shines on the island more than 300 days a year. The **meltem** wind blows there less violently than in the Cyclades, making the intense summer heat bearable. In the low season there is pleasant sunshine and winters are particularly mild. Since its beginnings, the island's tutelary god has been the sun, to whom the Colossus of Rhodes, its emblem, was dedicated. Yet again, the sun was responsible for the island's first name, **Helioússa** (from *helios*, meaning sun). In one of his *Odes*, Pindar tells how Rhodes was born, the result of the love between Helios the sun god and the nymph **Rhodia**. According to legend, three of their great grandchildren founded the first cities on the island, which were named after them: Líndos, Kámiros and Ialissós, three towns united round the sanctuary of Apollo, god of light.

## Birth of a prestigious city

The dominant influence was to be that of the **Dorians** who settled on the island in the 12C BC. Masters in the art of war, they also proved to be outstanding sailors. In the 9C BC the three leading city states on Rhodes – **Líndos**, **Kámiros** and **Ialissós** – united to found what soon became the Dorian Hexapolis (750 BC). There ensued a prosperous age that saw the Rhodian towns trading with the whole of the Middle East and the western Mediterranean.

From the moment the town of Rhodes was founded, the history of the island merged with that of its eponymous capital. In the late 5C BC the three city states joined to give rise to the **Rhodian Deme**, thus laying the early foundations for the town of Rhodes, which soon became a prestigious and ambitious city.

In the new world created by **Alexander the Great**, Rhodes was to experience three centuries of unprecedented influence. Between East and West, the island became a strategic point on the trade route linking the Hellenic world with Asia Minor, and its currency was valid everywhere. Founding its prosperity on a maritime economy, it armed itself with a powerful fleet that dominated the entire eastern Mediterranean, where the **Rhodian code** of navigation was adopted by all its neighbours.

Rhodes also became a brilliant centre of culture. The town had a famous school of sculpture and became home to the school of the Stoic philosopher **Panaetius**. Cicero and Caesar were among those who came to Rhodes to study.

But its unfortunate allegiance to Perseus, the last king of Macedon, led to the disintegration of its alliance with Rome, and Rhodes grew weaker. It was sacked by a Roman general in 42 BC, finally annexed by Rome in 297, and when the Roman Empire was divided up, it became Byzantine.

## Franks against Arabs

The Arab threat was making itself felt as early as the 7C. The eastern provinces of the ancient Hellenistic world were lost forever and the influence of Constantinople, which was destroyed in 1204 by Latins, in turn diminished. **Pirates** took advantage of this period of instability, plunging the whole region into decline. In 1306, however, the **Hospitallers of St John of Jerusalem** arrived in Rhodes (*see page 483*), moving their headquarters there, and calling themselves **Knights of Rhodes**. Great builders, they fortified the island and transformed the group of islands into an efficient chain of defence against the Turks. The multinational nature of the Order increased the cosmopolitanism that already existed on the islands, and the Dodecanese regained prosperity. However, the last Grand Master of Rhodes, the Frenchman **Villiers de L'Isle-Adam**, was unable to contain the considerable army of **Süleyman the Magnificent** during the terrible siege in 1522. While the knights withdrew to Malta, the Dodecanese once again became part of Asia Minor, under the Turks. Four centuries of domination began (1523-1911), but during that time, Rhodes and its satellite islands were able to keep a certain amount of administrative autonomy. With the end of the conflict between Italy and Turkey in 1911, the **Italians** took over the Dodecanese. Then in 1943, with the collapse of the fascist regime in Italy, the islands fell into the hands of the Germans, who in turn surrendered them to the British in 1945. Rhodes eventually became part of Greece in 1948.

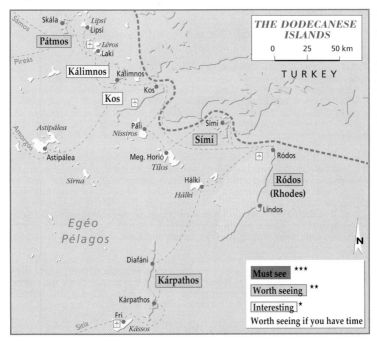

# RHODES TOWN★★★

Capital of Rhodes Island (Ródos) and of the district of the Dodecanese
Michelin map 980 fold 47 – Regional map page 479 – Pop 101 350
Allow at least 2 days

**Not to be missed**
The Knights' Quarter. A stroll through the alleyways of the medieval city.
Sunset from the top of Monte Smith.

**And remember...**
Stay in the medieval city, or in the pedestrian area in the modern town.
Enjoy the good quality restaurants.

The medieval city of Rhodes lies squeezed within its walls like a stone crescent. It is almost entirely encircled by the modern town, except to the east where it is lapped by the sea, and where the harbours of Emborió and Mandráki look towards Turkey. Arriving by boat, you have a superb view of the noble city with its ochre-coloured walls bristling with crenellations, towers, turrets and the odd tip of a minaret.

Within the ramparts, the maze of paved alleyways, arches and narrow passageways takes you right back to the Middle Ages. To the north, dominating the Hóra or Old Town, is the residential quarter of the knights, the Collachium, the site chosen by the Grand Masters of the Order to build their powerful palace-fortress. Outside this stronghold, losing yourself in the colourful alleys of the Hóra, here and there you will come across a lovely marble fountain, or hidden behind some ageless doorway, a little patio bathed in the scent of jasmine and bougainvillaea.

*To find your way in the Old Town, follow the public signposts rather than tourist maps, which are often misleading. Wear comfortable walking shoes as many of the streets are paved with pointed cobblestones.*

## The Knights' Quarter★★★ (Collachium) (Plan II)
*Plan II page 484. Allow half a day.*

### Palace of the Grand Masters★★★ (Paláti Megálon Magístron) (A1)
*Platia Kleovoúlou, 8am-7pm on weekdays, 8.30am-3pm Saturday and Sunday. Entrance fee. Allow 30min.* By way of a palace, the Grand Masters of the Order of St John built themselves a real military fortress. This was seriously damaged by an earthquake, soon followed by the explosion of a powder keg in 1856. It was then rebuilt by the Italians, in a style that did not always comply with the original Provençal Gothic architecture that recalled the Papal Palace in Avignon. However, the building has kept all its noble, impressive bearing.

The palace is built round a large square **courtyard**★★ surrounded by arcades paved with marble and punctuated by Roman statues. Beneath the courtyard are enormous **silos** once used for storing grain in anticipation of long sieges. Similarly, there are underground storerooms beneath the palace, where weapons and munitions were kept *(closed)*.

The tour of the **palace**★ itself takes in a succession of vast rooms with colonnades or pointed arches, often done up in the Victor Emmanuel III style, decorated with chests and **tapestries**, leaving space for **Greek and Roman mosaics**★★ that mostly come from Kos.

Do not miss the **underground rooms**★★ *(access from the courtyard, beneath the arcades)*, which house two extremely interesting exhibitions. One, devoted to **Antique Rhodes** *(allow 45min)*, displays various pieces of pottery, pearls and statues, as well as funerary ornaments, jewellery and utensils used in everyday life. The other *(a little smaller, allow 30min)* is on **Medieval Rhodes**, illustrated notably by beautiful 14C icons.

*As you leave the palace, turn left down Odós Ipotón.*

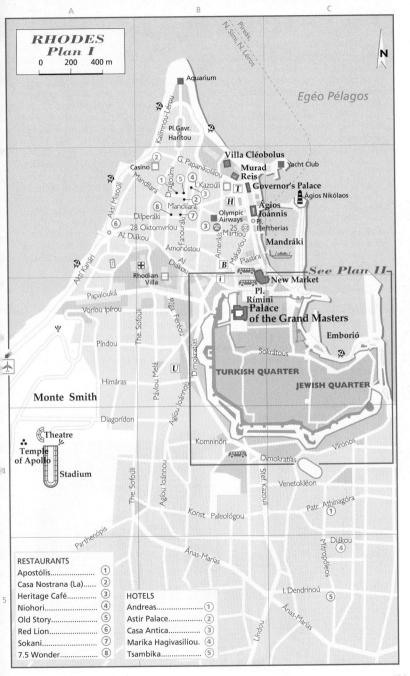

# RHODES
## Plan I
0    200    400 m

Pireás, N. Sími, N. Léros

Aquarium

Egéo Pélagos

Kalímnou-Lérou

Pl. Gavr.
Harítou

G. Papanikoláou

Casino

Villa Cléobolus

Murad
Reis

Yacht Club

Dragoúmi
I. Kazoúli

Governor's Palace

Mandílara

Ágios Nikólaos

Mandílara

Dilperáki

Olympic
Airways

Ágios
Ioánnis

Pl.
Eleftherías

28 Oktomvríou

Al. Diákou

Fanouráki

Amóhóstou

Amerikís
Martíou
25

Mandráki

Akti Miaoúli

Aktí Kanári

Rhodian
Villa

Makaríou
Plastíra

See Plan II

Papalouká

Voríou Ipírou

The Sofoúli

Ríga Feréou

New Market

Pl.
Rímini
Palace
of the Grand Masters

Píndou

Emborió

Sokrátous

Monte Smith

Pávlou Melá

Agíou Ioánnou

Himáras

TURKISH QUARTER

JEWISH QUARTER

Diagorídon

Theatre

Temple
of Apollo

Stadium

Komninón

Víronos

The Sofoúli

Agíou Ioánnou

Dimokratías

Venetokléon

Stef. Kazoúli

Parthenópis

Konst. Paleológou

Ánas-Marías

Dimokratías

Patr. Athinagóra

Díakou

Mitropóleos

Líndou

I. Dendrinoú

Ánas-Marías

## RESTAURANTS
Apostólis.................... ①
Casa Nostrana (La)...... ②
Heritage Café.............. ③
Niohori....................... ④
Old Story.................... ⑤
Red Lion.................... ⑥
Sokani........................ ⑦
7.5 Wonder................ ⑧

## HOTELS
Andreas...................... ①
Astir Palace................ ②
Casa Antica................ ③
Maríka Hagivasilíou.... ④
Tsambíka.................... ⑤

481

## Knights' Street*** (Odós Ipotón) (A1)

Lined by the inns of the different nationalities of the order of the knights (*see sidebar*) – sober buildings with smooth walls punctuated by arches – the street with its stone paving makes up a wonderful townscape, entirely 15C Gothic in character. As the street follows the route of an ancient road, it is straight, thus contrasting with the winding alleyways of the surrounding city. Once past **St John's Lodge**, an elegant portico with two wings that marks the entrance to the palace, you reach the **Provençal Inn** a little further down (*on the left*), linked by an arch to the **Spanish Inn**.

Still on the left, you come to the jewel of Odós Ipotón, the noble façade of the **French Inn**★★, the largest and most beautiful of all the inns. After the damage caused by the siege in 1480 and by an earthquake, the inn was largely modified in 1492. Today the inn houses a branch of the French Consulate. During office hours (*9am-12noon; closed Saturday and Sunday*), you can have a look at the exuberantly planted **garden**★. Further down on the left, you come to the **French Chapel**★ (Church of the Holy Trinity) (*Tuesday-Sunday, 8.30am-3pm; no charge*), recognisable by the small statue of the Virgin and Child in a **niche** on the façade.

Next comes the **Italian Inn**, and then, at the end of Odós Ipotón, standing opposite, is **St Mary's Cathedral**★★ (Our Lady of the Castle, Panagía) (*8.30am-3pm; closed Monday; entrance fee*), a wide building with three naves also known as the Byzantine Museum on account of its superb **Byzantine frescoes**★. It was built in the 11C and then modified by the knights in 1309, before being converted into a mosque by the Turks. There are lovely **mosaics** in the courtyard.

On leaving the church, you will see the **English Inn** on your left (*Platía Moussíou*). It faces the former **Knights' Hospital**, now a fascinating archaeological museum.

## Knights' Hospital★★ (Archaeological Museum) (A1)

*8am-7pm Tuesday-Saturday, 8am-2.30pm Sunday. Closed Monday. Entrance fee.* You enter this magnificent building through a wide **central courtyard**★★ surrounded by arcades. It is flanked by a **vaulted hallway**★★, the setting for a marble lion, a paleo-Christian mosaic and various sarcophagi. From here, a corridor leads to a secondary courtyard with **mosaics**.

Medieval Rhodes:
Odós Ipotón or Knights' Street

G. de Benoist/MICHELIN

Shops once stood on the ground floor, while the first floor, reached by a **grand staircase\***, housed the hospital services. The **Ward of the Sick\*** (Room I) is a huge hall with two naves that once contained about a hundred beds. A small **chapel\*** opposite juts out over the porch of the building, while along the walls are the **funerary plaques** of many of the knights, adorned with their coats-of-arms or bas-reliefs. The rather dull display-cases in the side rooms – 1 to 15 (*Arab numerals*) – show finds from excavations carried out

**The knights of the West**
First devoted to helping the sick and destitute on pilgrimages to the Holy Land, the religious Order of the Knights of St John of Jerusalem also became a military order in the 12C. Led by a Grand Master who was elected for life, the Order was made up of three social classes, knights (nobles), clerks and sergeants, and auxiliary soldiers responsible for ministering to the sick and carrying out domestic chores. From then on – apart from keeping the three vows of poverty, chastity and obedience, and helping the sick – the rules of membership included the defence of the Church and, most important of all, the struggle against the Infidel. The Order was divided into seven groups according to the languages spoken by the knights. Three of the groups were French – Provence, Auvergne, and France – making up the majority of the knights, and the rest were Spanish (later divided into Aragon and Castile), Italian, English, and German.

on the island during the Italian Period. It's better to spend time in **Rooms II to VI**, which contain the finest pieces, among them steles and statues from the Hellenistic Period of the Rhodian school. Here you will see notably the graceful **Aphrodite of Rhodes\*\*\*** (1C BC). There are other statues of Aphrodite, as well as a porphyry **Bacchus** and a statue of **Helios**, the sun god, the town's ancient emblem. Lastly, various pieces of marble, cannonballs and **mosaics** are mixed together in an attractive flower-filled courtyard.

*Retrace your steps by going up Odós Apélou to Platía Argirókastrou.*

### On Platía Argirókastrou (A1)
Here you can tour the colourful **Decorative Arts Museum** (*8.30am-3pm; closed Monday*), which displays all manner of items evoking various activities on the islands during the Turkish Period. There are ceramics from Nicaea (Iznik), faience, plates from Armenian workshops or from Líndos, **furniture and carved wooden objects** from Sími, crockery, and traditional costumes and **embroideries**.
Nearby you can visit the **Gallery of Modern Greek Art** (*daily, 8am-2pm except Sunday 8am-1pm; Thursday and Friday 5-8pm; closed Monday; entrance fee*) and, on the left, the **Arméria Palace** (A1). This was the first hospital in Rhodes and is adorned with the armorial bearings of one of the oldest Grand Masters, Roger de Pins.
Opposite, on the south side of Platía Sími, is the **Auvergne Inn** (Katálima Overnis) (B1). It was built in the 15C and consists of a covered gallery flanked by an outside staircase. Continuing around Platía Sími, you will see on the right the remains of the 3C BC **Temple of Aphrodite** hidden behind a grille.
There are two exits from the Collachium. One is through the **Arsenal Gate** (Píli Navarhíou) leading to the Commercial Harbour (*on the right*), and the other, opposite, is through the **Liberty Gate** (Píli Eleftherías), which the Italians built in 1924, leading to Mandráki harbour.

### A tour of the ramparts\*\*\*
*Only one departure time, 2.45pm, Tuesday and Saturday, all year round. Entrance on the left, before the courtyard of the Palace of the Grand Masters; allow 90min. Bring protection from the sun.* This is an ideal excursion to enable you to take in the whole of the medieval city and appreciate the colossal building work carried out by the knights. The perimeter walls, 4km long, were built in the early 14C to replace the Byzantine ramparts. They were consolidated and extended several times up until the 16C, and were up to 12m thick! Punctuated by towers bearing the white marble arms or

**Rhodes Town**

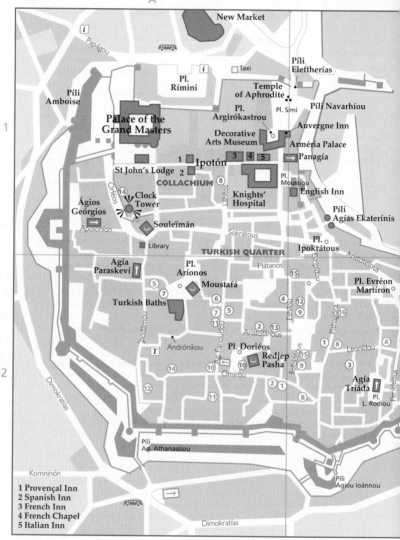

A

New Market

i Taxi

Pl. Rímini

Temple of Aphrodite

Pl. Simi

Píli Eleftherías

Píli Navarhíou

Píli Amboise

Palace of the Grand Masters

Pl. Argirókastrou

Decorative Arts Museum

Auvergne Inn

Arméria Palace

Panagía

1 Ipotón
St John's Lodge 2

3 4 5

COLLACHIUM

Pl. Moussiou

English Inn

Ágios Geórgios

Orféos

14 Clock Tower

Lahitos

8

Knights' Hospital

Píli Agías Ekaterínis

Apoloníon

Souleïmán

Sokrátous

Pl. Ipokrátous

Aristotélous

Library

TURKISH QUARTER

Agía Paraskeví

Pl. Aríonos

Plátanos

Euripídou

1

2

Poďímou

5

7

Moustafá

Turkish Baths

6

5

7

11

Andrónikou

T

Pl. Doriéos

Redjep Pasha

Aristofánous

2 13

15

Eshilou

4 12

9

Pl. Evréon Martíron

16

Pithagóra

1 6

Leonídou

4

14

10

Omírou

10

15

9

Sokrátous

3

Agía Triáda

2 1

8

Pl. L. Rodíou

Perikléous

12

11

Píli Ag. Athanassíou

Dimokratías

Komninón

1 Provençal Inn
2 Spanish Inn
3 French Inn
4 French Chapel
5 Italian Inn

Píli Agíou Ioánnou

Dimokratías

blazons of the successive Grand Masters, the walls benefit from the entire range of military architecture available at the time: there are embrasures for artillery, embedded loopholes for guns, jutting bastions, etc. The fortifications are further reinforced by a **double moat** between the Spanish Tower and Koskinoú Gate.

Each nation was assigned a combat post or **boulevard** that stretched between two towers. The **Amboise Gate★** (A1) (1512) flanked by two turrets is the most impressive of the city's gates. Cannon balls still embedded here and there in the wall on the Italian Tower and its curtain, testify to the violence of the second attack by the Turks

| RESTAURANTS | |
|---|---|
| Anakata | ① |
| Araliki | ② |
| Auberge (L') | ③ |
| Café Hammam | ④ |
| Cleo's | ⑤ |
| Despina's | ⑥ |
| Diafáni | ⑦ |
| Inside of the Wall | ⑧ |
| Mandala | ⑨ |
| Mango Bar | ⑩ |
| Marco Polo Café | ⑪ |
| Sea Star | ⑫ |
| Synaxaria | ⑬ |
| Clock Tower | ⑭ |
| Two Sisters | ⑮ |

| HOTELS | |
|---|---|
| Andreas | ① |
| Apollo | ② |
| Casa de la Serra | ③ |
| Eleni | ④ |
| Kastro | ⑤ |
| Lia | ⑥ |
| Marco Polo Mansion. | ⑦ |
| Minos | ⑧ |
| Niki's Rooms | ⑨ |
| Paris | ⑩ |
| Pink Elephant | ⑪ |
| S.Nikolis | ⑫ |
| Spot | ⑬ |
| Stathis | ⑭ |
| Teherani | ⑮ |
| Via Via | ⑯ |

(1522), when Süleyman the Magnificent's men took the town after a titanic siege that lasted six months. Apart from touring the ramparts, you can go on another pleasant walk, into the wide plant-filled **moat** laid out between the walls (*daily; free*).

## The Old Town** (Hóra) (Plan II)
*Rather than taking the main streets, Odós Sokrátous and Odós Aristotélous, which are full of tourists, go through the adjacent alleyways.*

The working-class district of the Hóra opens up south of the Collachium, marked off by Odós Sokrátous. This street follows the line of the walls that once closed off the Collachium to the south.
The medieval town is home to around 6 000 inhabitants, most of whom live very modestly. In some of the alleyways, the houses have their doors and windows open onto the street, showing plain interiors comprising one or two rooms at the most. People here live outside, and are not bothered by passers-by seeing them in the intimacy of their homes.

Before exploring the alleyways, climb up to the second floor of the **Clock Tower** (A1) (*daily in summer, 9am-10pm; entrance fee. The ticket includes access to the bar*) for the view. The tower was built in 1851 on the foundations of the Collachium's former watchtower. There is a lovely **panoramic view**\*\* of the Old Town.
From **Platía Ipokrátous** (B1), adorned with a **Turkish fountain**, Odós Aristotélous leads to **Platía Evréon Martíron** (B2), also with a pretty **fountain**, decorated with sea horses. The surrounding area is a maze of winding streets, where you'll come across shaded alleyways with plant-filled patios, or dazzlingly bright little squares.

### The Turkish Quarter** (Plan II)
The atmosphere becomes more oriental in the western part of the Old Town, where countless lively stalls hark back to the times of the old bazaar, each square has a fountain and the alleys are lined with vaulted houses whose façades are set off by

beautiful rows of arches. Furthermore, most of the Byzantine churches have been converted into mosques, their tapering minarets rising above the roofs.

Some of the former churches have gone back to their Greek names, such as the small **St George's Church** (Ágios Geórgios) (A1) *(at the end of Odós Orféos, make a detour right, into Odós Apoloníon)*, a fine building designed on a circular plan and reinforced with large **flying buttresses**. The same goes for the 15C **Agía Paraskeví** (A2), whose dome stands out at the bottom of Odós Ipodámou.

On the way, you pass the **Süleyman Mosque★** (Souleïmán) (A1), which marks the beginning of Odós Sokrátous. It was built after the 1522 siege and restored in the 19C, but has lost its minaret.

You really get a feel for Turkish Rhodes around the pleasant **Platía Aríonos** (A2) *(further south)*, which is shaded by plane trees. Lining it are the **Mustafa Mosque** (Dzamí Moustafá) and the majestic **Turkish Baths★**, both buildings dating from the 18C *(see "Other things to do", page 493)*.

Further south, at the bend in Odós Andrónikou, you pass the **open-air theatre** (A2), where various folk performances are held *(see "Other things to do", page 493)*. Then, if you go down Odós Ágios Fanouríou, lined with arcades, you come to **Platía Doriéos**, on which stands the **Redjep Pasha Mosque★** (A2), one of the town's oldest (16C).

### The Jewish Quarter★ (Plan II)

There is the same oriental atmosphere in the south-eastern part of the Old Town, in the shopping streets of the working-class Jewish Quarter. Odós Aristotélous, in particular, is the preserve of coppersmiths, whose stalls are sometimes set up beneath the pretty arches of Gothic houses.

Rhodes, streets in the Turkish Quarter

P. Fried/HOA QUI

The street leads into the **Square of the Jewish Martyrs** (Platía Evréon Martíron), dominated by the **Archbishop's Palace** (B2), a fine 15C building. The square, which is very close to the synagogue, has been named in memory of the 2 000 Jews deported from Rhodes.

There are also some Byzantine churches hidden among the alleyways in the district, some still with frescoes, often very damaged. On Platía Leonídou Rodíou, for instance, go into the **Church of the Holy Trinity★** (Agía Tríada) (B2) to see its **frescoes** and unusual **architecture**. The initial 15C Latin-cross plan had a domed chapel added in the north, while the southern nave was extended. The church was converted into a mosque, but all that remains of this is the base of a minaret that was destroyed during an earthquake.

Lastly, right over on the east side you come to the Commercial Harbour which is closed off by the **Windmill Gate** (Píli Mílon) (B1) and the powerful **St Catherine's Gate** (Píli Agías Ekaterínis) (B1). The first *(to the east)* owes its name to the many windmills that once lined the jetty (only one remains). The second, flanked by two crenellated and machicolated towers, has a fine **bas-relief★** of the Virgin and Child, crowned by the knights' blazons and the French coat of arms.

## Outside the walls (Plan I)

### In the harbour★

Rhodes port is divided into two deep harbours that extend east into **Akandia Bay**, anchorage for large cruise ships.

The **Commercial Harbour** (Emborió) (C3) opens out at the foot of the walls, protected to the right by the long ferry dock and to the left by a smaller port packed with fishing boats. To the north, separated by a long jetty also lined with **windmills**, is **Mandráki yachting harbour** (C2), an anchorage for pleasure craft, caiques, yachts and boats for excursions and scuba diving. It is also the hydrofoil dock.

At the end of the jetty rises the impressive **St Nicholas' Tower★** (C2) *(undergoing renovation, closed to the public)*, an advanced defence post built by the knights in the 15C and which today serves as a lighthouse. Perched on columns nearby are two bronze deer, **a buck and a roe** – the symbolic animals of Rhodes – watching over the town. According to tradition, the famous Colossus of Rhodes stood here, supposedly astride the harbour entrance, creating a giant arch. However, it is more likely that the work stood on the site of the Palace of the Grand Masters, formerly an ancient temple dedicated to Apollo.

### The modern town

Hugging the compact crescent of the medieval city, the modern town presents an unsightly face to the world, due in part to the uninspired town planning in the years under fascism.

On leaving Mandráki harbour, you first come to **Platía Rímini** (B3), which is adjoined by both the bus station and the main taxi rank. Dominated by the walls of the medieval city, the square forms the junction with the modern town. Behind it is the very lively, five-sided **New Market** (Néa Agorá) (B3).

From there, head northwards along the **Mandráki waterfront** (C2), where there are several fine examples of architecture from the Italian Period, in particular the **Church of Ágios Ioánnis** (B2), seat of the archbishopric, and the **Governor's Palace** (B2), a pale copy of the Doges' Palace in Venice.

On no account, however, should you miss the **Murad Reis Mosque★★** (B2) at the end of the quay *(to the left of the Yacht Club, access from the side nearest the port; no charge. Ask the warden to open up for*

### The Colossus of Rhodes

In 305 BC Demetrius Poliorcetes tried to lay siege to Rhodes, but in vain. Despite a considerable army and redoubtable siege engines, he had to give in to the unfailing resistance of the Rhodians. For consolation, he begged them to erect a monumental statue of Helios, the sun god, after whom the city was named. Financed by the sale of his war machines, he commissioned the workshop of Chares of Lindos to carry out the work. It took the latter twelve years to cast and assemble the gigantic bronze statue 31m high that was to be number among the Seven Wonders of the Ancient World. Alas, in 227 BC, an earthquake toppled the colossus, putting an end to its 56 years of existence. As the Oracle of Delphi interpreted this as a bad omen, the Rhodians never set it upright again. According to Pliny, however, even in pieces on the ground the statue was still extraordinary. The bits of bronze lay thus for a full nine centuries, until the Arab invasion in 654. They were then transported to Asia Minor – on the backs of 900 camels – to be sold to a Jewish merchant in Syria.

*you*). It is a haven of peace, left to its own devices far from the bustle of the city. In the adjoining **cemetery**\*, palms and eucalyptus shade the **graves** of Turkish dignitaries, sober oblong stones all lined up towards the east. The men's graves are topped by a carved turban, while the women's have a pine cone. At the back of the cemetery, hidden by the greenery, is the **Villa Cléobolus** (B2) (*closed to the public*) where the writer **Lawrence Durrell** lived from 1945 to 1947, during the short period when the island was under British administration. It was there that he wrote his *Reflections on a Marine Venus*, both an impressionistic, poetic novel, and an essay on Rhodes Island.

Beyond, you reach the northern tip of the town, a modern area with wide, well spaced out shopping streets. Some of them, with their bars, restaurants and night-clubs are extremely lively in the evening (*see "Having a drink", page 493*). For several decades, a large community of Scandinavians has been coming to this part of Rhodes for the summer. The Swedes were the first tourists to arrive here in large numbers in the 1950s and some of them have settled. This explains why some restaurant menus only appear in Swedish.

However, in the heart of this hectic district you will be able to find a picturesque little island of peace, marked off by several **pedestrian streets**\*, where it can be very pleasant to stay (*see "Where to stay", page 490*).

### Traces of ancient Rhodes (Plan I, A4)

*Around Monte Smith, less than 2km west of the Old Town. Allow 30min on foot, or take bus no 5 from Mandráki harbour. Free. Climb to the top preferably in the late afternoon.*
Founded in 408 BC, ancient Rhodes adopted the grid plan designed by **Hippodamus of Miletus** (*see page 36*). Laid out as straight as a die, the town stretched from the northern tip of the island to the site of the present Knights' Quarter and up to **Monte Smith**\*\*\* on which the acropolis was perched. The only remains of the ancient town are on the slopes of the mount. You can still see the remaining four Doric columns of the **Temple of Apollo**. But the most interesting buildings are the **stadium**\* and the ruins of the **gymnasium**\* (*close by*). The **theatre** nearby was entirely rebuilt by the Italians, and performances are given here every summer. The site also affords a superb **view**\*\* of the fortified town and the sea, all the way to the Turkish coast. You get an even better picture if you climb a little higher, up to the road dominating the shoreline. From there, the panorama takes in the whole of Ialissós Bay.

## Making the most of Rhodes Town

COMING AND GOING

**By air** – In the summer, there are plenty of scheduled and charter flights from Northern Europe. **Olympic Airways** connects Rhodes with Athens, Herakleion, Thessaloníki, Kássos, Kastellórizo, Kos and Kárpathos, as well as with several islands in the Cyclades.

Rhodes international airport is 16km from Rhodes Town, on the north-east coast near Paradíssi. In addition to taxis, there are regular buses to and from Rhodes Town (Platía Rímini), from 5.55am to 11.45pm from the airport to the town, and from 6am to 11pm in the opposite direction.

**By sea** – 4 ferry lines (including GA Ferries and DANE Sea Lines) connect the island with Piraeus, with stops respectively at Kos, Pátmos, Léros, Kálimnos, Páros, Amorgós, Astipálea, Níssiros, Tílos, Sími, Kastéllorizo, Hálki, Kássos, Kárpathos, Sitía, Ágios Nikólaos (Crete), Ikaría, Sámos, Chios, Lesbos, Límnos and Kavála.

From Rhodes two inter-island Dodecanese lines serve Sími, Tílos, Níssiros, Kos and Kastéllorizo in one direction, and Léros, Lipsí, Pátmos, Arkí, Agathoníssi, Pithagório (Sámos), Hálki, Diafáni (Kárpathos) and Kárpathos in the other direction.

You can also go by ferry to Cyprus (Limassol) or to Israel (Haifa).

The Flying Dolphin hydrofoils operate from April to October (when the sea is calm), linking Rhodes to some of the islands in the Aegean Sea. While they are twice as expensive as the ferries, they are a good deal faster. **Dodecanese Hydrofoil Company**, Platía Neoriou 6, ☎ (0241) 24 000.

The **EOT**, the municipal tourist office and the **harbourmaster's office** provide timetables.

### GETTING AROUND

Only certain local residents are allowed to use cars in the narrow alleyways of the Old Town. You must therefore get around on foot.

**By bus** – You can get to the main towns on the island from Rhodes Town, which has two interurban bus stations. The one on Platía Rímini serves the east coast: Kalithéa, Koskinoú, Faliráki, Kolímbia, Líndos, Genádi via Lárdos, Psínthos and Prasoníssi. For the west coast (Sálakos, Kámiros, Monólithos via Skála Kamírou and Émbonas), you should go to the bus station near the New Market.

**By taxi** – Taxi rank on Platía Rímini. Fares for the main destinations on the island are shown on a notice board. Prices go up at midnight.

**By rental car** – Plenty of car rental agents in Rhodes Town (particularly in the modern town, around Odós 28 Oktomvríou) but also in Ixiá, Triánda, Faliráki and Líndos. Compare prices and don't hesitate to use the competition as a bargaining counter, even in the high season. You can also easily hire scooters, motorcycles and bicycles.

### ADDRESS BOOK

**Tourist information** – **EOT**, on the corner of Odós Makaríou and Odós Papágou (Plan II, A1), ☎ (0241) 23 255 / 23 655, Monday to Friday, 7.30am-3pm. Professional service and useful advice, especially for accommodation (very efficient). Brochures, island map and town plan.

**Municipal tourist office**, Platía Rímini (Plan II, A1), ☎ (0241) 35 945. 8am-8pm, Sunday 8am-12noon; closed in the low season.

These two places distribute *Rodos News*, which provides tourist information in English.

**Bank / Currency exchange** – Banks are open Monday-Thursday, 8am-2pm, and Friday 8am-1.30pm. Plenty of cash dispensers in the town.

In the medieval city, **National Bank** and **Commercial Bank**, Platía Moussíou (Plan II, A1).

In the modern town, **National Bank** and **Alpha Credit Bank**, Platía Kíprou (Plan I, B2). **American Express**, represented by Rhodos Tours, Odós Amohóstou 18 (Plan I, B1), ☎ (0241) 21 010.

**Post office / Telephone** – **Main post office**, Platía Eleftherías (Plan I, B2), in Mandráki harbour. 7.30am-8pm, Saturday 7.30am-2pm, Sunday 9am-1pm.

**OTE**, Odós Amerikís 91 (Plan I, B2), 7am-11pm, ☎ (0241) 24 799.

**Internet** – There are several Internet cafés in the town, including **Rock Style**, Odós Dimokratías 7, and **Mango Bar**, Platía Doriéos 3, ☎ and Fax (0241) 248 77 / 28 324, karelas@rho.forthnet.gr

**Airline companies** – **Olympic Airways**, Odós Ieroú Lóhou (Plan I, B2), ☎ (0241) 24 571-3. **Air Greece**, Triton Holidays, Odós Plastíra 9 (Plan I, B2), ☎ (0241) 21 690, Fax (0241) 31 625.

**Travel agents** – **Minerva Travel**, Platía Sími 7 (Plan II, A1), ☎ (0241) 21 513 / 28 222. **Castellania Travel Service**, Odós Evripídou 17 (Plan II, B2), ☎ (0241) 75 860.

**Medical service** – **Papalouká Hospital**, north-west of the Old Town (Plan I, B2), ☎ (0241) 25 508.
**Ambulance**, ☎ (0241) 25 555 / 22 222.

**Tourist police** – Platía Moussíou (Plan II, A1), beside the EOT, ☎ (0241) 27 423.

**British consulate** – Odós Pávlou Melá 3 (Plan I, B3), ☎ (0241) 27 247. 9am-2pm, Monday to Friday.

**Left luggage** – **The New Market Pension**, Platía Rímini (Plan II, A1).

**Laundry** – **Lavomatique**, Odós 28 Oktomvríou 32 (Plan I, B2). **Express Servis**, Odós Dilperáki 97 (Plan I, B2).

## • Old Town

The medieval city with its pedestrian streets is the ideal place to stay, combining a central position, charm and peace and quiet (apart from scooters at night and the noisier tourist streets). The places to stay often have limited capacity and so it is essential to book in summer. The owners of small family guesthouses are not necessarily always at the reception. If this is the case when you arrive, wait for a little while or telephone the second number given with the addresses below. In low or mid-season, prices are 30 to 50% lower than in summer and can easily be negotiated.

*Around €24*

**Apollo**, Odós Omírou 28C, ☎ (0241) 32 003 / 63 398 – 8rm. 🏠 A small guesthouse with very attractive prices (be warned, it is often full). Modest rooms with basins, for 1 to 4 people. Shared bathroom and kitchen. Small terrace.

**Lia**, Platía Kleovoulinis 3 & 6, ☎ (0241) 26 209 / 20 371 – 16rm. The hotel is divided into two buildings, on either side of the street. Shared bathrooms, minimum decor. A good place if you are stuck, as there is more often room here than elsewhere.

**Hotel Kástro**, Platía Aríonos 14, ☎ (0241) 20 446 – 13rm. 🌙 ✗ 🏠 Right in the heart of the Turkish Quarter, in a quiet square. Pretty little terraces on the upper floors and a terrace on the roof. Plain, inexpensive rooms.

**Hotel Teheráni**, Odós Sofokléous 41B, ☎ (0241) 27 594 – 7rm. 🌙 ✗ A small, very quiet hotel in a good position. Friendly reception and reasonable prices. Fridge in the corridor. Open year round.

**Pension Minos**, Odós Omírou 5, ☎ (0241) 31 813 – 20rm. 🌙 ✗ 🏠 Shared bathrooms. Fridge available for clients. This pleasant, very clean, renovated guesthouse has spacious rooms and a lovely roof garden that affords a panoramic view of the Old Town. Breakfast extra. Good value for money.

**Hotel Státhis**, Odós Omírou 60, ☎ (0241) 24 357 – 10rm. 🌙 🏠 Stéphane Kefalás is very willing to be of help. If the hotel is really full, you can always, for a modest sum, sleep on the roof terrace under the stars. A very pleasant option as nights in Rhodes are extremely mild. The rooms themselves are rather small and timeworn, but clean. Breakfast is served on the terrace.

*Between €24 and €33*

**Casa de la Serra**, Odós Thísseos 38, ☎ (0241) 75 154 / 47 215 – 9rm. 🌙 ✗ 🏠 In the Jewish Quarter (near the ferry dock, through Windmill Gate, convenient for night departures). A 13C house with a beautiful façade and several terraces. The rooms are not all of the same quality, but some have pretty views. Clients may use the fridge on the first floor. No alcohol served in the bar. Breakfast extra. Open from April to October.

**Pension Eléni**, Odós Dimosthénous 25, ☎ (0241) 73 282 / 36 690 / 29 148 – 17rm. 🌙 🏠 🆑 A quiet, well-kept house in the Jewish Quarter with a flower-filled courtyard and rooms with kitchenettes. Open from April to the end of October.

🐝 **Hotel Via Via**, Odós Pithagóra 45, ☎ (0241) 77 027, ☎ and Fax (0241) 27 895 – 9rm. 🌙 ♪ ✗ 🏠 In Odós Lissipoú, an alley near Odós Pithagóra 45. The rooms are attractively decorated (ask for the most romantic one on the top floor, with a view across the roofs of the Old Town to the harbour). The rooms with private bathrooms are more expensive and have fridges and fans. Breakfast is extra. The hotel is expanding: a bar is planned, with Internet access. Open all year round.

🐝 **Pink Elephant**, Odós Irodótou 42, ☎ and Fax (0241) 22 469 – 9rm. 🌙 ♪ ✗ 🆑 In the southern part of the town near the walls, in a quiet area a little out-of-the-way (near the San Francisco taxi rank and a street – quite safe – frequented by prostitutes). A smart hotel with attractive faience decoration. No breakfast, but there's a small shared kitchen. Telephone and fax services. Very good value for money. Open from April to October.

**Hotel Spot**, Odós Perikléous 21, ☎ (0241) 34 737. 🌙 ✗ 🏠 In the Jewish Quarter. Cool, modest rooms and a little garden courtyard. Clients may use a fridge. Open from March to October.

**Pension Andreas**, Odós Omírou 28D, ☎ (0241) 34 156, Fax (0241) 74 285, andreasch@otenet.gr – 14rm. 🌙 🏠 🆑 A very popular guesthouse, with a relaxed atmosphere. The bar is open all day and there's a fine view of the town from

*The Dodecanese*

the terrace. Shared fridge and many services (taxi, car rental, fax). Open from 15 March to the end of October.

**Niki's Rooms to Let**, Odós Sofokléous 39, ☎ (0241) 25 115. 🍴 Have a look at several of the rooms as they are of different sizes, some quite spacious.

*Over €33*

**Hotel Paris**, Odós Agíou Fanouríou 88, ☎ (0241) 26 356 / 93 978, Fax (0241) 21 095 – 30rm. 🍴 ⚓ 🌿 🏠 CC A hotel with a large number of rooms in the heart of the Old Town. Quiet, with a lovely spacious garden courtyard. Open from May to October.

*Over €60*

**S Nikolís Hotel**, Odós Ipodámou 61, ☎ (0241) 34 561 / 36 238, Fax (0241) 32 034 – 8rm. 🍴 ⚓ 🔳 🌿 📺 🏠 CC The large garden and roof terrace with a panoramic view give the hotel its charm. Very comfortable rooms to boot. Breakfast included. Also has suites and fully equipped apartments.

🏨 **Marco Polo Mansion**, Odós Agíou Fanouríou 40-42, ☎ and Fax (0241) 25 562, marcopolomansion@hotmail.com – 7rm. 🍴 ⚓ 🌿 🏠 CC The most charming hotel in the Old Town of Rhodes. Even if you don't stay here, come for a look and a drink at the bar or in the courtyard. The hotel is in an old Turkish house, with a hammam, and has been restored and furnished in perfect taste by the owner, an Italian architect and decorator. Each room has its own theme. Ask to see the imperial or harem rooms. Breakfast is served in the delightful patio. Stays of one week preferred (3 days minimum). Taxi and fax services. Open from April to October.

● **Modern Town – north**

This is where most of the luxury hotels are concentrated (mainly along the beaches on the northern tip). There is, nonetheless, a charming little island of peace around the Kathopoúli, Amarándou and Konstandopédos alleyways. These form a picturesque quarter in a good position close to the beaches on the west, 10min on foot from the Old Town and in the immediate vicinity of night-spots. Among the hotels in the area are:

*Under €24*

🏨 **Tsambíka**, Odós Kathopoúli 38, ☎ (0241) 26 840 – 6rm and apartments.

🍴 🌿 🏠 A modest guesthouse in a very quiet street. Tsambíka, the friendly lady owner, only speaks Greek and a little Italian but you will easily be understood. There are studios and apartments with balconies (some with private bathrooms, kitchens, washing machines).

*Over €35*

🏨 **Casa Antica**, Odós Amarándou 8, ☎ (0241) 26 206 / 77 662 – 7rm. 🍴 🌿 🏠 A delightful yellow house with blue shutters, in a charming, quiet pedestrian street. You have breakfast in the peace of a beautiful garden terrace. Studios with kitchen facilities and balconies. Closed in November.

**Hotel Andréas**, Odós Konstandopédos 6, ☎ (0241) 29 334 / 28 489 – 7rm. 🍴 ⚓ 🌿 🏠 Another good place to stay, a little smarter and more expensive. Clean, tastefully decorated rooms with kitchenettes. Friendly reception and guaranteed peace and quiet. Open all year (groups in winter).

*Over €90*

**Grand Hotel Astir Palace**, Aktí Miaoúli, ☎ (0241) 26 284, Fax (0241) 35 589 / 32 217 – 390rm. 🍴 ⚓ 🔳 🌿 📺 ✖ ⚓ 🐾 💧 🏠 CC A luxury establishment overlooking the beach with every modern comfort and rooms with views of the sea.

● **Modern Town – south**

*Around €24*

**Maríka Hagivasilíou Rooms to Let**, Odós Athanasíou Diákou 28, ☎ (0241) 29 552 / 21 910 – 🍴 🌿 🏠 There are no signs indicating this very old, plain but clean family guesthouse. Located in a working area that sees few tourists, it has the advantage of being 5min on foot from the beaches on the east. The charming inner courtyard is scented with jasmine. There are different sized rooms, some with baths. We recommend the place for long stays – prices are very low in the low season, and negotiable.

**EATING OUT**

● **Old Town** (Plan II)

*Around €7.50*

🏨 **Diafáni**, Platía Aríonos 3 (A2), ☎ (0241) 26 053. Opposite the Turkish Baths. Copious portions of varied dishes (take a look in the kitchen), very good value for money.

**Two Sisters**, Odós Plátanos 49-50 (B2), ☎ (0241) 38 597. Friendly little restaurant run by a Turkish family. Peaceful terrace and good food.

**Déspina's**, Odós Agíou Fanouríou 30 (A2), ☎ (0241) 74 540. A tiny family-run taverna opening onto a very busy alleyway. Good, unpretentious, inexpensive home cooking. Quick service. Open all year round.

**Synaxariá**, Odós Aristofánous 47 (A2). A quiet, decent taverna. The owner prepares very reasonable dishes of the day.

*Between €9 and €15*
**Cleo's**, Odós Agíou Fanouríou 17 (A2), ☎ (0241) 28 415. cc A good Italian restaurant in the heart of the Old Town. Often full, although quite expensive. Only open in the evening, closed on Sunday.

*Around €15*
**Aralíki**, Odós Aristofánous 45 (A2). This stylish restaurant is run by two Italian sisters. Creative, tasty, Greek-Italian cooking. Very friendly welcome and good atmosphere. Closed on Sunday.

**Sea Star** (Pizaniás Kyriákos), Odós Sofokléous 24 (B2), ☎ (0241) 22 117 / 31 884. This place is reputed to be the best fish restaurant in town. Only serves grilled fish (prepared by the 75-year-old owner himself) and salads. Plain decor. Reasonable prices.

*Between €15 and €23*
**L'Auberge**, Odós Praxitélous 21 (B2), ☎ and Fax (0241) 34 292. A little out-of-the-way, in the south of the Old Town. Excellent cuisine (with a good list of French and Greek wines), impeccable service, unostentatious, friendly welcome, all at a very reasonable price. Temporary exhibitions are also held here. Only open in the evening, closed on Sunday.

**Inside of the Wall**, Odós Láhitos 13 (A1), ☎ (0241) 76 887. Although the restaurant is in the heart of a very touristy area it is not advertised and is only marked by a small green board, where its name is written in Greek, like its menu. Good food, inside terrace and bar (music in the evening, friendly atmosphere). Open in the evening in summer, midday and evening in winter.

● **Modern Town – north**
(Plan I, B2)
*Around €7.50*
**Niohori**, Odós Ioánni Kazoúli 29, ☎ (0241) 35 116. On the edge of the little island of peace in the modern town. Grilled specialities, salads and Greek dishes. Moderate prices.

*Between €9 and €15*
**La Casa Nostrana**, Odós Mandilará 28, ☎ (0241) 36 126. cc Wide choice of Italian dishes. Large terraces that can seat crowds of people. Only open in the evening.

*Between €15 and €23*
**7.5 Wonder** (Thávma), Odós Dilperáki 15, ☎ (0241) 39 805. cc A Swedish restaurant serving Scandinavian and Mediterranean specialities in a cosy setting with a tropical garden. Pleasant bar and professional service. Quite expensive, but very good. Only open in the evening.

● **Modern Town – south** (Plan I)
*Around €7.50*
**Apostólis**, near Odós Mitropóleos 49 (C4), ☎ (0241) 38 546. Unpretentious neighbourhood restaurant serving good Greek food. Quiet, pleasant interior. Open in the evening all year round.

*Between €15 and €23*
**Old Story**, Odós Mitropóleos 108 (C5), ☎ (0241) 32 421. cc Frequented mainly by local people. Pleasant setting, original decor, attentive service. Modern, carefully prepared Greek cuisine: grilled prawns with an orange and ouzo sauce, and grilled specialities. Booking essential.

HAVING A DRINK

The modern town is bursting with bars and night-clubs that draw a large crowd in summer. Most of the places are concentrated in the northern part of the town, mainly along the Diákou and Orfanídi thoroughfares, but also in streets such as Dilperáki, Rodíou, Dragoúmi, Fanouráki and Amarándou.

● **Old Town** (Plan II)
**Clock Tower**, Platía Orféos (A1). Daily. The bar closes at 10pm. The ticket for the tower includes a free drink at the terrace bar.

**Café Hamám**, Odós Eshílou 26 (A2), ☎ (0241) 33 242. In the evening you

The Dodecanese

can sip good cocktails and dance in vaulted cellars.

*Marco Polo Café*, Odós Agíou Fanouríou 40-42 (A2), ☎ (0241) 37 889. A café-bar that adjoins the hotel of the same name. Steps lead to the quiet garden in the inner courtyard where you can try good cocktails.

*Mango Bar*, Platía Doriéos 3 (A2), ☎ and Fax (0241) 248 77 / 28 324, karelas@rho.forthnet.gr Cocktails, long drinks, beer, etc, in a music bar with an Internet service. 7 rooms upstairs (but very noisy).

*Mandala*, Odós Sofokléous 38 (B2), ☎ (0241) 38 119. You can drink cocktails and also have something to eat (barbecues, salads, pasta, pizzas).

*Anakata*, Odós Pithagóra 79 (B2). An art gallery and a café in a pleasant courtyard with a relaxed atmosphere.

• **Modern Town** (Plan I)

*Red Lion*, Odós Orfanídou 9 (A2). Relaxing, English pub atmosphere, with modest prices.

*Sokani*, Odós Dilperáki 16 (B2), ☎ (0241) 38 926. A small bar that puts on numerous concerts in the season.

*Heritage Café*, Odós Martíou 25 (B2), ☎ (0241) 26 406. A Harley Davidson-style rock café-bar. Daily, all year round.

OTHER THINGS TO DO

**Son et lumière** – The life of the Knights of St John and the siege by Süleyman the Magnificent narrated in the green decor of the municipal gardens in Platía Rímini (Plan II, A1). Every evening. 3 performances on summer evenings, at 8.15pm, 9.15pm and 10.15pm. Fee.

**Folk performances** – The open-air theatre in Odós Andrónikou in the Old Town puts on song and dance performances in traditional costume. Pleasant setting. April to October on Monday, Wednesday and Friday at 9.30pm. Fee.

**Excursions** – Day trips by boat to Sími and Líndos (departure at 9am from Mandráki harbour, return at 6pm). For Turkey (Marmaris): 1hr crossing by ferry (departures at 8am and 3pm, return trips at 10am and 4pm), or by hydrofoil (April to October).
Caique excursion to Hálki from Skála Kamírou (1 departure a day at 2.30pm during the week and at 9am on Sunday. Return at 5.30am during the week and at 4pm on Sunday).

**Outdoor pursuits** – Rhodes Island lends itself particularly well to **water sports**, and there are several diving clubs in Rhodes Town in Mandráki harbour.

**Hammam** – Turkish baths in **Platía Aríonos**, in the Old Town (Plan II, A2). Separate reception for men and women. Tuesday 1-6pm, Wednesday and Friday 11am-6pm, Saturday 8am-6pm; closed Sunday and Monday (however, you should check the times). Modest prices. Bring sandals or flip-flops.

**Casino** – **Playboy Casino**, Odós Papanikoláou 4 (Plan I, B2), ☎ (0241) 97 500. People under 23 not allowed. Entrance fee. Open 24hr a day. Night-club.

**Aquarium** – On the northernmost tip of the island, north of the town (Plan I, B1). Daily, 9am-9pm. Rundown and poorly maintained.

SHOPPING GUIDE

**Arts and crafts** – The local arts and crafts – gold and silver jewellery, metalwork, leather goods and ceramics – are good quality. Don't hesitate to bargain, particularly in the Old Town (Odós Sokrátous and Odós Ipokrátous). Also plenty of shops in the modern town around Platía Kíprou and Odós Griva.

**Bookshops** – **The Academy Bookstore**, Odós Dragoúmi 7 (Plan I, B2) and **Moses Cohn**, Odós Themeli 83D.

# RHODES★★ (RÓDOS)
## TOUR OF THE ISLAND
A 296km tour starting from Rhodes Town
Michelin map 980 fold 47 – Regional map page 479 –Map of the island page 497
Allow at least 2 days to tour the island, not counting Rhodes Town

### Not to be missed
At least two of the island's three ancient towns: Kámiros and Líndos.
The unspoilt beaches in the south, and the quiet, cool hinterland.

### And remember...
Have no qualms about visiting Rhodes in the low season, even in winter.
For swimming, try the creeks at Kalithéa rather than crowded Ialissós Bay.

The further south you go from the crowded capital, the fewer the houses and hotels, and the wilder the terrain. The island stretches out over 77km, with a wide variety of landscapes. On the coast, rocks alternate with fine sand or pebble beaches. But strong winds blow on the windward west coast making the more sheltered east coast beaches with their calmer, clearer water a better option. Around the Atáviros massif, a rocky spine stretching in a north-south direction, are wooded valleys and fertile, well-watered agricultural plains where flowers burst into colour in springtime. Among them is the **rose**, the sacred flower of the sun god, and the supposed origin of the name Rhodes. However, if you were asked to choose a floral emblem for the island, you would probably think more of the crimson and orange **hibiscus** that you see flowering among the trees, or the fragrant jasmine, or even the pink and mauve bougainvillaea that cascades down village walls.

### Mass tourism
In the 1930s, the Italians, allied with the Germans, launched luxury tourism on Rhodes. But times have changed and the hotel business has become much more demo-cratic. For several decades, Rhodes has been attracting thousands of visitors, mainly from Northern Europe (Germany, Scandinavia and Britain). This has created a real industry that has unfortunately often had little respect for the coastal scenery and has adversely affected many traditions. During the summer months when tourism is at its height, there are certain places to be avoided as far as possible, including various parts of Rhodes Town, Líndos, and the coasts on the north-west and north-east of the island. Once the summer peak is over, Greek life comes into its own again, even in Rhodes Town, when there are fewer tourists, the sun is less strong and prices decrease.

*From the capital, two main roads lead off along the coasts, one heading south-west, the other south-east, to meet on the southern tip of the island. The tour we suggest below is by car (there are many fuel stations in the north, far fewer in the centre and south). You will be able to alternate between ancient cities, forest villages in the mountains, and little deserted beaches, thus escaping the long, straight, over-developed stretches of coast. You will easily be able to find somewhere to stay throughout the trip (see "Making the most of Rhodes Island", page 501).*

### The north★

*Head westwards out of Rhodes Town (from the modern town) and drive along the coast road for 8km. In Triánda, turn left towards Ialissós along a much less busy road (6km) that winds up the sides of Mt Filérimos.*

■ **Ialissós and Mt Filérimos★★** – *8am-7pm, Saturday, Sunday and Monday 8.30am-3pm. Fee. Allow 45min. Leave the ruins at the foot of the hill and climb directly to the acropolis on the top of Mt Filérimos. In the 15C BC, the Minoan coastal city of* **Achaia**

The Dodecanese

was destroyed by a natural disaster and was then transferred to the foot of the mountain. After invasion by the Dorians in the 10C BC the city was moved again, this time to the coast, near the village of **Kremastí**. It was then called Ialissós after a grandson of Helios, the sun god. The city prospered and formed an alliance with the two other Dorian cities on the island, Líndos and Kámiros. But in the 5C AD, the rapid growth of Rhodes Town brought about its decline and only the acropolis, an excellent strategic post, managed to outlive the city, surviving for several centuries. The Byzantines took refuge here during the occupation by the Genoese, who in turn were forced out by the Knights of St John. Then Süleyman the Magnificent based his camp here during the siege in 1522.

The site, which affords a wonderful **view\*\*** of the island and the sea, was also an important place of worship, as is borne out by several remains. The foundations of the **Doric temples** of Athena and Zeus Polieus (protector of the city) lie mixed up with stones from different periods: Hellenic, paleo-Christian, Frank and Byzantine. The knights built a vast monastery here, called **Moní Filérimos\*\*** (nearby), a fine 14C group of buildings (remodelled by the Italians) surrounded by pines and cypresses. Of this there remain the **cloisters\*** and a **church\***, dedicated to Our Lady of Filérimos, where you can see a lovely Byzantine **mosaic** of a fish. Below, take a look at the **underground chapel of Ágios Geórgios**, which contains 14C **frescoes\*** of saints. Unfortunately, their heads were burned by the Turks.

*Return to Triánda and take the coast road left for 10km. Then, 3km beyond Paradíssi, turn left again and keep going for 7km up to Butterfly Valley.*

■ **Butterfly Valley\*** (Petaloúdes) — *8.30am-7pm. Fee; parking area a little out-of-the way. Allow 1hr.* This is a famous natural curiosity. From June to September great clouds of red and brown **butterflies** arrive in the humid gorge, attracted by the sweet scent of the **liquidambar trees** (*Styrax* in Greek), the leaves of which are used to make incense. A shady path winds up the course of the river, through what would otherwise be an enchanting site were it not for the hordes of tourists, camcorders in hand, kneeling in the stream trying to catch the creatures' slightest wing movements.

*Return to the coast along the same road, go a further 7km west and turn left after Soroní. Go through the village of Eleoússa (11km), then continue to Profítis Ilías.*

■ 2km beyond **Eleoússa** and its strange church, appears the **Church of Ágios Nikólaos Fountouklí\***. The church and its fountain stand beside the road in a bucolic setting, opening onto a splendid **panorama\*\*** stretching to the coast. Topped by an unusual dome, the church is in a free-form Greek-cross plan with four conches and contains **frescoes** dating from the 10C and 14C.

■ The pleasant mountain road continues for 5km to **Mt Profítis Ilías** (798m), covered in thick pinewoods. When the Italians occupied the island, they built a small hill resort here. Today, only a few abandoned buildings remain, looking like Alpine chalets – the last house on the left as you leave the village once belonged to Mussolini. The place is quiet and cool with a soothing, slightly melancholy atmosphere, tempting for **walks\***. You have a choice of paths that disappear into the forest among the fragrant pines, cedars and cypresses. With a bit of luck you may even come across some deer.

*Continue for 8km. Bear right at the junction and drive 5.5km to the village of Sálakos (where you can stop). 8km further down you come to Kalavárda on the coast road, which you take southwards for 3km before turning left to Kámiros, 500m above.*

■ **Kámiros\*\*\*** — *8am-6.30pm. Closed Monday. Fee. Allow 1hr.* The ruins of the smallest of the three ancient cities on Rhodes are extremely charming. Scattered over a hillside sloping towards the sea, they are mainly from the Hellenistic Era, and their architectural unity is outstanding. They are set off by the **panorama\*\*** and the majesty of the setting, where the white marble blends in with the soft green of the pines, facing an azure blue sea.

Here better than anywhere else you get a clear idea of the way the city was organised in ancient times, with three sections: the agora, the residential quarter and the acropolis. The **agora**, a huge esplanade once surrounded by porticoes, formed the lower town. It was used for gatherings and was adorned by a fountain. Off it were the Roman **baths**, a **Temple to Apollo** (3C BC), as well as a **heroon**, a sanctuary dedicated to heroes and to gods, consisting of a sacrificial area with several altars. Beyond was the residential quarter, tiers of houses rising up the hillside and lining the city's main street. The street connected the agora with the acropolis, which was laid out on the highest terrace. Overlooking the agora (fine view) you can see a long **Doric portico**★ with fine columns standing above a series of large **cisterns** (5C-6C BC). These were fed by an ingenious system of water channels on the hillside. Further up is the acropolis, with the scattered remains of the **Temple of Athena**.

*Take the coast road left.*

■ Next you come to **Skála Kamírou** (17.5km), a charming fishing village with plenty of tavernas. This is where boats leave for **Hálki Island** (*daily connection, departure in the afternoon, return the next morning*).

On leaving the village, you will see on the right the ruins of **Kámiros Castle**, built by the knights on top of a rocky spur (superb **view**★★).

*Continue for 4.5km to Kritinía, where a narrow road climbs up to Émbonas (3km).*

■ The wine-growing village of **Émbonas**★ is built at the foot of Mt Atáviros – the bare peak which is the highest point on the island (1 215m) – with its whitewashed houses rising in tiered rows up the mountainside. The house of the poet **Iánnis Konstantákis**, hidden in the maze of white alleyways, contains a modest **Museum of Popular Arts and Traditions** (*entrance fee; no fixed times*). The lively streets of the modern town spread out below the old village.

Enthusiastic walkers may like to tackle **Mt Atáviros**★★ (*allow 3hr to reach the summit; you will find guides in the village*). The panoramic **view**★★★ from the top takes in the whole island.

■ Before reaching Monólithos, the road goes through **Siána** village (*17.5km from Émbonas to Monolithos*), renowned for its honey and its ouzo.

## Southern Rhodes★★

A symbolic line between Monólithos and Líndos (to the east) separates the north of the island from its southern tip. The drier, wilder south has a harsh landscape of steep rocks and bare plateaux crowned here and there by the ruins of fortresses built by the knights. The beautiful south has just as much to offer as the north but nonetheless remains off the beaten track, with fewer tourists (apart from Líndos).

■ **Monólithos**★★ – This isolated village high up in the cool of the hills enjoys an Olympian calm and a superb setting, not far from a wild coastline with deserted beaches. To the west, a road with numerous sea **views**★★ leads to **Monólithos Castle**★★ (2km), a real eagle's nest clinging to a rocky peak surrounded by greenery. This was built by the knights to watch over the sea, and also enjoys a magnificent **view**★★★.

Continue downhill (*for 4km*), and then drive along the shore where it is difficult to resist the **beaches at Foúrni**★★ (*on the left*) and **Agios Geórgios**★★ (*on the right*). With no amenities, they are among the most beautiful on the island, even if the sea is often rough.

*Return to Monólithos village, where a road leads south to Apolakiá (10.5km). From here, you can follow the coast to **Katavía** (18km) to enjoy a string of deserted (though often windy) beaches.*

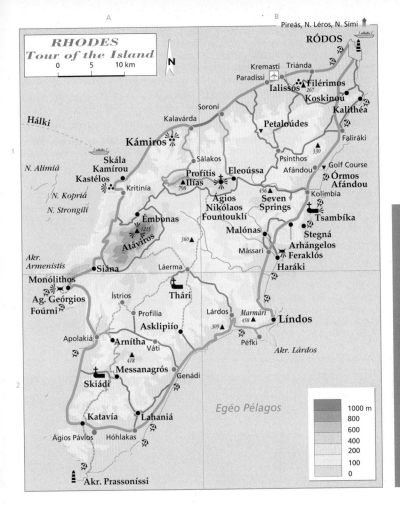

Alternatively, you could take the longer road inland (*27.5km*) that climbs in hairpin bends up into the hills where there is wonderful scenery, especially on the stretch between **Arnítha** and **Messanagrós**. You could make a short detour (*8km beyond Arnítha, to the right*) to see the charming, recently restored **Skiádi Monastery** dating from the Byzantine Era.

■ From Katavía you can head down to **Prassoníssi beach★★**, the southernmost point on the island (*6km, signposted*). The road crosses an unexpected area used for military manoeuvres and comes out, as if at the very ends of the earth, onto a long stretch of wind-battered sand. This is paradise for the many windsurfers who gather here (*windsurfing equipment for hire, but be careful as the winds are often violent and so the place is not suitable for beginners*). Right on the very tip of Rhodes is **Cape Prassoníssi★★**, a peninsula attached to the island by a thin tongue of sand often covered in water.

■ The road continues to the charming village of **Lahaniá**★ (*11.5km, signposted on the left*), where you can stop for a meal or spend the night. The alleyways in the old, sleepy lower part of the village are enlivened by the immaculate whitewash of **traditional houses**. The delightful **church square**★ shaded by plane trees tinkles with the sound of its many fountains – note the one covered in Turkish inscriptions.

*Head down to the coast road towards Genádi (9km from Lahaniá). The road runs beside a long, straight sandy* **beach** *that later turns to shingle, sheltered from the wind.*

*Continue beyond Genádi for 3.5km and turn left for the climb up to Asklipiío (3km).*

■ Perched on the heights, **Asklipiío**★ village has a fine **Byzantine church** dating from 1060, with walls covered in paintings (*ask a museum attendant to open the church for you*). Beside the church, a couple of small **museums** contain religious items and popular art (*no fixed times*).

*A poor road leads directly to Láerma, but it is wiser to return to the coast as far as Lárdos (8.5km), and from there take the road left to Láerma (12km). The road crosses a pinewood, which has unfortunately been partly burnt. 4km beyond Láerma, head first towards Profilía, then take a rather bumpy track left.*

■ **Thári Monastery**★, huddled at the bottom of an isolated valley that is difficult to reach, is well worth a visit (*free entry; modest clothes provided*). The serene, silent church has some beautiful **wall paintings**★ in the nave, the apse and the dome. In places they are superposed in four successive layers, and the oldest among them are believed to date from the 11C. You may be lucky enough to catch a rehearsal of liturgical chants.

*Return to Láerma and take the road to Lárdos, then skirt round the Mt Marmári Peninsula via Péfki to the town of Líndos (8km from Lárdos).*

Líndos, a citadel above the sea

# ■ Líndos★★

*There are 3 possible parking areas in Líndos: below the road above the police station if you're coming from the south, to the right of the road at the last crossroads if you're coming from Rhodes, and to the left of the square going down towards the north beach.*

In spite of the crowds, this fabulous site always manages to charm visitors. The acropolis is built on a steep-sided spur at a height of 116m, its ochre-coloured crenellations standing out against the sky. The massive walls snake round the hill, watching over the crystal water and the white houses in the little harbour huddled at its feet.

## Acropolis★★★

*8.30am-6.45pm, Monday 12.30pm-6.45pm, Saturday and Sunday, 8.30am-2.45pm. Fee. Allow 3hr. To avoid the crowds and the heat, come early in the morning or in the evening.*
The acropolis at Líndos was built between the 7C and 6C BC and was a place of worship in the Mycenaean Era. It was enlarged in Hellenistic times. Later, the Knights of St John built a fortress with a castle and garrison. This defensive role was maintained until the Ottoman Period.

Like those in ancient times, you climb up to it along a steep path punctuated with stairs. Beyond the first medieval gateway, steps lead down to the knights' administrative building, which is flanked by an ancient semicircular **exedra** (a seat in a rounded recess), hollowed out of the rock. Beside it, a **relief**, also carved out of the rock, features a ship's prow, which served as a base for the statue of one of Poseidon's priests. You then come to the ruins of the **Knights' Castle** and the adjoining Byzantine **church**, built in stone from different periods.

Standing on the highest terrace, the late-4C BC **sanctuary to Athena Lindia**★ marks the most sacred part of the acropolis. You get there by going up the monumental stairs of the propylaea flanked by majestic **Doric porticoes**★. Some of the columns

R. Mattès/MICHELIN

have been replaced in an upright position. From the top, there is a spectacular **view★★** over the sea and much of the lower town.

Note in particular **Mt Krána★** that rises up opposite the acropolis *(to the west)*. **Tombs** have been hollowed out of its sides, one dating from the Hellenistic Era and featuring the façade of a Doric temple. You can climb to the top of the rock *(access from the south-east along an alleyway in the village and then a path)*, where there is another magnificent **panorama★★**.

### Lower town★★

The lower town is literally invaded by groups in summer and subjected to well-instituted folk gambits – donkey rides, women selling local lace or faience, etc – so much so that you may be put off. Arm yourself with patience, however, as the place is worth lingering in. Move off quickly from the two or three main streets where the crowds concentrate and you will find a delightful maze of sloping alleyways, often connected by narrow stairs and lined with very old houses built between the 15C and 18C. These whitewashed buildings have beautifully kept courtyards paved with black and white pebbles. One of them, a **sea captain's mansion★** dating from the 17C is open to the public *(Odós Akrópoli 202)*. Also take a look inside the **Byzantine Church of the Virgin (Panagía)** *(beyond the square, up to the left)*, with its small paved pebble courtyard. It was built in the 15C and decorated with 17C and 18C **frescoes** *(Church museum, 9am-3pm)*. Lastly, heading towards St Paul's Bay you can see the remains of an **ancient theatre** on the north-east side of the hill.

## Return to the north
### Along the east coast

Beyond Líndos you gradually move into the busier atmosphere of the north of the island. The road to Rhodes Town passes crowded beaches and tourist villages on the edge of a long coastal plain dotted with olive trees.

■ On the way, you can stop at the fishing harbour of **Haráki** *(by forking right at Mássari)*. The imposing **Feraklós Castle★** (**view★**) built by the knights, dominates the harbour.

■ By making a short detour to the left of the road, you come to **Malónas**, a pretty village tucked away at the end of a rocky gorge that opens out onto a plain planted with cypress trees.

■ **Arhángelos★** *(27.5km from Líndos)*, a lively, commercial town, also has its own medieval castle, and the coast to either side is suitable for swimming. You might like to stop, for instance, at **Stegná★**, a small town in a pleasant setting sloping towards the sea, where there's a beach, a little harbour and some steep rocks.

A little further north, the fine sand on lovely **Tsambíka beach★** attracts a lot of people (too many) in summer. The **monastery** overlooking it affords a bird's eye **view★★** of the coast.

*7.5km beyond Arhángelos, turn left at Kolímbia (towards Eptá Pigés) and drive for another 3.5km.*

■ To get away from the heat, head a short distance inland to the cool **Seven Springs★** (Eptá Pigés), a charming wooded dale crisscrossed by myriad paths suitable for walking. A system of water channels, partly underground (into which the reckless may venture) conveys the water from the seven springs into a small **artificial lake**.

■ *Return to the coast road.* You soon reach **Afándou Bay** and its immense crescent of sand and pebbles sheltered from the wind. Afándou village, 5km from the beach, is renowned for its oriental-style **traditional carpets** *(you can visit a factory at the entrance to the village)*.

*Drive along the coast for another 7km, then bear right beyond Faliráki (fine sandy beach, but very popular), keeping within sight of the sea.*

■ You begin to enter the outskirts of Rhodes Town at **Kalithéa**\*\* (*10km from Rhodes Town, 20min by bus from Platía Néa Agora*), a spa built by the Italians in 1929. It has long been abandoned, and its dilapidated oriental-style buildings and baths laid out in a circle give it an old-fashioned charm. Nearby, for swimming there's a pretty **sandy beach** (*on the right*), and some small **rocky inlets**\*\* with pools of smooth, clear water.

■ Beyond Kalithéa (*5km*), have a look at the peaceful, flower-filled village of **Koskinoú**, with its elegant **neo-Classical houses**.

■ You now arrive at Rhodes Town. The huge **Rodíni Park** (*bus no 3 from Platía Néa Agora*) just outside is a pleasant place for a walk, with its small zoo, and its wine festival in summer. This is where the orator **Aeschines** (390-314 BC) is believed to have founded his School of Rhetoric. Very near here are the **Rhodes cemeteries**, where you can see some very old tombs, some dating as far back as the Hellenistic Era.

## — Making the most of Rhodes Island —

### ADDRESS BOOK (LÍNDOS)

**Tourist information** – You can get a plan of the town from the *municipal kiosk* on the square below the town.

**Tourist agencies** – In the town: *Pallas Travel*, ☏ (0244) 31 494. Also arranges rooms. *Líndos SunTours*, ☏ (0244) 31 333 / 31 353. Car rental.

### WHERE TO STAY

Much of the coast, especially in the north of the island, is being devoured by the tourist industry, with hotel chains, large complexes, etc. Be warned: as many large hotels deal with tour operators and are reserved for groups, it is sometimes difficult for independent travellers to find somewhere to stay in the high season. You will have more luck (and charm) with small hotels and rooms or studios to let. It is a good idea to stay in hill villages, where it is cooler in summer, and far more peaceful. Sálakos, Émbonas, Monólithos and Lahaniá, for instance, are pleasant places to stay, convenient for touring the island. Prices are higher in the north and on the coast. The least expensive hotels are more likely to be found in the inland villages in the south.

• **Ialissós** (B1)
Leofóros Ialissós, the avenue that runs beside the sea, has several gigantic luxury hotels, with every modern comfort but no charm. 90% of the hotels are less than 20 years old and disfigure the landscape.

*Over €33*
**Hotel Tákis**, Odós Themistokléous Sofoúli 8, ☏ (0241) 94 362 / 92 543, Fax (0241) 91 464 – 11rm. ⛩ ♟ ✕ TV CC 8km from Rhodes Town and 10min on foot from the beaches. Well-equipped rooms, with kitchenettes, balconies and safes. The few rooms that give onto the street are fairly noisy. A little English is spoken.

• **Sálakos** (A1)
*Under €24*
**Hotel Nymphi**, on the main road, ☏ (0246) 22 206 – 4rm. ⛩ ✕ ⌂ This white house with green shutters is one of the oldest hotels on the island. Quiet and well kept. Breakfast included. A good place to stay, and it is open all year.

• **Émbonas** (A1)
*Under €24*
**Hotel Vassilía**, at the western entrance to the village, on the left, ☏ and Fax (0246) 41 235 – 9rm. ⛩ ✕ Quiet, convenient for a stopover or a longer stay. Very clean well-equipped rooms (kitchenettes, fridges) with a lovely panoramic view of the sea and the mountain. Inexpensive (although breakfast is extra). Open year round.

• **Kalavárda** (A1)
*Around €24*
**Hotel Vouras**, near the main road, ☏ (0241) 40 003 – 12rm. ⛩ ✕ ⌂ Run by a farming couple (farm produce in the restaurant), the hotel has a mainly

German clientele. 3 apartments equipped with fridges and kitchens. Open all year. Reasonable prices.

### • Monólithos (A2)

*Under €24*

🍴**Thomás Hotel**, ☎ (0246) 61 291 / 22 741 – 10rm. ⌘ A quiet, modern hotel with clean, comfortable, spacious rooms with terraces and good facilities (fridges, kitchenettes) and also a fine view. Ideal as a base for walks and excursions. Very near Foúrni beach. Open year round. Excellent value for money.

### • Koskinoú (B1)

*Between €24 and €33*

**Irine Stoudios**, ☎ (0241) 61 944 – 7rm. ⌘ 禾 ⛩ The sea is 2.5km away and Rhodes Town 10km (direct bus). There's a garden, and the well-equipped rooms (kitchenettes) have balconies. A very quiet place, ideal for a prolonged family stay. Often full in summer.

### • Faliráki (B1)

*Campsite (around €12)*

**Faliráki Camping**, north of Afándou Bay, ☎ (0241) 85 516 / 85 358 – 125 pitches / 500 people. ⌘ ✕ ⛩ 禾 ⛩ cc A modern campsite (full in August) 16km from Rhodes Town (bus to Afándou or Líndos, those to Faliráki stop before). Clean, with good facilities and very comfortable, with a restaurant beside the swimming pool and numerous services (supermarket, laundry, television, video, telephone). It is best to have a car, however, to get away from the very popular beaches near the campsite.

### • Stegná (B1)

Rather than trying to stay in Líndos, which is full to bursting in summer, opt for Stegná, which is less than 20km from Líndos. You will find several tavernas and places to stay, and will be in quieter surroundings.

*Over €33*

🍴**Stegna Sun Studios (Kóstas Konstantoúras)**, as you go down the main road, 50m from the sea, on the right, ☎ (0244) 22 860, Fax (0244) 22 639 – 6rm. ⌘ 📖 ⛩ cc The rooms give onto a green, flower-filled garden and have balconies, fridges and air conditioning (extra). Very clean. Shared kitchen. A little noisy on account of the street.

### • Líndos (B2)

*Over €38*

**Pension Electra**, in the village, in the alleyway going down to the north beach, ☎ (0244) 31 266 – 11rm. ⌘ 📖 / 禾 ⛩ A large comfortable guesthouse, relatively quiet given the neighbourhood, with a huge garden and a wide terrace. Some rooms with showers and fridges, all with balconies. 2 shared kitchens. Essential to book well in advance in summer. Open from April to the end of October.

### • Apolakiá (A2)

*Under €24*

**Hotel Amalia**, ☎ (0244) 61 365 / 61 366, Fax (0244) 61 367 – 18rm. ⌘ 🖉 禾 ✕ ⛩ ⛱ In the centre of the town. A small, quiet, spacious hotel with a little garden courtyard. Moderate prices, breakfast extra. The swimming pool is not always in use. Open from April to the end of October.

## EATING OUT

In summer, it is quite difficult to find restaurants with character outside Rhodes Town that are not just for tourists. However, local people love going out to eat, mainly at the weekend and in the low season, so follow them!

### • Kalavárda (A1)

*Between €9 and €15*

🍴**Sea House**, coming from Rhodes Town it's on your right a little before you enter Kalavárda village, ☎ (0241) 40 120. Beside the sea, slightly set back from Kalavárda beach (well signposted). A restaurant that can cater for large numbers. Very pleasant setting with a big terrace (quite windy) shaded by an arbour. Superb view. Fresh fish specialities. Warm welcome. Open year round, lunch and dinner.

### • Émbonas (A1)

*Around €7*

Émbonas has numerous restaurants, including several traditional tavernas serving tasty fare.

🍴**Bakis Restaurant** (or "The Three Brothers"), ☎ (0246) 41 427. Go up into the alleyways in the upper village. This is a very good taverna serving traditional

The Dodecanese

recipes and a local wine. There's another Bakis restaurant, run by a brother, in the modern central part of the town where most of the restaurants are concentrated.

• **Haráki** (B1)
Several tavernas beside the sea.

*Over €15*
**Argo Restaurant**, at the end of Haráki beach, ☎ (0244) 51 410. Set between two bays, with a superb panoramic view. Unusually, and effectively, the tables are laid out in a circle. Fish, prawn and crayfish specialities. Quite expensive. Open for lunch and dinner.

• **Lahaniá** (A2)
*Around €7.50*
*Taverna Plátanos*, at the bottom of the village, in the old part (signposted), ☎ (0244) 46 027. In a peaceful square cooled by fountains. The wooden tables stand beneath a plane tree up against the church. Ducks come waddling round between the tables. No menu, but a daily special and grilled dishes. Lunch and dinner, year round. In winter, open weekends only.

• **Genádi** (A2)
*Between €9 and €15*
*Mezedákia*, heading towards Rhodes Town, 500m beyond Genádi, on the right and below the main road, ☎ (0244) 43 627. A rather poorly located fish restaurant but with a spacious setting. You eat very well here and are given a warm welcome. The owner is a fisherman and so the fish is very fresh. Lots of local diners on Sunday.

• **Líndos**
*Between €9 and €15*
**Agostinó's**, east of the lower town facing the police station, near the car park, ☎ (0244) 31 218. A little out of the centre. This is one of the rare restaurants

in Líndos that cater to a Greek clientele. Grilled dishes, house and Greek specialities, fish. Open from April to October, only in the evening (lunch only in May and June).

• **Pigi Psínthos** (B1)
*Around €7.50*
*Taverna Fasoúli*, below the town, ☎ (0241) 50 071. Meat dishes, especially grilled goat. A taverna that can cater for large numbers, mainly frequented by local people.

• **Koskinoú** (B1)
*Around €7.50*
**George**, in the main village square, opposite the school, ☎ (0241) 62 122. A family restaurant serving good Greek specialities, including tasty meat dishes. Friendly. English and German spoken. Open year round, lunch and dinner.

**OTHER THINGS TO DO**
The hotel complexes on the east coast (Faliráki, Tsambíka, Líndos) offer waterskiing. On some beaches you can hire pedalos, jet-skis, windsurfing boards, etc.
**Tennis**, in the major hotel complexes.
**Golf**, 18-hole course outside Afándou village, on the east coast, beside a sandy beach, ☎ (0241) 51 255 / 51 256.

**SHOPPING GUIDE**

**Arts and crafts** – **Oriental carpets** at Afándou, **embroidered goods** at Líndos, **faience** at Paradíssi, brightly coloured **leather boots** at Arhángelos.

**Wine** – At the entrance to Émbonas village take a look at the **Emery Wine Co-operative** (9am-4.20pm; closed weekends). The wine is very reasonable. Unfortunately, the bottles are often stored in the sun.

**Making the most of Rhodes Island**

# KÁLIMNOS ★

**Not to be missed**
The little harbour of Vathís and its fertile valley.
The north coast road and its superb panoramas, all the way to Emporiós.
And remember...
When looking for somewhere to stay, avoid the coast between Mirtiés and Massoúri.
Buy sponges directly from the factories.

Fishing and the sponge trade, the main activities on Kálimnos since time immemorial, are now being replaced by tourism, a new godsend that is not without its downside. The industry is already affecting the appearance of the island, with a whole portion of the west coast sacrificed to concrete. But Kálimnos is vast, and the terrain varied. The long coast road leading to the northern tip, for instance, has grandiose scenery all the way, with arid mountains plunging down to the sea. The harsh beauty of the heights gives way to oasis-like landscapes lower down: the fertile valley of Vathís and the long stretch of pines that runs from Póthia to Pánormos. These two green swathes, a refuge of shade and relative coolness, contrast pleasantly with the ochre-coloured rocks and the golden beaches.

## Sponge fishermen
Since Antiquity, there has been sponge fishing off the islands of Sími, Hálki and Kálimnos. But Kálimnos has made it its speciality. During the Ottoman Period, in exchange for a certain amount of independence, Kálimnos delivered sponges to

Kálimnos, the blue water of Vathís fjord

Sime/DIAF

The Dodecanese

Constantinople, thus paying its taxes in kind. As the areas they harvested began to decline, the island fishermen gradually left the Aegean to dive around Cyprus or along the North African coast from Egypt to Algeria where the season lasted from April to November.

Today fishing has almost been abandoned, apart from a few divers who faithfully keep to the tradition, and most of the sponges that you see in the shops are imported from Florida! On the other hand, the sponges are still processed in small

factories in Póthia. In order to keep just the skeleton of the animal – the part that we use – the sponges first have to rot in the sun, before being stamped on and then washed in sea water (the untreated brown sponges are rougher and more resistant than the light yellow ones that have been lightened chemically). Lastly, the men finish cutting the sponges with scissors, directly on the waterfront, before selling them.

## Póthia (Kálimnos)
*Allow a short half-day*

The island's capital, a large harbour in the shape of an amphitheatre, curves round a wide bay, its light-coloured houses reflected in the calm water. The town was founded in 1850 when the inhabitants left the fortified Horió, 2km inland, to benefit from an opening onto the sea. With its long noisy docks invaded by traffic, the impression Póthia gives to the world is that of an industrious town little bothered with tourists. In addition to its neo-Classical houses in pastel shades, the town also has soulless modern constructions. But many of the houses keep up their **blue and white façades** – the Greek national colours – an expression of the island's resistance to the Italian occupation (from 1912 to the Second World War), which itself followed four centuries of Turkish domination.

In the north-east of the town it is worth visiting the **Vouvalis mansion\***, converted into an **Archaeological Museum** (*signposted with arrows, 8.30am-2pm; closed Monday; 9am-2pm Sunday and during the holidays; entrance fee*). The opulent house built by a rich sponge merchant in the mid-19C has kept its period furniture.

To find out more about sponge fishing, go to the **Nautical Museum\*** (*8am-1.30pm, Saturday and Sunday 10am-12.30pm; entrance fee*), on the main quay. Photos, diving equipment, sponges and models of boats provide a sensitive account of the life and the work of sponge fishermen.

You can complement the visit by going to one of the **workshop-factories** that process the sponges. Some give onto the quays, near the landing-stage, others are in the alleyway that leads to the Archaeological Museum, and others still are right at the end of the quay towards Vathís.

Lastly, south-west of Póthia on the road up to the Ágios Sávvas Monastery, a very small **Museum of Popular Art and Traditions\*** depicts the daily life of a fisherman and his family in the late 19C. The museum is housed in the family home.

## Towards the west coast
### From Póthia to Massoúri

The road from Póthia to the west coast runs through a valley of pinewoods. As it leaves town, it passes the foot of the ruins of **Hrissohéria Castle\***, built by the knights on the top of a small rocky spur (*a little distance off the road to the left, 20min*

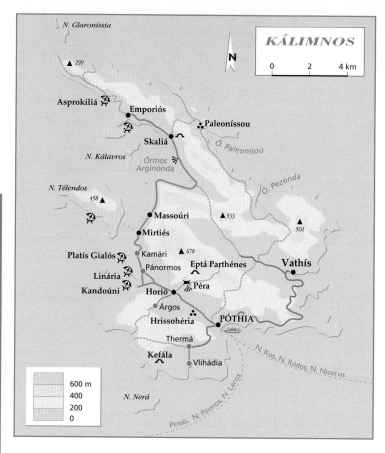

*on foot from Póthia*). Further on, the lovely **Cave of the Seven Virgins** (Eptá Parthénes) is unfortunately often closed to the public.

You then reach **Horió**, clinging to a hillside, the old capital of the island that still has a large population. On the right side of the hill steep steps lead to **Péra Castle**\*\* (Péra Kástro) (*8.30am-2pm; free*), a fortress with thick walls built by the Knights of St John. The site, an impressive jumble of rocks and ruined buildings, is being restored, particularly the small freshly painted **chapels** you see dotted about. The place is also worth visiting for the superb **viewpoint**\*\*\* over the valley, Póthia and the sea, all the way to the island of Kos.

The road comes out in the middle of the west coast. This is the most tourist-oriented part of the island, particularly around Pánormos, where the three beautiful **beaches of Kandoúni, Linária** and **Platís Gialós** follow one another in succession. As they face westwards, their sunsets are spectacular. But they are also overrun by developers and tour operators who have transformed the coast into a sea of concrete stretching from **Mirtiés** to **Massoúri** and beyond.

However, frequent caiques from Mirtiés harbour (*every 30min, from 8am to 12 midnight in summer*) enable you to escape to the more peaceful islet of **Télendos**\*. It lies facing the village, having become separated from Kálimnos during an earthquake in

535 AD. Apart from fine **beaches** skirted by a pleasant coast path, Télendos has two **monasteries**, several ancient ruins and a medieval fortress.

If you are interested in stalactites and stalagmites, take a boat trip south from Mirtiés to **Kefála Cave** (*also accessible from Póthia*).

### The coast road and the northern tip***

Beyond Massoúri, the buildings thankfully die out, and you can see the wonderfully wild landscape of the north of the island. From Arginónda Bay to the village of Emporiós, the coast road with its occasional oleanders overlooks the Aegean Sea, affording breathtaking **views***. At one point, you see a bare mountain like a sheer ochre wall splattered with sunlight plunging giddily into the deep blue sea.

On the way you can stop at **Skaliá** to visit a **cave** 100m from the village with a whole forest of concretions. From there you can also go on a **walk*** to the abandoned village at **Paleoníssou** (*1hr there*).

The road ends at **Emporiós****, a charming little coast town that has managed to keep its peaceful harmony in spite of the tourist crowds in the summer. Its beach, with shady tamarisk shrubs and clear water, is ideal for swimming, just like the one at **Asprokiliá** 150m further on.

## Vathís valley***
### 8km north-east of Pothía

Accessible by a coast road that is often subject to strong winds (*be careful if you are on a scooter*), Vathís lies at the seaward head of a fertile valley. This veritable oasis dotted with bright green orchards forms a striking contrast with the arid rocks around. The citrus plantations, including **tangerine groves**, give off a cool, fragrant scent. The valley follows a winding watercourse to the sea where it narrows and then opens onto **Vathís harbour*** nestling in the curve of a bay as steep-sided as a fjord. Tavernas line the waterfront, an ideal spot for a quiet evening.

## ——— Making the most of Kálimnos ———

#### COMING AND GOING

**By air** – An airport has been planned for a long time but is not yet open. There is one on Kos. From there you go to the neighbouring port at Mastihári to catch a shuttle boat to Kálimnos (Póthia) (travelling time: 30min).

**By sea** – From Póthia there are frequent ferry links with Piraeus (14hr crossing) and Thessaloníki. In peak season, there are good connections with Rhodes and the neighbouring islands (Kos, Pátmos, Léros, Lipsí, Sámos, Nissíros, etc), both by ferry and hydrofoil. The shipping companies are all concentrated on the western quays, near the ferry dock.

#### GETTING AROUND

**By bus** – The main bus station in Póthia is just south of the Cathedral. The buses, which are very cheap, run to all the main towns and resorts on the island. In summer, there are buses to Mirtiés-Massoúri, Vlihádia, Vathís and Emporiós. Tickets can be bought at travel agencies or at **Themis Mini Market**, east of the Cathedral.

**By taxi** – ☎ (0243) 50 300 / 50 303. Taxis are expensive. There is a rank at the ferry dock and on Platía Kíprou, 250m north of Póthia's main quay.

**By scooter** – You can easily tour Kálimnos by scooter, an economical, practical and pleasant means of transport. Watch out, however, for gusts of wind that can knock you off balance. Scooter rental outfits may be found along the waterfront in Póthia.

**By car** – Hiring a car is no problem but it is difficult to park, especially in Póthia. Opt for the more convenient two-wheelers. Plenty of car rental agencies in the harbour. As usual, check the brakes, fuel gauge, oil, etc.

### ADDRESS BOOK (PÓTHIA)

**Tourist information** – Tourist information kiosk in the north-east corner of the quayside, behind the statue of Poseidon, ☎ (0243) 23 140.

**Bank / Currency exchange** – **National Bank**, ☎ (0243) 28 553 and **Ionian Bank**, both on the main quay, west of the Cathedral.

**Post office / Telephone** – The **main post office** is 150m behind Platía Kíprou, ☎ (0243) 28 340. The **OTE** is just opposite.

**Police** – North of Platía Kíprou, ☎ (0243) 22 100.

**Harbourmaster's office** – On the ferry dock, ☎ (0243) 29 304.

**Medical service** – **Hospital** (emergencies), ☎ (0243) 28 851.

### WHERE TO STAY

• **Póthia**

*Under €27*

**Pension Panorma**, east of the harbour on the Vathís road, 400m beyond the Cathedral, ☎ (0243) 29 249, mobile 0944 865 084 – 5rm. ⁕ 🗶 Clean though rather noisy rooms with a fine view of the harbour. Prices are easily negotiable.

*Between €27 and €38*

**Hotel Panorama**, on the left side of the hill as you come up from the harbour, ☎ (0243) 23 138 – 13rm. ⁕🗥 In a high position overlooking the harbour (panoramic view of the bay). A quiet hotel with very clean comfortable rooms, together with a good reception and efficient service. The staff speak English. Moderate prices in the low season.

**Archontikó**, in the harbour, right over on the left next to the landing-stage, ☎ (0243) 24 051, Fax (0243) 24 149 – 10rm. ⁕ 🖉 🗶 The hotel has a rather pre-1940s charm about it, and is carefully managed by a delightful elderly couple. Beautiful view of the harbour, but a little noisy on account of the nearby quay. Italian and English spoken.

*Over €38*

**Villa Themelina**, in the north-east of the town opposite the Archaeological Museum, ☎ (0243) 22 682, Fax (0243) 23 920 – 25rm. ⁕ 🖉 🗶 🗥 All the charm of a traditional 19C mansion, in town but quiet. Pleasant swimming pool and garden. German spoken (the hotel is used by German groups). Breakfast included. Book well in advance.

• **Vathís**

*Under €27*

**Pension Manólis**, cross the little terrace of the Harbour Taverna and climb up for another 80m, ☎ (0243) 31 300 / 22 641- 6rm. ⁕ 🗥 A thoroughly charming guesthouse nestling in a pleasant setting among fig trees, olives and vines with an attractive view of the fjord. The son of the managers is also a taxi driver and tourist guide.

• **Pánormos**

Nearly all the standard, soulless hotels are concentrated round the three beaches at Platís Gialós, Linária and Kandoúni.

*Around €27*

**Pension Graziella**, in the town, ☎ (0243) 47 314 / 47 346 – 10rm. ⁕ The oldest hotel in the area. Rather antiquated, but quiet and set apart from the bustle of the beaches, which are 10min away on foot. The elderly owners will give you a very warm welcome. 1 single room, 4 doubles, 4 studios equipped with kitchen facilities and 1 family apartment. Inexpensive.

• **Télendos**

It is worth trying Télendos for accommodation. The pleasant islet is quieter than the coast opposite and has a good choice of guesthouses and tavernas.

*Around €27*

**Uncle George**, east of the quay, ☎ (0243) 47 502. ⁕ 🗶 A guesthouse beside the sea, with clean rooms and a good taverna (fish specialities).

• **Emporiós**

*Between €27 and €38*

**Harry's Paradise**, set back a little from the beach, 50m from the shore, ☎ (0243) 47 434 – 6rm. ⁕ 🖉 🗥 🗶 Rooms with kitchenettes and fridges. Good restaurant and very friendly welcome (English spoken).

## EATING OUT

Try the local delicacies, such as *keftédes* made with octopus, *ascidiés* (sea squirts) and *skordaliá* (mashed potatoes with garlic).

### • Póthia (Kálimnos harbour)

*Under €9*

🐚 **Restaurant Xeftéries**, in the centre of Póthia, in the street to the right of the Cathedral, ☎ (0243) 28 642. An old restaurant that looks like a canteen, serving very simple but good food in copious portions. Pleasant open-air dining room in the shade. Greek specialities but no fish. Choose from what's cooking in the kitchen. One of the best places for value for money. Open daily, lunch and dinner all year round.

*Between €9 and €15*

**Katerína's**, 150m from the harbour, before the taxi rank, on the right, ☎ (0243) 23 231. A family restaurant with terraces. Grilled dishes, Greek specialities, fish, pasta and pizza. Only open in the evening.

**Uncle Pétros**, the last restaurant at the very end of the quay on the right, ☎ (0243) 29 678. A fish restaurant popular with the locals, with a large terrace on the waterfront.

**Pizza Imia**, in the harbour on the left, ☎ (0243) 24 809. Good pizza served in a relaxed atmosphere.

### • Vathís

*Around €9*

🐚 **The Harbour Taverna**, on the Vathís quayside to the right, ☎ (0243) 31 206. The old men in the village come here for endless chats. Good atmosphere and friendly welcome. Fresh fish depending on the catch, and traditional Greek fare served in a typical setting. Open from May to October.

### • Pánormos

*Around €9*

🐚 **Marínos Restaurant**, outside the village on the left, on the Mirtiés road, ☎ (0243) 47 591. 🆑 Charmless decor, but the food, which includes Kálimnos specialities, is very good, inexpensive, and served in generous portions. The locals make no mistake: this is one of the few authentic restaurants in the area, and it has a quiet terrace. Open for lunch and dinner all year round.

### • Mirtiés (Melitsahás harbour)

*Between €9 and €15*

**Drosiá**, on the left of the little harbour at Melitsahás, just before Mirtiés, ☎ (0243) 48 745. An ouzo bar that also serves fresh fish. Open for lunch and dinner all year round.

### • Emporiós

*Between €9 and €15*

🐚 **Harry's Paradise**, the restaurant at the hotel of the same name, set back from the beach, ☎ (0243) 40 061 / 51 210. Without doubt the best in the area, with a lovely shady garden terrace.

**Artístico**, beside the beach, ☎ (0243) 40 115. A bar-restaurant run by a dynamic couple serving Greek and international food. Music in the evening, in a relaxed atmosphere. Open from March to October.

## OTHER THINGS TO DO

**Feasts & festivals** – Every Easter Sunday, the main square in Póthia bursts into life with major folk events.

**Scuba diving** – Enquire at **Aquanet Travel Agency**, on the waterfront in Póthia, ☎ (0243) 22 036.

**Stávros Valsamídis**, a scuba diving fan, runs a small diving club on Vlihádia beach in the south of the island. He has opened a museum for his marine finds (shells, amphorae, etc), ☎ (0243) 24 750 / 50 662, Fax (0243) 22 156.

**Boat trips** – Excursion boats in Póthia are grouped together on the west quay. From Vathís, there are daily trips to the beaches at Almyrés, Drasónda, Pezónda and Paleonísou, which can only be reached by sea.

**Hot springs – Thermá**, 2km south of Póthia, is renowned for its sulphur springs.

## SHOPPING GUIDE

Remember that the **sponges** sold on Kálimnos do not come from local waters. However, should you wish to buy some, you will find varied types and sizes in the many shops in the harbour, or you can buy them directly from the workshops where they are often cheaper. The island also produces some renowned **thyme honey**.

# KÁRPATHOS ★★

District of the Dodecanese – Michelin map 980 fold 46 – Regional map page 479
300km² – Pop 5 000

**Not to be missed**
The local specialities: loukoumádes, makaroúnes, thyme honey, etc.
The hill villages in the centre of the island, and especially those in the north,
Ólimbos and Diafáni, where you can look inside traditional houses.

**And remember...**
Make use of the superb beaches. The best ones are often the most difficult to get to,
especially on the east coast, so bring good walking shoes.

Kárpathos lies well out in the open sea at the tail end of the Dodecanese, halfway between Rhodes and Crete, and is a little less well served than its fellow islands. Long and narrow, it consists of a long, steep mountainous ridge narrowing from south to north. Though it is the second largest island in the Dodecanese, it has neither as prestigious a history as its large neighbour, nor any notable archaeological sites. It owes its interest and beauty simply to its unspoilt state. With limited urban development, a rugged and little exploited terrain, wild beaches – among the finest in the Aegean Sea – and panoramas to take your breath away, Kárpathos is definitely one of the most captivating islands in the Dodecanese.

## Tour of the island
*Allow 3 days, 2 if you have a car*

**A developing coastline...**
Many migrants who have made their fortune in the United States or Australia are returning to their homeland and investing in tourism. The island's coasts, particularly in the south, are gradually being changed, notably in the south-east around **Pigádia** (Kárpathos), the main harbour and the only large town on the island. This is where most of the island's activity is concentrated in summer, and modern buildings have already colonised the bay to the west of the harbour.
9km away to the south is the thriving resort of **Amopí**. Its recently constructed buildings rise in tiers up the hillside, hemming in a series of bays and little beaches that in times past were quite wild.
The small harbour of **Diafáni**, the only urban centre in the north-east of the island remains a lot more modest... and charming.

**...but unspoilt heights**
Elsewhere, in the mountains, Kárpathos is as it always was. Several ageless villages have hung on to their identity, and even if there is nothing special to detain the visitor, it is pleasant to stroll around them and experience something of the island's real spirit. From Pigádia, take the road that snakes across Kárpathos from east to west as far as Arkássa. You will pass a series of lost villages clinging to the mountain ridges.

■ Stop first at **Menetés**, a pretty hill village, and walk among its white houses set in a maze of silent alleyways.

■ Further west, you come to **Pilés** overlooking the sea. Another charming village that is also an excellent starting point for mountain walks (*see "Other things to do", below*).

■ Then you reach **Óthos**, a livelier place with its fine mansions, a modest market, and a number of tavernas. At the entrance to the village, go and see the local artist **Saunis Hapsis** in the tiny gallery where he sells his naïve paintings. He also has the keys to the small **Ethnographic Museum★★** – an outstanding reconstruction of a traditional interior – and will show you round.

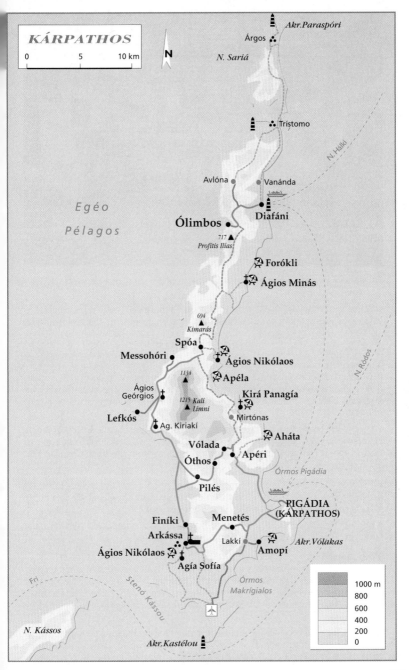

# KÁRPATHOS

0   5   10 km

N

Akr. Paraspóri

Árgos

N. Sariá

Trístomo

N. Hálki

Avlóna   Vanánda

Diafáni

Egéo
Pélagos

**Ólimbos**

717 ▲
*Profítis Ilías*

Forókli

Ágios Minás

694 ▲
*Kímarás*

Spóa

**Messohóri**

Ágios Nikólaos

1134 ▲

Apéla

Ágios
Geórgios

Kirá Panagía

1215 Kalí
▲ Límni

Mirtónas

**Lefkós**

Ag. Kiriakí

Aháta

**Vólada**

**Óthos**   Apéri

Órmos Pigádia

**Pilés**

**PIGÁDIA
(KÁRPATHOS)**

Finíki   **Menetés**

**Arkássa**

Lakkí   Akr. Vólakas

**Ágios Nikólaos**   **Amopí**

Agía Sofía

Órmos
Makrígialos

Frí

Stenó Kássou

| | 1000 m |
| --- | --- |
| | 800 |
| | 600 |
| | 400 |
| | 200 |
| | 0 |

N. Kássos

Akr. Kastélou

Traditional Kárpathos: a cosy interior at Diafáni

■ Before returning to Pigádia, stop at **Vólada**\* and **Apéri**\*, two large, prosperous villages, whose sparkling whitewashed houses spread out over the mountainside.

## Along the coast

### The west coast\*\*

Benefiting from plentiful sunshine, the west coast is beginning to develop in earnest. A magnificent **coast road** affords unequalled **views**\*\* over the mountain (which reaches a peak at 1 215m) and the sea, where the neighbouring island of Kássos stands out.

■ On the left before you reach the large village of **Arkássa**, by the **beach of Ágios Nikólaos**, have a look at the little **Agía Sofia Basilica**\*, which is fifteen centuries old. Built in the 5C, it has kept its **mosaics** and artefacts from the paleo-Christian Era.

■ A little further along the road you reach **Finíki**, a charming little fishing port.

■ The roads then climbs and runs above the coast for 15km before reaching **Lefkós**\*, a tourist resort. Lefkós has a superb **site**\*\* on a jagged rocky headland with a number of bays and beaches, behind which nestles the harbour.

■ Beyond **Messohóri**, a large village with white houses lining steep alleyways, the tarmac road ends at the village of **Spóa**.

### The east coast\*

The more rugged east coast has a wilder character, with a succession of submerged cliffs where fish abound, bays and beautiful long sandy beaches where few people go. Coming from Pigádia, on the right before you reach Apéri, you will find a drive-able track that heads down for 3km to **Aháta beach**\*\* (*small pebbles*), framed by the mountain.

After this, the road becomes more of an adventure: the **Apéri-Spóa stretch**\*\*\* along the coast is only practicable if you have a four-wheel-drive vehicle or a motorcycle, as the track is quite rough. But the trip is really worthwhile for the extremely beautiful, sometimes vertiginous, **panoramas**\*\*\* *(take advantage of the morning sun)*, and the best **beaches**\*\* on the island, including **Kirá Panagía** *(taverna and parasols)*, **Apéla** and **Ágios Nikólaos**.

## The northern tip\*\*
*First get to Spóa along the tarmac road on the west coast.* Isolated for many years, the north has remained the wildest area on the island, and you will be left with vivid memories of its breathtaking landscapes. The road from Spóa to Ólimbos is a track, but luckily with a firm surface, making it perfectly practicable.

On the way, if you like **deserted beaches** don't miss **Ágios Minás**\*\*\* or **Forókli**\*\*\*, two superb, forgotten coves that are difficult to reach *(even in a four-wheel-drive vehicle; you have to go down a stony track that is very steep in places)*, where the swimming is good.

And keep the best for the end: high up in the middle of nowhere, the fortified village of **Ólimbos**\*\*\* appears like a vision from another era. Here, life stopped in the Middle Ages. Since it was founded in 1420, the place barely seems to have changed. Most of the old women still wear the costume of long ago, consisting of a long black dress and a scarf, with the neck and cuffs embroidered in coloured patterns, and leather shoes or boots. Younger women prefer to dress in white. The kindly, hospitable inhabitants watch fiercely over their traditions, and they still use the very old local dialect, which has traces of the language spoken by the Dorians.

Don't hesitate to look at the **traditional house**\* open to the public. It consists of a single room with a central pillar, packed with folding beds, knick-knacks, and, above a wall sofa, icons and family photos.

The **windmills**\* above the village stand out against the sky. One of them is still used to grind the flour for making the village bread, which is baked in old wood-fired ovens outside.

Stay a little longer in the north, to see the quiet harbour of **Diafáni**\*\*, which comes to life when the ferries arrive. With its attractive traditional houses it is a very pleasant place to stay.

### COMING AND GOING

**By air** – The airport is on the southernmost tip of the island, 18km from Pigádia.

From Kárpathos, there are four flights a day to Rhodes and three a week to Athens. There's also a connection with Kássos, and with Sitía in Crete.

**By ferry** – On Saturday, a ferry arrives in Pigádia from Piraeus via Mílos, Sitía and Kássos. It then continues to Diafáni (in the north of the island), before going on to Hálki and Rhodes. The return is on Sunday, taking the same route.

On Wednesday, a ferry arrives in Pigádia from Piraeus via the Cyclades. It continues to Diafáni (in the north), then goes on to Hálki and Rhodes. Return trip on Thursday.

There is no hydrofoil connection.

### GETTING AROUND

**By bus** – The main bus station is in Pigádia, in Odós Dimokratías near the landing-stage. There are several buses a day to Amopí, Pilés via Apéri, Vólada and Óthos, to Finíki via Menetés and Arkássa, and to Lefkós. There are no buses from Pigádia to Ólimbos or Diafáni. To get to these two villages, you can either go by land (car or motorcycle), or by sea (see water-taxi below).

**By taxi** – Taxi rank near the quays, Odós Dimokratías, ☎ (0245) 22 705.

**By water-taxi** – Every day in summer, there's a ferry service between Pigádia and Diafáni (several departures in the morning, with a return in the late afternoon). The boats also do special excursions to the beaches on the east coast, stopping at Aháta, Kirá Panagía, Apéla, etc.

**By rental vehicle** – Hiring a vehicle is the best way to explore the mountain villages. For the Apéri-Spóa stretch along the magnificent coast road you must have a four-wheel-drive vehicle or a cross-country motorcycle. To get from Spóa to Ólimbos along the ridge, an ordinary car will be fine as long as you drive carefully. There are plenty of car rental places in Pigádia. **Safeway Rentals**, in the centre, near the town hall, ☎ (0245) 22 497, is one of the least expensive. Make sure you have enough fuel for the return trip, as there are only two fuel stations, both in the area around Pigádia.

### Address book (Pigádia)

**Tourist information** – There is no EOT agency. You can get information from travel agents, notably at **Kárpathos Travel**, Odós Dimokratías, ☎ (0245) 22 148 / 754, which gives helpful advice.

**Tourist police** – Near the post office, ☎ (0245) 22 218.

**Bank / Currency exchange** – **National Bank**, on the main quay.

**Post office / Telephone** – **Main post office**, at the corner of Odós 28 Oktomvríou and Odós Georgíou Loízou. **OTE**, Odós Ethnikís Anástasis.

**Medical service** – **Emergencies**, ☎ (0245) 22 228.

**Airline companies** – **Olympic Airways**, Odós Apodímon Karpáthou, ☎ (0245) 22 150 / 057.

### Where to stay

A large part of the island's hotel accommodation is in Pigádia. The resort at Amopí also has a fair number of good-quality hotels but they tend to be on top of each other and mainly work with package tour operators. On the rest of the island, you will be able to stay in villages in the middle of wonderful countryside. So it's a good idea to hire a car.

• **Pigádia**

*Around €27*

Mertonas Studios, on the hillside, to the left of the harbour as you come from the landing-stage, ☎ (0245) 22 622 – 14rm. Good value for money. Clean, comfortable, very well-equipped studios (fridges, kitchenettes) with balconies. Shared television room.

If you stay long enough, Eva, the friendly manager and "doctor of metaphysics", will share some of her unusual gifts with you.

**Hotel Kárpathos**, in the western part of the town, a short distance from the bus stop, ☎ (0245) 22 622 – 16rm. The owner is usually at the checkout counter in the small supermarket below. Clean and fairly inexpensive.

*Between €27 and €38*

**Pavilion Hotel**, in the town centre, on the hillside, ☎ (0245) 22 059 / 22 018, Fax (0245) 23 319. A huge, modern, comfortable but rather impersonal hotel.

• **Arkássa**

*Between €27 and €38*

**Gláros**, just beside Arkássa, on the Ágios Nikólaos beach, behind the little church of Agía Sofía, ☎ (0245) 61 015, Fax (0245) 61 016 – 5rm. The only hotel on this lovely sandy beach. The studios have large balconies giving onto the sea and have good facilities including kitchenettes.

• **Lefkós**

*Between €27 and €38*

**Hotel Krínos**, at the entrance to the built-up area, on the left, ☎ (0245) 71 410, Fax (0245) 71 413 – 29rm. This very comfortable hotel overlooks the sea and its rooms all have balconies with views. There are fridges and safes. Book three months ahead. Breakfast is extra. Car rental service.

**Sunset Studios**, on the right hand side of the harbour, ☎ (0245) 71 171, Fax (0245) 71 407 – 22rm. Studios with kitchen facilities and unrestricted views of Lefkós.

• **Ólimbos**

*Around €27*

**Hotel Aphrodite**, at the top of the village, ☎ (0245) 51 307 – 4rm. The owners of this little hotel also run the Parthenon restaurant (see below), which is a little higher up in the same street. Small, clean rooms with magnificent views of the sea and a windmill.

• **Diafáni**

*Under €27*

**Ánixis**, 20m up on the right from the quayside, ☎ (0245) 51 226 – 6rm. The owners of the restaurant of the same name let small, clean, simple rooms at very moderate prices.

*Around €27*
**Diafáni Palace**, 40m from the quayside, on the Ólimbos road, ☎ (0245) 51 210 – 9rm. A quiet hotel with clean rooms but a minimum amount of comfort. One of the rooms gives directly onto the roof terrace. Fish restaurant.

- **Kirá Panagía beach**

*Over €43*
**Kira Panagía**, ☎ and Fax (0245) 31 473 – 10 studios, 10 apartments. Ideal for families. Overlooking a delightful little beach with clear water. Access by car, taxi or boat from Pigádia. This top-quality hotel with every comfort caters for groups in summer, so it is best to reserve well ahead. Studios for 2 or 3 people, apartments for 2 to 4 people, and large self-catering apartments. Swimming pool 30m above the beach. Children's playground. Open from May to October.

**EATING OUT**

You should try the *loukoumádes* (fritters topped with honey and sprinkled with cinnamon) and *makaroúnes* (pasta).

- **Pigádia**

*Around €9*
**The Beautiful Kárpathos (or Koral)**, on the left of the quay, facing the landing-stage, ☎ (0245) 22 501. Very popular. You are given a friendly welcome and served copious dishes at reasonable prices. Specialities include *makaroúnes*, *stifádo* and meze.

**Romiós**, on the quay, to the west heading towards the beach, ☎ (0245) 23 771. Copious portions, varied dishes and mixed meat and vegetable salads at moderate prices.

- **Ólimbos**

*Between €9 and €15*
**Parthenon**, at the top of the village, ☎ (0245) 51 307. Pleasant roof terrace. Local Greek specialities.

- **Diafáni**

*Around €9*
**Restaurant Ánixis**, in an alleyway at right angles to the quay, on the right, ☎ (0245) 51 226. This is a simple, authentic restaurant that serves tasty home-style meals based on fresh produce: *dolmádes* with hibiscus leaves or delicious *loukoumádes*, served on a small terrace shaded by an arbour.

*Between €9 and €15*
**Restaurant Diafáni**, in the hotel of the same name (see "Where to stay" above), ☎ (0245) 51 210. The restaurant is run by a fisherman and serves fish and seafood specialities (octopus, crayfish).

- **Lefkós**

*Around €9*
**Small Paradise**, at the beginning of the built-up area, on the right, ☎ (0245) 71 184. Friendly atmosphere and good Greek food served on a shady terrace.

- **Finíki**

This tiny fishing port is a very pleasant place to spend an evening having dinner and watching the sunset.

*Between €9 and €15*
**Dimítrios Fisherman's Taverna**, ☎ (0245) 61 294. As the name suggests, the owner of the restaurant, which is popular with the locals, is a fisherman. So you are sure to eat very fresh fish and seafood (crayfish). Studios to let upstairs.

**HAVING A DRINK**

- **Pigádia**

The harbour is very lively in the evening and has plenty of bars.

**The Life of Angels**, in the main street above the quay, opposite a scuba-diving agency. Bar-taverna with a terrace overlooking the sea. Relaxed atmosphere and pleasant music.

- **Apéri**

**Platánia**, in the first village north-west of Pigádia, to the left of the main road, on the bend. Shaded by a large plane tree. A bar in an attractive, traditional 19C house. A popular meeting place with the village elders.

**OTHER THINGS TO DO**

**Feasts & festivals** – Easter is celebrated with great fervour. On Tuesday of Holy Week the men go on an icon procession through the villages, carrying the icons like crosses, strapped to their shoulders with scarves. Lamb feast on Easter Monday with music (*tsaboúna*, bagpipes, and *láouto*, lute).

# KOS ★

District of the Dodecanese – Michelin map 980 fold 46
Regional map page 479 – Map of the island page 518
290km² – Pop 26 379

### Not to be missed
For night owls, the hectic night-life in summer.
The site of the Asklepion (Asklipiío). The hill town of Kéfalos.
A swim at the foot of the Ágios Stéfanos Basilica.

### And remember...
Book your hotel in advance.
Avoid July and August if you want peace and quiet.

The island of Kos, the third largest in the Dodecanese, extends over about forty kilometres, less than 5km from the Turkish coast. Its western tip forms a hook, as though the island was afraid of drifting away. Indeed, Kos is in a class of its own. Unlike its fellow islands in the Dodecanese, it is a green, well-watered and prosperous land with a very mild climate. Even its relief is less rugged, with beautiful sandy coves ideal for swimming. Its history too has left a rich heritage of monuments, among them the outstanding Asklepion, a veritable medical centre of ancient times, or the many remains dotted about the modern town which recall the island's early splendour. But the

### The Father of Medicine

Hippocrates (c 460-377 BC), probably the son of a priest of Asklepios, was born in Kos where he studied medicine with Democritus. A tireless traveller, he went the length and breadth of Ancient Greece but devoted much of his career to teaching and practising at the Asklepion on Kos. He initiated treatment based on the clinical observation of symptoms, and advocated an overall approach to the human body, founded on the theory of the humours (body fluids such as blood, choler, etc). This theory was taken up by Galen (131-201 AD) a physician in Rome, and was to endure until the 17C. Considered the father of modern medicine, Hippocrates also laid down the philosophical foundations of medicine and its ethical code. The famous Hippocratic Oath, for instance, is what every doctor must take before beginning medical practice. All Hippocrates' treatises are collected in the "Corpus Hippocraticum", a vast anthology that he completed with several other authors.

source of the island's amazing popularity today, attracting in summer almost as many tourists as Rhodes, is its hectic night-life. Immense crowds, mainly trim young Scandinavians, transform Kos Town into a vast techno club every night, loud enough to shake the venerable old monuments to their very foundations.

### The island of the god of healing

The cult of Asklepios, the ancient god of medicine, is believed to have begun on Kos in the 14C BC with the arrival of the first Greek settlers. These either came from Thessaly – the original home of the god – or from Epidaurus, where there is another sanctuary dedicated to him. Whatever the case, there was already a large population on the island during the Mycenaean Era (15C-12C BC). Colonised by the Dorians (11C BC), the island then became a member of the **Dorian Hexapolis** (6C and 7C BC), and then, at the end of the Persian Wars, joined the **Athenian League**. Coming under Persian and then Athenian domination, the island recovered its autonomy in the late 4C BC and was occupied for a time by **Alexander the Great**. There began an unprecedented period of development, which was marked by the founding of a sanctuary – the Asklepion and its prestigious school of medicine – whose fame spread throughout the Ancient World. At the same time (366 BC) Kos changed its capital. The first, in the south-west of the island, was destroyed during the Peloponnesian

War (411 BC). The new city was moved to the north-west and grew rapidly. On the strength of its alliance with Rhodes and the protection of **Ptolemy II of Egypt** (who was born on Kos), the island soon blossomed through its trade in the Aegean Sea, earning a name for itself through the quality of its wines and silks.

Kos then came under Roman and then Byzantine domination, up until 1204 AD when Constantinople was taken by the crusaders. Later, after a brief occupation by the Genoese, Kos was given to the Knights of St John in the early 14C. The knights repelled two Turkish attacks, in 1457 and 1477, but then succumbed in 1522. After the fall of the Ottoman Empire the island was occupied by the **Italians** from 1912 until it became part of Greece in 1948. To the Italians we owe archaeological excavations and a large amount of restoration work.

### Kos Town★★
*Allow a good half-day*

Kos, the capital and main port of the island is a modern, spacious town with wide avenues shaded by pines and palm trees, where people get about on bicycles and scooters. Right in the centre, areas of **ancient ruins** (*free access*), whose white stones

Dome and minaret: the Haji Hassan Mosque

G. de Benoist/MICHELIN

blend in perfectly with the urban landscape, provide necessary breathing spaces. At a bend in the street or on a square, whole sections of the past rise up amid the modern surroundings.

The whole town is organised around the harbour, a circular roadstead defended on the east by an impressive bastion guarding the entrance to the channel and the many restaurants, bars and hotels that line the quays and avenues along the waterfront.

*Come up from the quayside in the vicinity of the castle either from Aktí Miaoúli on the right (the street with the tourist office), or from Aktí Koundourótou on the left.*

You reach **Platía Platánou**, a charming circular square paved with cobblestones and adorned with a pool for ablutions and a **Turkish fountain**. The square owes its name to **Hippocrates' Plane Tree★** that rises impressively in the middle, and which, according to legend, was planted by the doctor himself, who liked to teach in its shade. Be that as it may, the hollow tree has a very wide girth and is undeniably of a venerable age. It is in fact nearly 600 years old and believed to be the successor of the original tree that was planted here 2 400 years ago.

From here, take the footbridge straddling the old moat to the **Knights' Castle★★** (8.30am-3pm; closed Monday), a tremendous fortress whose two concentric sets of walls were built in the 15C, partly with stones from the Asklepion. From the **parapet walk★** you have a panoramic view that takes in the harbour, the sea and the Turkish coast a short distance away. You immediately understand the strategic value of the fort. Embedded in the outer wall are the **coats of arms** of the Grand Masters of Rhodes, Pierre d'Aubusson and Aimery d'Amboise. Those of the other knights are dotted about the inner wall. The moat within the inner wall now contains a **Museum**.

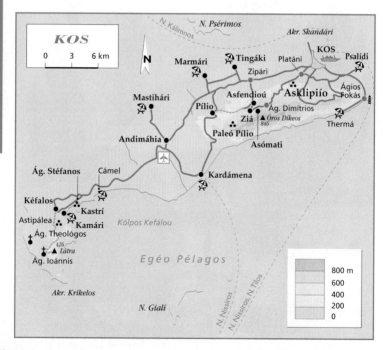

## The Agora and the Ancient Harbour District*

*Free access.* Go still further back in time by walking among the ruins of the ancient city, beginning with the agora and the harbour district. From the esplanade at the foot of the **Haji Hassan Mosque** *(closed down)* with its surviving **minaret**, you have a fine overall **view*** of the ruins. Now overrun with cats, the area was occupied by the buildings of the medieval town. But the district was subjected to numerous earthquakes and then entirely destroyed by one in 1933. This enabled archaeologists to excavate the ruins, uncovering part of the earlier Hellenistic town, including the **Temple to Heracles**, recognisable by its Corinthian columns, the propylaea of the **Temple to Aphrodite**, as well as a Roman mosaic. The agora, the heart of the ancient city, became the site for a small 15C church, **Ágios Konstandínos**. On the edge of a clump of trees **three chapels** mark off the eastern section of the excavations.

*Make your way to Liberty Square (Platía Eleftherías).* Bordered by the ruins of a mosque, **Platía Eleftherías** contains a covered market and the **Archaeological Museum**\*\* *(north of the square, 8.30am-3pm; closed Monday; entrance fee).* In spite of its small size, the museum houses a fine collection of **Hellenistic and Roman sculptures*** found on the island. Among them are a statue of Hippocrates, the head of a soldier under torture, an athlete holding a crown, a small head of Hermes, reliefs of funerary banquets, and a statuette of Eros.

## The western excavations**

*500m south of the main quay, free access.* Take a walk on either side of **Odós Grigoríou**, where a vast section of the ancient city stretches out, still under excavation. The walk is particularly enjoyable in the evening when the ruins are gently bathed in the fading light, or even at night, in the light of the moon. North of the street, an **ancient paved way*** crosses the district. You can still see the ruts hollowed out by chariot wheels. Several edifices stand out among the jumbled stones, among them a **baptistery**, **Roman baths**, a pool and latrines, Roman **mosaics** and **wall paintings**, the remains of a portico – a beautiful row of **Doric columns** – and even the outline of a **stadium**.

A little further east, opposite Odós Pávlou, lie the remains of a **Temple to Dionysus**, while on the other side of Odós Grigoríou you can see the **ancient theatre**. But the jewel of the district is the **Roman villa**\*\*\* *(8.30am-3pm; closed Monday),* an enormous patrician mansion dating from the 3C AD. Well preserved and partly restored by the Italians, it gives a good idea of what Roman daily life was like. The house is laid out around three inner courtyards, two of which have a peristyle. Several rooms have kept their **floor mosaics**\*\* and their **wall paintings**\*\*, a splendid sight. Excavations in the area around the villa have brought to light other remains, including some baths.

# The Asklepion*** (Asklipiío)

*5km from Kos Town. You can easily reach the site by bicycle, scooter or bus. Get there when it opens early in the morning to avoid the groups and the heat. 8.30am-3pm, 8.30am-7pm in summer. Closed Monday. Entrance fee. Allow 90min.*

The Asklepion, a huge sanctuary dedicated to the god **Asklepios** (Aesculapius in Latin), was founded in the late 4C BC, and then enlarged several times. Its medical school and treatment centre were renowned throughout the Ancient World, and many notables, first from Greece and then from the Roman Empire came here to recover their health. Today the only inmates are the big green lizards that scurry between the stones. The ruins, bristling with cypress and eucalyptus trees, stand on a magnificent **site**\*\*, rising in tiers on four immense terraces connected by monumental staircases. The higher you go, from esplanade to esplanade, the more the solemnity of the place strikes you, as it probably did visitors in ancient times.

The first terrace, in ruins, once held the **Roman baths**. You can make out one of the cooling baths.

**Kos**

A ramp leads up to the second terrace – the most spacious – which was lined by porticoes. It was here that **springs** welled up, containing properties such as iron and sulphur that people could benefit from in the adjoining **baths**.

Rising up in the middle of the third terrace is the **monumental altar to Asklepios**, surrounded by several shrines. There is an **Ionic Temple** (Temple B) dedicated to the god, where the treasures and the offerings left by the sick and pilgrims were kept, and a **Roman Temple** (Temple C), which was probably used for emperor worship. Seven of this temple's fine Corinthian columns have been stood upright.

Right at the top, on the last terrace, there once stood a large **Doric Temple** (Temple A) dedicated to Asklepios. This was a peripteral structure six columns broad by 11 long, made of white marble set off by black. Take the time to contemplate the superb **view\*\***, which encompasses the olive groves beyond the site, Kos Town, and the Turkish coast on the horizon.

From the Asklepion you can get to the village of **Ziá** (*see below*) along a beautiful ridge-top road. Three-quarters of its length (*8km*) consists of a rough stony track that is navigable in a four-wheel-drive vehicle or on foot if you are a keen walker. The **scenery\*\*\*** is really worth the effort.

## The beaches\*

Not far from Kos Town, the resort of **Psalídi**, south-east, has fine beaches, which, naturally enough, get very crowded. The same goes for the resorts along the north coast, such as **Tingáki** and **Marmári**, which are bordered by dunes and face the islands of Kálimnos and Psérimos. Try your luck a little further on, where the narrower **black sand** beaches attract far fewer people. **Mastihári**, for instance, is a pleasant fishing port.

### Around Kéfalos Bay\*

The area around the wide Bay of Kéfalos south-west of the island is a good place for swimming and touring. Before reaching Kamári, make sure you see the ruins of the 5C Byzantine basilica, **Ágios Stéfanos\*\***, isolated on a small cape pointing towards the picturesque islet of **Kastrí** (*from the road, go through the Club Med village*). The site is quite charming, with ancient columns standing right beside the water. If you gently rub aside the protective gravel that covers the ground, you will discover **mosaics\*** of birds. The place is also perfect for a swim. It is possible to swim out to the islet opposite (*but watch out for water-skiers*).

There are other good **beaches\*** dotted along the coast east of the basilica, with evocative, though hardly local names: Cámel, Paradise, Banana, Sunny and Magic. The further east you go, the fewer people there are (*access by road or on foot along the shore*).

Lastly, west of Ágios Stéfanos, there are still 5km of beaches on the bay, up to **Kamári harbour**, but they are entirely given over to tourism. The same goes for those round **Kardámena**, a large resort offering little of interest.

If you prefer less populated areas, head down to the **southern tip\*\*** to see the wildest landscapes on the island. Take the unsurfaced roads and you will come to creeks and beaches that are really deserted (*for instance, drive along the dirt track south of Kéfalos for 6km towards Ágios Theológos Monastery and follow the shore once you reach the restaurant of the same name*).

Kos, the elegant columns of Ágios Stéfanos, in Kéfalos Bay

## Villages in the interior*

*Short excursion (about 50km) from Zipári to Kéfalos*

**Mt Díkeos**, which reaches a height of 846m, is home to several forgotten villages whose white houses are gradually being abandoned by their owners who go off to find work on the coast.

■ One such village is **Asfendioú** (*about 3km from Zipári*), where delightful **Byzantine churches** are hidden in the narrow alleyways. **Ziá***, a little further on, nestles in the cool greenery of a forest. Unfortunately, the place features on all the tour operators' programmes. Tourists arrive by the coachload and the streets have been invaded by trashy souvenir shops. It is the spectacular sunsets that draw the crowds, and the village is also the starting point for Mt Díkeos (*2hr30min round trip*).

■ East of Ziá (*on the scenic road to Kos Town*), two other villages are also worth a visit: **Asómati**, where the oldest houses are being carefully restored, and **Ágios Dimítrios**, whose abandoned alleyways are full of silent charm, part melancholic, part serene.

*Return to Asfendioú and continue westwards up to the Marmári road.*

■ Overlooking the village of **Pílio** far below (*3km to the north*), are the meagre remains of the **medieval village of Pílio*** (Paleó Pílio), the capital of the island during the Byzantine Period. The trip here is mainly worthwhile for the beauty of the setting, an ideal place for a picnic as you admire the **landscape**★★. You can go for a short walk (*along the path to the left of the spring*) up to the ruins of the **citadel** that crowns the hill (*15min*).

*Continue westwards along the Kamári road to Andimáhia.*

■ Another pleasant site: the village and **fortress of Andimáhia**★★ (*3km east of Andimáhia town, along a dirt road, free access*), built by the Knights of Rhodes in the 15C. There are two **chapels**, and a path leads round the ramparts, immense stone walls snaking along the crest of the mountain. From the top, the **panorama**★★ stretches to the **Turkish peninsula of Knidos** to the south-east, and to the islands of Níssiros and Tílos further south.

■ The last part of the itinerary is to the peninsula that forms the south-western tip of the island. The old village of **Kéfalos**★★ stands isolated on the heights, perched on the edge of a limestone cliff that glows at sunset. From its position above Kamári Bay, it seems unaware of the tourist bustle along the coast at its feet. Life goes on in its drowsy streets as in the past. And you never tire of looking at the sea from the **Papavasílis windmill** or the remains of the **Knights' Fortress**.

## Making the most of Kos

### COMING AND GOING

**By air** – Daily connection with Athens and Rhodes, as well as with Sámos, Léros and Thessaloníki. Plenty of charters with direct flights from Northern Europe. The *airport* is near Andimáhia, 25km south-west of Kos Town, ☎ (0242) 51 225. An **Olympic Airways** bus leaves the company office 2hr before each flight. But as the airport is poorly served by city buses, you would do best to take a taxi (or share one) to Kos Town.

**By sea** – Daily ferry connections with Piraeus (12hr30min minimum travelling time) and Rhodes (4hr). Regular boats connect Kos with the other islands in the Dodecanese, as well as with Crete, the Cyclades, and the North and East Aegean Islands. Plenty of hydrofoils in summer to Rhodes, Sími, Pátmos, Léros, Níssiros and Sámos.

**Harbourmaster's office**, where Aktí Koundouriótou and Odós Megálou Alexándrou meet, ☎ (0242) 28 507.

Boat companies: **Koulias Travel Agency**, Aktí Koundouriótou, in the harbour, ☎ (0242) 26 985, **Aeolos Travel**, Odós Annétas Laoumtzí, ☎ (0242) 26 203.

## GETTING AROUND

**By bicycle or scooter** – The ideal way of getting around Kos Town, the Asklepion and the nearby beaches is to hire a **bicycle** or a **scooter**. There are dozens of rental places for these in Kos Town. On the other hand, if you want to cross the island using the main road that links Kos Town with Kéfalos (43km to the south-west), you should hire a **car** (or a **motorcycle**), as distances are long and the traffic heavy. Furthermore, the gusts of wind on the heights can be dangerous.

**By bus** – The bus station for services to the island's villages is behind the Olympic Airways office, in Odós Kleopátras, ☎ (0242) 22 292. There are several buses a day to Tingáki, Mastihári, Kardámena, Pilío, and Kéfalos via the beaches at Paradise, Ágios Stéfanos and Kamári. Local buses to the Asklepion, Lámbi and Ágios Fokás leave from the harbour (Aktí Koundouriótou).

**By taxi** – Taxi rank in the harbour, Aktí Koundouriótou, opposite the Knights' Castle, ☎ (0242) 22 777 / 23 333. For short distances.

## ADDRESS BOOK (KOS TOWN)

**Tourist information** – **Municipal tourist office**, Odós Vasiléos Georgíou 3, beside the hydrofoil jetty, ☎ (0242) 24 460 / 28 724, Fax (0242) 211 11. Open from May to October, 8am-9pm. Boat and bus timetables, maps and help with accommodation.

**Bank / Currency exchange** – You will easily find cash dispensers, particularly at the **National Bank**, Odós Antinavarhou, and at the **Ionian Bank**, Odós E Venizélou.

**Post office / Telephone** – **Main post office**, Odós E Venizélou 14, ☎ (0242) 22 250.
**OTE**, Odós Výronos 6L, ☎ (0242) 22 499.

**Tourist police** – In the large yellow building east of Hippocrates' Plane Tree, ☎ (0242) 22 666 / 28 277.

**Medical service** – **Emergencies / Hospital**, Odós Ippokrátous 32, ☎ (0242) 22 300.

**Airline companies** – **Olympic Airways**, Odós Vasiléos Pávlou 22, ☎ (0242) 28 330 / 28 331.

**Laundry** – **Happy Wash**, Odós Mitropólis 20. **Laundromat Center**, Odós Alikarnassoú 124.

## WHERE TO STAY

In addition to Kos Town, which has many hotels, most tourist accommodation is on the coast, particularly on the north-east of the island around Marmári, as well as along Kéfalos Bay and around Kardámena, a noisy resort with little appeal.

### • Kos Town

**Campsite**, 3.5km east of the town on the Ágios Fokás road, ☎ (0242) 23 275. Pleasant pitches beneath olive trees. Clean. Friendly welcome. Shared kitchen and bicycle rental. Around €12.

*Under €27*

**Pension Aléxis**, Odós Irodótou 9 & Odós Omírou, ☎ (0242) 28 798 / 25 594, Fax (0242) 25 797 – 14rm. 🚿 A simple place, with the advantage of being in the heart of the harbour district, less than 100m from the main quay. Rather spartan though reasonable rooms. Youthful atmosphere, with a friendly, helpful owner who sometimes organises boat excursions. Open from April to October.

*Between €27 and €38*

**Hotel Afendoúlis**, Odós Evripílou 1 ☎ (0242) 25 321, Fax (0242) 25 797 – 🍴📋✕📺🚿 CC In the south-eastern part of the modern town. A recently built, comfortable, clean hotel. Open from April to October.

**Hotel Hará**, Odós Hálkonos 6, ☎ (0242) 25 500 / 23 198 – 20rm. 🍴 Right near the shore. Fairly quiet in spite of the many bars and restaurants round about. Very clean, and efficiently run.

**Hotel Anna**, Odós E Venizélou 77, ☎ (0242) 23 030, Fax (0242) 23 886 – 21rm. 🍴 ✎ 🚿 Fairly quiet, except when spluttering scooters drive past. Ask for the rooms on the less noisy side. All the rooms have balconies. Pleasant little bar, friendly atmosphere.

**Hotel Paradise**, Odós Bouboulínas, ☎ (0242) 229 88, Fax (0242) 242 05 – 52rm. 🍴 ✎ ✕ CC In a quiet location 200m from the harbour and 300m from the beach (ask for the rooms that do not give onto the street). Some rooms have fridges. Fairly expensive but prices come down for long stays. Book at least 10 days ahead. Open from the end of May to the beginning of October.

*Over €45*
**Hotel Maritina**, Odós E Venizélou & Odós Výronos 19L, ☎ (0242) 23 511 / 23 513 / 27 301 / 27 303, Fax (0242) 26 124 – 83rm. ⌾ ♪ ▤ TV ♨ CC A top quality establishment benefiting from a good position in a quiet part of the ancient city (on the square facing the Temple to Dionysus). Comfortable, but lacks character. Indifferent reception. Breakfast extra. Open year round.

• **Kéfalos**

*Under €27*
In the old town, you can stay with local people in their own houses. There are no signs up, so you have to ask in tavernas. This can take time, but it is an inexpensive option and you will certainly meet friendly people. Among others, **Nákis**, ☎ (0242) 71 195, lets 4 rooms with bathrooms and kitchenettes, not far from the bus station.

• **Kéfalos Bay**

*Between €27 and €38*
**Panorama Studios**, on the Kéfalos road before you reach Ágios Stéfanos beach, up a track on the left (bus stop facing the track), ☎ (0242) 71 924, and in Kos Town, ☎ and Fax (0242) 71 524 – 17rm. ⌾ ♨ An appropriately named place built on the heights overlooking the whole of Kéfalos Bay, and benefiting from an unrestricted view. Unlike most hotel complexes of this kind in the bay, this one is quiet and does not work with tour operators. The very clean studios have kitchenettes with fridges, and balconies oriented to catch the sun right through to the evening. Breakfast included. English and German spoken. Open from March to October.
**Spring Studios**, Kamári harbour, ☎ (0242) 72 106 – 6 apartments. ⌾ ♨ At the far end of Kéfalos Bay, right at the end of the quay, 50m above the Faros restaurant. Quiet apartments with kitchenettes with fridges and terraces giving onto the sea.

• **Mastihári**
You will easily find rooms to let.

*Under €27*
**Studios Andreas**, on the western side of the village, ☎ (0242) 59 050 – 6rm. ⌾ Peaceful location on the heights overlooking the seafront. Four of the rooms have a lovely view of the sea. All of them have balconies.

**Irene Studios**, on the western side of the village, ☎ (0242) 51 269 / 29 398 – 5rm. ⌾ Just beside the studios above. Of similar standard, and even closer to the sea.

EATING OUT

• **Kos Town**
Kos Town has a large number of seasonal restaurants that are rather similar. Here are several places that stand out:

*Around €9*
⌾ **Antónis**, Odós Korytsas 1, ☎ (0242) 25 645. Set back a little, 500m from the sea. The restaurant is not much to look at, but it is extremely good: very fresh ingredients, and simple, tasty Greek dishes (such as *saganáki* flambé). In addition, this is one of the rare places not to be invaded by tourists in summer. Open all year, lunch and dinner.

*Between €9 and €15*
**Taverna Hiródion**, Odós Artemisías 27, ☎ (0242) 26 634. CC Near the Hotel Hará, on the eastern side of the modern town. Decent food, good value for money (chicken specialities). May to October, lunch and dinner.

**Olympiáda**, on the corner of Odós Pávlou and Odós Kleopátras, ☎ (0242) 23 031. CC Behind Olympic Airways. Traditional fare that you choose from the counter. Good value for money, so the place is popular. Open all year for lunch and dinner.

**Taverna Pétrino**, Platía Ioánnou Theológou, ☎ (0242) 27 251. CC Alongside the western excavations, to the right of the ancient gymnasium. A large, tastefully decorated terrace drowning in greenery. You eat by candlelight. Dinner only.

**Taverna Filoxénia**, on the corner of Odós Píndou & Odós Alikarnassoú, ☎ (0242) 24 967. CC A family taverna that is very tourist oriented, but serves decent food. Reasonable value for money (copious mixed dishes). April to October, lunch and dinner.

• **Kéfalos**
In the steep old village of Kéfalos perched on the heights, you can still find tiny tavernas that serve only the day's special, a tasty, authentic family dish. A good deal more reliable and enjoyable than most of the many beach restaurants that line Kéfalos Bay, recent places with a lot less soul (only open in summer).

- **Kamári (Kéfalos Bay)**
*Around €9*
**Stamatía**, on Kamári beach, ☎ (0242) 71 245. [CC] One of the oldest restaurants in the bay. At the end of Kamári beach beside the roundabout where the bus station road and the Kamári harbour road converge. Varied menu – fish, seafood, Greek specialities – and courteous reception. Lunch and dinner.
**Fáros**, in Kamári harbour, ☎ (0242) 71 240. At the end of Kéfalos Bay, at the end of the harbour, on the waterfront. Fish, seafood, Greek specialities and pasta, served in a pleasant setting just above a little beach. Lunch and dinner.

- **Marmári**
*Around €9*
**Apostólis**, bear right at the crossroads beyond Odós Linopólis 117. Halfway along the road that leads to Marmári, on the left, ☎ (0242) 41 403. Decent food and pleasant setting.

- **Mastihári**
The fishing harbour is renowned for its very good fish restaurants. Below are two of them, where you can try a wide choice of fish as well as Greek specialities.
*Around €9*
**Kalí Kardiá**, facing the harbour, west of the quay, ☎ (0242) 59 289. [CC] A popular, well-known place, fairly inexpensive. Lunch and dinner, April to the end of October.
**Seaside Restaurant**, at the beginning of the beach that faces west, ☎ (0242) 59 284. [CC] You eat in the cool of the sea breeze. Friendly reception. Open all year, lunch and dinner.

- **Ágios Theológos**
*Around €12*
**Ágios Theológos Restaurant**, on the south-west tip of the island, at the end of the peninsula, 500m before you reach the Ágios Theológos Monastery. The only restaurant in the vicinity is at the end of a 6km dirt track, in a beautiful wild setting with a lovely terrace looking onto the sea. A little more expensive than others given its remote location.

**HAVING A DRINK**
*Cafés, tearooms*
- **Kos Town**
In the town centre, you are spoilt for choice for cafés or somewhere to have a drink. The following is a delightful, unusual place:

**Café Theatráki**, Odós Grigoríou 5, ☎ (0242) 25 052. Snacks, pizza and ice cream. The bar with its swimming pool is to the west of the ancient theatre, in the middle of a wide lawn, certainly one of the pleasantest places in town. Cut off from the bustle of the centre, the relaxed, peaceful atmosphere contrasts with that of the overcrowded beaches. Ideal for sunbathing or a swim, with refreshments on the terrace. This is the place to come in the heat of the day or in the early evening.

*Bars, night-clubs*

- **Kos Town**

Hundreds of music bars and night-clubs vibrate to the blast of techno music. The evening usually begins in the ancient city district, on Aktí Koundouriótou, or around Odós Diákou, Odós Nafklírou and Odós Pávlou. It continues north of the harbour, in the large night-clubs at the end of Odós Avérof, about 1km from the harbour, notably at **Kalua**, or **Heaven** (Odós Zouroudi). There are also clubs where you can listen to rock music or modern Greek music, such as the **Hamam Club**, at the beginning of Aktí Koundouriótou, opposite the taxi rank.

**OTHER THINGS TO DO**

**Boat trips** – In summer, there is a daily ferry service to and from Bodrum (ancient Halicarnassus) on the Turkish coast. Departure 8.30am and return 4pm (1hr travelling time).

Plenty of excursions are also possible around the island or to neighbouring islands (day trips). Enquire at the harbour.

**Scuba diving** – Diving boats are lined up along the quays in Kos harbour. Very popular in summer. **Team Divers**, Odós Patakoú 3, ☎ (0242) 20 090.

**Hot springs** – The village of **Thermá**, 12km from Kos Town, has spa facilities.

**SHOPPING GUIDE**

**Arts and crafts** – The shops in Kos Town have ceramics, jewellery, woven articles, and all sorts of other items.

# PÁTMOS ★★

District of the Dodecanese – Michelin map 980 fold 34 – Regional map page 479
Map of the island page 528 – 34km² – Pop 2 665 – Allow at least a day

### Not to be missed
A walk at dusk through the alleyways of the hill town (Hóra).
St John's Monastery.
A swim at Psiliámos beach.

### And remember...
Avoid accommodation in noisy Skála if you are staying for several days.
A scooter is the best way of getting around the island.

St John's island, where the apostle had his revelations and wrote his *Apocalypse*, sees thousands of pilgrims and visitors every year. All of them – Orthodox Christians, Western Christians and lay people alike – come to visit the apostle's cave and the impressive Byzantine monastery dedicated to him. The eye is drawn automatically to the massive outline of the monastery standing on the heights in the middle of the island. But the mystical atmosphere of the two shrines now lives side by side with that of more profane pleasures, as Pátmos also caters to the tourist industry. Green and flower-filled in spring, dry and rocky in summer, the island has several faces, as you will discover when you explore its bays and beaches. Touring the place is all the more pleasant as Pátmos is a small island on a human scale. Distances are always short and getting about is easy, even on the winding roads in the hills. From the heights, the views are such that the island looks like a stone ship, completely encircled by the sea.

## A holy island
Mycenaeans, Dorians and Ionians all lived successively on the island. The Roman Empire deported its political undesirables here, including **St John the Evangelist**, who was exiled in 95-97 AD for preaching the Christian faith in Ephesus. A thousand years

Pátmos, St John's Monastery: the fortress of the Apocalypse

B. Kaufmann/MICHELIN

The Dodecanese

later (1088), Pátmos was given to the monk **Christódoulos Letrinós** by the Byzantine emperor Alexius I Comnenus so that he could found a monastery dedicated to St John. The monk's relics were brought to the island after his death in Ephesus, and soon attracted many pilgrims. From then on, the privileges granted to the monastery made Pátmos an important economic power, with sufficient naval strength to hold off raids by the pirates plundering the region. After the fall of Constantinople, the monastery was put under papal protection and so spared damage by the Turks when they took over the island in 1537. The monastery was shown the same respect by the Venetians, who nonetheless sacked the rest of the island in 1659. Having been spared the wars, the Monastery of St John the Divine could continue its activity, and in the 18C the important **School of Pátmos** was founded. Its teachings quickly gained fame and contributed to the awakening of national feeling. In spite of Greek independence in 1822, Pátmos remained under Ottoman domination until the Italian occupation in 1911, with the island only becoming part of Greece in 1948.

**John, the apostle of the End of the World**
St John the Evangelist, known as the Theologian by Orthodox Christians, referred to himself as "the one Jesus loved". He was in fact one of the first disciples of Jesus, and the last one to be with him: he was present at the Crucifixion, and was asked by Jesus to look after his mother. And so John took Mary to Ephesus, where he preached the Gospel of Christ with charisma. This success led Emperor Domitian to banish him to Pátmos in 95 AD. There he wrote his Apocalypse, his Gospel and his epistles. He then returned to Ephesus where he preached until his death, which took place towards the end of the reign of Trajan (98-117).

Today, while life on Pátmos no longer revolves exclusively around the monastery, a diffuse sense of spirituality reigns over the island. This is expressed during **religious festivals**, especially Orthodox Easter, which is celebrated here with great splendour and fervour. You will feel it during your walks, when, at a bend in the track or at the top of a hill, you will unfailingly come across some wayside shrine, oratory or chapel glinting in the sun.

## Tour of the island

■ **Skála** – The island's only harbour – for ferries, yachts and cruise ships – is a busy, noisy town, especially in summer with the influx of tourists. This is where you will find most of the hotels, restaurants and cafés on Pátmos, not forgetting the countless souvenir shops. But the place is still picturesque, especially along the waterfront, which stretches along sheltered quays to a small bay lined with colourful fishing boats. If you climb west of Skála up **Kastéli hill** *(20min on foot)*, you will have a fine **view**★★ of the surrounding islands, of the harbour's white houses huddled beside the blue water, and, of course, of the monastery.

■ **The cave of the Apocalypse**★ – *By bus, or on foot along a mule track (15min, descending from Hóra or climbing from Skála). Open May to September, 8am-1.30pm Monday, Wednesday, Friday and Saturday, 8am-1pm / 4-6pm Tuesday and Thursday, 8am-12noon / 4-6pm Sunday. Allow 15min.* On the winding track, halfway between Skála and Hóra, is a small, **fortified monastery**, built in the 17C and enlarged over later centuries. Hidden in a pinewood echoing to the sound of cicadas, the open, peaceful site affords lovely **views**★ of Skála Bay. It is difficult to believe that such a place, with its hibiscus and bougainvillaea, was the setting for St John's torment. Several steps, flanked by monks' cells, go down to the holy cave where according to tradition the apostle had his terrible visions of the *Apocalypse* and heard the great voice of God, "as of a trumpet". Transformed into a shrine, the cave contains a small niche hollowed out of the rock and ringed with metal where John laid his head to rest. There are also some **12C paintings** discovered in 1973.

■ **The Monastery of St John the Divine**★★★ (Ágios Ioánnis Theológos) – *8am-1.30pm Monday, Wednesday, Friday and Saturday, 8am-1pm / 4-6pm Tuesday and Thursday, 8am-12noon / 4-6pm Sunday. Entrance fee. Allow 1hr.* Visible from the sea, the crenellated walls of the monastery, a massively powerful setting for one of the most influential sanctuaries in Greece, rise above the white houses of Hóra like a crown of ochre-coloured stone.

Preceding the entrance to the fortress is a small **terrace**★ that looks over the town and affords a superb **view**★★ of Skála and the entire north of the island. The tiny **chapel** is dedicated to the Holy Apostles.

You enter the monastery through a narrow 12C gateway surmounted by a bell-tower. The central courtyard paved with black pebbles forms a narrow square. This is brightened up on the left side by the elegant arches of the **exonarthex** of the church, which contains some fine 17C and 19C **frescoes**. The gallery opens on to the **katholikón**★ (main church), the oldest part of the monastery, which is also decorated with frescoes. The church has a Greek-cross plan and is topped by a dome resting on a drum.

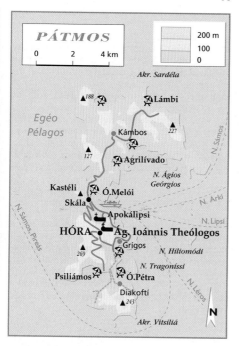

As monastery dogma held that one could not attend Mass more than once a day in the same church, there are no less than ten chapels within its walls. Two adjoin the main church: the **Chapel of Christódoulos**★, which contains the relics of the saint, a beautiful **iconostasis** and some **frescoes**, and the **Chapel of the Virgin**★★ with a very beautiful group of late-12C **frescoes**★★ and an **iconostasis** made of painted wood.

Don't miss the **Museum**★★ (Treasury) *(entrance fee)* on the other side of the courtyard. It has a wonderfully rich collection of rare items from the library, as well as Byzantine and post-Byzantine **icons**★★, a **chrysobul** (charter) giving an account of the founding of the monastery, beautifully illuminated Gospels, chalices, embroideries, vestments, etc. The library, unfortunately closed to the public, is one of the richest and oldest in the Byzantine world. It contains almost 4 000 works, including patriarchal bulls, parchment documents, manuscripts and rare books in Greek, Latin, Aramaic and Slav languages.

The rest of the building is a fine example of Byzantine monastery architecture, with a **kitchen** and a **refectory** *(temporarily closed for restoration)* decorated with many 12C and 13C **frescoes**, a storeroom, a cistern, a bakery and several chapels. Climb upstairs, where the first **terrace**★ gives an interesting view of the courtyard *(the upper terraces are unfortunately not accessible)*.

■ **Hóra**★★★ (Pátmos) – Unlike Skála, the hill town has distanced itself from the tourist frenzy, and while there may be the odd taverna, there are no hotels. Hóra has kept its **traditional architecture**, dating from the 16C and 17C. It forms a charm-

**The Dodecanese**

ing maze of stairways punctuated by covered passageways. The whitewashed alleyways are lined with little **arcaded houses★** or the more refined sea captains' neo-Classical mansions with pedimented doors and windows. In the north of the town (*on the right, up from the taxi rank*), go to the small square with the **town hall★** (an elegant neo-Classical building), where there is a lovely **view★★** over the Aegean. Nearby, you will be able to see the beautiful flower garden of the **Convent of Zoodóhos Pigí**, and its 17C frescoes.

### Niptiras, Easter on Pátmos

Pátmos, a holy island, is duty bound to celebrate Easter with fervour. On Maundy Thursday hundreds of worshippers go to Hóra to attend the Niptiras ceremony, which commemorates Christ's washing his disciples' feet before they gathered together for the Last Supper. The igoúmenos or superior washes the feet of twelve monks, a ritual performed in the past by all Byzantine emperors. On Easter Sunday, eggs painted red, symbolising the blood of Christ, are distributed to the faithful to mark the end of the Lenten fast.

## Swimming

The prevailing wind blows from the north-west, so you would do well to head for the more sheltered beaches on the east coast, which are also the most beautiful. There you will also find several holiday resorts that are quieter than Skála, notably in the deep cove around **Grígos Bay★★** (*by bus or caique from Skála*). You can relax, for instance, on **Pétra beach** (*follow the bay for 500m*), a sandy crescent fringed by marshland that faces the **islet of Tragoníssi**. Nearby stands a large, strangely shaped rock, which seems to have been inhabited by hermits, judging by the well and a small cave hollowed out of the rock. The **view★★** of the bay from the top is splendid. By continuing along the shore for another 300m, you come to a tiny **fishing harbour** hidden behind rocks, an attractive spot next to a small shipbuilding yard.

Another good choice for swimming is **Melói Bay★**, north-east of Skála. It has a large beach shaded by tamarisks, as does **Kámbos beach** a little further north. If solitude is what you are after, try the less crowded but windier beaches in the north of the island. One such is **Lámbi beach★**, covered in strange multicoloured pebbles smoothed by the tide.

There is also a charming beach at **Psiliámos★★** in the far south-west of the island. Inaccessible by road and therefore often deserted, it looks like somewhere at the ends of the earth. Discreet nudists sometimes camp rough here. Access is by caique (*from Skála or Grígos*), or alternatively on foot, a beautiful **walk★** along the coast starting east of Stávrou Bay (*beyond the isolated taverna and the farm, 20min on foot*).

## Making the most of Pátmos

### COMING AND GOING

Luckily, Pátmos does not have an airport. It is, however, possible to fly to the islands of Sámos, Léros, Kos, or Rhodes, where you can take a hydrofoil or a ferry. There are daily ferry connections with Piraeus and Rhodes, via Léros, Kálimnos and Kos. In summer the islands in the Dodecanese are well served by hydrofoil.

### GETTING AROUND

**By bus** – Plenty of convenient, inexpensive buses daily from Skála (station to the left of the tourist office) to Hóra (stop halfway at the Monastery of the Apocalypse), Grígos and Kámbos. From Hóra there are buses to Skála and Grígos (station 50m before the entrance to Hóra). No buses to Lámbi beach.

**By sea** – Water-taxis make daily trips to several of the island's beaches, which are not all accessible by road (enquire at the harbour).

**By taxi** – Taxi rank opposite the post office in Skála, and on the main square in Hóra, ☎ (0247) 31 225.

**By rental car** – Plenty of car and scooter rental places in Skála.

## ADDRESS BOOK (SKÁLA)

**Tourist information –** *Municipal information office* in the large white building opposite the landing-stage, ☎ (0247) 31 666 / 31 235 / 31 058. The **tourist police**, ☎ (0247) 31 303 and the **harbourmaster's office**, ☎ (0247) 31 231 are in the same building.

**Post office / Telephone –** *Main post office*, on the main square, right-hand side of the building mentioned above. **OTE** in a street at right angles to the quay, on the left, ☎ (0247) 31 399.

**Bank / Currency exchange –** *Commercial Bank*, ☎ (0247) 34 140. *National Bank*, ☎ (0247) 34 050.

**Medical service –** *Emergencies / Hospital*, ☎ (0247) 31 211.

**Laundry –** *Wash & Go*, at the new yacht dock.

## WHERE TO STAY

There is plenty of accommodation in Skála harbour, but the place is very crowded and noisy. Your best bet is to get away from the main quay and the adjacent streets. The situation is very different in the quiet, protected hilltop town of Hóra, which just has a few rooms in private houses. The resorts of Grígos, Melói and Kámbos can also be pleasant places for a holiday.

### • Skála

Go along the quays on the right for 300m, past the first pleasure craft dock and then up the alleyway on the left. You will find three quiet hotels side by side, set slightly back from the harbour.

*Around €24*

*Sydney*, behind the Australis Hotel, a little higher up on the left, ☎ (0247) 31 689 – 11rm. 🛏 🍴 An inexpensive guesthouse offering very good value for money. Very comfortable rooms with fridges. Mineral water and house wine kindly provided free of charge. April to October.

*Over €33*

*Villa Knossós*, just below the Australis Hotel, ☎ (0247) 32 189, Fax (0247) 32 284 – 7rm. 🛏 🍴 A quiet place with a flower garden. Rooms all have balconies, fridges and hotplates. Open from April to October.

*Over €38*

*Australis*, ☎ (0247) 31 576, Fax (0247) 32 284 – 20rm. 🛏 🍴 🍽 Set in a magnificent garden. Very comfortable, well-equipped rooms. Apartments for up to 6 people, with kitchens and televisions. A generous breakfast is included. The friendly owner, Fokas, speaks English and is extremely helpful. Scooter rental. April to October.

### • Melói

*Stéfanos campsite*, on Melói beach, to the left, ☎ (0247) 31 821 / 31 822 – 250 pitches maximum. 🛏 🍴 🍽 A clean, well laid out campsite on the shore. Bar-restaurant and a small shop. Scooter rental. Under €24 per pitch for two people.

### • Lámbi

*Around €24*

*Dolphin of Lámbi Beach*, ☎ (0247) 31 951 or (01) 864 66 04 (Athens) – 8rm. 🛏 🍴 🍽 🍴 **cc** The only place that lets rooms on the beach. Friendly welcome and moderate prices. Only open in summer (you should book).

### • Hóra

*Around €24*

There are very few rooms to let in the north-west part of the town (signposted). You should ask the locals. One place among others (no name), ☎ (0247) 31 963 – 5rm. 🛏 🍽 Shared kitchen. Two of the rooms share the same shower (convenient for a family). Shared facilities for the 3 others.

### • Grígos

The superb Grígos Bay is an ideal place for a quiet family holiday. There are plenty of hotel rooms and studios with kitchen facilities.

*Over €38*

*Hotel Athena*, facing the bay, on the heights, ☎ (0247) 31 859 / 68 977, Fax (0247) 32 859 – 14rm. 🛏 🍴 🍽 🍴 **cc** Spacious, clean, comfortable rooms, and a friendly welcome. Breakfast included. Television room. Only open in summer.

## EATING OUT

### • Skála

*Around €7.50*

*Ouzerí Khilimodi*, second alleyway on the left of the street that leads to

Hóra, ☎ (0247) 34 080. In a narrow lane adjoining a small garden. A very small, traditional taverna. Simple but tasty dishes. Friendly welcome. Only open in the evening, all year round.

**Restaurant Grigoris**, opposite the landing-stage, on the left side of the quay, ☎ (0247) 31 515. Very popular. Decent food.

*Between €7.50 and €15*

**Loikas**, on Skála's main thoroughfare, at right angles to the quay, 150m on the right, ☎ (0247) 32 515. cc A restaurant with a pleasant terrace where you eat grilled dishes and Greek specialities.

● **Hóra**

There are not many local restaurants, and they are very full at midday in summer.

*Between €9 and €15*

**Taverna Malkoni**, up from the taxi rank, on the left in the main street that climbs to the monastery, ☎ (0247) 32 115. cc Chicken specialities and traditional moussaká, served on a terrace. Lunch and dinner, April to October.

**Vagélis Restaurant**, on a little square, 150m on the left before the climb to the monastery, ☎ (0247) 31 967. Worthwhile for the lovely setting (2 terraces, one in the garden, the other on the street), and for the food (Greek specialities). Lunch and dinner. April to October.

*Around €23*

**Archontikó Restaurant**, Platía Xanthós (facing the town hall), ☎ and Fax (0247) 31 668 – cc Set in a traditional house. A renowned French restaurant that also serves Greek specialities. Friendly service. Dinner only.

● **Kámbos**

There are restaurants in the village, but you would do better down on the beach enjoying one of the waterfront terraces.

*Between €7.50 and €15*

**Restaurant Acrogiáli**, at the beginning of the beach, ☎ (0247) 32 590. Two terraces, one on the beach, the other more sheltered. The speciality is fresh farm lamb. April to October.

**Restaurant Kavorákia**, a little further along the same street that runs alongside the beach, ☎ (0247) 31 745. Large, pleasant terrace 15m from the water. Good value for money. Open from May to September.

● **Melói**

*Between €7.50 and €15*

**Restaurant Melói**, on the right side of the beach, ☎ (0247) 855 00. Open May to October. Terrace with an arbour. Greek specialities.

● **Lámbi**

*Between €7.50 and €15*

**Lámbi**, on the beach, ☎ (0247) 31 490. A little waterfront taverna serving fresh fish, and *saganáki* flambé with *Tsipouro*. From Easter to the end of September.

● **Grígos**

*Between €7.50 and €15*

**Taverna Stamátis**, in the middle of the harbour, just to the left as you arrive at the quay, ☎ (0247) 31 302. Very good reputation. They serve fresh fish, rabbit, and chicken with Parmesan. From 10 April to 10 October.

**HAVING A DRINK**

*Cafés and bars*

● **Skála**

**Adonis**, in the harbour, ☎ (0247) 32 040. A shady, spacious terrace that's particularly lively in the evening. Gives onto the harbour and onto the street.

**Arion**, next to the Adonis. A little trendier (techno music in the evening).

● **Hóra**

**Pyrgos Tower**, 100m below the last bend as you arrive in Hóra, ☎ (0247) 32 774. A little out of the way. A trendy music bar with an expensive restaurant, set in a large restored mansion that has numerous rooms and terraces and a lovely view of Skála. Every evening, from June to October.

**OTHER THINGS TO DO**

**Feasts & festivals – Holy Week** is an important occasion, especially Maundy Thursday and the Easter meal marking the end of Lent. On 27 July, the feast day of St Penteleímon is celebrated on the islet of Chilimódi. Kámbos village holds important ceremonies on 6 August for the Transfiguration and on 15 August for Assumption.

**Excursions –** The neighbouring islets of Lipsí, Agathoníssi and Arkí, with their fine beaches, are accessible by boat (departure from Skála in the morning, return in the evening).

# Sími ★★

District of the Dodecanese – Michelin map 980 fold 47 – Regional map page 479
Map of the island page 534 – 57km² – Pop 2 400

### Not to be missed
The hill town of Horió, at the top of a beautiful stairway.
Swimming from deserted beaches in unspoilt bays.

### And remember...
Compare and negotiate prices, as the island is expensive.
The roads are fairly bad, so be careful riding scooters.
Take water and a detailed map when you go walking (and pick aromatic herbs
such as thyme, wild marjoram, sage and rosemary).

Sími is an attractive little island in the Straits of Marmaris less than 5km from the Turkish coast. A touch of aristocratic charm makes it a refined holiday resort. Here, the carefully restored traditional houses have not given way to modern structures. Above Gialós harbour nestling in the curve of a sheltered bay, elegant neo-Classical houses with tiled roofs rise in tiers up to the old town, atop the hill overlooking the bay, forming a romantic picture.

The natural landscape is just as scenic. When you arrive from Rhodes (twenty kilometres away) or from Kos, the contrast is striking – no long stretches of beach, but a wild, jagged coastline of sheer cliffs and narrow creeks. This makes Sími a paradise for ramblers. The island with its small population, free-roaming goats and stray cats, has few tarmac roads. And even if the paths are seldom marked, it's a pleasure to wander along coastal paths to deserted bays, or along mountain ridges through pine-covered hills to valleys of olive trees, discovering the island's host of forgotten chapels.

## Decline
Sími had been renowned for its **shipbuilding** skills since Antiquity. In the late 19C, it was still building almost 500 boats a year, and the boats were so fast that the Ottoman postal service took on a whole fleet. The island also lived off its **sponge fishing**. The two lucrative activities brought prosperity to Sími, bestowing on it a certain amount of independence. But with the arrival of artificial sponges and the boom in steamship navigation, decline set in, becoming more pronounced under the Italian occupation and the damage wrought by the Second World War. Forced into exile, a large part of the population deserted the island, which today has ten times fewer inhabitants than it did last century. Sími owes its recent revival to tourism.

## Sími Town ★★★
*Allow half a day*

The capital of the island is divided into two parts: on the one hand, the lively, colourful harbour district, and on the other, the hilltop town with its fine pastel-coloured houses dotted among the cypress trees and bougainvillaea.

## Gialós harbour ★★
Most of the shops, restaurants and hotels are concentrated around Sími's harbour, the tourist hub of the island. Attractive black and white *Botsaloto* cobblestones (*see page 187*) decorate the squares and alleyways. During the day, this is where a joyful crowd mixes with the tourists arriving on boat excursions from Rhodes. But at nightfall the lower town recovers its peace and quiet, particularly because motorised traffic is then limited, if not banned. The quays lend themselves to cool evening strolls, past the splendid private yachts at anchor.

Boat lovers may be interested in the tiny **Maritime Museum** (*behind the harbour, 10.30am-3pm*), which has some fine models.

Sími: Horió harbour and its neo-Classical houses

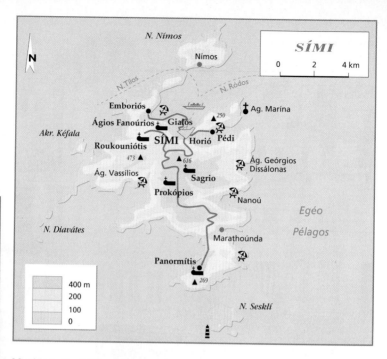

## Horió★★, the hilltop town

There's an attractive walk up to the town via a beautiful winding **stairway★★** made up of 400 steps, flanked by **neo-Classical houses★★★** dating from the 18C and 19C. These mansions have pastel façades in ochre or yellow and windows framed in brown. Many were abandoned for a long time and have been restored, even if most still seem to be unoccupied. Should you walk up in the blazing heat, several handy tavernas await you at the entrance to the old town. You then enter a maze of bright, quiet alleyways lined with more modest houses that have often been abandoned. Follow the blue arrows to the very elegant **Sími Museum★★** (*8.30am-3pm; closed Monday; entrance fee*), which contains statues and other paleo-Christian objects, 12C and 13C Byzantine pottery, beautiful **icons**, traditional costumes, etc.

Lastly, climb on up the right side of the hill to the **castle** (*signposted*) at the top. The fortress was built by the Knights of St John on the site of the ancient acropolis. Within its walls stands a church. From the top of the hill, you have a superb all-round **view★★**, especially of Gialós Bay.

## Around Sími

The west quay extends from Gialós harbour to the adjoining villages of **Haráni** and **Nos**. A small coast road then leads to the magnificent **Emboriós Bay★★** and to the large village of **Emboriós** (*4km west of Sími, allow 90min there and back on foot, or take one of the water-taxis that run every hour between 10am-2pm and 4-6pm*). The island's former commercial harbour is now a good place for a swim. Its quays are level with the water, ideal for diving or sunbathing, and there are also small pebble beaches round about.

You can also escape 2km east of Sími (*frequent buses*), to a fertile valley that opens onto the small fishing harbour of **Pédi**. This is very lively in summer, and has a **sandy beach**.

# Exploring the monasteries★★

*Often difficult to get to as they are not on tarmac roads. Bring a detailed map. Take a boat where possible (a pleasant option) or walk (with a hat and water).*

Monasteries abound on the island. They range from large complexes inhabited by monks to simple, deserted chapels – tiny white buildings lost among olive trees or perched on rocks. Many of them have outstanding **frescoes**, as Sími was the centre of a renowned school of religious painting in the 18C.

## St Michael of Panormítis (Moní Taxiárhou Mihaíl)
*Access by boat in 1hr from Sími harbour, departure between 10am and 12noon, return around 4-5pm. Access by road is difficult - 16km, including 8km along a track (see also "Getting around").*

The huge monastery on the south-western tip of the island is famous for its **miraculous icon** of St Michael, the patron saint of the island. It is therefore a popular place of pilgrimage *(with rooms to let, see "Where to stay")*, particularly on 8 November, the saint's feast day, and over Pentecost. Along the quay, the fishermen quietly repair their nets, unperturbed by the ferries from Rhodes and Sími.

The surrounding heights are home to roaming goats and to monks out walking. The monastery itself was built in the 18C and is unfortunately surrounded by massive modern buildings that provide accommodation for pilgrims. However, it is worth spending time in the **church**, to see its fine wooden **iconostasis★**, and in the **Museum of Religious and Folk Art★** *(open to fit in with the arrival of the boats; entrance fee)*, which is housed in a corner of the inner courtyard. It displays various objects of worship (icons, ex-votos, reliquaries, etc), as well as traditional costumes, tools and a reconstruction of an old-fashioned interior.

## St Michael Roukouniótis★ (Ágios Mikhaíl Roukouniótis)
*1hr on foot from Gialós. Also accessible by car (tarmac road). Ask the warden to open up for you.* Far more discreet than the former monastery, this small one in the west of the island is nonetheless a good deal richer. Its **church★** built in the 14C and reconstructed in the 16C has a magnificent **iconostasis★★** of St Michael, made of solid gold and silver. Note also the fine **painting** illustrating Abraham's hospitality, and the **pulpit** made of painted wood.

## And others...
*Buy a detailed map.* If you are interested in religious art and architecture, take the time to go and see the monasteries of **Ioánnis Sagrio** (12C) and **Prokópios** (14C), isolated in the middle of the island off the road leading to Panormítis. You could also take a pleasant walk to **Agios Fanoúrios**, starting from Gialós *(30min on foot)*.

---

# Making the most of Sími

### COMING AND GOING

**By sea** – Several boats (**Symi I** and **Symi II** are the least expensive) shuttle daily between Rhodes and Sími, either directly (in 2hr), or with a stop at Panormítis (3hr including 30min to tour the monastery). In summer there's a daily hydrofoil from Rhodes, and one 3 times a week from Kos (Monday, Friday and Saturday). 2 to 3 ferries a week connect Piraeus with Sími. However, it is simpler to go via Rhodes, which has far more connections. From Sími, there are regular links with the other islands in the Dodecanese.

### GETTING AROUND

**By bus and taxi** – The **bus station** (regular minibuses to Horió and Pédi beach) and **taxi rank**, ☎ (0241) 72 666, are on the east quay, which merges with the road to Horió.

**By scooter and motorcycle** – There are **scooter and motorcycle rental agencies** in the harbour (Gialós). A road runs almost the entire length of the island, from Emboriós to Panormítis. Be warned, only the first half of the road to Panormítis is tarmac, the rest is a rough track that is difficult to negotiate on a scooter. The only **fuel station** is right at the end of the east quay at Gialós.

## ADDRESS BOOK (GIALÓS)

**Tourist information** – Enquire at **Symi Tours** travel agency at the harbour, ☎ (0241) 71 307.

**Bank / Currency exchange** – **Ionian Bank** and **National Bank** are at the harbour. 8am-2pm, Monday to Friday.

**Post office / Telephone** – **Main post office**, on the western tip of the quay near the Clock Tower. **OTE**, up to the left of the main square.

**Medical service** – **Medical care**, ☎ (0241) 71 290 / 72 472.

**Police** – Next to the Clock Tower, ☎ (0241) 71 111.

**Harbourmaster's office** – In the white building next to the Clock Tower, ☎ (0241) 71 205.

## WHERE TO STAY

Sími is more expensive than Rhodes or Kos. Most of the hotels are in the luxury class and the restaurants are smart.

### • Gialós (harbour)

It is quite difficult to find inexpensive rooms in the lower town in summer. As soon as you arrive, ask the touts who await people getting off the boat.

*Between €27 and €38*

**Hotel Grace**, 150m behind the main square, set back from the harbour, ☎ (0241) 71 931 / 71 397 – 7rm. 📶 🖹 A quiet, comfortable seasonal hotel. Breakfast extra. The manager runs a jeweller's shop (FJ Coral) at the harbour.

*Over €45*

**Hotel Albatros**, right in the centre, in an alleyway at right angles to the main quay, ☎ (0241) 71 829 / 71 707, Fax (0241) 72 257 – 5rm. 📶 ✒ 🖹 A small renovated hotel impeccably run by helpful management. Open late March to mid-November.

The owners also run two lovely neo-Classical villas that have been attractively restored and divided into several apartments (2 to 5 people, ideal for a family or group) with hotel service. **Villa Thalassa** and **Villa Symeria** are at the end of the east quay, respectively beside the quay and a little uphill. 📶 ✒ 🖹 ✕

**Opera House**, at the back of the lower town up behind the church, 150m from the main quay, ☎ (0241) 71 856 / 72 034, Fax (0241) 72 035 – 5rm and 19 apartments. 📶 🖹 🛁 🆑 A quiet complex away from the busy harbour, consisting of well-equipped rooms, studios and apartments in villas set around a garden. Very convenient for families or groups of friends. Open all year. Be warned, prices almost double in summer.

*Over €90*

**Alíki Hotel**, at the end of the west quay, beyond the Clock Tower, ☎ (0241) 71 665, Fax (0241) 71 655 – 15rm. 📶 ✒ 🖹 ✕ 🛁 🆑 A charming hotel on the waterfront, slightly removed from the busy centre. Has a large bar and a roof garden. Open all year.

### • Horió (upper town)

Far quieter than the harbour, the upper town is a pleasant place for a holiday.

*Between €27 and €38*

**Hotel Fiona**, on the right of the road coming up from the harbour, near the pedestrian street, ☎ and Fax (0241) 72 088, symi-vis@otenet.gr – 11rm. 📶 🛁 Recognisable by the flags. A quiet, clean hotel in a beautiful setting with a fine view of the sea. Small courtyard, balconies. Breakfast included. Open all year.

### • Emboriós

Emboriós Bay is very sheltered and therefore ideal for a quiet stay at the seaside.

*Under €27*

**Metapontis** (the home of Maria Perouli), near the small landing-stage, ☎ (0241) 71 820 – 4rm. 📶 ✕ 🛁 This peaceful little guesthouse-taverna with its family atmosphere is only open in high season.

### • Panormítis

*Under €15*

**Panormítis Monastery**, ☎ (0241) 71 581. The monastery has about a hundred rooms for pilgrims and other visitors. The rooms have no hot water but have basic facilities (some with kitchens), and are in the two large white buildings facing onto the sea. Without necessarily going on retreat, this is a good place to spend a few very peaceful days. Enquire at the manager's office (to the right of the church on the first floor). Open all year.

- **Pédi**

You will find several hotels and apartments to let around the beach and the harbour.

## EATING OUT

- **Gialós (lower town)**

*Between €9 and €15*

**Meraklís**, behind the main quay, ☎ (0241) 71 003. `CC` A traditional taverna with moderate prices and a friendly welcome. Often crowded.

*Around €15*

**Taverna Ouzerí Dimítris**, right at the end of the east quay, ☎ (0241) 72 207. The whole family helps in the restaurant, with the father grilling fish on the quayside. Pleasant setting though often windy. Fresh fish. Prices vary depending on the type of fish.

**Mythos**, on the east quay, ☎ (0241) 71 488. One of the best restaurants in the harbour, with several tables on the waterfront in an elegant setting. The place is fairly windy, but quiet in the evening. Fresh fish, carefully prepared dishes. Only open for dinner.

*Over €30*

**Restaurant Mylopetre**, to the left of the square behind the little bridge, ☎ (0241) 72 333. A peaceful, attractive place laid out in an old mill. Two Hellenistic tombs have been unearthed just beneath the dining room! Traditional and modern Mediterranean fare based on fresh produce. Expensive, but the food, like the decor, is refined. Only open for dinner.

- **Horió (upper town)**

The upper town has several rather expensive restaurants and tavernas, grouped around the square and the pedestrian street.

*Between €9 and €15*

**Georgio's Taverna**, at the top of the large stairway, below and to the left of the square, ☎ (0241) 71 984. Fresh produce, Greek specialities. Covered terrace.

- **Emboriós**

*Between €9 and €15*

**Metapontis**, on the quayside, ☎ (0241) 71 820. A pleasant family restaurant adjoining the guesthouse (see *"Where to stay"*).

- **Panormítis**

*Between €9 and €15*

**Panormion**, at the beginning of the quay, ☎ (0241) 71 305. The only restaurant in Panormítis. Greek specialities and fish dishes. Open from March to November.

- **Pédi**

Pédi has 4 restaurants all in the same category.

*Between €9 and €15*

**Kamares**, at the end of the beach to the right, ☎ (0241) 72 016. Decent fare, with fish and seafood, served in a beautiful setting. Open from April to October.

## OTHER THINGS TO DO

**Boat trips** – Water-taxis from Gialós harbour go to the **beaches** at Pédi, Geórgios Dissálonas, Nanoú, Marathoúnda and Ágio Vassílios, and to the islet of Sesklí in the south.

In summer, caiques also leave from Pédi for the beaches, and from Panormítis for the islets of Nímos in the north and Sesklí in the south.

# INDEX

**Kárpathos** (Dodec): sight or place described in the text
*Venizélos (Elefthérios):* historical figure
Ouzo: practical information or term explained in the text
Abbreviations:　　(Cre): Crete　　　　　(Aeg): North Aegean
　　　　　　　　　(Cyc): Cyclades　　　　(Sar): Saronic Gulf
　　　　　　　　　(Dodec): Dodecanese　(Spor): Sporades

# H

# L

# MAPS AND PLANS

## Manufacture Française des Pneumatiques Michelin

Société en commandite par actions au capital de 304 000 000 EUR
Place des Carmes-Déchaux – 63000 Clermont-Ferrand (France)
R.C.S. Clermont-Fd B 855 200 507

© Michelin et Cie, Propriétaires-éditeurs, 2001
Dépôt légal novembre 2001 – ISBN 2-06-100059-2 – ISSN 0763-1383
No part of this publication may be reproduced in any form
without the prior permission of the publisher.

**Printed in France 11-2001/1.1**
Typesetting: Nord Compo – Villeneuve d'Ascq
Printing: IME – Baume-les-Dames

**Cover photography:**
An islander from Crete (P. de Wilde/HOA QUI)
Mýkonos (H. Le Gac/MICHELIN)
Knossós (detail of a fresco) (B. Perousse/MICHELIN)

**Michelin Travel Publications**
39 Clarendon Road, Watford Herts WD17 1JA
☎ 01923 205 240 – www.ViaMichelin.com

These helpless creatures are not only unhoused, but often driven off the land, no one remaining on the lands being allowed to lodge or harbour them. Or they, perhaps, linger about the spot, and frame some temporary shelter out of the materials of their old homes against a broken wall, or behind a ditch or fence, or in a bog-hole (scalps as they are called), places totally unfit for human habitations; they crowd into some of the few neighbouring cabins still left standing, when allowed to do so, as lodgers, where such numbers usually congregate that disease, together with the privations of other kinds which they endure, before long carry them off. As soon as one horde of houseless and all but naked paupers are dead, or provided for in the workhouse, another wholesale eviction doubles the number, who in their turn pass through the same ordeal of wandering from house to house, or burrowing in bogs or behind ditches, till broken down by privation and exposure to the elements, they seek the workhouse, or die by the roadside.

...ther drove them to seek the workhouse. These were ...le to whom ten miles away was 'foreign', who might ...r have travelled from their home place all their lives.

...ext to Clare, the worst area for evictions was County ..., the scene of ten per cent of all evictions between 1849 ...854. Among the worst landlords was the Earl of Lucan, ...owned over 60,000 acres, and had once said that 'he ...d not breed paupers to pay priests'. He removed over ...tenants in the parish of Ballinrobe alone, and restocked ...eared land as grazing farms. The Marquis of Sligo was ...n evicting landlord, but he claimed to be selective, only ...g rid of the idle and dishonest. He cleared about one-...r of his tenants altogether.

...e of the evictions might have taken place earlier if it ...t been for fear of the threats of the secret societies, but ...ere now greatly weakened by the Famine. However, ...e was still occasionally taken, and seven landlords ...ot, six fatally, during the autumn and winter of 1847.

debts themselves. The Marquis of Sligo owed £1,650 to Westport Union, in 1848; he could only pay it by borrowing, and his debts and mortgages already came to £6,000 per year. But Captain Arthur Kennedy, a Poor Law inspector in Kilrush, County Clare, later said: '...there were days in that western county when I came back from some scene of eviction so maddened by the sights of hunger and misery I had seen in the day's work that I felt disposed to take the gun from behind my door and shoot the first landlord I met.'

There had been some clearances in 1846, but the great wave of evictions came in 1847. There were also thousands of 'voluntary' surrenders, where tenants simply surrendered possession of their patch of land and began to beg, usually heading for the nearest town. Of course these were just as much evictions as the official ones — there was precious little 'voluntary' about them. In other cases tenants were persuaded to accept a small sum of money, and sometimes they helped to tear down their poor dwellings themselves. They were cheated into believing the workhouse would take them in.

One of the worst areas for evictions was West Clare, as landlords turned thousands of families onto the road and demolished their inadequate cabins. In April 1848, Captain Kennedy calculated that 1,000 houses had been levelled since November, with an average of six people to each house. In Birr, County Offaly, a man called Denis Duffy was evicted, although he was ill: 'Duffy was brought out and laid under a shed, covered with turf, which was once used as a pig cabin, and his house thrown down. The landlord, not deeming the possession to be complete while the pig cabin remained entire, ordered the roof to be removed, and poor Duffy, having no friend to shelter him, remained under the open air for two days and two nights, until death put an end to his sufferings'.

The evicted families would shelter in ditches, until bad

| No. | DENOMINATIONS. | TENANTS. | Rent, when due. | Arrears. | Half-Year's Rent. | Half Year's Rent Charge, in lieu of tithe, due 1 may 1847 |
|---|---|---|---|---|---|---|
| | | Forward | 5928 4 4 | 7630 7 1 | 441 7 4 | |
| 367 365 | Spa + Ballinaberlagh | Duggan Patrick | 18 0 0 | 6 0 0 | | |
| 368 366 | " | p⁰ Duggan John | 12 0 0 | 6 0 0 | | |
| 369 367 | " | p⁰ Lynch Thomas | 56 0 0 | 18 0 0 | | |
| 370 368 | " | p⁰ Lynch James | 44 0 0 | 11 0 0 | | |
| 371 369 | " | p⁰ Hourly Timothy | 23 8 0 | 5 17 0 | | |
| 372 370 | " | p⁰ Concoian John | 24 0 0 | 8 0 0 | | |
| 373 371 | " | p⁰ Toby Denis | 28 16 11 | 9 0 0 | | |
| 374 372 | " | p⁰ Toby Mary | 40 0 0 | 9 0 0 | | |
| 375 373 | " | p⁰ Markue John | 41 16 0 | 7 12 0 | | |
| 376 374 | " | p⁰ Mahoney Denis | 21 0 0 | 21 0 0 | | |
| 377 375 | " | p⁰ Leahy John | 30 0 0 | 10 0 0 | | |
| 378 376 | " | p⁰ Murray Martin Denis | 51 0 0 | 13 0 0 | | |
| 379 377 | " | p⁰ Murphy Martin | 32 0 0 | 8 0 0 | | |
| 380 378 | " | p⁰ Murphy Martin | 4 15 0 | 4 15 0 | | |
| 381 379 | " | p⁰ Leahy James | 39 0 0 | 13 0 0 | | |
| 382 380 | " | p⁰ Cronin Michael | 27 12 0 | 8 0 0 | | |
| 383 381 | " | p⁰ Murphy John Martin | 44 0 0 | 8 0 0 | | |
| 384 382 | " | p⁰ Murphy Sabin | 26 8 0 | 8 16 0 | | |
| 385 383 | " | p⁰ Murphy Martin | 20 10 0 | 10 0 0 | | |
| 386 384 | " | p⁰ Murphy John Michl | 41 12 0 | 10 0 0 | | |

*Left: Ejectment of Irish tenantry, Illustrated London N...*
*Above: extract from rental of the Earl of Midleton's e...*
*7 August 1847. Transcript of the right hand column...*

| No 368 | Received notice to quit |
| No 369 | Two of the tenants, Jeremi... their portion of arrear will... |
| No 370 | Tenant dead notice to qui... |
| No 372 | Tenant removed arrear lo... |
| No 373 | Arrear lost tenant sent to... |
| No 375, 376 and 377 | Notices to quit at March... |
| No 379 | Arrear lost tenant sent t... |
| No 380 | Received notice to quit... |
| No 381 | Arrear lost tenant sent f... |
| No 382 & 384 | Notices to quit at Marc... |
| No 386 | To be removed by eje... |
| No 387 | Arrear lost tenant sen... |
| No 390 & 391 | Notices given to quit... |

Ten other occupiers of land, though without tenants, were also murdered. Lord Clarendon was alarmed that this meant rebellion, and he asked for special powers to combat crime.

Lord John Russell was not sympathetic to this appeal, believing that the landlords themselves were largely responsible for the tragedy in the first place. He remarked, '...It is quite true that landlords in England would not like to be shot like hares and partridges...but neither does any landlord in England turn out fifty persons at once and burn their houses over their heads, giving them no provision for the future.' However, a compromise was reached, and a Crime and Outrage Act was passed in December, 1847. Extra troops were sent to Ireland, and regulations about carrying arms were tightened.

# Emigration

Not all the landlords who evicted tenants threw them on the side of the road. Emigration from Ireland had been common for some time, and there now began some 'assisted emigration', whereby landlords gave their tenants enough money for a passage to America or Canada. Some landlords even hired ships to transport them. One-quarter of a million people left Ireland in 1847 (about 5,000 of them landlord-assisted) and 200,000 or more every year for the next five years.

Only three or four per cent of emigrants overall were helped by landlords, but others got aid from charities, or had been sent money by family members who had gone already.

By the time this massive shift of population had begun to die down, almost two million people had left the small island of Ireland forever. At first, the landlords who helped people to go were praised for their efforts, but by 1848 there was a

change of tone. Priests, politicians and newspapers began to attack this enforced exile, accusing Britain of trying to annihilate the population.

Between 1815 and the start of the Famine, almost 1.5 million Irish people had already left Ireland, mainly going to England, the United States, Canada and Australia. The difference between this earlier emigration and the Famine-driven flood was that those who had left by choice, seeking a better life, were mainly the young and strong, 70 per cent of them aged between 16 and 34.

By contrast, the millions who fled from the Famine contained large numbers of the very old and the very young, and were often weakened by fever and want before they even started. In those days, the journey to such countries as the United States was exhausting and full of hardship, even if the conditions were good, and you had to be fit for it.

The earlier emigrations, after 1815, had been caused by poor economic conditions after the Napoleonic War, and had been encouraged by cheap sailings. There was a large amount of trade between America and Britain, but the ships returning to America were often almost empty. Emigrants were a profitable way to fill these ships. Better routes to Canada were being opened up as well, and English

*Dormitory life between decks on the emigrant ship.*

*Facing page: The Ocean Monarch, an emigrant ship which caught fire and sank off Liverpool on 24 August 1848. It had just set sail for America with 306 people on board. 178 were lost in the shipwreck. Illustrated London News, 2 September 1848. The Ocean Monarch was one of 59 emigrant ships to America which sank in the years 1847-53.*

> *Kilcock, Co Kildare, threatening note sent to*
> *James Flanagan on 6 January 1848*

Sir — We the people of the district that you collected the Poor Rates in, in either Boush or Innismacthesant, or any other part that you collect the Poor Rate in, or take up any distress, or drives any person's cattle for the Rates, we will be under the necessity of shooting you in the open daylight, for we may as well loose our lives as to loose our support; so if you don't like this warning we give you, take your own advice, for we are determined to stop you or any other person that will come to collect them till the times mend.

        James Flanagan,
           There is your doom,
             so if like it
              continue.

*The Government Medical Inspector's Office at Liverpool, Illustrated London News, 6 July 1850*

shipowners began to get in on the traffic. By 1831, you could go from Newry (County Down) to Liverpool and then to New York for only three pounds.

This was still a large sum of money, so many emigrants just went as far as Britain. The largest proportion of these early emigrants were of Scots Presbyterian stock, from Ulster, because the linen industry there was declining. The English Poor Law provided Outdoor Relief more freely than in Ireland, and the food was better. Steam passenger ferries began to cross the Irish Sea during the 1820s, and the competition among ports and among ferry companies kept prices low. The ferries were often overcrowded, as passengers made a last-minute rush to get on board. The shipping companies delayed proper regulation as long as they could, because it would cut profits.

Between 1846 and 1852, over one million people left Ireland. Emigration continued to drain the country, once the pattern had been established. It is estimated that four million left between 1851 and 1910, and at least one-fifth of this

LETTER FROM AN IRISH EMIGRANT TO LORD MONTEAGLE.

Melbourne, Port Philip,
20th of March, 1848.

My Lord,

I, as in duty bound, feel called upon to inform your Lordship how the Emigrants who obtained a passage through your lordship's intercession are situated. All the Girls are employed in the Town of Melbourne, at the rate of Twenty-five to Twenty-six pounds per annum; they are all in respectable places. Thos. Sheahan is employed in the Town adjoining, attending Bricklayers at Four Shillings and Six pence per day—John Enraght on Public work, at the same rate. The general hire for Labourers of every description, my lord, is from Twenty-eight to Thirty-two pounds per annum, with board and lodgings. There is nothing in such demand in this Colony as Male and Female Servants: I was employed myself, my lord, on board the Lady Peel, by the Colonial Doctor, filling up forms of agreement between Masters and Servants, so that I had an opportunity of knowing all the particulars concerning wages, term of employment, occupation, &c. &c.

I would mention all, but I consider your lordship will feel satisfied when you know they are all in good situations, and with respectable masters and mistresses. ⌄ I have seen a good deal of the Emigrants whom I knew at home, that obtained a passage through your lordship's intercession, about eleven years ago, some of them live in the Town of Melbourne, and are living comfortably. Ellen Shanahan (Loughill), is married to one Rockford, in this Town, and keeps a Hotel. Maurice Connors, of Foynes, is living in this Town, and has as much money spared as exempts him from personal labour. I have heard from some more of them who live in the Country, and as far as I can learn, my lord, they are living independently. Ellen Sheahan is just going up to her brother accompanied by her first cousin, Daniel Mulcare, of Clounlikard, himself and his brother has lived some time in this Town, and kept a Grocer's Shop. They have acted the part of a brother to me, my lord, they gave me the best of entertainment, and procured a situation for me with one Mr. Ham, a Surveyor. I am going up the Country to the Avoca River to survey a Station; my wages are Twenty-one pounds for six months. Mr. Hurley has sent for his nephew and his aunt, they are on their way up by this time. I expect, my lord, to be able to remit some money to your lordship in recompense for the expenses incurred on my and my sisters' account by your lordship, as well as some relief to my poor mother, brothers and sister. I hope, my lord, this humble but imperfect epistle will find your Lordship, Lady Monteagle, Mr. Spring Rice, and all his family in good health. Any information I can give your lordship respecting the interior of this Country, will not be lost sight of on my part. Mr. Thos. Ham, of Great Collins Street, Melbourne, would forward any commands to me, my lord, if your lordship should want any more information concerning any of the late or former Emigrants. Every thing in this Colony, my lord, is from three to four times as dear here as it is in England or Ireland, except Bread, Beef, Mutton, &c., the best of which is obtained at Three half-pence to Two-pence per lb.

I am, My Lord, with profound veneration,
Your Lordship's most devoted Servant,
P. DANAHER,

P.S. My Sisters also, my lord, beg leave to return their most sincere thanks to your Lordship and Lady Monteagle.

John Flanagan and Wife are both employed by a man of the name of Murphy, a Brewer, about twelve miles out in the Country, wages Fifty pounds per annum.

*Letter sent to Lord Monteagle by a tenant whose passage to Australia he had paid, telling how well he and other emigrants from Shanagolden were faring. This letter was printed in circular form to encourage emigration.*

emigration was to Britain. Thousands flooded into Liverpool, creating huge problems of overcrowding and disease, and three-quarters of those who sailed across the Atlantic left from this port. The size of the remittances sent back home was notable; between 1848 and 1870, over sixteen million pounds arrived in Ireland from the USA.

## Hazards of Emigration

Because so many people had already emigrated over the previous decades, emigration was seen as a common-sense response to the appalling conditions at home. In most European countries, emigration was the last resort in bad economic conditions, but in Ireland emigration began in a matter of months after the first crop failure. Newspapers carried advertisements, placards were pasted up everywhere — the passenger companies were determined to encourage large numbers to travel.

One of the strongest 'pull' factors was the stream of letters home, praising the new life and urging family members to follow. Of course, emigrants who had not done well in their new homes soon lost touch with their families out of shame, so the letters that did arrive may have given a slightly unrealistic picture of the fine prospects. Once the Famine had tightened its grip, it was not just the poor who emigrated. Merchants and tradesmen, watching the economy collapse, were being crippled by heavy taxation. Large numbers of the entrepreneurial class began to leave as well.

Until 1850, when iron-hulled screw steamers were introduced, it took at least a month to cross the Atlantic. Travellers were given a basic minimum of food and water, but had to provide anything else themselves. The packed holds were a fertile ground for typhus. Only a very small number of these vessels were wrecked, but the wrecks were widely reported and vividly described, adding to the fears of the trip.

The worst death rate among emigrants occurred in 1847, when the notorious 'coffin ships' travelled to Canada; of over 100,000 emigrants making this trip, one-sixth died on board ship or soon after landing. Possibly about 5 per cent of the Famine emigrants died; the normal death rate, however, was about 2 per cent.

Ships' officers described the appalling conditions: '...friendless emigrants stowed away like bales of cotton, and packed like slaves in a slave ship; confined in a place that, during storm time, must be closed against both light and air, who can do no cooking, nor warm so much as a cup of water... Passengers are cut off from the most indispensable conveniences of a civilised dwelling... We had not been at sea one week, when to hold your head down the fore-hatchway was like holding it down a suddenly opened cess pool'.

Despite all the reasons to be afraid of the journey, nothing could stop desperate people determined to go. They would have to face seasickness, insanitary accommodation, violent fellow passengers and often the hostility of the crew, as well as rotten food and foul water, and they would have to fight off the crooks and touts who tried to rob and cheat them both before and after the journey. 'Trappers' or confidence tricksters hung around the ports in Ireland and Liverpool to rob the unwary and illiterate travellers, and 'runners' waited at the other end, to entice them into 'boarding-houses' which were no more than robbers' dens.

An example of the notorious 'coffin ships' was the barque *Elizabeth and Sarah*, which sailed from County Mayo in July 1846, heading for Canada. She carried 276 persons, instead of the 212 listed, and had only 8,700 gallons of water for the

*Above: Overcrowded emigrant ship leaving Ireland*

### William Steuart Trench

I shall not readily forget the scenes that occurred in Kenmare when I returned, and announced that I was prepared at Lord Lansdowne's expense to send to America every one now in the poor-house who was chargeable to his lordship's estate, and who desired to go; leaving each to select what port in America he pleased — whether Boston, New York, New Orleans or Quebec.

The announcement at first was scarcely credited; it was considered by the paupers to be too good news to be true. But when it began to be believed and appreciated, a rush was made to get away at once.

Two hundred each week were selected of those apparently most suited for emigration: and having arranged their slender outfit, a steady man, on whom I could depend, Mr. Jeremiah O'Shea, was employed to take charge of them on their journey to Cork, and not to leave them nor allow them to scatter, until he saw them safely on board the emigrant ship.

voyage, instead of the 12,532 gallons she should have had. Each passenger was entitled to be given 7 lbs of provisions each week, but none was ever distributed. The 276 passengers shared 32 berths, and there was no sanitary facility of any kind. The voyage took eight weeks, because the captain took the wrong course, and by the time the ship broke down and was towed into the St Lawrence river in September, 42 people had died.

By this time the authorities in Canada and the United States thought they knew what to expect from the emigrant ships — thousands of emigrants had arrived already, and their numbers and poverty had caused the passing of various Passenger Acts, forbidding emigrants who had no money or subsistence to land. But no-one expected the 'ship fever' of 1847, that is, the typhus fever which now crossed the Atlantic as well.

In 1847, the St Lawrence river, the entrance route to Canada, stayed frozen over until May, much later than usual. The first ship which then arrived at Grosse Ile, the quarantine station, had 84 cases of fever on board (nine had died). They had all come from Ireland, via Britain. The quarantine hospital could only accommodate 200 people, but eight more ships arrived carrying 430 fever cases, and three days later seventeen more ships. By May 26, thirty vessels waited at Grosse Ile to be cleared, with 10,000 emigrants on board. By May 31 this had risen to forty ships, stretching two miles down the river.

Conditions became intolerable. Tents were hastily erected on land, but patients were often left for days on the ships without treatment. Most of the ships had not one healthy person on board, and those who had escaped fever were weakened by starvation. Processions of boats carried the sick and dead from the ships, flinging them on the beach to crawl to the hospital if they could.

By the middle of the summer, it was impossible to

quarantine people properly, and they were allowed to stay on the ships for fifteen days, instead of spending ten days in the hospital. This meant the sick and healthy were still cooped up together, and fever spread as before. By the end of July, quarantine efforts had been abandoned, and the hordes of emigrants were just sent on inland. The result was that Quebec and Montreal later suffered widespread fever epidemics.

After 1848, stricter controls were enforced, and the emigrant death rates fell dramatically. A monument on Grosse Ile, at the site of the emigrant cemetery, bears the inscription, 'In this secluded spot lie the mortal remains of 5,294 persons, who, flying from pestilence and famine in Ireland in the year 1847, found in America but a grave.'

The United States had responded with great generosity to the appeals from famine-stricken Ireland, and thousands of dollars in aid had been sent, as well as food supplies and clothing. However, the American authorities were appalled at the sudden influx of starving, impoverished emigrants, too ill and weak to work, and were more successful than the Canadians at enforcing the Passenger Acts. Ships which arrived with destitute passengers were forbidden to land them, and were turned back to sea, to the despair of those on board. Many of these ships then headed to Canada instead.

The Irish were not welcome emigrants. Apart from their poverty and the fever they often carried, they had no suitable skills or trades, and most of them were so weakened they were unfit for work of any kind, even the unskilled agricultural labour they had been used to. They tended to drift to the slums of the large cities, supporting themselves by unskilled labour. Often they drank, to cover the despair and loneliness of unsuccessful emigration, and fighting was frequent. Child mortality was huge; in Boston, 61 percent of children died under the age of five between 1841 and 1845, even before the new wave of emigrants began to arrive.

The Irish tended to congregate in 'Irish quarters', and they stayed in the cities — only about ten per cent moved on to rural areas. They were fodder for the political bosses, and became notorious for drunken rows and violent crime. It took a long time for the Famine emigrants to overcome their disadvantages, and to begin to make a positive contribution to the countries they had reached.

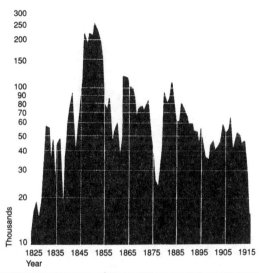

*Chart showing Irish overseas emigration, 1825-1915. Numbers leaving the United Kingdom per annum.*

*Below: Cork Harbour, the point of departure for many.*

*Above: Emigrants at Cork: a scene on the quay*
*Below: Accommodation was often a cramped space between decks, Illustrated*
*London News, July 1850*

# CHAPTER 9

## 1848–49

## Crop fails again

The potato crop of 1847 was not affected by blight, because weather conditions were too dry, but the crop itself, though sound, was far too small to make any difference to the ongoing tragedy. Enormous efforts were therefore made to increase the 1848 crop, and farmers strained to plant as

*Sligo Union 19 February 1848*

A boy of 14, named James Foley ... left the Killanummery hospital on 22nd January, being a week convalescent after fever; he received from the doctor who had been in charge of the hospital, which was at that time ordered to be closed, a ticket of admission to the hospital at Manorhamilton; the boy, instead of going there, returned to his father, who, fearing contagion, would not admit him among his other children, and probably from want of shelter, in addition to his weak state of health, the poor boy perished in the inclement weather, or it might have been from a relapse. The father was in the receipt of out-door relief for himself and his children, including the boy James, and he did not report either his being in hospital, or his subsequent condition to the relieving officer.

many potatoes as possible.

The total acreage of potatoes in 1848 was three times more than that in 1847, but that summer was extremely wet. The blight raged again, and the crop was lost. The Quakers were asked to re-establish soup kitchens, but refused. Their workers were physically exhausted and their resources had almost run out. Besides, they felt that free alms were damaging to the people in the long run.

# Young Ireland rebellion

During all this time of increasing hopelessness and despair, one group of men was still actively working towards revolution, believing that the only answer was for Ireland to be in a position of independence. These were the Young Irelanders, who had broken from Daniel O'Connell's Repeal Movement in 1846 because they were not convinced by his doctrine of 'moral force', and wanted radical solutions to Ireland's problems.

A mood of revolution was sweeping over Europe in 1848, with rebellions in Austria and Italy. In France, the monarchy was overthrown and a republic was proclaimed (again). The British government was growing increasingly nervous of the Chartists, a working-class movement seeking civil rights.

The Young Irelanders began to form 'revolutionary clubs' all over Ireland, seeking the overthrow of the state.

This movement for change coincided with a new tenant rights movement, spearheaded by James Fintan Lalor and supported by John Mitchel, son of a Presbyterian, and a spellbinding orator. Lalor held that the land should belong to the community as a whole, and that tenants were entitled to secure tenure and fixed rents. He hoped to achieve this change peacefully, through a national rent strike. However, this movement was before its time; the people were too broken by misfortune to care, and the landlords were vehemently opposed to tenant right. Mitchel began to consider violent revolution as the only means of change, and founded a firebrand newspaper called the *United Irishman* in January 1848.

The government, galvanised by the threat of rebellion, sent 10,000 troops into Ireland. Leaders of the movement, including Mitchel, William Smith O'Brien and Thomas

*'The Union!' by Thomas Rowlandson, 1801*

Francis Meagher ('Meagher of the Sword') were arrested and charged with sedition, but were released on bail. O'Brien and Meagher went to Paris, seeking aid, but had no success — the new French government did not want to antagonise Britain. Meanwhile the Catholic Church was working against them through the parish priests, who were very influential. Pope Pius IX forbade priests to engage in political activities, and suspended Father Kenyon, in Tipperary, who had pledged himself to Young Ireland.

In May 1848 O'Brien and Meagher were tried, but the prosecutions failed and they were freed. However, when Mitchel came to trial, the jury was 'packed', and troops filled the street outside. He was found guilty, and sentenced to transportation to Australia for fourteen years, with hard labour in the penal colonies. After the trial, his comrades began to plan a rebellion, collecting money and arms.

It seems extraordinary that they could have expected such a project to succeed. Destitution was worse than ever, and beggars were pouring into every town. Jail had become a place of safety, because at least food was available there, and people were so desperate that they were committing crimes so that they could be transported — anything to get away from a country which seemed cursed. Besides, the plotters were very badly organised. Every move they made seems to have been known to the police, and was even described in the newspapers.

*Thomas Francis Meagher ('of the Sword') who was sentenced to transportation after the 1848 rebellion. From Tasmania, he later escaped to the USA.*

The new Treason Felony Act came into force in July, and Meagher was arrested again, along with another leader, Charles Gavan Duffy. Dublin, Cork, Waterford and Drogheda were put under martial law, and a bill suspending Habeas Corpus was rushed through the British Parliament. The Young Irelanders now had to decide whether to drop their plans for a rebellion, or start it prematurely, before it was ready.

When it eventually happened, the rebellion collapsed. There had been no plans, no strategy, and the only responses were from counties Kilkenny, Limerick and Tipperary. On 30 July William Smith O'Brien, with forty armed men, and about a hundred peasants armed with stones, took part in the only real event of the 1848 rebellion, the 'Battle of Ballingarry', in Tipperary. There the rebels found themselves surrounded by police, and were trapped in the garden of Widow McCormack. Smith O'Brien escaped on a stolen police horse, and the remaining rebels fled.

Smith O'Brien later wrote bitterly, '...the people preferred to die of starvation at home, or to flee as voluntary exiles to other lands, rather than to fight for their lives and liberties.' He seems to have had no idea of the effects of starvation, or of how badly the spirit of the people had been broken.

## Breakdown of Administration

One effect of the rebellion, of course, was to cause the well of private charity to dry up. If the Irish were so ungrateful as to bite the hand that was trying to feed them, then let them starve. The Poor Law Unions now owed the government about £260,000, and the British Association, which had been paying out £13,000 a week in aid, ran out of funds on 1 July 1848. Gradually the relief system wound down, as the whole weight of assistance fell on the Unions, and the British administrators such as Routh went home. The Society of Friends still gave what help they could, but they were fighting a losing battle.

Trevelyan wrote to the Poor Law Commissioners, insisting that a rate of 5 shillings in the pound had to be struck so that costs could be covered, but Commissioner Twisleton eventually forced him to agree a rate of 3 shillings, complaining that even that could hardly be collected. Trevelyan, however, obviously felt that the Commissioners were trying to get as much money from the state as they could, without using their own resources properly. In September, he told them that Treasury grants to distressed Unions were to come to an end, and there would be no more issues of free clothing.

The wave of emigration now became a torrent, as people gave up hope of remaining alive in Ireland. Trevelyan refused to be alarmed: 'If small farmers go, and then landlords are induced to sell portions of their estates to persons who will invest capital, we shall at last arrive at something like a satisfactory settlement of the country'.

Land was being left waste everywhere, and landowners who despaired of selling simply went, abandoning their estates. No buyers could be found for large estates crumbling under a weight of debt. Trade was at a standstill, and the smaller towns were being abandoned for the cities. An appeal to Lord John Russell said, 'We shall be left a pauper warren...the Queen being the matron of the largest union workhouse ever yet founded.'

Trevelyan, always opposed to Outdoor Relief, had managed to get the numbers receiving it reduced by 200,000. People were brought to workhouses screaming for food, and the buildings were surrounded by crowds of people, who threatened those inside, and seemed ready to riot. Lord Clarendon pleaded for help to Sir George Grey, the Home Secretary, but got the answer: 'It may be that if numerous deaths should occur the Government would be blamed, but there is such an indisposition to spend more money on Ireland, that the Government will assuredly be severely

There can be no doubt in a pious mind, that there is a ruling hand guiding all the affairs of men. Prayer, the Christian knows, 'moves the hand that moves the Universe', and it would be an outrage on both reason and revelation, for the creatures of earth to question the right of the Omnipotent to do whatever seems to him right in the government of the world he has made. It is impious to think that God could or would do any thing wrong; but, at the same time, it would be highly impertinent in us to wish to know all the reasons that God may have for doing what he sometimes does, in this dark world of ours. We know that nothing happens without cause; and it follows, as a matter of course, that the potato blight, which appeared so suddenly and so destructively, at the very time Ireland was threatened with an insurrection of the lower orders against the higher, was sent as an arrest to prevent a greater evil, by the infliction of a lesser evil; and the facility with which God put a stop to the Repeal movement, and the revolutionary schemes of the Young Irelanders, should make survivors to feel the truth of that pithy saying: 'Man's extremity is God's opportunity'.

blamed if they advance money to pay debts...'

The government had decided to follow Trevelyan's proposed system of 'operation of natural causes', in other words to do nothing. Lord John Russell wrote: 'We have subscribed, worked, visited, clothed, for the Irish, millions of money, years of debate, etc., etc., etc. The only return is rebellion and calumny. Let us not grant, lend, clothe, etc., any more, and see what that will do...British people think this.'

The Poor Law rules were being strictly applied, including the labour test requiring eight hours' work a day from able-bodied men. Each applicant received one pound of meal a day, and the cost of keeping one person alive for 34 weeks was estimated to be £1. Twisleton, compiling the Poor

*Constabulary of Ireland.*

What can be more absurd — what can be more wicked, than for men professing attachment to an imperial Constitution to answer claims now put forward for state assistance to the unprecedented necessities of Ireland, by talking of Ireland being a drain upon the *English* treasury? ... If the Union be not a mockery, there exists no such thing as an English treasury. The exchequer is the exchequer of the United Kingdom.

Ireland has been deprived, by the Union with England, of all separate power of action. She cannot do now, as in the days of her parliament she might have done — draw upon her own resources, or pledge her own credit, for objects of national importance. Irish men were told, indeed, that in consenting to a Union which would make them partners with a great and opulent nation, like England, they would have all the advantages that might be expected to be realised. How are these pledges to be fulfilled, if the partnership is only to be one of loss, and never of profit to us? If, bearing our share of all imperial burdens — when calamity falls upon us we are to be told that we then recover our separate existence as a nation, just so far as to disentitle us to the state assistance which any portion of a nation, visited with such a calamity, had the right to expect from the governing power? If Cornwall had been visited with the scenes that have desolated Cork, would similar arguments have been used? Would men have stood up and denied that Cornwall was entitled to have the whole country share the extraordinary loss?

Law Commission annual report, left out this calculation, in case it was said 'we were slowly murdering the peasantry by the scantiness of our relief'.

In December 1848, Clarendon wrote to Trevelyan: '...the statements I have received from (credible) eyewitnesses exceed all I have ever heard of horrible misery, except perhaps that of shipwrecked mariners on a yacht or desert island'.

# Rate-in-Aid

1849 was perhaps the worst year of the Great Famine. The rural population had been decimated by fever and starvation. Twenty-two Unions were ruined or bankrupt, and a further forty or fifty were on the brink of collapse. Ballina, County Mayo owed more than £18,000, and had 21,000 people on outdoor relief. In Bantry, County Cork, 2,327 people and 600 children were crammed into two workhouses. People who had paid rates of 13 shillings were now being asked for £13. At this point even *The Times* newspaper, which had always opposed Irish aid, called for 'exceptional relief'. Again Trevelyan offered money to the Quakers to re-establish soup kitchens, and again they refused.

As yet another solution, Trevelyan brought forward a scheme called 'rate-in-aid'. This meant that the more prosperous Unions would have to come to the aid of the distressed ones. The Treasury would also lend £100,000 for further relief. Lord Lansdowne reacted with horror to this 'scheme of confiscation, by which the weak would not be saved, but the strong be involved in general ruin.'

The whole country came together in anger — what was the point of the Act of Union, if Ireland now had to stand completely alone? Why couldn't help be given by English and Scottish Poor Law Unions as well? Twisleton resigned from the Poor Law Commissioners, because the government seemed to be trying to exterminate the population. The Rate-in-Aid Act was passed in May 1849, and the sum to be levied was assessed at a total of £322. 552. 11 shillings.

If blight and famine fell upon the South of France, the whole common revenue of the kingdom would certainly be largely employed in setting the people to labour upon works of public utility; in purchasing and storing for sale, at a cheap rate, such quantities of foreign corn as might be needed, until the season of distress should pass over, and another harvest should come. If Yorkshire and Lancashire had sustained a like calamity in England, there is no doubt such measures as these would have been taken promptly and liberally. And we know that the English Government is not slow to borrow money for great public objects, when it suits British policy so to do. They borrowed twenty million sterling to give away to their slaveholding colonists for a mischievous whim.

\* \* \*

It will be easy to appreciate the feelings which then prevailed in the two islands — in Ireland, a vague and dim sense that we were somehow robbed; in England, a still more vague and blundering idea, that an impudent beggar was demanding their money, with a scowl in his eye and a threat upon his tongue.

\* \* \*

In addition to the proceeds of the new Poor law, Parliament appropriated a further sum of £50,000, to be applied in giving work in some absolutely pauper districts where there was no hope of ever raising rates to repay it. £50,000 was just the sum which was that same year voted out of the English and Irish revenue to improve the buildings of the British Museum.

\* \* \*

In this year (1847) it was that the Irish famine began to be a world's wonder, and men's hearts were moved in the uttermost ends of the earth by the recital of its horrors. The London *Illustrated News* began to be adorned with engravings of tottering windowless hovels in Skibbereen, and elsewhere, with naked wretches dying on a truss of wet straw; and the constant language of English ministers and members of Parliament created the impression abroad that Ireland was in need of *alms*, and nothing but alms; whereas Irishmen themselves uniformly protested that what they required was a repeal of the Union, so that the English might cease to devour their substance.

THE CAUSES OF EMIGRATION FROM IRELAND.

*The Lady's Newspaper,* 1849.

To the Irish peasantry, who, more than any other people of Europe, are accustomed to bestow care and attention on the funeral of their friends and relatives, the Cholera in its necessity for speedy interment, was increased in Terrors tenfold. The honours which they were wont to lavish on the dead — the ceremonial of the wake — the mingled merriment and sorrow — the profusion with which they spent the hoarded gains of hard-working labour — and lastly, the long train to the churchyard, evidencing the respect entertained for the departed, should all be foregone; for had not prudence forbid their assembling in numbers, and thus incurring the chances of contagion, which, whether real or not, they firmly believed in, the work of death was too widely disseminated to make such gatherings possible. Each one had someone to lament within the limits of his own family, and private sorrow left little room for public sympathy.

# Cholera

In December 1848, a man infected with Asiatic cholera had come from Edinburgh to Belfast. He died in hospital there, but cases of cholera began to appear in the workhouse to which he had gone first. Gradually it was carried all over Ireland, and the epidemic reached a peak in May. Advice was given on hospitals and dispensaries, but there was no money to help cholera victims; it was all going to the starving.

Clarendon wrote desperately to Lord John Russell, 'Surely this is a state of things to justify you asking the House of Commons for an advance, for I don't think there is another legislature in Europe that would disregard such suffering as now exists in the west of Ireland, or coldly persist in a policy of extermination.' By the end of the cholera epidemic, 36,000 people had died of the disease.

By June 1849, 768,902 people were on Outdoor Relief, and Irish Unions owed more than £450,000. Discipline had broken down, and clothing distribution had stopped. Queen Victoria contributed £500 to a private fund launched by members of the government, which collected £10,000. But now the Quakers left Ireland, unable to continue. They made it plain that private charity could no longer cope, that the basic essential was for the land system to be completely reformed, and that 'the government alone could raise the funds and carry out the measures necessary in many districts to save the lives of the people'. In all, the Society of Friends had spent £200,000.

# CHAPTER 10

## 1849

## Encumbered Estates Act

The plight of the landlords finally made some impression on the government, which realised that something had to be done to allow the system of agriculture to be revived. As long as the estates were crushed by debt, no money would be put into the land, and the value of Irish land had fallen drastically.

The Encumbered Estates Act was passed in July 1849. Under this act, landlords could sell their estates without having to pay off their debts first. A tribunal could order the sale of encumbered land, even if the landlord did not agree, and could grant secure titles to new buyers. It was hoped that the estates would be taken over by English entrepreneurs, who would run them more efficiently, but of 7,489 buyers (up to 1857) only 4 per cent were of this type. Most of them were Irish, from the landed gentry and the professions.

The result of the Encumbered Estates Act, from the point

---

*Journal of Elizabeth Smith
during Queen Victoria's visit, 1849*

---

The rain was extremely unfortunate as it prevented all the fun we selects had promised ourselves in visiting the different places of amusement. The gentlemen indeed braved the weather, leaving the *few* ladies collected in the market house to enjoy the excellent musick of Kavanagh's Band without any chance of dancing to it, for they were wanted to keep order in the hotel, carve for the awkward, serve the drink and so on, and they served too much drink, as long before mid-night there was hardly a sober man and long before daybreak there were hundreds drunken. It was wonderful that no accident happened among them; the gentlemen and a few others kept order. *Our* party was hurt by the Queen, so many had gone in to see her enter Dublin. She was enthusiastically received, showed herself most gracefully and abundantly and was in high good-humour. She has grown very fat, was much sunburned, and too plainly dressed to please the Irish. As she did not come in state there was no procession to signify. The illuminations must have been quite spoiled by the rain. Today she visits all that is worth seeing in the city.

---

of view of the ordinary peasant, was a new and vicious wave of evictions. The buyers of land expected to find that land empty, so that they could get on with their own plans, usually the expansion of grazing. If they found people still clinging to it, they cleared them ruthlessly. Indeed, the land was often advertised with this deliberate intention. The prospectus for the Martin estate in Galway stated: '... it is believed many changes advantageous to a purchaser have since taken place [since 1847], and that the same tenants by name and in number will not be found on the land.'

*Our Welcome*
*(Elizabeth Varian, published in The Nation)*

... We dare not bid thee welcome! hark to that mad appeal —
Our brother's blood for vengeance calls, whilst we ignobly kneel.
'Twere fitting work for rugged hand to strew with flowers thy way
And tattered rags would well befit a nation's holiday!
Hark! to the famine cries, the shrieks of stalwart men struck down,
Crushed in their manhood's noble prime, in all their fair renown;
Thy helpless sister's wailing, the moan of infancy!
Then ask thy conscience, Lady, what welcome waits for thee?

*Queen's College, Cork, during Queen Victoria's visit, 3 August 1849.*
*Lithograph by W. Scraggs from drawing by N.M Cummins*

Kilrush Union, Co Clare, 21 December 1849
(Simon Boland, Relieving Officer)

Thomas Brown, of Tullogower, five in family, were living on turnips supplied by his neighbours; his wife could not use the turnips; I found her in a very weak state ....

John O'Brien, of Moyadda, eight in family, lives in a hut built in a bog; the hut is not much larger than a pigsty, the wet pouring in through the walls of it; he is sick in bed, I believe with fever ... he cannot be taken to the workhouse, as a horse and car could not get to his cabin, and men would not venture to take him out in fever ....

William Buckley of Kilcarrol, six in family ... I found old Buckley nearly dead of dysentery; his son had weaving to do, but was not able to do it with the hunger. I gave them the last shilling I had ....

*From a report to the Poor Law Commissioners*

# Royal Visit

Lord Clarendon, Lord Lieutenant of a devastated country, with millions dead and dying and all commercial activity grinding to a halt, decided that a Royal Visit would be good for morale. Whatever about Irish opinions of the government, Queen Victoria herself was quite popular, and the country needed to be given some confidence for the future. Trade was at rock-bottom.

Attitudes to the royal visit were mixed. When people were starving, and the funds of the Dublin Central Relief Committee were completely finished, it seemed a great waste of money to be providing banquets and pageants. On the other hand, perhaps it would raise spirits a bit, and reassure people that they were not forgotten overseas. At any rate, the plans went ahead.

The visit began on 1 August, and went off very well. Crowds of thin and ragged people greeted the Queen (who travelled with her husband, Prince Albert, and some of their children); there was an air of excitement, and they were cheered on their way. A banquet was held at the Vice-Regal Lodge (cleaned up for the occasion), and a huge military spectacle took place in the Phoenix Park. Writing to her uncle, the King of the Belgians, Victoria noted: 'You see more ragged and wretched people here than I ever saw anywhere else.' The royal family visited Cork as well, and were welcomed enthusiastically. The Queen wrote: 'We ... stepped on shore at *Cove*, a small place, to enable them to call it *Queen's Town*: the enthusiasm is immense...'

The climax of the visit was the departure from Kingstown (now Dún Laoghaire, County Dublin) on 10 August 1849. Crowds waved off the royal vessel, and the Queen said that she left Ireland 'with real regret'. The visit had brought some welcome colour and pleasure into Irish lives, however briefly, but of course it had no long-term effect. Clarendon was left with a bill for £2,000.

# Famine's aftermath

By 1850, the worst of the Famine was over, and the potato crop was recovering its former strength, although blight still struck at intervals. The Famine affected many future generations, however, and left echoes for years afterwards.

The number of people who died, generally reckoned at one to one-and-a-half million, will never be known. The last census before the Famine, in 1841, had been deficient in many respects, and part of the problem of distributing food in isolated areas lay in the unexpected discovery of large numbers of people who had not been recorded before. The huge numbers of deaths meant that record-keeping almost stopped — no-one could keep up with them, and hundreds died absolutely unknown and unmissed, because their families had gone before them.

The lowest population loss through death and emigration was in Leinster, the most prosperous province in Ireland, and Ulster came next. Munster and Connacht, the poorer provinces, lost between 23% and 28% of their populations. The counties with the highest death rates were Sligo, Galway and Mayo, followed by Tipperary. One in nine of the population died, and children under 10 and old people over 60, who were one-third of the population, accounted for three-fifths of all deaths.

Some improvements took place in the land system as a result of the Famine. It was more efficient that the smaller farms were to be replaced by larger holdings — the number of holdings of less than 5 acres was halved — but this efficiency had been purchased at great cost. A franchise reform act in 1850 gave the vote to thousands of farmers, mostly those who held 12 acres or more, and they could now act collectively for change. Dairy farming increased greatly in importance, and cattle farmers grew prosperous. However, the landless tenants remained poor and insecure, and still basically dependent on the potato, for another thirty years.

The total costs to the British government of the Famine amounted to £8.1 million, between 1845 and 1850. Less than half of this was grants from the Treasury; the rest was from Treasury loans, which were supposed to be repaid.

*Above: Priest blessing emigrants in 1851, the year of greatest emigration when over a quarter of a million people left Ireland.*
*Below: 'The emigration agents' office — the passage money paid', 1851*

However, less than £600,000 had been repaid by 1850, when the debts were consolidated and refinanced. All debts were cancelled completely in 1853, when Ireland was brought into the British income tax net.

However, these huge outlays must be looked at in context. Britain's expenditure on its national defence costs had averaged about £16 million per year since 1815, and its average annual tax revenue was about £53 million. It should also be noted that many contemporary voices, in parliament and elsewhere, argued that the government was not providing anything like enough money for the size of the tragedy. In fact, the greatest assistance to Famine relief came from Ireland itself, through Poor Rate collections, and money contributed by some landlords. At least £1 million was also collected through private charity.

The Famine led to a breakdown of Irish rural society, partly through the greatly increased emigration — about one million emigrated, but again records are very incomplete, and there is no way of judging the full extent. Age-old traditions and folk ways were wiped out, and whole communities disappeared. In 1845, around three million people were Irish-speakers, but this dropped to below two million in 1850. The famine period itself was marked by a dramatic decline in the birth-rate, and far fewer marriages.

The population began to replace itself fairly quickly, once conditions improved, and within a generation many communities had built themselves up again. But the traditional stories of hunger and misery were passed down from one generation to another, fuelling anger against Britain, seen as the author of it all.

This was, in fact, probably the most long-lasting effect of the Great Famine and it acted as a spur to the rebellions and land agitation which broke out at intervals until the end of the century. Another lasting effect, of course, was the Irish diaspora. The large numbers of emigrants provided fertile ground for efforts to win Irish independence, and spread elements of Irish culture far and wide.

Attitudes in Britain, on the other hand, were more mixed. There had been a great outpouring of charity from all over the country, but some commentators were inclined to blame the Irish for being lazy, shiftless, rebellious and ungrateful. Some so-called Christian writers felt that a merciful Providence had acted to clear the land of such worthless rogues, but William Bennett, a Quaker, wrote: 'Is this to be regarded in the light of a Divine dispensation and punishment? Before we can safely arrive at such a conclusion, we must be satisfied that human agency and legislation, individual oppressions, and social relationships have had no hand in it.'

# EPILOGUE

The effects of the Great Famine were far-reaching, and include the vast diaspora of emigrants who spread as far as Australia, Canada and the United States, and the pervasive distrust that has influenced relations between Ireland and Britain ever since.

The descriptions of the Famine, and of the deaths and despair which it engendered, are indeed appalling, and can lead to a kind of numbness — it becomes unbearable to read about any further skeletal bodies, overcrowded and noxious workhouse dormitories, desperate and starving hordes, called 'paupers' rather than a more dignified term, overturning soup boilers and trampling over weaker sufferers in the agony of severe hunger.

You find yourself thinking that of course it was terrible, but it could not happen now — we do things better. But it does happen now, and is happening still, and the old arguments are still trotted out about how famine aid is not appropriate, how it doesn't reach the right people, how it demoralises the ability of communities to look after themselves. Technological developments, the ease of modern transport and communications, all the advantages the nineteenth century didn't have, do not seem to have made any difference to the universal human ability to delay, to confuse, to prevaricate, to discriminate, to excuse the inexcusable.

These descriptions are not just part of history. The listless, apathetic groups staring at the ground, the pits filled with dozens of dead, can still be seen in other parts of the world. We have learned less than we should from the Great Irish Famine.

# BIBLIOGRAPHY

I was commissioned to write this book as a short history of the Famine, listing the main events in readable form. Of necessity, a lot of detail has had to be left out, and the list of books below is intended to refer interested readers to more detailed historical works.

The most easily accessible primary source is the collection of reprints of nineteenth-century Parliamentary Papers, which was produced by Irish University Press from the late 1960s. Eight volumes of these reprints deal with the Famine period, and they contain Poor Law Guardians' reports, Relief Committees' letters, and all kinds of material relating to the various relief efforts, with many harrowing accounts from all over Ireland. I am grateful to the Gilbert Library, Pearse Street, Dublin, for access to these.

I relied heavily, of course, on material about the Famine published by established historians, and based on solid original research. A basic text is Volume V of *A New History of Ireland* (Dublin, 1989), called *Ireland Under the Union I: 1801 -70*, edited by W.E. Vaughan. This contains eight chapters dealing with the Famine period by James S. Donnelly Jr, and chapters on emigration by David Fitzpatrick and Patrick J. O'Farrell. Equally useful material, relevant to the Famine in Northern Ireland, is to be found in *A History of Ulster* (Blackstaff Press, 1992) by Jonathan Bardon.

The most well-known book on the Famine, of course, is *The Great Hunger, Ireland 1845-1849*, by Cecil Woodham-Smith, originally published in 1962. This is a very detailed account of the Famine, but some of the conclusions have been challenged by later research. Another older book on the subject is *The Great Famine, Studies in Irish History 1845-52*, edited by R.D. Edwards and T.D. Williams, and published by Browne and Nolan in 1956.

More up-to-date research can be found in *The Famine in Ireland* by Mary Daly, published by the Dublin Historical Association in 1986. Cormac Ó Gráda, an economic historian, published *The Great Irish Famine* in 1989 (Gill and Macmillan). Austin Bourke, a meteorologist, devoted years of study to the history of the potato and its importance in the Irish pre-Famine economy, and has published *'The Visitation of God'? The Potato and the Great Irish Famine* (Lilliput Press, 1993). If you are interested in Irish emigration, Graham Davis's book *The Irish in Britain 1815-1914* (Gill and Macmillan, 1991), should be consulted.

Anyone interested in Famine history should try to visit Ireland's first Famine Museum, newly-opened in Strokestown House, Strokestown, Co. Roscommon. The Mahon family of Strokestown House were evicting landlords, and one of them was murdered.

For eye-witness accounts, one book to consult is *The Great Irish Famine*, written by Canon John O'Rourke and originally published in 1874. It was reprinted by Veritas Publications in 1989. Another contemporary account can be found in *Irish Journals of Elizabeth Smith 1840-1850* (Oxford, 1980) edited by David Thomson and M. McGusty.

I would also recommend *A Diary of the Irish Famine*, edited by K.D.M. Snell, (Irish Academic Press, 1994) which reprints a contemporary diary kept by Alexander Somerville.

William Carleton's *The Black Prophet*, cited here, is a powerful nineteenth-century novel published immediately after the Famine. Liam O'Flaherty's *Famine* is the classic novel of the Irish Famine, based on original research by the author.

# Other Works Consulted

Benson, A.C. and Viscount Esher (eds.), *The Letters of Queen Victoria (1837-1861)*, Vol. II, London, 1908

Boyce, D. George, *Ireland 1828-1923, From Ascendancy to Democracy*, Blackwater Press, 1992

Boyce, D. George, *Nineteenth Century Ireland, The Search for Stability*, Gill and Macmillan, 1990

Deane, Seamus (ed.), *Field Day Anthology of Irish Writing, Vol. 2*, Derry, 1991

Mangan, James J., *Gerald Keegan's Famine Diary: Journey to a New World*, Wolfhound Press, 1992

Mokyr, Joel, *Why Ireland Starved: A Quantitative and Analytical History of the Irish Economy, 1800-1850*, Allen and Unwin, 1985

Mokyr, Joel and Ó Gráda, Cormac, *New Developments in Irish Population History, 1700-1850*, Centre for Economic Research, University College Dublin, Working Paper 17, 1983

Morash, Christopher (ed.), *The Hungry Voice: The Poetry of the Irish Famine*, Irish Academic Press, 1989

Murphy, Ignatius, *The Diocese of Killaloe 1800-1850*, Four Courts Press, 1992

Ó Gráda, Cormac, *'For Irishmen to Forget?' Recent Research on the Great Irish Famine*, Centre for Economic Research, University College Dublin, Working Paper WP88/7, 1988

Robins, Joseph, *The Lost Children, A Study of Charity Children in Ireland 1700-1900*, Institute of Public Administration, 1980

Speed, P.F. *The Potato Famine and the Irish Emigrants*, Longman, 1976

**Illustration credits**

Colour pages: Quaker tapestry courtesy of the Quaker Tapestry Scheme; William Burke Kerwan paintings courtesy of the National Library of Ireland; 'Another deserted village' and 'The dying drag the dead' courtesy of Sister Anne Therese Dillen OSU; 'Emigrants at Cork' courtesy of the Department of Irish Folklore, University College Dublin; Jeanne Rynhart statue courtesy of Bord Fáilte; 'Queen Victoria leaves Kingstown', 'Nora Dooday' and 'Eliza Morrison' from the National Library of Ireland; folk park ship courtesy of the Ulster American Folk Park; Mission Dolores gravestone courtesy of Seamus Cashman; 'Economic Pressure' by Seán Keating courtesy of the Crawford Municipal Gallery, Cork.

Special thanks to Bord Fáilte and *Ireland of the Welcomes* magazine for assistance in the preparation of illustration.

Sincere thanks to the following for documents and illustrations: Public Records Office of Ireland and the State Paper Office for pages 19, 20, 26, 27, 32, 41, 42, 48, 53, 58, 59, 63, 67, 68, 69, 73, 80, 88, 89, 96, 97, 103

John Gough, Conna for photographs on pages 35, 41

*Illustrated London News*, pages 6, 22, 32, 38, 53, 58, 63, 69, 88, 96, 100, 101, 102, 106, 110, 131

*Irish Journals of Elizabeth Smith 1840-1850* (Oxford, 1980), edited by David Thomson and M. McGusty, pages 11, 55, 64, 72, 75, 126

Bord Fáilte and *Ireland of the Welcomes* magazine, pages 106, 109, 123, 140-141

*Overleaf: Continuing emigration — Departure of Irish emigrants at Clifden, County Galway, 1853*

# INDEX